MAJOR

MODERN

ESSAYISTS

MAJOR MODERN ESSAYISTS

Second Edition

edited by

Gilbert H. Muller

The City University of New York,
LaGuardia

with

Alan F. Crooks

The American University

A BLAIR PRESS BOOK

Prentice
Hall

PRENTICE HALL, Upper Saddle River, New Jersey 07458

Library of Congress Cataloging-in-Publication Data

Major modern essayists / edited by Gilbert H. Muller and Alan F.
  Crooks. — 2nd ed.
      p.   cm.
    "A Blair Press book."
    Includes index.
    ISBN 0-13-497983-4 (pbk.)
    1. English essays—20th century.   2. American essays—20th
  century.   I. Muller, Gilbert H.   II. Crooks, Alan F.
  PR1367.M345 1994
  824'.9108—dc20   93-20970
                                                            CIP

Cover design: Design Lab
Production coordinator: Bob Anderson
Photo editor: Lori Morris-Nantz
Photo research: Joelle Burrows

Cover Art:
"Arcades" (After Walter Benjamin) by R. B. Kitaj, 1972–74.
Oil on canvas, 60 × 60. Photo courtesy Marlborough Fine Art, London.

Acknowledgements appear on pages 477–80, which constitute a continuation of
the copyright page.

Blair Press
The Statler Building
20 Park Plaza, Suite 1113
Boston, MA 02116-4399

 © 1994 by Prentice-Hall, Inc.
Upper Saddle River, New Jersey 07458

Printed in the United States of America
10   9

ISBN 0-13-497983-4

Prentice-Hall International (UK) Limited, *London*
Prentice-Hall of Australia Pty. Limited, *Sydney*
Prentice-Hall Canada Inc., *Toronto*
Prentice-Hall Hispanoamericana, S.A., *Mexico*
Prentice-Hall of India Private Limited, *New Delhi*
Prentice-Hall of Japan, Inc., *Tokyo*
Prentice-Hall Asia Pte. Ltd., *Singapore*
Editora Prentice-Hall do Brasil, Ltda., *Rio de Janeiro*

Preface

Those who are familiar with the first edition of *Major Modern Essayists* should find this new edition particularly exciting, for not only are most of the classroom-proven essayists—Woolf, White, Orwell, Thomas, Baldwin, Selzer, Didion, Atwood, Kingston, Gould, Rodriguez, Walker, and Dillard—still included, but their selections have been "finetuned" to better demonstrate each essayist's wide range of styles and techniques. To that end, we have replaced a few essays by individual writers that seemed too similar to each other in subject or tone, and we have added more recent and, we hope, more relevant essays by several of the writers retained from the first edition. We have also added two of the most respected and thought-provoking American essayists currently writing, Cynthia Ozick and Barry Lopez.

Continuing the tradition established by its predecessor, the second edition restricts the number of essayists to a small group of outstanding writers in order to provide three to five complete selections by each. This in-depth treatment allows students to perceive writers working in a wide variety of prose forms and in different voices. Moreover, this edition provides further evidence that writing styles and authorial visions are shaped in response to different cultural contexts. The essays included in this edition address a wide variety of issues on the twentieth-century's multicultural landscape. Indeed, the essays again treat so many topics and range over so much global terrain that the book could comfortably serve as a multicultural, cross-disciplinary reader. There are essays dealing with archeology, education, ecology, European history, contemporary politics, sociology, geography, literature, psychology, religion, medicine, and more. Students should have no trouble responding to Lewis Thomas's provocative essay on contemporary medicine or to Margaret Atwood's powerful statement concerning the female body. Issues such as intercultural relations are addressed in a variety of ways: they permeate George Orwell's masterful recounting of shooting an elephant in Burma; they provide a unique focal point for James Baldwin's experience in a small Swiss village; and they are central to Cynthia Ozick's powerful personal memoir of growing up in Brooklyn. Within all of these essays as well as others making up the collection can be discerned a celebration of life that underlies the essayists' challenge to any divisive force threatening the human community.

With the addition of the new "Global Voices" section, the second edition of *Major Modern Essayists* demonstrates that the world of the essay is not limited to any particular nationality or language. Included in the new section are ten essays by ten internationally acclaimed writers, two of them winners of the Nobel Prize for Literature. There are, for example, essays examining aspects of American culture by Octavio Paz (Mexico) and Umberto Eco (Italy); an essay analyzing South Africa's racial crisis by that country's premier writer, Nadine Gordimer; and a personal memoir describing coming of age in Soviet-controlled Czechoslovakia by its former president, Vaclav Havel. These provocative international voices provide marvelous bases for energetic discussions linking students to the international community of which they are a part.

This new edition of *Major Modern Essayists* again reflects the fact that writing does not—and, indeed, cannot—exist in a formal or aesthetic vacuum (something students must recognize in their own approach to writing) and that essays achieving the highest standards of excellence must be understood in their own terms, in relation to each other, and in relation to the social pressures of the age. All the essays of this edition, like those of its predecessor, reflect a "fierce attachment to an idea," as Virginia Woolf described the essayists' stance. And being passionately committed to an idea is not a bad starting point for college writers, who may be trying out their own ideas for the first time.

We again hope that the book's flexible, pluralistic design will liberate teachers, who can use the collection in any number of ways as they design their courses. There is very little interference, and the apparatus is minimal. As in the first edition, we have provided an alternate thematic table of contents and a rhetorical index to accommodate various approaches to the teaching of writing.

For students, we have again included a substantial introduction to each essayist that places the writer in his or her cultural and rhetorical contexts. And every essay is once again followed by four categories of questions: "Purpose and Meaning," "Language and Style," "Strategy and Structure," and "Thinking and Writing." These questions are designed to promote thoughtful reading, meaningful discussion, and clear writing.

Finally, we hope that students and teachers alike will enjoy reading this new edition of *Major Modern Essayists* as much as we enjoyed assembling it. We hope, as well, that it aptly illustrates the exceptional flexibility of the essay as a literary form. Within the essays of this collection, students will find a wide variety of issues and questions upon which to reflect. More importantly, perhaps, they will find in the essays ideas of significance and relevance that will evoke their own responses as writers.

Acknowledgements

This edition, much like its predecessor, has been the work of a team—a cooperative venture. Motivated by the enthusiastic response to the first edition, we have attempted to make this edition of *Major Modern Essayists* an even stronger, more widely usable textbook. If we have succeeded in our endeavor, a good deal of the credit belongs to the dynamo publisher of Blair Press, Nancy Perry, whose insights were central to the revision process. Credit also belongs to LeeAnn Einert, editorial assistant, and Sue Brown, editor for this project. Their efficiency, cheerfulness, and editorial skills consistently kept the focus on quality and the project on the tightest of schedules.

The collection owes a great deal as well to those who reviewed the first edition of *Major Modern Essayists* and made suggestions as to authors and titles to include in the second edition: Nancy K. Barry, Luther College; Jean W. Cash, James Madison University; Laura Cuozzo, University of New Hampshire; Jane Dominik, San Joaquin Delta College; Richard J. Farrell, University of New Haven; Francis L. Fennell, Loyola University, Chicago; Sharon J. Hamilton, Indiana University, Indianapolis; Douglas Hesse, Illinois State University; Michael Keller, Virginia Commonwealth University; Marion Boyle Petrillo, Bloomsburg University; William H. Roberts, University of Massachusetts, Lowell; Timothy Martin, Rutgers University, Camden; Emily Seelbinder, Queens College; Debra Spark, Tufts University; Gary Tate, Texas Christian University; and Phyllis C. Whitesell, Franklin & Marshall College. They will see that their suggestions were followed wherever possible.

GILBERT H. MULLER

ALAN F. CROOKS

I especially want to thank those people at The American University who became involved with *Major Modern Essayists* through my participation in the second edition: my friend and Associate Dean of the College of Arts and Sciences, Kay Mussell, whose personal support made my work on this project possible; my chief advisor, Kermit Moyer,

Chair of the Literature Department, whose wonderful sensitivity pointed me in new directions; my colleague and confidant, Harvey Grossinger, who kept me rational at critical moments; and my Writing Center tutors, especially my assistant, Tim Fisher, who bravely put up with my mania during the whole process.

Finally, I want to thank my wife, Leah Henry, and my son, David, for their endurance and understanding when it counted most.

A. F. C.

Contents

BARRY LOPEZ   381

GLOBAL VOICES

Alternate Thematic Contents

ETHICS AND RELIGION

HISTORY AND POLITICS

HUMOR AND SATIRE

LANGUAGE AND LITERATURE

LEISURE AND SPORT

THE MINORITY EXPERIENCE

THE NATURAL WORLD

PERSONAL IDENTITY

SCIENCE AND TECHNOLOGY

WOMEN'S EXPERIENCES

VIRGINIA WOOLF

"Human nature changed in or about December 1910," Virginia Woolf once observed in attempting to define the modern sensibility. She was alluding to the Post-Impressionist Exhibition organized by art critic Roger Fry—an exhibition of modernist art by Manet, Gauguin, Cézanne, and Van Gogh that had been greeted with howls of contempt by the English public. Nevertheless, Woolf along with other artists and writers understood that new forms and techniques were needed to capture modern reality.

Virginia Stephen Woolf, born in London on January 25, 1882, is one of the modern era's most esteemed novelists and essayists. She was the daughter of the celebrated critic, philosopher, and biographer Leslie Stephen. The Stephen house pulsed with the conversation and conviviality of such distinguished guests as Robert Louis Stevenson, Oliver Wendell Holmes, Thomas Hardy, and John Ruskin. Lively and sociable, educated largely at home in her father's enormous library, Woolf grew up, as the critic David Daiches remarked, taking culture for granted. She took pride in being a member of the intellectual elite, but as her essay "Middlebrow" demonstrates, she could be witty and good-humored in her examination of the importance of intelligence as an index of culture.

Woolf's mother, Julia, died in 1895, precipitating the child's first nervous breakdown at the age of thirteen. Her father's death in 1904 led to a second breakdown and a suicide attempt. After Sir Leslie's death, Virginia settled with her sister and two brothers in Bloomsbury, where, with an independent income, she turned to writing. In Leonard Woolf, whom she married in 1912 after a friendship of eight years, she found a source of stability within the liberating but volatile environment of the Bloomsbury group of artists, writers, and intellectuals that consisted of E. M. Forster, John Maynard Keynes, T. S. Eliot, and others.

Woolf began her career as an essayist, becoming a reviewer for the *Times Literary Supplement* and publishing criticism in English and American journals. With the founding of the Hogarth Press by the Woolfs in 1917, Virginia Woolf became, in T. S. Eliot's words, "the centre. . .of literary life in London." Possessed of daring imagination, wide erudition, and extraordinary stylistic gifts, Woolf published several novels—*Mrs. Dolloway* (1925), *To the Lighthouse* (1927), *Orlando* (1928), and *The Waves* (1931). Yet even as Woolf established herself as a pioneer of modern experimental fiction and one of England's foremost novelists, she also secured her reputation as a major modern essayist.

Woolf's essays, collected in *The Common Reader* (1925, 1932), *The Death of the Moth* (1942), *The Moment and Other Essays* (1947), *The Captain's Death-Bed* (1950), *Granite and Rainbow* (1958), and the four-volume *Collected Essays* (1958), are noted for their range, vitality, and insight. "Whether you are writing a review or a love letter," Woolf maintained, "the great thing is to be confronted with a very vivid idea of your subject." Woolf can be opinionated, resistant, and radical, as she shows us in "Professions for Women"; she can also be highly evocative and poetic, as she is in "Leslie Stephen" and "The Death of the Moth."

"Have I the power of conveying the true reality?" Virginia Woolf asked. "Or do I write essays about myself?" Woolf speaks to the readers in a smooth, conversational suggestive voice. She reveals herself but also sums up an entire era's social and political turmoil between the two world wars. Her many essays and two books on women's liberation—*A Room of One's Own* (1928) and *Three Guineas* (1938)—make her a decidedly contemporary figure, but they should be seen against a broader attempt to defend culture and intellectual freedom. Ultimately the ravages of World War II pressed too many horrors, as Woolf admitted, on her eyes and on her fragile psyche. The Woolf's London home was bombed, their library destroyed. In Sussex on the morning of March 28, 1941, Virginia Woolf arose, wrote a tender note to her husband—"so perfectly good"—and then walked down to the River Ouse where, leaving her cane on the bank, she walked into the water and drowned.

Professions for Women

When your secretary invited me to come here, she told me that your Society is concerned with the employment of women and she suggested that I might tell you something about my own professional experiences. It is true I am a woman; it is true I am employed; but what professional experiences have I had? It is difficult to say. My profession is literature; and in that profession there are fewer experiences for women than in any other, with the exception of the stage—fewer, I mean, that are peculiar to women. For the road was cut many years ago—by Fanny Burney, by Aphra Behn, by Harriet Martineau, by Jane Austen, by George Eliot—many famous women, and many more unknown and forgotten, have been before me, making the path smooth, and regulating my steps. Thus, when I came to write, there were very few material obstacles in my way. Writing was a reputable and harmless occupation. The family peace was not broken by the scratching of a pen. No demand was made upon the family purse. For ten and sixpence one can buy paper enough to write all the plays of Shakespeare—if one has a mind that way. Pianos and models, Paris, Vienna, and Berlin, masters and mistresses, are not needed by a writer. The cheapness of writing paper is, of course, the reason why women have succeeded as writers before they have succeeded in the other professions.

But to tell you my story—it is a simple one. You have only got to figure to yourselves a girl in a bedroom with a pen in her hand. She had only to move that pen from left to right—from ten o'clock to one. Then it occurred to her to do what is simple and cheap enough after all—to slip a few of those pages into an envelope, fix a penny stamp in the corner, and drop the envelope into the red box at the corner. It was thus that I became a journalist; and my effort was rewarded on the first day of the following month—a very glorious day it was for me—by a letter from an editor containing a cheque for one pound ten shillings and sixpence. But to show you how little I deserve to be called a professional woman, how little I know of the struggles and difficulties of such lives, I have to admit that instead of spending that sum upon bread and butter, rent, shoes and stockings, or butcher's bills, I went out and bought a cat—a beautiful cat, a Persian cat, which very soon involved me in bitter disputes with my neighbors.

What could be easier than to write articles and to buy Persian cats with the profits? But wait a moment. Articles have to be about something. Mine, I seem to remember, was about a novel by a famous man.

4

And while I was writing this review, I discovered that if I were going to review books I should need to do battle with a certain phantom. And the phantom was a woman, and when I came to know her better I called her after the heroine of a famous poem. The Angel in the House. It was she who used to come between me and my paper when I was writing reviews. It was she who bothered me and wasted my time and so tormented me that at last I killed her. You who come of a younger and happier generation may not have heard of her—you may not know what I mean by The Angel in the House. I will describe her as shortly as I can. She was intensely sympathetic. She was immensely charming. She was utterly unselfish. She excelled in the difficult arts of family life. She sacrificed herself daily. If there was chicken, she took the leg; if there was a draught she sat in it—in short she was so constituted that she never had a mind or a wish of her own, but preferred to sympathize always with the minds and wishes of others. Above all—I need not say it—she was pure. Her purity was supposed to be her chief beauty—her blushes, her great grace. In those days—the last of Queen Victoria—every house had its Angel. And when I came to write I encountered her with the very first words. The shadow of her wings fell on my page; I heard the rustling of her skirts in the room. Directly, that is to say, I took my pen in my hand to review that novel by a famous man, she slipped behind me and whispered: "My dear, you are a young woman. You are writing about a book that has been written by a man. Be sympathetic; be tender; flatter; deceive; use all the arts and wiles of our sex. Never let anybody guess that you have a mind of your own. Above all, be pure." And she made as if to guide my pen. I now record the one act for which I take some credit to myself, though the credit rightly belongs to some excellent ancestors of mine who left me a certain sum of money—shall we say five hundreds pounds a year?—so that it was not necessary for me to depend solely on charm for my living. I turned upon her and caught her by the throat. I did my best to kill her. My excuse if I were to be had up at a court of law, would be that I acted in self-defence. Had I not killed her she would have killed me. She would have plucked the heart out of my writing. For as I found directly I put pen to paper, you cannot review even a novel without having a mind of your own, without expressing what you think to be the truth about human relations, morality, sex. And all these questions, according to the Angel of the House cannot be dealt with freely and openly by women; they must charm, they must conciliate, they must—to put it bluntly—tell lies if they are to succeed. Thus, whenever I felt the shadow of her wing or the radiance of her halo upon my page, I took up the inkpot and flung it at her. She died hard. Her fictitious nature was of great assistance to her. It is far harder to kill a phantom than a reality. She was always creeping back when I thought I had despatched her. Though I flatter myself that I killed her in the end, the struggle was severe; it took much time that had better have been spent upon learning Greek grammar; or in roaming the world in search of adventures. But it was a real experience; it was an experience that was bound to befall all women writers at that time. Killing the Angel in the House was part of the occupation of a woman writer.

But to continue my story. The Angel was dead; what then remained? You may say that what remained was a simple and common object—a young woman in a bedroom with an inkpot. In other words, now that she had rid herself of falsehood, that young woman had only to be herself. Ah, but what is "herself"? I mean, what is a woman? I assure you, I do not know. I do not believe that you know. I do not believe that anybody can know until she has expressed herself in all the arts and professions open to human skill. That indeed is one of the reasons why I have come here—out of respect for you, who are in process of showing us by your experiments what a woman is, who are in process of providing us, by your failures and successes, with that extremely important piece of information.

But to continue the story of my professional experiences. I made one pound ten and six by my first review; and I bought a Persian cat with the proceeds. Then I grew ambitious. A Persian cat is all very well, I said; but a Persian cat is not enough. I must have a motor-car. And it was thus that I became a novelist—for it is a very strange thing that people will give you a motor-car if you will tell them a story. It is a still stranger thing that there is nothing so delightful in the world as telling stories. It is far pleasanter than writing reviews of famous novels. And yet, if I am to obey your secretary and tell you my professional experiences as a novelist, I must tell you about a very strange experience that befell me as a novelist. And to understand it you must try first to imagine a novelist's state of mind. I hope I am not giving away professional secrets if I say that a novelist's chief desire is to be as unconscious as possible. He has to induce in himself a state of perpetual lethargy. He wants life to proceed with the utmost quiet and regularity. He wants to see the same faces, to read the same books, to do the same things day after day, month after month, while he is writing, so that nothing may break the illusion in which he is living—so that nothing may disturb or disquiet the mysterious nosings about, feelings round, darts, dashes, and sudden discoveries of that very shy and illusive spirit, the imagination. I suspect that this state is the same both for men and women. Be that as it may, I want you to imagine me writing a novel in a state of trance. I want you to figure to yourselves a girl sitting with a pen in her hand, which for minutes, and indeed for hours, she never dips into the inkpot. The image that comes to my mind when I think of this girl is the image of a fisherman lying sunk in dreams on the verge of a deep lake with a rod held out over the water. She was letting her imagination

4

5

sweep unchecked round every rock and cranny of the world that lies submerged in the depths of our unconscious being. Now came the experience that I believe to be far commoner with women writers than with men. The line raced through the girl's fingers. Her imagination had rushed away. It had sought the pools, the depths, the dark places where the largest fish slumber. And then there was a smash. There was an explosion. There was foam and confusion. The imagination had dashed itself against something hard. The girl was roused from her dream. She was indeed in a state of the most acute and difficult distress. To speak without figure, she had thought of something, something about the body, about the passion, which it was unfitting for her as a woman to say. Men, her reason told her, would be shocked. The consciousness of what men will say of a woman who speaks the truth about her passions had roused her from her artist's state of unconsciousness. She could write no more. The trance was over. Her imagination could work no longer. This I believe to be a very common experience with women writers—they are impeded by the extreme conventionality of the other sex. For though men sensibly allow themselves great freedom in these respects, I doubt that they realize or can control the extreme severity with which they condemn such freedom in women.

These then were two very genuine experiences of my own. These were two of the adventures of my professional life. The first—killing the Angel in the House—I think I solved. She died. But the second, telling the truth about my own experiences as a body, I do not think I solved. I doubt that any woman has solved it yet. The obstacles against her are still immensely powerful—and yet they are very difficult to define. Outwardly, what is simpler than to write books? Outwardly, what obstacles are there for a woman rather than for a man? Inwardly, I think, the case is very different; she has still many ghosts to fight, many prejudices to overcome. Indeed it will be a long time still, I think, before a woman can sit down to write a book without finding a phantom to be slain, a rock to be dashed against. And if this is so in literature, the freest of all professions for women, how is it in the new professions which you are now for the first time entering?

Those are the questions that I should like, had I time, to ask you. And indeed, if I have laid stress upon these professional experiences of mine, it is because I believe that they are, though in different forms, yours also. Even when the path is nominally open—when there is nothing to prevent a woman from being a doctor, a lawyer, a civil servant—there are many phantoms and obstacles, as I believe, looming in her way. To discuss and define them is I think of great value and importance; for thus only can the labour be shared, the difficulties be solved. But besides this, it is necessary also to discuss the ends and the aims for which we are fighting, for which we are doing battle with these formidable obstacles. Those aims cannot be taken for granted; they must be perpetually questioned and examined. The whole position, as I see it—here in this hall surrounded by women practising for the first time in history I know not how many different professions—is one of extraordinary interest and importance. You have won rooms of your own in the house hitherto exclusively owned by men. You are able, though not without great labour and effort, to pay the rent. You are earning your five hundred pounds a year. But this freedom is only a beginning; the room is your own, but it is still bare. It has to be furnished; it has to be decorated; it has to be shared. How are you going to furnish it, how are you going to decorate it? With whom are you going to share it, and upon what terms? These, I think are questions of the utmost importance and interest. For the first time in history you are able to ask them; for the first time you are able to decide for yourselves what the answers should be. Willingly would I stay and discuss those questions and answers—but not tonight. My time is up; and I must cease.

1931

Purpose and Meaning

1. What expectations does the title of this essay create for the reader? Do you think the title is an accurate reflection of the essay's thesis? Can you think of a better one?

2. Who is Woolf's immediate audience? Is the tone of the essay appropriate for its readers? Explain your answer.

3. By mentioning the list of women writers in the first paragraph, what assumptions has Woolf made about her audience's educational and cultural background?

Language and Style

1. Why is the "Angel in the House" an appropriate way for Woolf to describe an adversary that got in the way of her writing? How does this extended image strengthen the thesis of the essay?

2. Woolf writes of struggling to overcome obstacles created by a male-dominated society. Yet she uses the pronouns *he* (paragraph 5) to describe novelists in general. Does the pronoun, as it is used here, indicate gender? What does this usage indicate about the author's assumptions about language? What can we infer about the essay's historical and cultural context from the use of this pronoun? Why might contemporary women writers choose a different one?

3. Is the word *room* (paragraph 7) used figuratively, literally, or in both ways? Explain your answer.

Strategy and Structure

1. In paragraph 1, Woolf describes the physical requirements and the act of writing in straightforward terms. Is this description important for the overall thesis of the essay, or is it extraneous? How does the description affect the structure of the essay? How does it prepare the audience for what is to follow?

2. In paragraph 6, Woolf poses some questions for her audience. What is her purpose in doing this? How does it change the writer audience relationship? How does it prepare readers for the concluding paragraph?

Thinking and Writing

1. Have women today overcome the second of the "adventures" Woolf describes in paragraph 6? Write an essay arguing for or against the thesis that a contemporary woman today is free to express "her own experiences as a body."

2. What professions other than writing possess a strong, inner, psychological dimension as well as an external, concrete one? Write an essay that describes a field of endeavor that requires both dimensions.

3. Think of an audience (for instance, fellow students, children, a college graduating class), and draw upon your experiences to tailor a speech that imparts a lesson to that particular audience. For example, what would you say about college life at your institution to a group of prospective students to encourage them to enroll at your institution?

Leslie Stephen

By the time that his children were growing up the great days of my father's life were over. His feats on the river and on the mountains had been won before they were born. Relics of them were to be found lying about the house—the silver cup on the study mantelpiece; the rusty alpenstocks that leant against the bookcase in the corner; and to the end   1 of his days he would speak of great climbers and explorers with a peculiar mixture of admiration and envy. But his own years of activity were over, and my father had to content himself with pottering about the Swiss valleys or taking a stroll across the Cornish moors.

That to potter and to stroll meant more on his lips than on other people's is becoming obvious now that some of his friends have given their own version of those expeditions. He would start off after breakfast alone, or with one companion. Shortly before dinner he would return. If the walk had been successful, he would have out his great map and commemorate a new short cut in red ink. And he was quite capable, it appears, of striding all day across the moors without speaking more than a word or two to his companion. By that time, too, he had written the *History of English Thought in the Eighteenth Century*, which is said by some to be his masterpiece; and the *Science of Ethics*—the book which interested him most; and *The Playground of Europe*, in which is to be found "The Sunset on Mont Blanc"—in his opinion the best thing he ever wrote.

He still wrote daily and methodically, though never for long at a time. In London he wrote in the large room with three long windows at the top of the house. He wrote lying almost recumbent in a low rocking chair which he tipped to and fro as he wrote, like a cradle, and as he wrote he smoked a short clay pipe, and he scattered books round him in a circle. The thud of a book dropped on the floor could be heard in the room beneath. And often as he mounted the stairs to his study with his firm, regular tread he would burst, not into song, for he was entirely unmusical, but into a strange rhythmical chant, for verse of all kinds, both "utter trash," as he called it, and the most sublime words of Milton and Wordsworth stuck in his memory, and the act of walking or climbing seemed to inspire him to recite whichever it was that came uppermost or suited his mood.

But it was his dexterity with his fingers that delighted his children before they could potter along the lanes at his heels or read his books. He would twist a sheet of paper beneath a pair of scissors and out would drop an elephant, a stag, or a monkey with trunks, horns, and tails delicately and exactly formed. Or, taking a pencil, he would draw beast after beast—an art that he practised almost unconsciously as he read, so that the fly-leaves of his books swarm with owls and donkeys as if to illustrate the "Oh, you ass!" or "Conceited dunce," that he was wont to scribble impatiently in the margin. Such brief comments, in which one may find the germ of the more temperate statements of his essays, recall some of the characteristics of his talk. He could be very silent, as his friends have testified. But his remarks, made suddenly in a low voice between the puffs of his pipe, were extremely effective. Sometimes with one word—but his one word was accompanied by a gesture of the hand—he would dispose of the tissue of exaggerations which his own sobriety seemed to provoke. "There are 40,000,000 unmarried women in London alone!" Lady Ritchie once informed him. "Oh, Annie, Annie!" my father exclaimed in tones of horrified but affectionate rebuke. But Lady Ritchie, as if she enjoyed being rebuked, would pile it up even higher next time she came.

The stories he told to amuse his children of adventures in the Alps—but accidents only happened, he would explain, if you were so foolish as to disobey your guides—or of those long walks, after one of which, from Cambridge to London on a hot day, "I drank, I am sorry to say, rather more than was good for me," were told very briefly, but with a curious power to impress the scene. The things that he did not say were always there in the background. So, too, though he seldom told anecdotes, and his memory for facts was bad, when he described a person—and he had known many people, both famous and obscure—he would convey exactly what he thought of him in two or three words. And what he thought might be the opposite of what other people thought. He had a way of upsetting established reputations and disregarding conventional values that could be disconcerting, and sometimes perhaps wounding, though no one was more respectful of any feeling that seemed to him genuine. But when, suddenly opening his bright blue eyes, and rousing himself from what had seemed complete abstraction, he gave his opinion, it was difficult to disregard it. It was a habit, especially when deafness made him unaware that this opinion could be heard, that had its inconveniences.

"I am the most easily bored of men," he wrote, truthfully as usual: and when, as was inevitable in a large family, some visitor threatened to stay not merely for tea but also for dinner, my father would express his anguish at first by twisting and untwisting a certain lock of hair. Then he would burst out, half to himself, half to the powers above, but quite audibly, "Why can't he go? Why can't he go?" Yet such is the charm of simplicity—and did he not say, also truthfully, that "bores are the salt of the earth"?—that the bores seldom went, or, if they did, forgave him and came again.

Too much, perhaps, has been said of his silence; too much stress has been laid upon his reserve. He loved clear thinking; he hated sentimentality and gush; but this by no means meant that he was cold and unemotional, perpetually critical and condemnatory in daily life. On the contrary, it was his power of feeling strongly and of expressing his feeling with vigour that made him sometimes so alarming as a companion. A lady, for instance, complained of the wet summer that was spoiling her tour in Cornwall. But to my father, though he never called himself a democrat, the rain meant that the corn was being laid; some poor man was being ruined; and the energy with which he expressed his sympathy—not with the lady—left her discomfited. He had something of the same respect for farmers and fishermen that he had for climbers and explorers. So, too, he talked little of patriotism, but during the South African War—and all wars were hateful to him—he lay awake thinking that he heard the guns on the battlefield. Again, neither his reason nor his cold common sense helped to convince him that a child could be late for dinner without having been maimed or killed in an accident. And not all his mathematics together with a bank balance which he insisted must be ample in the extreme, could persuade him, when it came to signing a cheque, that the whole family was not "shooting Niagara to ruin," as he put it. The pictures that he would draw of old age and the bankruptcy court, of ruined men of letters who have to support large families in small houses at Wimbledon (he owned a very small house at Wimbledon) might have convinced those who complain of his understatements that hyperbole was well within his reach had he chosen.

Yet the unreasonable mood was superficial, as the rapidity with which it vanished would prove. The cheque-book was shut; Wimbledon and the workhouse were forgotten. Some thought of a humorous kind made him chuckle. Taking his hat and his stick, calling for his dog and his daughter, he would stride off into Kensington Gardens, where he had walked as a little boy, where his brother Fitzjames and he had made beautiful bows to young Queen Victoria and she had swept them a curtsey, and so, round the Serpentine, to Hyde Park Corner, where he had once saluted the great Duke himself; and so home. He was not then in the least "alarming"; he was very simple, very confiding; and his silence, though one might last unbroken from the Round Pond to the Marble Arch, was curiously full of meaning, as if he were thinking half aloud, about poetry and philosophy and people he had known. 8

He himself was the most abstemious of men. He smoked a pipe 9
perpetually, but never a cigar. He wore his clothes until they were too shabby to be tolerable; and he held old-fashioned and rather puritanical views as to the vice of luxury and the sin of idleness. The relations between parents and children today have a freedom that would have been impossible with my father. He expected a certain standard of behaviour, even of ceremony, in family life. Yet if freedom means the right to think one's own thoughts and to follow one's own pursuits, then no one respected and indeed insisted upon freedom more completely than he did. His sons, with the exception of the Army and Navy, should follow whatever professions they chose; his daughters, though he cared little enough for the higher education of women, should have the same liberty. If at one moment he rebuked a daughter sharply for smoking a cigarette— smoking was not in his opinion a nice habit in the other sex—she had only to ask him if she might become a painter, and he assured her that

so long as she took her work seriously he would give her all the help he could. He had no special love for painting; but he kept his word. Freedom of that sort was worth thousands of cigarettes.

It was the same with the perhaps more difficult problem of litera-   10
ture. Even today there may be parents who would doubt the wisdom of allowing a girl of fifteen the free run of a large and quite unexpurgated library. But my father allowed it. There were certain facts—very briefly, very shyly he referred to them. Yet "Read what you like," he said, and all his books, "mangy and worthless," as he called them, but certainly they were many and various, were to be had without asking. To read what one liked because one liked it, never to pretend to admire what one did not—that was his only lesson in the art of reading. To write in the fewest possible words, as clearly as possible, exactly what one meant—that was his only lesson in the art of writing. All the rest must be learnt for oneself. Yet a child must have been childish in the extreme not to feel that such was the teaching of a man of great learning and wide experience, though he would never impose his own views or parade his own knowledge. For, as his tailor remarked when he saw my father walk past his shop up Bond Street, "There goes a gentleman that wears good clothes without knowing it."

In those last years, grown solitary and very deaf, he would some-   11
times call himself a failure as a writer; he had been "jack of all trades, and master of none." But whether he failed or succeeded as a writer, it is permissible to believe that he left a distinct impression of himself on the minds of his friends. Meredith saw him as "Phoebus Apollo turned fasting friar" in his earlier days; Thomas Hardy, years later, looked at the "spare and desolate figure" of the Schreckhorn and thought of

> him,
> Who scaled its horn with ventured life and limb,
> Drawn on by vague imaginings, maybe,
> Of semblance to his personality
> In its quaint glooms, keen lights, and rugged trim.

But the praise he would have valued most, for though he was an agnostic nobody believed more profoundly in the worth of human relationships, was Meredith's tribute after his death: "He was the one man to my knowledge worthy to have married your mother." And Lowell, when he called him "L.S., the most lovable of men," has best described the quality that makes him, after all these years, unforgettable.

1931

Purpose and Meaning

1. As a descriptive portrait, this essay is rather unusual for its limited use of physical detail. What characteristics does Woolf choose to emphasize? How do they fit her thesis? In what ways, if any, is her thesis similar to that of Alice Walker's "Father"?

2. Woolf writes of her father's "old fashioned" and "puritanical" views concerning parental-child relations to reach one of her more important points concerning her father's character. What is that quality, and how is it reflected in this essay?

3. Woolf recalls her father calling himself a failure as a writer. She refuses to judge his success, saying only that he left a "distinct impression" of himself on the minds of his friends (paragraph 11). The issue of professional success is less important to Woolf than other measures of "success." Why does Woolf refrain from expressing a judgment? Explain your answer.

Language and Style

1. Woolf writes that her father gave her one lesson in the art of writing. What was it? Does this essay in any way reflect that lesson?

2. How does this essay compare in style to Woolf's other writings represented in this collection? How is it different?

3. Examine the long sentences in paragraph 5. How do they work within the paragraph? What do they add to the style of the essay?

Strategy and Structure

1. Throughout this essay, Woolf recalls several anecdotal incidents. Are these diversions appropriate to her strategy? Why? What do they lend to the essay?

2. How does Wolf structure her paragraphs to present her father's character?

3. How does Woolf's opening affect the reader's expectations of the essay's development? How effective is the opening? Would the essay lose or gain in impact if it were changed?

Thinking and Writing

1. Write an essay that discusses the ways in which Woolf uses both style and subject matter to allow the character of her father to emerge for the reader.

2. Emulating Woolf's approach, write an essay in which you explore your relationship with one of your parents. As she has done, compare the public image of your father or mother with an intimate one.

○●○●○●○●○●○●○●○●○●○●○●○

The Death of the Moth

Moths that fly by day are not properly to be called moths; they do   1
not excite that pleasant sense of dark autumn nights and ivy-blossom
which the commonest yellow underwing asleep in the shadow of the
curtain never fails to rouse in us. They are hybrid creatures, neither gay
like butterflies nor sombre like their own species. Nevertheless the present specimen, with his narrow hay-coloured wings, fringed with a tas-
sel of the same colour, seemed to be content with life. It was a pleasant
morning, mid-September, mild, benignant, yet with a keener breath than
that of the summer months. The plough was already scoring the field
opposite the window, and where the share had been, the earth was
pressed flat and gleamed with moisture. Such vigour came rolling in
from the fields and the down beyond that it was difficult to keep the
eyes strictly turned upon the book. The rooks too were keeping one of
their annual festivities; soaring round the tree-tops until it looked as if a
vast net with thousands of black knots in it has been cast up into the air;
which, after a few moments sank slowly down upon the trees until
every twig seemed to have a knot at the end of it. Then, suddenly, the
net would be thrown into the air again in a wider circle this time, with
the utmost clamour and vociferation, as though to be thrown into the air
and settle slowly down upon the tree-tops were a tremendously exciting
experience.

The same energy which inspired the rooks, the ploughmen, the   2
horses, and even, it seemed, the lean bare-backed downs, sent the moth
fluttering from side to side of his square of the window-pane. One could
not help watching him. One was, indeed, conscious of a queer feeling of
pity for him. The possibilities of pleasure seemed that morning so enormous and so various that to have only a moth's part in life, and a day
moth's at that, appeared a hard fate, and his zest in enjoying his meagre
opportunities to the full, pathetic. He flew vigorously to one corner of
his compartment, and, after waiting there a second, flew across to the
other. What remained for him but to fly to a third corner and then to a
fourth? That was all he could do, in spite of the size of the downs, the
width of the sky, the far-off smoke of houses, and the romantic voice,
now and then, of a steamer out at sea. What he could do he did.
Watching him, it seemed as if a fibre, very thin but pure, of the enormous energy of the world had been thrust into his frail and diminutive

body. As often as he crossed the pane, I could fancy that a thread of vital light became visible. He was little or nothing but life.

Yet, because he was so small, and so simple a form of the energy that was rolling in at the open window and driving its way through so many narrow and intricate corridors in my own brain and in those of other human beings, there was something marvelous as well as pathetic about him. It was as if someone had taken a tiny bead of pure life and decking it as lightly as possible with down and feathers, had set it dancing and zigzagging to show us the true nature of life. Thus displayed one could not get over the strangeness of it. One is apt to forget all about life, seeing it humped and bossed and garnished and cumbered so that it has to move with the greatest circumspection and dignity. Again, the thought of all that life might have been had he been born in any other shape caused one to view his simple activities with a kind of pity.

3

After a time, tired by his dancing apparently, he settled on the window ledge in the sun, and the queer spectacle being at an end, I forgot about him. Then, looking up, my eye was caught by him. He was trying to resume his dancing, but seemed either so stiff or so awkward that he could only flutter to the bottom of the window-pane; and when he tried to fly across it he failed. Being intent on other matters I watched these futile attempts for a time without thinking, unconsciously waiting for him to resume his flight, as one waits for a machine, that has stopped momentarily, to start again without considering the reason for its failure. After perhaps a seventh attempt he slipped from the wooden ledge and fell, fluttering his wings, on to his back on the window-sill. The helplessness of his attitude roused me. It flashed upon me that he was in difficulties; he could no longer raise himself; his legs struggled vainly. But, as I stretched out a pencil, meaning to help him to right himself, it came over me that the failure and awkwardness were the approach of death. I laid the pencil down again.

4

The legs agitated themselves once more. I looked as if for the enemy against which he struggled. I looked out of doors. What had happened there? Presumably it was midday, and work in the fields had stopped. Stillness and quiet had replaced the previous animation. The birds had taken themselves off to feed in the brooks. The horses stood still. Yet the power was there all the same, massed outside indifferent, impersonal, not attending to anything in particular. Somehow it was opposed to the little hay-coloured moth. It was useless to try to do anything. One could only watch the extraordinary efforts made by those tiny legs against an oncoming doom which could, had it chosen, have submerged an entire city, not merely a city, but masses of human beings; nothing, I knew, had any chance against death. Nevertheless after a pause of exhaustion the legs fluttered again. It was superb this last protest, and so frantic that he succeeded at last in righting himself. One's sympathies, of course, were all on the side of life. Also, when there was

5

nobody to care or to know, this gigantic effort on the part of an insignificant little moth, against a power of such magnitude, to retain what no one else valued or desired to keep, moved one strangely. Again, somehow, one saw life, a pure bead. I lifted the pencil again, useless though I knew it to be. But even as I did so, the unmistakable tokens of death showed themselves. The body relaxed, and instantly grew stiff. The struggle was over. The insignificant little creature now knew death. As I looked at the dead moth, this minute wayside triumph of so great a force over so mean an antagonist filled me with wonder. Just as life had been strange a few minutes before, so death was now as strange. The moth having righted himself now lay most decently and uncomplainingly composed. O yes, he seemed to say, death is stronger than I am.

1942

Purpose and Meaning

1. What was your initial response to the title of this essay? How did your response change after you read the essay?

2. What is Woolf's thesis in this essay? Does the tone of the essay suggest a death scene? Does the author maintain an emotional attitude, a rational attitude, or a combination toward the subject matter? How does this attitude affect the reader's understanding of death?

3. What religious or spiritual overtones does Woolf use in handling the subject matter? How do these overtones relate to the thesis of the essay?

Language and Style

1. The author uses the pronoun *one* to describe her own observations and reflections about the scene. What does her word choice suggest about her point of view? How does her use of *one* affect our own attitude toward the writer and her subject?

2. Locate and discuss places in the essay where Woolf combines literal and figurative descriptions.

3. Personification is the description of something nonhuman in human terms. Locate examples of this technique in the essay. For each example, explain what Woolf gains by using personification.

4. Woolf makes several references to abstract concepts such as "pure life," "energy," and "power." Why are these appropriate words for what she is describing? Give examples of other abstractions in the essay.

Strategy and Structure

1. The opening paragraph of this essay is quite long. Why did Woolf give so much attention to the scene outside the window?

2. The moth undergoes a dramatic change during the essay. What changes happen to it from paragraph to paragraph? Similarly, the author seems to undergo a change in her relationship to the moth. Explore the author's change by studying each paragraph individually. Is the change emotional, spiritual, or religious?

3. In the final paragraph of the first essay ("Professions for Women"), Woolf asserts that a woman needs a room in which to flourish and achieve. How does "The Death of the Moth" demonstrate the relationship between having one's own space and the opportunity to be creative?

Thinking and Writing

1. For Woolf, an apparently insignificant event became an occasion for a meditative essay on life, death, nature, and human development. Select a seemingly insignificant event in your own life, and describe it in a way that makes the reader understand that the episode was actually quite important.

2. Do you know of any events or objects that seem to embody principles of life itself? Select a specific object or event (for example, a storm, a bridge, a painting), and compare it to a principle (disorder, structure, harmony).

E. B. WHITE

Perhaps the most distinguished American essayist of our time, Elwyn Brooks White was born in Mount Vernon, New York, on July 11, 1899. The youngest of six children, White, from an early age, treated life in the twentieth century as a wondrous, joyful adventure. "I was a skinny kid but hard," he stated, a latter-day Huck Finn preoccupied by questions of "life, love, war, girls." He was also a child writer, publishing his first work at the age of ten in the *Ladies Home Journal*.

From Mount Vernon High School to Cornell University; from his half-century at the *New Yorker* to his half-century of marriage to Katharine Angell White; from his apartment in New York City to his farm in North Brooklin, Maine, E. B. White molded the American essay to suit his witty, open-minded, democratic vision of the national experience. He specialized, as he stated in a letter to his brother Stanley Hart White, in "the small things of the day, the trivial matters of the heart, the inconsequential but near things of this living." Although White could, in his own words, sound off at times, notably against "progress" and bureaucracy, his typical posture is that of a writer enamored of the discrete particulars of this world. He attends to detail—a treasured camp in "Once More to the Lake," an old car in "Farewell, My Lovely!" a landscape in "Walden," a country schoolhouse in "Education," a circus in the South in "The Ring of Time." White does not let an essay out of his hands until he has captured in it a certain sharp, vibrant physicality of the world. His conversational manner and easy prose style are actually precise, formal instruments with which he measures the wondrous pulse of humanity and earth.

White's mature vision and style emerged during his years as an editor and writer for the *New Yorker*, which he joined as a part-timer in 1927, when the magazine was in its infancy. From 1927 to 1938, White worked at the *New Yorker* in a variety of capacities, writing satirical sketches, essays, poems, editorials, reviews, cartoon captions, and newsbreaks. Many of his contributions appeared anonymously in the magazine's delightful "Talk of the Town" section. White shaped the "New Yorker style"—witty and wise, above all graceful and urbane—more than any other contributor. In 1929, White published two books, *The Lady Is Cold* and, with his friend James Thurber, *Is Sex Necessary?* That same year, he married Katharine S. Angell, the fiction editor of the *New Yorker*.

In early 1938, the Whites left New York to live on a saltwater farm at Allen Cove on the Maine coast, and for years they divided their time between city and country. While continuing to contribute to the *New Yorker*, White also wrote a column for *Harper's* that resulted in *One Man's Meat* (1942). With the publication of *Stuart Little* (1945), *Charlotte's Web* (1952), and *The Trumpet of the Swan* (1972), White achieved fame as a writer of books for children. With his former teacher, William Strunk, Jr., he developed *The Elements of Style* (1959), a concise, lucid guide to writing. His collected *Letters* (1976), *Essays* (1977), and *Poems and Sketches* (1981) are monuments to his career.

When White received the Gold Medal for Essays and Criticism from the National Institute of Arts and Letters in 1960, the presenter, Marchette Chute, captured his achievement. "Of all the gifts he has given us," she stated, "the best gift is himself. He has permitted us to meet a man who is both cheerful and wise, the owner of an uncommon sense that is lit by laughter. When he writes of large subjects he does not make them larger and windier than they are, and when he writes of small things they are never insignificant. He is, in fact, a civilized human being—an order of man that has always been distinguished for its rarity." White received many other awards, including honorary degrees from Harvard and Yale and, from John F. Kennedy in 1963, the first Presidential Medal of Freedom.

White's beloved wife, Katharine, died in 1977. "She seemed beautiful to me the first time I saw her," he wrote in a letter, "and she seemed beautiful when I gave her the small kiss that was goodbye." White had once observed in a *New Yorker* column that we live in a changed world, but in his own life he opted for the old values and loyalties, for reverence and celebration, and above all, for humor—for humor, as he once observed, "is a handy tool on the writer's workbench." E. B. White died in 1985.

Farewell, My Lovely !

(An aging male kisses an old flame good-bye, circa 1936)*

I see by the new Sears Roebuck catalogue that it is still possible to   1
buy an axle for a 1909 Model T Ford, but I am not deceived. The great
days have faded, the end is in sight. Only one page in the current catalogue is devoted to parts and accessories for the Model T; yet everyone remembers springtimes when the Ford gadget section was larger than men's
clothing, almost as large as household furnishings. The last Model T was
built in 1927, and the car is fading from what scholars call the American
scene—which is an understatement, because to a few million people who
grew up with it, the old Ford practically *was* the American scene.

It was the miracle God had wrought. And it was patently the sort   2
of thing that could only happen once. Mechanically uncanny, it was like
nothing that had ever come to the world before. Flourishing industries
rose and fell with it. As a vehicle, it was hard-working, commonplace,
heroic, and it often seemed to transmit those qualities to the persons
who rode in it. My own generation identifies it with Youth, with its
gaudy, irretrievable excitements; before it fades into the mist, I would
like to pay it the tribute of the sigh that is not a sob, and set down random entries in a shape somewhat less cumbersome than a Sears
Roebuck catalogue.

The Model T was distinguished from all other makes of cars by the   3
fact that its transmission was of a type known as planetary—which was
half metaphysics, half sheer friction. Engineers accepted the word "planetary" in its epicyclic sense, but I was always conscious that it also
meant "wandering," "erratic." Because of the peculiar nature of this
planetary element, there was always, in Model T, a certain dull rapport
between engine and wheels, and even when the car was in a state
known as neutral, it trembled with a deep imperative and tended to inch
forward. There was never a moment when the bands were not faintly
egging the machine on. In this respect it was like a horse, rolling the bit
on its tongue, and country people brought to it the same technique they
used with draft animals.

*This piece originally appeared in the *New Yorker* over the pseudonym Lee
Strout White. It was suggested by a manuscript submitted by Richard L. Strout,
of the *Christian Science Monitor*, and Mr. Strout, an amiable collaborator, has
kindly allowed me to include it in this collection. The piece was published as a
little book by G. P. Putnam's Sons in 1936, *Farewell to Model T*.

Its most remarkable quality was its rate of acceleration. In its palmy   4
days the Model T could take off faster than anything on the road. The reason was simple. To get under way, you simply hooked the third finger of
the right hand around a lever on the steering column, pulled down hard,
and shoved your left foot forcibly against the low-speed pedal. These
were simple, positive motions; the car responded by lunging forward
with a roar. After a few seconds of this turmoil, you took your toe off the
pedal, eased up a mite on the throttle, and the car, possessed of only two
forward speeds, catapulted directly into high with a series of ugly jerks
and was off on its glorious errand. The abruptness of this departure was
never equaled in other cars of the period. The human leg was (and still is)
incapable of letting in a clutch with anything like the forthright abandon
that used to send Model T on its way. Letting in a clutch is a negative,
hesitant motion, depending on delicate nervous control; pushing down
the Ford pedal was a simple, country motion—an expansive act, which
came as natural as kicking an old door to make it budge.

The driver of the old Model T was a man enthroned. The car, with   5
top up, stood seven feet high. The driver sat on top of the gas tank,
brooding it with his own body. When he wanted gasoline, he alighted,
along with everything else in the front seat; the seat was pulled off, the
metal cap unscrewed, and a wooden stick thrust down to sound the liquid in the well. There were always a couple of these sounding sticks
around in the ratty sub-cushion regions of a flivver. Refueling was more
of a social function then, because the driver had to unbend, whether he
wanted to or not. Directly in front of the driver was the windshield—
high, uncompromisingly erect. Nobody talked about air resistance, and
the four cylinders pushed the car through the atmosphere with a simple
disregard of physical law.

There was this about a Model T: the purchaser never regarded his   6
purchase as a complete, finished product. When you bought a Ford, you
figured you had a start—a vibrant, spirited framework to which could
be screwed an almost limitless assortment of decorative and functional
hardware. Driving away from the agency, hugging the new wheel between your knees, you were already full of creative worry. A Ford was
born naked as a baby, and a flourishing industry grew up out of correct-
ing its rare deficiencies and combatting its fascinating diseases. Those
were the great days of lily-painting. I have been looking at some old
Sears Roebuck catalogues, and they bring everything back so clear.

First you bought a Ruby Safety Reflector for the rear, so that your   7
posterior would glow in another's car's brilliance. Then you invested
thirty-nine cents in some radiator Moto Wings, a popular ornament
which gave the Pegasus touch to the machine and did something god-
like to the owner. For nine cents you bought a fanbelt guide to keep the
belt from slipping off the pulley.

You bought a radiator compound to stop leaks. This was as much a [8]
part of everybody's equipment as aspirin tablets are of a medicine cabinet. You bought special oil to prevent chattering, a clamp-on dash light, a patching outfit, a tool box which you bolted to the running board, a sun visor, a steering-column brace to keep the column rigid, and a set of emergency containers for gas, oil, and water—three thin, disc-like cans which reposed in a case on the running board during long, important journeys—red for gas, gray for water, green for oil. It was only a beginning. After the car was about a year old, steps were taken to check the alarming disintegration. (Model T was full of tumors, but they were benign.) A set of anti-rattlers (ninety-eight cents) was a popular panacea. You hooked them on to the gas and spark rods, to the brake pull rod, and to the steering-rod connections. Hood silencers, of black rubber, were applied to the fluttering hood. Shock-absorbers and snubbers gave "complete relaxation." Some people bought rubber pedal pads, to fit over the standard metal pedals. (I didn't like these, I remember.) Persons of a suspicious or pugnacious turn of mind bought a rear-view mirror; but most Model T owners weren't worried by what was coming from behind because they would soon enough see it out in front. They rode in a state of cheerful catalepsy. Quite a large mutinous clique among Ford owners went over to a foot accelerator (you could buy one and screw it to the floor board), but there was a certain madness in these people, because the Model T, just as she stood, had a choice of three foot pedals to push, and there were plenty of moments when both feet were occupied in the routine performance of duty and when the only way to speed up the engine was with the hand throttle.

Gadget bred gadget. Owners not only bought ready-made gadgets, [9]
they invented gadgets to meet special needs. I myself drove my car directly from the agency to the blacksmith's, and had the smith affix two enormous iron brackets to the port running board to support an army trunk.

People who owned closed models builded along different lines: [10]
they bought ball grip handles for opening doors, window antirattlers, and deluxe flower vases of the cut-glass antisplash type. People with delicate sensibilities garnished their car with a device called the Donna Lee Automobile Disseminator—a porous vase guaranteed, according to Sears, to fill the car with a "faint clean odor of lavender." The gap between open cars and closed cars was not as great then as it is now: for $11.95, Sears Roebuck converted your touring car into a sedan and you went forth renewed. One agreeable quality of the old Fords was that they had no bumpers, and their fenders softened and wilted with the years and permitted the driver to squeeze in and out of tight places.

Tires were 30 × 3½, cost about $12, and punctured readily. [11]

Everybody carried a Jiffy patching set, with a nutmeg grater to roughen the tube before the goo was spread on. Everybody was capable of putting on a patch, expected to have to, and did have to.

During my association with Model T's, self-starters were not a prevalent accessory. They were expensive and under suspicion. Your car came equipped with a serviceable crank, and the first thing you learned was how to Get Results. It was a special trick, and until you learned it (usually from another Ford owner, but sometimes by a period of appalling experimentation) you might as well have been winding up an awning. The trick was to leave the ignition switch off, proceed to the animal's head, pull the choke (which was a little wire protruding through the radiator) and give the crank two or three nonchalant upward lifts. Then, whistling as though thinking about something else, you would saunter back to the driver's cabin, turn the ignition on, return to the crank, and this time, catching it on the down stroke, give it a quick spin with plenty of that. If this procedure was followed, the engine almost always responded—first with a few scattered explosions, then with a tumultuous gunfire, which you checked by racing around to the driver's seat and retarding the throttle. Often, if the emergency brake hadn't been pulled all the way back, the car advanced on you the instant the first explosion occurred and you would hold it back by leaning your weight against it. I can still feel my old Ford nuzzling me at the curb, as though looking for an apple in my pocket.   12

In zero weather, ordinary cranking became an impossibility, except for giants. The oil thickened, and it became necessary to jack up the rear wheels, which, for some planetary reason, eased the throw.   13

The lore and legend that governed the Ford were boundless. Owners had their own theories about everything; they discussed mutual problems in that wise, infinitely resourceful way old women discuss rheumatism. Exact knowledge was pretty scarce, and often proved less effective than superstition. Dropping a camphor ball into the gas tank was a popular expedient; it seemed to have a tonic effect on both man and machine. There wasn't much to base exact knowledge on. The Ford driver flew blind. He didn't know the temperature of his engine, the speed of his car, the amount of his fuel, or the pressure of his oil (the old Ford lubricated itself by what was amiably described as the "splash system"). A speedometer cost money and was an extra, like a windshield wiper. The dashboard of the early models was bare save for an ignition key; later models, grown effete, boasted an ammeter which pulsated alarmingly with the throbbing of the car. Under the dash was a box of coils, with vibrators which you adjusted, or thought you adjusted. Whatever the driver learned of his motor, he learned not through instru-   14 ments but through sudden developments. I remember that the timer was one of the vital organs about which there was ample doctrine. When everything else had been checked, you "had a look" at the timer. It was an extravagantly odd little device, simple in construction, mysterious in function. It contained a roller, held by a spring, and there were four contact points on the inside of the case against which, many people believed, the roller rolled. I have had a timer apart on a sick Ford many times. But I never really knew what I was up to—I was just showing off before God. There were almost as many schools of thought as there were timers. Some people, when things went wrong, just clenched their teeth and gave the timer a smart crack with a wrench. Other people opened it up and blew on it. There was a school that held that the timer needed large amounts of oil; they fixed it by frequent baptism. And there was a school that was positive it was meant to run dry as a bone; these people were continually taking it off and wiping it. I remember once spitting into a timer; not in anger, but in a spirit of research. You see, the Model T driver moved in the realm of metaphysics. He believed his car could be hexed.

One reason the Ford anatomy was never reduced to an exact science was that, having "fixed" it, the owner couldn't honestly claim that the treatment had brought about the cure. There were too many authenticated cases of Fords fixing themselves—restored naturally to health after a short rest. Farmers soon discovered this, and it fitted nicely with their draft-horse philosophy: "Let 'er clear off and she'll snap into it again."   15

A Ford owner had Number One Bearing constantly in mind. This bearing, being at the front end of the motor, was the one that always burned out, because the oil didn't reach it when the car was climbing hills. (That's what I was always told, anyway.) The oil used to recede and leave Number One dry as a clam flat; you had to watch that bearing like a hawk. It was like a weak heart—you could hear it start knocking, and that was when you stopped to let her cool off. Try as you would to keep the oil supply right, in the end Number One always went out. "Number One Bearing burned out on me and I had to have her replaced," you would say, wisely; and your companions always had a lot to tell about how to protect and pamper Number One to keep her alive.   16

Sprinkled not too liberally among the millions of amateur witch doctors who drove Fords and applied their own abominable cures were the heaven-sent mechanics who could really make the car talk. These professionals turned up in undreamed-of spots. One time, on the banks of the Columbia River in Washington, I heard the rear end go out of my Model T when I was trying to whip it up a steep incline onto the deck of a ferry. Something snapped; the car slid backward into the mud. It seemed to me like the end of the trail. But the captain of the ferry, observing the withered remnant, spoke up.   17

"What's got her?" he asked.   18

"I guess it's the rear end," I replied, listlessly. The captain leaned   19
over the rail and stared. Then I saw that there was a hunger in his eyes
that set him off from other men.

"Tell you what," he said, carelessly, trying to cover up his eager-   20
ness, "Let's pull the son of a bitch up onto the boat, and I'll help you fix
her while we're going back and forth on the river."

We did just this. All that day I plied between the towns of Pasco   21
and Kennewick, while the skipper (who had once worked in a Ford
garage) directed the amazing work of resetting the bones of my car.

Springtime in the heyday of the Model T was a delirious season.   22
Owning a car was still a major excitement, roads were still wonderful
and bad. The Fords were obviously conceived in madness: any car
which was capable of going from forward into reverse without any perceptible mechanical hiatus was bound to be a mighty challenging thing
to the human imagination. Boys used to veer them off the highway into
a level pasture and run wild with them, as though they were cutting up
with a girl. Most everybody used the reverse pedal quite as much as the
regular foot brake—it distributed the wear over the bands and wore
them all down evenly. That was the big trick, to wear all the bands
down evenly, so that the final chattering would be total and the whole
unit scream for renewal.

The days were golden, the nights were dim and strange. I still re-   23
call with trembling those loud, nocturnal crises when you drew up to a
signpost and raced the engine so the lights would be bright enough to
read destinations by. I have never been really planetary since. I suppose
it's time to say good-bye. Farewell, my lovely!

1936

Purpose and Meaning

1. According to White, what is the underlying property of the Model T that
   makes it so appealing? Why does he describe its mechanics in glowing
   terms?

2. In paragraph 1, White refers to the "great days" in American history. What
   is the significance of the word *great*? What era is he referring to? What was
   life like then, particularly in the realm of technology? Notice the reference
   to the time the essay was written (1936). What were the historical and social contexts of that era?

3. White uses considerable hyperbole in the first three paragraphs. He says
   the Model T "practically *was* the American scene"; "It was the miracle God

had wrought"; its transmission was "half metaphysics." How do these observations help determine the tone of the essay?

Language and Style

1. White's descriptions suggest that the Model T had a life of its own. (For example, in paragraph 14, White refers to the auto's "vital organs.") Specifically, where and how does the author use personification to transmit this impression?

2. We easily recognize humor in television and film comedies and in jokes comedians tell. What stylistic elements make this essay humorous? In reading the essay, how long did it take until you became aware of its comic tone? What specific elements made you aware of this tone?

Strategy and Structure

1. How does White employ process analysis to organize large segments of this essay?

2. Why does White divide the essay into three sections?

3. How does White structure paragraph 14 so that it is an effective unit of writing? How does the opening sentence of the paragraph contribute to its unity?

4. Study the opening sentences of each paragraph. Which of these serve as the topic for the rest of the paragraph? Is this strategy an effective means of structuring an essay? Explain.

Thinking and Writing

1. Discuss the concept of nostalgia in class. What makes an object or era nostalgic? Consider some of the nostalgic interests people have in society today: old movies, out-of-fashion clothes, antique television sets and radios, the fifties. Select one of these or something else nostalgic of your own choosing and describe what makes it so. Making a list of its properties may be an effective means of brainstorming the subject.

2. Examine the work of a contemporary writer of humor (for example, Clive James's essay in this book). Write an essay evaluating what makes the writing funny.

3. Interview one of your parents or someone from your parents' generation about his or her childhood or youth. Focus on those things, people, or events that are recalled with nostalgia. Ask what role these things played in the person's life. Then write an account of your findings.

o🔴o🔴o🔴o🔴o

Walden

Miss Nims, take a letter to Henry David Thoreau. Dear Henry: I   1
thought of you the other afternoon as I was approaching Concord doing
fifty on Route 62. That is a high speed at which to hold a philosopher in
one's mind, but in this century we are a nimble bunch.

On one of the lawns in the outskirts of the village a woman was   2
cutting the grass with a motorized lawn mower. What made me think of
you was that the machine had rather got away from her, although she
was game enough, and in the brief glimpse I had of the scene it appeared to me that the lawn was mowing the lady. She kept a tight grip
on the handles, which throbbed violently with every explosion of the
one-cylinder motor, and as she sheered around bushes and lurched
along at a reluctant trot behind her impetuous servant, she looked like a
puppy who had grabbed something that was too much for him.
Concord hasn't changed much, Henry; the farm implements and the animals still have the upper hand.

I may as well admit that I was journeying to Concord with the de-   3
liberate intention of visiting your woods; for although I have never knelt
at the grave of a philosopher nor placed wreaths on moldy poets, and
have often gone a mile out of my way to avoid some place of historical
interest, I have always wanted to see Walden Pond. The account which
you left of your sojourn there is, you will be amused to learn, a docu-
ment of increasing pertinence; each year it seems to gain a little head-
way, as the world loses ground. We may all be transcendental yet,
whether we like it or not. As our common complexities increase, any tale
of individual simplicity (and yours is the best written and the cockiest)
acquires a new fascination; as our goods accumulate, but not our well-
being, your report of an existence without material adornment takes on
a certain awkward credibility.

My purpose in going to Walden Pond, like yours, was not to live   4
cheaply or to live dearly there, but to transact some private business
with the fewest obstacles. Approaching Concord, doing forty, doing
forty-five, doing fifty, the steering wheel held snug in my palms, the
highway held grimly in my vision, the crown of the road now serving
me (on the righthand curves), now defeating me (on the lefthand
curves), I began to rouse myself from the stupefaction which a day's
motor journey induces. It was a delicious evening, Henry, when the
whole body is one sense, and imbibes delight through every pore, if I

may coin a phrase. Fields were richly brown where the harrow, drawn by the stripped Ford, had lately sunk its teeth; pastures were green; and overhead the sky had that same everlasting great look which you will find on Page 144 of the Oxford pocket edition. I could feel the road entering me, through tire, wheel, spring, and cushion; shall I not have intelligence with earth too? Am I not partly leaves and vegetable mold myself?—a man of infinite horsepower, yet partly leaves.

Stay with me on 62 and it will take you into Concord. As I say, it 5 was a delicious evening. The snake had come forth to die in a bloody S on the highway, the wheel upon its head, its bowels flat now and exposed. The turtle had come up too to cross the road and die in the attempt, its hard shell smashed under the rubber blow, its intestinal yearning (for the other side of the road) forever squashed. There was a sign by the wayside which announced that the road had a "cotton surface." You wouldn't know what that is, but neither, for that matter, did I. There is a cryptic ingredient in many of our modern improvements—we are awed and pleased without knowing quite what we are enjoying. It is something to be traveling on a road with a cotton surface.

The civilization round Concord today is an odd distillation of city, 6 village, farm, and manor. The houses, yards, fields look not quite suburban, not quite rural. Under the bronze beech and the blue spruce of the departed baron grazes the milch goat of the heirs. Under the porte-cochère stands the reconditioned station wagon; under the grape arbor sit the puppies for sale. (But why do men degenerate ever? What makes families run out?)

It was June and everywhere June was publishing her immemorial 7 stanza; in the lilacs, in the syringa, in the freshly edged paths and the sweetness of moist beloved gardens, and the little wire wickets that preserve the tulips' front. Farmers were already moving the fruits of their toil into their yards, arranging the rhubarb, the asparagus, the strictly fresh eggs on the painted stands under the little shed roofs with the patent shingles. And though it was almost a hundred years since you had taken your ax and started cutting out your home on Walden Pond, I was interested to observe that the philosophical spirit was still alive in Massachusetts: in the center of a vacant lot some boys were assembling the framework of a rude shelter, their whole mind and skill concentrated in the rather inauspicious helter-skeleton of studs and rafters. They too were escaping from town, to live naturally, in a rich blend of savagery and philosophy.

That evening, after supper at the inn, I strolled out into the twilight 8 to dream my shapeless transcendental dreams and see that the car was locked up for the night (first open the right front door, then reach over, straining, and pull up the handles of the left rear and the left front till you hear the click, then the handle of the right rear, then shut the right front but open it again, remembering that the key is still in the ignition switch, remove the key, shut the right front again with a bang, push the tiny keyhole cover to one side, insert key, turn, and withdraw). It is what we all do, Henry. It is called locking the car. It is said to confuse thieves and keep them from making off with the laprobe. Four doors to lock behind one robe. The driver himself never uses a laprobe, the free movement of his legs being vital to the operation of the vehicle; so that when he locks the car it is a pure and unselfish act. I have in my life gained very little essential heat from laprobes, yet I have ever been at pains to lock them up.

The evening was full of sounds, some of which would have stirred your memory. The robins still love the elms of New England villages at sundown. There is enough of the thrush in them to make song inevitable at the end of day, and enough of the tramp to make them hang round the dwellings of men. A robin, like many another American, dearly loves a white house with green blinds. Concord is still full of them. 9

Your fellow-townsmen were stirring abroad—not many afoot, most of them in their cars; and the sound which they made in Concord at evening was a rustling and a whispering. The sound lacks steadfastness and is wholly unlike that of a train. A train, as you know who lived so near the Fitchburg line, whistles once or twice sadly and is gone, trailing a memory in smoke, soothing to ear and mind. Automobiles, skirting a village green, are like flies that have gained the inner ear—they buzz, cease, pause, start, shift, stop, halt, brake, and the whole effect is a nervous polytone curiously disturbing. 10

As I wandered along, the toc toc of ping pong balls drifted from an attic window. In front of the Reuben Brown house a Buick was drawn up. At the wheel, motionless, his hat upon his head, a man sat, listening to Amos and Andy on the radio (it is a drama of many scenes and without an end). The deep voice of Andrew Brown, emerging from the car, although it originated more than two hundred miles away, was unstrained by distance. When you used to sit on the shore of your pond on Sunday morning, listening to the church bells of Acton and Concord, you were aware of the excellent filter of the intervening atmosphere. Science has attended to that, and sound now maintains its intensity without regard for distance. Properly sponsored, it goes on forever. 11

A fire engine, out for a trial spin, roared past Emerson's house, hot with readiness for public duty. Over the barn roofs the martins dipped and chittered. A swarthy daughter of an asparagus grower, in culottes, shirt, and bandanna, pedalled past on her bicycle. It was indeed a delicious evening, and I returned to the inn (I believe it was your house once) to rock with the old ladies on the concrete veranda. 12

Next morning early I started afoot for Walden, out Main Street and down Thoreau, past the depot and the Minuteman Chevrolet Company. The morning was fresh, and in a bean field along the way I flushed an agriculturalist, quietly studying his beans. Thoreau Street soon joined 13

Number 126, an artery of the State. We number our highways nowadays, our speed being so great we can remember little of their quality or character and are lucky to remember their number. (Men have an indistinct notion that if they keep up this activity long enough all will at length ride somewhere, in next to no time.) Your pond is on 126.

I knew I must be nearing your woodland retreat when the Golden   14
Pheasant lunchroom came into view—Sealtest ice cream, toasted sandwiches, hot frankfurters, waffles, tonics, and lunches. Were I the proprietor, I should add rice, Indian meal, and molasses—just for old time's sake. The Pheasant, incidentally, is for sale: a chance for some nature lover who wishes to set himself up beside a pond in the Concord atmosphere and live deliberately, fronting only the essential facts of life on Number 126. Beyond the Pheasant was a place called Walden Breezes, an oasis whose porch pillars were made of old green shutters sawed into lengths. On the porch was a distorting mirror, to give the traveler a comical image of himself, who had miraculously learned to gaze in an ordinary glass without smiling. Behind the Breezes, in a sun-parched clearing, dwelt your philosophical descendants in their trailers, each trailer the size of your hut, but all grouped together for the sake of congeniality. Trailer people leave the city, as you did, to discover solitude and in any weather, at any hour of the day or night, to improve the nick of time; but they soon collect in villages and get bogged deeper in the mud than ever. The camp behind Walden Breezes was just rousing itself to the morning. The ground was packed hard under the heel, and the sun came through the clearing to bake the soil and enlarge the wry smell of cramped housekeeping. Cushman's bakery truck had stopped to deliver an early basket of rolls. A camp dog, seeing me in the road, barked petulantly. A man emerged from one of the trailers and set forth with a bucket to draw water from some forest tap.

Leaving the highway I turned off into the woods toward the pond,   15
which was apparent through the foliage. The floor of the forest was strewn with dried old oak leaves and *Transcripts*. From beneath the flattened popcorn wrapper (*granum explosum*) peeped the frail violet. I followed a footpath and descended to the water's edge. The pond lay clear and blue in the morning light, as you have seen it so many times. In the shallows a man's waterlogged shirt undulated gently. A few flies came out to greet me and convoy me to your cove, past the No Bathing signs on which the fellows and the girls had scrawled their names. I felt strangely excited suddenly to be snooping around your premises, tiptoeing along watchfully, as though not to tread by mistake upon the intervening century. Before I got to the cove I heard something which seemed to me quite wonderful: I heard your frog, a full, clear *troonk*, guiding me, still hoarse and solemn, bridging the years as the robins had bridged them in the sweetness of the village evening. But he soon quit, and I came on a couple of young boys throwing stones at him.

Your front yard is marked by a bronze tablet set in a stone. Four   16
small granite posts, a few feet away, show where the house was. On top
of the tablet was a pair of faded blue bathing trunks with a white stripe.
Back of it is a pile of stones, a sort of cairn, left by your visitors as a tribute I suppose. It is a rather ugly little heap of stones, Henry. In fact the
hillside itself seems faded, browbeaten; a few tall skinny pines, bare of
lower limbs, a smattering of young maples in suitable green, some
birches and oaks, and a number of trees felled by the last big wind. It
was from the bole of one of these fallen pines, torn up by the roots, that I
extracted the stone which I added to the cairn—a sentimental act in
which I was interrupted by a small terrier from a nearby picnic group,
who confronted me and wanted to know about the stone.

I sat down for a while on one of the posts of your house to listen to   17
the bluebottles and the dragonflies. The invaded glade sprawled shabby
and mean at my feet, but the flies were tuned to the old vibration. There
were the remains of a fire in your ruins, but I doubt that it was yours;
also two beer bottles trodden into the soil and become part of earth. A
young oak had taken root in your house, and two or three ferns, un-
rolling like the ticklers at a banquet. The only other furnishings were a
DuBarry pattern sheet, a page torn from a picture magazine, and some
crusts in wax paper.

Before I quit I walked clear round the pond and found the place   18
where you used to sit on the northeast side to get the sun in the fall, and
the beach where you got sand for scrubbing your floor. On the eastern
side of the pond, where the highway borders it, the State has built dressing rooms for swimmers, a float with diving towers, drinking fountains
of porcelain, and rowboats for hire. The pond is in fact a State Preserve,
and carries a twenty-dollar fine for picking wild flowers, a decree signed
in all solemnity by your fellow-citizens Walter C. Wardwell, Erson B.
Barlow, and Nathaniel I. Bowditch. There was a smell of creosote where
they had been building a wide wooden stairway to the road and the
parking area. Swimmers and boaters were arriving; bodies plunged vigorously into the water and emerged wet and beautiful in the bright air.
As I left, a boatload of town boys were splashing about in mid-pond,
kidding and fooling, the young fellows singing at the tops of their lungs
in a wild chorus:

> Amer-ica, Amer-i-ca, God shed his grace on thee,
> And crown thy good with brotherhood
> From sea to shi-ning sea!

I walked back to town along the railroad, following your custom.   19
The rails were expanding noisily in the hot sun, and on the slope of the
roadbed the wild grape and the blackberry sent up their creepers to the
track.

The expense of my brief sojourn in Concord was: 20

Canvas shoes..............................	$1.95	
Baseball bat	.25	} gifts to take back
Left-handed fielder's glove........	1.25	to a boy
Hotel and meals..........................	4.25	
In all	$7.70	

As you see, this amount was almost what you spent for food for eight   20
months. I cannot defend the shoes or the expenditure for shelter and
food: they reveal a meanness and grossness in my nature which you
would find contemptible. The baseball equipment, however, is the kind
of impediment with which you were never on even terms. You must remember that the house where you practiced the sort of economy which I
respect was haunted only by mice and squirrels. You never had to cope
with a shortstop.

1939

Purpose and Meaning

1. White opens this essay with a directive to "Miss Nims" to take a letter to
   Henry David Thoreau. How appropriate is the opening to White's thesis?
   How effectively does the opening contribute to the essay's tone?

2. In paragraph 2, White mentions that Concord has undergone little change
   since Thoreau's time, yet he notes that the natural world is also much the
   same as it was then (paragraphs 9 and 15). What has changed? How are
   those changes central to White's thesis?

3. In this essay, White meticulously details his observations while at Walden
   Pond, a technique he also uses in "Once More to the Lake." How does his
   use of fine detail differ in the two essays?

Language and Style

1. White often alludes to Thoreau's *Walden* throughout his essay of the same
   title. What assumptions about his audience is White making by doing this?

2. White uses particularly vivid verbs in this essay. Find several of the memorable ones, and discuss what they add to the overall effectiveness of the
   essay. If they were changed, would the effectiveness of the essay be
   changed? How?

3. In several places, White chooses figurative language in describing his experience at Walden. How effective is such usage in making his point? Does it add to or detract from the essay? Explain your answer.

4. Explain White's use of the word *transcripts* in paragraph 14. How does it contribute to the essay's tone?

Strategy and Structure

1. White uses several different organizational patterns in this essay. How are paragraphs 3 and 4 structured? How is paragraph 8 structured? How does his use of several patterns strengthen the essay's effectiveness?

2. How does the essay's loose chronological pattern work with White's strategy?

3. How does the final paragraph contribute to the essay's overall structure?

Thinking and Writing

1. Like many of White's other essays, "Walden" makes significant observations about contemporary society. Discuss the similarities and differences between White's observations in "Walden" with those of Barry Lopez in "The Stone Horse."

2. Develop an essay in which you describe the effects of visitors upon a particular scenic location that you know well.

3. Using White's format as a model, write a letter to an American writer in which you ironically comment on a particularly effective evocation of a landscape, such as Mark Twain's description of the Mississippi river in *Old Times on the Mississippi* or in *Huckleberry Finn*.

○●○●○●○●○●○●○

Education

I have an increasing admiration for the teacher in the country school where we have a third-grade scholar in attendance. She not only undertakes to instruct her charges in all the subjects of the first three grades, but she manages to function quietly and effectively as a guardian of their health, their clothes, their habits, their mothers, and their snowball engagements. She has been doing this sort of Augean task for twenty years, and is both kind and wise. She cooks for the children on the stove that heats the room, and she can cool their passions or warm their soup with equal competence. She conceives their costumes, cleans up their messes, and shares their confidences. My boy already regards his teacher as his great friend, and I think tells her a great deal more than he tells me.

The shift from city school to country school was something we worried about quietly all last summer. I have always rather favored public school over private school, if only because in public school you meet a greater variety of children. This bias of mine, I suspect, is partly an attempt to justify my own past (I never knew anything but public schools) and partly an involuntary defense against getting kicked in the shins by a young ceramist on his way to the kiln. My wife was unacquainted with public schools, never having been exposed (in her early life) to anything more public than the washroom of Miss Winsor's. Regardless of our backgrounds, we both knew that the change in schools was something that concerned not us but the scholar himself. We hoped it would work out all right. In New York our son went to a medium-priced private institution with semi-progressive ideas of education and modern plumbing. He learned fast, kept well, and we were satisfied. It was an electric, colorful, regimented existence with moments of pleasurable pause and giddy incident. The day the Christmas angel fainted and had to be carried out by one of the Wise Men was educational in the highest sense of the term. Our scholar gave imitations of it around the house for weeks afterward, and I doubt if it ever goes completely out of his mind.

His days were rich in formal experience. Wearing overalls and an old sweater (the accepted uniform of the private seminary), he sallied forth at morn accompanied by a nurse or a parent and walked (or was pulled) two blocks to a corner where the school bus made a flag stop. This flashy vehicle was as punctual as death: seeing us waiting at the cold curb, it would sweep to a halt, open its mouth, suck the boy in, and spring away with an angry growl. It was a good deal like a train picking up a bag of mail. At school the scholar was worked on for six or seven hours by half a dozen teachers and a nurse, and was revived on orange juice in mid-morning. In a cinder court he played games supervised by an athletic instructor, and in a cafeteria he ate lunch worked out by a dietitian. He soon learned to read with gratifying facility and discernment and to make Indian weapons of a semi-deadly nature. Whenever one of his classmates fell low of a fever the news was put on the wires and there were breathless phone calls to physicians, discussing periods of incubation and allied magic.

In the country all one can say is that the situation is different and somehow more casual. Dressed in corduroys, sweatshirts, and short rubber boots, and carrying a tin dinner-pail, our scholar departs at crack of dawn for the village school, two and a half miles down the road, next to the cemetery. When the road is open and the car will start, he makes the journey by motor, courtesy of his old man. When the snow is deep or the motor is dead or both, he makes it on the hoof. In the afternoons he walks or hitches all or part of the way home in fair weather, gets transported in foul. The schoolhouse is a two-room frame building, bungalow type, shingles stained a burnt brown with weather-resistant stain. It has a chemical toilet in the basement and two teachers above stairs. One takes the first three grades, the other the fourth, fifth, and sixth. They have little or no time for individual instruction, and no time at all for the esoteric. They teach what they know themselves, just as fast and as hard as they can manage. The pupils sit still at their desks in class, and do their milling around outdoors during recess.

There is no supervised play. They play cops and robbers (only they   5
call it "Jail") and throw things at one another—snowballs in winter, rose hips in fall. It seems to satisfy them. They also construct darts, pinwheels, and "pick-up sticks" (jackstraws), and the school itself does a brisk trade in penny candy, which is for sale right in the classroom and which contains "surprises." The most highly prized surprise is a fake cigarette, made of cardboard, fiendishly lifelike.

The memory of how apprehensive we were at the beginning is still   6
strong. The boy was nervous about the change too. The tension, on that first fair morning in September when we drove him to school, almost blew the windows out of the sedan. And when later we picked him up on the road, wandering along with his little blue lunch-pail, and got his laconic report "All right" in answer to our inquiry about how the day had gone, our relief was vast. Now, after almost a year of it, the only difference we can discover in the two school experiences is that in the country he sleeps better at night—and *that* probably is more the air than the education. When grilled on the subject of school-in-country *vs.* school-in-city, he replied that the chief difference is that the day seems to go much quicker in the country. "Just like lightning," he reported.

1939

Purpose and Meaning

1. To what does the title specifically refer: White's child's education? White's own education? education in a general sense? What clues in the essay lead you to this conclusion?

2. How do the diverse roles that White's son's teacher performs compare with the functions of today's teachers? What activities described in paragraph 1 and in other paragraphs "date" the essay?

3. Why does White favor public schools?

4. Although the author does not mention his economic or social status directly, what clues does he provide that indicate his background? Does he implicitly assume that the reader is of the same background as he? What evidence is there in the essay for your answer?

Language and Style

1. In paragraph 2, White mentions that "the day the Christmas angel fainted and had to be carried out by one of the Wise Men was educational in the highest sense of the term." What does he mean by "educational"? Does this experience fulfill the requirements of your own definition of "educational"?

2. Today, discussions of education are often heated and argumentative. What contributes to the calm, even-tempered tone of this essay? Is it the difference in attitude toward education then and now? Is it a question of style? Explain your answer.

3. Some of White's sentences are lengthy without being confusing. Consider the following from paragraph 3: "Wearing overalls and an old sweater (the accepted uniform of the private seminary), he sallied forth at morn accompanied by a nurse or a parent and walked (or was pulled) two blocks to a corner where the school bus made a flag stop." Does this sentence demonstrate "good" writing? If so, why? If not, why not? Find other lengthy sentences in the essay and analyze them for clarity. Note how phrases relate to the basic subject-verb pattern of the sentence.

4. Consider the syntax and vocabulary in the following sentence from paragraph 2 and discuss how they are characteristic of White's prose style: "It was an electric, colorful, regimented existence with moments of pleasurable pause and giddy incident."

Strategy and Structure

1. The opening focuses on a teacher. However, she is not mentioned again in the essay. Why does White introduce the essay's subject matter in this way? Is it confusing or is it effective?

2. How does White employ comparison and contrast to advance his argument? What, specifically, is compared, and what contrasted?

3. What does the response in the last sentence "Just like lightning . . . " reveal about the son's educational development? Why do you suppose White ended the essay with it?

Thinking and Writing

1. Imagine that the last paragraph of White's essay has been destroyed. Write your own conclusion to the essay, imitating the style of the author. Compare your version to the original. How are they similar or different in terms of tone, syntax, vocabulary, and voice?

2. Write an essay describing one type of informal education that children receive today that differs from the type White's son received. For example, what type of education does one receive from television? city streets? video games?

3. Write an essay comparing urban, suburban, and rural education in America today. Draw conclusions about the superiority of one to the others.

○●○●○●○●○●○●○●○●○●○●○●○●○

Once More to the Lake

One summer, along about 1904, my father rented a camp on a lake in Maine and took us all there for the month of August. We all got ringworm from some kittens and had to rub Pond's Extract on our arms and legs night and morning, and my father rolled over in a canoe with all his clothes on; but outside of that the vacation was a success and from then on none of us ever thought there was any place in the world like that lake in Maine. We returned summer after summer—always on August 1 for one month. I have since become a salt-water man, but sometimes in summer there are days when the restlessness of the tides and the fearful cold of the sea water and the incessant wind that blows across the afternoon and into the evening make me wish for the placidity of a lake in the woods. A few weeks ago this feeling got so strong I bought myself a couple of bass hooks and a spinner and returned to the lake where we used to go, for a week's fishing and to revisit old haunts.

I took along my son, who had never had any fresh water up his nose and who had seen lily pads only from train windows. On the journey over to the lake I began to wonder what it would be like. I wondered how time would have marred this unique, this holy spot—the coves and streams, the hills that the sun set behind, the camps and the paths behind the camps. I was sure that the tarred road would have found it out, and I wondered in what other ways it would be desolated. It is strange how much you can remember about places like that once you allow your mind to return into the grooves that lead back. You remember one thing, and that suddenly reminds you of another thing. I guess I remembered clearest of all the early mornings, when the lake was cool and motionless, remembered how the bedroom smelled of the lumber it was made of and of the wet woods whose scent entered through the screen. The partitions in the camp were thin and did not extend clear to the top of the rooms, and as I was always the first up I would dress softly so as not to wake the others, and sneak out into the sweet outdoors and start out in the canoe, keeping close along the shore in the long shadows of the pines. I remembered being very careful never to rub my paddle against the gunwale for fear of disturbing the stillness of the cathedral.

The lake had never been what you would call a wild lake. There 3 were cottages sprinkled around the shores, and it was in farming country although the shores of the lake were quite heavily wooded. Some of the cottages were owned by nearby farmers, and you would live at the shore and eat your meals at the farmhouse. That's what our family did. But although it wasn't wild, it was a fairly large and undisturbed lake and there were places in it that, to a child at least, seemed infinitely remote and primeval.

I was right about the tar; it led to within half a mile of the shore. 4 But when I got back there, with my boy, and we settled into a camp near a farmhouse and into the kind of summertime I had known, I could tell that it was going to be pretty much the same as it had been before—I knew it, lying in bed the first morning, smelling the bedroom and hearing the boy sneak quietly out and go off along the shore in a boat. I began to sustain the illusion that he was I, and therefore, by simple transposition, that I was my father. This sensation persisted, kept cropping up all the time we were there. It was not an entirely new feeling, but in this setting it grew much stronger. I seemed to be living a dual existence. I would be in the middle of some simple act. I would be picking up a bait box or laying down a table fork, or I would be saying something, and suddenly it would be not I but my father who was saying the words or making the gesture. It gave me a creepy sensation.

We went fishing the first morning. I felt the same damp moss cov- 5 ering the worms in the bait can, and saw the dragonfly alight on the tip of my rod as it hovered a few inches from the surface of the water. It was the arrival of this fly that convinced me beyond any doubt that everything was as it always had been, that the years were a mirage and that there had been no years. The small waves were the same, chucking the rowboat under the chin as we fished at anchor, and the boat was the same boat, the same color green and the ribs broken in the same places, and under the floorboards the same fresh-water leavings and débris— the dead helgramite, the wisps of moss, the rusty discarded fishhook, the dried blood from yesterday's catch. We stared silently at the tips of our rods, at the dragonflies that came and went. I lowered the tip of mine into the water, tentatively, pensively dislodging the fly, which darted two feet away, poised, darted two feet back, and came to rest again a little farther up the rod. There had been no years between the ducking of this dragonfly and the other one—the one that was part of memory. I looked at the boy, who was silently watching his fly, and it was my hands that held his rod, my eyes watching. I felt dizzy and didn't know which rod I was at the end of.

We caught two bass, hauling them in briskly as though they were   6
mackerel, pulling them over the side of the boat in a businesslike manner without any landing net, and stunning them with a blow on the back
of the head. When we got back for a swim before lunch, the lake was exactly where we had left it, the same number of inches from the dock, and
there was only the merest suggestion of a breeze. This seemed an utterly
enchanted sea, this lake you could leave to its own devices for a few
hours and come back to, and find that it had not stirred, this constant
and trustworthy body of water. In the shallows, the dark, water-soaked
sticks and twigs, smooth and old, were undulating in clusters on the bottom against the clean ribbed sand, and the track of the mussel was plain.
A school of minnows swam by, each minnow with its small individual
shadow, doubling the attendance, so clear and sharp in the sunlight.
Some of the other campers were in swimming, along the shore, one of
them with a cake of soap, and the water felt thin and clear and unsub-
stantial. Over the years there had been this person with the cake of soap,
this cultist, and here he was. There had been no years.

Up to the farmhouse to dinner through the teeming, dusty field,   7
the road under our sneakers was only a two-track road. The middle
track was missing, the one with the marks of the hooves and the
splotches of dried, flaky manure. There had always been three tracks to
choose from in choosing which track to walk in; now the choice was nar-
rowed down to two. For a moment I missed terribly the middle alternative. But the way led past the tennis court, and something about the way
it lay there in the sun reassured me; the tape had loosened along the
backline, the alleys were green with plantains and other weeds, and the
net (installed in June and removed in September) sagged in the dry
noon, and the whole place steamed with midday heat and hunger and
emptiness. There was a choice of pie for dessert, and one was blueberry
and one was apple, and the waitresses were the same country girls,
there having been no passage of time, only the illusion of it as in a
dropped curtain—the waitresses were still fifteen; their hair had been
washed, that was the only difference—they had been to the movies and
seen the pretty girls with the clean hair.

Summertime, oh, summertime, pattern of life indelible, the fade-   8
proof lake, the woods unshatterable, the pasture with the sweetfern and
the juniper forever and ever, summer without end; this was the background, and the life along the shore was the design, the cottagers with
their innocent and tranquil design, their tiny docks with the flagpole and
the American flag floating against the white clouds in the blue sky, the
little paths over the roots of the trees leading from camp to camp and the
paths leading back to the outhouses and the can of lime for sprinkling,
and at the souvenir counters at the store the miniature birch-bark canoes
and the postcards that showed things looking a little better than they

looked. This was the American family at play, escaping the city heat, wondering whether the newcomers in the camp at the head of the cove were "common" or "nice," wondering whether it was true that the people who drove up for Sunday dinner at the farmhouse were turned away because there wasn't enough chicken.

It seemed to me, as I kept remembering all this, that those times and those summers had been infinitely precious and worth saving. There had been jollity and peace and goodness. The arriving (at the beginning of August) had been so big a business in itself, at the railway station the farm wagon drawn up, the first smell of the pine-laden air, the first glimpse of the smiling farmer, and the great importance of the trunks and your father's enormous authority in such matters, and the feel of the wagon under you for the long ten-mile haul, and at the top of the last long hill catching the first view of the lake after eleven months of not seeing this cherished body of water. The shouts and cries of the other campers when they saw you, and the trunks to be unpacked, to give up their rich burden. (Arriving was less exciting nowadays, when you sneaked up in your car and parked it under a tree near the camp and took out the bags and in five minutes it was all over, no fuss, no loud wonderful fuss about trunks.) 9

Peace and goodness and jollity. The only thing that was wrong now, really, was the sound of the place, an unfamiliar nervous sound of the outboard motors. This was the note that jarred, the one thing that would sometimes break the illusion and set the years moving. In those other summertimes all motors were inboard; and when they were at a little distance, the noise they made was a sedative, an ingredient of summer sleep. They were one-cylinder and two-cylinder engines, and some were make-and-break and some were jump-spark, but they all made a sleepy sound across the lake. The one-lungers throbbed and fluttered, and the twin-cylinder ones purred and purred, and that was a quiet sound, too. But now the campers all had outboards. In the daytime, in the hot mornings, these motors made a petulant, irritable sound; at night, in the still evening when the afterglow lit the water, they whined about one's ears like mosquitoes. My boy loved our rented outboard, and his great desire was to achieve single-handed mastery over it, and authority, and he soon learned the trick of choking it a little (but not too much), and the adjustment of the needle valve. Watching him I would remember the things you could do with the old one-cylinder engine with the heavy flywheel, how you could have it eating out of your hand if you got really close to it spiritually. Motorboats in those days didn't have clutches, and you would make a landing by shutting off the motor at the proper time and coasting in with a dead rudder. But there was a way of reversing them, if you learned the trick, by cutting the switch and putting it on again exactly on the final dying revolution of the flywheel, so that it would kick back against compression and begin reversing. Approaching 10 dock in a strong following breeze, it was difficult to slow up sufficiently by the ordinary coasting method, and if a boy felt he had complete mastery over his motor, he was tempted to keep it running beyond its time and then reverse it a few feet from the dock. It took a cool nerve, because if you threw the switch a twentieth of a second too soon you would catch the flywheel when it still had speed enough to go up past center, and the boat would leap ahead, charging bull-fashion at the dock.

We had a good week at the camp. The bass were biting well and the sun shone endlessly, day after day. We would be tired at night and lie down in the accumulated heat of the little bedrooms after the long hot day and the breeze would stir almost imperceptibly outside and the smell of the swamp drift in through the rusty screens. Sleep would come easily and in the morning the red squirrel would be on the roof, tapping out his gay routine. I kept remembering everything, lying in bed in the mornings—the small steamboat that had a long rounded stern like the lip of a Ubangi, and how quietly she ran on the moonlight sails, when the older boys played their mandolins and the girls sang and we ate doughnuts dipped in sugar, and how sweet the music was on the water in the shining night, and what it had felt like to think about girls then. After breakfast we would go up to the store and the things were in the same place—the minnows in a bottle, the plugs and spinners disarranged and pawed over by the youngsters from the boys' camp, the Fig Newtons and the Beeman's gum. Outside, the road was tarred and cars stood in front of the store. Inside, all was just as it had always been, except there was more Coca-Cola and not so much Moxie and root beer and birch beer and sarsaparilla. We would walk out with the bottle of pop apiece and sometimes the pop would backfire up our noses and hurt. We explored the streams, quietly, where the turtles slid off the sunny logs and dug their way into the soft bottom; and we lay on the town wharf and fed worms to the tame bass. Everywhere we went I had trouble making out which was I, the one walking at my side, the one walking in my pants.

One afternoon while we were there at that lake a thunderstorm came up. It was like the revival of an old melodrama that I had seen long ago with childish awe. The second-act climax of the drama of the electrical disturbance over a lake in America had not changed in any important respect. This was the big scene, still the big scene. The whole thing was so familiar, the first feeling of oppression and heat and a general air around the camp of not wanting to go very far away. In midafternoon (it was all the same) a curious darkening of the sky, and a lull in everything that had made life tick; and then the way the boats suddenly swung the other way at their moorings with the coming of a breeze out of the new quarter, and the premonitory rumble. Then the kettle drum, then the snare, then the bass drum and cymbals, then crackling light against the dark, and the gods grinning and licking their chops

11

12

in the hills. Afterward the calm, the rain steadily rustling in the calm lake, the return of light and hope and spirits, and the campers running out in joy and relief to go swimming in the rain, their bright cries perpetuating the deathless joke about how they were getting simply drenched, and the children screaming with delight at the new sensation of bathing in the rain, and the joke about getting drenched linking the generations in a strong indestructible chain. And the comedian who waded in carrying an umbrella.

When the others went swimming, my son said he was going in, too. He pulled his dripping trunks from the line where they had hung all through the shower and wrung them out. Languidly, and with no thought of going in, I watched him, his hard little body, skinny and bare, saw him wince slightly as he pulled up around his vitals the small, soggy, icy garment. As he buckled the swollen belt, suddenly my groin felt the chill of death. 13

1941

Purpose and Meaning

1. White's son is silent throughout the essay, yet his presence is essential to its thesis. How does the son affect the author's perspective during his trip? In what way would White's experience have been different had he gone alone?

2. Not much seems to have changed at the lake since White visited it as a boy. Does White endow this fact with any significance, or is it simply a neutral observation? Elaborate on your answer.

3. The lake elicits poignant memories for White. What is the purpose of his recording these memories? Why is it significant that he is writing down his observations and reflections so meticulously? What might White's response have been to the question, "Why bother writing about this experience?"

Language and Style

1. What is the effect of describing nature specifically and concretely yet in a way that strongly evokes the senses? Find some especially vivid sensory details.

2. In paragraph 2, White calls the lake "this holy spot." Locate other examples of this elevated diction. How do they affect the tone of the essay? What is the overall effect when White combines this "high" diction with more colloquial language? Find examples of this juxtaposition.

3. Repetition is a device often used for literary effect. Notice the use of the

word *same* in paragraph 5. How does its repetition contribute to the tone of the paragraph?

4. White is describing a common scene of American life, a visit to the countryside. But his writing style is anything but typical. Paragraph 8, for example, begins with a ten-line sentence that contains unusual syntax. Read the sentence aloud to sense the rhythm of it. How does this and other long sentences contribute to the essay's mood?

Strategy and Structure

1. The author seems to write about nature with great facility, yet his essay is actually very carefully constructed. Which paragraphs constitute the introduction, body, and conclusion? How do they connect? What theme is introduced in paragraph 12?

2. Locate instances of comparison and contrast in this essay. Why does White mix comparison and description?

3. How does White develop the lake as a symbol?

4. What is the significance of the last sentence of the essay? How does it contribute to the overall organization of the piece?

Thinking and Writing

1. Explore the function and effect of figurative language—allusion, analogy, simile, personification, metaphor—in "Once More to the Lake."

2. How are the generations linked in White's essay? Review all the passages in the work that describe this linkage. Write a brief analysis of each reference the author makes to generations.

3. Write an essay on one memorable place that you have revisited. As in White's essay, try to capture the original feeling and the newer one.

○●○●○●○●○●○●○●○●○

The Ring of Time

After the lions had returned to their cages, creeping angrily   1
through the chutes, a little bunch of us drifted away and into an open
doorway nearby, where we stood for a while in semidarkness, watching
a big brown circus horse go harumphing around the practice ring. His

trainer was a woman of about forty, and the two of them, horse and woman, seemed caught up in one of those desultory treadmills of afternoon from which there is no apparent escape. The day was hot, and we kibitzers were grateful to be briefly out of the sun's glare. The long rein, or tape, by which the woman guided her charge counterclockwise in his dull career formed the radius of their private circle, of which she was the revolving center; and she, too, stepped a tiny circumference of her own, in order to accommodate the horse and allow him his maximum scope. She had on a short-skirted costume and a conical straw hat. Her legs were bare and she wore high heels, which probed deep into the loose tanbark and kept her ankles in a state of constant turmoil. The great size and meekness of the horse, the repetitious exercise, the heat of the afternoon, all exerted a hypnotic charm that invited boredom; we spectators were experiencing a languor—we neither expected relief nor felt entitled to any. We had paid a dollar to get into the grounds, to be sure, but we had got our dollar's worth a few minutes before, when the lion trainer's whiplash had got caught around a toe of one of the lions. What more did we want for a dollar?

Behind me I heard someone say, "Excuse me, please," in a low   2
voice. She was halfway into the building when I turned and saw her—a girl of sixteen or seventeen, politely threading her way through us onlookers who blocked the entrance. As she emerged in front of us, I saw that she was barefoot, her dirty little feet fighting the uneven ground. In most respects she was like any of two or three dozen showgirls you encounter if you wander about the winter quarters of Mr. John Ringling North's circus, in Sarasota—cleverly proportioned, deeply browned by the sun, dusty, eager, and almost naked. But her grave face and the naturalness of her manner gave her a sort of quick distinction and brought a new note into the gloomy octagonal building where we had all cast our lot for a few moments. As soon as she had squeezed through the crowd, she spoke a word or two to the older woman, whom I took to be her mother, stepped to the ring, and waited while the horse coasted to a stop in front of her. She gave the animal a couple of affectionate swipes on his enormous neck and then swung herself aboard. The horse immediately resumed his rocking canter, the woman goading him on, chanting something that sounded like "Hop! Hop!"

In attempting to recapture this mild spectacle, I am merely acting   3
as recording secretary for one of the oldest of societies—the society of those who, at one time or another, have surrendered, without even a show of resistance, to the bedazzlement of a circus rider. As a writing man, or secretary, I have always felt charged with the safekeeping of all unexpected items of worldly or unwordly enchantment, as though I might be held personally responsible if even a small one were to be lost. But it is not easy to communicate anything of this nature. The circus

comes as close to being the world in microcosm as anything I know; in a way, it puts all the rest of show business in the shade. Its magic is universal and complex. Out of its wild disorder comes order; from its rank smell rises the good aroma of courage and daring; out of its preliminary shabbiness comes the final splendor. And buried in the familiar boasts of its advance agents lies the modesty of most of its people. For me the circus is at its best before it has been put together. It is at its best at certain moments when it comes to a point, as through a burning glass, in the activity and destiny of a single performer out of so many. One ring is always bigger than three. One rider, one aerialist, is always greater than six. In short, a man has to catch the circus unawares to experience its full impact and share its gaudy dream.

The ten-minute ride the girl took achieved—as far as I was concerned, who wasn't looking for it, and quite unbeknownst to her, who wasn't even striving for it—the thing that is sought by performers everywhere, on whatever stage, whether struggling in the tidal currents of Shakespeare or bucking the difficult motion of a horse. I somehow got the idea she was just cadging a ride, improving a shining ten minutes in the diligent way all serious artists seize free moments to hone the blade of their talent and keep themselves in trim. Her brief tour included only elementary postures and tricks, perhaps because they were all she was capable of, perhaps because her warmup at this hour was unscheduled and the ring was not rigged for a real practice session. She swung herself off and on the horse several times, gripping his mane. She did a few knee-stands—or whatever they are called—dropping to her knees and quickly bouncing back upon her feet again. Most of the time she simply rode in a standing position, well aft on the beast, her hands hanging easily at her sides, her head erect, her straw-colored ponytail lightly brushing her shoulders, the blood of exertion showing faintly through the tan of her skin. Twice she managed a one-foot stance—a sort of ballet pose, with arms outstretched. At one point the neck strap of her bathing suit broke and she went twice around the ring in the classic attitude of a woman making minor repairs to a garment. The fact that she was standing on the back of a moving horse while doing this invested the matter with a clownish significance that perfectly fitted the spirit of the circus— jocund, yet charming. She just rolled the strap into a neat ball and stowed it inside her bodice while the horse rocked and rolled beneath her in dutiful innocence. The bathing suit proved as self-reliant as its owner and stood up well enough without benefit of strap.

The richness of the scene was in its plainness, its natural condition—of horse, of ring, of girl, even to the girl's bare feet that gripped the bare back of her proud and ridiculous mount. The enchantment grew not out of anything that happened or was performed but out of something that seemed to go round and around and around with the girl, attending her, a steady gleam in the shape of a circle—a ring of ambition, of happiness, of youth. (And the positive pleasures of equilibrium under difficulties.) In a week or two, all would be changed, all (or almost all) lost: the girl would wear makeup, the horse would wear gold, the ring would be painted, the bark would be clean for the feet of the horse, the girl's feet would be clean for the slippers that she'd wear. All, all would be lost.

As I watched with the others, our jaws adroop, our eyes alight, I became painfully conscious of the element of time. Everything in the hideous old building seemed to take the shape of a circle, conforming to the course of the horse. The rider's gaze, as she peered straight ahead, seemed to be circular, as though bent by force of circumstance; then time itself began running in circles, and so the beginning was where the end was, and the two were the same, and one thing ran into the next and time went round and around and got nowhere. The girl wasn't so young that she did not know the delicious satisfaction of having a perfectly behaved body and the fun of using it to do a trick most people can't do, but she was too young to know that time does not really move in a circle at all. I thought: "She will never be as beautiful as this again"—a thought that made me acutely unhappy—and in a flash my mind (which is too much of a busybody to suit me) had projected her twenty-five years ahead, and she was now in the center of the ring, on foot, wearing a conical hat and high-heeled shoes, the image of the older woman, holding the long rein, caught in the treadmill of an afternoon long in the future. "She is at that enviable moment in life [I thought] when she believes she can go once around the ring, make one complete circuit, and at the end be exactly the same age as at the start." Everything in her movements, her expression, told you that for her the ring of time was perfectly formed, changeless, predictable, without beginning or end, like the ring in which she was traveling at this moment with the horse that wallowed under her. And then I slipped back into my trance, and time was circular again—time, pausing quietly with the rest of us, so as not to disturb the balance of a performer.

Her ride ended as casually as it had begun. The older woman stopped the horse, and the girl slid to the ground. As she walked toward us to leave, there was a quick, small burst of applause. She smiled broadly, in surprise and pleasure; then her face suddenly regained its gravity and she disappeared through the door.

It has been ambitious and plucky of me to attempt to describe what is indescribable, and I have failed, as I knew I would. But I have discharged my duty to my society; and besides, a writer, like an acrobat, must occasionally try a stunt that is too much for him. At any rate, it is worth reporting that long before the circus comes to town, its most notable performances have already been given. Under the bright lights of the finished show, a performer need only reflect the electric candle power that is directed upon him; but in the dark and dirty old training rings and in the makeshift cages, whatever light is generated, whatever excitement, whatever beauty, must come from original sources—from internal fires of professional hunger and delight, from the exuberance and gravity of youth. It is the difference between planetary light and the combustion of stars.

The South is the land of the sustained sibilant. Everywhere, for the appreciative visitor, the letter "s" insinuates itself in the scene: in the sound of sea and sand, in the singing shell, in the heat of sun and sky, in the sultriness of the gentle hours, in the siesta, in the stir of birds and insects. In contrast to the softness of its music, the South is also cruel and hard and prickly. A little striped lizard, flattened along the sharp green bayonet of a yucca, wears in its tiny face and watchful eye the pure look of death and violence. And all over the place, hidden at the bottom of their small sandy craters, the ant lions lie in wait for the ant that will stumble into their trap. (There are three kinds of lions in this region: the lions of the circus, the ant lions, and the Lions of the Tampa Lions Club, who roared their approval of segregation at a meeting the other day—all except one, a Lion named Monty Gurwit, who declined to roar and thereby got his picture in the paper.) 9

The day starts on a note of despair: the sorrowing dove, alone on its telephone wire, mourns the loss of night, weeps at the bright perils of the unfolding day. But soon the mockingbird wakes and begins an early rehearsal, setting the dove down by force of character, running through a few slick imitations, and trying a couple of original numbers into the bargain. The redbird takes it from there. Despair gives way to good humor. The Southern dawn is a pale affair, usually, quite different from our northern daybreak. It is a triumph of gradualism; night turns to day imperceptibly, softly, with no theatrics. It is subtle and undisturbing. As a first light seeps in through the blinds I lie in bed half awake, despairing with the dove, sounding the A for the brothers Alsop. All seems lost, all seems sorrowful. Then a mullet jumps in the bayou outside the bedroom window. It falls back into the water with a smart smack. I have asked several people why the mullet incessantly jump and I have received a variety of answers. Some say the mullet jump to shake off a parasite that annoys them. Some say they jump for the love of jumping—as the girl on the horse seemed to ride for the love of riding (although she, too, like all artists, may have been shaking off some parasite that fastens itself to the creative spirit and can be got rid of only by fifty turns around a ring while standing on a horse). 10

In Florida at this time of year, the sun does not take command of 11 the day until a couple of hours after it has appeared in the east. It seems to carry no authority at first. The sun and the lizard keep the same schedule; they bide their time until the morning has advanced a good long way before they come fully forth and strike. The cold lizard waits astride his warming leaf for the perfect moment; the cold sun waits in his nest of clouds for the crucial time.

On many days, the dampness of the air pervades all life, all living.   12
Matches refuse to strike. The towel, hung to dry, grows wetter by the hour. The newspaper, with its headlines about integration, wilts in your hand and falls limply into the coffee and the egg. Envelopes seal themselves. Postage stamps mate with one another as shamelessly as grasshoppers. But most of the time the days are models of beauty and wonder and comfort, with the kind sea stroking the back of the warm sand. At evening there are great flights of birds over the sea, where the light lingers; the gulls, the pelicans, the terns, the herons stay aloft for half an hour after land birds have gone to roost. They hold their ancient formations, wheel and fish over the Pass, enjoying the last of day like children playing outdoors after suppertime.

To a beachcomber from the North, which is my present status, the   13
race problem has no pertinence, no immediacy. Here in Florida I am a guest in two houses—the house of the sun, the house of the State of Florida. As a guest, I mind my manners and do not criticize the customs of my hosts. It gives me a queer feeling, though, to be at the center of the greatest social crisis of my time and see hardly a sign of it. Yet the very absence of signs seems to increase one's awareness. Colored people do not come to the public beach to bathe, because they would not be made welcome there; and they don't fritter away their time visiting the circus, because they have other things to do. A few of them turn up at the ball-park, where they occupy a separate but equal section of the left-field bleachers and watch Negro players on the visiting Braves team using the same bases as the white players, instead of separate (but equal) bases. I have had only two small encounters with "color." A colored woman named Viola, who had been a friend of my wife's sister years ago, showed up one day with some laundry of ours that she had consented to do for us, and with the bundle she brought a bunch of nasturtiums, as a sort of natural accompaniment to the delivery of clean clothes. The flowers seemed a very acceptable thing and I was touched by them. We asked Viola about her daughter, and she said she was at Kentucky State College, studying voice.

The other encounter was when I was explaining to our cook, who   14
is from Finland, the mysteries of bus travel in the American Southland. I showed her the bus stop, armed her with a timetable, and then, as a matter of duty, mentioned the customs of the Romans. "When you get on

the bus," I said, "I think you'd better sit in one of the front seats—the seats in back are for colored people." A look of great weariness came into her face, as it does when we use too many dishes, and she replied, "Oh, I know—isn't it silly!"

Her remark, coming as it did all the way from Finland and landing on this sandbar with a plunk, impressed me. The Supreme Court said nothing about silliness, but I suspect it may play more of a role than one might suppose. People are, if anything, more touchy about being thought silly than they are about being thought unjust. I note that one of the arguments in the recent manifesto of Southern Congressmen in support of the doctrine of "separate but equal" was that it had been founded on "common sense." The sense that is common to one generation is uncommon to the next. Probably the first slave ship, with Negroes lying in chains on its decks, seemed commonsensical to the owners who operated it and to the planters who patronized it. But such a vessel would not be in the realm of common sense today. The only sense that is common, in the long run, is the sense of change—and we all instinctively avoid it, and object to the passage of time, and would rather have none of it.

The Supreme Court decision is like the Southern sun, laggard in its early stages, biding its time. It has been the law in Florida for two years now, and the years have been like the hours of the morning before the sun has gathered its strength. I think the decision is as incontrovertible and warming as the sun, and, like the sun, will eventually take charge.

But there is certainly a great temptation in Florida to duck the passage of time. Lying in warm comfort by the sea, you receive gratefully the gift of the sun, the gift of the South. This is true seduction. The day is a circle—morning, afternoon, and night. After a few days I was clearly enjoying the same delusion as the girl on the horse—that I could ride clear around the ring of day, guarded by wind and sun and sea and sand, and be not a moment older.

P.S. (April 1962).   When I first laid eyes on Fiddler Bayou, it was wild land, populated chiefly by the little crabs that gave it its name, visited by wading birds and by an occasional fisherman. Today, houses ring the bayou, and part of the mangrove shore has been bulkheaded with a concrete wall. Green lawns stretch from patio to water's edge, and sprinklers make rainbows in the light. But despite man's encroachment, Nature manages to hold her own and assert her authority: high tides and high winds in the gulf sometimes send the sea crashing across the sand barrier, depositing its wrack on lawns and ringing everyone's front door bell. The birds and the crabs accommodate themselves quite readily to the changes that have taken place; every day brings herons to hunt around among the roots of the mangroves, and I have discovered that I can approach to within about eight feet of a Little Blue Heron simply by entering the water and swimming slowly toward him. Apparently he has decided that when I'm in the water, I am without guile—possibly even desirable, like a fish.

The Ringling circus has quit Sarasota and gone elsewhere for its hibernation. A few circus families still own homes in the town, and every spring the students at the high school put on a circus, to let off steam, work off physical requirements, and provide a promotional spectacle for Sarasota. At the drugstore you can buy a postcard showing the bed John Ringling slept in. Time has not stood still for anybody but the dead, and even the dead must be able to hear the acceleration of little sports cars and know that things have changed.   19

From the all-wise *New York Times*, which has the animal kingdom ever in mind, I have learned that one of the creatures most acutely aware of the passing of time is the fiddler crab himself. Tiny spots on his body enlarge during daytime hours, giving him the same color as the mud-bank he explores and thus protecting him from his enemies. At night the spots shrink, his color fades, and he is almost invisible in the light of the moon. These changes are synchronized with the tides, so that each day they occur at different hour. A scientist who experimented with the crabs to learn more about the phenomenon discovered that even when they are removed from their natural environment and held in confinement, the rhythm of their bodily change continues uninterrupted, and they mark the passage of time in their laboratory prison, faithful to the tides in their fashion.   20

1956

Purpose and Meaning

1. How does the title of the essay provide a clue to its thesis? How does the "ring" of time connect with the circus? What is White's purpose in establishing this connection? To whom is he writing, and why?

2. In paragraph 6, the author says he "became painfully conscious of the element of time." What is the significance of the word *painfully* in this paragraph? Are there other places in the essay that suggest this particular perception?

3. Consider the first sentence of paragraph 5: "The richness of the scene was in its plainness . . . " Isn't this self-contradictory? How does the rest of the paragraph support this opening observation?

4. Paragraph 13 mentions the idea of a "separate but equal" racial doctrine. How do the author's observations on the issue relate to his reflections on time?

Language and Style

1. The author describes at length the young acrobat's practice session on her horse. Yet in paragraph 8, he states, "It has been ambitious and plucky of me to attempt to describe what is indescribable, and I have failed." Reread the sections of the essay pertaining to the acrobat. How successful is White in describing her practice session? Why does he say it is "indescribable"? Has he really failed to describe the event? In what sections of the essay do you find his description most successful?

2. In paragraph 9, the author not only states that the letter *s* somehow is appropriate for the South, but also uses many words in the paragraph that begin with *s*. What is the effect of this technique?

3. How many suggestions of circularity or images of rings can you find in the essay? How do these images contribute to the organization of the essay as a whole?

Strategy and Structure

1. This essay appears to be divided into two sections (excluding the postscript). Where do these sections begin and end? Why does the author divide them in this way? What is the focus of each, and how is each one related to all the others?

2. The essay begins with an image of lions and ends with a description of crabs. What is the purpose for this organizational strategy?

3. What is the point of the postscript (written six years after the main text)?

Thinking and Writing

1. The author claims that there is "a great temptation in Florida to duck the passage of time." Yet images of Florida in 1956 and today show it as anything but timeless or unaffected by change. Select a place with great contrasts; then write an essay comparing and contrasting two aspects of this locale. Examples might be "The Two New Yorks," "The Two Californias," and so forth.

2. The last sentence of paragraph 8 says that the difference between a circus rehearsal and performance is like the difference between "planetary light and the combustion of stars." Develop an essay that investigates the differences between rehearsal and performance in an activity that you know well.

3. White claims he is acting as a "recording secretary" (paragraph 3) in his role as a writer. Write an essay evaluating White's role or function in "The Ring of Time" and his purpose. Does he record objectively, offer commentary, or do both?

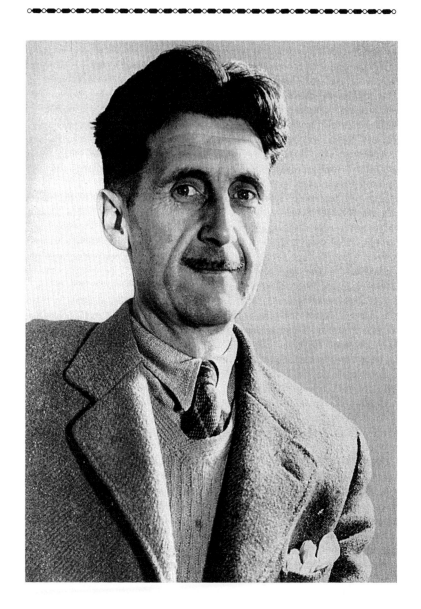

GEORGE ORWELL

George Orwell, the pen name of Eric Blair, was born in 1903 in Motihari, Bengal, India, the son of English parents. His father, a minor civil servant in the Opium Department of the Indian Customs Service, retired when his son was relatively young. Nevertheless, with considerable hardship, the family sent him to England for his education—a poor boy at fashionable British schools. Blair attended Eton on a scholarship and then, on the advice of a tutor, accepted a position with the Indian Imperial Police in Burma. Five years later, increasingly mistrustful of English imperialism, which he termed "a racket," Blair quit to become a writer. As George Orwell—the man who gave us such terms as "newspeak," "doublethink," and "big brother"—he demonstrated the ways in which we can transform "political writing into an art."

As a political writer, George Orwell was—in the words of the esteemed English essayist and fiction writer V. S. Pritchett—"the conscience of his generation." Orwell, a rather idiosyncratic socialist at odds with many of the ideological movements of the left of the 1930s and 1940s, came to his social and political convictions through experience. His disdain for British imperialism, seen in classic essays like "A Hanging" and "Shooting an Elephant," reflects the start of his intellectual journey in India and Burma in the 1920s. His early struggle to be a writer, an eight-year period of privation he spent as a dishwasher, a tramp, a tutor, and a bookshop assistant, is recorded in *Down and Out in Paris and London* (1935). His firsthand Depression-era reports on the English working class resulted in *The Road To Wigan Pier* (1937). Orwell's memorable *Homage to Catalonia* (1938), based on his participation in the Spanish Civil War, where as a volunteer in the Trotskyite People's Militia he was wounded severely in the neck, indicts both the political right and left for their rigid orthodoxies. His last books, the celebrated fable *Animal Farm* (1945) and the classic dystopian novel, *Nineteen Eighty-four* (1950), published a year before his death from pulmonary tuberculosis, are towering attacks on totalitarianism and lust for power exhibited by big government.

Orwell's "sense of injustice," as he confessed in "Why I Write," was the stimulant for his writing. Lionel Trilling stated that Orwell "immediately put his mind to work the politics that he had experienced. He told the truth, and told it in an exemplary way, quietly, simply, with due warning to the readers that it was only one man's truth." Orwell himself, near the end of his life, acknowledged that he had a talent for facing unpleasant facts and powerfully conveying them to his audience. His essays, collected by his second wife, Sonia Orwell, in four volumes, *The Collected Essays, Journalism and Letters* (1968), are lucid reflections on an age that witnessed two world wars, the Great Depression, Stalinism and Fascism, and the emergence of the Cold War. Orwell illuminated these major events, exposing their terrors. For the imagination, as he observed, "like certain wild animals, will not breed in captivity."

A Hanging

It was in Burma, a sodden morning of the rains. A sickly light, like 1
yellow tinfoil, was slanting over the high walls into the jail yard. We
were waiting outside the condemned cells, a row of sheds fronted with
double bars, like small animal cages. Each cell measured about ten feet
by ten and was quite bare within except for a plank bed and a pot for
drinking water. In some of them brown silent men were squatting at the
inner bars, with their blankets draped round them. These were the condemned men, due to be hanged within the next week or two.

One prisoner had been brought out of his cell. He was a Hindu, a 2
puny wisp of a man, with a shaven head and vague liquid eyes. He had
a thick, sprouting moustache, absurdly too big for his body, rather like
the moustache of a comic man on the films. Six tall Indian warders were
guarding him and getting him ready for the gallows. Two of them stood
by with rifles and fixed bayonets, while the others handcuffed him,
passed a chain through his handcuffs and fixed it to their belts, and
lashed his arms tight to his sides. They crowded very close about him,
with their hands always on him in a careful, caressing grip, as though all
the while feeling him to make sure he was there. It was like men handling a fish which is still alive and may jump back into the water. But he
stood quite unresisting, yielding his arms limply to the ropes, as though
he hardly noticed what was happening.

Eight o'clock struck and a bugle call, desolately thin in the wet air, 3
floated from the distant barracks. The superintendent of the jail, who
was standing apart from the rest of us, moodily prodding the gravel
with his stick, raised his head at the sound. He was an army doctor, with
a grey toothbrush moustache and a gruff voice. "For God's sake hurry
up, Francis," he said irritably. "The man ought to have been dead by this
time. Aren't you ready yet?"

Francis, the head jailer, a fat Dravidian in a white drill suit and 4
gold spectacles, waved his black hand. "Yes sir, yes sir," he bubbled.
"All iss satisfactorily prepared. The hangman iss waiting. We shall proceed."

"Well, quick march, then. The prisoners can't get their breakfast till 5
this job's over."

We set out for the gallows. Two warders marched on either side of 6
the prisoner, with their rifles at the slope; two others marched close
against him, gripping him by arm and shoulder, as though at once pushing and supporting him. The rest of us, magistrates and the like, followed behind. Suddenly, when we had gone ten yards, the procession
stopped short without any order or warning. A dreadful thing had hap-

pened—a dog, come goodness knows whence, had appeared in the yard. It came bounding among us with a loud volley of barks, and leapt round us wagging its whole body, wild with glee at finding so many human beings together. It was a large woolly dog, half Airedale, half pariah. For a moment it pranced round us, and then, before anyone could stop it, it had made a dash for the prisoner and, jumping up, tried to lick his face. Everyone stood aghast, too taken aback even to grab at the dog.

"Who let that bloody brute in here?" said the superintendent angrily. "Catch it, someone!"   7

A warder, detached from the escort, charged clumsily after the dog, but it danced and gambolled just out of his reach, taking everything as part of the game. A young Eurasian jailer picked up a handful of gravel and tried to stone the dog away, but it dodged the stones and came after us again. Its yaps echoed from the jail walls. The prisoner, in the grasp of the two warders, looked on incuriously, as though this was another formality of the hanging. It was several minutes before someone managed to catch the dog. Then we put my handkerchief through its collar and moved off once more, with the dog still straining and whimpering.   8

It was about forty yards to the gallows. I watched the bare brown back of the prisoner marching in front of me. He walked clumsily with his bound arms, but quite steadily, with that bobbing gait of the Indian who never straightens his knees. At each step his muscles slid neatly into place, the lock of hair on his scalp danced up and down, his feet printed themselves on the wet gravel. And once, in spite of the men who gripped him by each shoulder, he stepped slightly aside to avoid a puddle on the path.   9

It is curious, but till that moment I had never realized what it means to destroy a healthy, conscious man. When I saw the prisoner step aside to avoid the puddle I saw the mystery, the unspeakable wrongness, of cutting a life short when it is in full tide. This man was not dying, he was alive just as we are alive. All the organs of his body were working—bowels digesting food, skin renewing itself, nails growing, tissues forming—all toiling away in solemn foolery. His nails would still be growing when he stood on the drop, when he was falling through the air with a tenth-of-a-second to live. His eyes saw the yellow gravel and the grey walls, and his brain still remembered, foresaw, reasoned—reasoned even about puddles. He and we were a party of men walking together, seeing, hearing, feeling, understanding the same world; and in two minutes, with a sudden snap, one of us would be gone—one mind less, one world less.   10

The gallows stood in a small yard, separate from the main grounds of the prison, and overgrown with tall prickly weeds. It was a brick erection like three sides of a shed, with planking on top, and above that two   11 beams and a crossbar with the rope dangling. The hangman, a grey-haired convict in the white uniform of the prison, was waiting beside his machine. He greeted us with a servile crouch as we entered. At a word from Francis the two warders, gripping the prisoner more closely than ever, half led half pushed him to the gallows and helped him clumsily up the ladder. Then the hangman climbed up and fixed the rope round the prisoner's neck.

We stood waiting, five yards away. The warders had formed in a 12 rough circle round the gallows. And then, when the noose was fixed, the prisoner began crying out to his god. It was a high, reiterated cry of "Ram! Ram! Ram! Ram!" not urgent and fearful like a prayer or cry for help, but steady, rhythmical, almost like the tolling of a bell. The dog answered the sound with a whine. The hangman, still standing on the gallows, produced a small cotton bag like a flour bag and drew it down over the prisoner's face. But the sound, muffled by the cloth, still persisted, over and over again: "Ram! Ram! Ram! Ram! Ram!"

The hangman climbed down and stood ready, holding the lever. 13 Minutes seemed to pass. The steady, muffled crying from the prisoner went on and on. "Ram! Ram! Ram!" never faltering for an instant. The superintendent, his head on his chest, was slowly poking the ground with his stick; perhaps he was counting the cries, allowing the prisoner a fixed number—fifty, perhaps, or a hundred. Everyone had changed color. The Indians had gone grey like bad coffee, and one or two of the bayonets were wavering. We looked at the lashed, hooded man on the drop, and listened to his cries—each cry another second of life; the same thought was in all our minds: oh, kill him quickly, get it over, stop that abominable noise!

Suddenly the superintendent made up his mind. Throwing up his 14 head he made a swift motion with his stick. "Chalo!" he shouted almost fiercely.

There was a clanking noise, and then dead silence. The prisoner had 15 vanished, and the rope was twisting on itself. I let go of the dog, and it galloped immediately to the back of the gallows; but when it got there it stopped short, barked, and then retreated into a corner of the yard, where it stood among the weeds, looking timorously out at us. We went round the gallows to inspect the prisoner's body. He was dangling with his toes pointed straight downwards, very slowly revolving, as dead as a stone.

The superintendent reached out with his stick and poked the bare 16 brown body; it oscillated slightly. "*He's* all right," said the superintendent. He backed out from under the gallows, and blew out a deep breath. The moody look had gone out of his face quite suddenly. He glanced at his wrist-watch. "Eight minutes past eight. Well, that's all for this morning, thank God."

The warders unfixed bayonets and marched away. The dog, 17 sobered and conscious of having misbehaved itself, slipped after them.

We walked out of the gallows yard, past the condemned cells with their waiting prisoners, into the big central yard of the prison. The convicts, under the command of warders armed with lathis, were already receiving their breakfast. They squatted in long rows, each man holding a tin pannikin, while two warders with buckets marched round ladling out rice; it seemed quite a homely, jolly scene, after the hanging. An enormous relief had come upon us now that the job was done. One felt an impulse to sing, to break into a run, to snigger. All at once everyone began chattering gaily.

The Eurasian boy walking beside me nodded towards the way we   18 had come, with a knowing smile: "Do you know, sir, our friend [he meant the dead man] when he heard his appeal had been dismissed, he pissed on the floor of his cell. From fright. Kindly take one of my cigarettes, sir. Do you not admire my new silver case, sir? From the boxwalah, two rupees eight annas. Classy European style."

Several people laughed—at what, nobody seemed certain.   19

Francis was walking by the superintendent, talking garrulously: 20 "Well, sir, all hass passed off with the utmost satisfactoriness. It was all finished—flick! like that. It iss not always so—oah, no! I have known cases where the doctor wass obliged to go beneath the gallows and pull the prissoner's legs to ensure decease. Most disagreeable!"

"Wriggling about, eh? That's bad," said the superintendent.   21

"Ach, sir, it iss worse when they become refractory! One man, I re-   22 call, clung to the bars of hiss cage when we went to take him out. You will scarcely credit, sir, that it took six warders to dislodge him, three pulling at each leg. We reasoned with him. 'My dear fellow,' we said, 'think of all the pain and trouble you are causing to us!' But no, he would not listen! Ach, he wass very troublesome!"

I found that I was laughing quite loudly. Everyone was laughing.   23 Even the superintendent grinned in a tolerant way. "You'd better all come out and have a drink," he said quite genially. "I've got a bottle of whiskey in the car. We could do with it."

We went through the big double gates of the prison into the road.   24 "Pulling at his legs!" exclaimed a Burmese magistrate suddenly, and burst into a loud chuckling. We all began laughing again. At that moment Francis' anecdote seemed extraordinarily funny. We all had a drink together, native and European alike, quite amicably. The dead man was a hundred yards away.

1931

Purpose and Meaning

1. By this narrative account, Orwell intends to persuade. What is his persuasive purpose, and what evidence in the text supports this purpose?

2. Orwell never mentions the condemned man's crime. Explain why this

omission was intentional. How does the omission illuminate the essay's theme?

3. Does Orwell approach his subject matter emotionally, objectively, analytically, or in a combination of any of these? How does the essay's brief title suggest the author's tone? What is ironic about such a terse title?

4. Orwell describes the dog at some length. Why does he devote so much of the essay to the animal? Why are the soldiers and officials so disturbed by its behavior?

Language and Style

1. Analyze Orwell's use of the first-person point of view. Is Orwell a participant in or observer of the action?

2. Orwell uses adjectives such as *sodden, sickly, limply,* and adverbs such as *desolately* and *moodily* in paragraphs 1 through 3. How do these descriptive words contribute to the mood of the narrative? What is this mood? How else is description used in later paragraphs to maintain this mood?

3. Compare Orwell's writing style to White's. How do their sentence structures compare in terms of syntax, figurative language, and length? Do you prefer one style to the other? If so, why?

Strategy and Structure

1. How does Orwell frame his narrative in this essay? How does he handle action, setting, and time?

2. Orwell intersperses his story with bits of dialogue. How does the dialogue contribute to the overall effect? What effect does the description of the prisoner's prayer have on the reader?

3. Paragraph 10, a moral reflection upon the hanging, temporarily breaks up the narrative flow of the story. Is this an effective rhetorical strategy? Should Orwell have placed the paragraph at the conclusion of the essay instead? Justify your answer.

4. Is the last part of the essay—after the prisoner has been hanged—anticlimactic? What is Orwell's purpose in including this section? Why has Orwell written so much dialogue into the last five paragraphs? Is the content of what the speakers are saying significant, or is it something else?

Thinking and Writing

1. Orwell was, among other things, a journalist. Does this piece of writing remind you more of a newspaper article or an essay? Discuss in class the differences between the two. Try describing one incident in two ways: the

first, in purely objective terms; the second, as a means to advance a theme or thesis.

2. We learn much about the inner feelings of the people in this essay from what they say. Analyze the dialogue in "A Hanging" and what it reveals about the characters.

3. Write a narrative account that reveals your own attitude toward capital punishment.

4. Write an essay comparing "A Hanging" and White's "The Ring of Time." Attempt to explain how each essay arrives at a political statement about the human condition.

Shooting an Elephant

In Moulmein, in Lower Burma, I was hated by large numbers of people—the only time in my life that I have been important enough for this to happen to me. I was sub-divisional police officer of the town, and in an aimless, petty kind of way anti-European feeling was very bitter. No one had the guts to raise a riot, but if a European woman went through the bazaars alone somebody would probably spit betel juice over her dress. As a police officer I was an obvious target and was baited whenever it seemed safe to do so. When a nimble Burman tripped me up on the football field and the referee (another Burman) looked the other way, the crowd yelled with hideous laughter. This happened more than once. In the end the sneering yellow faces of young men that met me everywhere, the insults hooted after me when I was at a safe distance, got badly on my nerves. The young Buddhist priests were the worst of all. There were several thousands of them in the town and none of them seemed to have anything to do except stand on street corners and jeer at Europeans.

All this was perplexing and upsetting. For at that time I had already made up my mind that imperialism was an evil thing and the sooner I chucked up my job and got out of it the better. Theoretically—and secretly, of course—I was all for the Burmese and all against their oppressors, the British. As for the job I was doing, I hated it more bitterly than I can perhaps make clear. In a job like that you see the dirty work of Empire at close quarters. The wretched prisoners huddling in the stinking cages of the lock-ups, the grey, cowed faces of the long-term convicts, the scarred buttocks of the men who had been flogged with bamboos—all these oppressed me with an intolerable sense of guilt. But I could get nothing into perspective. I was young and ill-educated and I had had to think out my problems in the utter silence that is imposed on every Englishman in the East. I did not even know that the British Empire is dying, still less did I know that it is a great deal better than the younger empires that are going to supplant it. All I knew was that I was stuck between my hatred of the empire I served and my rage against the evil-spirited little beasts who tried to make my job impossible. With one part of my mind I thought of the British Raj as an unbreakable tyranny, as something clamped down, *in saecula saeculorum*, upon the will of prostrate peoples; with another part I thought that the greatest joy in the world would be to drive a bayonet into a Buddhist priest's guts. Feelings like these are the normal by-products of imperialism; ask any Anglo-Indian official, if you can catch him off duty.

One day something happened which in a roundabout way was enlightening. It was a tiny incident in itself, but it gave me a better glimpse than I had had before of the real nature of imperialism—the real motives for which despotic governments act. Early one morning the sub-inspector at a police station the other end of the town rang me up on the phone and said that an elephant was ravaging the bazaar. Would I please come and do something about it? I did not know what I could do, but I wanted to see what was happening and I got on to a pony and started out. I took my rifle, an old ·44 Winchester and much too small to kill an elephant, but I thought the noise might be useful *in terrorem*. Various Burmans stopped me on the way and told me about the elephant's doings. It was not, of course, a wild elephant, but a tame one which had gone "must." It had been chained up as tame elephants always are when their attack of "must" is due, but on the previous night it had broken its chain and escaped. Its mahout, the only person who could manage it when it was in that state, had set out in pursuit, but he had taken the wrong direction and was now twelve hours' journey away, and in the morning the elephant had suddenly reappeared in the town. The Burmese population had no weapons and were quite helpless against it. It had already destroyed somebody's bamboo hut, killed a cow and raided some fruit-stalls and devoured the stock; also it had met the municipal rubbish van, and, when the driver jumped out and took to his heels, had turned the van over and inflicted violence upon it.

The Burmese sub-inspector and some Indian constables were waiting for me in the quarter where the elephant had been seen. It was a very poor quarter, a labyrinth of squalid bamboo huts, thatched with palm-leaf, winding all over a steep hillside. I remember that it was a cloudy stuffy morning at the beginning of the rains. We began questioning the people as to where the elephant had gone, and, as usual, failed to get any definite information. That is invariably the case in the East; a story always sounds clear enough at a distance, but the nearer you get to the scene of events the vaguer it becomes. Some of the people said that the elephant had gone in one direction, some said that he had gone in another, some professed not even to have heard of any elephant. I had almost made up my mind that the whole story was a pack of lies, when we heard yells a little distance away. There was a loud, scandalised cry of "Go away, child! Go away this instant!" and an old woman with a switch in her hand came round the corner of a hut, violently shooing away a crowd of naked children. Some more women followed, clicking their tongues and exclaiming; evidently there was something there that the children ought not to have seen. I rounded the hut and saw a man's dead body sprawling in the mud. He was an Indian, a black Dravidian coolie, almost naked, and he could not have been dead many minutes. The people said that the elephant had come suddenly upon him round the corner of the hut, caught him with its trunk, put its foot on his back and ground him into the earth. This was the rainy season and the ground was soft, and his face had scored a trench a foot deep and a couple of yards long. He was lying on his belly with arms crucified and head sharply twisted to one side. His face was coated with mud, the eyes wide open, the teeth bared and grinning with an expression of unendurable agony. (Never tell me, by the way, that the dead look peaceful. Most of the corpses I have seen looked devilish.) The friction of the great beast's foot had stripped the skin from his back as neatly as one skins a rabbit. As soon as I saw the dead man I sent an orderly to a friend's house nearby to borrow an elephant rifle. I had already sent back the pony, not wanting it to go mad with fright and throw me if it smelled the elephant.

The orderly came back in a few minutes with a rifle and five cartridges, and meanwhile some Burmans had arrived and told us that the elephant was in the paddy fields below, only a few hundred yards away. As I started forward practically the whole population of the quarter flocked out of their houses and followed me. They had seen the rifle and were all shouting excitedly that I was going to shoot the elephant. They had not shown much interest in the elephant when he was merely ravaging their homes, but it was different now that he was going to be shot. It was a bit of fun to them, as it would be to an English crowd; besides, they wanted the meat. It made me vaguely uneasy. I had no intent of shooting the elephant—I had merely sent for the rifle to defend myself if necessary—and it is always unnerving to have a crowd following you. I marched down the hill, looking and feeling a fool, with the rifle over my shoulder and an evergrowing army of people jostling at my heels. At the bottom, when you got away from the huts, there was a metalled road and beyond that a miry waste of paddy fields a thousand yards across, not yet ploughed but soggy from the first rains and dotted with coarse grass.

The elephant was standing eighty yards from the road, his left side towards us. He took not the slightest notice of the crowd's approach. He was tearing up bunches of grass, beating them against his knees to clean them and stuffing them into his mouth.

I had halted on the road. As soon as I saw the elephant I knew with perfect certainty that I ought not to shoot him. It is a serious matter to shoot a working elephant—it is comparable to destroying a huge and costly piece of machinery—and obviously one ought not to do it if it can possibly be avoided. And at that distance, peacefully eating, the elephant looked no more dangerous than a cow. I thought then and I think now what his attack of "must" was already passing off; in which case he would merely wander harmlessly about until the mahout came back and caught him. Moreover, I did not in the least want to shoot him. I decided that I would watch him for a little while to make sure that he did not turn savage again, and then go home.

But at that moment I glanced round at the crowd that had followed me. It was an immense crowd, two thousand at the least and growing every minute. It blocked the road for a long distance on either side. I looked at the sea of yellow faces above the garish clothes—faces all happy and excited over this bit of fun, all certain that the elephant was going to be shot. They were watching me as they would watch a conjuror about to perform a trick. They did not like me, but with the magical rifle in my hands I was momentarily worth watching. And suddenly I realised that I should have to shoot the elephant after all. The people expected it of me and I had got to do it; I could feel their two thousand wills pressing me forward, irresistibly. And it was at this moment, as I stood there with the rifle in my hands, that I first grasped the hollowness, the futility of the white man's dominion in the East. Here was I, the white man with his gun, standing in front of the unarmed native crowd—seemingly the leading actor of the piece; but in reality I was only an absurd puppet pushed to and fro by the will of those yellow faces behind. I perceived in this moment that when the white man turns tyrant it is his own freedom that he destroys. He becomes a sort of hollow, posing dummy, the conventionalised figure of a sahib. For it is the condition of his rule that he shall spend his life in trying to impress the "natives" and so in every crisis he has got to do what the "natives" expect of him. He wears a mask, and his face grows to fit it. I had got to shoot the elephant. I had committed myself to doing it when I sent for the rifle. A sahib has got to act like a sahib; he has got to appear resolute, to know his own mind and do definite things. To come all that way, rifle in hand, with two thousand people marching at my heels, and then to trail feebly away, having done nothing—no that was impossible. The crowd would laugh at me. And my whole life, every white man's life in the East, was one long struggle not to be laughed at.

But I did not want to shoot the elephant. I watched him beating his bunch of grass against his knees, with that preoccupied grandmotherly air that elephants have. It seemed to me that it would be murder to shoot him. At that age I was not squeamish about killing animals, but I had never shot an elephant and never wanted to. (Somehow it always seems worse to kill a *large* animal.) Besides, there was the beast's owner to be considered. Alive, the elephant was worth at least a hundred pounds; dead, he would only be worth the value of his tusks—five pounds, possibly. But I had got to act quickly. I turned to some experienced-looking Burmans who had been there when we arrived, and asked them how the elephant had been behaving. They all said the same thing: he took no notice of you if you left him alone, but he might charge if you went too close to him. 8

It was perfectly clear to me what I ought to do. I ought to walk up to within, say, twenty-five yards of the elephant and test his behaviour. If he charged I could shoot, if he took no notice of me it would be safe to leave him until the mahout came back. But also I knew that I was going to do no such thing. I was a poor shot with a rifle and the ground was soft mud into which one would sink at every step. If the elephant charged and I missed him, I should have about as much chance as a toad under a steam-roller. But even then I was not thinking particularly of my own skin, only the watchful yellow faces behind. For at that moment, with the crowd watching me, I was not afraid in the ordinary sense, as I would have been if I had been alone. A white man mustn't be frightened in front of "natives"; and so, in general, he isn't frightened. The sole thought in my mind was that if anything went wrong those two thousand Burmans would see me pursued, caught, trampled on and reduced to a grinning corpse like that Indian up the hill. And if that happened it was quite probable that some of them would laugh. That would never do. There was only one alternative. I shoved the cartridges into the magazine and lay down on the road to get a better aim. 9

The crowd grew very still, and a deep, low, happy sigh, of people who see the theatre curtain go up at last, breathed from innumerable throats. They were going to have their bit of fun after all. The rifle was a beautiful German thing with cross-hair sights. I did not then know that in shooting an elephant one should shoot to cut an imaginary bar running from ear-hole to ear-hole. I ought therefore, as the elephant was sideways on, to have aimed straight at his ear-hole; actually I aimed several inches in front of this, thinking the brain would be further forward. 10

When I pulled the trigger I did not hear the bang or feel the kick—one never does when a shot goes home—but I heard the devilish roar of glee that went up from the crowd. In that instant, in too short a time, one would have thought, even for the bullet to get there, a mysterious, terrible change had come over the elephant. He neither stirred nor fell, but 11 every line of his body had altered. He looked suddenly stricken, shrunken, immensely old, as though the frightful impact of the bullet had paralysed him without knocking him down. At last, after what seemed a long time—it might have been five seconds, I dare say—he sagged flabbily to his knees. His mouth slobbered. An enormous senility seemed to have settled upon him. One could have imagined him thousands of years old. I fired again into the same spot. At the second shot he did not collapse but climbed with desperate slowness to his feet and stood weakly upright, with legs sagging and head drooping. I fired a third time. That was the shot that did for him. You could see the agony of it jolt his whole body and knock the last remnant of strength from his legs. But in falling he seemed for a moment to rise, for as his hindlegs collapsed beneath him he seemed to tower upwards like a huge rock toppling, his trunk reaching skyward like a tree. He trumpeted, for the first and only time. And then down he came, his belly towards me, with a crash that seemed to shake the ground even where I lay.

I got up. The Burmans were already racing past me across the 12 mud. It was obvious that the elephant would never rise again, but he was not dead. He was breathing very rhythmically with long rattling gasps, his great mound of a side painfully rising and falling. His mouth was wide open—I could see far down into caverns of pale pink throat. I waited a long time for him to die, but his breathing did not weaken. Finally I fired my two remaining shots into the spot where I thought his heart must be. The thick blood welled out of him like red velvet, but still he did not die. His body did not even jerk when the shots hit him, the tortured breathing continued without a pause. He was dying, very slowly and in great agony, but in some world remote from me where not even a bullet could damage him further. I felt that I had got to put an end to that dreadful noise. It seemed dreadful to see the great beast lying there, powerless to move and yet powerless to die, and not even to be able to finish him. I sent back for my small rifle and poured shot after shot into his heart and down his throat. They seemed to make no impression. The tortured gasps continued as steadily as the ticking of a clock.

In the end I could not stand it any longer and went away. I heard 13 later that it took him half an hour to die. Burmans were arriving with dahs and baskets even before I left, and I was told they had stripped his body almost to the bones by the afternoon.

Afterwards, of course, there were endless discussions about the 14 shooting of the elephant. The owner was furious, but he was only an Indian and could do nothing. Besides, legally I had done the right thing, for a mad elephant has to be killed, like a mad dog, if its owner fails to control it. Among the Europeans opinion was divided. The older men said I was right, the younger men said it was a damn shame to shoot an elephant for killing a coolie, because an elephant was worth more than any damn Coringhee coolie. And afterwards I was very glad that the coolie had been killed; it put me legally in the right and it gave me a sufficient pretext for shooting the elephant. I often wondered whether any of the others grasped that I had done it solely to avoid looking a fool.

1936

Purpose and Meaning

1. Orwell quite clearly states the thesis of this essay. What sentence reveals it?

2. Why do the Burmese hate Orwell? What is Orwell's attitude toward those who hate him?

3. In paragraph 2, Orwell refers to the British Empire and "the younger empires that are going to supplant it." To what historical context is he referring? What other specific allusions in the essay suggest the period in which the action occurs?

4. What relevance does this essay have beyond the historical period in which it was written?

Language and Style

1. The killing of the elephant is described in great detail (paragraph 11). Why does Orwell devote so much attention to the act? How does it compare to the execution of the condemned man in "A Hanging"?

2. Orwell describes the Burmese as "evil-spirited little beasts" in paragraph 2. What other dehumanizing terms does Orwell use to characterize them? In paragraph 7, he feels "two thousand wills pressing me forward." How does this description depersonalize the crowd? Where else are the Burmese portrayed in this manner? What type of relationship does this portrayal set up between Orwell and the colonized?

3. Orwell's style in this essay is a complex mixture of slang, Latinisms, imagery, metaphors, and similes. Locate examples of each, and explain their overall effect.

Strategy and Structure

1. The first two paragraphs are a general reflection on Orwell's experience in Burma and his attitudes toward imperialism. Paragraph 3 begins the narrative. What is the purpose and effect of this organizational strategy?

2. At the beginning of paragraph 10, Orwell states that the crowd behaved like "people who see the theatre curtain go up at last." How do the preceding paragraphs prepare us for this culminating moment?

3. Identify when Orwell uses irony and paradox in this essay.

4. How does the concluding paragraph capture the main conflicts in this narrative?

Thinking and Writing

1. Has an incident in your life ever served to illustrate a general principle about the world you live in? Develop a personal narrative that presents such a relationship. Pay careful attention to how you integrate the specific details of the event with your general insights.

2. Orwell's social, political, and cultural perspective toward the Burmese greatly influences the way he describes them. In an essay, discuss how the status of an individual affects the attitude of that individual toward others.

3. Orwell claims that he was "only an absurd puppet pushed to and fro" and that at the time he was "young and ill-educated" and had "to think out [his] problems in . . . utter silence." Consider Orwell's role in the narrative. Did he have a choice in whether to kill the elephant or not? Develop an argumentative essay advancing your point of view.

o●○●○●○●○●○●○●○●○●○●○●○●○

Politics and the English Language

Most people who bother with the matter at all would admit that the English language is in a bad way, but it is generally assumed that we cannot by conscious action do anything about it. Our civilization is decadent and our language—so the argument runs—must inevitably share in the general collapse. It follows that any struggle against the abuse of language is a sentimental archaism, like preferring candles to electric light or hansom cabs to aeroplanes. Underneath this lies the half-conscious belief that language is a natural growth and not an instrument which we shape for our own purposes.

Now, it is clear that the decline of a language must ultimately have political and economic causes: it is not due simply to the bad influence of this or that individual writer. But an effect can become a cause, reinforcing the original cause and producing the same effect in an intensified form, and so on indefinitely. A man may take to drink because he feels himself to be a failure, and then fail all the more completely because he drinks. It is rather the same thing that is happening to the

English language. It becomes ugly and inaccurate because our thoughts are foolish, but the slovenliness of our language makes it easier for us to have foolish thoughts. The point is that the process is reversible. Modern English, especially written English, is full of bad habits which spread by imitation and which can be avoided if one is willing to take the necessary trouble. If one gets rid of these habits one can think more clearly, and to think clearly is a necessary first step towards political regeneration: so that the fight against bad English is not frivolous and is not the exclusive concern of professional writers. I will come back to this presently, and I hope that by that time the meaning of what I have said here will have become clearer. Meanwhile, here are five specimens of the English language as it is now habitually written.

These five passages have not been picked out because they are especially bad—I could have quoted far worse if I had chosen—but because they illustrate various of the mental vices from which we now suffer. They are a little below the average, but are fairly representative samples. I number them so that I can refer back to them when necessary:

> (1) I am not, indeed, sure whether it is not true to say that the Milton who once seemed not unlike a seventeenth-century Shelley had not become, out of an experience ever more bitter in each year, more alien [*sic*] to the founder of that Jesuit sect which nothing could induce him to tolerate.
>
> Professor Harold Laski
(Essay in Freedom of Expression)

> (2) Above all, we cannot play ducks and drakes with a native battery of idioms which prescribes such egregious collocations of vocables as the Basic *put up with* for *tolerate* or *put at a loss* for *bewilder*.
>
> Professor Lancelot Hogben (Interglossa)

> (3) On the one side we have the free personality: by definition it is not neurotic, for it has neither conflict nor dream. Its desires, such as they are, are transparent, for they are just what institutional approval keeps in the forefront of consciousness; another institutional pattern would alter their number and intensity; there is little in them that is natural, irreducible, or culturally dangerous. But on the other side, the social bond itself is nothing but the mutual reflection of these self-secure integrities. Recall the definition of love. Is not this the very picture of a small academic? Where is there a place in this hall of mirrors for either personality or fraternity?
>
> Essay on psychology in Politics (New York)

> (4) All the "best people" from the gentlemen's clubs, and all the frantic fascist captains, united in common hatred of Socialism and bestial horror of the rising tide of the mass revolutionary movement, have turned to acts of provocation, to foul incendiarism, to medieval legends of poisoned wells,

3

to legalize their own destruction of proletarian organizations, and rouse the agitated petty-bourgeoisie to chauvinistic fervor on behalf of the fight against the revolutionary way out of the crisis.

Communist pamphlet

(5) If a new spirit is to be infused into this old country, there is one thorny and contentious reform which must be tackled, and that is the humanization and galvanization of the B.B.C. Timidity here will bespeak canker and atrophy of the soul. The heart of Britain may be sound and of strong beat, for instance, but the British lion's roar at present is like that of Bottom in Shakespeare's *Midsummer Night's Dream*—as gentle as any sucking dove. A virile new Britain cannot continue indefinitely to be traduced in the eyes or rather ears, of the world by the effete languors of Langham Place, brazenly masquerading as "standard English." When the Voice of Britain is heard at nine o'clock, better far and infinitely less ludicrous to hear aitches honestly dropped than the present priggish, inflated, inhibited, school-ma'amish arch braying of blameless bashful mewing maidens!

Letter in *Tribune*

Each of these passages has faults of its own, but, quite apart from avoidable ugliness, two qualities are common to all of them. The first is staleness of imagery; the other is lack of precision. The writer either has a meaning and cannot express it, or he inadvertently says something else, or he is almost indifferent as to whether his words mean anything or not. This mixture of vagueness and sheer incompetence is the most marked characteristic of modern English prose, and especially of any kind of political writing. As soon as certain topics are raised, the concrete melts into the abstract and no one seems able to think of turns of speech that are not hackneyed: prose consists less and less of *words* chosen for the sake of their meaning, and more and more of *phrases* tacked together like the sections of a prefabricated hen-house. I list below, with notes and examples, various of the tricks by means of which the work of prose-construction is habitually dodged:

Dying metaphors. A newly invented metaphor assists thought by evoking a visual image, while on the other hand a metaphor which is technically "dead" (e.g. *iron resolution*) has in effect reverted to being an ordinary word and can generally be used without loss of vividness. But in between these two classes there is a huge dump of worn-out metaphors which have lost all evocative power and are merely used because they save people the trouble of inventing phrases for themselves. Examples are: *Ring the changes on, take up the cudgels for, toe the line, ride roughshod over, stand shoulder to shoulder with, play into the hands of, no axe to grind, grist to the mill, fishing in troubled waters, on the order of the day, Achilles' heel, swan song, hotbed.* Many of these are used without knowledge of their meaning (what is a "rift," for instance?), and incompatible metaphors are frequently mixed, a sure sign that the writer is not interested in what he is saying. Some metaphors now current have been twisted out of their original meaning without those who use them even being aware of the fact. For example, *toe the line* is sometimes written *tow the line*. Another example is the *hammer and the anvil*, now always used with the implication that the anvil gets the worst of it. In real life it is always the anvil that breaks the hammer, never the other way about: a writer who stopped to think what he was saying would be aware of this, and would avoid perverting the original phrase.

Operators or verbal false limbs. These save the trouble of picking out   6
appropriate verbs and nouns, and at the same time pad each sentence with extra syllables which give it an appearance of symmetry. Characteristic phrases are *render inoperative, militate against, make contact with, be subjected to, give rise to, give grounds for, have the effect of, play a leading part (role) in, make itself felt, take effect, exhibit a tendency to, serve the purpose of, etc., etc*. The keynote is the elimination of simple verbs. Instead of being a single word, such as *break, stop, spoil, mend, kill*, a verb becomes a *phrase*, made up of a noun or adjective tacked on to some general-purpose verb such as *prove, serve, form, play, render*. In addition, the passive voice is wherever possible used in preference to the active, and noun constructions are used instead of gerunds (*by examination of* instead of *by examining*). The range of verbs is further cut down by means of the -*ize* and *de*-formations, and the banal statements are given an appearance of profundity by means of the *not un*-formation. Simple conjunctions and prepositions are replaced by such phrases as *with respect to, having regard to, the fact that, by dint of, in view of, in the interests of, on the hypothesis that*; and the ends of sentences are saved by anticlimax by such resounding common-places as *greatly to be desired, cannot be left out of account, a development to be expected in the near future, deserving of serious consideration, brought to a satisfactory conclusion*, and so on and so forth.

Pretentious diction. Words like *phenomenon, element, individual* (as   7
noun), *objective, categorical, effective, virtual, basic, primary, promote, constitute, exhibit, exploit, utilize, eliminate, liquidate*, are used to dress up simple statement and give an air of scientific impartiality to biased judgments. Adjectives like *epoch-making, epic, historic, unforgettable, triumphant, age-old, inevitable, inexorable, veritable*, are used to dignify the sordid processes of international politics, while writing that aims at glorifying war usually takes on an archaic color, its characteristic words being: *realm, throne, chariot, mailed fist, trident, sword, shield, buckler, banner, jack-boot, clarion*. Foreign words and expressions such as *cul de sac, ancien régime, deus ex machina, mutatis mutandis, status quo, gleichschaltung,*

weltanschauung, are used to give an air of culture and elegance. Except for the useful abbreviations *i.e., e.g.,* and *etc.,* there is no real need for any of the hundreds of foreign phrases now current in English. Bad writers, and especially scientific, political and sociological writers, are nearly always haunted by the notion that Latin or Greek words are grander than Saxon ones, and unnecessary words like *expedite, ameliorate, predict, extraneous, deracinated, clandestine, subaqueous* and hundreds of others constantly gain ground from their Anglo-Saxon opposite numbers.* The jargon peculiar to Marxist writing (*hyena, hangman, cannibal, petty bourgeois, these gentry, lacquey, flunkey, mad dog, White Guard,* etc.) consists largely of words and phrases translated from Russian, German or French; but the normal way of coining a new word is to use a Latin or Greek root with the appropriate affix and, where necessary, the size formation. It is often easier to make up words of this kind (*deregionalize, impermissible, extramarital, nonfragmentary* and so forth) than to think up the English words that will cover one's meaning. The result, in general, is an increase in slovenliness and vagueness.

Meaningless words. In certain kinds of writing, particularly in art criticism and literary criticism, it is normal to come across long passages which are almost completely lacking in meaning.† Words like *romantic, plastic, values, human, dead, sentimental, natural, vitality,* as used in art criticism, are strictly meaningless, in the sense that they not only do not point to any discoverable object, but are hardly ever expected to do so by the reader. When one critic writes, "The outstanding feature of Mr. X's work is its living quality," while another writes, "The immediately striking thing about Mr. X's work is its peculiar deadness," the reader accepts this as a simple difference of opinion. If words like *black* and *white* were involved, instead of the jargon words *dead* and *living,* he would see at once that language was being used in an improper way.

8

---

*An interesting illustration of this is the way in which the English flower names which were in use till very recently are being ousted by Greek ones, *snapdragon* becoming *antirrhinum, forget-me-not* becoming *myosotis,* etc. It is hard to see any practical reason for this change of fashion: it is probably due to an instinctive turning-away from the more homely word and a vague feeling that the Greek word is scientific.

†Example: "Comfort's catholicity of perception and image, strangely Whitemanesque in range, almost the exact opposite in aesthetic compulsion, continues to evoke that trembling atmospheric accumulative hinting at a cruel, an inexorably serene timelessness . . . . Wrey Gardiner scores by aiming at simple bull's-eyes with precision. Only they are not so simple, and through this contented sadness runs more than the surface bitter-sweet of resignation." (*Poetry Quarterly.*)

Many political words are similarly abused. The word *Fascism* has now no meaning except in so far as it signifies "something not desirable." The words *democracy, socialism, freedom, patriotic, realistic, justice*, have each of them several different meanings which cannot be reconciled with one another. In the case of a word like *democracy*, not only is there no agreed definition, but the attempt to make one is resisted from all sides. It is almost universally felt that when we call a country democratic we are praising it: consequently the defenders of every kind of régime claim that it is a democracy, and fear that they might have to stop using the word if it were tied down to any one meaning. Words of this kind are often used in a consciously dishonest way. That is, the person who uses them has his own private definition, but allows his hearer to think he means something quite different. Statements like *Marshal Pétain was a true patriot, The Soviet Press is the freest in the world, The Catholic Church is opposed to persecution*, are almost always made with intent to deceive. Other words used in variable meanings, in most cases more or less dishonestly, are: *class, totalitarian, science, progressive, reactionary, bourgeois, equality.*

Now that I have made this catalogue of swindles and perversions, 9 let me give another example of the kind of writing that they lead to. This time it must of its nature be an imaginary one. I am going to translate a passage of good English into modern English of the worst sort. Here is a well-known verse from *Ecclesiastes:*

"I returned and saw under the sun, that the race is not to the swift, 10 nor the battle to the strong, neither yet bread to the wise, nor yet riches to men of understanding, nor yet favour to men of skill; but time and chance happeneth to them all."

Here it is in modern English: 11

"Objective considerations of contemporary phenomena compels 12 the conclusion that success or failure in competitive activities exhibits no tendency to be commensurate with innate capacity, but that a considerable element of the unpredictable must invariably be taken into account."

This is a parody, but not a very gross one. Exhibit (3), above, for in- 13 stance, contains several patches of the same kind of English. It will be seen that I have not made a full translation. The beginning and ending of the sentence follow the original meaning fairly closely, but in the middle the concrete illustrations—race, battle, bread—dissolve into the vague phrase "success or failure in competitive activities." This had to be so, because no modern writer of the kind I am discussing—no one capable of using phrases like "objective consideration of contemporary phenomena"—would ever tabulate his thoughts in that precise and detailed way. The whole tendency of modern prose is away from concreteness.

Now analyse these two sentences a little more closely. The first contains forty-nine words but only sixty syllables, and all its words are those of everyday life. The second contains thirty-eight words of ninety syllables: eighteen of its words are from Latin roots, and one from Greek. The first sentence contains six vivid images, and only one phrase ("time and chance") that could be called vague. The second contains not a single fresh, arresting phrase, and in spite of its ninety syllables it gives only a shortened version of the meaning contained in the first. Yet without a doubt it is the second kind of sentence that is gaining ground in modern English. I do not want to exaggerate. This kind of writing is not yet universal, and outcrops of simplicity will occur here and there in the worst-written page. Still, if you or I were told to write a few lines on the uncertainty of human fortunes, we should probably come much nearer to my imaginary sentence than to the one from *Ecclesiastes*.

As I have tried to show, modern writing at its worst does not consist of picking out words for the sake of their meaning and inventing images in order to make the meaning clearer. It consists in gumming together long strips of words which have already been set in order by someone else, and making the results presentable by sheer humbug. The attraction of this way of writing is that it is easy. It is easier—even quicker, once you have the habit—to say *In my opinion it is not an unjustifiable assumption that* than to say *I think*. If you use ready-made phrases, you not only don't have to hunt about for words; you also don't have to bother with the rhythms of your sentences, since these phrases are generally so arranged as to be more or less euphonious. When you are composing in a hurry—when you are dictating to a stenographer, for instance, or making a public speech—it is natural to fall into a pretentious, Latinized style. Tags like *a consideration which we should do well to bear in mind* or *a conclusion to which all of us would readily assent* will save many a sentence from coming down with a bump. By using stale metaphors, similes and idioms, you save much mental effort, at the cost of leaving your meaning vague, not only for your reader but for yourself. This is the significance of mixed metaphors. The sole aim of a metaphor is to call up a visual image. When these images clash—as in *The Fascist octopus has sung its swan song, the jackboot is thrown into the melting pot*—it can be taken as certain that the writer is not seeing a mental image of the objects he is naming; in other words he is not really thinking. Look again at the examples I gave at the beginning of this essay. Professor Laski (1) uses five negatives in fifty-three words. One of these is superfluous, making nonsense of the whole passage, and in addition there is the slip *alien* for *akin*, making further nonsense, and several avoidable pieces of clumsiness which increase the general vagueness. Professor Hogben (2) plays ducks and drakes with a battery which is able to write prescriptions, and, while disapproving of the everyday phrase *put up with*, is unwilling to look *egregious* up in the dictionary and see what it means; (3), if one takes an uncharitable attitude towards it, is simply meaningless: probably one could work out its intended meaning by reading the whole of the article in which it occurs. In (4), the writer knows more or less what he wants to say, but an accumulation of stale phrases chokes him like tea leaves blocking a sink. In (5), words and meaning have almost parted company. People who write in this manner usually have a general emotional mean-ing—they dislike one thing and want to express solidarity with another—but they are not interested in the detail of what they are saying. A scrupulous writer, in every sentence that he writes, will ask himself at least four questions, thus: What am I trying to say? What words will ex-press it? What image or idiom will make it clearer? Is this image fresh enough to have an effect? And he will probably ask himself two more: Could I put it more shortly? Have I said anything that is avoidably ugly? But you are not obliged to go to all this trouble. You can shirk it by sim-ply throwing your mind open and letting the ready-made phrases come crowding in. They will construct your sentences for you—even think your thoughts for you, to a certain extent—and at need they will perform the important service of partially concealing your meaning even from yourself. It is at this point that the special connection between politics and the debasement of language becomes clear.

In our time it is broadly true that political writing is bad writing. Where it is not true, it will generally be found that the writer is some kind of rebel, expressing his private opinions and not a "party line." Orthodoxy, of whatever color, seems to demand a lifeless, imitative style. The political dialects to be found in pamphlets, leading articles, mani-festos, White Papers and the speeches of under-secretaries do, of course, vary from party to party, but they are all alike in that one almost never finds in them a fresh, vivid, home-made turn of speech. When one watches some tired hack on the platform mechanically repeating the fa-miliar phrases—*bestial atrocities, iron heel, bloodstained tyranny, free peoples of the world, stand shoulder to shoulder*—one often has a curious feeling that one is not watching a live human being but some kind of dummy: a feel-ing which suddenly becomes stronger at moments when the light catches the speaker's spectacles and turns them into blank discs which seem to have no eyes behind them. And this is not altogether fanciful. A speaker who uses that kind of phraseology has gone some distance towards turn-ing himself into a machine. The appropriate noises are coming out of his larynx, but his brain is not involved as it would be if he were choosing his words for himself. If the speech he is making is one that he is accus-tomed to make over and over again, he may be almost unconscious of what he is saying, as one is when one utters the responses in church. And this reduced state of consciousness, if not indispensable, is at any rate fa-vorable to political conformity.

15

In our time, political speech and writing are largely the defence of the indefensible. Things like the continuance of British rule in India, the Russian purges and deportation, the dropping of the atom bombs on Japan, can indeed be defended, but only by arguments which are too brutal for most people to face, and which do not square with the professed aims of political parties. Thus political language has to consist largely of euphemism, question-begging and sheer cloudy vagueness. Defenceless villages are bombarded from the air, the inhabitants driven out into the countryside, the cattle machine-gunned, the huts set on fire with incendiary bullets: this is called *pacification*. Millions of peasants are robbed of their farms and sent trudging along the roads with no more than they can carry: this is called *transfer of population* or *rectification of frontiers*. People are imprisoned for years without trial, or shot in the back of the neck or sent to die of scurvy in Arctic lumber camps: this is called *elimination of unreliable elements*. Such phraseology is needed if one wants to name things without calling up mental pictures of them. Consider for instance some comfortable English professor defending Russian totalitarianism. He cannot say outright, "I believe in killing off your opponents when you can get good results by doing so." Probably, therefore, he will say something like this:

"While freely conceding that the Soviet régime exhibits certain features which the humanitarian may be inclined to deplore, we must, I think, agree that a certain curtailment of the right to political opposition is an unavoidable concomitant of transitional periods, and that the rigors which the Russian people have been called upon to undergo have been amply justified in the sphere of concrete achievement."

The inflated style is itself a kind of euphemism. A mass of Latin words falls upon the facts like soft snow, blurring the outlines and covering up all the details. The great enemy of clear language is insincerity. When there is a gap between one's real and one's declared aims, one turns as it were instinctively to long words and exhausted idioms, like a cuttlefish squirting out ink. In our age there is no such thing as "keeping out of politics." All issues are political issues, and politics itself is a mass of lies, evasions, folly, hatred and schizophrenia. When the general atmosphere is bad, language must suffer. I should expect to find—this is a guess which I have not sufficient knowledge to verify—that the German, Russian and Italian languages have all deteriorated in the last ten or fifteen years, as a result of dictatorship.

But if thought corrupts language, language can also corrupt thought. A bad usage can spread by tradition and imitation, even among people who should and do know better. The debased language that I have been discussing is in some ways very convenient. Phrases like *a not unjustifiable assumption, leaves much to be desired, would serve no good purpose, a consideration which we should do well to bear in mind*, are a continuous temptation, a packet of aspirins always at one's elbow. Look back through this essay, and for certain you will find that I have again and again committed the very faults I am protesting against. By this morning's post I have received a pamphlet dealing with conditions in Germany. The author tells me that he "felt impelled" to write it. I open it at random, and here is almost the first sentence that I see: "[The Allies] have an opportunity not only of achieving a radical transformation of Germany's social and political structure in such a way as to avoid a nationalistic reaction in Germany itself, but at the same time of laying the foundations of a co-operative and unified Europe." You see, he "feels impelled" to write—feels, presumably, that he has something new to say—and yet his words, like cavalry horses answering the bugle, group themselves automatically into the familiar dreary pattern. This invasion of one's mind by ready-made phrases (*lay the foundations, achieve a radical transformation*) can only be prevented if one is constantly on guard against them, and every such phrase anaesthetizes a portion of one's brain.

I said earlier that the decadence of our language is probably cur-   20
able. Those who deny this would argue, if they produced an argument at all, that language merely reflects existing social conditions, and that we cannot influence its development by any direct tinkering with words and constructions. So far as the general tone or spirit of a language goes, this may be true, but it is not true in detail. Silly words and expressions have often disappeared, not through any evolutionary process but owing to the conscious action of a minority. Two recent examples were *explore every avenue* and *leave no stone unturned*, which were killed by the jeers of a few journalists. There is a long list of flyblown metaphors which could similarly be got rid of if enough people would interest themselves in the job; and it should also be possible to laugh the *not un*-formation out of existence,* to reduce the amount of Latin and Greek in the average sentence, to drive out foreign phrases and strayed scientific words, and, in general, to make pretentiousness unfashionable. But all these are minor points. The defence of the English language implies more than this, and perhaps it is best to start by saying what it does *not* imply.

To begin with it has nothing to do with archaism, with the sal-   21
vaging of obsolete words and turns of speech, or with the setting up of a "standard English" which must never be departed from. On the contrary, it is especially concerned with the scrapping of every word or idiom which has outworn its usefulness. It has nothing to do with correct grammar and syntax, which are of no importance so long as one

---

*One can cure oneself of the *not un*-formation by memorizing this sentence: *A not unblack dog was chasing a not unsmall rabbit across a not ungreen field.*

makes one's meaning clear, or with the avoidance of Americanisms, or with having what is called a "good prose style." On the other hand it is not concerned with fake simplicity and the attempt to make written English colloquial. Nor does it even imply in every case preferring the Saxon word to the Latin one, though it does imply using the fewest and shortest words that will cover one's meaning. What is above all needed is to let the meaning choose the word, and not the other way about. In prose, the worst thing one can do with words is to surrender to them. When you think of a concrete object, you think wordlessly, and then, if you want to describe the thing you have been visualizing you probably hunt about till you find the exact words that seem to fit it. When you think of something abstract you are more inclined to use words from the start, and unless you make a conscious effort to prevent it, the existing dialect will come rushing in and do the job for you, at the expense of blurring or even changing your meaning. Probably it is better to put off using words as long as possible and get one's meaning as clear as one can through pictures or sensations. Afterwards one can choose—not simply *accept*—the phrases that will best cover the meaning, and then switch round and decide what impression one's words are likely to make on another person. This last effort of the mind cuts out all stale or mixed images, all prefabricated phrases, needless repetitions, and humbug and vagueness generally. But one can often be in doubt about the effect of a word or a phrase, and one needs rules that one can rely on when instinct fails. I think the following rules will cover most cases:

i. Never use a metaphor, simile or other figure of speech which you are used to seeing in print.

ii. Never use a long word where a short one will do.

iii. If it is possible to cut a word out, always cut it out.

iv. Never use the passive where you can use the active.

v. Never use a foreign phrase, a scientific word or a jargon word if you can think of an everyday English equivalent.

vi. Break any of these rules sooner than say anything outright barbarous.

These rules sound elementary, and so they are, but they demand a deep change of attitude in anyone who has grown used to writing in the style now fashionable. One could keep all of them and still write bad English, but one could not write the kind of stuff that I quoted in those five specimens at the beginning of this article.

I have not here been considering the literary use of language, but merely language as an instrument for expressing and not for concealing or preventing thought. Stuart Chase and others have come near to claiming that all abstract words are meaningless, and have used this as a pretext for advocating a kind of political quietism. Since you don't know what Fascism is, how can you struggle against Fascism? One need not swallow such absurdities as this, but one ought to recognize that the present political chaos is connected with the decay of language, and that one can probably bring about some improvement by starting at the verbal end. If you simplify your English, you are freed from the worst follies of orthodoxy. You cannot speak any of the necessary dialects, and when you make a stupid remark its stupidity will be obvious, even to yourself. Political language—and with variations this is true of all political parties, from Conservatives to Anarchists—is designed to make lies sound truthful and murder respectable, and to give an appearance of solidity to pure wind. One cannot change this all in a moment, but one can at least change one's own habits, and from time to time one can even, if one jeers loudly enough, send some wornout and useless phrase—some *jackboot, Achilles' heel, hotbed, melting pot, acid test, veritable inferno* or other lump of verbal refuse—into the dustbin where it belongs.

1946

Purpose and Meaning

1. In what sense is the word *politics* used in the title? What is the significance of this word in terms of the thesis of the essay?

2. What is the historical and political context of this essay? What conditions in Orwell's time contributed to using English "in a bad way"?

3. According to Orwell, what is it about the nature of language that makes it so difficult to break bad writing habits and acquire good ones? Why, for example, does Orwell use the generic *he*?

Language and Style

1. Orwell discusses four major attributes of poor writing: dying metaphors, operators, pretentious diction, and meaningless words. Is Orwell's own writing in this essay free of these devices? Choose any of Orwell's other essays in this book, and apply his own standards to it.

2. Orwell claims that good English has "nothing to do with correct grammar and syntax . . . as long as one makes one's meaning clear." Examine the syntax of the following sentence from paragraph 2: "But an effect can become a cause, reinforcing the original cause and producing the same effect in an intensified form, and so on indefinitely." Using Orwell's criteria for good writing, can you call this a clear sentence? Are Orwell's grammar and syntax clear throughout the essay? Justify your response.

3. Orwell provides us with a writing lesson in this essay. What is his tone as a teacher? How did you arrive at your opinion?

Strategy and Structure

1. Study the first two paragraphs of this essay. How well do they establish Orwell's basic argument? What specific rhetorical devices does Orwell use to introduce his subject?

2. Orwell uses an abundance of examples for every point he tries to demonstrate about bad writing. Does he need so many to get his point across? Would fewer examples make the essay clearer and more concise? What effect was Orwell trying to create on the reader by including such an extensive catalog?

3. Orwell interrupts the serious tone of his essay with an example of a passage he "translated" from the Bible. What is the purpose of this example? Why is the passage a good device for maintaining the reader's interest? Do you agree that it is not a "very gross" parody? Explain your answer.

4. Explain the importance of definition and hypothetical reasoning in the structure of this essay.

Thinking and Writing

1. Using Orwell's four categories of bad writing, write an argumentative essay using examples from contemporary politics and media to demonstrate that English remains a dangerously bankrupt language.

2. Try your hand at writing a parody of poor writing. Select a paragraph from this essay or any of the other essays by Orwell in this book, and create a specimen of bad prose. Afterward, study the result. What makes the writing unclear, pretentious, or meaningless?

3. Write an extended definition of a "meaningless" term that is abused frequently or used hypocritically in the United States today. You might want to check the annual "doublespeak" awards.

o━●○━●○━●○━●○━●○━●○━●○━●○━●○━●○━●○━●○

Antisemitism in Britain

There are about 400,000 known Jews in Britain, and in addition   1
some thousands or, at most, scores of thousands of Jewish refugees who have entered the country from 1934 onwards. The Jewish population is almost entirely concentrated in half a dozen big towns and is mostly employed in the food, clothing and furniture trades. A few of the big mo-

nopolies, such as the ICI, one or two leading newspapers and at least one big chain of department stores are Jewish-owned or partly Jewish-owned, but it would be very far from the truth to say that British business life is dominated by Jews. The Jews seem, on the contrary, to have failed to keep up with the modern tendency towards big amalgamations and to have remained fixed in those trades which are necessarily carried out on a small scale and by old-fashioned methods.

I start off with these background facts, which are already known to any well-informed person, in order to emphasise that there is no real Jewish "problem" in England. The Jews are not numerous or powerful enough, and it is only in what are loosely called "intellectual circles" that they have any noticeable influence. Yet it is generally admitted that anti-semitism is on the increase, that it has been greatly exacerbated by the war, and that humane and enlightened people are not immune to it. It does not take violent forms (English people are almost invariably gentle and law-abiding), but it is ill-natured enough, and in favourable circumstances it could have political results. Here are some samples of antisemitic remarks that have been made to me during the past year or two:

> Middle-aged office employee: "I generally come to work by bus. It takes longer, but I don't care about using the Underground from Golders Green nowadays. There's too many of the Chosen Race travelling on that line."

> Tobacconist (woman): "No, I've got no matches for you. I should try the lady down the street. *She's* always got matches. One of the Chosen Race, you see."

> Young intellectual, Communist or near-Communist: "No, I do *not* like Jews. I've never made any secret of that. I can't stick them. Mind you, I'm not antisemitic, of course."

> Middle-class woman: "Well, no one could call me antisemitic, but I do think the way these Jews behave is too absolutely stinking. The way they push their way to the head of queues, and so on. They're so abominably selfish. I think they're responsible for a lot of what happens to them."

> Milk roundsman: "A Jew don't do no work, not the same as what an Englishman does. 'E's too clever. We work with this 'ere" (flexes his biceps). "They work with that there" (taps his forehead).

> Chartered accountant, intelligent, left-wing in an undirected way: "These bloody Yids are all pro-German. They'd change sides tomorrow if the Nazis got here. I see a lot of them in my business. They admire Hitler at the bottom of their hearts. They'll always suck up to anyone who kicks them."

> Intelligent woman, on being offered a book dealing with antisemitism and German atrocities: "Don't show it to me, *please* don't show it to me. It'll only make me hate the Jews more than ever."

I could fill pages with similar remarks, but these will do to go on with. Two facts emerge from them. One—which is very important and which I must return to in a moment—is that above a certain intellectual level people are ashamed of being antisemitic and are careful to draw a distinction between "antisemitism" and "disliking Jews." The other is that antisemitism is an irrational thing. The Jews are accused of specific offences (for instance, bad behaviour in food queues) which the person speaking feels strongly about, but it is obvious that these accusations merely rationalise some deep-rooted prejudice. To attempt to counter them with facts and statistics is useless, and may sometimes be worse than useless. As the last of the above-quoted remarks shows, people can remain antisemitic, or at least anti-Jewish, while being fully aware that their outlook is indefensible. If you dislike somebody, you dislike him and there is an end of it: your feelings are not made any better by a recital of his virtues.

It so happens that the war has encouraged the growth of anti-semitism and even, in the eyes of many ordinary people, given some jus-tification for it. To begin with, the Jews are one people of whom it can be said with complete certainty that they will benefit by an Allied victory. Consequently the theory that "this is a Jewish war" has a certain plausi-bility, all the more so because the Jewish war effort seldom gets its fair share of recognition. The British Empire is a huge heterogeneous organi-sation held together largely by mutual consent, and it is often necessary to flatter the less reliable elements at the expense of the more loyal ones. To publicise the exploits of Jewish soldiers, or even to admit the exis-tence of a considerable Jewish army in the Middle East, rouses hostility in South Africa, the Arab countries and elsewhere: it is easier to ignore the whole subject and allow the man in the street to go on thinking that Jews are exceptionally clever at dodging military service. Then again, Jews are to be found in exactly those trades which are bound to incur unpopularity with the civilian public in war-time. Jews are mostly con-cerned with selling food, clothes, furniture and tobacco—exactly the commodities of which there is a chronic shortage, with consequent over-charging, black-marketing and favouritism. And again, the common charge that Jews behave in an exceptionally cowardly way during air raids was given a certain amount of colour by the big raids of 1940. As it happened, the Jewish quarter of Whitechapel was one of the first areas to be heavily blitzed, with the natural result that swarms of Jewish refugees distributed themselves all over London. If one judged merely from these war-time phenomena, it would be easy to imagine that anti-semitism is a quasi-rational thing, founded on mistaken premises. And naturally the antisemite thinks of himself as a reasonable being. Whenever I have touched on this subject in a newspaper article, I have always had a considerable "come-back," and invariably some of the let-ters are from well-balanced, middling people—doctors, for example—

with no apparent economic grievance. These people always say (as Hitler says in *Mein Kampf*) that they started out with no anti-Jewish prejudice but were driven into their present position by mere observation of the facts. Yet one of the marks of antisemitism is an ability to believe stories that could not possibly be true. One could see a good example of this in the strange accident that occurred in London in 1942, when a crowd, frightened by a bomb-burst nearby, fled into the mouth of an Underground station, with the result that something over a hundred people were crushed to death. The very same day it was repeated all over London that "the Jews were responsible." Clearly, if people will believe this kind of thing, one will not get much further by arguing with them. The only useful approach is to discover *why* they can swallow absurdities on one particular subject while remaining sane on others.

But now let me come back to that point I mentioned earlier—that there is widespread awareness of the prevalence of antisemitic feeling, and unwillingness to admit sharing it. Among educated people, antisemitism is held to be an unforgivable sin and in a quite different category from other kinds of racial prejudice. People will go to remarkable lengths to demonstrate that they are *not* antisemitic. Thus, in 1943 an intercession service on behalf of the Polish Jews was held in a synagogue in St John's Wood. The local authorities declared themselves anxious to participate in it, and the service was attended by the mayor of the borough in his robes and chain, by representatives of all the churches, and by detachments of RAF, Home Guards, nurses, Boy Scouts and what not. On the surface it was a touching demonstration of solidarity with the suffering Jews. But it was essentially a *conscious* effort to behave decently be people whose subjective feelings must in many cases have been very different. That quarter of London is partly Jewish, antisemitism is rife there, and, as I well knew, some of the men sitting round me in the synagogue were tinged by it. Indeed, the commander of my own platoon of Home Guards, who had been especially keen beforehand that we should "make a good show" at the intercession service, was an ex-member of Mosley's Blackshirts. While this division of feeling exists, tolerance of mass violence against Jews, or, what is more important, antisemitic legislation, are not possible in England. It is not at present possible, indeed, that antisemitism should *become respectable*. But this is less of an advantage than it might appear.

One effect of the persecutions in Germany has been to prevent antisemitism from being seriously studied. In England a brief inadequate survey was made by Mass Observation a year or two ago, but if there has been any other investigation of the subject, then its findings have been kept strictly secret. At the same time there has been conscious suppression, by all thoughtful people, of anything likely to wound Jewish susceptibilities. After 1934 the "Jew joke" disappeared as though by

5

6

magic from postcards, periodicals and the music-hall stage, and to put an unsympathetic Jewish character into a novel or short story came to be regarded as antisemitism. On the Palestine issue, too, it was *de rigueur* among enlightened people to accept the Jewish case as proved and avoid examining the claims of the Arabs—a decision which might be correct on its own merits, but which was adopted primarily because the Jews were in trouble and it was felt that one must not criticise them. Thanks to Hitler, therefore, you had a situation in which the press was in effect censored in favour of the Jews while in private antisemitism was on the up-grade, even, to some extent, among sensitive and intelligent people. This was particularly noticeable in 1940 at the time of the internment of the refugees. Naturally, every thinking person felt that it was his duty to protest against the wholesale locking-up of unfortunate foreigners who for the most part were only in England because they were opponents of Hitler. Privately, however, one heard very different sentiments expressed. A minority of the refugees behaved in an exceedingly tactless way, and the feeling against them necessarily had an antisemitic undercurrent, since they were largely Jews. A very eminent figure in the Labour Party—I won't name him, but he is one of the most respected people in England—said to me quite violently: "We never asked these people to come to this country. If they choose to come here, let them take the consequences." Yet this man would as a matter of course have associated himself with any kind of petition or manifesto against the internment of aliens. This feeling that antisemitism is something sinful and disgraceful, something that a civilised person does not suffer from, is unfavourable to a scientific approach, and indeed many people will admit that they are frightened of probing too deeply into the subject. They are frightened, that is to say, of discovering not only that antisemitism is spreading, but that they themselves are infected by it.

To see this in perspective one must look back a few decades, to the days when Hitler was an out-of-work house-painter whom nobody had heard of. One would then find that though antisemitism is sufficiently in evidence now, it is probably *less* prevalent in England than it was thirty years ago. It is true that antisemitism as a fully thought-out racial or religious doctrine has never flourished in England. There has never been much feeling against intermarriage, or against Jews taking a prominent part in public life. Nevertheless, thirty years ago it was accepted more or less as a law of nature that a Jew was a figure of fun and—though superior in intelligence—slightly deficient in "character." In theory a Jew suffered from no legal disabilities, but in effect he was debarred from certain professions. He would probably not have been accepted as an officer in the navy, for instance, nor in what is called a "smart" regiment in the army. A Jewish boy at a public school almost invariably had a bad time. He could, of course, live down his Jewishness if he was exceptionally charming or athletic, but it was an initial disability comparable to a stammer or a birthmark. Wealthy Jews tended to disguise themselves under aristocratic English or Scottish names, and to the average person it seemed quite natural that they should do this, just as it seems natural for a criminal to change his identity if possible. About twenty years ago, in Rangoon, I was getting into a taxi with a friend when a small ragged boy of fair complexion rushed up to us and began a complicated story about having arrived from Colombo on a ship and wanting money to get back. His manner and appearance were difficult to "place," and I said to him:

"You speak very good English. What nationality are you?"   8

He answered eagerly in his chi-chi accent: "I am a *Joo*, sir!"   9

And I remember turning to my companion and saying, only partly   10
in joke, "He admits it openly." All the Jews I had known till then were people who were ashamed of being Jews, or at any rate preferred not to talk about their ancestry, and if forced to do so tended to use the word "Hebrew."

The working-class attitude was no better. The Jew who grew up in   11
Whitechapel took it for granted that he would be assaulted, or at least hooted at, if he ventured into one of the Christian slums nearby, and the "Jew joke" of the music halls and the comic papers was almost consistently ill-natured.* There was also literary Jew-baiting, which in the hands of Belloc, Chesterton and their followers reached an almost continental level of scurrility. Non-Catholic writers were sometimes guilty of the same thing in a milder form. There has been a perceptible antisemitic strain in English literature from Chaucer onwards, and without even getting up from this table to consult a book I can think of passages which *if written now* would be stigmatised as antisemitism, in the works of Shakespeare, Smollett, Thackeray, Bernard Shaw, H. G. Wells, T. S. Eliot, Aldous Huxley and various others. Offhand, the only English writers I can think of who, before the days of Hitler, made a definite effort to stick up for Jews are Dickens and Charles Reade. And however little the average intellectual may have agreed with the opinions of Belloc and Chesterton, he did not acutely disapprove of them.

*It is interesting to compare the "Jew joke" with that other stand-by of the music halls, the "Scotch joke," which superficially it resembles. Occasionally a story is told (e.g. the Jew and the Scotsman who went into a pub together and both died of thirst) which puts both races on an equality, but in general the Jew is credited *merely* with cunning and avarice while the Scotsman is credited with physical hardihood as well. This is seen, for example, in the story of the Jew and the Scotsman who go together to a meeting which has been advertised as free. Unexpectedly there is a collection, and to avoid this the Jew faints and the Scotsman carries him out. Here the Scotsman performs the athletic feat of carrying the other. It would seem vaguely wrong if it were the other way about.

Chesterton's endless tirades against Jews, which he thrust into stories and essays upon the flimsiest pretexts, never got him into trouble—indeed Chesterton was one of the most generally respected figures in English literary life. Anyone who wrote in that strain *now* would bring down a storm of abuse upon himself, or more probably would find it impossible to get his writings published.

If, as I suggest, prejudice against Jews has always been pretty widespread in England, there is no reason to think that Hitler has genuinely diminished it. He has merely caused a sharp division between the politically conscious person who realises that this is not a time to throw stones at the Jews, and the unconscious person whose native antisemitism is increased by the nervous strain of the war. One can assume, therefore, that many people who would perish rather than admit to antisemitic feelings are secretly prone to them. I have already indicated that I believe antisemitism to be essentially a neurosis, but of course it has its rationalisations, which are sincerely believed in and are partly true. The rationalisation put forward by the common man is that the Jew is an exploiter. The partial justification for this is that the Jew, in England, is generally a small businessman—that is to say a person whose depredations are more obvious and intelligible than those of, say, a bank or an insurance company. Higher up the intellectual scale, antisemitism is rationalised by saying that the Jew is a person who spreads disaffection and weakens national morale. Again there is some superficial justification for this. During the past twenty-five years the activities of what are called "intellectuals" have been largely mischievous. I do not think it an exaggeration to say that if the "intellectuals" had done their work a little more thoroughly, Britain would have surrendered in 1940. But the disaffected intelligentsia inevitably included a large number of Jews. With some plausibility it can be said that the Jews are the enemies of our native culture and our national morale. Carefully examined, the claim is seen to be nonsense, but there are always a few prominent individuals who can be cited in support of it. During the past few years there has been what amounts to a counter-attack against the rather shallow Leftism which was fashionable in the previous decade and which was exemplified by such organisations as the Left Book Club. This counterattack (see for instance such books as Arnold Lunn's *The Good Gorilla* or Evelyn Waugh's *Put Out More Flags*) has an antisemitic strain, and it would probably be more marked if the subject were not so obviously dangerous. It so happens that for some decades past Britain has had no nationalist intelligentsia worth bothering about. But British nationalism, i.e. nationalism of an intellectual kind, may revive, and probably will revive if Britain comes out of the present war greatly weakened. The young intellectuals of 1950 may be as naively patriotic as those of 1914. In that case the kind of antisemitism which flourished among the anti-

Dreyfusards in France, and which Chesterton and Belloc tried to import into this country, might get a foothold.

I have no hard-and-fast theory about the origins of antisemitism. 13
The two current explanations, that it is due to economic causes, or on the other hand, that it is a legacy from the Middle Ages, seem to me unsatisfactory, though I admit that if one combines them they can be made to cover the facts. All I would say with confidence is that antisemitism is part of the larger problem of nationalism, which has not yet been seriously examined, and that the Jew is evidently a scapegoat, though *for what* he is a scapegoat we do not yet know. In this essay I have relied almost entirely on my own limited experience, and perhaps every one of my conclusions would be negatived by other observers. The fact is that there are almost no data on this subject. But for what they are worth I will summarise my opinions. Boiled down, they amount to this:

There is more antisemitism in England than we care to admit, and 14
the war has accentuated it, but it is not certain that it is on the increase if one thinks in terms of decades rather than years.

It does not at present lead to open persecution, but it has the effect 15
of making people callous to the sufferings of Jews in other countries.

It is at bottom quite irrational and will not yield to argument. 16

The persecutions in Germany have caused much concealment of 17
antisemitic feeling and thus obscured the whole picture.

The subject needs serious investigation. 18

Only the last point is worth expanding. To study any subject scien- 19
tifically one needs a detached attitude, which is obviously harder when one's own interests or emotions are involved. Plenty of people who are quite capable of being objective about sea urchins, say, or the square root of 2, become schizophrenic if they have to think about the sources of their own income. What vitiates nearly all that is written about antisemitism is the assumption in the writer's mind that *he himself* is immune to it. "Since I know that antisemitism is irrational," he argues, "it follows that I do not share it." He thus fails to start his investigation in the one place where he could get hold of some reliable evidence—that is, in his own mind.

It seems to me a safe assumption that the disease loosely called na- 20
tionalism is now almost universal. Antisemitism is only one manifestation of nationalism, and not everyone will have the disease in that particular form. A Jew, for example, would not be antisemitic: but then many Zionist Jews seem to me to be merely antisemites turned upside-down, just as many Indians and Negroes display the normal colour prejudices in an inverted form. The point is that something, some psychological vitamin, is lacking in modern civilisation, and as a result we are all more or less subject to this lunacy of believing that whole races or nations are mysteriously good or mysteriously evil. I defy any modern in-

tellectual to look closely and honestly into his own mind without coming upon nationalistic loyalties and hatreds of one kind or another. It is the fact that he can feel the emotional tug of such things, and yet see them dispassionately for what they are, that gives him his status as an intellectual. It will be seen, therefore, that the starting point for any investigation of antisemitism should not be "Why does this obviously irrational belief appeal to other people?" but "Why does antisemitism appeal to *me*? What is there about it that I feel to be true?" If one asks this question one at least discovers one's own rationalisations, and it may be possible to find out what lies beneath them. Antisemitism should be investigated—and I will not say by antisemites, but at any rate by people who know that they are not immune to that kind of emotion. When Hitler has disappeared a real enquiry into this subject will be possible, and it would probably be best to start not by debunking antisemitism, but by marshalling all the justifications for it that can be found, in one's own mind or anybody else's. In that way one might get some clues that would lead to its psychological roots. But that antisemitism will be definitively *cured*, without curing the larger disease of nationalism, I do not believe.

1945

Purpose and Meaning

1. Orwell's title flatly states the topic of the essay. In what way does the wording affect the reader's expectations of his purpose? How effective is the title?

2. What relevance does this essay, written in 1945, have for us today? Is it only of historical interest? Explain your answer.

3. What is Orwell's purpose in using the quoted statements in paragraph 2? What do they add to his argument? What, if anything, would be lost if they were removed?

Language and Style

1. As he does in other essays in this collection, Orwell includes an anecdote recalling a personal experience in Rangoon. How is he using the anecdote? What, if anything, does the anecdote add to the overall effectiveness of the essay?

2. In the course of the essay, Orwell shifts pronoun subjects. What is gained or lost by these shifts? How does the shifting affect the direction of the argument?

3. Orwell begins paragraph 5 with a conjunction. Is this an effective word choice? Examine the effectiveness of other transitions that Orwell uses in

the essay. Could the coherence be improved by using different words and phrases?

Strategy and Structure

1. In "Why I Write," which was written a year after this essay, Orwell says that he consciously tried to make political writing into an art and that his starting point was always a feeling of injustice. In what ways is this essay an example of a combination of art and politics? Has Orwell succeeded in his attempt to combine the two kinds of writing?

2. How does Orwell structure his argument? Is it deductive? inductive? both? Explain your answer.

3. What kinds of evidence does Orwell marshal to support his premises? How effective is his use of the testimonial evidence in paragraph 2?

Thinking and Writing

1. Develop an essay in which you expand on Orwell's assertion that nationalism is a cause of antisemitism and other prejudices.

2. Orwell says that antisemitism is "an irrational thing" and that it is useless to attempt to counter it with facts. Are there other irrational beliefs that resist fact? How can these beliefs be countered, if not by reason and fact?

3. Write an essay in which you argue for or against nationalism as a concern in contemporary America.

◦●◦●◦●◦●◦●◦●◦●◦

Why I Write

From a very early age, perhaps the age of five or six, I knew that when I grew up I should be a writer. Between the ages of about seventeen and twenty-four I tried to abandon this idea, but I did so with the consciousness that I was outraging my true nature and that sooner or later I should have to settle down and write books.

I was the middle child of three, but there was a gap of five years on either side, and I barely saw my father before I was eight. For this and other reasons I was somewhat lonely, and I soon developed disagreeable mannerisms which made me unpopular throughout my schooldays. I had the lonely child's habit of making up stories and holding conversations with imaginary persons, and I think from the very start my literary ambitions were mixed up with the feeling of being isolated and under-valued. I knew that I had a facility with words and a power of facing un-pleasant facts, and I felt that this created a sort of private world in which I could get my own back for my failure in everyday life. Nevertheless the volume of serious—i.e. seriously intended—writing which I pro-duced all through my childhood and boyhood would not amount to half a dozen pages. I wrote my first poem at the age of four or five, my mother taking it down to dictation. I cannot remember anything about it except that it was about a tiger and the tiger had "chair-like teeth"—a good enough phrase, but I fancy the poem was a plagiarism of Blake's "Tiger, Tiger." At eleven, when the war of 1914–18 broke out, I wrote a patriotic poem which was printed in the local newspaper, as was an-other, two years later, on the death of Kitchener. From time to time, when I was a bit older, I wrote bad and usually unfinished "nature poems" in the Georgian style. I also, about twice, attempted a short story which was a ghastly failure. That was the total of the would-be serious work that I actually set down on paper during all those years.

However, throughout this time I did in a sense engage in literary   3
activities. To begin with there was the made-to-order stuff which I pro-duced quickly, easily and without much pleasure to myself. Apart from school work, I wrote *vers d'occasion*, semicomic poems which I could turn out at what now seems to me astonishing speed—at fourteen I wrote a whole rhyming play, in imitation of Aristophanes, in about a week—and helped to edit school magazines, both printed and in manu-script. These magazines were the most pitiful burlesque stuff that you could imagine, and I took far less trouble with them than I now would with the cheapest journalism. But side by side with all this, for fifteen years or more, I was carrying out a literary exercise of a quite different kind: this was the making up of a continuous "story" about myself, a sort of diary existing only in the mind. I believe this is a common habit of children and adolescents. As a very small child I used to imagine that I was, say, Robin Hood, and picture myself as the hero of thrilling ad-ventures, but quite soon my "story" ceased to be narcissistic in a crude way and became more and more a mere description of what I was doing and the things I saw. For minutes at a time this kind of thing would be running through my head: "He pushed the door open and entered the room. A yellow beam of sunlight, filtering through the muslin curtains, slanted on to the table, where a matchbox, half open, lay beside the inkpot. With his right hand in his pocket he moved across to the win-dow. Down in the street a tortoise-shell cat was chasing a dead leaf," etc. etc. This habit continued till I was about twenty-five, right through my non-literary years. Although I had to search, and did search, for the right words, I seemed to be making this descriptive effort almost against my will, under a kind of compulsion from outside. The "story" must, I

suppose, have reflected the styles of the various writers I admired at different ages, but so far as I remember it always had the same meticulous descriptive quality.

When I was about sixteen I suddenly discovered the joy of mere words, i.e. the sounds and associations of words. The lines from *Paradise Lost*,

> So hee with difficulty and labour hard
> Moved on: with difficulty and labour hee,

which do not now seem to be so very wonderful, sent shivers down my backbone; and the spelling "hee" for "he" was an added pleasure. As for the need to describe things, I knew all about it already. So it is clear what kind of books I wanted to write, in so far as I could be said to want to write books at that time. I wanted to write enormous naturalistic novels with unhappy endings, full of detailed descriptions and arresting similes, and also full of purple passages in which words were used partly for the sake of their sound. And in fact my first completed novel, *Burmese Days*, which I wrote when I was thirty but projected much earlier, is rather that kind of book.

I give all this background information because I do not think one can assess a writer's motives without knowing something of his early development. His subject matter will be determined by the age he lives in—at least this is true in tumultuous, revolutionary ages like our own—but before he ever begins to write he will have acquired an emotional attitude from which he will never completely escape. It is his job, no doubt, to discipline his temperament and avoid getting stuck at some immature stage, or in some perverse mood: but if he escapes from his early influences altogether, he will have killed his impulse to write. Putting aside the need to earn a living, I think there are four great motives for writing, at any rate for writing prose. They exist in different degrees in every writer, and in any one writer the proportions will vary from time to time, according to the atmosphere in which he is living. They are:

1. Sheer egoism. Desire to seem clever, to be talked about, to be remembered after death, to get your own back on grown-ups who snubbed you in childhood, etc. etc. It is humbug to pretend that this is not a motive, and a strong one. Writers share this characteristic with scientists, artists, politicians, lawyers, soldiers, successful businessmen—in short, with the whole top crust of humanity. The great mass of human beings are not acutely selfish. After the age of about thirty they abandon individual ambition—in many cases, indeed, they almost abandon the sense of being individuals at all—and live chiefly for others, or are simply smothered under drudgery. But there is also the minority of gifted,

wilful people who are determined to live their own lives to the end, and writers belong in this class. Serious writers, I should say, are on the whole more vain and self-centered than journalists, though less interested in money.

2. Aesthetic enthusiasm. Perception of beauty in the external world, or, on the other hand, in words and their right arrangement. Pleasure in the impact of one sound on another, in the firmness of good prose or the rhythm of a good story. Desire to share an experience which one feels is valuable and ought not to be missed. The aesthetic motive is very feeble in a lot of writers, but even a pamphleteer or a writer of textbooks will have pet words and phrases which appeal to him for nonutilitarian reasons; or he may feel strongly about typography, width of margins, etc. Above the level of a railway guide, no book is quite free from aesthetic considerations.

3. Historical impulse. Desire to see things as they are, to find out true facts and store them up for the use of posterity.

4. Political purpose—using the word "political" in the widest possible sense. Desire to push the world in a certain direction, to alter other people's idea of the kind of society that they should strive after. Once again, no book is genuinely free from political bias. The opinion that art should have nothing to do with politics is itself a political attitude.

It can be seen how these various impulses must war against one another, and how they must fluctuate from person to person and from time to time. By nature—taking your "nature" to be the state you have attained when you are first adult—I am a person in whom the first three motives would outweigh the fourth. In a peaceful age I might have written ornate or merely descriptive books, and might have remained almost unaware of my political loyalties. As it is I have been forced into becoming a sort of pamphleteer. First I spent five years in an unsuitable profession (the Indian Imperial Police, in Burma), and then I underwent poverty and the sense of failure. This increased my natural hatred of authority and made me for the first time fully aware of the existence of the working classes, and the job in Burma had given me some understanding of the nature of imperialism: but these experiences were not enough to give me an accurate political orientation. Then came Hitler, the Spanish civil war, etc. By the end of 1935 I had still failed to reach a firm decision. I remember a little poem that I wrote at that date, expressing my dilemma:

> A happy vicar I might have been
> Two hundred years ago,
> To preach upon eternal doom
> And watch my walnuts grow;

But born, alas, in an evil time,
I missed that pleasant haven,
For the hair has grown on my upper lip
And the clergy are all clean-shaven.

And later still the times were good,
We were so easy to please,
We rocked our troubled thoughts to sleep
On the bosoms of the trees.

All ignorant we dared to own
The joys we now dissemble;
The greenfinch on the apple bough
Could make my enemies tremble.

But girls' bellies and apricots,
Roach in a shaded stream,
Horses, ducks in flight at dawn,
All these are a dream.

It is forbidden to dream again;
We maim our joys or hide them;
Horses are made of chromium steel
And little fat men shall ride them.

I am the worm who never turned,
The eunuch without a harem;
Between the priest and the commissar
I walk like Eugene Aram;

And the commissar is telling my fortune
While the radio plays,
But the priest has promised an Austin Seven,
For Duggie always pays.

I dreamed I dwelt in marble halls,
And woke to find it true;
I wasn't born for an age like this;
Was Smith? Was Jones? Were you?

The Spanish war and other events in 1936–37 turned the scale and thereafter I knew where I stood. Every line of serious work that I have written since 1936 has been written, directly or indirectly, *against* totalitarianism and *for* democratic Socialism, as I understand it. It seems to me nonsense, in a period like our own, to think that one can avoid writing of such subjects. Everyone writes of them in one guise or another. It is simply a question of which side one takes and what approach one follows.

And the more one is conscious of one's political bias, the more chance one has of acting politically without sacrificing one's aesthetic and intellectual integrity.

What I have most wanted to do throughout the past ten years is to   11
make political writing into an art. My starting point is always a feeling of partisanship, a sense of injustice. When I set down to write a book, I do not say to myself, "I am going to produce a work of art." I write it because there is some lie that I want to expose, some fact to which I want to draw attention, and my initial concern is to get a hearing. But I could not do the work of writing a book, or even a long magazine article, if it were not also an aesthetic experience. Anyone who cares to examine my work will see that even when it is downright propaganda it contains much that a full-time politician would consider irrelevant. I am not able, and I do not want, completely to abandon the world-view that I acquired in childhood. So long as I remain alive and well I shall continue to feel strongly about prose style, to love the surface of the earth, and to take pleasure in solid objects and scraps of useless information. It is no use trying to suppress that side of myself. The job is to reconcile my ingrained likes and dislikes with the essentially public, non-individual activities that this age forces on all of us.

It is not easy. It raises problems of construction and of language,   12
and it raises in a new way the problem of truthfulness. Let me give just one example of the cruder kind of difficulty that arises. My book about the Spanish civil war, *Homage to Catalonia*, is, of course, a frankly political book, but in the main it is written with a certain detachment and regard for form. I did try very hard in it to tell the whole truth without violating my literary instincts. But among other things it contains a long chapter, full of newspaper quotations and the like, defending the Trotskyists who were accused of plotting with Franco. Clearly such a chapter, which after a year or two would lose its interest for any ordinary reader, must ruin the book. A critic whom I respect read me a lecture about it. "Why did you put in all that stuff?" he said. "You've turned what might have been a good book into journalism." What he said was true, but I could not have done otherwise. I happened to know, what very few people in England had been allowed to know, that innocent men were being falsely accused. If I had not been angry about that I should never have written the book.

In one form or another this problem comes up again. The problem   13
of language is subtler and would take too long to discuss. I will only say that of late years I have tried to write less picturesquely and more exactly. In any case I find that by the time you have perfected any style of writing, you have always outgrown it. *Animal Farm* was the first book in which I tried, with full consciousness of what I was doing, to fuse political purpose and artistic purpose into one whole. I have not written a

novel for seven years, but I hope to write another fairly soon. It is bound to be a failure, every book is a failure, but I know with some clarity what kind of book I want to write.

Looking back through the last page or two, I see that I have made it   14 appear as though my motives in writing were wholly public-spirited. I don't want to leave that as the final impression. All writers are vain, selfish and lazy, and at the very bottom of their motives there lies a mystery. Writing a book is a horrible, exhausting struggle, like a long bout of some painful illness. One would never undertake such a thing if one were not driven on by some demon whom one can neither resist nor understand. For all one knows that demon is simply the same instinct that makes a baby squall for attention. And yet it is also true that one can write nothing readable unless one constantly struggles to efface one's own personality. Good prose is like a window pane. I cannot say with certainty which of my motives are the strongest, but I know which of them deserve to be followed. And looking back through my work, I see that it is invariably where I lacked a political purpose that I wrote lifeless books and was betrayed into purple passages, sentences without meaning, decorative adjectives and humbug generally.

1946

Purpose and Meaning

1. In the final paragraph, Orwell states that no one would write a book "if one were not driven on by some demon." Tracing Orwell's autobiographical sketch from the beginning, find those "demons" that seem to have driven him to write.

2. Examine the four motives that Orwell lists as to why a writer writes. How do these motives correspond to Orwell's own experience as a developing writer?

3. In paragraph 9, the author states "no book is genuinely free from political bias" and "that art should have nothing to do with politics is itself a political attitude." How do you reconcile this seeming contradiction? If Orwell is correct, in what way are any one of the authors in this anthology political writers?

4. In paragraph 13, Orwell says "every book is a failure." What did he mean by "failure"? If this statement is true, why would Orwell—or anyone else for that matter—write?

Language and Style

1. Orwell states in the final paragraph that "one can write nothing readable unless one constantly struggles to efface one's personality." What can you

say about the tone, diction, or mood in "A Hanging" or "Shooting an Elephant" that provides evidence of this effacement?

2. In paragraph 3, Orwell quotes a passage he wrote during his youth. How does it compare to his writing as an adult? What makes Orwell's adult writing more mature?

3. The author makes quite a few references to other authors, writing genres, particular works of writing (including his own), and historical events. How does this knowledge add to our appreciation of the essay?

Strategy and Structure

1. Orwell enumerates the main motives for writing. How does listing them by number affect Orwell's authority? Would the impact or effect have differed if he had not numbered them?

2. Why do you think Orwell has inserted the poem in the essay? Why couldn't the sentiments in the poem have been expressed as succinctly in prose? How does the poem affect the unity of the essay? What does the poem contribute to the essay?

3. Does Orwell's conclusion summarize or add to the information he has already provided? How does the emphasis Orwell places in the final sentence create a strong ending? How does this emphasis help iterate the theme of the essay?

Thinking and Writing

1. Has any experience (or experiences) in your own life influenced your choice of major or of a career? Write an essay exploring this relationship.

2. Follow up on Orwell's assertion that the social and political climate of the times influenced the type of writer he became. Conduct research on Orwell and his times. Then write an extended essay exploring this influence of events on Orwell's literary career.

3. To what specific type of writing is Orwell referring in this essay? Does the function of writing affect one's motivation for writing? Consider such forms of writing as instruction manuals, textbooks, newspaper articles, and college research papers. How do their functions influence the motivation behind the writing of them? Select a particular type of writing, and compose an essay enumerating the motives an author would have for writing it.

LEWIS THOMAS

No one surveys the vast spectrum of contemporary science, medicine, technology, and culture more eloquently than Dr. Lewis Thomas—since 1973 researcher, professor, director, and chancellor of the Memorial Sloan-Kettering Cancer Center in New York City. Born in 1913 in Flushing, New York, the son of a doctor, Thomas received his undergraduate education at Princeton University and his M.D. from Harvard. He wrote poetry at Princeton and published verse during the Great Depression. He also wrote more than two hundred articles on pathology, his specialty, for professional medical journals. At the age of fifty-seven, after teaching at Johns Hopkins, Tulane, the University of Minnesota, and NYU, where he became dean of the medical school, he began his career as an essayist, writing a monthly column for the *New England Journal of Medicine.*

When Thomas, who at the time was dean of the Yale medical school, undertook his monthly column, "Notes of a Biology Watcher," he intended merely to offer twelve-hundred-word reports on current topics of interest in medical and biological science. Yet his clarity, precision, wit, and graceful style, combined with a reverence for the worldly, human estate, soon earned him a broad, popular audience. For Thomas, writing is a labor of love. "We have language," he writes, "and can find metaphors as skillfully and precisely as ribosomes make proteins." He wrestles playfully with language, as we see in "Notes on Punctuation," but turns it typically toward an affirmation of life.

Thomas collected twenty-nine of his columns in *The Lives of a Cell: Notes of a Biology Watcher* (1974). To his surprise, it became a best-seller; clearly the reading public was intrigued by a scientist who could write engaging, persuasive prose about varied and complex topics. Whether comparing people with machines, as in "Computers," or reflecting upon science and the medical profession, as he does in "The Tucson Zoo" and "Becoming a Doctor," Thomas finds ways to celebrate humanity "embedded in nature." In 1975, Thomas received the National Book Award in Arts and Letters for his first essay collection. His subsequent essay collections include *The Medusa and the Snail* (1979) and *Late Night Thoughts on Listening to Mahler's Ninth Symphony* (1983). *The Youngest Science* (1983) is Thomas's memoir of his father's medical career and his own decision to become a physician. Another collection of essays, *The Fragile Species*, was published in 1992.

Thomas seems to astonish himself as much as he does his readers. "I get surprised by an idea that I hadn't anticipated getting, which is a little bit like being in a laboratory. Including, in fact, that the outcome in writing essays, like the outcome in a laboratory, often turns out to be a dud." This bemused, self-effacing, and analogical reflection scarcely obscures Thomas's prominence as the dean of American science writers—a group also represented in this book by Richard Selzer and Stephen Jay Gould. Yet at times—as we sense in his essay "The Tucson Zoo"—Thomas seems somewhat closer to Annie Dillard, another writer in this anthology, in his meditative, philosophical explorations of first and last things. Whether somber or playful, Thomas remains forever in awe of natural creation, offering in his essays a startling statement to the mysteries and marvels of life.

Computers

You can make computers that are almost human. In some respects they are superhuman; they can beat most of us at chess, memorize whole telephone books at a glance, compose music of a certain kind and write obscure poetry, diagnose heart ailments, send personal invitations to vast parties, even go transiently crazy. No one has yet programmed a computer to be of two minds about a hard problem, or to burst out laughing, but that may come. Sooner or later, there will be real human hardware, great whirring, clicking cabinets intelligent enough to read magazines and vote, able to think rings around the rest of us.

Well, maybe, but not for a while anyway. Before we begin organizing sanctuaries and reservations for our software selves, lest we vanish like the whales, here is a thought to relax with.

Even when technology succeeds in manufacturing a machine as big as Texas to do everything we recognize as human, it will still be, at best, a single individual. This amounts to nothing, practically speaking. To match what we can do, there would have to be 3 billion of them with more coming down the assembly line, and I doubt that anyone will put up the money, much less make room. And even so, they would all have to be wired together, intricately and delicately, as we are, communicating with each other, talking incessantly, listening. If they weren't *at* each other this way, all their waking hours, they wouldn't be anything like human, after all. I think we're safe, for a long time ahead.

It is in our collective behavior that we are most mysterious. We won't be able to construct machines like ourselves until we've understood this, and we're not even close. All we know is the phenomenon: we spend our time sending messages to each other, talking and trying to listen at the same time, exchanging information. This seems to be our most urgent biological function; it is what we do with our lives. By the time we reach the end, each of us has taken in a staggering store, enough to exhaust any computer, much of it incomprehensible, and we generally manage to put out even more than we take in. Information is our source of energy; we are driven by it. It has become a tremendous enterprise, a kind of energy system on its own. All 3 billion of us are being connected by telephones, radios, television sets, airplanes, satellites, harangues on public-address systems, newspapers, magazines, leaflets dropped from great heights, words got in edgewise. We are becoming a grid, a circuitry around the earth. If we keep at it, we will become a computer to end all computers, capable of fusing all the thoughts of the world into a syncytium.

Already, there are no closed, two-way conversations. Any word   5
you speak this afternoon will radiate out in all directions, around town
before tomorrow, out and around the world before Tuesday, accelerat-
ing to the speed of light, modulating as it goes, shaping new and unexpected messages, emerging at the end as an enormously funny
Hungarian joke, a fluctuation in the money market, a poem, or simply a
long pause in someone's conversation in Brazil.

We do a lot of collective thinking, probably more than any other   6
social species, although it goes on in something like secrecy. We don't
acknowledge the gift publicly, and we are not as celebrated as the insects, but we do it. Effortlessly, without giving it a moment's thought,
we are capable of changing our language, music, manners, morals, entertainment, even the way we dress, all around the earth in a year's turning. We seem to do this by general agreement, without voting or even
polling. We simply think our way along, pass information around, exchange codes disguised as art, change our minds, transform ourselves.

Computers cannot deal with such levels of improbability, and it is   7
just as well. Otherwise, we might be tempted to take over the control of
ourselves in order to make long-range plans, and that would surely be
the end of us. It would mean that some group or other, marvelously intelligent and superbly informed, undoubtedly guided by a computer,
would begin deciding what human society ought to be like, say, over the
next five hundred years or so, and the rest of us would be persuaded,
one way or another, to go along. The process of social evolution would
then grind to a standstill, and we'd be stuck in today's rut for a millen-
nium.

Much better we work our way out of it on our own, without gover-   8
nance. The future is too interesting and dangerous to be entrusted to any
predictable, reliable agency. We need all the fallibility we can get. Most
of all, we need to preserve the absolute unpredictability and total improbability of our connected minds. That way we can keep open all the
options, as we have in the past.

It would be nice to have better ways of monitoring what we're up   9
to so that we could recognize change while it is occurring, instead of
waking up as we do now to the astonished realization that the whole
century just past wasn't what we thought it was, at all. Maybe computers can be used to help in this, although I rather doubt it. You can make
simulation models of cities, but what you learn is that they seem to be
beyond the reach of intelligent analysis; if you try to use common sense
to make predictions, things get more botched up than ever. This is interesting, since a city is the most concentrated aggregation of humans, all
exerting whatever influence they can bring to bear. The city seems to
have a life of its own. If we cannot understand how this works, we are
not likely to get very far with human society at large.

Still, you'd think there would be some way in. Joined together, the   10
great mass of human minds around the earth seems to behave like a coherent, living system. The trouble is that the flow of information is
mostly one-way. We are all obsessed by the need to feed information in,
as fast as we can, but we lack sensing mechanisms for getting anything
much back. I will confess that I have no more sense of what goes on in
the mind of mankind than I have for the mind of an ant. Come to think
of it, this might be a good place to start.

1974

Purpose and Meaning

1. Is the title of this essay appropriate? What is the thesis of this essay? Is the
   essay really about computers? Explain. Why be concerned with such an
   issue in the 1990s?

2. What property or properties distinguish human beings from computers?
   Does Thomas believe that computers will one day become like human beings?

3. In paragraphs 4 and 10, Thomas emphasizes the importance of information. How does he define this elusive word?

Language and Style

1. In his essay "Why I Write," George Orwell claims that all writers share an
   aesthetic enthusiasm, a "pleasure in the impact of one sound on another, in
   the firmness of good prose or the rhythm of a good story." What stylistic
   techniques used in this essay suggest that Thomas shares that aesthetic enthusiasm? Identify and discuss specific passages to support your answer.

2. Notice Thomas's choice of pronouns. He uses *you* and *we* throughout. To
   whom do these words refer? How does his choice of pronouns influence
   the relationship between the writer and the reader? How does it affect the
   overall tone of the essay?

3. Paragraphs 4 and 5 have sentences that include a long series of items.
   Locate and analyze these two sentences. Do they contribute to the unique
   voice of the writer? What other atypical syntax can you find in the essay?

Strategy and Structure

1. Thomas cites few specific names, dates, statistics, or events in this essay.
   How does the absence of this evidence determine the tone of his argument? Does Thomas's propensity toward writing in general terms affect
   the strength of his argument?

2. What points of contrast between computers and human beings does Thomas establish to structure his argument?

3. Thomas seems to alternate between familiar phrases like "burst out laughing" (paragraph 1) and unusual ones like "software selves" (paragraph 2). Can you find other examples of these two extremes? What rhetorical function might this strategy have on the essay as a whole?

4. Paragraph 5 is nearly all one sentence. Is this sentence too long? What relationship is there between the length and structure of this sentence and its content?

5. Thomas concludes the essay ironically. What does he suggest by this unusual ending? If the last sentence of the essay had been deleted, how would it have influenced the impact of the work?

Thinking and Writing

1. Argue for or against the proposition that technology ultimately will make much human behavior unnecessary or obsolete. Specify the behaviors.

2. In paragraph 8, Thomas states, "We need all the fallibility we can get." What does he mean? Develop and write an argument either supporting or rejecting this view.

3. How are computers and human beings similar to and different from one another? Brainstorm the idea by compiling two lists: one listing the attributes of human beings, the other of computers. Using these lists as a starting point, write an essay comparing and contrasting the two.

○●○●○●○●○●○●○●○●○●○

The Tucson Zoo

Science gets most of its information by the process of reductionism, exploring the details, then the details of the details, until all the smallest bits of the structure, or the smallest parts of the mechanism, are laid out for counting and scrutiny. Only when this is done can the investigation be extended to encompass the whole organism or the entire system. So we say.

Sometimes it seems that we take a loss, working this way. Much of today's public anxiety about science is the apprehension that we may forever be overlooking the whole by an endless, obsessive preoccupation with the parts. I had a brief, personal experience of this misgiving one afternoon in Tucson, where I had time on my hands and visited the zoo, just outside the city. The designers there have cut a deep pathway between two small artificial ponds, walled by clear glass, so when you stand in the center of the path you can look into the depths of each pool, and at the same time you can regard the surface. In one pool, on the right side of the path, is a family of otters; on the other side, a family of beavers. Within just a few feet from your face, on either side, beavers and otters are at play, underwater and on the surface, swimming toward your face and then away, more filled with life than any creatures I have ever seen before, in all my days. Except for the glass, you could reach across and touch them.

I was transfixed. As I now recall it, there was only one sensation in   3
my head: pure elation mixed with amazement at such perfection. Swept off my feet, I floated from one side to the other, swiveling my brain, staring astounded at the beavers, then at the otters. I could hear shouts across my corpus callosum, from one hemisphere to the other. I remember thinking, with what was left in charge of my consciousness, that I wanted no part of the science of beavers and otters; I wanted never to know how they performed their marvels; I wished for no news about the physiology of their breathing, the coordination of their muscles, their vision, their endocrine systems, their digestive tracts. I hoped never to have to think of them as collections of cells. All I asked for was the full hairy complexity, then in front of my eyes, of whole, intact beavers and otters in motion.

It lasted, I regret to say, for only a few minutes, and then I was   4
back in the late twentieth century, reductionist as ever, wondering about the details by force of habit, but not, this time, the details of otters and beavers. Instead, me. Something worth remembering had happened in my mind, I was certain of that; I would have put it somewhere in the brain stem; maybe this was my limbic system at work. I became a behavioral scientist, an experimental psychologist, an ethologist, and in the instant I lost all the wonder and the sense of being overwhelmed, I was flattened.

But I came away from the zoo with something, a piece of news   5
about myself: I am coded, somehow, for otters and beavers. I exhibit instinctive behavior in their presence, when they are displayed close at hand behind glass simultaneously below water and at the surface. I have receptors for this display. Beavers and otters possess a "releaser" for me, in the terminology of ethology, and the releasing was my experience. What was released? Behavior. What behavior? Standing, swiveling flabbergasted, feeling exultation and a rush of friendship. I could not, as the result of the transaction, tell you anything more about beavers and otters

than you already know. I learned nothing new about them. Only about me, and I suspect also about you, maybe about human beings at large: we are endowed with genes which code out our reaction to beavers and otters, maybe our reaction to each other as well. We are stamped with stereotyped, unalterable patterns of response, ready to be released. And the behavior released in us, by such confrontations, is, essentially, a surprised affection. It is compulsory behavior and we can avoid it only by straining with the full power of our conscious minds, making up conscious excuses all the way. Left to ourselves, mechanistic and autonomic, we hanker for friends.

Everyone says, stay away from ants. They have no lessons for us; 6 they are crazy little instruments, inhuman, incapable of controlling themselves, lacking manners, lacking souls. When they are massed together, all touching, exchanging bits of information held in their jaws like memoranda, they become a single animal. Look out for that. It is a debasement, a loss of individuality, a violation of human nature, an unnatural act.

Sometimes people argue this point of view seriously and with deep 7 thought. Be individuals, solitary and selfish, is the message. Altruism, a jargon word for what used to be called love, is worse than weakness, it is sin, a violation of nature. Be separate. Do not be a social animal. But this is a hard argument to make convincingly when you have to depend on language to make it. You have to print up leaflets or publish books and get them bought and sent around, you have to turn up on television and catch the attention of millions of other human beings all at once, and then you have to say to all of them, all at once, all collected and paying attention: be solitary; do not depend on each other. You can't do this and keep a straight face.

Maybe altruism is our most primitive attribute, out of reach, be- 8 yond our control. Or perhaps it is immediately at hand, waiting to be released, disguised now, in our kind of civilization, as affection or friendship or attachment. I don't see why it should be unreasonable for all human beings to have strands of DNA coiled up in chromosomes, coding out instincts for usefulness and helpfulness. Usefulness may turn out to be the hardest test of fitness for survival, more important than aggression, more effective, in the long run, than grabbiness. If this is the sort of information biological science holds for the future, applying to us as well as to ants, then I am all for science.

One thing I'd like to know most of all: when those ants have made 9 the Hill, and are all there, touching and exchanging, and the whole mass begins to behave like a single huge creature, and *thinks*, what on earth is that thought? And while you're at it, I'd like to know a second thing: when it happens, does any single ant know about it? Does his hair stand on end?

Purpose and Meaning

1. Why is the title of this essay appropriate? How does it affect Thomas's thesis? What is the essay's thesis?

2. In paragraphs 1, 2, and 4, Thomas appears to argue against reductionism; however, in paragraph 8, he states that he is "for science." What changes his mind?

3. In paragraphs 7 and 8, Thomas discusses altruism. How does he use this concept to support his major point? Is he changing the term's dictionary meaning in any way? How?

4. In the closing paragraph, Thomas asks two questions about ants. Explain whether this type of ending for the essay is or is not effective and appropriate.

Language and Style

1. What assumptions is Thomas making about his audience by his choice of language?

2. Paragraph 1 is comprised of three sentences, each progressively shorter. What is Thomas's purpose for using such an arrangement? Discuss the effectiveness of the technique.

3. In "Computers," Thomas uses the pronouns *you* and *we* throughout the essay. However, in this essay, he uses *I, me,* and *my* extensively in the essay's first half but then shifts to *you* and *we* for most of the second half. How does this shift affect the essay's purpose and tone?

4. In paragraphs 6 and 7, Thomas uses several commands. In what ways do they affect the essay's tone? Would the essay gain or lose any of its effectiveness if these commands were changed to declarative sentences? Explain your answer.

Strategy and Structure

1. What techniques does Thomas use to advance his argument?

2. At what point in the essay does Thomas begin to generalize from his experience at the zoo? How does the shift affect the coherence of the essay?

3. Paragraph 5 begins with the conjunction *but.* Is such usage appropriate to the essay? Does it mark other structural shifts as well as acting simply as a transitional word? Explain your answer.

Thinking and Writing

1. Write an essay in which you discuss some of the specific anxieties about science's methodology that Thomas mentions in paragraph 2.

2. Develop an essay in which you refute Thomas's argument that separatism, individuality, and selfishness are not viable human conditions.

3. Transport yourself to the twenty-second century, and discuss the effect of the future scientific discovery that reveals the presence of DNA strands or chromosomal codes for "usefulness" and "helpfulness" projected by Thomas in paragraph 8.

○●○●○●○●○●○●○●○●○●○●○●○●○

Notes on Punctuation

There are no precise rules about punctuation (Fowler lays out some   1
general advice (as best he can under the complex circumstances of English prose (he points out, for example, that we possess only four stops (the comma, the semicolon, the colon and the period (the question mark and exclamation point are not, strictly speaking, stops; they are indicators of tone (oddly enough, the Greeks employed the semicolon for their question mark (it produces a strange sensation to read a Greek sentence which is a straightforward question: Why weepest thou; (instead of Why weepest thou? (and, of course, there are parentheses (which are surely a kind of punctuation making this whole matter much more complicated by having to count up the left-handed parentheses in order to be sure of closing with the right number (but if the parentheses were left out, with nothing to work with but the stops, we would have considerably more flexibility in the deploying of layers of meaning than if we tried to separate all the clauses by physical barriers (and in the latter case, while we might have more precision and exactitude for our meaning, we would lose the essential flavor of language, which is its wonderful ambiguity))))))))))).

The commas are the most useful and usable of all the stops. It is   2
highly important to put them in place as you go along. If you try to come back after doing a paragraph and stick them in the various spots that tempt you you will discover that they tend to swarm like minnows into all sorts of crevices whose existence you hadn't realized and before you know it the whole long sentence becomes immobilized and lashed up squirming in commas. Better to use them sparingly, and with affection, precisely when the need for each one arises, nicely, by itself.

I have grown fond of semicolons in recent years. The semicolon   3
tells you that there is still some question about the preceding full sentence; something needs to be added; it reminds you sometimes of the

Greek usage. It is almost always a greater pleasure to come across a semicolon than a period. The period tells you that that is that; if you didn't get all the meaning you wanted or expected, anyway you got all the writer intended to parcel out and now you have to move along. But with a semicolon there you get a pleasant little feeling of expectancy; there is more to come; read on; it will get clearer.

Colons are a lot less attractive, for several reasons: firstly, they give   4 you the feeling of being rather ordered around, or at least having your nose pointed in a direction you might not be inclined to take if left to yourself, and, secondly, you suspect you're in for one of those sentences that will be labeling the points to be made: firstly, secondly and so forth, with the implication that you haven't sense enough to keep track of a sequence of notions without having them numbered. Also, many writers use this system loosely and incompletely, starting out with number one and number two as though counting off on their fingers but then going on and on without the succession of labels you've been led to expect, leaving you floundering about searching for the ninethly or seventeenthly that ought to be there but isn't.

Exclamation points are the most irritating of all. Look! they say,   5 look at what I just said! How amazing is my thought! It is like being forced to watch someone else's small child jumping up and down crazily in the center of the living room shouting to attract attention. If a sentence really has something of importance to say, something quite remarkable, it doesn't need a mark to point it out. And if it is really, after all, a banal sentence needing more zing, the exclamation point simply emphasizes its banality!

Quotation marks should be used honestly and sparingly, when   6 there is a genuine quotation at hand, and it is necessary to be very rigorous about the words enclosed by the marks. If something is to be quoted, the *exact* words must be used. If part of it must be left out because of space limitations, it is good manners to insert three dots to indicate the omission, but it is unethical to do this if it means connecting two thoughts which the original author did not intend to have tied together. Above all, quotation marks should not be used for ideas that you'd like to disown, things in the air so to speak. Nor should they be put in place around clichés; if you want to use a cliché you must take full responsibility for it yourself and not try to fob it off on anon., or on society. The most objectionable misuse of quotation marks, but one which illustrates the dangers of misuse in ordinary prose, is seen in advertising, especially in advertisements for small restaurants, for example "just around the corner," or "a good place to eat." No single, identifiable, citable person ever really said, for the record, "just around the corner," much less "a good place to eat," least likely of all for restaurants of the type that use this type of prose.

The dash is a handy device, informal and essentially playful, telling you that you're about to take off on a different tack but still in some way connected with the present course—only you have to remember that the dash is there, and either put a second dash at the end of the notion to let the reader know that he's back on course, or else end the sentence, as here, with a period.   7

The greatest danger in punctuation is for poetry. Here it is necessary to be as economical and parsimonious with commas and periods as with the words themselves, and any marks that seem to carry their own subtle meanings, like dashes and little rows of periods, even semicolons and question marks, should be left out altogether rather than inserted to clog up the thing with ambiguity. A single exclamation point in a poem, no matter what else the poem has to say, is enough to destroy the whole work.   8

The things I like best in T. S. Eliot's poetry, especially in the *Four Quartets*, are the semicolons. You cannot hear them, but they are there, laying out the connections between the images and the ideas. Sometimes you get a glimpse of a semicolon coming, a few lines farther on, and it is like climbing a steep path through woods and seeing a wooden bench just at a bend in the road ahead, a place where you can expect to sit for a moment, catching your breath.   9

Commas can't do this sort of thing; they can only tell you how the different parts of a complicated thought are to be fitted together, but you can't sit, not even take a breath, just because of a comma,   10

1979

Purpose and Meaning

1. How is Thomas's approach to the subject of punctuation different from the standard textbook method? What level of competence does he assume on the part of the reader for him or her to appreciate the tone and content of the essay?

2. Is Thomas's purpose to instruct, entertain, show off, or a combination of these? How does his approach demonstrate that he is an expert in the subject matter?

3. What does punctuation mean to Thomas? What does he value in punctuation?

Language and Style

1. What is the first indication that Thomas is approaching the subject in a humorous way? When did you first realize that nature of his approach?

2. Does Thomas give us a clue to his attitude about punctuation in the tone of the essay? Does his style imply that proper punctuation is something immutable? something subject to change? something to be feared? to be respected? to be experimented with?

3. In paragraph 2, Thomas states that without proper usage, commas "tend to swarm like minnows into all sorts of crevices." Where else does Thomas endow punctuation marks with animate qualities? What is there about prose writing that lends itself to depicting punctuation marks in this way?

Strategy and Structure

1. Study the first paragraph. Does Thomas's use of parentheses make sense? Are they used appropriately "in the deploying of layers of meaning"?

2. Thomas is using the same humorous approach in paragraphs 1 and 7. What is this strategy? What makes it funny?

3. While Thomas is being clever in his use of examples to illustrate his major points on punctuation, the essay's basic organization is quite conventional. How does Thomas create a coherent essay? How does each paragraph fit into the scheme? How do the topic sentences help give coherence to the paragraphs?

Thinking and Writing

1. Rewrite paragraph 1 without using any parentheses. Compare both versions. How do they differ in meaning and effect? Does the version without parentheses have the "wonderful ambiguity" Thomas suggests? Similarly, add commas in the long sentence in paragraph 2 that is devoid of them, and compare both versions.

2. Select one of Thomas's other essays in this book, and analyze his use of punctuation in several of its paragraphs. Does this essay reflect Thomas's advice on punctuation? Write an essay demonstrating that Thomas's use of punctuation conforms, or does not conform, to his personal views on it.

3. Argue for or against the proposition that English teachers are too strict and conventional in the way they teach punctuation. Use examples, illustrations, and personal experience.

○●○●○●○●○●○●○●○●○●○●○

Becoming a Doctor

Doctors, dressed up in one professional costume or another, have   1
been in busy practice since the earliest records of every culture on earth.
It is hard to think of a more dependable or enduring occupation, harder
still to imagine any future events leading to its extinction. Other
trades—goldsmithing, embalming, cathedral architecture, hexing, even

philosophy—have had their ups and downs and times of vanishing, but doctoring has been with us since we stumbled into language and society, and will likely last forever, or for as long as we become ill and die, which is to say forever.

What is it that we expected from our shamans, millennia ago, and still require from the contemporary masters of the profession? To *do* something, that's what.

The earliest sensation at the onset of illness, often preceding the recognition of identifiable symptoms, is apprehension. Something has gone wrong, and a glimpse of mortality shifts somewhere deep in the mind. It is the most ancient of our fears. Something must be done, and quickly. Come, please, and help, or go, please, and find help. Hence, the profession of medicine.

You might expect that such a calling, with origins in deepest antiquity, would by this time have at hand an immense store of traditional dogma, volumes and volumes of it, filled with piece after piece of old wisdom, tested through the ages. It is not so. Volumes do exist, of course, but all of them are shiny new, and nearly all the usable knowledge came in a few months ago. Medical information does not, it seems, build on itself; it simply replaces structures already set in place, like the New York skyline. Medical knowledge and technical savvy are biodegradable. The sort of medicine that was practiced in Boston or New York or Atlanta fifty years ago would be as strange to a medical student or interne today as the ceremonial dance of a !Kung San tribe would seem to a rock festival audience in Hackensack.

I take it further. The dilemma of modern medicine, and the underlying central flaw in medical education and, most of all, in the training of internes, is this irresistible drive to do something, anything. It is expected by patients and too often agreed to by their doctors, in the face of ignorance. And, truth to tell, ignorance abounds side by side with the neat blocks of precise scientific knowledge brought into medicine in recent years.

It is no new thing. In 1876, on the occasion of the country's first centennial, a book entitled *A Century of American Medicine, 1776–1876*, was published. The five authors were indisputable authorities in their several fields, from the faculties of Harvard, Columbia, and Jefferson Medical College. The book is a summary of the major achievements in American medicine of the previous century. The optimistic last sentence in the book is perhaps more telling than the writers may have realized: "It is better to have a future than a past." A very large part of the past in that century of medicine was grim.

Early on, there was no such thing as therapeutic science, and beyond the efforts by a few physicians to classify human diseases and record the natural history of clinical phenomena, no sort of reliable empirical experience beyond anecdotes. Therapeutics was a matter of trial and error, with the trials based on guesswork and the guesses based mostly on a curious dogma inherited down the preceding centuries from Galen. Galen himself (c. 130–c. 200) had guessed wildly, and wrongly, in no less than five hundred treatises on medicine and philosophy, that everything about human disease could be explained by the misdistribution of "humors" in the body. Congestion of the various organs was the trouble to be treated, according to Galen, and by the eighteenth century the notion had been elevated to a routine cure-all, or anyway treat-all: remove the excess fluid, one way or another. The ways were direct and forthright: open a vein and take away a pint or more of blood at a sitting, enough to produce faintness and a bluish pallor, place suction cups on the skin to draw out lymph, administer huge doses of mercury or various plant extracts to cause purging, and if all else failed induce vomiting. George Washington perhaps died of this therapy at the age of sixty-six. Hale and hearty, he had gone for a horseback ride in the snow, later in the day had a fever and a severe sore throat, took to his bed, and called in his doctors. His throat was wrapped in poultices, he was given warm vinegar and honey to gargle, and over the next two days he was bled from a vein for about five pints of blood. His last words to his physician were, "Pray take no more trouble about me. Let me go quietly."

Beginning around the 1830s, medicine looked at itself critically, [8] and began to change. Groups of doctors in Boston, Paris, and Edinburgh raised new questions, regarded as heretical by most of their colleagues, concerning the real efficacy of the standard treatments of the day. Gradually, the first example of science applied to clinical practice came somewhat informally into existence. Patients with typhoid fever and delirium tremens, two of the most uniformly fatal illnesses of the time, were divided into two groups. One was treated by bleeding, cupping, purging, and the other athletic feats of therapy, while the other group received nothing more than bed rest, nutrition, and observation. The results were unequivocal and appalling, and by the mid-nineteenth century medical treatment began to fall out of fashion and the era known as "therapeutic nihilism" was well launched.

The great illumination from this, the first revolution in medical [9] practice in centuries, was the news that there were many diseases that are essentially self-limited. They would run their predictable course, if left to run that course without meddling, and, once run, they would come to an end and certain patients would recover by themselves. Typhoid fever, for example, although an extremely dangerous and potentially fatal illness, would last for five or six weeks of fever and debilitation, but at the end about 70 percent of the patients would get well again. Lobar pneumonia would run ten to fourteen days and then, if lucky, previously healthy patients, the famous "crisis" would take place and the patients would recover overnight. Patients with the frightening manifestations of delirium tremens only needed to be confined to a dark room for a few days, and then were ready to come out into the world and drink again. Some were doomed at the outset, of course, but not all. The new lesson was that treating them made the outcome worse rather than better.

It is difficult to imagine, from this distance, how overwhelming this news was to most physicians. The traditional certainty had been that every disease was aimed toward a fatal termination, and without a doctor and his energetic ministrations, or barring miraculous intervention by a higher force, all sick people would die of their disease. To recognize that this was not so, and that with rare exceptions (rabies the most notable one) many sick people could get well by themselves, went against the accepted belief of the time. It took courage and determination, and time, to shake off the old idea. 10

Looking back over the whole embarrassing record, the historians of that period must be hard put to it for explanations of the steadily increasing demand, decade after decade, for more doctors, more clinics and hospitals, more health care. You might think that people would have turned away from the medical profession, or abandoned it. Especially since, throughout the last half of the nineteenth century and the full first third of this one, there was so conspicuously little that medicine had to offer in the way of effective drugs or indeed any kind of technology. Opium, digitalis, quinine, and bromides (for the "nerves") were the mainstays. What else did physicians do during all those years that kept their patients calling and coming? 11

Well, they did a lot of nontechnology, and it was immensely effective. Mainly, they made diagnoses, explained matters to the patient and family, and then stood by, taking responsibility. To be sure, there were skeptics and critics all around, but they had always been around. Montaigne wrote bluntly, concerning doctors: "I have known many a good man among them, most worthy of affection. I do not attack them, but their art. It is only fear of pain and death, and a reckless search for cures, which blinds us. It is pure cowardice that makes us so gullible." Molière made delightful fun of doctors in his century. Dickens had some affection but no great respect for the doctors, most of them odd, bumbling eccentrics, who turned up as minor but essential characters in all his novels. Shaw was a scathing critic of medicine and its pretensions, clear into modern times. 12

But the public regard, and loyalty, somehow held. It is exemplified by a memorial tablet in the north wall of St. James Church in Piccadilly, in honor of Sir Richard Bright (1789–1858), the discoverer of the kidney disease which still bears his name, and a not-atypical Harley Street prac- 13 titioner during the period of transition from the try-anything to the just-observe schools of medicine. The plaque reads, in part,

> Sacred to the memory of Sir Richard Bright, M.D. D.C.L.
> Physician Extraordinary to the Queen
>
> He Contributed to Medical Science Many Scientific Discoveries
> And Works of Great Value
> And Died While In the Full Practice of His Profession
> After a Life of Warm Affection
> Unsullied Purity
> And Great Usefulness

This is what nineteenth-century people expected their doctors to   14
be, and believed most of them were in real life. The expectation survives to this day, but the reality seems to have undergone a change, in the public mind anyway.

There are many very good physicians around, as gifted and sought   15
after as Bright was in his time, unquestionably better equipped by far to deal with life-threatening illnesses, trained to a level of comprehension of disease mechanisms beyond any nineteenth-century imagination, but "warm affection" and "unsullied purity" have an anachronistic sound these days, and even "great usefulness" is open to public questioning. The modern doctor is literally surrounded by items of high technology capable of preventing or reversing most of the ailments that used to kill people in their youth and middle years—most spectacularly, the bacterial and viral infections chiefly responsible for the average life expectancy of less than forty-five years in Bright's day. But medicine's agenda still contains a long list of fatal or incapacitating diseases, mostly the chronic disabilities of older people, and there is still no technology for these, not even yet a clear understanding of their underlying mechanisms.

The unequivocal successes include miliary tuberculosis, tertiary   16
syphilis of the brain and heart, poliomyelitis, the childhood contagions, septicemias, typhoid, rheumatic fever and valvular heart disease, and most of the other great infectious diseases, now largely under control or already conquered. This was the result of the second big transformation in medicine, starting about fifty years ago with the introduction of the sulfonamides, penicillin, and the other antibiotics, gifts straight from science. The revolution continues in full force, thanks to what is now called the "biological revolution," but it is still in its early stages. With new technologies of fantastic power, such as recombinant DNA and monoclonal antibodies, disease mechanisms that were blank mysteries, totally inaccessible just a few years back, are now at least open to direct scrutiny in detail. The prospects for comprehending the ways in which cancer works, as well as other illnesses on what is becoming a long list,

are now matters of high confidence and excitement among the younger researchers within the universities and in industrial laboratories.

But the future is not yet in sight, and medicine is still stuck, for an unknowable period, with formidable problems beyond the reach of therapy or prevention. The technologies for making an accurate diagnosis have been spectacularly effective, and at the same time phenomenally complex and expensive. This new activity is beginning to consume so much of the time of the students and internes, and the resources of the hospitals in which they do their work, that there is less and less time for the patient. Instead of the long, leisurely ceremony of history-taking, and the equally long ritual of the complete physical examination, and then the long explanations of what has gone wrong and a candid forecast of what may lie ahead, the sick person perceives the hospital as an enormous whirring machine, with all the professionals—doctors, nurses, medical students, aides, and porters—out in the corridors at a dead run. Questionnaires, fed into computers along with items analyzing the patient's financial capacity to pay the bills, have replaced part of the history. Blood samples off to the laboratory, the CAT scan, and Nuclear Magnetic Resonance machines are relied upon as more dependable than the physical examination. 17

Everyone, even the visitors, seems pressed for time. There is never enough time, the whole place is overworked to near collapse, out of breath, bracing for the next irremediable catastrophe—the knife wounds in the emergency ward, the flat lines on the electroencephalogram, the cardiac arrests, and always everywhere on every ward and in every room the dying. The Hippocratic adage "Art is long, Life is short" is speeded up to a blur. 18

Everyone is too busy, urgently doing something else, and there is no longer enough time for the old meditative, speculative ward rounds or the amiable conversations at bedside. The house staff, all of them—internes, residents, junior fellows in for the year on NIH training fellowships—are careening through the corridors on their way to the latest "code" (the euphemism for the nearly dead or the newly dead, who too often turn out to be, in the end, the same), or deciphering computer messages from the diagnostic laboratories, or drawing blood and injecting fluids, or admitting in a rush the newest patient. The professors are elsewhere, trying to allocate their time between writing out their research requests (someone has estimated that 30 percent of a medical school faculty's waking hours must be spent composing grant applications), doing or at least supervising the research in their laboratories, seeing their own patients (the sustenance of a contemporary clinical department has become significantly dependent on the income brought in by the faculty's collective private practice), and worrying endlessly about tenure (and 19 parking). About the only professionals who are always on the wards, watching out for the unforeseen, talking and listening to the patients' families, are the nurses, who somehow manage, magically, to hold the place together for all its tendency to drift toward shambles.

I have only two proposals, more like obsessive wishes for the future than a recipe for the present. My first hope is for removal of substantial parts of the curriculum in the first two years, making enough room for a few courses in medical ignorance, so that students can start out with a clear view of the things medicine does not know. My second hope is for more research into the mechanisms of that still-unsolved list of human diseases. The trouble with medicine today is that we simply do not know enough, we are still a largely ignorant profession, faced by an array of illnesses which we do not really understand, unable to do much beyond trying to make the right diagnosis, shoring things up whenever we can by one halfway technology or another (the transplantation of hearts, kidneys, livers, and lungs are the only measures available when we lack any comprehension of the events responsible for the prior destruction of such organs). A great deal of the time and energy expended in a modern hospital is taken up by efforts to put off endgame.

We will be obliged to go on this way and at steadily increasing expense, as far as I can see, until we are rid of disease—at least rid of the ailments which now dominate the roster and fill the clinics and hospitals. This is not asking for as much as it sounds. We will never be free of our minor, self-limited ills, nor should we be planning on postponing dying beyond the normal human span of living—the seventies and eighties for most of us, the nineties for the few more (or less) lucky among us. But there is a great deal we will be able to do as soon as we have learned what to do, both for curing and preventing. It can never be done by guessing, as the profession learned in earlier centuries. Nor can very much be changed by the trendy fashions in changed "life-styles," all the magazine articles to the contrary; dieting, jogging, and thinking different thoughts may make us feel better while we are in good health, but they will not change the incidence or outcome of most of our real calamities. We are obliged, like it or not, to rely on science for any hope of solving such biological puzzles as Alzheimer's disease, schizophrenia, cancer, coronary thrombosis, stroke, multiple sclerosis, diabetes, rheumatoid arthritis, cirrhosis, chronic nephritis, and now, topping the list, AIDS. When we have gained a clear comprehension, in detail, of what has gone wrong in each of these, medicine will be earning its keep, in spades.

1992

Purpose and Meaning

1. How does Thomas's thesis differ from that which the essay's title suggests? How is the thesis reflected in the essay?

2. What does Thomas suggest is wrong with contemporary medical training? How does his historical summary of the medical profession relate to his purpose?

3. What is Thomas's purpose in quoting the words of a memorial plaque in paragraph 13? How does the wording of the plaque reflect Thomas's major point?

Language and Style

1. In paragraph 4, Thomas argues that most medical knowledge is new. What techniques does he use to support that assertion? How does his language reflect his assumptions about his audience?

2. What is Thomas's reason for referring to Montaigne, Molière, Dickens, and Shaw in paragraph 12? What, if anything, do these critics have to do with his assertions about medical training?

3. How would you characterize the essay's tone: subjective or objective? Support your opinion by pointing out particular places in the essay that reveal Thomas's attitude toward his subject.

4. Examine the sentences of paragraph 19. How do their structures support the paragraph's subject matter? How do they contribute to the effectiveness of the paragraph?

5. How effective is Thomas's final image presented in the essay's last paragraph? Would removing it affect the strength of the argument? Explain your answer.

Strategy and Structure

1. Unlike "Computers," this essay draws upon specific dates, events, people, and books. How does Thomas use these materials? What do they contribute to the effectiveness of the essay?

2. How does Thomas structure the essay to provide a coherent progression of paragraphs?

3. How does Thomas's word choice contribute to his general strategy?

Thinking and Writing

1. Using the same techniques as Thomas in paragraph 20, write an essay in which you make proposals for a curriculum change in another field of study.

2. Thomas maintains that modern medical centers tend to "drift toward shambles." Write an essay in which you describe another institution that may be considered to be drifting into a similar state of chaos.

3. In paragraph 21, Thomas argues that activities such as dieting, jogging, or thinking different thoughts will not change the outcomes of real medical calamities. In an essay, argue for or against changes of life-style as possible ways of preventing major medical calamities.

JAMES BALDWIN

Langston Hughes once referred to James Baldwin as "thought-provoking, tantalizing, irritating, abusing and amusing. And he uses words as the sea uses waves, to grow and beat, advance and retreat, rise and take a bow in disappearing." Indeed, Baldwin, who was born in Harlem in 1924, had many voices and a rhythmical, highly poetic prose style. Passionate, probing, controversial, Baldwin—as novelist, short story writer, dramatist, and, above all, essayist—probed the American consciousness in more than fifteen books from the perspective of what he termed in *The Fire Next Time* (1963), our "racial nightmare."

Part of Baldwin's power and greatness was his willingness to expose candidly his own psychic consciousness within the dual dialectics of race and sexuality, for he was an African American and a homosexual. Forced to react to multiple bigotries, Baldwin developed extraordinary methods, notably in his essays, for conveying the harrowing, personal pain of his situation, the implication of this pain for America's social fabric, and a transcendent faith that we cannot surrender to despair. As Baldwin asserts in the introduction to one of his essay collections, *Nobody Knows My Name* (1961), "One can only face in others what one can face in oneself. On this confrontation depends the measure of our wisdom and our compassion."

From childhood, raised in a fundamentalist Christian household with a stern and fanatical stepfather, Baldwin sensed his isolation and his calling as a writer. From 1924 to 1942, Baldwin lived in Harlem, attending Frederick Douglass Junior High School and DeWitt Clinton High School. In junior high, he studied under famed poet Countee Cullen and published material in the school newspaper. In "Autobiographical Notes" and "Fifth Avenue, Uptown," Baldwin offers autobiographical and sociological analyses of the nature of the Harlem ghetto that shaped his early life and threatened to entrap him.

Baldwin did break with the ghetto and also with his brief career as a young evangelical minister. Shortly after graduation, he left Harlem, going first to New Jersey and then to Greenwich Village, determined, as he once put it, to fight the devil in order to be a writer. For six years, aided by Saxton and Rosenwald fellowships for writers, he toiled with scant success. Then, in 1948, Baldwin sailed for Europe on a one-way ticket, beginning his adult years of transcendental voyaging in France, Switzerland, and Turkey, with one notable period from 1957 to 1965 back in the United States, where he became an eloquent crusader and lecturer for the civil rights movement. Baldwin's early years in Europe gave him a global perspective on racial and cultural issues as revealed in "Stranger in the Village," as well as an inspiring burst of creativity. During his first phase overseas, from 1948 to 1957, he published the novels *Go Tell It on the Mountain* (1953) and *Giovanni's Room* (1956) along with his magisterial collection of essays, *Notes of a Native Son* (1955). Subsequent works—the powerful essay *The Fire Next Time* (1963), the play *Blues for Mister Charley* (1964), and the novel *Another Country* (1967)—are among his most militant, filled with the apocalyptic overtones characteristic of the American 1960s. From the civil rights era to the end of his life in 1987, Baldwin's steady output was consciously political, treating such topics as the American criminal justice system in *If Beale Street Could Talk* (1974) and the Atlanta child murders in *Evidence of Things Not Seen* (1985).

Baldwin's essays have been collected in *The Price of the Ticket: Collected Nonfiction 1948–1985*, a testament to his towering reputation in the genre. Early in his career, he had declared that he wanted to be "an honest man and a good writer." With searing honesty and intense autobiographical introspection, his essays, owing much to the hellfire and brimstone oratory of his evangelical youth, move from emotion to logical abstraction. These essays seek what is good and honest in human nature. For life is a journey and each person must pay the price of the ticket. Moreover, as Baldwin declares on the last page of *The Price of the Ticket*, "We are a part of each other."

Autobiographical Notes

I was born in Harlem thirty-one years ago. I began plotting novels   1
at about the time I learned to read. The story of my childhood is the
usual bleak fantasy, and we can dismiss it with the restrained observation that I certainly would not consider living it again. In those days my
mother was given to the exasperating and mysterious habit of having
babies. As they were born, I took them over with one hand and held a
book with the other. The children probably suffered, though they have
since been kind enough to deny it, and in this way I read *Uncle Tom's
Cabin* and *A Tale of Two Cities* over and over and over again; in this way,
in fact, I read just about everything I could get my hands on—except the
Bible, probably because it was the only book I was encouraged to read. I
must also confess that I wrote—a great deal—and my first professional
triumph, in any case, the first effort of mine to be seen in print, occurred
at the age of twelve or thereabouts, when a short story I had written
about the Spanish revolution won some sort of prize in an extremely
short-lived church newspaper. I remember the story was censored by
the lady editor, though I don't remember why, and I was outraged.

Also wrote plays, and songs, for one of which I received a letter of   2
congratulations from Mayor La Guardia, and poetry, about which the
less said, the better. My mother was delighted by all these goings-on,
but my father wasn't; he wanted me to be a preacher. When I was fourteen I became a preacher, and when I was seventeen I stopped. Very
shortly thereafter I left home. For God knows how long I struggled with
the world of commerce and industry—I guess they would say they
struggled with *me*—and when I was about twenty-one I had enough
done of a novel to get a Saxton Fellowship. When I was twenty-two the
fellowship was over, the novel turned out to be unsalable, and I started
waiting on tables in a Village restaurant and writing book reviews—
mostly, as it turned out, about the Negro problem, concerning which the
color of my skin made me automatically an expert. Did another book, in
company with photographer Theodore Pelatowski, about the storefront
churches in Harlem. This book met exactly the same fate as my first—
fellowship, but no sale. (It was a Rosenwald Fellowship.) By the time I
was twenty-four I had decided to stop reviewing books about the Negro
problem—which, by this time, was only slightly less horrible in print
than it was in life—and I packed my bags and went to France, where I
finished, God knows how, *Go Tell It on the Mountain*.

Any writer, I suppose, feels that the world into which he was born   3 is nothing less than a conspiracy against the cultivation of his talent—which attitude certainly has a great deal to support it. On the other hand, it is only because the world looks on his talent with such a frightening indifference that the artist is compelled to make his talent important. So that any writer, looking back over even so short a span of time as I am here forced to assess, finds that the things which hurt him and the things which helped him cannot be divorced from each other; he could be helped in a certain way only because he was hurt in a certain way; and his help is simply to be enabled to move from one conundrum to the next—one is tempted to say that he moves from one disaster to the next. When one begins looking for influences one finds them by the score. I haven't thought much about my own, not enough anyway; I hazard that the King James Bible, the rhetoric of the store-front church, something ironic and violent and perpetually understated in Negro speech—and something of Dickens' love for bravura—have something to do with me today; but I wouldn't stake my life on it. Likewise, innumerable people have helped me in many ways; but finally, I suppose, the most difficult (and most rewarding) thing in my life has been the fact that I was born a Negro and was forced, therefore, to effect some kind of truce with this reality. (Truce, by the way, is the best one can hope for.)

One of the difficulties about being a Negro writer (and this is not 4 special pleading, since I don't mean to suggest that he has it worse than anybody else) is that the Negro problem is written about so widely. The bookshelves groan under the weight of information, and everyone therefore considers himself informed. And this information, furthermore, operates usually (generally, popularly) to reinforce traditional attitudes. Of traditional attitudes there are only two—For or Against—and I, personally, find it difficult to say which attitude has caused me the most pain. I am speaking as a writer; from a social point of view I am perfectly aware that the change from ill-will to good-will, however motivated, however imperfect, however expressed, is better than no change at all.

But it is part of the business of the writer—as I see it—to examine 5 attitudes, to go beneath the surface, to tap the source. From this point of view the Negro problem is nearly inaccessible. It is not only written about so widely; it is written about so badly. It is quite possible to say that the price a Negro pays for becoming articulate is to find himself, at length, with nothing to be articulate about. ("You taught me language," says Caliban to Prospero, "and my profit on't is I know how to curse.") Consider: the tremendous social activity that this problem generates imposes on whites and Negroes alike the necessity of looking forward, of working to bring about a better day. This is fine, it keeps the waters troubled; it is all, indeed, that has made possible the Negro's progress. Nevertheless, social affairs are not generally speaking the writer's prime concern, whether they ought to be or not; it is absolutely necessary that he establish between himself and these affairs a distance which will allow, at least, for clarity, so that before he can look forward in any meaningful sense, he must first be allowed to take a long look back. In the context of the Negro problem neither whites nor blacks, for excellent reasons of their own, have the faintest desire to look back; but I think that the past is all that makes the present coherent, and further, that the past will remain horrible for exactly as long as we refuse to assess it honestly.

I know, in any case, that the most crucial time in my own develop-   6
ment came when I was forced to recognize that I was a kind of bastard of the West; when I followed the line of my past I did not find myself in Europe but in Africa. And this meant that in some subtle way, in a really profound way, I brought to Shakespeare, Bach, Rembrandt, to the stones of Paris, to the cathedral at Chartres, and to the Empire State Building, a special attitude. These were not really my creations, they did not contain my history; I might search in them in vain forever for any reflection of myself. I was an interloper; this was not my heritage. At the same time I had no other heritage which I could possibly hope to use—I had certainly been unfitted for the jungle or the tribe. I would have to appropriate these white centuries. I would have to make them mine—I would have to accept my special attitude, my special place in this scheme—otherwise I would have no place in *any* scheme. What was the most difficult was the fact that I was forced to admit something I had always hidden from myself, which the American Negro has had to hide from himself as the price of his public progress; that I hated and feared white people. This did not mean that I loved black people; on the contrary, I despised them, possibly because they failed to produce Rembrandt. In effect, I hated and feared the world. And this meant, not only that I thus gave the world an altogether murderous power over me, but also that in such a self-destroying limbo I could never hope to write.

One writes out of one thing only—one's own experience.   7
Everything depends on how relentlessly one forces from this experience the last drop, sweet or bitter, it can possibly give. This is the only real concern of the artist, to recreate out of the disorder of life that order which is art. The difficulty then, for me, of being a Negro writer was the fact that I was, in effect, prohibited from examining my own experience too closely by the tremendous demands and the very real dangers of my social situation.

I don't think the dilemma outlined above is uncommon. I do think,   8
since writers work in the disastrously explicit medium of language, that it goes a little way towards explaining why, out of the enormous resources of Negro speech and life, and despite the example of Negro music, prose written by Negroes has been generally speaking so pallid

and so harsh. I have not written about being a Negro at such length because I expect that to be my only subject, but only because it was the gate I had to unlock before I could hope to write about anything else. I don't think that the Negro problem in America can be even discussed coherently without bearing in mind its context; its context being the history, traditions, customs, the moral assumptions and preoccupations of the country; in short, the general social fabric. Appearances to the contrary, no one in America escapes its effects and everyone in America bears some responsibility for it. I believe this the more firmly because it is the overwhelming tendency to speak of this problem as though it were a thing apart. But in the work of Faulkner, in the general attitude and certain specific passages in Robert Penn Warren, and, most significantly, in the advent of Ralph Ellison, one sees the beginnings—at least—of a more genuinely penetrating search. Mr. Ellison, by the way, is the first Negro novelist I have ever read to utilize in language, and brilliantly, some of the ambiguity and irony of Negro life.

About my interests: I don't know if I have any, unless the morbid   9 desire to own a sixteen-millimeter camera and make experimental movies can be so classified. Otherwise, I love to eat and drink—it's my melancholy conviction that I've scarcely ever had enough to eat (this is because it's *impossible* to eat enough if you're worried about the next meal)—and I love to argue with people who do not disagree with me too profoundly, and I love to laugh. I do *not* like bohemia, or bohemians, I do not like people whose principal aim is pleasure, and I do not like people who are *earnest* about anything. I don't like people who like me because I'm a Negro; neither do I like people who find in the same accident grounds for contempt. I love America more than any other country in the world, and, exactly for this reason, I insist on the right to criticize her perpetually. I think all theories are suspect, that the finest principles may have to be modified, or may even be pulverized by the demands of life, and that one must find, therefore, one's own moral center and move through the world hoping that this center will guide one aright. I consider that I have many responsibilities, but none greater than this: to last, as Hemingway says, and get my work done.

I want to be an honest man and a good writer.   10

1963

Purpose and Meaning

1. What is Baldwin's main purpose here? Summarize the essay's thesis in a few sentences.

2. What special burden does Baldwin feel he carries as a result of having been

born black? What was his strategy in coping with this burden? Baldwin also states that being born an African American was the "most rewarding thing in my life." Why does he feel this way?

3. Baldwin states, "The price a Negro pays for becoming articulate is to find himself, at length, with nothing to be articulate about." What does this mean? How does Baldwin's own writing disprove the universality of this statement?

Language and Style

1. In paragraph 3, Baldwin states as one of his influences the "ironic and violent and perpetually understated in Negro speech." How can the following quotations be placed into these categories: "The story of my childhood is the usual bleak fantasy (paragraph 1); " . . . poetry, about which the less said, the better" (paragraph 2); "I love to argue with people who do not disagree with me too profoundly" (paragraph 9). Can you find statements that have a similar tone?

2. Consider how these two sentences begin: "Also wrote plays, and songs . . . " (paragraph 2); "Did another book . . . " (paragraph 2). How do they contribute to the tone of the essay? Do they seem to have the quality of "notes" as expressed in the title?

3. How often does Baldwin make didactic statements? How do these affect the tone of the essay? Consider these two as examples: "One of the difficulties about being a Negro writer is that the Negro problem is written about so widely" (paragraph 4); and "One writes out of one thing only—one's own experience" (paragraph 7). Are these assertions (and others) based on fact, opinion, emotion, or a combination of these? Find other examples of didactic statements.

Strategy and Structure

1. This essay might be divided into three parts. Baldwin's description of his early years, his reflections on the role and struggles of the writer in general and the black writer in particular, and a concluding section that describes his interests. How do these sections complement one another? Do they give us a well-rounded picture of the author until the age of thirty-one? Are there any glaring omissions?

2. Examine the topic sentences of each paragraph. How do they contribute to structuring the array of ideas that Baldwin presents? How do they aid in the essay's coherence?

3. The concluding one-sentence paragraph is intentionally terse. How does it contribute to the organizational strength of the essay? Is it a good conclusion? Does it simply summarize, or does it add a new dimension to what has gone before it?

Thinking and Writing

1. In paragraph 9, Baldwin states, "I love America more than any other country in the world, and, exactly for this reason, I insist on the right to criticize it." Develop an essay in which you defend or criticize this proposition.

2. Write your own essay entitled "Autobiographical Notes." Include both facts of your life and reflections on what you have observed about life.

3. In paragraph 9, Baldwin states that "one must find . . . one's own moral center." What does Baldwin mean by "moral center"? Develop an essay in which you present an extended definition of the term. What is it? How is it acquired? What is its purpose? What happens to a person who lacks one?

Fifth Avenue, Uptown

A letter from Harlem

There is a housing project standing now where the house in which we grew up once stood, and one of those stunted city trees is snarling where our doorway used to be. This is on the rehabilitated side of the avenue. The other side of the avenue—for progress takes time—has not been rehabilitated yet and it looks exactly as it looked in the days when we sat with our noses pressed against the windowpane, longing to be allowed to go "across the street." The grocery store which gave us credit is still there, and there can be no doubt that it is still giving credit. The people in the project certainly need it—far more, indeed, than they ever needed the project. The last time I passed by, the Jewish proprietor was still standing among his shelves, looking sadder and heavier but scarcely any older. Farther down the block stands the shoe-repair store in which our shoes were repaired until reparation became impossible and in which, then, we bought all our "new" ones. The Negro proprietor is still in the window, head down, working at the leather. 1

These two, I imagine, could tell a long tale if they would (perhaps they would be glad to if they could), having watched so many, for so long, struggling in the fishhooks, the barbed wire, of this avenue. 2

The avenue is elsewhere the renowned and elegant Fifth. The area I am describing, which, in today's gang parlance, would be called "the turf," is bounded by Lenox Avenue on the west, the Harlem River on the east, 135th Street on the north, and 130th Street on the south. We never lived beyond these boundaries; this is where we grew up. Walking 3 along 145th Street, for example, familiar as it is, and similar, does not have the same impact because I do not know any of the people on the block. But when I turn east on 131st Street and Lenox Avenue, there is first a soda-pop joint, then a shoeshine "parlor," then a grocery store, then a dry cleaners', then the houses. All along the street there are people who watched me grow up, people who grew up with me, people I watched grow up along with my brothers and sisters; and, sometimes in my arms, sometimes underfoot, sometimes at my shoulder—or on it—their children, a riot, a forest of children, who include my nieces and nephews.

When we reach the end of this long block, we find ourselves on wide, filthy, hostile Fifth Avenue, facing that project which hangs over the avenue like a monument to the folly, and the cowardice, of good intentions. All along the block, for anyone who knows it, are immense human gaps, like craters. These gaps are not created merely by those who have moved away, inevitably into some other ghetto; or by those who have risen, almost always into a greater capacity for self-loathing and self-delusion; or yet by those who, by whatever means—the Second World War, the Korean war, a policeman's gun or billy, a gang war, a brawl, madness, an overdose of heroin, or, simply, unnatural exhaustion—are dead. I am talking about those who are left, and I am talking principally about the young. What are they doing? Well, some, a minority, are fanatical churchgoers, members of the more extreme of the Holy Roller sects. Many, many more are "moslems," by affiliation or sympathy, that is to say that they are united by nothing more—and nothing less—than a hatred of the white world and all its works. They are present, for example, at every Buy Black street-corner meeting—meetings in which the speaker urges his hearers to cease trading with white men and establish a separate economy. Neither the speaker nor his hearers can possibly do this, or course, since the Negroes do not own General Motors or RCA or the A&P, nor indeed, do they own more than a wholly insufficient fraction of anything else in Harlem (those who *do* own anything are more interested in their profits than in their fellows). But these meetings nevertheless keep alive in the participators a certain pride of bitterness without which, however futile this bitterness may be, they could scarcely remain alive at all. Many have given up. They stay home and watch the TV screen, living on the earnings of their parents, cousins, brothers, or uncles, and only leave the house to go to the movies or to the nearest bar. "How're you making it?" one may ask, running into them along the block, or in the bar. "Oh, I'm TV-ing it"; with the saddest, sweetest, most shamefaced of smiles, and from a great distance. This distance one is compelled to respect; anyone who has traveled so far will not easily be dragged again into the world. There are further retreats, of course, than the TV screen or the bar. There are those who are simply sitting on their stoops, "stoned," animated for a moment only, and hideously, by the approach of someone who may lend them the money for a "fix." Or by the approach of someone from whom they can purchase it, one of the shrewd ones, on the way to prison or just coming out.

And the others, who have avoided all of these deaths, get up in the morning and go downtown to meet "the man." They work in the white man's world all day and come home in the evening to this fetid block. They struggle to instill in their children some private sense of honor or dignity which will help the child to survive. This means, of course, that they must struggle, stolidly, incessantly, to keep this sense alive in themselves, in spite of the insults, the indifference, and the cruelty they are certain to encounter in their working day. They patiently browbeat the landlord into fixing the heat, the plaster, the plumbing; this demands prodigious patience; nor is patience usually enough. In trying to make their hovels habitable, they are perpetually throwing good money after bad. Such frustration, so long endured, is driving many strong, admirable men and women whose only crime is color to the very gates of paranoia.

One remembers them from another time—playing handball in the playground, going to church, wondering if they were going to be promoted at school. One remembers them going off to war—gladly, to escape this block. One remembers their return. Perhaps one remembers their wedding day. And one sees where the girl is now—vainly looking for salvation from some other embittered, trussed, and struggling boy—and sees the all-but-abandoned children in the streets.

Now I am perfectly aware that there are other slums in which white men are fighting for their lives, and mainly losing. I know that blood is also flowing through those streets and that the human damage there is incalculable. People are continually pointing out to me the wretchedness of white people in order to console me for the wretchedness of blacks. But an itemized account of the American failure does not console me and it should not console anyone else. That hundreds of thousands of white people are living, in effect, no better than the "niggers" is not a fact to be regarded with complacency. The social and moral bankruptcy suggested by this fact is the bitterest, most terrifying kind.

The people, however, who believe that this democratic anguish has some consoling value are always pointing out that So-and-So, white, and So-and-So, black, rose from the slums into the big time. The existence—the public existence—of, say, Frank Sinatra and Sammy Davis, Jr., proves to them that America is still the land of opportunity and that inequalities vanish before the determined will. It proves nothing of the sort. The determined will is rare—at the moment, in this country, it is unspeakably rare—and the inequalities suffered by the many are in no way justified by the rise of a few. A few have always risen—in every country, every era, and in the teeth of regimes which can by no stretch of the imagination be thought of as free. Not all of these people, it is worth remembering, left the world better than they found it. The determined will is rare, but it is not invariably benevolent. Furthermore, the American equation of success with the big times reveals an awful disrespect for human life and human achievement. This equation has placed our cities among the most dangerous in the world and has placed our youth among the most empty and most bewildered. The situation of our youth is not mysterious. Children have never been very good at listening to their elders, but they have never failed to imitate them. They must, they have no other models. That is exactly what our children are doing. They are imitating our immorality, our disrespect for the pain of others.

All other slum dwellers, when the bank account permits it, can   9
move out of the slum and vanish altogether from the eye of persecution. No Negro in this country has ever made that much money and it will be a long time before any Negro does. The Negroes in Harlem, who have no money, spend what they have in such gimcracks as they are sold. These include "wider" TV screens, more "faithful" hi-fi sets, more "powerful" cars, all of which, of course, are obsolete long before they are paid for. Anyone who has ever struggled with poverty knows how extremely expensive it is to be poor; and if one is a member of a captive population, economically speaking, one's feet have simply been placed on the treadmill forever. One is victimized, economically, in a thousand ways—rent, for example, or car insurance. Go shopping one day in Harlem—for anything—and compare Harlem prices and quality with those downtown.

The people who have managed to get off this block have only got   10
as far as a more respectable ghetto. This respectable ghetto does not even have the advantages of the disreputable one—friends, neighbors, a familiar church, and friendly tradesmen; and it is not, moreover, in the nature of any ghetto to remain respectable long. Every Sunday, people who have left the block take the lonely ride back, dragging their increasingly discontented children with them. They spend the day talking, not always with words, about the trouble they've seen and the trouble—one must watch their eyes as they watch their children—they are only too likely to see. For children do not like ghettos. It takes them nearly no time to discover exactly why they are there.

The projects in Harlem are hated. They are hated almost as much   11
as policemen, and this is saying a great deal. And they are hated for the same reason: both reveal, unbearably, the real attitude of the white

world, no matter how many liberal speeches are made, no matter how many lofty editorials are written, no matter how many civil-rights commissions are set up.

The projects are hideous, of course, there being a law, apparently   12
respected throughout the world, that popular housing shall be as cheerless as a prison. They are lumped all over Harlem, colorless, bleak, high, and revolting. The wide windows look out on Harlem's invincible and indescribable squalor: the Park Avenue railroad tracks, around which, about forty years ago, the present dark community began; the unrehabilitated houses, bowed down, it would seem, under the great weight of frustration and bitterness they contain; the dark, the ominous schoolhouses from which the child may emerge maimed, blinded, hooked, or enraged for life; and the churches, churches, block upon block of churches, niched in the walls like cannon in the walls of a fortress. Even if the administration of the projects were not so insanely humiliating (for example: one must report raises in salary to the management, which will then eat up the profit by raising one's rent; the management has the right to know who is staying in your apartment; the management can ask you to leave, at their discretion), the projects would still be hated because they are an insult to the meanest intelligence.

Harlem got its first private project, Riverton*—which is now, natu-   13
rally, a slum—about twelve years ago because at that time Negroes were not allowed to live in Stuyvesant Town. Harlem watched Riverton go up, therefore, in the most violent bitterness of spirit, and hated it long before the builders arrived. They began hating it at about the time people began moving out of their condemned houses to make room for this additional proof of how thoroughly the white world despised them. And they had scarcely moved in, naturally, before they began smashing windows, defacing walls, urinating in the elevators, and fornicating in the playgrounds. Liberals, both white and black, were appalled at the spectacle. I was appalled by the liberal innocence—or cynicism, which comes out in practice as much the same thing. Other people were delighted to be able to point to proof positive that nothing could be done to better the lot of the colored people. They were, and are, right in one

*The inhabitants of Riverton were much embittered by this description; they have, apparently, forgotten how their project came into being; and have repeatedly informed me that I cannot possibly be referring to Riverton, but to another housing project which is directly across the street. It is quite clear, I think, that I have no interest in accusing any individuals or families of the depredations herein described: but neither can I deny the evidence of my own eyes. Nor do I blame anyone in Harlem for making the best of a dreadful bargain. But anyone who lives in Harlem and imagines that he has *not* struck this bargain, or that what he takes to be his status (in whose eyes?) protects him against the common pain, demoralization, and danger, is simply self-deluded.

respect: that nothing can be done as long as they are treated like colored people. The people in Harlem know they are living there because white people do not think they are good enough to live anywhere else. No amount of "improvement" can sweeten this fact. Whatever money is now being earmarked to improve this, or any other ghetto, might as well be burnt. A ghetto can be improved in one way only: out of existence.

Similarly, the only way to police a ghetto is to be oppressive. None 14 of the Police Commissioner's men, even with the best will in the world, have any way of understanding the lives led by the people they swagger about in twos and threes controlling. Their very presence is an insult, and it would be, even if they spent their entire day feeding gumdrops to children. They represent the force of the white world, and that world's real intentions are, simply, for that world's criminal profit and ease, to keep the black man corraled up here, in his place. The badge, the gun in the holster, and the swinging club make vivid what will happen should his rebellion become overt. Rare, indeed, is the Harlem citizen, from the most circumspect church member to the most shiftless adolescent, who does not have a long tale to tell of police incompetence, injustice, or brutality. I myself have witnessed and endured it more than once. The businessmen and racketeers also have a story. And so do the prostitutes. (And this is not, perhaps, the place to discuss Harlem's very complex attitude toward black policemen, nor the reasons, according to Harlem, that they are nearly all downtown.)

It is hard, on the other hand, to blame the policeman, blank, good- 15 natured, thoughtless, and insuperably innocent, for being such a perfect representative of the people he serves. He, too, believes in good intentions and is astounded and offended when they are not taken for the deed. He has never, himself, done anything for which to be hated—which of us has?—and yet he is facing, daily and nightly, people who would gladly see him dead, and he knows it. There is no way for him not to know it: there are few things under heaven more unnerving than the silent, accumulating contempt and hatred of a people. He moves through Harlem, therefore, like an occupying soldier in a bitterly hostile country; which is precisely what, and where, he is, and is the reason he walks in twos and threes. And he is not the only one who knows why he is always in company: the people who are watching him know why, too. Any street meeting, sacred or secular, which he and his colleagues uneasily cover has as its explicit or implicit burden the cruelty and injustice of the white domination. And these days, of course, in terms increasingly vivid and jubilant, it speaks of the end of that domination. The white policeman standing on a Harlem street corner finds himself at the very center of the revolution now occurring in the world. He is not prepared for it—naturally, nobody is—and, what is possibly much more to the point, he is exposed, as few white people are, to the anguish of the black people around him. Even if he is gifted with the merest mustard grain of imagination, something must seep in. He cannot avoid observing that some of the children, in spite of their color, remind him of children he has known and loved, perhaps even of his own children. He knows that he certainly does not want *his* children living this way. He can retreat from his uneasiness in only one direction: into a callousness which very shortly becomes second nature. He becomes more callous, the population becomes more hostile, the situation grows more tense, and the police force is increased. One day, to everyone's astonishment, someone drops a match in the powder keg and everything blows up. Before the dust has settled or the blood congealed, editorials, speeches, and civil-rights commissions are loud in the land, demanding to know what happened. What happened is that Negroes want to be treated like men.

Negroes want to be treated like men: a perfectly straightforward state- 16 ment, containing only seven words. People who have mastered Kant, Hegel, Shakespeare, Marx, Freud, and the Bible find this statement utterly impenetrable. The idea seems to threaten profound, barely conscious assumptions. A kind of panic paralyzes their features, as though they found themselves trapped on the edge of a steep place. I once tried to describe to a very well-known American intellectual the conditions among Negroes in the South. My recital disturbed him and made him indignant; and he asked me in perfect innocence, "Why don't all the Negroes in the South move North?" I tried to explain what *has* happened, unfailingly, whenever a significant body of Negroes move North. They do not escape Jim Crow: they merely encounter another, not-less-deadly variety. They do not move to Chicago, they move to the South Side; they do not move to New York, they move to Harlem. The pressure within the ghetto causes the ghetto walls to expand, and this expansion is always violent. White people hold the line as long as they can, and in as many ways as they can, from verbal intimidation to physical violence. But inevitably the border which has divided the ghetto from the rest of the world falls into the hands of the ghetto. The white people fall back bitterly before the black horde; the landlords make a tidy profit by raising the rent, chopping up the rooms, and all but dispensing with the upkeep; and what has once been a neighborhood turns into a "turf." This is precisely what happened when the Puerto Ricans arrived in their thousands—and the bitterness thus caused is, as I write, being fought out all up and down those streets.

Northerners indulge in an extremely dangerous luxury. They seem 17 to feel that because they fought on the right side during the Civil War, and won, they have earned the right merely to deplore what is going on in the South, without taking any responsibility for it; and that they can ignore what is happening in northern cities because what is happening in Little Rock or Birmingham is worse. Well, in the first place, it is not possible for anyone who has not endured both to know which is "worse." I know Negroes who prefer the South and white southerners, because "At least there, you haven't got to play any guessing games." The guessing games referred to have driven more than one Negro into the narcotics ward, the madhouse, or the river. I know another Negro, a man very dear to me, who says, with conviction and with truth, "The spirit of the South is the spirit of America." He was born in the North and did his military training in the South. He did not, as far as I can gather, find the South "worse"; he found it, if anything, all too familiar. In the second place, though, even if Birmingham *is* worse, no doubt Johannesburg, South Africa, beats it by several miles, and Buchenwald was one of the worst things that ever happened in the entire history of the world. The world has never lacked for horrifying examples; but I do not believe that these examples are meant to be used as justification for our own crimes. This perpetual justification empties the heart of all human feeling. The emptier our hearts become, the greater will be our crimes. Thirdly, the South is not merely an embarrassingly backward region, but a part of this country, and what happens there concerns every one of us.

As far as the color problem is concerned, there is but one great dif-   18
ference between the southern white and the northerner: the southerner remembers, historically and in his own psyche, a kind of Eden in which he loved black people and they loved him. Historically, the flaming sword laid across this Eden is the Civil War. Personally, it is the southerner's sexual coming of age, when, without any warning, unbreakable taboos are set up between himself and his past. Everything, thereafter, is permitted him except the love he remembers and has never ceased to need. The resulting, indescribable torment affects every southern mind and is the basis of the southern hysteria.

None of this is true for the northerner. Negroes represent nothing   19
to him personally, except, perhaps, the dangers of carnality. He never sees Negroes. Southerners see them all the time. Northerners never think about them whereas southerners are never really thinking of anything else. Negroes are, therefore, ignored in the North and are under surveillance in the South, and suffer hideously in both places. Neither the southerner nor northerner is able to look on the Negro simply as a man. It seems to be indispensable to the national self-esteem that the Negro be considered either as a kind of ward (in which case we are told how many Negroes, comparatively, bought Cadillacs last year and how few, comparatively, were lynched), or as a victim (in which case we are promised that he will never vote in our assemblies or go to school with our kids). They are two sides of the same coin and the South will not

change—*cannot* change—until the North changes. The country will not change until it reexamines itself and discovers what it really means by freedom. In the meantime, generations keep being born, bitterness is increased by incompetence, pride, and folly, and the world shrinks around us.

It is a terrible, an inexorable, law that one cannot deny the human-   20
ity of another without diminishing one's own: in the face of one's victim, one sees oneself. Walk through the streets of Harlem and see what we, this nation, have become.

1960

Purpose and Meaning

1. What connotations are conveyed by the title? In what way does it implicate its intended audience? Why did Baldwin write a letter to people who lived only a short distance from him?

2. Whom is Baldwin addressing in this "letter"? What attitude toward black society does Baldwin presume his audience has?

3. In paragraph 10, Baldwin states, "The people who have managed to get off this block have only got as far as a more respectable ghetto." What does he mean? What additional information in the essay supports this observation?

Language and Style

1. Is the diction of the essay typical of most letters? Explain your answer.

2. Baldwin often writes long, substantive sentences. Consider this one from paragraph 12: "The wide windows look out on Harlem's invincible and indescribable squalor: the Park Avenue railroad tracks, around which, about forty years ago, the present dark community began; the unrehabilitated houses, bowed down, it would seem, under the great weight of frustration and bitterness they contain; the dark, the ominous schoolhouses from which the child may emerge maimed, blinded, hooked, or enraged for life; and the churches, churches, block upon block of churches, niched in the walls like cannon in the walls of a fortress." Study its syntax, vocabulary, and rhythm. Reading the sentence aloud may be helpful. What distinctive voice emerges in the writing? Locate other sentences in this essay that display the writer's voice.

3. Paragraph 2 is a single sentence. Would it have been easier to understand if Baldwin had divided it into several sentences? What was his purpose in writing one long sentence?

Strategy and Structure

1. Paragraph 8 offers an argument condemning the "American dream." How does Baldwin support his argument? How persuasive is he?

2. Paragraph 11 marks a new section of the essay. How does paragraph 11 denote a new mood? If you were to give this second section a title, what would it be?

3. Is the progression of Baldwin's argument a result of explanation, emotion, description, or a combination of these? How effective is the final paragraph as a culmination of Baldwin's overall theme?

Thinking and Writing

1. In paragraph 9, Baldwin states, "All other slum dwellers, when the bank account permits it, can move out of the slum and vanish altogether from the eye of persecution. No Negro in this country has ever made that much money and it will be a long time before any Negro does." Has this situation changed since 1960, the year this essay was published? Argue for or against the proposition that Baldwin's statement is no longer true.

2. Follow Baldwin's suggestion in the final sentence of his essay. Walk through a poor neighborhood, and write an essay in which you analyze the mood and health of the area by observing its people, its physical features, and its activities. Contrast this to a walk through an upper-middle-class neighborhood. How do you assess "what America has become"?

3. Baldwin claims that many people find the phrase "Negroes want to be treated like men" utterly impenetrable. Taking Baldwin's own reasoning as a foundation, argue for or against this thesis.

Stranger in the Village

From all available evidence no black man had ever set foot in this tiny Swiss village before I came. I was told before arriving that I would probably be a "sight" for the village; I took this to mean that people of my complexion were rarely seen in Switzerland, and also that city people are always something of a "sight" outside of the city. It did not occur to me—possibly because I am an American—that there could be people anywhere who had never seen a Negro.

It is a fact that cannot be explained on the basis of the inaccessibility of the village. The village is very high, but it is only four hours from Milan and three hours from Lausanne. It is true that it is virtually unknown. Few people making plans for a holiday would elect to come here. On the other hand, the villagers are able, presumably, to come and go as they please—which they do: to another town at the foot of the mountain, with a population of approximately five thousand, the nearest place to see a movie or go to the bank. In the village there is no movie house, no bank, no library, no theater; very few radios, one jeep, one station wagon; and, at the moment, one typewriter, mine, an invention which the woman next door to me here had never seen. There are about six hundred people living here, all Catholic—I conclude this from the fact that the Catholic church is open all year round, whereas the Protestant chapel, set off on a hill a little removed from the village, is open only in the summertime when the tourists arrive. There are four or five hotels, all closed now, and four or five *bistros*, of which, however, only two do any business during the winter. These two do not do any great deal, for life in the village seems to end around nine or ten o'clock. There are a few stores, butcher, baker, *épicerie*, a hardware store, and a money-changer—who cannot change travelers' checks, but must send them down to the bank, an operation which takes two or three days. There is something called the *Ballet Haus*, closed in the winter and used for God knows what, certainly not ballet, during the summer. There seems to be only one schoolhouse in the village, and this for the quite young children; I suppose this to mean that their older brothers and sisters at some point descend from these mountains in order to complete their education—possibly, again, to the town just below. The landscape is absolutely forbidding, mountains towering on all four sides, ice and snow as far as the eye can reach. In this white wilderness, men and women and children move all day, carrying washing, wood, buckets of milk or water, sometimes skiing on Sunday afternoons. All week long boys and young men are to be seen shoveling snow off the rooftops, or dragging wood down from the forest in sleds.

The village's only real attraction, which explains the tourist season, is the hot spring water. A disquietingly high proportion of these tourists are cripples, or semicripples, who come year after year—from other parts of Switzerland, usually—to take the waters. This lends the village, at the height of the season, a rather terrifying air of sanctity, as though it were a lesser Lourdes. There is often something beautiful, there is always something awful, in the spectacle of a person who has lost one of his faculties, a faculty he never questioned until it was gone, and who struggles to recover it. Yet people remain people, on crutches or indeed on deathbeds; and wherever I passed, the first summer I was here, among the native villagers or among the lame, a wind passed with me—of astonishment, curiosity, amusement, and outrage. That first summer I

3

stayed two weeks and never intended to return. But I did return in the winter, to work; the village offers, obviously, no distractions whatever and has the further advantage of being extremely cheap. Now it is winter again, a year later, and I am here again. Everyone in the village knows my name, though they scarcely ever use it, knows that I come from America—though, this, apparently, they will never really believe: black men come from Africa—and everyone knows that I am the friend of the son of a woman who was born here, and that I am staying in their chalet. But I remain as much a stranger today as I was the first day I arrived, and the children shout *Neger! Neger!* as I walk along the streets.

It must be admitted that in the beginning I was far too shocked to have any real reaction. In so far as I reacted at all, I reacted by trying to be pleasant—it being a great part of the American Negro's education (long before he goes to school) that he must make people "like" him. This smile-and-the-world-smiles-with-you routine worked about as well in this situation as it had in the situation for which it was designed, which is to say that it did not work at all. No one, after all, can be liked whose human weight and complexity cannot be, or has not been, admitted. My smile was simply another unheard-of phenomenon which allowed them to see my teeth—they did not, really, see my smile and I began to think that, should I take to snarling, no one would notice any difference. All of the physical characteristics of the Negro which had caused me, in America, a very different and almost forgotten pain were nothing less than miraculous—or infernal—in the eyes of the village people. Some thought my hair was the color of tar, that it had the texture of wire, or the texture of cotton. It was jocularly suggested that I might let it all grow long and make myself a winter coat. If I sat in the sun for more than five minutes some daring creature was certain to come along and gingerly put his fingers on my hair, as though he were afraid of an electric shock, or put his hand on my hand, astonished that the color did not rub off. In all of this, in which it must be conceded there was the charm of genuine wonder and in which there was certainly no element of intentional unkindness, there was yet no suggestion that I was human: I was simply a living wonder.

I knew that they did not mean to be unkind, and I know it now; it is necessary, nevertheless, for me to repeat this to myself each time that I walk out of the chalet. The children who shout *Neger!* have no way of knowing the echoes this sound raises in me. They are brimming with good humor and the more daring swell with pride when I stop to speak with them. Just the same, there are days when I cannot pause and smile, when I have no heart to play with them: when, indeed, I mutter sourly to myself, exactly as I muttered on the streets of a city these children have never seen, when I was no bigger than these children are now: *Your* mother *was a nigger.* Joyce is right about history being a nightmare—but it may be the nightmare from which no one *can* awaken. People are trapped in history and history is trapped in them.

There is a custom in the village—I am told it is repeated in many villages—of "buying" African natives for the purpose of converting them to Christianity. There stands in the church all year round a small box with a slot for money, decorated with a black figurine, and into this box the villagers drop their francs. During the *carnaval* which precedes Lent, two village children have their faces blackened—out of which bloodless darkness their blue eyes shine like ice—and fantastic horsehair wigs are placed on their blond heads; thus disguised, they solicit among the villagers for money for the missionaries in Africa. Between the box in the church and the blackened children, the village "bought" last year six or eight African natives. This was reported to me with pride by the wife of one of the *bistro* owners and I was careful to express astonishment and pleasure at the solicitude shown by the village for the souls of black folk. The *bistro* owner's wife beamed with a pleasure far more genuine than my own and seemed to feel that I might now breathe more easily concerning the souls of at least six of my kinsmen.

I tried not to think of these so lately baptized kinsmen, of the price paid for them, or the peculiar price they themselves would pay, and said nothing about my father, who having taken his own conversion too literally never, at bottom, forgave the white world (which he described as heathen) for having saddled him with a Christ in whom, to judge at least from their treatment of him, they themselves no longer believed. I thought of white men arriving for the first time in an African village, strangers there, as I am a stranger here, and tried to imagine the astounded populace touching their hair and marveling at the color of their skin. But there is a great difference between being the first white man to be seen by Africans and being the first black man to be seen by whites. The white man takes the astonishment as tribute, for he arrives to conquer and to convert the natives, whose inferiority in relation to himself is not even to be questioned; whereas I, without a thought of conquest, find myself among a people whose culture controls me, has even, in a sense, created me, people who have cost me more in anguish and rage than they will ever know, who yet do not even know of my existence. The astonishment with which I might have greeted them, should they have stumbled into my African village a few hundred years ago, might have rejoiced their hearts. But the astonishment with which they greet me today can only poison mine.

And this is so despite everything I may do to feel differently, despite my friendly conversations with the *bistro* owner's wife, despite their three-year-old son who has at last become my friend, despite the *saluts* and *bonsoirs* which I exchange with people as I walk, despite the fact that I know that no individual can be taken to task for what history is doing, or has done. I say that the culture of these people controls me—but they can scarcely be held responsible for European culture. America comes out of Europe, but these people have never seen America, nor have most of them seen more of Europe than the hamlet at the foot of their mountain. Yet they move with an authority which I shall never have; and they regard me, quite rightly, not only as a stranger in their village but as a suspect latecomer, bearing no credentials, to everything they have—however unconsciously—inherited.

For this village, even were it incomparably more remote and in-credibly more primitive, is the West, the West onto which I have been so strangely grafted. These people cannot be, from the point of view of power, strangers anywhere in the world; they have made the modern world, in effect, even if they do not know it. The most illiterate among them is related, in a way that I am not, to Dante, Shakespeare, Michelangelo, Aeschylus, Da Vinci, Rembrandt, and Racine; the cathe-dral at Chartres says something to them which it cannot say to me, as in-deed would New York's Empire State Building, should anyone here ever see it. Out of their hymns and dances come Beethoven and Bach. Go back a few centuries and they are in their full glory—but I am in Africa, watching the conquerors arrive. 9

The rage of the disesteemed is personally fruitless, but it is also ab-solutely inevitable; this rage, so generally discounted, so little under-stood even among the people whose daily bread it is, is one of the things that makes history. Rage can only with difficulty, and never entirely, be brought under the domination of the intelligence and is therefore not susceptible to any arguments whatever. This is a fact which ordinary representatives of the *Herrenvolk*, having never felt this rage and being unable to imagine it, quite fail to understand. Also, rage cannot be hid-den, it can only be dissembled. This dissembling deludes the thought-less, and strengthens rage and adds, to rage, contempt. There are, no doubt, as many ways of coping with the resulting complex of tensions as there are black men in the world, but no black man can hope ever to be entirely liberated from this internal warfare—rage, dissembling, and contempt having inevitably accompanied his first realization of the power of white men. What is crucial here is that, since white men repre-sent in the black man's world so heavy a weight, white men have for black men a reality which is far from being reciprocal; and hence all black men have toward all white men an attitude which is designed, re-ally, either to rob the white man of the jewel of his naïveté, or else to make it cost him dear. 10

The black man insists, by whatever means he finds at his disposal, that the white man cease to regard him as an exotic rarity and recognize him as a human being. This is a very charged and difficult moment, for there is a great deal of will power involved in the white man's naïveté. 11

Most people are not naturally reflective any more than they are naturally malicious, and the white man prefers to keep the black man at a
certain human remove because it is easier for him thus to preserve his
simplicity and avoid being called to account for crimes committed by his
forefathers, or his neighbors. He is inescapably aware, nevertheless, that
he is in a better position in the world than black men are, nor can he
quite put to death the suspicion that he is hated by black men therefore.
He does not wish to be hated, neither does he wish to change places, and
at this point in his uneasiness he can scarcely avoid having recourse to
those legends which white men have created about black men, the most
usual effect of which is that the white man finds himself enmeshed, so to
speak, in his own language which describes hell, as well as the attributes
which lead one to hell, as being as black as night.

Every legend, moreover, contains its residuum of truth, and the   12
root function of language is to control the universe by describing it. It is
of quite considerable significance that black men remain, in the imagination, and in overwhelming numbers in fact, beyond the disciplines of
salvation; and this despite the fact that the West has been "buying"
African natives for centuries. There is, I should hazard, an instantaneous
necessity to be divorced from this so visibly unsaved stranger, in whose
heart, moreover, one cannot guess what dreams of vengeance are being
nourished; and, at the same time, there are few things on earth more attractive than the idea of the unspeakable liberty which is allowed the
unredeemed. When, beneath the black mask, a human being begins to
make himself felt one cannot escape a certain awful wonder as to what
kind of human being it is. What one's imagination makes of other people is dictated, of course, by the laws of one's own personality and it is
one of the ironies of black-white relations that, by means of what the
white man imagines the black man to be, the black man is enabled to
know who the white man is.

I have said, for example, that I am as much a stranger in this vil-   13
lage today as I was the first summer I arrived, but this is not quite true.
The villagers wonder less about the texture of my hair than they did
then, and wonder rather more about me. And the fact that their wonder
now exists on another level is reflected in their attitudes and in their
eyes. There are the children who make those delightful, hilarious, sometimes astonishingly grave overtures of friendship in the unpredictable
fashion of children; other children, having been taught that the devil is a
black man, scream in genuine anguish as I approach. Some of the older
women never pass without a friendly greeting, never pass, indeed, if it
seems that they will be able to engage me in conversation; other women
look down or look away or rather contemptuously smirk. Some of the
men drink with me and suggest that I learn how to ski—partly, I gather,
because they cannot imagine what I would look like on skis—and want

to know if I am married, and ask questions about my *métier*. But some of the men have accused *le sale nègre*—behind my back—of stealing wood and there is already in the eyes of some of them that peculiar, intent, paranoiac malevolence which one sometimes surprises in the eyes of American white men, when, out walking with their Sunday girl, they see a Negro male approach.

There is a dreadful abyss between the streets of this village and the streets of the city in which I was born, between the children who shout *Neger!* today and those who shouted *Nigger!* yesterday—the abyss is experience, the American experience. The syllable hurled behind me today expresses, above all, wonder: I am a stranger here. But I am not a stranger in America and the same syllable riding on the American air expresses the war my presence has occasioned in the American soul.   14

For this village brings home to me this fact: that there was a day, and not really a very distant day, when Americans were scarcely Americans at all but discontented Europeans, facing a great unconquered continent and strolling, say, into a marketplace and seeing black men for the first time. The shock this spectacle afforded is suggested, surely, by the promptness with which they decided that these black men were not really men but cattle. It is true that the necessity on the part of the settlers of the New World of reconciling their moral assumptions with the fact—and the necessity—of slavery enhanced immensely the charm of this idea, and it is also true that this idea expresses, with a truly American bluntness, the attitude which to varying extents all masters have had toward all slaves.   15

But between all former slaves and slave-owners and the drama which begins for Americans over three hundred years ago at Jamestown, there are at least two differences to be observed. The American Negro slave could not suppose, for one thing, as slaves in past epochs had supposed and often done, that he would ever be able to wrest the power from his master's hands. This was a supposition which the modern era, which was to bring about such vast changes in the aims and dimensions of power, put to death; it only begins, in unprecedented fashion, and with dreadful implications, to be resurrected today. But even had this supposition persisted with undiminished force, the American Negro slave could not have used it to lend his condition dignity, for the reason that this supposition rests on another: that the slave in exile yet remains related to his past, has some means—if only in memory—of revering and sustaining the forms of his former life, is able, in short, to maintain his identity.   16

This was not the case with the American Negro slave. He is unique among the black men of the world in that his past was taken from him, almost literally, at one blow. One wonders what on earth the first slave found to say to the first dark child he bore. I am told that there are   17

Haitians able to trace their ancestry back to African kings, but any American Negro wishing to go back so far will find his journey through time abruptly arrested by the signature on the bill of sale which served as the entrance paper for his ancestor. At the time—to say nothing of the circumstances—of the enslavement of the captive black man who was to become the American Negro, there was not the remotest possibility that he would ever take power from his master's hands. There was no reason to suppose that his situation would ever change, nor was there, shortly, anything to indicate that his situation had ever been different. It was his necessity, in the words of E. Franklin Frazier, to find a "motive for living under American culture or die." The identity of the American Negro comes out of this extreme situation, and the evolution of this identity was a source of the most intolerable anxiety in the minds and the lives of his masters.

For the history of the American Negro is unique also in this: that the question of his humanity, and of his rights therefore as a human being, became a burning one for several generations of Americans, so burning a question that it ultimately became one of those used to divide the nation. It is out of this argument that the venom of the epithet *Nigger!* is derived. It is an argument which Europe has never had, and hence Europe quite sincerely fails to understand how or why the argument arose in the first place, why its effects are so frequently disastrous and always so unpredictable, why it refuses until today to be entirely settled. Europe's black possessions remained—and do remain—in Europe's colonies, at which remove they represented no threat whatever to European identity. If they posed any problem at all for the European conscience, it was a problem which remained comfortingly abstract: in effect, the black man, *as a man*, did not exist for Europe. But in America, even as a slave, he was an inescapable part of the general social fabric and no American could escape having an attitude toward him. Americans attempt until today to make an abstraction of the Negro, but the very nature of these abstractions reveals the tremendous effects the presence of the Negro has had on the American character.

When one considers the history of the Negro in America it is of the greatest importance to recognize that the moral beliefs of a person, or a people, are never really as tenuous as life—which is not moral—very often causes them to appear; these create for them a frame of reference and a necessary hope, the hope being that when life has done its worst they will be enabled to rise above themselves and to triumph over life. Life would scarcely be bearable if this hope did not exist. Again, even when the worst has been said, to betray a belief is not by any means to have put oneself beyond its power; the betrayal of a belief is not the same thing as ceasing to believe. If this were not so there would be no moral standards in the world at all. Yet one must also recognize that morality is based on ideas and that all ideas are dangerous—dangerous because ideas can only lead to action and where the action leads no man can say. And dangerous in this respect: that confronted with the impossibility of remaining faithful to one's beliefs, and the equal impossibility of becoming free of them, one can be driven to the most inhuman excesses. The ideas on which American beliefs are based are not, though Americans often seem to think so, ideas which originated in America. They came out of Europe. And the establishment of democracy on the American continent was scarcely as radical a break with the past as was the necessity, which Americans faced, of broadening this concept to include black men.

This was, literally, a hard necessity. It was impossible, for one [20] thing, for Americans to abandon their beliefs, not only because these beliefs alone seemed able to justify the sacrifices they had endured and the blood that they had spilled, but also because these beliefs afforded them their only bulwark against a moral chaos as absolute as the physical chaos of the continent it was their destiny to conquer. But in the situation in which Americans found themselves, these beliefs threatened an idea which, whether or not one likes to think so, is the very warp and woof of the heritage of the West, the idea of white supremacy.

Americans have made themselves notorious by the shrillness and [21] the brutality with which they have insisted on this idea, but they did not invent it; and it has escaped the world's notice that those very excesses of which Americans have been guilty imply a certain, unprecedented uneasiness over the idea's life and power, if not, indeed, the idea's validity. The idea of white supremacy rests simply on the fact that white men are the creators of civilization (the present civilization, which is the only one that matters; all previous civilizations are simply "contributions" to our own) and are therefore civilization's guardians and defenders. Thus it was impossible for Americans to accept the black man as one of themselves, for to do so was to jeopardize their status as white men. But not so to accept him was to deny his human reality, his human weight and complexity, and the strain of denying the overwhelmingly undeniable forced Americans into rationalizations so fantastic that they approached the pathological.

At the root of the American Negro problem is the necessity of the [22] American white man to find a way of living with the Negro in order to be able to live with himself. And the history of this problem can be reduced to the means used by Americans—lynch law and law, segregation and legal acceptance, terrorization and concession—either to come to terms with this necessity, or to find a way around it, or (most usually) to find a way of doing both these things at once. The resulting spectacle, at once foolish and dreadful, led someone to make the quite accurate observation that "the Negro-in-America is a form of insanity which overtakes white men."

In this long battle, a battle by no means finished, the unforeseeable   23
effects of which will be felt by many future generations, the white man's
motive was the protection of his identity: the black man was motivated
by the need to establish an identity. And despite the terrorization which
the Negro in America endured and endures sporadically until today, despite the cruel and totally inescapable ambivalence of his status in his
country, the battle for his identity has long ago been won. He is not a
visitor to the West, but a citizen there, an American; as American as the
Americans who despise him, the Americans who fear him, the
Americans who love him—the Americans who became less than themselves, or rose to be greater than themselves by virtue of the fact that the
challenge he represented was inescapable. He is perhaps the only black
man in the world whose relationship to white men is more terrible, more
subtle, and more meaningful than the relationship of bitter possessed to
uncertain possessor. His survival depended, and his development depends, on his ability to turn his peculiar status in the Western world to
his own advantage and, it may be, to the very great advantage of that
world. It remains for him to fashion out of his experience that which will
give him sustenance, and a voice.

The cathedral at Chartres, I have said, says something to the people   24
of this village which it cannot say to me; but it is important to understand that this cathedral says something to me which it cannot say to
them. Perhaps they are struck by the power of the spires, the glory of the
windows; but they have known God, after all, longer than I have known
him, and in a different way, and I am terrified by the slippery bottom-
less well to be found in the crypt, down which heretics were hurled to
death, and by the obscene, inescapable gargoyles jutting out of the stone
and seeming to say that God and the devil can never be divorced. I
doubt that the villagers think of the devil when they face a cathedral because they have never been identified with the devil. But I must accept
the status which myth, if nothing else, gives me in the West before I can
hope to change the myth.

Yet, if the American Negro has arrived at his identity by virtue of   25
the absoluteness of his estrangement from his past, American white men
still nourish the illusion that there is some means of recovering the
European innocence, of returning to a state in which black men do not
exist. This is one of the greatest errors Americans can make. The identity
they fought so hard to protect has, by virtue of that battle, undergone a
change: Americans are as unlike any other white people in the world as
it is possible to be. I do not think, for example, that it is too much to suggest that the American vision of the world—which allows so little reality, generally speaking, for any of the darker forces in human life, which
tends until today to paint moral issues in glaring black and white—owes
a great deal to the battle waged by Americans to maintain between
themselves and black men a human separation which could not be

bridged. It is only now beginning to be borne in on us—very faintly, it must be admitted, very slowly, and very much against our will—that this vision of the world is dangerously inaccurate, and perfectly useless. For it protects our moral high-mindedness at the terrible expense of weakening our grasp of reality. People who shut their eyes to reality simply invite their own destruction, and anyone who insists on remaining in a state of innocence long after that innocence is dead turns himself into a monster.

The time has come to realize that the interracial drama acted out on the American continent has not only created a new black man, it has created a new white man, too. No road whatever will lead Americans back to the simplicity of this European village where white men still have the luxury of looking on me as a stranger. I am not, really, a stranger any longer for any American alive. One of the things that distinguishes Americans from other people is that no other people has ever been so deeply involved in the lives of black men, and vice versa. This fact faced, with all its implications, it can be seen that the history of the American Negro problem is not merely shameful, it is also something of an achievement. For even when the worst has been said, it must also be added that the perpetual challenge posed by this problem was always, somehow, perpetually met. It is precisely this black-white experience which may prove of indispensable value to us in the world we face today. This world is white no longer, and it will never be white again.

1953

Purpose and Meaning

1. How does Baldwin use his experience in the Swiss village to reinforce his thesis? Is the thesis stated or implied?

2. According to Baldwin, what is the primary difference between his treatment in the village and his treatment in America? Why is that difference important?

3. What does Baldwin consider the basic belief that was being threatened by the presence of black men in America? Who is responsible for that idea, according to the author? What is Baldwin's purpose in discussing it?

Language and Style

1. How does Baldwin's word choice affect the essay? Discuss the effect of the language on the essay's thesis.

2. How do Baldwin's structurally complex sentences affect the reader's perception of the argument's strengths?

3. Would you classify this essay as formal and objective or informal and subjective? Explain your answer.

Strategy and Structure

1. As he does in "Autobiographical Notes," in this essay Baldwin combines a personal experience with his reflections on the role and fate of African Americans. How does his strategy differ in the two essays?

2. In paragraphs 1 through 8, Baldwin uses the pronoun subject *I* extensively. In paragraphs 9, 10, and 11, the dominant pronoun is *he*. How does the pronoun shift function in Baldwin's strategy?

3. How does paragraph 13 function in the overall design of the essay?

Thinking and Writing

1. In an essay, compare what Baldwin says about rage to what Orwell says about antisemitism. How are the two statements similar? Are the ideas related in terms of cause and effect?

2. In an essay, discuss how Lewis Thomas might respond to Baldwin's statement that "most people are not naturally reflective."

3. In an essay or in class discussion, compare Baldwin's statement about the black man's struggle to Virginia Woolf's argument concerning English women in "Professions for Women."

4. In "If Black English Isn't a Language, Then Tell Me, What Is?" Baldwin says that a language comes into existence by means of "brutal necessity" (paragraph 7). In "Stranger in the Village," he says that the "function of language is to control the universe by describing it" (paragraph 12). In an essay, discuss the two statements on language. Are they mutually supportive? How is language used to "control" the universe?

If Black English Isn't a Language, Then Tell Me, What Is?

The argument concerning the use, or the status, or the reality, of   1
black English is rooted in American history and has absolutely nothing to do with the question the argument supposes itself to be posing. The

argument has nothing to do with language itself but with the role of language. Language, incontestably, reveals the speaker. Language, also, far more dubiously, is meant to define the other—and, in this case, the other is refusing to be defined by a language that has never been able to recognize him.

People evolve a language in order to describe and thus control   2
their circumstances or in order not to be submerged by a situation that they cannot articulate. (And if they cannot articulate it, they are submerged.) A Frenchman living in Paris speaks a subtly and crucially different language from that of the man living in Marseilles; neither sounds very much like a man living in Quebec; and they would all have great difficulty in apprehending what the man from Guadeloupe, or Martinique, is saying, to say nothing of the man from Senegal—although the "common" language of all these areas is French. But each has paid, and is paying, a different price for this "common" language, in which, as it turns out, they are not saying, and cannot be saying, the same things: They each have very different realities to articulate, or control.

What joins all languages, and all men, is the necessity to confront   3
life, in order, not inconceivably, to outwit death: The price for this is the acceptance, and achievement, of one's temporal identity. So that, for example, though it is not taught in the schools (and this has the potential of becoming a political issue) the south of France still clings to its ancient and musical Provençal, which resists being described as a "dialect." And much of the tension in the Basque countries, and in Wales, is due to the Basque and Welsh determination not to allow their languages to be destroyed. This determination also feeds the flames in Ireland for among the many indignities the Irish have been forced to undergo at English hands is the English contempt for their language.

It goes without saying, then, that language is also a political instru-   4
ment, means, and proof of power. It is the most vivid and crucial key to identity. It reveals the private identity, and connects one with, or divorces one from, the larger, public, or communal identity. There have been, and are, times and places, when to speak a certain language could be dangerous, even fatal. Or, one may speak the same language, but in such a way that one's antecedents are revealed, or (one hopes) hidden. This is true in France, and is absolutely true in England: The range (and reign) of accents on that damp little island make England coherent for the English and totally incomprehensible for everyone else. To open your mouth in England is (if I may use black English) to "put your business in the street." You have confessed your parents, your youth, your school, your salary, your self-esteem, and, alas, your future.

Now, I do not know what white Americans would sound like if   5
there had never been any black people in the United States, but they would not sound the way they sound. *Jazz*, for example, is a very spe-

cific sexual term, as in *jazz me, baby*, but white people purified it into the Jazz Age. *Sock it to me*, which means, roughly, the same thing, has been adopted by Nathaniel Hawthorne's descendants with no qualms or hesitations at all, along with *let it all hang out* and *right on! Beat to his socks*, which was once the black's most total and despairing image of poverty, was transformed into a thing called the Beat Generation, which phenomenon was, largely, composed of *uptight*, middle-class white people, imitating poverty, trying to *get down*, to get *with it*, doing their *thing*, doing their despairing best to be *funky*, which we, the blacks, never dreamed of doing—we were funky, baby, like *funk* was going out of style.

Now, no one can eat his cake, and have it, too, and it is late in the day to attempt to penalize black people for having created a language that permits the nation its only glimpse of reality, a language without which the nation would be even more *whipped* than it is.

I say that the present skirmish is rooted in American history, and it is. Black English is the creation of the black diaspora. Blacks came to the United States chained to each other, but from different tribes. Neither could speak the other's language. If two black people, at that bitter hour of the world's history, had been able to speak to each other, the institution of chattel slavery could never have lasted as long as it did. Subsequently, the slave was given, under the eye, and the gun, of his master, Congo Square, and the Bible—or, in other words, and under those conditions, the slave began the formation of the black church, and it is within this unprecedented tabernacle that black English began to be formed. This was not, merely, as in the European example, the adoption of a foreign tongue, but an alchemy that transformed ancient elements into a new language: *A language comes into existence by means of brutal necessity, and the rules of the language are dictated by what the language must convey.*

There was a moment, in time, and in this place, when my brother, or my mother, or my father, or my sister, had to convey to me, for example, the danger in which I was standing from the white man standing just behind me, and to convey this with a speed and in a language, that the white man could not possibly understand, and that, indeed, he cannot understand, until today. He cannot afford to understand it. This understanding would reveal to him too much about himself and smash that mirror before which he has been frozen for so long.

Now, if this passion, this skill, this (to quote Toni Morrison) "sheer intelligence," this incredible music, the mighty achievement of having brought a people utterly unknown to, or despised by "history"—to have brought this people to their present, troubled, troubling, and unassailable and unanswerable place—if this absolutely unprecedented journey does not indicate that black English is a language, I am curious to know what definition of languages is to be trusted.

A people at the center of the western world, and in the midst of so 10 hostile a population, has not endured and transcended by means of what is patronizingly called a "dialect." We, the blacks, are in trouble, certainly, but we are not inarticulate because we are not compelled to defend a morality that we know to be a lie.

The brutal truth is that the bulk of the white people in America 11 never had any interest in educating black people, except as this could serve white purposes. It is not the black child's language that is despised. It is his experience. A child cannot be taught by anyone who despises him, and a child cannot afford to be fooled. A child cannot be taught by anyone whose demand, essentially, is that the child repudiate his experience, and all that gives him sustenance, and enter a limbo in which he will no longer be black, and in which he knows that he can never become white. Black people have lost too many black children that way.

And, after all, finally, in a country with standards so untrustwor- 12 thy, a country that makes heroes of so many criminal mediocrities, a country unable to face why so many of the nonwhite are in prison, or on the needle, or standing, futureless, in the streets—it may very well be that both the child, and his elder, have concluded that they have nothing whatever to learn from the people of a country that has managed to learn so little.

1979

Purpose and Meaning

1. According to Baldwin, how should a language be defined?

2. Where in essay does Baldwin "prove" that black English is a language? In your own words, restate the gist of his argument.

3. In paragraph 4, Baldwin says that "language is also a political instrument." What does this mean? How does he support this contention?

Language and Style

1. In paragraph 1, Baldwin refers to black Americans as "the other." In paragraph 5, Baldwin refers to white Americans as "Nathaniel Hawthorne's descendants." What is he suggesting in these descriptions?

2. Do the references Baldwin makes in paragraphs 3 to 5 concerning the importance of language to other societal groups strengthen his authority as a writer on the subject? Is there anything in Baldwin's tone that gives him his authority?

3. Baldwin states that "a language comes into existence by means of brutal necessity" (paragraph 7). Where does he refer to the brutality of America toward blacks?

4. Study paragraph 9, which is a single sentence. How many ideas does Baldwin present? How does he join these ideas together? How does the structure of this paragraph contribute to Baldwin's assertive voice?

Strategy and Structure

1. Observe the way Baldwin begins paragraphs. What devices does he use to keep his argument moving? How do they serve in connecting one paragraph to the next?

2. In paragraph 5, approximately halfway through the essay, Baldwin presents several terms from black English that have influenced standard English. How do his choice of examples and their placement contribute to the structure of the essay?

3. How does Baldwin culminate his argument in the concluding paragraph? What is the intended emotional effect on the audience? To leave them frustrated? angry? motivated? What is Baldwin suggesting about the future of black English? What is Baldwin suggesting about the future of America?

Thinking and Writing

1. Examine your own speech. Jot down any words or expressions you regularly use that originate from black English. Write an essay explaining what function they serve in your vocabulary.

2. Develop an essay in which you argue for or against the proposition that every English-speaking person should have a right to his or her own dialect.

3. Do you use a different "language" in different situations? For example, how does your vocabulary differ when you speak with your friends, teachers, parents, employers, and so on? Select two groups with whom you regularly come into contact, and write an essay comparing and contrasting your language choices when communicating with them.

4. Compare Baldwin's vision of the modern world and the artist's role in it with that of George Orwell.

CYNTHIA OZICK

Widely acknowledged as a master prose stylist, Cynthia Ozick was born in New York City on April 17, 1928, to Russian Jewish parents. She grew up in the Bronx, where her father owned a drugstore, an upbringing she recalls in "A Drugstore in Winter." She received her B.A. from New York University in 1949 and an M.A. the following year from Ohio State University. After a self-imposed literary apprenticeship lasting sixteen years, she published *Trust*, her first novel, in 1966. The three collections of short fiction that followed—*The Pagan Rabbi and Other Stories* (1971), *Bloodshed and Three Novellas* (1976), and *Levitation: Five Fictions* (1982)—established her as a major contemporary writer and won her numerous national awards. Her second and third novels, *The Cannibal Galaxy* (1983) and *The Messiah of Stockholm* (1987), clearly confirmed her brilliance as storyteller and stylistic virtuoso.

Ozick recalls in the foreword to *Art and Ardor* (1983) that when she was preparing this collection of essays, she was truly surprised to discover she had written over one hundred nonfiction pieces. And although she contends that she "never meant to write essays," they have nonetheless appeared in *Commentary*, *Judaism*, *Mademoiselle*, *Ms.*, the *New York Times*, and other periodicals. Her second essay collection, *Metaphor and Memory*, was published in 1989.

Whether reflections on personal experiences or meditative analyses of books, people, or Judaic history and culture, such as "Of Christian Heroism," Ozick's essays are always informed by an intelligence of the highest order, a quality she still has difficulty accepting. Considered a "failure" during her early school years and taken seriously only by her mother at the outset of her writing career, Ozick finds it astonishing that she is often considered by readers as "too brainy" and is hurt by the notion that she is inaccessible to readers.

A declared and dedicated feminist since the age of five and a half, Ozick first addressed the feminist cause in 1965, when, she recalls, "there was no glimmer of a woman's movement in sight." Not always in the movement's mainstream, Ozick draws her essential feminist ideas from the Torah, which, she maintains, addresses the very heart of feminism in its condemnation of anyone's using a human being. This, Ozick points out, "is what feminism is about." It is with this tenet that she has continued to challenge the movement's assumptions of "new truths," as she calls them, with her incisive observations over nearly two decades.

Ozick admits in "The Seam of the Snail" that she is an "exacting perfectionist" who takes little interest in anything but flawless sentences. "I treat each sentence with the respect I would give to a line of a poem," she once told a *Contemporary Authors* interviewer. "I will not let it go until it is as 'perfect' as I can make it." That intensity and respect for written language results in a prose style that is so precise that removing a single word would seemingly destroy the entire structure of a sentence. Yet when asked where a sense of style comes from, she admits to not having any final answer: "Style is craft plus something spooky. I have many other intentions and everything I write comes out this crabbed Ozick sentence. That's just fingerprint or color of eye or brain snowflake or something. It's just something one can't help."

A Drugstore in Winter

This is about reading; a drugstore in winter; the gold leaf on the dome of the Boston State House; also loss, panic, and dread.

First, the gold leaf. (This part is a little like a turn-of-the-century pulp tale, though only a little. The ending is a surprise, but there is no plot.) Thirty years ago I burrowed in the Boston Public Library one whole afternoon, to find out—not out of curiosity—how the State House got its gold roof. The answer, like the answer to most Bostonian questions, was Paul Revere. So I put Paul Revere's gold dome into an "article," and took it (though I was just as scared by recklessness then as I am now) to the *Boston Globe*, on Washington Street. The Features Editor had a bare severe head, a closed parenthesis mouth, and silver Dickensian spectacles. He made me wait, standing, at the side of his desk while he read; there was no bone in me that did not rattle. Then he opened a drawer and handed me fifteen dollars. Ah, joy of Homer, joy of Milton! Grub Street bliss!

The very next Sunday, Paul Revere's gold dome saw print. Appetite for more led me to a top-floor chamber in Filene's department store: Window Dressing. But no one was in the least bit dressed—it was a dumbstruck nudist colony up there, a mob of naked frozen enigmatic manikins, tall enameled skinny ladies with bald breasts and skulls, and legs and wrists and necks that horribly unscrewed. Paul Revere's dome paled beside this gold mine! A sight—mute numb Walpurgisnacht—easily worth another fifteen dollars. I had a Master's degree (thesis topic: "Parable in the Later Novels of Henry James") and a job as an advertising copywriter (9 a.m. to 6 p.m. six days a week, forty dollars per week; if you were male and had no degree at all, sixty dollars). Filene's Sale Days—Crib Bolsters! LullaBuys! Jonnie-Mops! Maternity Skirts with Expanding Invisible Trick Waist! And a company show; gold watches to mark the retirement of elderly Irish salesladies; for me the chance to write song lyrics (to the tune of "On Top of Old Smoky") honoring our Store. But "Mute Numb Walpurgisnacht in Secret Downtown Chamber" never reached the *Globe*. Melancholy and meaning business, the Advertising Director forbade it. Grub Street was bad form, and I had to promise never again to sink to another article. Thus ended my life in journalism.

Next: reading, and certain drugstore winter dusks. These come together. It is an aeon before Filene's, years and years before the Later Novels of Henry James. I am scrunched on my knees at a round glass table near a plate glass door on which is inscribed, in gold leaf Paul Revere never put there, letters that must be read backward: PARK VIEW PHARMACY There is an evening smell of late coffee from the fountain, and all the librarians are lined up in a row on the tall stools, sipping and chattering. They have just stepped in from the cold of the Traveling Library, and so have I. The Traveling Library is a big green truck that stops, once every two weeks, on the corner of Continental Avenue, just a little way in from Westchester Avenue, not far from a house that keeps a pig. Other houses fly pigeons from their roofs, other yards have chickens, and down on Mayflower there is even a goat. This is Pelham Bay, the Bronx, in the middle of the Depression, all cattails and weeds, such a lovely place and tender hour! Even though my mother takes me on the subway far, far downtown to buy my winter coat in the frenzy of Klein's on Fourteenth Street, and even though I can recognize the heavy power of a quarter, I don't know it's the Depression. On the trolley on the way to Westchester Square I see the children who live in the boxcar strangely set down in an empty lot some distance from Spy Oak (where a Revolutionary traitor was hanged—served him right for siding with redcoats); the lucky boxcar children dangle their stick-legs from their train-house maw and wave; how I envy them! I envy the orphans of the Gould Foundation, who have their own private swings and seesaws. Sometimes I imagine I am an orphan, and my father is an impostor pretending to be my father.

My father writes in his prescription book: *#59330 Dr. O'Flaherty* [5] *Pow .60/ #59331 Dr. Mulligan Gtt .65/ #59332 Dr. Thron Tab .90.* Ninety cents! A terrifically expensive medicine; someone is really sick. When I deliver a prescription around the corner or down the block, I am offered a nickel tip. I always refuse, out of conscience; I am, after all, the Park View Pharmacy's own daughter, and it wouldn't be seemly. My father grinds and mixes powders, weighs them out in tiny snowy heaps on an apothecary scale, folds them into delicate translucent papers or meticulously drops them into gelatin capsules.

In the big front window of the Park View Pharmacy there is a star- [6] tling display—goldfish bowls, balanced one on the other in amazing pyramids. A German lady enters, one of my father's cronies—his cronies are both women and men. My quiet father's eyes are water-color blue, he wears his small skeptical quiet smile and receives the neighborhood's life-secrets. My father is discreet and inscrutable. The German lady pokes a punchboard with a pin, pushes up a bit of rolled paper, and cries out—she has just won a goldfish bowl, with two swimming goldfish in it! Mr. Jaffe, the salesman from McKesson & Robbins, arrives, trailing two mists: winter steaminess and the animal fog of his cigar,*

*Mr. Matthew Bruccoli, another Bronx drugstore child, has written to say that he remembers with certainty that Mr. Jaffe did not smoke. In my memory the cigar is somehow there, so I leave it.

which melts into the coffee smell, the tarpaper smell, the eerie honeyed tangled drugstore smell. Mr. Jaffe and my mother and father are intimates by now, but because it is the 1930s, so long ago, and the old manners still survive, they address one another gravely as Mr. Jaffe, Mrs. Ozick, Mr. Ozick. My mother calls my father Mr. O, even at home, as in a Victorian novel. In the street my father tips his hat to ladies. In the winter his hat is a regular fedora; in the summer it is a straw boater with a black ribbon and a jot of blue feather.

What am I doing at this round glass table, both listening and not listening to my mother and father tell Mr. Jaffe about their struggle with "Tessie," the lion-eyed landlady who has just raised, threefold, in the middle of that Depression I have never heard of, the Park View Pharmacy's devouring rent? My mother, not yet forty, wears bandages on her ankles, covering oozing varicose veins; back and forth she strides, dashes, runs, climbing cellar stairs or ladders; she unpacks cartoons, she toils behind drug counters and fountain counters. Like my father, she is on her feet until one in the morning, the Park View's closing hour. My mother and father are in trouble, and I don't know it. I am too happy. I feel the secret center of eternity, nothing will ever alter, no one will ever die. Through the window, past the lit goldfish, the gray oval sky deepens over our neighborhood wood, where all the dirt paths lead down to seagull-specked water. I am familiar with every frog-haunted monument: Pelham Bay Park is thronged with WPA art—statuary, fountains, immense rococo staircases cascading down a hillside, Bacchus-faced stelae—stone Roman glories afterward mysteriously razed by an avenging Robert Moses. One year—how distant it seems now, as if even the climate is past returning—the bay froze so hard that whole families, mine among them, crossed back and forth to City Island, strangers saluting and calling out in the ecstasy of the bright trudge over such a sudden wilderness of ice.

In the Park View Pharmacy, in the winter dusk, the heart in my body is revolving like the goldfish fleet-finned in their clear bowls. The librarians are still warming up over their coffee. They do not recognize me, though only half an hour ago I was scrabbling in the mud around the two heavy boxes from the Traveling Library—oafish crates tossed with a thump to the ground. One box contains magazines—*Boy's Life*, *The American Girl*, *Popular Mechanix*. But the other, the other! The other transforms me. It is tumbled with storybooks, with clandestine intimations and transfigurations. In school I am a luckless goosegirl, friendless and forlorn. In P.S. 71 I carry, weighty as a cloak, the ineradicable knowledge of my scandal—I am cross-eyed, dumb, an imbecile at arithmetic; in P.S. 71 I am publicly shamed in Assembly because I am caught not singing Christmas carols; in P.S. 71 I am repeatedly accused of deicide. But in the Park View Pharmacy, in the winter dusk, branches blackening in the park across the road, I am driving in rapture through the Violet Fairy Book and the Yellow Fairy Book, insubstantial chariots snatched from the box in the mud. I have never been *inside* the Traveling Library; only grownups are allowed. The boxes are for the children. No more than two books may be borrowed, so I have picked the fattest ones, to last. All the same, the Violet and the Yellow are melting away. Their pages dwindle. I sit at the round glass table, dreaming, dreaming. Mr. Jaffe is murmuring advice. He tells a joke about Wrong-Way Corrigan. The librarians are buttoning up their coats. A princess, captive of an ogre, receives a letter from her swain and hides it in her bosom. I can visualize her bosom exactly—she clutches it against her chest. It is a tall and shapely vase, with a hand-painted flower on it, like the vase on the secondhand piano at home.

I am incognito. No one knows who I truly am. The teachers in P.S. 71 don't know. Rabbi Meskin, my *cheder* teacher, doesn't know. Tessie the lion-eyed landlady doesn't know. Even Hymie the fountain clerk can't know—though he understands other things better than anyone: how to tighten roller skates with a skatekey, for instance, and how to ride a horse. On Friday afternoons, when the new issue is out, Hymie and my brother fight hard over who gets to see *Life* magazine first. My brother is older than I am, and doesn't like me; he builds radios in his bedroom, he is already W2LOM, and operates his transmitter (*da-di-da-dit, da-da-di-da*) so penetratingly on Sunday mornings that Mrs. Eva Brady, across the way, complains. Mrs. Eva Brady has a subscription to *The Writer*; I fill a closet with her old copies. How to Find a Plot. Narrative and Character, the Writer's Tools. Because my brother has his ham license, I say, "I have a license too." "What kind of license?" my brother asks, falling into the trap. "Poetic license," I reply; my brother hates me, but anyhow his birthday presents are transporting: one year *Alice in Wonderland, Pinocchio* the next, then *Tom Sawyer*. I go after Mark Twain, and find *Joan of Arc* and my first satire, *Christian Science*. My mother surprises me with *Pollyanna*, the admiration of her Lower East Side childhood, along with *The Lady of the Lake*. Mrs. Eva Brady's daughter Jeannie has outgrown her Nancy Drews and Judy Boltons, so on rainy afternoons I cross the street and borrow them, trying not to march away with too many—the child of immigrants, I worry that the Bradys, true and virtuous Americans, will judge me greedy or careless. I wrap the Nancy Drews in paper covers to protect them. Old Mrs. Brady, Jeannie's grandmother, invites me back for more. I am so timid I can hardly speak a word, but I love her dark parlor; I love its black bookcases. Old Mrs. Brady sees me off, embracing books under an umbrella; perhaps she divines who I truly am. My brother doesn't care. My father doesn't notice. I think my mother knows. My mother reads the *Saturday Evening Post* and the *Woman's Home Companion*; sometimes the *Ladies'*

Home Journal, but never *Good Housekeeping*. I read all my mother's magazines. My father reads *Drug Topics* and *Der Tog*, the Yiddish daily. In Louie Davidowitz's house (waiting our turn for the rabbi's lesson, he teaches me chess in *cheder*) there is a piece of furniture I am in awe of: a shining circular table that is also a revolving bookshelf holding a complete set of Charles Dickens. I borrow *Oliver Twist*. My cousins turn up with *Gulliver's Travels, Just So Stories, Don Quixote*, Oscar Wilde's *Fairy Tales*, uncannily different from the usual kind. Blindfolded, I reach into a Thanksgiving grabbag and pull out *Mrs. Leicester's School*, Mary Lamb's desolate stories of rejected children. Books spill out of rumor, exchange, miracle. In the Park View Pharmacy's lending library I discover, among the nurse romances, a browning, brittle miracle: *Jane Eyre*. Uncle Morris comes to visit (*his* drugstore is on the other side of the Bronx) and leaves behind, just like that, a three-volume Shakespeare. Peggy and Betty Provan, Scottish sisters around the corner, lend me their *Swiss Family Robinson*. Norma Foti, a whole year older, transmits a rumor about Louisa May Alcott; afterward I read *Little Women* a thousand times. Ten thousand! I am no longer incognito, not even to myself. I am Jo in her "vortex"; not Jo exactly, but some Jo-of-the-future. I am under an enchantment: who I truly am must be deferred, waited for and waited for. My father, silently filling capsules, is grieving over his mother in Moscow. I write letters in Yiddish to my Moscow grandmother, whom I will never know. I will never know my Russian aunts, uncles, cousins. In Moscow there is suffering, deprivation, poverty. My mother, threadbare, goes without a new winter coat so that packages can be sent to Moscow. Her fiery justice-eyes are semaphores I cannot decipher.

Some day, when I am free of P.S. 71, I will write stories; meanwhile, in winter dusk, in the Park View, in the secret bliss of the Violet Fairy Book, I both see and do not see how these grains of life will stay forever, papa and mama will live forever, Hymie will always turn my skatekey. 10

Hymie, after Italy, after the Battle of the Bulge, comes back from the war with a present: *From Here to Eternity*. Then he dies, young. Mama reads *Pride and Prejudice* and every single word of Willa Cather. Papa reads, in Yiddish, all of Sholem Aleichem and Peretz. He reads Malamud's *The Assistant* when I ask him to. 11

Papa and mama, in Staten Island, are under the ground. Some other family sits transfixed in the sun parlor where I read *Jane Eyre* and *Little Women* and, long afterward, *Middlemarch*. The Park View Pharmacy is dismantled, turned into a Hallmark card shop. It doesn't matter! I close my eyes, or else only stare, and everything is in its place again, and everyone. 12

A writer is dreamed and transfigured into being by spells, wishes, goldfish, silhouettes of trees, boxes of fairy tales dropped in the mud, 13 uncles' and cousins' books, tablets and capsules and powders, papa's Moscow ache, his drugstore jacket with his special fountain pen in the pocket, his beautiful Hebrew paragraphs, his Talmudist's rationalism, his Russian-Gymnasium Latin and German, mama's furnace-heart, her masses of memoirs, her paintings of autumn walks down to the sunny water, her braveries, her reveries, her old, old school hurts.

A writer is buffeted into being by school hurts—Orwell, Forster, Mann!—but after a while other ambushes begin: sorrows, deaths, disappointments, subtle diseases, delays, guilts, the spite of the private haters of the poetry side of life, the snubs of the glamorous, the bitterness of those for whom resentment is a daily gruel, and so on and so on; and then one day you find yourself leaning here, writing at that selfsame round glass table salvaged from the Park View Pharmacy—writing this, an impossibility, a summary of how you came to be where you are now, and where, God knows, is that? Your hair is whitening, you are a well of tears, what you meant to do (beauty and justice) you have not done, papa and mama are under the earth, you live in panic and dread, the future shrinks and darkens, stories are only vapor, your inmost craving is for nothing but an old scarred pen, and what, God knows, is that?

1982

Purpose and Meaning

1. Ozick opens this essay with a one-sentence paragraph. How does her intent differ from her announcement of the essay's subject? What is her central concern?

2. How effective is this essay as a personal memoir? In what ways is it a commentary on memory?

3. The essay's last two paragraphs are composed essentially of long lists, or catalogs. What is their purpose? How do they function? How do they relate to Ozick's central purpose?

Language and Style

1. Ozick's sentences are often rich and uniquely styled. Select several examples of sentences that have unusual syntax and descriptive density, and comment on their contribution to the essay's effectiveness.

2. Paragraph 9 is filled with titles of books and magazines. What is Ozick's purpose in citing them? How do they assist the reader in developing an image of the author as a child?

3. Notice Ozick's shift of personal pronouns in the closing paragraph. How effective is the shift? What does it contribute to the essay's purpose?

4. Isolate and comment on Ozick's use of similes in descriptions. What do they add to the effectiveness of the descriptions? What other use of figurative language can you find?

Strategy and Structure

1. The present tense is dominant in this essay. How effective is such a strategy? Why?

2. Examine the opening sentences of paragraphs 2 and 4. How effective are they? Why do you think Ozick chose not to repeat this technique in the remainder of the essay?

3. Notice the extreme length of paragraph 9. How effective is it? As a reader, do you find it hard to follow? Why? If it were broken up into two or more shorter paragraphs, would the essay's structure be adversely affected? Why?

Thinking and Writing

1. Using the present tense, write an essay describing memories of your own childhood that played a significant part in establishing who and what you are. Include five or six sentences imitating some of the structures Ozick uses in this essay.

2. Write an essay in which you discuss the effects of particular books on the development of your personality.

3. We all have several identities in our daily lives; we are different people at home than we are at school, for instance. Write an essay in which you contrast the identity you have at home from that which you have at school.

○●○●○●○●○●○●○●○●○●○●○●○●○

The Seam of the Snail

In my Depression childhood, whenever I had a new dress, my cousin Sarah would get suspicious. The nicer the dress was, and especially the more expensive it looked, the more suspicious she would get. Finally she would lift the hem and check the seams. This was to see if the dress had been bought or if my mother had sewed it. Sarah could always tell. My mother's sewing had elegant outsides, but there was something catch-as-catch-can about the insides. Sarah's sewing, by contrast, was as impeccably finished inside as out; not one stray thread dangled.

My uncle Jake built meticulous grandfather clocks out of rosewood; he was a perfectionist, and sent to England for the clockworks. My mother built serviceable radiator covers and a serviceable cabinet, with hinged doors, for the pantry. She built a pair of bookcases for the living room. Once, after I was grown and in a house of my own, she fixed the sewer pipe. She painted ceilings, and also landscapes; she reupholstered chairs. One summer she planted a whole yard of tall corn. She thought herself capable of doing anything, and did everything she imagined. But nothing was perfect. There was always some clear flaw, never visible head-on. You had to look underneath, where the seams were. The corn thrived, though not in rows. The stalks elbowed one another like gossips in a dense little village.

"Miss Brrrroooobaker," my mother used to mock, rolling her Russian r's, whenever I crossed a t she had left uncrossed, or corrected a word she had misspelled, or became impatient with a v that had tangled itself up with a w in her speech. ("Vvventriloquist," I would say. "Vvventriloquist," she would obediently repeat. And the next time it would come out "wiolinist.") Miss Brubaker was my high school English teacher, and my mother invoked her name as an emblem of raging finical obsession. "Miss Brrrroooobaker," my mother's voice hoots at me down the years, as I go on casting and recasting sentences in a tiny handwriting on monomaniacally uniform paper. The loops of my mother's handwriting—it was the Palmer Method—were as big as soup bowls, spilling generous splashy ebullience. She could pull off, at five minutes' notice, a satisfying dinner for ten concocted out of nothing more than originality and panache. But the napkin would be folded a little off center, and the spoon might be on the wrong side of the knife. She was an optimist who ignored trifles; for her, God was not in the details but in the intent. And all these culinary and agricultural efflorescences were extracurricular, accomplished in the crevices and niches of a fourteen-hour business day. When she scribbled out her family memoirs, in heaps of dog-eared notebooks, or on the backs of old bills, or on the margins of last year's calendar, I would resist typing them; in the speed of the chase she often omitted words like "the," "and," "will." The same flashing and bountiful hand fashioned and fired ceramic pots, and painted brilliant autumn views and vases of imaginary flowers and ferns, and decorated ordinary Woolworth platters with lavish enameled gardens. But bits of the painted petals would chip away.

Lavish: my mother was as lavish as nature. She woke early and saturated the hours with work and inventiveness, and read late into the night. She was all profusion, abundance, fabrication. Angry at her children, she would run after us whirling the cord of the electric iron, like a lasso or a whip; but she never caught us. When, in seventh grade, I was afraid of failing the Music Appreciation final exam because I could not tell the difference between "To a Wild Rose" and "Barcarole," she got the idea of sending me to school with a gauze sling rigged up on my writing arm, and an explanatory note that was purest fiction. But the sling kept slipping off. My mother gave advice like mad—she boiled over with so much passion for the predicaments of strangers that they turned into permanent cronies. She told intimate stories about people I had never heard of.

Despite the gargantuan Palmer loops (or possibly because of 5 them), I have always known that my mother's was a life of—intricately abashing word!—excellence: insofar as excellence means ripe generosity. She burgeoned, she proliferated; she was endlessly leafy and flowering. She wore red hats, and called herself a gypsy. In her girlhood she marched with the suffragettes and for Margaret Sanger and called herself a Red. She made me laugh, she was so varied: like a tree on which lemons, pomegranates, and prickly pears absurdly all hang together. She had the comedy of prodigality.

My own way is a thousand times more confined. I am a pinched 6 perfectionist, the ultimate fruition of Miss Brubaker; I attend to crabbed minutiae and am self-trammeled through taking pains. I am a kind of human snail, locked in and condemned by my own nature. The ancients believed that the moist track left by the snail as it crept was the snail's own essence, depleting its body little by little; the farther the snail toiled, the smaller it became, until it finally rubbed itself out. That is how perfectionists are. Say to us Excellence, and we will show you how we use up our substance and wear ourselves away, while making scarcely any progress at all. The fact that I am an exacting perfectionist in a narrow strait only, and nowhere else, is hardly to the point, since nothing matters to me so much as a comely and muscular sentence. It is my narrow strait, this snail's road; the track of the sentence I am writing now; and when I have eked out the wet substance, ink or blood, that is its mark, I will begin the next sentence. Only in treading out sentences am I perfectionist; but then there is nothing else I know how to do, or take much interest in. I miter every pair of abutting sentences as scrupulously as Uncle Jake fitted one strip of rosewood against another. My mother's worldly and bountiful hand has escaped me. The sentence I am writing is my cabin and my shell, compact, self-sufficient. It is the burnished horizon—a merciless planet where flawlessness is the single standard, where even the inmost seams, however hidden from a laxer eye, must meet perfection. Here "excellence" is not strewn casually from a tipped cornucopia, here disorder does not account for charm, here trifles rule like tyrants.

I measure my life in sentences pressed out, line by line, like the lus- 7 trous ooze on the underside of the snail, the snail's secret open seam, its wound, leaking attar. My mother was too mettlesome to feel the force of a comma. She scorned minutiae. She measured her life according to what poured from the horn of plenty, which was her own seamless, ample, cascading, elastic, susceptible, inexact heart. My narrower heart rides between the tiny twin horns of the snail, dwindling as it goes.

And out of this thinnest thread, this ink-wet line of words, must rise a visionary fog, a mist, a smoke, forging cities, histories, sorrows, quagmires, entanglements, lives of sinners, even the life of my furnace-hearted mother: so much wilderness, waywardness, plenitude on the head of the precise and impeccable snail, between the horns. (Ah, if this could be!)   8

1985

Purpose and Meaning

1. How clearly does the essay's title express Ozick's main concern in this essay? How does she use the opening anecdote in relation to her central concern?

2. What is the distinguishing characteristic of her mother to which Ozick draws the reader's attention? How does she use that characteristic to reach conclusions about herself?

3. What is Ozick's intent in enclosing the essay's final sentence in parentheses? Given the essay's major concern, how effective is such a technique?

Language and Style

1. Ozick's descriptions are often built around figurative language, particularly similes and metaphors. What do they add to the overall effectiveness of the essay?

2. What kinds of modification does Ozick tend to use? What kinds of modifiers does she rely on in describing her mother in paragraph 3? Are they different from those she uses in describing herself? Explain your answer.

3. Ozick refers to her own stylistic concerns in paragraphs 6 and 7. Select several sentences that bear testimony to her being an "exacting perfectionist," and discuss their structures.

Strategy and Structure

1. What organizational strategy does Ozick use to structure this essay? What other strategies are evident?

2. In paragraph 6, Ozick calls her sentences "self-sufficient." What does she mean? What assumptions about her strategy can you draw from her own comments about her sentences?

Thinking and Writing

1. Develop an essay in which you explore the differences between yourself and one of your parents. Concentrate on a single essential difference, supporting that quality with concrete examples.

2. Ozick concentrates her self-analysis on a single element: the sentence. Write a short descriptive essay of approximately 300 words in which you analyze a single characteristic of yours that seems to dominate your personality. Try to include a single analogy, such as Ozick does in this essay.

3. Write an essay in which you describe an important friend or teacher in your life. In your description of this person, use vivid verbs and figurative language to draw the reader's attention to specific characteristics.

Of Christian Heroism

There is a story about Clare Boothe Luce complaining that she was bored with hearing about the Holocaust. A Jewish friend of hers said he perfectly understood her sensitivity in the matter; in fact, he had the same sense of repetitiousness and fatigue, hearing so often about the Crucifixion.

Herbert Gold, "Selfish Like Me"

I

Of the great European murder of six million Jews, and the murderers themselves, there is little to say. The barbaric years when Jews were hunted down for sport in the middle of the twentieth century have their hellish immortality, their ineradicable infamy, and will inflame the nightmares—and (perhaps) harrow the conscience—of the human race until the sun burns out and takes our poor earth-speck with it. Of the murder and the murderers everything is known that needs to be known: how it was done, who did it, who helped, where it was done, and when, and why. Especially why: the hatred of a civilization that teaches us to say No to hatred.

Three "participant" categories of the Holocaust are commonly named: murderers, victims, bystanders.* Imagination demands a choosing. Which, of this entangled trio, are we? Which are we most likely to have become? Probably it is hardest of all to imagine ourselves victims. After all, we were here and not there. Or we were Gentiles and not Jews or Gypsies. Or we were not yet born. But if we had already been born, if we were there and not here, if we were Jews and not Gentiles . . .

"If" is the travail of historians and philosophers, not of the ordinary human article. What we can be sure of without contradiction—we can be sure of it because we *are* the ordinary human article—is that, difficult as it might be to imagine ourselves among the victims, it is not in us even to begin to think of ourselves as likely murderers. The "banality of evil" is a catchword of our generation; but no, it is an unusual, an exceptional, thing to volunteer for the S.S.; to force aged Jews to their knees to scrub the gutter with their beards; to empty Zyklon B canisters into the hole in the roof of the gas chamber; to enact those thousand thousand atrocities that lead to the obliteration of a people and a culture.

The victims take our pity and our horror, and whatever else we can, in our shame, cede to their memory. But they do not puzzle us. It does not puzzle us that the blood of the innocent cries up from the ground—how could it be otherwise? Even if humanity refuses to go on remembering, the voices crushed in the woods and under the fresh pavements of Europe press upward. The new plants that cover the places where corpses were buried in mass pits carry blood in their dew. Basement-whispers trouble the new blocks of flats that cover the streets where the flaming Warsaw Ghetto fell. The heavy old sideboards of the thirties that once stood in Jewish dining rooms in certain neighborhoods of Berlin and Vienna are in Catholic and Protestant dining rooms now, in neighborhoods where there are no longer any Jews; the great carved legs of these increasingly valued antiques groan and remember the looting. The books that were thrown onto bonfires in the central squares of every German city still send up their flocks of quivering phantom letters.

All that—the looting, the shooting, the herding, the forced marches, the gassing, the torching of synagogues, the cynicism, the mendacity, the shamelessness, the truncheons, the bloodthirstiness, the fanaticism, the opportunism, the Jews of Europe as prey, their dehumanization, the death factories, the obliteration of a civilization, the annihilation of a people—all that it is possible to study, if not to assimilate. Pious

*We owe the perception of these categories to Raul Hilberg's book, *Perpetrators, Victims, Bystanders*.

Jews, poor Jews, secular Jews, universalist Jews, baptized Jews, Jews who were storekeepers, or doctors, or carpenters, or professors, or teamsters, Jewish infants and children—all annihilated. Thousands upon thousands of Jewish libraries and schools looted and destroyed. Atrocity spawns an aftermath—perhaps an afterlife. In the last four decades the documents and the testimonies have been heaped higher and higher— yet a gash has been cut in the world's brain that cannot be healed by memorial conferences or monuments. Lamentation for the martyred belongs now to the history of cruelty and to the earth. There is no paucity of the means to remember; there may be a paucity of the will to remember. Still, we know what we think of the murders and the murderers. We are not at a loss to know how to regard them.

But what of the bystanders? They were not the criminals, after all. For the bystanders we should feel at least the pale warmth of recognition—call it self-recognition. And nowadays it is the bystanders whom we most notice, though at the time, while the crimes were in progress, they seemed the least noticeable. We notice them now because they are the ones we can most readily identify with. They are the ones imagination can most readily accommodate. A bystander is like you and me, the ordinary human article—what normal man or woman or adolescent runs to commit public atrocities? The luck of the draw (the odds of finding oneself in the majority) saves the bystander from direct victimhood: the Nuremberg "racial" laws, let us say, are what exempt the bystander from deportation. The bystander is, by definition, not a Jew or a Gypsy. The bystander stays home, safe enough if compliant enough. The bystander cannot be charged with taking part in any evil act; the bystander only watches as the evil proceeds. One by one, and suddenly all at once, the Jewish families disappear from their apartments in building after building, in city after city. The neighbors watch them go. One by one, and suddenly all at once, the Jewish children disappear from school. Their classmates resume doing their sums.

The neighbors are decent people—decent enough for ordinary purposes. They cannot be blamed for not being heroes. A hero—like a murderer—is an exception and (to be coarsely direct) an abnormality, a kind of social freak. No one ought to be expected to become a hero. Not that the bystanders are, taken collectively, altogether blameless. In the Germany of the thirties it was they—because there were so many of them—who created the norm. The conduct of the bystanders—again because there were so many of them—defined what was common and what was uncommon, what was exceptional and what was unexceptional, what was heroic and what was quotidian. If the bystanders in all their numbers had not been so docile, if they had not been so conciliatory, or, contrariwise, if they had not been so "inspired" (by slogans and rabble-rousers and uniforms and promises of national glory), if they had

not acquiesced both through the ballot box and alongside the parades—
if, in short, they had not been *so many*—the subject of heroism would
never have had to arise.

When a whole population takes on the status of bystander, the vic-   8
tims are without allies; the criminals, unchecked, are strengthened; and
only then do we need to speak of heroes. When a field is filled from end
to end with sheep, a stag stands out. When a continent is filled from end
to end with the compliant, we learn what heroism is. And alas for the society that requires heroes.

Most of us, looking back, and identifying as we mainly do with the   9
bystanders—because it is the most numerous category, into which simple demographic likelihood thrusts us; or because surely it is the easiest
category, the most recognizably human, if not the most humane—will
admit to some perplexity, a perplexity brought on by hindsight. Taken
collectively, as I dared to do a moment ago, the bystanders are culpable.
But taking human beings "collectively" is precisely what we are obliged
to do. Then consider the bystanders not as a group, not as a stereotype,
but one by one. If the bystander is the ordinary human article, as we
have agreed, what can there be to puzzle us? This one, let us say, is a
good and zealous hater (no one can deny that hating belongs to the ordinary human article), encouraged by epaulets, posters, flashy rhetoric,
and pervasive demagoguery. And this one is an envious malcontent,
lustful for a change of leadership. And this one is a simple patriot. And
this one, unemployed, is a dupe of the speechmakers. Such portraits,
both credible and problematical, are common enough. But let us concede
that most of the bystanders were quiet citizens who wanted nothing
more than to get on with their private lives: a portrait entirely palatable
to you and me. The ordinary human article seeks nothing more complex
than the comforts of indifference to public clamor of any kind.
Indifference is a way of sheltering oneself from evil; who would interpret such unaggressive sheltering as a contribution to evil? The ordinary
human article hardly looks to get mixed up in active and wholesale
butchery of populations; what rational person would want to accuse the
bystander—who has done no more than avert her eyes—of a hardness-
of-heart in any way approaching that of the criminals? That would be a
serious lie—a distortion both of fact and of psychological understanding.

Yet it is the nature of indifference itself that bewilders. How is it   10
that indifference, which on its own does no apparent or immediate positive harm, ends by washing itself in the very horrors it means to have
nothing to do with? Hoping to confer no hurt, indifference finally grows
lethal; why is that? Can it be that indifference, ostensibly passive, har-
bors an unsuspected robustness? The act of turning toward—while carrying a club—is an act of brutality; but the act of turning away, however
empty-handed and harmlessly, remains nevertheless an *act*. The whole

truth may be that the idea of human passivity is nothing but the illusion of wistful mortals; and that waking into the exigencies of our own time—whichever way we turn, toward or away—implies action. To be born is to be compelled to act.

One of the most curious (and mephitic) powers of indifference is 11 its retroactive capacity: it is possible to be indifferent *nunc pro tunc*. I am thinking of a few sentences I happened to be shown the other day: they were from the pen of a celebrated author who was commenting on a piece of so-called "Holocaust writing." "These old events," she complained, "can rake you over only so much, and then you long for a bit of satire on it all. Like so many others of my generation"—she was a young adult during the forties—"who had nothing to do with any of it, I've swallowed all the guilt I can bear, and if I'm going to be lashed, I intend to save my skin for more recent troubles in the world."

Never mind the odd protestation of innocence where nothing has 12 been charged—what secret unquiet lies within this fraying conscience? What is odder still is that a statement of retroactive indifference is represented as a commitment to present compassion. As for present compassion, does anyone doubt that there is enough contemporary suffering to merit one's full notice? Besides, a current indifference to "these old events" seems harmless enough now; the chimneys of Dachau and Birkenau and Belsen have been cold for the last forty-five years. But does this distinguished figure—a voice of liberalism as well as noteworthy eloquence—suppose that indifference to "old events" frees one for attention to new ones? In fact, indifference to past suffering is a sure sign that there will be indifference to present suffering. Jaded feelings have little to do with the staleness of any event. To be "jaded" is to decline to feel at all.

And that is perhaps the central point about indifference, whether 13 retroactive or current. Indifference is not so much a gesture of looking away—of choosing to be passive—as it is an active disinclination to feel. Indifference shuts down the humane, and does it deliberately, with all the strength deliberateness demands. Indifference is as determined—and as forcefully muscular—as any blow. For the victims on their way to the chimneys, there is scarcely anything to choose between a thug with an uplifted truncheon and the decent citizen who will not lift up his eyes.

II

We have spoken of three categories: criminal, victim, bystander. 14 There is a fourth category—so minuscule that statistically it vanishes. Fortunately it is not a category that can be measured by number—its measure is metaphysical and belongs to the sublime. "Whoever saves a single life," says the Talmud, "is as one who has saved an entire world."

This is the category of those astounding souls who refused to stand by as their neighbors were being hauled away to the killing sites. They were willing to see, to judge, to decide. Not only did they not avert their eyes—they set out to rescue. They are the heroes of Nazified Europe. They are Polish, Italian, Romanian, Russian, Hungarian, French, Yugoslavian, Swiss, Swedish, Dutch, Spanish, German. They are Catholic and Protestant. They are urban and rural; educated and uneducated; sophisticated and simple; they include nuns and socialists. And whatever they did, they did at the risk of their lives.

It is typical of all of them to deny any heroism. "It was only decent," they say. But no: most people are decent; the bystanders were decent. The rescuers are somehow raised above the merely decent. When the rescuers declare that heroism is beside the point, it is hard to agree with them. 15

There is, however, another view, one that takes the side of the rescuers. Under the steady Jerusalem sun stands a low and somber building known as Yad Vashem: a memorial to the Six Million, a place of mourning, a substitute for the missing headstones of the victims; there are no graveyards for human beings ground into bone meal and flown into evanescent smoke. But Yad Vashem is also a grove of celebration and honor: a grand row of trees, one for each savior, marks the valor of the Christian rescuers of Europe, called the Righteous Among the Nations. Mordechai Paldiel, the director of the Department for the Righteous at Yad Vashem, writing in *The Jerusalem Post* not long ago, offered some arresting reflections on the "normality" of goodness: 16

> We are somehow determined to view these benefactors as heroes: hence the search for underlying motives. The Righteous persons, however, consider themselves as anything but heroes, and regard their behavior during the Holocaust as quite normal. How to resolve this enigma?
>
> For centuries we have undergone a brain-washing process by philosophers who emphasized man's despicable character, highlighting his egotistic and evil disposition at the expense of other attributes. Wittingly or not, together with Hobbes and Freud, we accept the proposition that man is essentially an aggressive being, bent on destruction, involved principally with himself, and only marginally interested in the needs of others...
>
> Goodness leaves us gasping, for we refuse to recognize it as a natural human attribute. So off we go on a long search for some hidden motivation, some extraordinary explanation, for such peculiar behavior.
>
> Evil is, by contrast, less painfully assimilated. There is no comparable search for the reason for its constant manifestation (although in earlier centuries theologians pondered this issue).
>
> We have come to terms with evil. Television, movies and the printed word have made evil, aggression and egotism household terms and unconsciously acceptable to the extent of making us immune to displays of evil. There is a danger that the evil of the Holocaust will be absorbed in a

similar manner; that is, explained away as further confirmation of man's inherent disposition to wrongdoing. It confirms our visceral feeling that man is an irredeemable beast, who needs to be constrained for his own good.

In searching for an explanation of the motivations of the Righteous Among the Nations, are we not really saying: what was wrong with them? Are we not, in a deeper sense, implying that their behavior was something other than normal? . . . Is acting benevolently and altruistically such an outlandish and unusual type of behavior, supposedly at odds with man's inherent character, as to justify a meticulous search for explanations? Or is it conceivable that such behavior is as natural to our psychological constitution as the egoistic one we accept so matter-of-factly?

It is Mr. Paldiel's own goodness that leaves me gasping. How I [17] want to assent to his thesis! How alluring it is! His thesis asserts that it is the rescuers who are in possession of the reality of human nature, not the bystanders; it is the rescuers who are the ordinary human article. "In a place where there are no human beings, *be* one"—it is apparent that the rescuers were born to embody this rabbinic text. It is not, they say, that they are exceptions; it is that they are human. They are not to be considered "extraordinary," "above the merely decent."

Yet their conduct emphasizes—exemplifies—the exceptional. [18]

For instance: [19]

Giorgio Perlasca, an Italian from Padua, had a job in the Spanish [20] Embassy in Budapest. When the Spanish envoy fled before the invading Russians, Perlasca substituted the Spanish "Jorge" for the Italian "Giorgio" and passed himself off as the Spanish chargé d'affaires. He carried food and powdered milk to safe houses under the Spanish flag, where several hundred Jews at a time found a haven. He issued protective documents that facilitated the escape of Jews with Spanish passes. "I began to feel like a fish in water," he said of his life as an impostor: the sole purpose of his masquerade was to save Jews. And he saved thousands.

Bert Berchove was a Dutch upholsterer who lived with his wife [21] and two children in a large apartment over his shop, in a town not far from Amsterdam. At first he intended to help only his wife's best friend, who was Jewish; her parents had already been deported. Berchove constructed a hiding place in the attic, behind a false wall. Eventually thirty-seven Jews were hidden there.

In a Dominican convent near Vilna, seven nuns and their mother [22] superior sheltered a number of Jews who had escaped from the ghetto, including some poets and writers. The fugitives were disguised in nuns' habits. The sisters did not stop at hiding Jews: they scoured the countryside for weapons to smuggle into the ghetto.

Who will say that the nuns, the upholsterer, and the impostor are [23] not extraordinary in their altruism, their courage, the electrifying boldness of their imaginations? How many nuns have we met who would think of dressing Jewish poets in wimples? How many upholsterers do we know who would actually design and build a false wall? Who among us would dream of fabricating a fake diplomatic identity in order to save Jewish lives? Compassion, it is clear, sharpens intuition and augments imagination.

For me, the rescuers are *not* the ordinary human article. Nothing   24
would have been easier than for each and every one of them to have remained a bystander, like all those millions of their countrymen in the nations of Europe. It goes without saying that the bystanders, especially in the occupied lands, had troubles enough of their own, and hardly needed to go out of their way to acquire new burdens and frights. I do not—cannot—believe that human beings are, without explicit teaching, naturally or intrinsically altruistic. I do not believe, either, that they are naturally vicious, though they can be trained to be. The truth (as with most truths) seems to be somewhere in the middle: most people are born bystanders. The ordinary human article does not want to be disturbed by extremes of any kind—not by risks, or adventures, or unusual responsibility.

And those who undertook the risks, those whose bravery steeped   25
them in perilous contingencies, those whose moral strength urged them into heart-stopping responsibility—what (despite their demurrals) are they really, if not the heroes of our battered world? What other name can they possibly merit? In the Europe of the most savage decade of the twentieth century, not to be a bystander was the choice of an infinitesimal few. These few are more substantial than the multitudes from whom they distinguished themselves; and it is from these undeniably heroic and principled few that we can learn the full resonance of civilization.

1992

Purpose and Meaning

1. Although the title clearly announces Ozick's primary concern, only the second half of the essay actually deals with heroism. What is her purpose in spending approximately one-half of the essay discussing other topics?

2. In "The Tucson Zoo," Lewis Thomas discusses altruism. How might he respond to Ozick's discussion of natural altruism in paragraph 22? Which of the two authors is more convincing? Why? How might Mordechai Paldiel, who is mentioned in paragraph 16 of Ozick's essay, respond to Thomas and to Ozick?

3. What does Ozick mean in paragraph 3 when she says that "if" is not the travail of the ordinary human article? Who, according to Ozick, is the ordinary human article?

Language and Style

1. Ozick's sentences in this essay are often long, complex structures, such as the last two sentences of paragraph 7. Locate other sentences in the essay that resemble those of paragraph 7, and discuss what they reveal about Ozick's style.

2. Compare Ozick's approach to abstract and concrete language in this essay with that of her approach in "The Seam of the Snail." What differences in language and diction are evident? What differences are there in tone between the two essays?

3. How does paragraph 4 differ in language from most of the essay's other paragraphs? Does the tone also change? What is Ozick's strategy in this paragraph?

Strategy and Structure

1. What organizational strategy does Ozick employ as the basic structure for this essay? What sorts of materials does she use to develop her thesis?

2. Why does Ozick bother to use the long quotation from Mordechai Paldiel's *Jerusalem Post* article? Would the essay gain or lose impact if it were removed or paraphrased? How does the quotation affect the essay's thesis?

3. This essay is formally divided into two parts, each approximately the same length. How effective is the structure, considering Ozick's thesis? Would another strategy have worked equally well? Explain your answer.

Thinking and Writing

1. Review Ozick's discussion of heroism, and write an essay in which you develop your own view of the term in a contemporary context. Adopt the strategies Ozick uses in the second part of this essay.

2. Write an essay in which you discuss positive characteristics of what Ozick calls the "ordinary human article" when not placed in the context of the Holocaust.

3. In paragraph 17, Ozick cites a line from a rabbinic text: "In a place where there are no human beings, *be* one." Select a contemporary situation you perceive to be without human beings, and develop an essay in which you analyze and define the participants such as Ozick does in this essay.

RICHARD SELZER

Richard Selzer is a surgeon and a writer—an essayist who writes compassionately and often starkly about mortality and the transitory nature of life. Born in Troy, New York, in 1928, the son of a family practitioner, he was educated at Union College, Albany Medical College, and Yale. He practiced general surgery in New Haven from 1960 to the 1980s and was on the faculty of the Yale School of Medicine. In 1986, as he admits in an essay in this collection, he turned in the scalpel for the pen.

Selzer is in the great modern tradition of the physician-author that includes such major figures as Chekhov, William Carlos Williams, and his contemporary Lewis Thomas. His essays, collected in *Mortal Lessons* (1977), *Confessions of a Knife* (1979), *Letters to a Young Doctor* (1982), and *Taking the World in for Repairs* (1986), contain the pathos and subtle narrative force of a Chekhov story, as we witness in "The Masked Marvel's Last Toehold" and his memorable essay on AIDS, "A Mask on the Face of Death," which originally appeared in *Life* magazine. At the same time, in essays like "Lessons from the Art," Selzer imbues the surgeon's craft with the vivid coloring of a Williams poem. With Selzer, we can find ourselves—often uncomfortably—inside the patient, learning more about our fragile lives than we might care to imagine. Yet Selzer's compassion for the living and the dead, his precise technical gifts, and his bizarre sense of humor as he dissects the human condition make him one of the most daring and distinctive writers today.

Although he is no frequenter of churches—indeed, he calls himself an infidel—Selzer in his essays invites us to faith and to heroism. Selzer likens religious faith to "perfect pitch," and it is his own fine-tuning of the essayist's art that makes his work sparkle with literary magic. As a surgeon, he "has grown accustomed to primordial dramas, organic events involving flesh, blood, and violence." Yet it is precisely Selzer's intimacy with the stark realities of the operating room that compels him to erect an affirmative—almost sacred—vision of life. Whether interviewing prostitutes infected with the AIDS virus in Haiti, or analyzing his own experiences as a surgeon, Selzer finds ways to convey a sacred vision of life. Fitzhugh Mullan, writing of Selzer in the *New York Times Book Review* (August 29, 1982) said, "his marvelous insight and potent imagery make his tales of surgery and medicine both works of art and splendid tools of instruction."

Perhaps the loss of ritual in the act of surgery is what led Selzer, as he acknowledges in "The Pen and the Scalpel," to move gradually from one profession into another. Always fond of metaphor, Selzer has often likened surgery to varieties of faith and worship, yet ultimately he finds the surgeon-as-priest comparison to be somewhat specious, since surgery today is lacking in religious ecstasy. If ritual, as he once wrote, has receded from the act of surgery, then Selzer seems to find it in the craft of writing.

As a teacher of writing at Yale, recipient of the National Magazine Award for essays in 1975 and the American Medical Writers Award in 1984, and guest lecturer and fellow at numerous universities, Selzer in recent years has had the opportunity to serve as literary shaman. His lyrical voice invites us to insight and to vision.

Lessons from the Art

With trust the surgeon approaches the operating table. To be sure, 1
he is impeccably trained. He has stood here so many times before. The
belly that presents itself to him this morning, draped in green linen and
painted with red disinfectant, is little different from those countless others he has entered. It is familiar terrain, to be managed. He watches it
rise and fall in the regular rhythm of anesthesia. Vulnerable, it returns
his trust, asks but his excellence, his clever ways. With a blend of arrogance and innocence the surgeon makes his incision, expecting a particular organ to be exactly where he knows it to be. He has seen it there, in
just that single place, over and again. He has aimed his blade for that
very spot, found the one artery he seeks, the one vein, captured them in
his hemostats, ligated them, and cut them safely; then on to the next,
and the one after that, until the sick organ falls free into his waiting
hand—mined.

But this morning, as the surgeon parts the edges of the wound with 2
his retractor, he feels uncertain, for in that place where he *knows* the duct
to be, there is none. Only masses of scar curtained with blood vessels of
unimagined fragility. They seem to rupture even as he studies them, as
though it is the abrasion of the air that breaks them. Blood is shed into
the well of the wound. It puddles upon the banks of scar, concealing the
way inward. The surgeon sees this, and knows that the fierce wind of inflammation has swept this place, burying the tubes and canals he seeks.
It is an alien land. Now all is forestial, swampy. The surgeon suctions
away the blood, even as he does so, new red trickles; his eyes are full of
it; he cannot see. He advances his fingers into the belly, feeling the walls
of scar, running the tips gently over each eminence, into each furrow,
testing the roll of the land, probing for an opening, the smallest indenta-
tion that will accept his pressure, and invite him to follow with his instruments. There is none. It is terra incognita. Hawk-eyed, he peers,
waiting for a sign, a slight change in color, that would declare the line of
a tube mounding from its sunken position. There is no mark, no trail left
by some earlier explorer.

At last he takes up his scissors and forceps and begins to dissect, 3
millimetering down and in. The slightest step to either side may be the
bit of excess that will set off avalanche or flood. And he is *alone*. No matter how many others crowd about the mouth of the wound, no matter
their admiration and encouragement, it is *he* that rappels this crevasse,
dangles in this dreadful place, and he is *afraid*—for he knows well the
worth of this belly, that it is priceless and irreplaceable.

"Socked in," he says aloud. His language is astronaut terse. The [4]
others are silent. They know the danger, but they too have given him
their reliance. He speaks again.

"The common bile duct is bricked up in scar . . . the pancreas [5]
swollen about it . . . soup." His voice is scarcely more than the movement of his lips. The students and interns must strain to hear, as though
the sound comes from a great distance. They envy him his daring, his
dexterity. They do not know that he envies them their safe footing, their
distance from the pit.

The surgeon cuts. And all at once there leaps a mighty blood. As [6]
when from the hidden mountain ledge a pebble is dislodged, a pebble
behind whose small slippage the whole of the avalanche is pulled. Now
the belly is a vast working lake in which it seems both patient and surgeon will drown. He speaks.

"Pump the blood in. Faster! Faster! Jesus! We are losing him." [7]

And he stands there with his hand sunk in the body of his patient, [8]
leaning with his weight upon the packing he has placed there to occlude
the torn vessel, and he watches the transfusion of new blood leaving the
bottles one after the other and entering the tubing. He knows it is not
enough, that the shedding outraces the donation.

At last the surgeon feels the force of the hemorrhage slacken be- [9]
neath his hand, sees that the suction machine has cleared the field for
him to see. He can begin once more to approach that place from which
he was driven. Gently he teases the packing from the wound so as not to
jar the bleeding alive. He squirts in saline to wash away the old stains.
Gingerly he searches for the rent in the great vein. Then he hears.

"I do not have a heartbeat." It is the man at the head of the table who [10]
speaks. "The cardiogram is flat," he says. Then, a moment later . . . "This
man is dead."

Now there is no more sorrowful man in the city, for this surgeon [11]
has discovered the surprise at the center of his work. It is death.

The events of this abdomen have conspired to change him, for no [12]
man can travel back from such darkness and be the same as he was.

As much from what happens *outside* the human body as within [13]
that place that for him has become the image of his mind, the surgeon
learns.

It is Korea. 1955. [14]

I am awakened by a hand on my chest, jostling. [15]

"Sir Doc! Sir Doc!" It is Jang, the Korean man who assists me. [16]

I open my eyes. Not gladly. To awaken here, in this place, in this [17]
time, is to invite despair.

"Boy come. Gate. Very scared. His brother bad sick. Pain belly. You [18]
come?"

O God, I think, let it not be appendicitis. I do not know how many   19
more anesthesia-less operations I have left in me. Not many, I think. For
I can no longer bear the gagged mouths, the trembling, frail bodies
strapped to the table, round and round with the wide adhesive tape
from neck to ankles, with a space at the abdomen for the incision. Nor
the knuckles burning white as they clutch the "courage stick" thrust into
their hands at the last minute by a mamasan. Nor the eyes, slant and
roving, enkindled with streaky lights. Something drags at my arms, tangles my fingers. They grow ponderous at the tips.

"Couldn't they bring him here?"   20

"No, Sir Doc. Too very sick."   21

It is midnight. I force myself to look at the boy who will guide us.   22
He is about ten years old, small, thin, and with a festoon of snot connecting one nostril to his upper lip. It gives a harelip effect.

We are four in the ambulance. Jang, Galloway the driver, the boy,   23
and myself. A skinny bare arm points up into the mountains where I
know the road is narrow, winding. There are cliffs.

"We'll go up the stream bed," says Galloway. "It's still dry, and   24
safer. Far as we can, then tote in."

I make none of these decisions. The ambulance responds to the   25
commands of the boy like a huge trained beast. Who would have
thought a child to have so much power in him? Soon we are in the dry
gully of the stream. It is slow. Off in the distance there is a torch. It
swings from side to side like the head of a parrot. A signal. We move on.

The first cool wind plays with the hair, blows the lips dry, bright-   26
ens the tops of cigarettes, then skips away. In a moment it returns. Its
strength is up.

"Rain start today," says Jang.   27

"Today?"   28

"Now," says Galloway. A thrum hits the windshield, spreads to   29
the roof, and we are enveloped in rain. A flashlight floats morosely off to
one side, ongoing. There is shouting in Korean.

Now we are suckstepping through rice paddies, carrying the litter   30
and tarps. We arrive at the house.

A sliding paper door opens. It is like stepping into a snail shell. On   31
the floor mat lies a boy, he is a little smaller than the other. He wears
only a loose-fitting cotton shirt out of which his head sticks like a fifth
limb. His face is as tightly drawn as a fist. Flies preen there. His eyes
rove in their fissures like a pendulum. I kneel. Heat rises from the skin
in a palpable cloud. The ribbed bellows of the chest work above the
swollen taut abdomen. Tight parts shine, I think. Knuckles and blisters
and a belly full of pus. I lay my hand on the abdomen. It helps me. I
grow calm. Still, my fingers inform of the disease packaged there,
swarming, lapping in untouched corners. For one moment, I long to

leave it there, encased. To let it out, to cut it open, is to risk loosing it over the earth, an oceanic tide.

The abdomen is rigid, guarded. *Défense musculaire*, the French call it. You could bounce a penny on it. The slight pressure of my hand causes pain, and the child raises one translucent hand to ward me off. *Peritonitis*. Fluttering at the open lips, a single bubble expands and contracts with each breath. A soul budding there. 32

Outside, the sound of the rain has risen. There is anger in it. We place the boy on the litter, cover him with the tarpaulin. The door is slid open, twists of water skirl from the roof. 33

"Don't run," I say. "No jouncing." 34

The two men and the litter disappear like a melting capital H. I bow to the family of the child. Their faces are limp, flaccid; the muscles, skin, lips, eyelids—everything still. I recognize it as woe. The mother hunkers by the pallet gazing at the door. Fine colonies of sweat, like seed pearls, show upon her nose; strapped to her back, an infant twists its head away from hers in sleep. The father stands by the door. His breath is rich with kimchi, he seems to be listening. I am relieved to thrust myself into the rain. 35

Once again we are in the ambulance. 36

"The bumps," I say. "They hurt him." I need not have said that. The others knew. 37

There is no longer a stream bed. Where it had been, a river rushes. It has many mouths. It is maniacal. In the morning the fields below will be flooded. We drive into the torrent because . . . there is nothing else to do. We hear his little grunts, the "hic" at the end of each breath, and we enter the river. In a minute the water is at the running board, sliding back and forth on the floor. We move out to the middle. It is deeper there. In the back of the vehicle, Jang hovers over the litter, bracing it with his body. All at once, I feel the impact of the wave, like the slap of a giant tail. We are silent as the ambulance goes over on its side. We are filling with water. I push with my boots against Galloway's body, and open the door. I climb out onto the side of the ambulance. 38

"Pass him out. Give him here." 39

The moaning white figure is held up. He is naked save for the shirt. I hold him aloft. I am standing on the red cross. The others climb out. We huddle as the water screens the surface around where we stand. Then we are *in*. Rolling over and over, choking. I see the boy fly from my hands, watch him rise into the air, as in slow motion, his shirt-ends fluttering, the wind whipping the cloth. For an instant, he hangs there, his small bare arms raised, his fingers waving airily. Then he is a fish, streaking whitely, now ducking, now curving above. At last, he is a twig, turning lazily, harbored. When we reach him, he is on his back, the water rolling in and out of his mouth, his cracked head ribboning the water with blood. 40

All that night we walk, carrying the body in turns. The next day 41
the father arrives. We give him the body, and I listen as Jang tells him
the story of the drowning. We do not look at each other.

A man of letters lies in the intensive care unit. A professor, used to 42
words, and students. He has corrected the sentences of many. He understands punctuation. One day in his classroom he was speaking of Emily
Dickinson when suddenly he grew pale, and a wonder sprang upon his
face, as though he had just, for the first time, *seen* something, understood
something that had eluded him all his life. It was the look of the Wound,
the struck blow that makes no noise, but happens in the depths somewhere, unseen. His students could not have known that at that moment
his stomach had perforated, that even as he spoke, its contents were is-
suing forth into his peritoneal cavity like a horde of marauding goblins.
From the blackboard to the desk he reeled, fell across the top of it, and
turning his face to one side, he vomited up his blood, great gouts and
gobbets of it, as though having given his class the last of his spirit, he
now offered them his fluid and cells.

In time, he was carried to the operating room, this man whom I 43
had known, who had taught me poetry. I took him up, in my hands, and
laid him open, and found from where he bled. I stitched it up, and ban-
daged him, and said later, "Now you are whole."

But it was not so, for he had begun to die. And I could not keep him 44
from it, not with all my earnestness, so sure was his course. From surgery
he was taken to the intensive care unit. His family, his students were
stopped at the electronic door. They could not pass, for he had entered a
new state of being, a strange antechamber where they may not go.

For three weeks he has dwelt in that House of Intensive Care, 45
punctured by needles, wearing tubes of many calibers in all of his ori-
fices, irrigated, dialyzed, insufflated, pumped, and drained . . . and feeling every prick and pressure the way a lover feels desire spring acutely
to his skin.

In the room a woman moves. She is dressed in white. Lovingly she 46
measures his hourly flow of urine. With hands familiar, she delivers
oxygen to his nostrils and counts his pulse as though she were telling
beads. Each bit of his decline she records with her heart full of grief,
shaking her head. At last, she turns from her machinery to the simple
touch of the flesh. Sighing, she strips back the sheet, and bathes his
limbs.

The man of letters did not know this woman before. Preoccupied 47
with dying, he is scarcely aware of her presence now. But this nurse is
his wife in his new life of dying. They are close, these two, intimate,
depending one upon the other, loving. It is a marriage, for although
they own no shared past, they possess this awful, intense present, this
matrimonial now, that binds them as strongly as any promise.

A man does not know whose hands will stroke from him the last 48
bubbles of his life. That alone should make him kinder to strangers.

I stand by the bed where a young woman lies, her face postopera- 49
tive, her mouth twisted in palsy, clownish. A tiny twig of the facial
nerve, the one to the muscles of her mouth, has been severed. She will be
thus from now on. The surgeon had followed with religious fervor the
curve of her flesh; I promise you that. Nevertheless, to remove the tumor
in her cheek, I had cut the little nerve.

Her young husband is in the room. He stands on the opposite side 50
of the bed, and together they seem to dwell in the evening lamplight,
isolated from me, private. Who are they, I ask myself, he and this wry-
mouth I have made, who gaze at and touch each other so generously,
greedily? The young woman speaks.

"Will my mouth always be like this?" she asks. 51

"Yes," I say, "it will. It is because the nerve was cut." 52

She nods, and is silent. But the young man smiles. 53

"I like it," he says. "It is kind of cute." 54

All at once I *know* who he is. I understand, and I lower my gaze. 55
One is not bold in an encounter with a god. Unmindful, he bends to kiss
her crooked mouth, and I so close I can see how he twists his own lips to
accommodate to hers, to show her that their kiss still works. I remember
that the gods appeared in ancient Greece as mortals, and I hold my
breath and let the wonder in.

Far away from the operating room, the surgeon is taught that some 56
deaths are undeniable, that this does not deny their meaning. To *perceive*
tragedy is to wring from it beauty and truth. It is a thing beyond mere
competence and technique, or the handsomeness to precisely cut and
stitch. Further, he learns that love can bloom in the stoniest desert, an intensive care unit, perhaps.

These are things of longest memory, and like memory, they cut. 57
When the patient becomes the surgeon, he goes straight for the soul.

I do not know when it was that I understood that it is precisely this 58
hell in which we wage our lives that offers us the energy, the possibility
to care for each other. A surgeon does not slip from his mother's womb
with compassion smeared upon him like the drippings of his birth. It is
much later that it comes. No easy shaft of grace this, but the cumulative
murmuring of the numberless wounds he has dressed, the incisions he
has made, all the sores and ulcers and cavities he has touched in order to
heal. In the beginning it is barely audible, a whisper, as from many
mouths. Slowly it gathers, rises from the streaming flesh until, at last, it
is a pure *calling*—an exclusive sound, like the cry of certain solitary
birds—telling that out of the resonance between the sick man and the

one who tends him there may spring that profound courtesy that the religious call Love.

1976

Purpose and Meaning

1. "Lessons from the Art" describes four wide-ranging medical cases. What are these cases, and what is Selzer's purpose in separating them with simple double spacing? What is the central lesson that Selzer learns from his experiences?

2. In paragraph 56, Selzer says, "To *perceive* tragedy is to wring from it beauty and truth." What form of beauty does Selzer find in his cases? How does he depict the events he describes as beautiful? What does he mean by tragedy?

Language and Style

1. In paragraphs 2 and 3, Selzer uses figurative language to describe the patient: "the fierce wind of inflammation has swept this place"; "all is forestial, swampy"; "It is terra incognita." What is the extended image he is using in these paragraphs? What image does he use to portray the role of the surgeon?

2. Selzer describes the sick Korean boy's disease as "swarming, lapping in untouched corners" and "to let it out is to risk loosing it over the earth, an oceanic tide" (paragraph 31). To what is Selzer comparing the disease? How does his description connect the boy's illness with the weather outside the hut? What fear does Selzer express in this paragraph that comes true in an unexpected way?

3. In the third section of the essay, Selzer refers to the intensive care unit as the "House of Intensive Care." What does this suggest about its purpose and function? How does the description of the nurse and her duties contribute to this purpose?

4. Selzer is as careful with the art of writing as with the art of surgery. Study the following sentences: "As much from what happens *outside* the human body as within that place that for him has become the image of his mind, the surgeon learns" (paragraph 13); "The surgeon had followed with religious fervor the curve of her flesh; I promise you that" (paragraph 49). How does their unique syntax contribute to the tone of the essay?

5. Read the following aloud: "I do not know when it was that I understood that it is precisely this hell in which we wage our lives that offers us the en-

ergy, the possibility to care for each other" (paragraph 58). How does the sound of the words contribute to the poetic quality of this sentence?

Strategy and Structure

1. The first and last sections are written in the third person *he*, and the middle sections are written in the first person. What is the purpose of this organizational strategy? How does the use of first or third person affect the tone of each section?

2. Section 1 begins with a terse, unexpected sentence. What effect is Selzer trying to achieve with this strategy? How does the sentence compare to the final one of section 1?

3. Section 4 is quite short. How does the length of this section correspond to what occurs in it?

Thinking and Writing

1. Select five to ten sentences from the essay that have a particularly interesting syntax, sound, or imagery. In an essay of your own, discuss these aspects of Selzer's style.

2. Reread "Lessons from the Art" carefully. Then write an essay listing the small lessons and the overall lesson Selzer learned as a surgeon.

3. In the final paragraph, Selzer explains that the experiences of a surgeon accumulate into "a pure *calling*." What other professions resemble a religious mission in their intensity? Select any profession you wish, and write an essay explaining why it transcends the category of "profession."

The Masked Marvel's Last Toehold

Morning rounds.

On the fifth floor of the hospital, in the west wing, I know that a   1
man is sitting up in his bed, waiting for me. Elihu Koontz is seventy-five, and he is diabetic. It is two weeks since I amputated his left leg just below the knee. I walk down the corridor, but I do not go straight into his room. Instead, I pause in the doorway. He is not yet aware of my

presence, but gazes down at the place in the bed where his leg used to be, and where now there is the collapsed leg of his pajamas. He is totally absorbed, like an athlete appraising the details of his body. What is he thinking, I wonder. Is he dreaming the outline of his toes. Does he see there his foot's incandescent ghost? Could he be angry? Feel that I have taken from him something for which he yearns now with all his heart? Has he forgotten so soon the pain? It was a pain so great as to set him apart from all other men, in a red-hot place where he had no kith or kin. What of those black gorilla toes and the soupy mess that was his heel? I watch him from the doorway. It is a kind of spying, I know.

Save for a white fringe open at the front, Elihu Koontz is bald. The hair has grown too long and is wilted. He wears it as one would wear a day-old laurel wreath. He is naked to the waist, so that I can see his breasts. They are the breasts of Buddha, inverted triangles from which the nipples swing, dark as garnets. 2

I have seen enough. I step into the room, and he sees that I am there. 3

"How did the night go, Elihu?" 4

He looks at me for a long moment. "Shut the door," he says. 5

I do, and move to the side of the bed. He takes my left hand in both of his, gazes at it, turns it over, then back, fondling, at last holding it up to his cheek. I do not withdraw from this loving. After a while he relinquishes my hand, and looks up at me. 6

"How is the pain?" I ask. 7

He does not answer, but continues to look at me in silence. I know at once that he has made a decision. 8

"Ever hear of The Masked Marvel?" He says this in a low voice, almost a whisper. 9

"What?" 10

"The Masked Marvel," he says. "You never heard of him?" 11

"No." 12

He clucks his tongue. He is exasperated. 13

All at once there is a recollection. It is dim, distant, but coming near. 14

"Do you mean the wrestler?" 15

Eagerly, he nods, and the breasts bob. How gnomish he looks, oval as the huge helpless egg of some outlandish lizard. He has very long arms, which, now and then, he unfurls to reach for things—a carafe of water, a get-well card. He gazes up at me, urging. He *wants* me to remember. 16

"Well . . . yes," I say. I am straining backward in time. "I saw him wrestle in Toronto long ago." 17

"Ha!" He smiles. "You saw *me*." And his index finger, held rigid and upright, bounces in the air. 18

The man has said something shocking, unacceptable. It must be 19
challenged.

"You?" I am trying to smile. 20

Again that jab of the finger. "You saw *me*." 21

"No," I say. But even then, something about Elihu Koontz, those 22
prolonged arms, the shape of his head, the sudden agility with which he
leans from his bed to get a large brown envelope from his nightstand,
something is forcing me toward a memory. He rummages through his
papers, old newspaper clippings, photographs, and I remember . . .

It is almost forty years ago. I am ten years old. I have been sent to 23
Toronto to spend the summer with relatives. Uncle Max has bought two
tickets to the wrestling match. He is taking me that night.

"He isn't allowed," says Aunt Sarah to me. Uncle Max has angina. 24

"He gets too excited," she says. 25

"I wish you wouldn't go, Max," she says. 26

"You mind your own business," he says. 27

And we go. Out into the warm Canadian evening. I am not only 28
abroad, I am abroad in the *evening!* I have never been taken out in the
evening. I am terribly excited. The trolleys, the lights, the horns. It is a
bazaar. At the Maple Leaf Gardens, we sit high and near the center. The
vast arena is dark except for the brilliance of the ring at the bottom.

It begins. 29

The wrestlers circle. They grapple. They are all haunch and 30
paunch. I am shocked by their ugliness, but I do not show it. Uncle Max
is exhilarated. He leans forward, his eyes unblinking, on his face a look
of enormous happiness. One after the other, a pair of wrestlers enter the
ring. The two men join, twist, jerk, tug, bend, yank, and throw. Then
they leave and are replaced by another pair. At last it is the main event.
"The Angel vs. The Masked Marvel."

On the cover of the program notes, there is a picture of The Angel 31
hanging from the limb of a tree, a noose of thick rope around his neck.
The Angel hangs just so for an hour every day, it is explained, to
strengthen his neck. The Masked Marvel's trademark is a black stocking
cap with holes for the eyes and mouth. He is never seen without it,
states the program. No one knows who The Masked Marvel really is!

"Good," says Uncle Max. "Now you'll see something." He is fid- 32
geting, waiting for them to appear. They come down separate aisles,
climb into the ring from opposite sides. I have never seen anything like
them. It is The Angel's neck that first captures the eye. The shaved nape
rises in twin columns to puff into the white hood of a sloped and bosse-
lated skull that is too small. As though, strangled by the sinews of that
neck, the skull had long since withered and shrunk. The thing about The
Angel is the absence of any mystery in his body. It is simply *there*. A

monosyllabic announcement. A grunt. One looks and knows everything at once, the fat thighs, the gigantic buttocks, the great spine from which hang knotted ropes and pale aprons of beef. And that prehistoric head. He is all of a single hideous piece, The Angel is. No detachables.

The Masked Marvel seems dwarfish. His fingers dangle kneeward.   33
His short legs are slightly bowed as if under the weight of the cask they are forced to heft about. He has breasts that swing when he moves! I have never seen such breasts on a man before.

There is a sudden ungraceful movement, and they close upon one   34
another. The Angel stoops and hugs The Marvel about the waist, locking his hands behind The Marvel's back. Now he straightens and lifts The Marvel as though he were uprooting a tree. Thus he holds him, then stoops again, thrusts one hand through The Marvel's crotch, and with the other grabs him by the neck. He rears and . . . The Marvel is aloft! For a long moment, The Angel stands as though deciding where to make the toss. Then throws. Was that board or bone that splintered there? Again and again, The Angel hurls himself upon the body of The Masked Marvel.

Now The Angel rises over the fallen Marvel, picks up one foot in   35
both of his hands, and twists the toes downward. It is far beyond the tensile strength of mere ligament, mere cartilage. The Masked Marvel does not hide his agony, but pounds and slaps the floor with his hand, now and then reaching up toward The Angel in an attitude of supplication. I have never seen such suffering. And all the while his black mask rolls from side to side, the mouth pulled to a tight slit through which issues an endless hiss that I can hear from where I sit. All at once, I hear a shouting close by.

"Break it off! Tear off a leg and throw it up here!"   36

It is Uncle Max. Even in the darkness I can see that he is gray. A   37
band of sweat stands upon his upper lip. He is on his feet now, panting, one fist pressed at his chest, the other raised warlike toward the ring. For the first time I begin to think that something terrible might happen here. Aunt Sarah was right.

"Sit down, Uncle Max," I say. "Take a pill, please."   38

He reaches for the pillbox, gropes, and swallows without taking   39
his gaze from the wrestlers. I wait for him to sit down.

"That's not fair," I say, "twisting his toes like that."   40

"It's the toehold," he explains.   41

"But it's not *fair*," I say again. The whole of the evil is laid open for   42
me to perceive. I am trembling.

And now The Angel does something unspeakable. Holding the   43
foot of The Marvel at full twist with one hand, he bends and grasps the mask where it clings to the back of The Marvel's head. And he pulls. He is going to strip it off! Lay bare an ultimate carnal mystery! Suddenly it

is beyond mere physical violence. Now I am on my feet, shouting into the Maple Leaf Gardens.

"Watch out," I scream. "Stop him. Please, somebody, stop him."   44

Next to me, Uncle Max is chuckling.   45

Yet The Masked Marvel hears me, I know it. And rallies from his   46
bed of pain. Thrusting with his free heel, he strikes The Angel at the back of the knee. The Angel falls. The Masked Marvel is on top of him, pinning his shoulders to the mat. One! Two! Three! And it is over. Uncle Max is strangely still. I am gasping for breath. All this I remember as I stand at the bedside of Elihu Koontz.

Once again, I am in the operating room. It is two years since I am-   47
putated the left leg of Elihu Koontz. Now it is his right leg which is gangrenous. I have already scrubbed. I stand to one side wearing my gown and gloves. And . . . *I am masked.* Upon the table lies Elihu Koontz, pinned in a fierce white light. Spinal anesthesia has been administered. One of his arms is taped to a board placed at a right angle to his body. Into this arm, a needle has been placed. Fluid drips here from a bottle overhead. With his other hand, Elihu Koontz beats feebly at the side of the operating table. His head rolls from side to side. His mouth is pulled into weeping. It seems to me that I have never seen such misery.

An orderly stands at the foot of the table, holding Elihu Koontz's   48
leg aloft by the toes so that the intern can scrub the limb with antiseptic solutions. The intern paints the foot, ankle, leg, and thigh, both front and back, three times. From a corner of the room where I wait, I look down as from an amphitheater. Then I think of Uncle Max yelling, "Tear off a leg. Throw it up here." And I think that forty years later I am making the catch.

"It's not fair," I say aloud. But no one hears me. I step forward to   49
break The Masked Marvel's last toehold.

Purpose and Meaning

1. Consider the effectiveness of the essay's title. What does it reveal about Selzer's purpose?

2. What role does Selzer's own feelings play in the overall design of the essay? Would the essay lose anything if the personal memories were removed?

3. Although the essay purports to deal with an amputation of a patient's leg, is it also about something else? How does the last bit of dialogue reveal Selzer's ultimate purpose?

Language and Style

1. Selzer often uses figurative language in descriptions. Select several examples, and discuss their function in the overall design of this essay.
2. Selzer sometimes shifts from metaphoric to formal, technical language to describe physical characteristics. What is the effect of such shifts?
3. The sentences in this essay are often short and direct by design. Would the essay lose or gain in impact if they were lengthened?
4. Most of the essay is written in the active voice. However, in paragraph 47 Selzer shifts to the passive voice. How does this shift function in the scene being described?
5. How does this essay differ in language and diction from "A Mask on the Face of Death"?

Strategy and Structure

1. How many sections are there in this essay? How does each function? Is this strategy the most effective one Selzer could have chosen? How else might the essay be structured?
2. How does the extensive use of direct dialogue serve Selzer in achieving his desired effect? How would removing the dialogue affect the success of the essay?

Thinking and Writing

1. Write an essay about an experience at a sporting event that has later affected you in a significant way. Use active verbs and present tense to convey the immediacy of the experience and metaphoric language to strengthen your point.
2. In an essay or in class discussion, examine the ironies of seemingly superhuman athletes whose careers have been adversely affected by disease.

A Mask on the Face of Death

It is ten o'clock at night as we drive up to the Copacabana, a dilapidated brothel on the rue Dessalines in the red-light district of Port-au-Prince. My guide is a young Haitian, Jean-Bernard. Ten years before, J-B tells me, at the age of fourteen, "like every good Haitian boy" he had been brought here by his older cousins for his *rite de passage*. From the car to the entrance, we are accosted by a half dozen men and women for sex. We enter, go down a long hall that breaks upon a cavernous room with a stone floor. The cubicles of the prostitutes, I am told, are in an attached wing of the building. Save for a red-purple glow from small lights on the walls, the place is unlit. Dark shapes float by, each with a blindingly white stripe of teeth. Latin music is blaring. We take seats at the table farthest from the door. Just outside, there is the rhythmic lapping of the Caribbean Sea. About twenty men are seated at the tables or lean against the walls. Brightly dressed women, singly or in twos or threes, stroll about, now and then exchanging banter with the men. It is as though we have been deposited in act two of Bizet's *Carmen*. If this place isn't Lillas Pastia's tavern, what is it?

Within minutes, three light-skinned young women arrive at our table. They are very beautiful and young and lively. Let them be Carmen, Mercedes and Frasquita. 2

"I want the old one," says Frasquita, ruffling my hair. The women laugh uproariously. 3

"Don't bother looking any further," says Mercedes. "We are the prettiest ones." 4

"We only want to talk," I tell her. 5

"Aaah, aaah," she crows. "*Massissi*. You are *massissi*." It is the contemptuous Creole term for homosexual. If we want only to talk, we must be gay. Mercedes and Carmen are slender, each weighing one hundred pounds or less. Frasquita is tall and hefty. They are dressed for work: red taffeta, purple chiffon and black sequins. Among them a thousand gold bracelets and earrings multiply every speck of light. Their bare shoulders are like animated lamps gleaming in the shadowy room. Since there is as yet no business, the women agree to sit with us. J-B orders beer and cigarettes. We pay each woman $10. 6

"Where are you from?" I begin. 7

"We are Dominican." 8

"Do you miss your country?" 9

"Oh, yes, we do." Six eyes go muzzy with longing. "Our country is the most beautiful in the world. No country is like the Dominican. And it doesn't stink like this one." 10

"Then why don't you work there? Why come to Haiti?" 11

"Santo Domingo has too many whores. All beautiful, like us. All light-skinned. The Haitian men like to sleep with light women." 12

"Why is that?" 13

"Because always, the whites have all the power and the money. The black men can imagine they do, too, when they have us in bed." 14

Eleven o'clock. I looked around the room that is still sparsely peopled with men. 15

"It isn't getting any busier," I say. Frasquita glances over her shoul-   16
der. Her eyes drill the darkness.

"It is still early," she says.   17

"Could it be that the men are afraid of getting sick?" Frasquita is   18
offended.

"Sick! They do not get sick from us. We are healthy, strong. Every   19
week we go for a checkup. Besides, we know how to tell if we are getting sick."

"I mean sick with AIDS." The word sets off a hurricane of taffeta,   20
chiffon and gold jewelry. They are all gesticulation and fury. It is
Carmen who speaks.

"AIDS!" Her lips curl about the syllable. "There is no such thing. It   21
is a false disease invented by the American government to take advantage of the poor countries. The American President hates poor people, so
now he makes up AIDS to take away the little we have." The others nod
vehemently.

"*Mira, mon cher.* Look, my dear," Carmen continues. "One day the   22
police came here. Believe me, they are worse than the *tonton macoutes*
with their submachine guns. They rounded up one hundred and five of
us and they took our blood. That was a year ago. None of us have died,
you see? We are all still here. *Mira,* we sleep with all the men and we are
not sick."

"But aren't there some of you who have lost weight and have diar-   23
rhea?"

"One or two, maybe. But they don't eat. That is why they are   24
weak."

"Only the men die," says Mercedes. "They stop eating, so they die.   25
It is hard to kill a woman."

"Do you eat well?"   26

"Oh, yes, don't worry, we do. We eat like poor people, but we eat."   27
There is a sudden scream from Frasquita. She points to a large rat that
has emerged from beneath the table.

"My God!" she exclaims. "It is big like a pig." They burst into   28
laughter. For a moment the women fall silent. There is only the restlessness of their many bracelets. I give them each another $10.

"Are many of the men here bisexual?"   29

"Too many. They do it for money. Afterward, they come to us."   30
Carmen lights a cigarette and looks down at the small lace handkerchief
she has been folding and unfolding with immense precision on the table.
All at once she turns it over as though it were the ace of spades.

"*Mira, blanc . . .* look, white man," she says in a voice suddenly full   31
of foreboding. Her skin too seems to darken to coincide with the tone of
her voice.

"*Mira,* soon many Dominican women will die in Haiti!"   32

"Die of what?"   33

She shrugs. "It is what they do to us."   34

"Carmen," I say, "if you knew that you had AIDS, that your blood   35
was bad, would you still sleep with men?" Abruptly, she throws back
her head and laughs. It is the same laughter with which Frasquita had
greeted the rat at our feet. She stands and the others follow.

"*Méchant!* You wicked man," she says. Then, with terrible solem-   36
nity, "You don't know anything."

"But you are killing the Haitian men," I say.   37

"As for that," she says, "everyone is killing everyone else." All at   38
once, I want to know everything about these three—their childhood,
their dreams, what they do in the afternoon, what they eat for lunch.

"Don't leave," I say. "Stay a little more." Again, I reach for my wal-   39
let. But they are gone, taking all the light in the room with them—
Mercedes and Carmen to sit at another table where three men have been
waiting. Frasquita is strolling about the room. Now and then, as if captured by the music, she breaks into a few dance steps, snapping her fingers, singing to herself.

Midnight. And the Copacabana is filling up. Now it is like any   40
other seedy nightclub where men and women go hunting. We get up to
leave. In the center a couple are dancing a *méringue*. He is the most
graceful dancer I have ever watched; she, the most voluptuous. Together
they seem to be riding the back of the music as it gallops to a precisely
sexual beat. Closer up, I see that the man is short of breath, sweating. All
at once, he collapses into a chair. The woman bends over him, coaxing,
teasing, but he is through. A young man with a long polished stick
blocks my way.

"I come with you?" he asks. "Very good time. You say yes? Ten   41
dollars? Five?"

I have been invited by Dr. Jean William Pape to attend the AIDS   42
clinic of which he is the director. Nothing from the outside of the low
whitewashed structure would suggest it as a medical facility. Inside, it is
divided into many small cubicles and a labyrinth of corridors. At nine
a.m. the hallways are already full of emaciated silent men and women,
some sitting on the few benches, the rest leaning against the walls. The
only sounds are subdued moans of discomfort interspersed with
coughs. How they eat us with their eyes as we pass.

The room where Pape and I work is perhaps ten feet by ten. It con-   43
tains a desk, two chairs and a narrow table that is covered with a sheet
that will not be changed during the day. The patients are called in one at
a time, asked how they feel and whether there is any change in their
symptoms, then examined on the table. If the patient is new to the clinic,
he or she is questioned about sexual activities.

A twenty-seven-year-old man whose given name is Miracle enters.   44

He is wobbly, panting, like a groggy boxer who has let down his arms and is waiting for the last punch. He is neatly dressed and wears, despite the heat, a heavy woolen cap. When he removes it, I see that his hair is thin, dull reddish and straight. It is one of the signs of AIDS in Haiti, Pape tells me. The man's skin is covered with a dry itchy rash. Throughout the interview and examination he scratches himself slowly, absentmindedly. The rash is called prurigo. It is another symptom of AIDS in Haiti. This man has had diarrhea for six months. The laboratory reports that the diarrhea is due to an organism called cryptosporidium, for which there is no treatment. The telltale rattling of the tuberculous moisture in his chest is audible without a stethoscope. He is like a leaky cistern that bubbles and froths. And, clearly, exhausted.

"Where do you live?" I ask.   45

"Kenscoff." A village in the hills above Port-au-Prince.   46

"How did you come here today?"   47

"I came on the *tap-tap.*" It is the name given to the small buses that   48
swarm the city, each one extravagantly decorated with religious slogans, icons, flowers, animals, all painted in psychedelic colors. I have never seen a *tap-tap* that was not covered with passengers as well, riding outside and hanging on. The vehicles are little masterpieces of contagion, if not of AIDS then of the multitude of germs which Haitian flesh is heir to. Miracle is given a prescription for a supply of Sera, which is something like Gatorade, and told to return in a month.

"*Mangé kou bêf,*" says the doctor in farewell. "Eat like an ox." What   49
can he mean? The man has no food or money to buy any. Even had he food, he has not the appetite to eat or the ability to retain it. To each departing patient the doctor will say the same words—"*Mangé kou bêf.*" I see that it is his way of offering a hopeful goodbye.

"Will he live until his next appointment?" I ask.   50

"No." Miracle leaves to catch the *tap-tap* for Kenscoff.   51

Next is a woman of twenty-six who enters holding her right hand   52
to her forehead in a kind of permanent salute. In fact, she is shielding her eye from view. This is her third visit to the clinic. I see that she is still quite well nourished.

"Now, you'll see something beautiful, tremendous," the doctor   53
says. Once seated upon the table, she is told to lower her hand. When she does, I see that her right eye and its eyelid are replaced by a hugh fungating ulcerated tumor, a side product of her AIDS. As she turns her head, the cluster of lymph glands in her neck to which the tumor has spread is thrown into relief. Two years ago she received a blood transfusion at a time when the country's main blood bank was grossly contaminated with AIDS. It has since been closed down. The only blood available in Haiti is a small supply procured from the Red Cross.

"Can you give me medicine?" the woman wails.   54

"No."   55

"Can you cut it away?"   56

"No."   57

"Is there radiation therapy?" I ask.   58

"No."   59

"Chemotherapy?" The doctor looks at me in what some might call   60
weary amusement. I see that there is nothing to do. She has come here
because there is nowhere else to go.

"What will she do?"   61

"Tomorrow or the next day or the day after that she will climb up   62
into the mountains to seek relief from the *houngan*, the voodoo priest,
just as her slave ancestors did two hundred years ago."

Then comes a frail man in his thirties, with a strangely spiritual-   63
ized face, like a child's. Pus runs from one ear onto his cheek, where it
has dried and caked. He has trouble remembering, he tells us. In fact, he
seems confused. It is from toxoplasmosis of the brain, an effect of his
AIDS. This man is bisexual. Two years ago he engaged in oral sex with
foreign men for money. As I palpate the swollen glands of his neck, a
mosquito flies between our faces. I swat at it, miss. Just before coming to
Haiti I had read that the AIDS virus had been isolated from a certain
mosquito. The doctor senses my thought.

"Not to worry," he says. "So far as we know there has never been a   64
case transmitted by insects."

"Yes," I say. "I see."   65

And so it goes until the last, the thirty-sixth AIDS patient has been   66
seen. At the end of the day I am invited to wash my hands before leaving. I go down a long hall to a sink. I turn on the faucets but there is no
water.

"But what about *you*?" I ask the doctor. "You are at great personal   67
risk here—the tuberculosis, the other infections, no water to wash. . ."
He shrugs, smiles faintly and lifts his hands palm upward.

We are driving up a serpiginous steep road into the barren moun-   68
tains above Port-au-Prince. Even in the bright sunshine the countryside
has the bloodless color of exhaustion and indifference. Our destination is
the Baptist Mission Hospital, where many cases of AIDS have been reported. Along the road there are slow straggles of schoolchildren in blue
uniforms who stretch out their hands as we pass and call out, "Give me
something." Already a crowd of outpatients has gathered at the entrance
to the mission compound. A tour of the premises reveals that in contrast
to the aridity outside the gates, this is an enclave of productivity, lush
with fruit trees and poinsettia.

The hospital is clean and smells of creosote. Of the forty beds less   69
than a third are occupied. In one male ward of twelve beds, there are

two patients. The chief physician tells us that last year he saw ten cases of AIDS each week. Lately the number has decreased to four or five.

"Why is that?" we want to know.   70

"Because we do not admit them to the hospital, so they have   71
learned not to come here."

"Why don't you admit them?"   72

"Because we would having nothing but AIDS here then. So we   73
send them away."

"But I see that you have very few patients in bed."   74

"That is also true."   75

"Where do the AIDS patients go?"   76

"Some go to the clinic in Port-au-Prince or the general hospital in   77
the city. Others go home to die or to the voodoo priest."

"Do the people with AIDS know what they have before they come   78
here?"

"Oh, yes, they know very well, and they know there is nothing to   79
be done for them."

Outside, the crowd of people is dispersing toward the gate. The   80
clinic has been canceled for the day. No one knows why. We are conducted to the office of the reigning American pastor. He is a tall, handsome Midwesterner with an ecclesiastical smile.

"It is voodoo that is the devil here." He warms to his subject. "It is   81
a demonic religion, a cancer on Haiti. Voodoo is worse than AIDS. And
it is one of the reasons for the epidemic. Did you know that in order for
a man to become a *houngan* he must perform anal sodomy on another
man? No, of course you didn't. And it doesn't stop there. The *houngans*
tell the men that in order to appease the spirits they too must do the
same thing. So you have ritualized homosexuality. That's what is
spreading the AIDS." The pastor tells us of a nun who witnessed two
acts of sodomy in a provincial hospital where she came upon a man sexually assaulting a houseboy and another man mounting a male patient
in his bed.

"Fornication," he says. "It is Sodom and Gomorrah all over again,   82
so what can you expect from these people?" Outside his office we are
shown a cage of terrified, cowering monkeys to whom he coos affection-
ately. It is clear that he loves them. At the car, we shake hands.

"By the way," the pastor says, "what is your religion? Perhaps I am   83
a kinsman?"

"While I am in Haiti," I tell him, "it will be voodoo or it will be   84
nothing at all."

Abruptly, the smile breaks. It is as though a crack had suddenly   85
appeared in the face of an idol.

From the mission we go the general hospital. In the heart of Port-   86 au-Prince, it is the exact antithesis of the immaculate facility we have just left—filthy, crowded, hectic and staffed entirely by young interns and residents. Though it is associated with a medical school, I do not see any members of the faculty. We are shown around by Jocelyne, a young intern in a scrub suit. Each bed in three large wards is occupied. On the floor about the beds, hunkered in the posture of the innocent poor, are family members of the patients. In the corridor that constitutes the emergency room, someone lies on a stretcher receiving an intravenous infusion. She is hardly more than a cadaver.

"Where are the doctors in charge?" I ask Jocelyne. She looks at me questioningly.   87

"We are in charge."   88

"I mean your teachers, the faculty."   89

"They do not come here."   90

"What is wrong with that woman?"   91

"She has had diarrhea for three months. Now she is dehydrated." I   92
ask the woman to open her mouth. Her throat is covered with the white plaques of thrush, a fungus infection associated with AIDS.

"How many AIDS patients do you see here?"   93

"Three or four a day. We send them home. Sometimes the families   94
abandon them, then we must admit them to the hospital. Every day, then, a relative comes to see if the patient has died. They want to take the body. That is important to them. But they know very well that AIDS is contagious and they are afraid to keep them at home. Even so, once or twice a week the truck comes to take away the bodies. Many are children. They are buried in mass graves."

"Where do the wealthy patients go?"   95

"There is a private hospital called Canapé Vert. Or else they go to   96
Miami. Most of them, rich and poor, do not go to the hospital. Most are never diagnosed."

"How do you know these people have AIDS?"   97

"We don't know sometimes. The blood test is inaccurate. There are   98
many false positives and false negatives. Fifteen percent of those with the disease have negative blood tests. We go by their infections—tuberculosis, diarrhea, fungi, herpes, skin rashes. It is not hard to tell."

"Do they know what they have?"   99

"Yes. They understand at once and they are prepared to die."   100

"Do the patients know how AIDS is transmitted?"   101

"They know, but they do not like to talk about it. It is taboo. Their   102
memories do not seem to reach back to the true origins of their disaster. It is understandable, is it not?"

"Whatever you write, don't hurt us any more than we have already been hurt." It is a young Haitian journalist with whom I am drink-   103 ing a rum punch. He means that any further linkage of AIDS and Haiti in the media would complete the economic destruction of the country. The damage was done early in the epidemic when the Centers for Disease Control in Atlanta added Haitians to the three other high-risk groups—hemophiliacs, intravenous drug users and homosexual and bisexual men. In fact, Haitians are no more susceptible to AIDS than anyone else. Although the CDC removed Haitians from special scrutiny in 1985, the lucrative tourism on which so much of the country's economy was based was crippled. Along with tourism went much of the foreign business investment. Worst of all was the injury to the national pride. Suddenly Haiti was indicated as the source of AIDS in the western hemisphere.

What caused the misunderstanding was the discovery of a large 104 number of Haitian men living in Miami with AIDS antibodies in their blood. They denied absolutely they were homosexuals. But the CDC investigators did not know that homosexuality is the strongest taboo in Haiti and that no man would ever admit to it. Bisexuality, however, is not uncommon. Many married men and heterosexually oriented males will occasionally seek out other men for sex. Further, many, if not most, Haitian men visit female prostitutes from time to time. It is not difficult to see that once the virus was set loose in Haiti, the spread would be swift through both genders.

Exactly how the virus of AIDS arrived is not known. Could it have 105 been brought home by the Cuban soldiers stationed in Angola and thence to Haiti, about fifty miles away? Could it have been passed on by the thousands of Haitians living in exile in Zaire, who later returned home or immigrated to the United States? Could it have come from the American and Canadian homosexual tourists, and, yes, even some U.S. diplomats who have traveled to the island to have sex with impoverished Haitian men all too willing to sell themselves to feed their families? Throughout the international gay community Haiti was known as a good place to go for sex.

On a private tip from an official at the Ministry of Tourism, J-B and 106 I drive to a town some fifty miles from Port-au-Prince. The hotel is owned by two Frenchmen who are out of the country, one of the staff tells us. He is a man of about thirty and clearly he is desperately ill. Tottering, short of breath, he shows us about the empty hotel. The furnishings are opulent and extreme—tiger skins on the wall, a live leopard in the garden, a bedroom containing a giant bathtub with gold faucets. Is it the heat of the day or the heat of my imagination that makes these walls echo with the painful cries of pederasty?

The hotel where we are staying is in Pétionville, the fashionable 107 suburb of Port-au-Prince. It is the height of the season but there are no tourists, only a dozen or so French and American businessmen. The swimming pool is used once or twice a day by a single person. Otherwise, the water remains undisturbed until dusk, when the fruit bats come down to drink in midswoop. The hotel keeper is an American. He is eager to set me straight on Haiti.

"What did and should attract foreign investment is a combination 108 of reliable weather, an honest and friendly populace, low wages and multilingual managers."

"What spoiled it?" 109

"Political instability and a bad American press about AIDS." He 110 pauses, then adds: "To which I hope you won't be contributing."

"What about just telling the truth?" I suggest. 111

"Look," he says, "there is no more danger of catching AIDS in 112 Haiti than in New York or Santo Domingo. It is not where you are but what you do that counts." Agreeing, I ask if he had any idea that much of the tourism in Haiti during the past few decades was based on sex.

"No idea whatsoever. It was only recently that we discovered that 113 that was the case."

"How is it that you hoteliers, restaurant owners and the Ministry 114 of Tourism did not know what *tout* Haiti knew?"

"Look. All I know is that this is a middle-class, family-oriented 115 hotel. We don't allow guests to bring women, or for that matter men, into their rooms. If they did, we'd ask them to leave immediately."

At five a.m. the next day the telephone rings in my room. A Creole- 116 accented male voice.

"Is the lady still with you, sir?" 117

"There is no lady here." 118

"In your room, sir, the lady I allowed to go up with a package?" 119

"There is no lady here, I tell you." 120

At seven a.m. I stop at the front desk. The clerk is a young man. 121

"Was it you who called my room at five o'clock?" 122

"Sorry," he says with a smile. "It was a mistake, sir. I meant to ring the 123 room next door to yours." Still smiling, he holds up his shushing finger.

Next to Dr. Pape, director of the AIDS clinic, Bernard Liautaud, a 124 dermatologist, is the most knowledgeable Haitian physician on the subject of the epidemic. Together, the two men have published a dozen articles on AIDS in international medical journals. In our meeting they present me with statistics:

There are more than one thousand documented cases of AIDS in Haiti, 125 and as many as one hundred thousand carriers of the virus.

Eighty-seven percent of AIDS is now transmitted heterosexually. While it 126 is true that the virus was introduced via the bisexual community, that route has decreased to 10 percent or less.

Sixty percent of the wives or husbands of AIDS patients tested positive for 127 the antibody.

Fifty percent of the prostitutes tested in the Port-au-Prince area are in- 128 fected.

Eighty percent of the men with AIDS have had contact with prostitutes. 129

The projected number of active cases in four years is ten thousand. (Since 130 my last visit, the Haitian Medical Association broke its silence on the epidemic by warning that one million of the country's six million people could be carriers by 1992.)

The two doctors have more to tell. "The crossing over of the plague 131 from the homosexual to the heterosexual community will follow in the United States within two years. This, despite the hesitation to say so by those who fear to sow panic among your population. In Haiti, because bisexuality is more common, there was an early crossover into the general population. The trend, inevitably, is the same in the two countries."

"What is there to do, then?" 132

"Only education, just as in America. But here the Haitians reject the 133 use of condoms. Only the men who are too sick to have sex are celibate."

"What is to be the end of it?" 134

"When enough heterosexuals of the middle and upper classes die, 135 perhaps there will be the panic necessary for the people to change their sexual lifestyles."

This evening I leave Haiti. For two weeks I have fastened myself to 136 this lovely fragile land like an ear pressed to the ground. It is a country to break a traveler's heart. It occurs to me that I have not seen a single jogger. Such a public expenditure of energy while everywhere else strength is ebbing—it would be obscene. In my final hours, I go to the Cathédral of Sainte Trinité, the inner walls of which are covered with murals by Haiti's most renowned artists. Here are all the familiar Bible stories depicted in naiveté and piety, and all in such an exuberance of color as to tax the capacity of the retina to receive it, as though all the vitality of Haiti had been turned to paint and brushed upon these walls. How to explain its efflorescence at a time when all else is lassitude and inertia? Perhaps one day the plague will be rendered in poetry, music, painting, but not now. Not now.

1987

Purpose and Meaning

1. In the essay's title, to what does the word *mask* refer? What significance does "mask" have for the thesis of the essay?

2. What is Selzer's stance toward the AIDS epidemic in Haiti? Does he make

any moral judgments? Is Selzer an objective observer? What seems to be his purpose for writing? How does his stance suggest a model for the reader?

Language and Style

1. Selzer uses images of light and dark to describe the prostitutes in the first section—for example, "Dark shapes float by, each with a blindingly white stripe of teeth" (paragraph 1); "Their bare shoulders are like animated lamps gleaming in the shadowy room" (paragraph 6); "They are gone, taking all the light in the room with them" (paragraph 39). What does this say about Selzer's attitude toward the women? What irony is there in these descriptions, considering the prostitutes' role in the transmission of AIDS?

2. Compare the descriptions of places and people with those in Selzer's "Lessons from the Art." How is it different from this one in diction and vocabulary?

3. In the concluding paragraph, Selzer states, "For two weeks I have fastened myself to this lovely fragile land like an ear pressed to the ground." How has the breadth of Selzer's investigation, the exactness of the recorded dialogue, and the clarity of his descriptions all contributed to the truth of this simile?

Strategy and Structure

1. The beginning of each of the eight sections of the essay establishes where Selzer is and whom he is with. How does this information contribute to the coherence of the essay? How does it help create transitions from one section to the next?

2. Does Selzer's recording of dialogue seem truthful? Why do you think he uses so much direct speech in this essay? How does it compare in quality and quantity to the dialogue in his previous essays in this collection? By what means does Selzer seem to recall the actual conversations he had? Did he tape record them? Or does he just have a good memory? Is he giving us the gist of the conversations instead of the actual words?

3. As in his previous two essays, Selzer composes this one as a series of vignettes centering on a common theme. How does this structural choice challenge the reader's comprehension? What critical talents must the reader possess to appreciate the full import of the essay?

Thinking and Writing

1. To improve your skill at writing dialogue, keep a "dialogue journal" for a week, recording conversations you hear among schoolmates, friends, and relatives. After a week, rewrite the conversations so they have maximum effectiveness. Then compare them to the dialogue in this essay. How does

your dialogue differ from Selzer's in terms of dramatic effect, realism, and attention to detail?

2. How successful is the interview method in uncovering people's attitudes about a controversial subject? Select a site, such as a school or place of business, and conduct four or five interviews about a particular issue. Use these interviews as the basis for an essay.

3. Study the means Selzer uses to investigate the AIDS phenomenon in Haiti. In an essay of your own, explain the various methods he used. Whom did he interview? What did he observe? What conclusions did he draw? What were his overall failings and accomplishments as a medical investigator?

○●○●○●○●○●○●○●○●○●○●○●○●○●○

The Pen and the Scalpel

I had been a general surgeon for 15 years when, at the age of 40, 1 the psychic energy for writing inexplicably appeared. It was an appearance that was to knock over my life. For 15 years I had studied, practiced and taught surgery at the Yale School of Medicine, all the while enjoying the usefulness and the *handsomeness* of the craft. For the next 16 years, until my recent retirement, I would practice both surgery and writing. But where to fit in the writing when all of my days and half of my nights were fully engaged? Certainly not evenings. In the evening, one visits with one's next-of-kin; in the evening one helps with homework; in the evening, if one is so inclined, one has a martini. Instead, I became the first adult in the state of Connecticut to go to bed in the evening. Having slept from 8:30 p.m. to 1 in the morning, I rose, went down to the kitchen, put on a pot of tea and wrote in longhand (a typewriter would disturb the household) until 3 o'clock. Then it was back upstairs and to sleep until 6 in the morning, when I began the day's doctoring. Plenty of sleep, only divided by two hours, when I was alone with my pen, and all the light in the world gathered upon a sheet of paper. In this way, I wrote three collections of stories, essays and memoirs.

Time was when in the professions—medicine and law—to patron- 2 ize the arts was respectable; to practice them was not. For a surgeon it was even more questionable. Who wants to know, after all, what a surgeon does in his spare time? When it became known how I was spending my wild nights, my colleagues at the hospital were distressed. "Come, come" they coaxed in (more or less) the words of the poet Richard Wilbur, "Forsake those roses of the mind, and tend the true, the moral flower." But because the subject of my writings was my work as a doctor, the two seemed inseparable. The one fertilized the other. Why, I wondered, doesn't every surgeon write? A doctor walks in and out of a dozen short stories a day. It is irresistible to write them down. When, at last, the time came to make a choice between my two passions, it had already been made for me. Listen:

In the operating room, the patient must be anesthetized in order 3
that he feel no pain. The surgeon too must be "anesthetized" in order to remain at some distance from the event: when he cuts the patient, his own flesh must not bleed. It is this seeming lack of feeling that gives the surgeon the image of someone who is out of touch with his humanity, a person wanting only to cut, to perform. I assure you that it is the image only. A measure of insulation against the laying open of the bodies of his fellow human beings is necessary for the well-being of both patient and doctor. In surgery, if nowhere else, dispassion is an attribute. But the surgeon-writer is not anesthetized. He remains awake; sees everything; censors nothing. It is his dual role to open and repair the body of his patient and to report back to the waiting world in the keenest language he can find. By becoming a writer, I had stripped off the protective carapace. It was time to go. A surgeon can unmake himself; a writer cannot.

A Faustian bargain, you say? Perhaps, but, truth to tell, New 4
Haven had begun to seem rather like the Beast With a Thousand Gallbladders. And where is it graven in stone that, once having been ordained, a surgeon must remain at the operating table until the scalpel slips from his lifeless fingers? Nor had I any wish to become like the old lion whose claws are long since blunt but not the desire to use them. Still, one does not walk away from the workbench of one's life with a cheery wave of the hand. In the beginning, I felt a strange sense of dislocation. As though I were standing near a river whose banks were flowing while the stream itself stood still. Only now, after two years, have I ceased to have attacks of longing for the labor that so satisfied and uplifted my spirit. Then, too, there was the risk that by withdrawing from the hospital, with its rich cargo of patients and those who tend them, I would be punished as a writer, suffer from impotence of the pen. A writer turns his back upon his native land at his own peril. Besides, to begin the life of a writer at the age of 56 is to toil under the very dart of death. As did another doctor-writer, John Keats, I too "have fears that I may cease to be before my pen has gleaned my teeming brain."

In medicine, there is a procedure called transillumination. If, in a 5
darkened room, a doctor holds a bright light against a hollow part of the

body, he will see through the outer tissues to the structures within that cavity—arteries, veins, projecting shelves of bone. In such a ruby gloom he can distinguish among a hernia, a hydrocele of the scrotum and a tumor of the testicle. Or he can light up a sinus behind the brow. Unlike surgery, which opens the body to direct examination, transillumination gives an indirect vision, calling into play the simplest perceptions of the doctor. To write about a patient is like transillumination. You hold the lamp of language against his body and gaze through the covering layers at the truths within.

At first glance, it would appear that surgery and writing have little in common, but I think that is not so. For one thing, they are both sub-celestial arts; as far as I know, the angels disdain to perform either one. In each of them you hold a slender instrument that leaves a trail wherever it is applied. In one, there is the shedding of blood; in the other it is ink that is spilled upon a page. In one, the scalpel is restrained; in the other, the pen is given rein. The surgeon sutures together the tissues of the body to make whole what is sick or injured; the writer sews words into sentences to fashion a new version of human experience. A surgical operation is rather like a short story. You make the incision, rummage around inside for a bit, then stitch up. It has a beginning, a middle and an end. If I were to choose a medical specialist to write a novel, it would be a psychiatrist. They tend to go on and on. And on.

Despite that I did not begin to write until the middle of my life, I think I must always have been a writer. Like my father who was a general practitioner during the Depression in Troy, N.Y., and who wrote a novel. It was all about a prostitute with a heart of gold (her name was Goldie!) and the doctor who first saves her life, then falls in love with her. Mother read it and told him: "Keep it away from the children."

Father's office was on the ground floor of an old brownstone, and we lived upstairs. At night, after office hours, my brother Billy and I (we were 10 and 9 years old) would sneak downstairs to Father's darkened consultation room and there, shamefaced, by the light of a candle stub, we would take down from the shelves his medical textbooks. Our favorite was "The Textbook of Obstetrics and Gynecology."

It was there that I first became aware of the rich language of medicine. Some of the best words began with the letter C. *Carcinoma*, I read, and thought it was that aria from "Rigoletto" that mother used to sing while she washed and dried the dishes. *Cerebellum*. I said the word aloud, letting it drip off the end of my tongue like melted chocolate. And I read *choledochojejunostomy*, which later I was to learn as the name of an operation. All those syllables marching off in my mind to that terminal *y*! If that was the way surgeons talked, I thought, I would be one of them, and live forever in a state of mellifluous rapture. I do not use these words in my writing, but I do try to use language that evokes the sounds of the body—the *lub-dup, lub-dup* of the garrulous heart, the gasp and wheeze of hard breathing, all the murmur and splash of anatomy and physiology. And I have tried to make use of the poetic potential in scientific language. Here, from my diary, this specimen:

> How gentle the countryside near Troy, with much farming everywhere. 10
> Farming gives a sense of health to the land. It is replenishing to watch at dusk as the herd of cattle flows like a giant amoeba toward the barn. First one cow advances. She pauses. Another pseudopodium is thrust ahead, pulling the others behind it until all of the cytoplasm, trailing milk, is inside the barn. All along the banks of the Hudson River, oak, elm and locust trees have grown very tall. The bark of the locust is thrown into deep folds coated with lichen and moss. So old are these trees that, without the least wind, one will drop off a quite large branch as if to shed a part of its burden. This letting-fall doesn't seem to do the tree any harm. It is more an anatomical relinquishment of a part so that the whole might remain healthy. Much as a diabetic will accept amputation of a gangrenous toe in order that he might once again walk on his foot. How clever of these locust trees to require no surgeon for their trimmage, only their own corporeal wisdom.

1988

Purpose and Meaning

1. Does the title of this essay prepare us for Selzer's purpose and approach to the subject? Would your expectations have been different if the title of the essay had been "Memories of a Surgeon-Writer"?

2. This essay first appeared in the *New York Times Magazine*. In paragraph 1, Selzer describes what "one" normally does in the evening. What do his examples suggest about author-reader backgrounds? What other elements of the essay reveal the assumptions the author has made about readers' cultural, social, and economic background?

Language and Style

1. Like doctor-writer John Keats, Selzer is a bit of a poet. Discuss these instances of figurative language: "rich cargo of patients" (paragraph 4); "ruby gloom" (paragraph 5); "a writer sews words into sentences" (paragraph 6). Identify some of the poetic devices in the essay. How does the figurative language change from paragraph 3 to paragraph 6? from paragraph 8 to paragraph 10? Why do these shifts occur?

2. In paragraph 9, Selzer gives examples of several medical terms and talks about the "poetic potential in scientific language." What elements in his own writing are poetic?

3. Explain how the following sentences create a tone appropriate to Selzer's subject and audience: "Time was when in the professions—medicine and law—to patronize the arts was respectable; to practice them was not" (paragraph 2); "He remains awake; sees everything; censors nothing" (paragraph 3); "How gentle the countryside near Troy, with much farming everywhere" (paragraph 10).

Strategy and Structure

1. The opening paragraph of the essay contains biographical and factual information. Many of the following paragraphs are more general, addressing the nature of writing, surgery, and Selzer's emotional conflict in choosing between the two. Then the author reverts to specifics toward the end, finishing the essay with a "specimen" from his diary. What effect does this organizational structure achieve? How does the structure contribute to Selzer's thesis?

2. One special rhetorical strategy in writing is analogy—finding similarities between two different things. Locate some of Selzer's analogies.

3. In the final paragraph, Selzer provides an excerpt from his journal in which he muses on the beauty and elegance of nature. How does this passage synthesize elements of the essay's form and content?

Thinking and Writing

1. Selzer expresses several doubts and fears concerning his decision to become a writer. How significant is experience for a writer? Argue for or against his decision to become a full-time writer.

2. Write an essay using analogy. The "signifier"—that is, the subject being used to describe another subject—may be a sport, an art or craft, or an occupation. The "signified"—that is, the subject being described—may be a topic such as love, life, marriage, or friendship.

3. Study Selzer's four essays in this section, and conduct additional research on the author. Drawing on this material, write an essay on how Selzer's first profession has influenced his writing.

JOAN DIDION

In her essay "Why I Write," developed originally as an address to the faculty at the University of California at Berkeley, Joan Didion acknowledges that she took the title from an essay by George Orwell (included in this book). Like Orwell, she functions, in her writing, as the conscience of her generation. Both authors attack received opinion and bankrupt ideology. Both are militant writers seeking to expose shoddy thinking and blatant lying with a style that is crisp, concrete, and clear. Both are superb at creating nonfiction of stupendous narrative and descriptive strength.

Didion was born in Sacramento, California, in 1934, educated in Sacramento schools and, from 1952 to 1956, at the University of California at Berkeley. The physical, psychological, and cultural landscape of California has been a dominant element in both her fiction and nonfiction. For example, in her first essay collection, *Slouching Towards Bethlehem* (1968), is a section subtitled "Lifestyles in the Golden Land." That section contains eight journalistic feature articles that treat the American West as an emblem for the national experience and the American character. As she indicates in "Marrying Absurd," "Las Vegas is the most extreme and allegorical of American settlements." Personal essays, such as "On Self-Respect," also appear in Didion's classic first collection and continue the theme initiated by its Yeatsean title—that the center of contemporary civilization cannot hold. Nevertheless, Didion, with sophistication, perception, and ironic nuance, forces herself, as she declares in her preface, "to come to terms with disorder" and thereby assert her worth as a writer.

As a writer—and notably as an essayist—Joan Didion is in a league by herself. Critic John Leonard once wrote that "nobody writes better English prose than Joan Didion. Try to rearrange one of her sentences, and you've realized that the sentence was inevitable." Precise and unsentimental, she has a talent, as did Orwell, for the minute, telling detail. The sharpness of her imagery, she explains in "Why I Write," centers on observed details—the picture in her mind—which, she says, dictates its arrangement into words. The resulting precision of her images can be appreciated in her keenly drawn portraits, such as "Georgia O'Keeffe." Indeed, in all her essay collections—*Slouching Towards Bethlehem; The White Album* (1979), her second essay collection; *Salvador* (1983); and *Miami* (1987)—she invariably offers unforgettable portraits of people and places caught in the absurdity and terror of the times.

As "In Bed" clearly demonstrates, Didion also engages in relentless self-scrutiny. Readers of her essays learn more than they might feel comfortable with about her depression, her "migraine personality," her marriage to writer John Gregory Dunne, their drinking, and their daily lives in Brentwood Park, a section of Los Angeles. Even readers of her novels—among them *Run River* (1963) and *Play It As It Lays* (1970), which was nominated for a National Book Award—will find in their characters images of the volatile author. Her last collection of essays, *After Henry*, was published in 1992.

Didion's introspective impulse is a major literary strength, for it opens her to the feelings and attitudes of others. Dubbed by her California friends "the Kafka of Brentwood Park," Joan Didion is a wise and often witty purveyor of the postures of contemporary alienation. For Didion, even the myth of the American Eden, the Golden Land, contains within it what she has termed "the unspeakable peril of the everyday," which she locates in the tension between the innocence and evil in the American grain.

Marrying Absurd

To be married in Las Vegas, Clark County, Nevada, a bride must
swear that she is eighteen or has parental permission and a bridegroom
that he is twenty-one or has parental permission. Someone must put up
five dollars for the license. (On Sundays and holidays, fifteen dollars.
The Clark County Courthouse issues marriage licenses at any time of the
day or night except between noon and one in the afternoon, between
eight and nine in the evening, and between four and five in the morning.) Nothing else is required. The State of Nevada, alone among these
United States, demands neither a premarital blood test nor a waiting period before or after the issuance of a marriage license. Driving in across
the Mojave from Los Angeles, one sees the signs way out on the desert,
looming up from that moonscape of rattlesnakes and mesquite, even before the Las Vegas lights appear like a mirage on the horizon: "GETTING
MARRIED? Free License Information First Strip Exit." Perhaps the Las
Vegas wedding industry achieved its peak operational efficiency between 9:00 p.m. and midnight of August 26, 1965, an otherwise unremarkable Thursday which happened to be, by Presidential order, the
last day on which anyone could improve his draft status merely by getting married. One hundred and seventy-one couples were pronounced
man and wife in the name of Clark County and the State of Nevada that
night, sixty-seven of them by a single justice of the peace, Mr. James A.
Brennan. Mr. Brennan did one wedding at the Dunes and the other
sixty-six in his office, and charged each couple eight dollars. One bride
lent her veil to six others. "I got it down from five to three minutes," Mr.
Brennan said later of his feat. "I could've married them *en masse*, but
they're people, not cattle. People expect more when they get married."

What people who get married in Las Vegas actually do expect—
what, in the largest sense, their "expectations" are—strikes one as a curious and self-contradictory business. Las Vegas is the most extreme and
allegorical of American settlements, bizarre and beautiful in its venality
and in its devotion to immediate gratification, a place the tone of which
is set by mobsters and call girls and ladies' room attendants with amyl
nitrite poppers in their uniform pockets. Almost everyone notes that
there is no "time" in Las Vegas, no night and no day and no past and no
future (no Las Vegas casino, however, has taken the obliteration of the
ordinary time sense quite so far as Harold's Club in Reno, which for a
while issued, at odd intervals in the day and night, mimeographed "bul-
letins" carrying news from the world outside); neither is there any logi-

cal sense of where one is. One is standing on a highway in the middle of a vast hostile desert looking at an eighty-foot sign which blinks "STAR-DUST" or "CAESAR'S PALACE." Yes, but what does that explain? This geographical implausibility reinforces the sense that what happens there has no connection with "real" life; Nevada cities like Reno and Carson are ranch towns, Western towns, places behind which there is some historical imperative. But Las Vegas seems to exist only in the eye of the beholder. All of which makes it an extraordinarily stimulating and interesting place, but an odd one in which to want to wear a candlelight satin Priscilla of Boston wedding dress with Chantilly lace insets, tapered sleeves and a detachable modified train.

And yet the Las Vegas wedding business seems to appeal to precisely that impulse. "Sincere and Dignified Since 1954," one wedding chapel advertises. There are nineteen such wedding chapels in Las Vegas, intensely competitive, each offering better, faster, and, by implication, more sincere services than the next: Our Photos Best Anywhere, Your Wedding on A Phonograph Record, Candlelight with Your Ceremony, Honeymoon Accommodations, Free Transportation from Your Motel to Courthouse to Chapel and Return to Motel, Religious or Civil Ceremonies, Dressing Rooms, Flowers, Rings, Announcements, Witnesses Available, and Ample Parking. All of these services, like most others in Las Vegas (sauna baths, payroll-check cashing, chinchilla coats for sale or rent) are offered twenty-four hours a day, seven days a week, presumably on the premise that marriage, like craps, is a game to be played when the table seems hot.

But what strikes one most about the Strip chapels, with their wishing wells and stained-glass paper windows and their artificial bouvardia, is that so much of their business is by no means a matter of simple convenience, of late-night liaisons between show girls and baby Crosbys. Of course there is some of that. (One night about eleven o'clock in Las Vegas I watched a bride in an orange minidress and masses of flame-colored hair stumble from a Strip chapel on the arm of her bridegroom, who looked the part of the expendable nephew in movies like *Miami Syndicate*. "I gotta get the kids," the bride whimpered. "I gotta pick up the sitter, I gotta get to the midnight show." "What you gotta get," the bridegroom said, opening the door of a Cadillac Coupe de Ville and watching her crumple on the seat, "is sober.") But Las Vegas seems to offer something other than "convenience"; it is merchandising "niceness," the facsimile of proper ritual, to children who do not know how else to find it, how to make the arrangements, how to do it "right." All day and evening long on the Strip, one sees actual wedding parties, waiting under the harsh lights at a crosswalk, standing uneasily in the parking lot of the Frontier while the photographer hired by The Little

Church of the West ("Wedding Place of the Stars") certifies the occasion, takes the picture: the bride in a veil and white satin pumps, the bridegroom usually in a white dinner jacket, and even an attendant or two, a sister or a best friend in hot-pink *peau de soie*, a flirtation veil, a carnation nosegay. "When I Fall in Love It Will Be Forever," the organist plays, and then a few bars of Lohengrin. The mother cries; the stepfather, awkward in his role, invites the chapel hostess to join them for a drink at the Sands. The hostess declines with a professional smile; she has already transferred her interest to the group waiting outside. One bride out, another in, and again the sign goes up on the chapel door: "One moment please—Wedding."

I sat next to one such wedding party in a Strip restaurant the last   5
time I was in Las Vegas. The marriage had just taken place; the bride still wore her dress, the mother her corsage. A bored waiter poured out a few swallows of pink champagne ("on the house") for everyone but the bride, who was too young to be served. "You'll need something with more kick than that," the bride's father said with heavy jocularity to his new son-in-law; the ritual jokes about the wedding night had a certain Panglossian character, since the bride was clearly several months pregnant. Another round of pink champagne, this time not on the house, and the bride began to cry. "It was just as nice," she sobbed, "as I hoped and dreamed it would be."

1967

Purpose and Meaning

1. What makes getting married in Las Vegas absurd? What is Didion's purpose in this essay? What assumptions do we have about marriage that make the Las Vegas practice seem absurd?

2. What is Didion's thesis? How effective is the title in suggesting the thesis? What alternative title could you give it that would summarize the author's thesis?

3. What does Didion mean in paragraph 2 when she says that "Las Vegas is the most extreme and allegorical of American settlements"?

Language and Style

1. Reread paragraph 2. Note the way in which Didion describes the atmosphere of Las Vegas. In what way do the syntax and length of her sentences

help create a sense of this atmosphere? Study, in particular, the sentence that begins, "Almost everyone notes that there is no 'time' in Las Vegas . . . "

2. In paragraph 2, Didion states that what people expect in Las Vegas is "a curious and self-contradictory business." How are Mr. Brennan's comments in paragraph 1 about marriage a self-contradiction? Where else does Didion use irony to provide evidence of this self-contradiction?

3. In paragraphs 3 and 4, Didion is quite specific in her itemization, listing the many signs that advertise the marriage services in Las Vegas, car models, and song titles. How does this attention to detail contribute to the portrayal of merchandising that goes on in the city?

Strategy and Structure

1. Is Didion's theme made clear in the introduction? What is the effect of starting the essay as if we had jumped into it in the middle?

2. Paragraph 2 makes almost no reference to marriage. Is there little connection between it and paragraph 1? What function does paragraph 2 serve in the overall scheme of the essay?

3. Didion uses narration, description, and exposition in her essay. Which paragraphs coincide with which of these three forms? Does this blend of forms contribute to or detract from the impact of the essay?

4. The essay's conclusion describes a brief incident that Didion witnessed. How effective was it to conclude the essay this way? Why does the essay end with a direct quotation? Would it have been more effective to summarize the theme of the essay in the conclusion?

Thinking and Writing

1. Select a place that has special significance to you. Write an essay in which you reveal your attitude about this place in the way you present it. Try to avoid stating a specific thesis about the place, but instead allow the description and narration to convey your main meaning.

2. Compare your own image of Las Vegas or Atlantic City with that of Didion. What elements have shaped your image?

3. Select from among television shows, theme parks, circuses, or shopping malls. Then write an expository essay explaining the techniques one of these places uses to manipulate or satisfy your expectations of it. What are your desires and expectations? What methods, techniques, props, and timing does the place use to influence us?

On Self-Respect

Once, in a dry season, I wrote in large letters across two pages of a   1
notebook that innocence ends when one is stripped of the delusion that
one likes oneself. Although now, some years later, I marvel that a mind
on the outs with itself should have nonetheless made painstaking record
of its every tremor, I recall with embarrassing clarity the flavor of those
particular ashes. It was a matter of misplaced self-respect.

I had not been elected to Phi Beta Kappa. This failure could   2
scarcely have been more predictable or less ambiguous (I simply did not
have the grades), but I was unnerved by it; I had somehow thought myself a kind of academic Raskolnikov, curiously exempt from the cause-
effect relationships which hampered others. Although even the humor-
less nineteen-year-old that I was must have recognized that the situation
lacked real tragic stature, the day that I did not make Phi Beta Kappa
nonetheless marked the end of something, and innocence may well be
the word for it. I lost the conviction that lights would always turn green
for me, the pleasant certainty that those rather passive virtues which had
won me approval as a child automatically guaranteed me not only Phi
Beta Kappa keys but happiness, honor, and the love of a good man; lost
a certain touching faith in the totem power of good manners, clean hair,
and proven competence on the Stanford-Binet scale. To such doubtful
amulets had my self-respect been pinned, and I faced myself that day
with the nonplused apprehension of someone who has come across a
vampire and has no crucifix at hand.

Although to be driven back upon oneself is an uneasy affair at best,   3
rather like trying to cross a border with borrowed credentials, it seems
to me now the one condition necessary to the beginnings of real self-respect. Most of our platitudes notwithstanding, self-deception remains
the most difficult deception. The tricks that work on others count for
nothing in that very well-lit back alley where one keeps assignations
with oneself: no winning smiles will do here, no prettily drawn lists of
good intentions. One shuffles flashily but in vain through one's marked
cards—the kindness done for the wrong reason, the apparent triumph
which involved no real effort, the seemingly heroic act into which one
had been shamed. The dismal fact is that self-respect has nothing to do
with the approval of others—who are, after all, deceived easily enough;
has nothing to do with reputation, which, as Rhett Butler told Scarlett
O'Hara, is something people with courage can do without.

To do without self-respect, on the other hand, is to be an unwilling 4
audience of one to an interminable documentary that details one's failings, both real and imagined, with fresh footage spliced in for every
screening. *There's the glass you broke in anger, there's the hurt on X's face;
watch now, this next scene, the night Y came back from Houston, see how you
muff this one.* To live without self-respect is to lie awake some night, beyond the reach of warm milk, phenobarbital, and the sleeping hand on
the coverlet, counting up the sins of commission and omission, the trusts
betrayed, the promises subtly broken, the gifts irrevocably wasted
through sloth or cowardice or carelessness. However long we postpone
it, we eventually lie down alone in that notoriously uncomfortable bed,
the one we make ourselves. Whether or not we sleep in it depends, of
course, on whether or not we respect ourselves.

To protest that some fairly improbable people, some people who 5
could not possibly respect themselves, seem to sleep easily enough is to miss
the point entirely, as surely as those people miss it who think that self-
respect has necessarily to do with not having safety pins in one's underwear. There is a common superstition that "self-respect" is a kind of
charm against snakes, something that keeps those who have it locked in
some unblighted Eden, out of strange beds, ambivalent conversations,
and trouble in general. It does not at all. It has nothing to do with the
face of things, but concerns instead a separate peace, a private reconciliation. Although the careless, suicidal Julian English in *Appointment in
Samarra* and the careless, incurably dishonest Jordan Baker in *The Great
Gatsby* seem equally improbable candidates for self-respect, Jordan
Baker had it, Julian English did not. With that genius for accommoda-
tion more often seen in women than in men, Jordan took her own measure, made her own peace, avoided threats to that peace: "I hate careless
people," she told Nick Carraway. "It takes two to make an accident."

Like Jordan Baker, people with self-respect have the courage of 6
their mistakes. They know the price of things. If they choose to commit
adultery, they do not then go running, in an access of bad conscience, to
receive absolution from the wronged parties; nor do they complain unduly of the unfairness, the undeserved embarrassment, of being named
co-respondent. In brief, people with self-respect exhibit a certain toughness, a kind of moral nerve; they display what was once called *character*,
a quality which, although approved in the abstract, sometimes loses
ground to other, more instantly negotiable virtues. The measure of its
slipping prestige is that one tends to think of it only in connection with
homely children and United States senators who have been defeated,
preferably in the primary, for reelection. Nonetheless, character—the
willingness to accept responsibility for one's own life—is the source
from which self-respect springs.

Self-respect is something that our grandparents, whether or not 7 they had it, knew all about. They had instilled in them, young, a certain discipline, the sense that one lives by doing things one does not particularly want to do, by putting fears and doubts to one side, by weighing immediate comforts against the possibility of larger, even intangible, comforts. It seemed to the nineteenth century admirable, but not remarkable, that Chinese Gordon put on a clean white suit and held Khartoum against the Madhi; it did not seem unjust that the way to free land in California involved death and difficulty and dirt. In a diary kept during the winter of 1846, an emigrating twelve-year-old named Narcissa Cornwall noted coolly: "Father was busy reading and did not notice that the house was being filled with strange Indians until Mother spoke about it." Even lacking any clue as to what Mother said, one can scarcely fail to be impressed by the entire incident: the father reading, the Indians filing in, the mother choosing the words that would not alarm, the child duly recording the event and noting further those particular Indians were not, "fortunately for us," hostile. Indians were simply part of the *donnée.*

In one guise or another, Indians always are. Again, it is a question 8 of recognizing that anything worth having has its price. People who respect themselves are willing to accept the risk that the Indians will be hostile, that the venture will go bankrupt, that the liaison may not turn out to be one in which *every day is a holiday because you're married to me.* They are willing to invest something of themselves; they may not play at all, but when they do play, they know the odds.

That kind of self-respect is a discipline, a habit of mind that can 9 never be faked but can be developed, trained, coaxed forth. It was once suggested to me that, as an antidote to crying, I put my head in a paper bag. As it happens, there is a sound physiological reason, something to do with oxygen, for doing exactly that, but the psychological effect alone is incalculable: it is difficult in the extreme to continue fancying oneself Cathy in *Wuthering Heights* with one's head in a Food Fair bag. There is a similar case for all the small disciplines, unimportant in themselves; imagine maintaining any kind of swoon, commiserative or carnal, in a cold shower.

But those small disciplines are valuable only insofar as they repre- 10 sent larger ones. To say that Waterloo was won on the playing fields of Eton is not to say that Napoleon might have been saved by a crash program in cricket; to give formal dinners in the rain forest would be pointless did not the candlelight flickering on the liana call forth deeper, stronger disciplines, values instilled long before. It is a kind of ritual, helping us to remember who and what we are. In order to remember it, one must have known it.

To have that sense of one's intrinsic worth which constitutes self- 11 respect is potentially to have everything: the ability to discriminate, to love and to remain indifferent. To lack it is to be locked within oneself, paradoxically incapable of either love or indifference. If we do not respect ourselves, we are on the one hand forced to despise those who have so few resources as to consort with us, so little perception as to remain blind to our fatal weaknesses. On the other, we are peculiarly in thrall to everyone we see, curiously determined to live out—since our self-image is untenable—their false notions of us. We flatter ourselves by thinking this compulsion to please others an attractive trait: a gist for imaginative empathy, evidence of our willingness to give. *Of course* I will play Francesca to your Paolo, Helen Keller to anyone's Annie Sullivan: no expectation is too misplaced, no role too ludicrous. At the mercy of those we cannot but hold in contempt, we play roles doomed to failure before they are begun, each defeat generating fresh despair at the urgency of divining and meeting the next demand made upon us.

It is the phenomenon sometimes called "alienation from self." In its   12
advanced stages, we no longer answer the telephone, because someone might want something; that we could say *no* without drowning in self-reproach is an idea alien to this game. Every encounter demands too much, tears the nerves, drains the will, and the specter of something as small as an unanswered letter arouses such disproportionate guilt that answering it becomes out of the question. To assign unanswered letters their proper weight, to free us from the expectations of others, to give us back to ourselves—there lies the great, the singular power of self-respect. Without it, one eventually discovers the final turn of the screw: one runs away to find oneself, and finds no one at home.

1961

Purpose and Meaning

1. According to Didion, what is self-respect? Is one born with it, or is it developed later? What are the benefits of having self-respect?

2. In the first two paragraphs, Didion describes a momentous time in her life when her innocence ended. What caused this end of innocence? What was its effect on her? What is its relationship to self-respect?

3. What type of audience is Didion writing for? How do you know?

Language and Style

1. In paragraph 1, Didion uses three images that suggest a somber time in her life: "a dry season," "stripped of the delusion," and "particular ashes." How do these images establish the tone of the essay? How do they relate to Didion's concept of self-respect?

2. In paragraph 2, Didion uses three supernatural images: "totem power," "doubtful amulets," and "crucifix at hand." What is the relevance of these images to Didion's thesis? Why are they used as images of the lack of self-respect? In what way do they represent Didion's unique writing style? What other patterns of imagery, simile, and metaphor can you detect in the essay?

3. Study this rather long sentence in paragraph 6: "If they choose to commit adultery, they do not then go running, in an access of bad conscience, to receive absolution from the wronged parties; nor do they complain unduly of the unfairness, the undeserved embarrassment, of being named co-respondent." How many ideas does Didion cover in this sentence? What gives the sentence its complexity? What gives it its strength? How is it representative of other sentences in the essay? Reread the essay to find similar examples of Didion's syntax. What are the similarities between the sentence here and others?

Strategy and Structure

1. Study the three sections of the essay. Why has Didion divided the essay in this way? What is the relationship of each part to the others?

2. Examine paragraphs 3 and 4. What are the central images of each? How do these central images give the paragraphs their unity?

3. Didion makes some literary and historical references in her essay. What purpose do these references serve? With how many of these were you familiar? Do they contribute to or detract from her argument? Explain your answer.

4. How does Didion develop her extended definition of self-respect in this essay?

Thinking and Writing

1. How does Didion support her thesis: through example? anecdote? facts? personal experience? Make a list of her supporting points, dividing them into appropriate categories. Then write an essay on how the methods she uses to support her argument are appropriate to the subject matter.

2. In paragraph 6, Didion compares self-respect to the concept of character. Write an essay defining and describing the concept of character, employing the same kinds of supports that Didion uses.

3. There are numerous self-help books—many of them best-sellers—that claim to offer guidelines to achieve self-respect, self-realization, and personal success. Argue for or against the proposition that one can learn self-respect by following the instructions in a book.

∘●∘●∘●∘●∘

In Bed

Three, four, sometimes five times a month, I spend the day in bed with a migraine headache, insensible to the world around me. Almost every day of every month, between these attacks, I feel the sudden irrational irritation and the flush of blood into the cerebral arteries which tell me that migraine is on its way, and I take certain drugs to avert its arrival. If I did not take the drugs, I would be able to function perhaps one day in four. The physiological error called migraine is, in brief, central to the given of my life. When I was 15, 16, even 25, I used to think that I could rid myself of this error by simply denying it, character over chemistry. "Do you have headaches *sometimes? frequently? never?*" the application forms would demand. "Check one." Wary of the trap, wanting whatever it was that the successful circumnavigation of that particular form could bring (a job, a scholarship, the respect of mankind and the grace of God), I would check one. "*Sometimes,*" I would lie. That in fact I spent one or two days a week almost unconscious with pain seemed a shameful secret, evidence not merely of some chemical inferiority but of all my bad attitudes, unpleasant tempers, wrongthink.

For I had no brain tumor, no eyestrain, no high blood pressure, nothing wrong with me at all: I simply had migraine headaches, and migraine headaches were, as everyone who did not have them knew, imaginary. I fought migraine then, ignored the warnings it sent, went to school and later to work in spite of it, sat through lectures in Middle English and presentations to advertisers with involuntary tears running down the right side of my face, threw up in washrooms, stumbled home by instinct, emptied ice trays onto my bed and tried to freeze the pain in my right temple, wished only for a neurosurgeon who would do a lobotomy on house call, and cursed my imagination.

It was a long time before I began thinking mechanistically enough to accept migraine for what it was: something with which I would be living, the way some people lived with diabetes. Migraine is something more than the fancy of a neurotic imagination. It is an essentially hereditary complex of symptoms, the most frequently noted but by no means the most unpleasant of which is a vascular headache of blinding severity, suffered by a surprising number of women, a fair number of men (Thomas Jefferson had migraine, and so did Ulysses S. Grant, the day he accepted Lee's surrender), and by some unfortunate children as young as two years old. (I had my first when I was eight. It came on during a

1

2

3

fire drill at the Columbia School in Colorado Springs, Colorado. I was taken first home and then to the infirmary at Peterson Field, where my father was stationed. The Air Corps doctor prescribed an enema.) Almost anything can trigger a specific attack of migraine: stress, allergy, fatigue, an abrupt change in barometric pressure, a contretemps over a parking ticket. A flashing light. A fire drill. One inherits, of course, only the predisposition. In other words I spent yesterday in bed with a headache not merely because of my bad attitudes, unpleasant tempers and wrongthink but because both my grandmothers had migraine, my father has migraine and my mother has migraine.

No one knows precisely what it is that is inherited. The chemistry   4
of migraine, however, seems to have some connection with the nerve hormone named serotonin, which is naturally present in the brain. The amount of serotonin in the blood falls sharply at the onset of migraine, and one migraine drug, methysergide, or Sansert, seems to have some effect on serotonin. Methysergide is a derivative of lysergic acid (in fact Sandoz Pharmaceuticals first synthesized LSD-25 while looking for a migraine cure), and its use is hemmed about with so many contraindications and side effects that most doctors prescribe it only in the most incapacitating cases. Methysergide, when it is prescribed, is taken daily, as a preventive; another preventive which works for some people is old-fashioned ergotamine tartrate, which helps to constrict the swelling blood vessels during the "aura," the period which in most cases precedes the actual headache.

Once an attack is under way, however, no drug touches it.   5
Migraine gives some people mild hallucinations, temporarily blinds others, shows up not only as a headache but as a gastrointestinal disturbance, a painful sensitivity to all sensory stimuli, an abrupt overpowering fatigue, a strokelike aphasia, and a crippling inability to make even the most routine connections. When I am in a migraine aura (for some people the aura lasts fifteen minutes, for others several hours), I will drive through red lights, lose the house keys, spill whatever I am holding, lose the ability to focus my eyes or frame coherent sentences, and generally give the appearance of being on drugs, or drunk. The actual headache, when it comes, brings with it chills, sweating, nausea, a debility that seems to stretch the very limits of endurance. That no one dies of migraine seems, to someone deep into an attack, an ambiguous blessing.

My husband also has migraine, which is unfortunate for him but   6
fortunate for me: perhaps nothing so tends to prolong an attack as the accusing eye of someone who has never had a headache. "Why not take a couple of aspirin," the unafflicted will say from the doorway, or "I'd have a headache, too, spending a beautiful day like this inside with all the shades drawn." All of us who have migraine suffer not only from the

attacks themselves but from this common conviction that we are perversely refusing to cure ourselves by taking a couple of aspirins, that we are making ourselves sick, that we "bring it on ourselves." And in the most immediate sense, the sense of why we have a headache this Tuesday and not last Thursday, of course we often do. There certainly is what doctors call a "migraine personality," and that personality tends to be ambitious, inward, intolerant of error, rather rigidly organized, perfectionist. "You don't look like a migraine personality," a doctor once said to me. "Your hair's messy. But I suppose you're a compulsive housekeeper." Actually my house is kept even more negligently than my hair, but the doctor was right nonetheless: perfectionism can also take the form of spending most of a week writing and rewriting and not writing a single paragraph.

But not all perfectionists have migraine, and not all migrainous   7
people have migraine personalities. We do not escape heredity. I have tried in most of the available ways to escape my own migrainous hereditary (at one point I learned to give myself two daily injections of histamine with a hypodermic needle, even though the needle so frightened me that I had to close my eyes when I did it), but I still have migraine. And I have learned how to live with it, learned when to expect it, and how to outwit it, even how to regard it, when it does come, as more friend than lodger. We have reached a certain understanding, my migraine and I. It never comes when I am in real trouble. Tell me that my house is burned down, my husband has left me, that there is gunfighting in the streets and panic in the banks, and I will not respond by getting a headache. It comes instead when I am fighting not an open but a guerrilla war with my own life, during weeks of small household confusions, lost laundry, unhappy help, canceled appointments, on days when the telephone rings too much and I get no work done and the wind is coming up. On days like that my friend comes uninvited.

And once it comes, now that I am wise in its ways, I no longer fight   8
it. I lie down and let it happen. At first every small apprehension is magnified, every anxiety a pounding terror. Then the pain comes, and I concentrate only on that. Right there is the usefulness of migraine, there in that imposed yoga, the concentration on the pain. For when the pain recedes, ten or twelve hours later, everything goes with it, all the hidden resentments, all the vain anxieties. The migraine has acted as a circuit breaker, and the fuses have emerged intact. There is a pleasant convalescent euphoria. I open the windows and feel the air, eat gratefully, sleep well. I notice the particular nature of a flower in a glass on the stair landing. I count my blessings.

1968

Purpose and Meaning

1. How effectively does Didion's title relate to her purpose? Is the title itself effective? Considering her thesis, what might be a better one?

2. In view of the essay's subject matter, what does Didion mean in the concluding four-word sentence?

3. How might Didion respond if you asked her, "Why write about this topic?" What is the significance to her life?

Language and Style

1. How are the sentences of paragraph 2 typical of Didion's style? Do any other paragraphs in the essay contain similar sentences? How would you characterize her style in this essay?

2. Examine Didion's use of parenthetical information in paragraphs 1, 3, 4, and 7. Are her subject and tone best served by this usage? What, if anything, might be lost or gained if they were removed?

3. In paragraph 7, Didion extends the definition of her term "migraine personality" in a figurative way. How does the extended term affect the essay's design?

4. What is Didion's purpose in devoting paragraph 4 to a discussion of specific drugs? How does her word choice affect the essay's tone?

Strategy and Structure

1. How does the essay's opening paragraph relate to Didion's main purpose?

2. Where in the essay does Didion's purpose become clear to the reader? What techniques does she use to support her main thesis?

3. How do the topics of paragraphs 3, 4, and 5 relate to the essay's overall design?

Thinking and Writing

1. Adopting a structure similar to Didion's, write an essay in which you discuss a friend or relative's coping mechanisms developed as a result of a medical condition or personality trait.

2. There are many situations and events that often lead to people being accused of "bringing it on themselves." In an essay, discuss the appropriateness of such a charge, and support your argument with specific and relevant data.

◦●◦●◦●◦●◦●◦●◦●◦

Why I Write

Of course I stole the title for this talk, from George Orwell. One
reason I stole it was that I like the sound of the words: *Why I Write*.
There you have three short unambiguous words that share a sound, and
the sound they share is this:

I

I

I

In many ways writing is the act of saying *I*, of imposing oneself
upon other people, of saying *listen to me, see it my way, change your mind.*
It's an aggressive, even a hostile act. You can disguise its aggressiveness
all you want with veils of subordinate clauses and qualifiers and tentative subjunctives, with ellipses and evasions—with the whole manner of
intimating rather than claiming, of alluding rather than stating—but
there's no getting around the fact that setting words on paper is the tactic of a secret bully, an invasion, an imposition of the writer's sensibility
on the reader's most private space.

I stole the title not only because the words sounded right but because they seemed to sum up, in a no-nonsense way, all I have to tell
you. Like many writers I have only this one "subject," this one "area":
the act of writing. I can bring you no reports from any other front. I may
have other interests: I am "interested," for example, in marine biology,
but I don't flatter myself that you would come out to hear me talk about
it. I am not a scholar. I am not in the least an intellectual, which is not to
say that when I hear the word "intellectual" I reach for my gun, but only
to say that I do not think in abstracts. During the years when I was an
undergraduate at Berkeley I tried, with a kind of hopeless late-adoles-
cent energy, to buy some temporary visa into the world of ideas, to forge
for myself a mind that could deal with the abstract.

In short I tried to think. I failed. My attention veered inexorably
back to the specific, to the tangible, to what was generally considered, by
everyone I knew then and for that matter have known since, the peripheral. I would try to contemplate the Hegelian dialectic and would find
myself concentrating instead on a flowering pear tree outside my window and the particular way the petals fell on my floor. I would try to
read linguistic theory and would find myself wondering instead if the

lights were on in the bevatron up the hill. When I say that I was wondering if the lights were on in the bevatron you might immediately suspect, if you deal in ideas at all, that I was registering the bevatron as a political symbol, thinking in shorthand about the military-industrial complex and its role in the university community, but you would be wrong. I was only wondering if the lights were on in the bevatron, and how they looked. A physical fact.

I had trouble graduating from Berkeley, not because of this inability to deal with ideas—I was majoring in English, and I could locate the house-and-garden imagery in "The Portrait of a Lady" as well as the next person, "imagery" being by definition the kind of specific that got my attention—but simply because I had neglected to take a course in Milton. For reasons which now sound baroque I needed a degree by the end of that summer, and the English department finally agreed, if I would come down from Sacramento every Friday and talk about the cosmology of "Paradise Lost," to certify me proficient in Milton. I did this. Some Fridays I took the Greyhound bus, other Fridays I caught the Southern Pacific's City of San Francisco on the last leg of its transcontinental trip. I can no longer tell you whether Milton put the sun or the earth at the center of the universe in "Paradise Lost," the central question of at least one century and a topic about which I wrote 10,000 words that summer, but I can still recall the exact rancidity of the butter in the City of San Francisco's dining car, and the way the tinted windows on the Greyhound bus cast the oil refineries around Carquinez Straits into a grayed and obscurely sinister light. In short my attention was always on the periphery, on what I could see and taste and touch, on the butter, and the Greyhound bus. During those years I was traveling on what I knew to be a very shaky passport, forged papers: I knew that I was no legitimate resident in any world of ideas. I knew I couldn't think. All I knew then was what I couldn't do. All I knew then was what I wasn't, and it took me some years to discover what I was.

Which was a writer.

By which I mean not a "good" writer or a "bad" writer but simply a writer, a person whose most absorbed and passionate hours are spent arranging words on pieces of paper. Had my credentials been in order I would never have become a writer. Had I been blessed with even limited access to my own mind there would have been no reason to write. I write entirely to find out what I'm thinking, what I'm looking at, what I see and what it means. What I want and what I fear. Why did the oil refineries around Carquinez Straits seem sinister to me in the summer of 1956? Why have the night lights in the bevatron burned in my mind for twenty years? *What is going on in these pictures in my mind?*

When I talk about pictures in my mind I am talking, quite specifically, about images that shimmer around the edges. There used to be an illustration in every elementary psychology book showing a cat drawn by a patient in varying stages of schizophrenia. This cat had a shimmer around it. You could see the molecular structure breaking down at the very edges of the cat: the cat became the background and the background the cat, everything interacting, exchanging ions. People on hallucinogens describe the same perception of objects. I'm not a schizophrenic, nor do I take hallucinogens, but certain images do shimmer for me. Look hard enough, and you can't miss the shimmer. It's there. You can't think too much about these pictures that shimmer. You just lie low and let them develop. You stay quiet. You don't talk to many people and you keep your nervous system from shorting out and you try to locate the cat in the shimmer, the grammar in the picture.

Just as I meant "shimmer" literally I mean "grammar" literally. 9 Grammar is a piano I play by ear, since I seem to have been out of school the year the rules were mentioned. All I know about grammar is its infinite power. To shift the structure of a sentence alters the meaning of that sentence, as definitely and inflexibly as the position of a camera alters the meaning of the object photographed. Many people know about camera angles now, but not so many know about sentences. The arrangement of words matters, and the arrangement you want can be found in the picture in your mind. The picture dictates the arrangement. The picture dictates whether this will be a sentence with or without clauses, a sentence that ends hard or a dying-fall sentence, long or short, active or passive. The picture tells you how to arrange the words and the arrangement of the words tells you, or tells me, what's going on in the picture. *Nota bene:*

It tells you.   10

You don't tell it.   11

Let me show you what I mean by pictures in the mind. I began 12 "Play It As It Lays" just as I have begun each of my novels, with no notion of "character" or "plot" or even "incident." I had only two pictures in my mind, more about which later, and a technical intention, which was to write a novel so elliptical and fast that it would be over before you noticed it, a novel so fast that it would scarcely exist on the page at all. About the pictures: the first was of white space. Empty space. This was clearly the picture that dictated the narrative intention of the book—a book in which anything that happened would happen off the page, a "white" book to which the reader would have to bring his or her own bad dreams—and yet this picture told me no "story," suggested no situation. The second picture did. This second picture was of something actually witnessed. A young woman with long hair and a short white halter dress walks through the casino at the Riviera in Las Vegas at one in the morning. She crosses the casino alone and picks up a house telephone. I watch her because I have heard her paged, and recognize her name: she is a minor actress I see around Los Angeles from time to time, in places like Jax and once in a gynecologist's office in the Beverly Hills Clinic, but have never met. I know nothing about her. Who is paging her? Why is she here to be paged? How exactly did she come to this? It was precisely this moment in Las Vegas that made "Play It As It Lays" begin to tell itself to me, but the moment appears in the novel only obliquely, in a chapter which begins:

"Maria made a list of things she would never do. She would never: walk through the Sands or Caesar's alone after midnight. She would never: ball at a party, do S-M unless she wanted to, borrow furs from Abe Lipsey, deal. She would never: carry a Yorkshire in Beverly Hills." 13

That is the beginning of the chapter and that is also the end of the chapter, which may suggest what I meant by "white space." 14

I recall having a number of pictures in my mind when I began the novel I just finished, "A Book of Common Prayer." As a matter of fact one of these pictures was of that bevatron I mentioned, although I would be hard put to tell you a story in which nuclear energy figured. Another was a newspaper photograph of a hijacked 707 burning on the desert in the Middle East. Another was the night view from a room in which I once spent a week with paratyphoid, a hotel room on the Colombian coast. My husband and I seemed to be on the Colombian coast representing the United States of America at a film festival (I recall invoking the name "Jack Valenti" a lot, as if its reiteration could make me well), and it was a bad place to have fever, not only because my indisposition offended our hosts but because every night in this hotel the generator failed. The lights went out. The elevator stopped. My husband would go to the event of the evening and make excuses for me and I would stay alone in this hotel room, in the dark. I remember standing at the window trying to call Bogotá (the telephone seemed to work on the same principle as the generator) and watching the night wind come up and wondering what I was doing eleven degrees off the equator with a fever of 103. The view from that window definitely figures in "A Book of Common Prayer," as does the burning 707, and yet none of these pictures told me the story I needed. 15

The picture that did, the picture that shimmered and made these other images coalesce, was the Panama airport at 6 a.m. I was in this airport only once, on a plane to Bogotá that stopped for an hour to refuel, but the way it looked that morning remained superimposed on everything I saw until the day I finished "A Book of Common Prayer." I lived in that airport for several years. I can still feel the hot air when I step off the plane, can see the heat already rising off the tarmac at 6 a.m. I can feel my skirt damp and wrinkled on my legs. I can feel the asphalt stick to my sandals. I remember the big tail of a Pan American plane floating motionless down at the end of the tarmac. I remember the sound of a slot machine in the waiting room. I could tell you that I remember a particular woman in the airport, an American woman, a *norteamericana*, a 16 thin *norteamericana* about 40 who wore a big square emerald in lieu of a wedding ring, but there was no such woman there.

I put this woman in the airport later. I made this woman up, just as I later made up a country to put the airport in, and a family to run the country. This woman in the airport is neither catching a plane nor meeting one. She is ordering tea in the airport coffee shop. In fact she is not simply "ordering" tea but insisting that the water be boiled, in front of her, for twenty minutes. Why is this woman in this airport? Why is she going nowhere, where has she been? Where did she get that big emerald? What derangement, or disassociation, makes her believe that her will to see the water boiled can possibly prevail?

"She had been going to one airport or another for four months, one could see it, looking at the visas on her passport. All those airports where Charlotte Douglas's passport had been stamped would have looked alike. Sometimes the sign on the tower would say 'Bienvenidos' and sometimes the sign on the tower would say 'Bienvenue,' some places were wet and hot and others dry and hot, but at each of these airports the pastel concrete walls would rust and stain and the swamp off the runway would be littered with the fuselages of cannibalized Fairchild F-227's and the water would need boiling.

"I knew why Charlotte went to the airport even if Victor did not.

"I knew about airports."

These lines appear about halfway through "A Book of Common Prayer," but I wrote them during the second week I worked on the book, long before I had any idea where Charlotte Douglas had been or why she went to airports. Until I wrote these lines I had no character called "Victor" in mind: the necessity for mentioning a name, and the name "Victor," occurred to me as I wrote the sentence. *I knew why Charlotte went to the airport* sounded incomplete. *I knew why Charlotte went to the airport even if Victor did not* carried a little more narrative drive. Most important of all, until I wrote these lines I did not know who "I" was, who was telling the story. I had intended until that moment that the "I" be no more than the voice of the author, a 19th-century omniscient narrator. But there it was:

"I knew why Charlotte went to the airport even if Victor did not.

"I knew about airports."

This "I" was the voice of no author in my house. This "I" was someone who not only knew why Charlotte went to the airport but also knew someone called "Victor." Who was Victor? Who was this narrator? Why was this narrator telling me this story? Let me tell you one thing about why writers write: had I known the answer to any of these questions I would never have needed to write a novel.

1976

Purpose and Meaning

1. Compare Didion's reasons for writing with those Orwell offers in his "Why I Write" essay. How do their reasons differ? How are they similar?

2. In paragraph 2, Didion likens writing to an aggressive act. In what way is this particular essay an example of this? How does this fact influence Didion's attitude toward her audience and her "talk"?

3. What does Didion mean in the final sentence of the essay? How closely does this sentence relate to the reasons for writing she enumerates in paragraph 7?

Language and Style

1. Didion claims to have "stolen" the title from Orwell because it sums up what she has to say about writing—specifically, that writing "is the act of saying I." In what way is the word *I* significant in this essay? What special tone does it give the essay that confirms Didion's statement in paragraph 2 that writing is "an imposition of the writer's sensibility on the reader's most private space"?

2. In paragraph 9, Didion explains how a "picture dictates the arrangement" of a sentence. Taking the types of sentences she specifies in this paragraph, find examples of each in Didion's previous essays. How do the arrangements of the sentences you found determine the picture the sentence is describing?

3. In paragraph 14, Didion states that she intends paragraph 13 to serve as an example of her goal to create a "white space." In what way is the example (which she states is one entire chapter from the book) an effective illustration of her goal?

4. Consider the excerpt from *A Book of Common Prayer* that constitutes paragraphs 18 through 20. How does the writer's voice in this excerpt from Didion's fiction resemble or differ from the voice of her nonfiction essays?

Strategy and Structure

1. What is Didion's purpose in graphically illustrating the three *I* sounds in the title "Why I Write"?

2. What is the purpose and effect of paragraphs 10 and 11? How do the paragraphs serve as a transition for the paragraphs that precede and follow them?

3. What is the purpose of repeating the dialogue from *A Book of Common Prayer* in paragraphs 22 and 23? How does this excerpt prepare the reader for the concluding paragraph?

Thinking and Writing

1. In paragraph 4, Didion states that her "attention veered inexorably back to the specific." Are you a person who focuses on physical facts, on ideas and the abstract, or on both? Write an essay entitled "How I Think." What are you doing when you are "thinking," as opposed to daydreaming? Provide personal examples, illustrations, and anecdotes to support your view.

2. Why do *you* write? What kinds of satisfaction do you gain from writing? Write an essay developing this theme. If you hate to write, write an essay with the title, "Why I Don't Write."

3. Using the information Didion provides in paragraph 9 concerning the importance of the arrangement of words in her writing, write an expository essay in which you discuss the role of Didion's syntax in her writing style. Use the other four essays by Didion in this anthology to gather your examples.

4. Compare and contrast the essays entitled "Why I Write" by Orwell and Didion.

◦━◦━◦━◦━◦━◦━◦━◦━◦━◦━◦

Georgia O'Keeffe

"Where I was born and where and how I have lived is unimportant," Georgia O'Keeffe told us in the book of paintings and words published in her ninetieth year on earth. She seemed to be advising us to forget the beautiful face in the Stieglitz photographs. She appeared to be dismissing the rather condescending romance that had attached to her by then, the romance of extreme good looks and advanced age and deliberate isolation. "It is what I have done with where I have been that should be of interest." I recall an August afternoon in Chicago in 1973 when I took my daughter, then seven, to see what Georgia O'Keeffe had done with where she had been. One of the vast O'Keeffe "Sky Above Clouds" canvases floated over the back stairs in the Chicago Art Institute that day, dominating what seemed to be several stories of empty light, and my daughter looked at it once, ran to the landing, and kept on looking. "Who drew it," she whispered after a while. I told her. "I need to talk to her," she said finally.

My daughter was making, that day in Chicago, an entirely unconscious but quite basic assumption about people and the work they do. She was assuming that the glory she saw in the work reflected a glory in its maker, that the painting was the painter as the poem is the poet, that every choice one made alone—every word chosen or rejected, every brush stroke laid or not laid down—betrayed one's character. *Style is character.* It seemed to me that afternoon that I had rarely seen so instinctive an application of this familiar principle, and I recall being pleased not only that my daughter responded to style as character but that it was Georgia O'Keeffe's particular style to which she responded: this was a hard woman who had imposed her 192 square feet of clouds on Chicago.

"Hardness" has not been in our century a quality much admired in   3
women, nor in the past twenty years has it even been in official favor for men. When hardness surfaces in the very old we tend to transform it into "crustiness" or eccentricity, some tonic pepperiness to be indulged at a distance. On the evidence of her work and what she has said about it, Georgia O'Keeffe is neither "crusty" nor eccentric. She is simply hard, a straight shooter, a woman clean of received wisdom and open to what she sees. This is a woman who could early on dismiss most of her contemporaries as "dreamy," and would later single out one she liked as "a very poor painter." (And then add, apparently by way of softening the judgment: "I guess he wasn't a painter at all. He had no courage and I believe that to create one's own world in any of the arts takes courage.") This is a woman who in 1939 could advise her admirers that they were missing her point, that their appreciation of her famous flowers was merely sentimental. "When I paint a red hill," she observed coolly in the catalogue for an exhibition that year, "you say it is too bad that I don't always paint flowers. A flower touches almost everyone's heart. A red hill doesn't touch everyone's heart." This is a woman who could describe the genesis of one of her most well-known paintings—the "Cow's Skull: Red, White and blue" owned by the Metropolitan—as an act of quite deliberate and derisive orneriness. "I thought of the city men I had been seeing in the East," she wrote. "They talked so often of writing the Great American Novel—the Great American Play—the Great American Poetry. . . . So as I was painting my cow's head on blue I thought to myself, 'I'll make it an American painting. They will not think it great with the red stripes down the sides—Red, White and Blue—but they will notice it.' "

The city men. The men. They. The words crop up again and again as   4
this astonishingly aggressive woman tells us what was on her mind when she was making her astonishingly aggressive paintings. It was those city men who stood accused of sentimentalizing her flowers: "I made you take time to look at what I saw and when you took time to really notice my flower you hung all your associations with flowers on my flower and you write about my flower as if I think and see what you

think and see—and I don't. *And I don't.* Imagine those words spoken, and the sound you hear is *don't tread on me.* "The men" believed it impossible to paint New York, so Georgia O'Keeffe painted New York. "The men" didn't think much of her bright color, so she made it brighter. The men yearned toward Europe so she went to Texas, and then New Mexico. The men talked about Cézanne, "long involved remarks about the 'plastic quality' of his form and color," and took one another's long involved remarks, in the view of this angelic rattlesnake in their midst, altogether too seriously. "I can paint one of those dismal- colored paintings like the men," the woman who regarded herself always as an outsider remembers thinking one day in 1922, and she did: a painting of a shed "all low-toned and dreary with the tree beside the door." She called this act of rancor "The Shanty" and hung it in her next show. "The men seemed to approve of it," she reported fifty-four years later, her contempt undimmed. "They seemed to think that maybe I was beginning to paint. That was my only low-toned dismal-colored painting."

Some women fight and others do not. Like so many successful guerrillas in the war between the sexes, Georgia O'Keeffe seems to have been equipped early with an immutable sense of who she was and a fairly clear understanding that she would be required to prove it. On the surface her upbringing was conventional. She was a child on the Wisconsin prairie who played with china dolls and painted watercolors with cloudy skies because sunlight was too hard to paint and, with her brother and sisters, listened every night to her mother read stories of the Wild West, of Texas, of Kit Carson and Billy the Kid. She told adults that she wanted to be an artist and was embarrassed when they asked what kind of artist she wanted to be: she had no idea "what kind." She had no idea what artists did. She had never seen a picture that interested her, other than a pen-and-ink Maid of Athens in one of her mother's books, some Mother Goose illustrations printed on cloth, a tablet cover that showed a little girl with pink roses, and the painting of Arabs on horseback that hung in her grandmother's parlor. At thirteen, in a Dominican convent, she was mortified when the sister corrected her drawing. At Chatham Episcopal Institute in Virginia she painted lilacs and sneaked time alone to walk out to where she could see the line of the Blue Ridge Mountains on the horizon. At the Art Institute in Chicago she was shocked by the presence of live models and wanted to abandon anatomy lessons. At the Art Students League in New York one of her fellow students advised her that, since he would be a great painter and she would end up teaching painting in a girls' school, any work of hers was less important than modeling for him. Another painted over her work to show her how the Impressionists did trees. She had not before heard how the Impressionists did trees and she did not much care.

At twenty-four she left all those opinions behind and went for the first time to live in Texas, where there were no trees to paint and no one to tell her how not to paint them. In Texas there was only the horizon she craved. In Texas she had her sister Claudia with her for a while, and in the late afternoons they would walk away from town and toward the horizon and watch the evening star come out. "That evening star fascinated me," she wrote. "It was in some way very exciting to me. My sister had a gun, and as we walked she would throw bottles into the air and shoot as many as she could before they hit the ground. I had nothing but to walk into nowhere and the wide sunset space with the star. Ten watercolors were made from that star." In a way one's interest is compelled as much by the sister Claudia with the gun as by the painter Georgia with the star, but only the painter left us this shining record. Ten watercolors were made from that star.

1976

Purpose and Meaning

1. Didion opens this essay with a direct quotation by O'Keeffe. Why is this particular quotation effective as an opening? How does it relate to Didion's intended purpose?

2. Throughout the essay, Didion quotes extensively from O'Keeffe's own writing. How does she use the quotations to illuminate the artist's character?

3. What impressions of the subject stand out in this brief portrait? What qualities is Didion emphasizing? Which is most important to Didion: the art or the artist? Why?

Language and Style

1. Examine the modifiers Didion uses in paragraphs 3 and 4 to characterize O'Keeffe. How are they different from those a reader might expect to characterize a woman artist? What is Didion stressing by their usage?

2. What assumption is Didion making about her audience by word choice and tone?

3. How effective is the beginning of paragraph 4? How does Didion use this opening in the remainder of the paragraph? How effective is that usage?

Strategy and Structure

1. How does Didion's strategy echo the "familiar principle: style is character" (paragraph 2)?

2. How does Didion integrate the anecdote about her visit to the Chicago Art Institute? How does it affect the essay's overall design?

3. As she does in "On Self-Respect," Didion, in this essay, refers to particular people and places. What do such references contribute to her purpose?

Thinking and Writing

1. Write an essay in which you discuss a person whose special relationship to a particular landscape played a dominant role in that person's life.

2. Develop an essay in which you argue that specific geographical areas do or do not have a significant impact on an individual's personality.

3. After examining several O'Keeffe paintings at a museum or in a book, write an essay that supports or refutes Didion's characterization of O'Keeffe as being "astonishingly aggressive."

MARGARET ATWOOD

Born in Ottawa, Canada, in 1939, Margaret Eleanor Atwood began writing juvenile poems at the age of six and published her first work at the age of eighteen. Today she is a major literary talent, the author of some thirty volumes of poetry, fiction, and essays that have been translated into more than a dozen languages. She lives in Toronto with novelist Graeme Gibson and their daughter, Jess.

Atwood graduated from the University of Toronto in 1961—the same year that she was awarded the E. J. Pratt Medal for her poetry collection *Double Persephone*. In her laconic autobiographical essay "Great Unexpectations," which first appeared in *Ms.* magazine in 1987, Atwood alludes to the force of literature in her life during this period, to the need for literary models, and to her vocation as a writer. After receiving her M.A. degree from Radcliffe College in 1962, Atwood returned to Toronto to teach. At the age of twenty-seven, she received the Governor-General's Award for Poetry for *The Circle Game*. Her major poetry collections are *Selected Poems: 1965–1975* and *Selected Poems II: 1976–1986*.

Critics have described the uniqueness of Atwood's writing with such phrases as "violent dualities," "life mostly as wounds," and "distinctly dystopian." She is indeed a serious writer concerned with the struggles of women and men. Still, her writings—particularly those appearing here—are not without humor and joy. Even as Atwood, in her critical study *Survival: A Thematic Guide to Canadian Literature* (1972), speaks of a Canadian national sensibility that is "undeniably somber and negative," she locates subtle, powerful, and complex ways to affirm existence, as she does in the search for personal and national identity in her essay "Travels Back."

Tensions between art and life, the modern and the primitive, Canada and the United States, and most especially women and men are recurring themes in Atwood's work. She is a feminist writer ("Why the hell not!" she once exclaimed), a distinction earned with the publication of her first novel, *The Edible Woman*, in 1970. But her feminism has been generally on such personal terms as to avoid quick and easy categorization as can be seen in "The Female Body," included in this collection. *Surfacing* (1972), *Lady Oracle* (1976), *Life Before Man* (1979), *Bodily Harm* (1982), *The Handmaid's Tale* (1986), and *Cat's Eye* (1989) are her prominent publications containing feminist themes. Perhaps her fiercest and most outwardly feminist work is her dystopian novel *The Handmaid's Tale*, in which the United States bears a likeness to the novel's Republic of Gilead, where women are reduced to slave status and men are their brutal masters.

Atwood's essays and articles, some of them collected in *Second Words* (1982), reflect the essential vision in her work in all genres: the need to hold, to survive in a chaotic age. She brings a tough, resilient phrasing to both her enthusiasm for life's little riches and her abhorrence of contemporary forms of victimization. In her best essays, including those in this collection, she takes the reader on quite personal journeys as she seeks to define her place in the world as a woman and as a Canadian.

○●○●○●○●○●○●○●○

Travels Back

Three hours past midnight, Highway 17 between Ottawa and 1
North Bay, November. I'm looking out the Greyhound bus window at
the almost nothing I can see. Coffee taste still with me from the Ottawa
station, where I was marooned four hours because someone in Toronto
mixed up the schedules; I sat writing letters and trying not to watch as
the waitresses disposed of a tiny wizened drunk. "I been all over the
world, girlie," he told them as they forced his coat on him, "I been places
you never seen."

The headlights pick out asphalt, snow-salted road borders, dark 2
trees as we lean round the frequent bends. What I picture is that we'll
pass the motel, which they said was on the highway outside Renfrew—
but *which* side?—and I'll have to walk, a mile maybe carrying the two
suitcases full of my own books I'm lugging around because there may
not be any bookstores, who in Toronto knows? A passing truck,
Canadian Content squashed all over the road, later the police wondering
what I was doing there anyway, as I am myself at this moment.
Tomorrow at nine (nine!) I'm supposed to be giving a poetry reading in
the Renfrew high school. Have fun in Renfrew, my friends in Toronto
said with, I guess, irony before I left.

I'm thinking of summer, a swimming pool in France, an acquain- 3
tance of mine floating on his back and explaining why bank managers in
Canada shouldn't be allowed to hang Group of Seven pictures on their
walls—it's a false image, all nature, no people—while a clutch of as-
sorted Europeans and Americans listen incredulously.

"I mean, *Canada*," one of them drawls. "I think they should give it 4
to the United States, then it would be good. All except Quebec, they
should give that to France. You should come and live here. I mean, you
don't really live *there* any more."

We get to Renfrew finally and I step off the bus into six inches of 5
early snow. He was wrong, this if anywhere is where I live. Highway 17
was my first highway, I travelled along it six months after I was born,
from Ottawa to North Bay and then to Temiskaming, and from there
over a one-track dirt road into the bush. After that, twice a year, north
when the ice went out, south when the snow came, the time between
spent in tents; or in the cabin built by my father on a granite point a mile
by water from a Quebec village so remote that the road went in only two
years before I was born. The towns I've passed and will pass—Arnprior,
Renfrew, Pembroke, Chalk River, Mattawa, the old gingerbread man-

sions in each of them built on lumber money and the assumption that the forest would never give out—they were landmarks, way stations. That was 30 years ago though and they've improved the highway, now there are motels. To me nothing but the darkness of the trees is familiar.

I didn't spend a full year in school until I was 11. Americans usu-   6
ally find this account of my childhood—woodsy, isolated, nomadic—less surprising than do Canadians: after all, it's what the glossy magazine ads say Canada is supposed to be like. They're disappointed when they hear I've never lived in an igloo and my father doesn't say "On, huskies!" like Sergeant Preston on the defunct (American) radio program, but other than that they find me plausible enough. It's Canadians who raise eyebrows. Or rather the Torontonians. It's as though I'm a part of their own past they find disreputable or fake or just can't believe ever happened.

I've never read at a high school before. At first I'm terrified, I chew   7
Tums,while the teacher introduces me, remembering the kinds of things we used to do to visiting dignitaries when I was in high school: rude whispers, noises, elastic bands and paper clips if we could get away with it. Surely they've never heard of me and won't be interested: we had no Canadian poetry in high school and not much of anything else Canadian. In the first four years we studied the Greeks and Romans and the Ancient Egyptians and the Kings of England, and in the fifth we got Canada in a dull blue book that was mostly about wheat. Once a year a frail old man would turn up and read a poem about a crow; afterward he would sell his own books (as I'm about to do), autographing them in his thin spidery handwriting. That was Canadian poetry. I wonder if I look like him, vulnerable, misplaced and redundant. Isn't the real action—the *real* action—their football game this afternoon?

Question period: Do you have a message? Is your hair really like   8
that, or do you get it done? Where do you get the ideas? How long does it take? What does it *mean*? Does it bother you, reading your poems out loud like that? It would bother me. What is the Canadian identity? Where can I send my poems? To get them published.

They are all questions with answers, some short, some long. What   9
astonishes me is that they ask them at all, that they want to talk: at my high school you didn't ask questions. And they *write*, some of them. Inconceivable. It wasn't like that, I think, feeling very old, in my day.

In Deep River I stay with my second cousin, a scientist with the   10
blue inhuman eyes, craggy domed forehead and hawk nose of my maternal Nova Scotian relatives. He takes me through the Atomic Research Plant, where he works; we wear white coats and socks to keep from being contaminated and watch a metal claw moving innocent-looking

lethal items—pencils, a tin can, a Kleenex—behind a 14-inch leaded glass window. "Three minutes in there," he says, "will kill you." The fascination of invisible force.

After that we examine beaver damage on his property and he tells 11 me stories about my grandfather, before there were cars and radios. I like these stories, I collect them from all my relatives, they give me a link, however tenuous, with the past and with a culture made up of people and their relationships and their ancestors rather than objects in a landscape. This trip I learn a new story: my grandfather's disastrous muskrat farm. It consisted of a fence built carefully around a swamp, the idea being that it would be easier to gather in the muskrats that way; though my cousin says he trapped more muskrat outside the fence than my grandfather ever did inside it. The enterprise failed when a farmer dumped out some of his apple spray upstream and the muskrats were extinguished; but the Depression hit and the bottom fell out of the muskrat market anyway. The fence is still there.

Most of the stories about my grandfather are success stories, but I 12 add this one to my collection: when totems are hard to come by, failure stories have their place. "Do you know," I say to my cousin, repeating a piece of lore recently gleaned from my grandmother, "that one of our ancestresses was doused as a witch?" That was in New England; whether she sank and was innocent or swam and was guilty isn't recorded.

Out his living-room window, across the Ottawa River, solid trees, 13 is my place. More or less.

Freezing rain overnight; I make it to the next poetry reading 14 pulling my suitcases on a toboggan two miles over thin ice.

I reach North Bay, an hour later because of the sleet. That evening I 15 read at the Oddfellows' Hall, in the basement. The academics who have organized the reading are nervous, they think no one will come, there's never been a poetry reading in North Bay before. In a town where everyone's seen the movie, I tell them, you don't have to worry, and in fact they spent the first fifteen minutes bringing in extra chairs. These aren't students, there are all kinds of people, old ones, young ones, a friend of my mother's who used to stay with us in Quebec, a man whose uncle ran the fishing camp at the end of the lake . . .

In the afternoon I was interviewed for the local TV station by a 16 stiff-spined man in a tight suit. "What's this," he said, dangling one of my books nonchalantly by the corner to show the viewers that poetry isn't his thing, he's virile really, "a children's book?" I suggested that if he wanted to know what was inside it he might try reading it. He became enraged and said he had never been so insulted, and Jack McClelland hadn't been mean like that when *he* was in North Bay. In place of the interview they ran a feature on green noodles.

Later, 30 poetry readings later. Reading a poem in New York that   17
has an outhouse in it and having to define outhouse (and having the two
or three people come up furtively afterwards and say that they, too,
once . . .). Meeting a man who has never seen a cow; who has never, in
fact, been outside the city of New York. Talking then about whether
there is indeed a difference between Canada and the U.S. (I been places
you never seen . . .). Trying to explain, in Detroit, that in Canada for
some strange reason it isn't just other poets who come to poetry readings. ("You mean . . . people like *our mothers* read poetry?") Having
someone tell me that maybe what accounts for the "strength" of my
work is its fetching "regional" qualities—"you know, like Faulkner . . ."

In London, Ontario, the last poetry reading of the year and per-   18
haps, I'm thinking, for ever, I'm beginning to feel like a phonograph. A
lady: "I've never felt less like a Canadian since all this nationalism came
along." Another lady, very old, with astonishing sharp eyes: "Do you
think in metaphor?" Someone else: "What is the Canadian identity?"
That seems to be on people's minds.

How to keep all this together in your head, my head. Because   19
where I live is where everyone lives: it isn't just a place or a region,
though it is also that (and I could have put in Vancouver and Montreal,
where I lived for a year each, and Edmonton where I lived for two, and
Lake Superior and Toronto . . .). It's a space composed of images, experiences, the weather, your own past and your ancestors', what people say
and what they look like and how they react to what you're doing, important events and trivial ones, the connections among them not always
obvious. The images come from outside, they are *there*, they are the
things we live with and must deal with. But the judgements and the connections (what does it *mean*?) have to be made inside your head and
they are made with words: good, bad, like, dislike, whether to go,
whether to stay, whether to live there any more. For me that's partly
what writing is: an exploration of where in reality I live.

I think Canada, more than most countries, is a place you choose to   20
live in. It's easy for us to leave, and many of us have. There's the U.S.
and England, we've been taught more about their histories than our
own, we can blend in, become permanent tourists. There's been a kind
of standing invitation here to refuse authenticity to your actual experience, to think life can be meaningful or important only in "real" places
like New York or London or Paris. And it's a temptation: the swimming
pool in France is nothing if not detached. The question is always, Why
stay? and you have to answer that over and over.

I don't think Canada is "better" than any other place, any more   21
than I think Canadian literature is "better"; I live in one and read the
other for a simple reason: they are mine, with all the sense of territory

that implies. Refusing to acknowledge where you come from—and that must include the noodle man and his hostilities, the anti-nationalist lady and her doubts—is an act of amputation: you may become free floating, a citizen of the world (and in what other country is that an ambition?) but only at the cost of arms, legs or heart. By discovering your place your discover yourself.

But there's another image, fact, coming from the outside that I have   22 to fit in. This territory, this thing I have called "mine," may not be mine much longer. Part of the much-sought Canadian identity is that few nationals have done a more enthusiastic job of selling their country than have Canadians. Of course there are buyers willing to exploit, as they say, our resources; there always are. It is our eagerness to sell that needs attention. Exploiting resources and developing potential are two different things: one is done from without by money, the other from within, by something I hesitate only for a moment to call love.

1973

Purpose and Meaning

1. A sense of place is prominent in Atwood's essay. Primarily, the places are Canadian towns and provinces. In paragraph 2, Atwood tells how her friends ironically advise her to "have fun in Renfrew." In paragraph 4, she contrasts France with Canada and quotes a companion who says Canada should be given to the United States. How do these early characterizations of Canada prepare us for Atwood's thesis?

2. What does the interaction between Atwood and the television station interviewer, in paragraph 16, reveal about the author? What point is she making about cultural attitudes toward women, and women writers in particular? How does she want her audience to respond to this incident?

3. Would a reader have to be Canadian to appreciate "Travels Back"? Why or why not? If you are not Canadian, what have you learned about Canada from this essay? What was your previous perception of Canada? Has this essay changed or amplified it?

Language and Style

1. The first sentence of "Travels Back" is a fragment; it contains subjects but no verb. What tone does Atwood create when she uses fragments?

2. How would you characterize Atwood's diction? Is the writing style objective or subjective? Explain your answer.

3. In paragraph 19, Atwood writes that where she lives "isn't just a place. . . . It's a space composed of images, experiences, the weather, your own past and your ancestors', what people say and what they look like and how

they react to what you're doing, important events and trivial ones, the connections among them not always obvious." Look over the essay again and note how these items—images in particular—are represented. What is their stylistic effect? What does Atwood mean when she writes that writing is in part "an exploration of where in reality I live"?

Strategy and Structure

1. What connections do you perceive between the beginning and ending paragraphs of this essay?

2. This essay is an exploration of home and how Atwood considers writing itself to be part of that exploration. In what ways is the essay exploratory instead of telling? How does the journal format lend itself to exploration?

3. Many of Atwood's paragraphs begin with references to a change of place: France (paragraph 3), Renfrew (paragraph 5), high school (paragraph 7), Deep River (paragraph 10), and so forth. How do these changes help create a sense of movement, as is reflected in the essay's title?

4. In what way might this essay be considered an extended definition? What is being defined, and how is the definition structured?

Thinking and Writing

1. In paragraph 21, Atwood writes, "By discovering your place you discover yourself." Write an essay using Atwood's format in which you explore your home town or neighborhood, or where you live now.

2. Over the next week, keep a log noting all of your travels and changes of place. Characterize each place and reflect upon it in a paragraph or two. At the end of the week, evaluate your writing, and see what you have discovered about yourself.

3. Atwood sets up several comparisons of places in her essay. Notice the specific elements she compares. Then select two places that you know well, and write a comparative essay on them.

Great Unexpectations

In 1960 I was nineteen years old. I was in third-year college in   1
Toronto, Ontario, which was not then known as People City or The Paris of the Northeast; but as Hogtown, which was not an inaccurate descrip-

tion. I had never eaten an avocado or been on an airplane or encountered a croissant or been south of Vermont. Panty hose had not yet hit the market; neither had the Pill. We were still doing garter belts and repression. Abortion was not a word you said out loud, and lesbians might as well have been mythological hybrids, like Sphinxes; in any case I was quite certain I had never met one. I wanted to be—no, worse—was determined to be, was convinced I was—a writer. I was scared to death.

I was scared to death for a couple of reasons. For one thing, I was Canadian, and the prospects for being a Canadian and a writer, both at the same time, in 1960, were dim. The only writers I had encountered in high school had been dead and English, and in university we barely studied American writers, much less Canadian ones. Canadian writers, it was assumed—by my professors, my contemporaries, and myself— were a freak of nature, like duck-billed platypuses. Logically they ought not to exist, and when they did so anyway, they were just pathetic imitations of the real thing. This estimate was borne out by statistics: for those few who managed, despite the reluctance of publishers, to struggle into print (five novels in English in 1960), two hundred copies of a book of poetry was considered average to good, and a thousand made a novel a Canadian best seller. I would have to emigrate, I concluded gloomily. I faced a future of scrubbing restaurant floors in England—where we colonials could go, then, much more easily than we could to the United States—writing masterpieces in a freezing cold garret at night, and getting T.B., like Keats. Such was my operatic view of my own future.

But it was more complicated than that, because, in addition to being a Canadian, I was also a woman. In some ways this was an advantage. Being a male writer in Canada branded you a sissy, but writing was not quite so unthinkable for a woman, ranking as it did with flower painting and making roses out of wood. As one friend of my mother's put it, trying to take a cheerful view of my eccentricity, "Well, that's nice dear, because you can do it at home, can't you?" She was right, as it turned out, but at that moment she aroused nothing but loathing in my adolescent soul. Home, hell. It was garret or nothing. What did she think I was, inauthentic? However, most people were so appalled by my determination to be a writer that no one even thought of saying I couldn't because I was a girl. That sort of thing was not said to me until later, by male writers, by which time it was too late.

Strangely, no one was pushing early marriage, not in my case. Canada, being a cultural backwater, had not been swept by the wave of Freudianism that had washed over the United States in the fifties— Canadian women were not yet expected to be fecund and passive in order to fulfill themselves—and there were still some bluestockings around in the educational system, women who warned us not to get silly about boys too soon and throw away our chances. What my elders had in mind for me was more along academic lines. Something, that is to say, with a salary.

But, since gender is prior to nationality, the advantages of being a Canadian woman writer were canceled out by the disadvantages of being a woman writer. I'd read the biographies, which were not encouraging. Jane Austen never married Mr. Darcy. Emily Brontë died young, Charlotte in childbirth. George Eliot never had children and was ostracized for living with a married man. Emily Dickinson flitted; Christina Rossetti looked at life through the wormholes in a shroud. Some had managed to combine writing with what I considered to be a normal life—Mrs. Gaskell, Harriet Beecher Stowe—but everyone knew they were second rate. My choices were between excellence and doom on the one hand, and mediocrity and cosiness on the other. I gritted my teeth, set my face to the wind, gave up double dating, and wore horn-rims and a scowl so I would not be mistaken for a puffball.

It was in this frame of mind that I read Robert Graves's *The White Goddess*, which further terrified me. Graves did not dismiss women. In fact he placed them right at the center of his poetic theory; but they were to be inspirations rather than creators, and a funny sort of inspiration at that. They were to be incarnations of the White Goddess herself, alternately loving and destructive, and men who got involved with them ran the risk of disembowelment or worse. A woman just might—might, mind you—have a chance of becoming a decent poet, but only if she too took on the attributes of the White Goddess and spent her time seducing men and then doing them in. All this sounded a little strenuous, and appeared to rule out domestic bliss. It wasn't my idea of how men and women should get on together—raking up leaves in the backyard, like my mom and dad—but who was I to contradict the experts? There was no one else in view giving me any advice on how to be a writer, though female. Graves was it.

That would be my life, then. To the garret and the T.B. I added the elements of enigma and solitude. I would dress in black. I would learn to smoke cigarettes, although they gave me headaches and made me cough, and drink something romantic and unusually bad for you, such as absinthe. I would live by myself, in a suitably painted attic (black) and have lovers whom I would discard in appropriate ways, though I drew the line at bloodshed. (I was, after all, a nice Canadian girl.) I would never have children. This last bothered me a lot, as before this I had always intended to have some, and it seemed unfair, but White Goddesses did not have time for children, being too taken up with cannibalistic sex, and Art came first. I would never, never own an automatic washer-dryer. Sartre, Samuel Beckett, Kafka, and Ionesco, I was sure, did not have major appliances, and these were the writers I most admired. I had no concrete ideas about how the laundry would get done, but it would only be my own laundry, I though mournfully—no fuzzy sleepers, no tiny T-shirts—and such details could be worked out later.

I tried out the garrets, which were less glamorous than expected; so 8 was England, and so were the cigarettes, which lasted a mere six months. There wasn't any absinthe to be had, so I tried bad wine, which made me sick. It began to occur to me that maybe Robert Graves didn't have the last word on women writers, and anyway I wanted to be a novelist as well as a poet, so perhaps that would let me off the homicide. Even though Sylvia Plath and Anne Sexton had been setting new, high standards in self-destructiveness for female poets, and people had begun asking me not whether but when I was going to commit suicide (the only authentic woman poet is a dead woman poet?), I was wondering whether it was really all that necessary for a woman writer to be doomed, any more than it was necessary for a male writer to be a drunk. Wasn't all of this just some sort of postromantic collective delusion? If Shakespeare could have kids and avoid suicide, then so could I, dammit. When Betty Friedan and Simone de Beauvoir came my way, like shorebirds heralding land, I read them with much interest. They got a lot right, for me, but there was one thing they got wrong. They were assuring me that I didn't have to get married and have children. But what I wanted was someone to tell me I could.

And so I did. The marriage and the children came in two lots—the 9 marriage with one, child with another—but they did come. This is the part that will sound smug, I suppose, but I also suppose it's not that much smugger than my black-sweatered, garter-belted, black-stockinged, existential pronouncements at the age of nineteen. I now live a life that is pretty close to the leaves-in-the-backyard model I thought would have been out of bounds forever. Instead of rotting my brains with absinthe, I bake (dare I admit it?) chocolate chip cookies, and I find that doing the laundry with the aid of my washer-dryer is one of the more relaxing parts of my week. I worry about things like remembering Parents' Day at my daughter's school and running out of cat food, though I can only afford these emotional luxuries with the aid of some business assistants and a large man who likes kids and cats and food, and has an ego so solid it isn't threatened by mine. This state of affairs was not achieved without struggle, some of it internal—did an addiction to knitting brand me as an inauthentic writer?—but it was reached. The White Goddess still turns up in my life, but mainly as a fantasy projection on the part of certain male book reviewers, who seem to like the idea of my teeth sinking into some cringing male neck. I think of this as fifties nostalgia.

As for writing, yes. You *can* do it at home. 10

1987

Purpose and Meaning

1. What were the major obstacles to Atwood's becoming a writer? What is her purpose in cataloging these obstacles? What thesis emerges from her inventory of obstacles?

2. Atwood has observed that Canada has a "national inferiority complex." How is this trait reflected in "Great Unexpectations" and also in "Travels Back"?

3. What expectations does the author have of her readers? How do you know?

Language and Style

1. Although Atwood writes about serious problems, her style and tone tend to be breezy, ironic, and humorous. Cite and explain examples of her method.

2. Consider the similes "lesbians might as well have been mythological hybrids, like Sphinxes" (paragraph 1) and "Canadian writers . . . were a freak of nature, like duck-billed platypuses" (paragraph 2). What do these similes have in common? How do they advance Atwood's thesis?

Strategy and Structure

1. Atwood's introductory paragraph offers a striking and graphic overview of the year 1960. What effect do the details have on the reader? In what way do they involve us in the writer's emerging dilemma?

2. What sorts of evidence to support her thesis does Atwood provide in this essay? How does she organize it? How effective is it in supporting her thesis?

3. How does Atwood employ comparison and contrast to advance her essay? What are the major points of comparison?

4. Do you find the one-sentence conclusion to be effective or ineffective? Explain your answer.

Thinking and Writing

1. How do both "Great Unexpectations" and "Travels Back" explore questions of identity, place, and potential loss of self? Write an essay on this topic.

2. Write an autobiographical essay based on Atwood's example in which you describe a specific time in your life when you decided to do something against all odds.

3. Why does Atwood focus so much in the latter part of her essay on the White Goddess? Is the White Goddess metaphor still operative in culture today? Write an argumentative essay on this issue.

The Female Body

> ... entirely devoted to the subject of "The Female Body." Knowing how well you have written on this topic ... this capacious topic ...
>
> letter from *Michigan Quarterly Review*

1

I agree, it's a hot topic. But only one? Look around, there's a wide range. Take my own, for instance.

I get up in the morning. My topic feels like hell. I sprinkle it with water, brush parts of it, rub it with towels, powder it, add lubricant. I dump in the fuel and away goes my topic, my topical topic, my controversial topic, my capacious topic, my limping topic, my nearsighted topic, my topic with back problems, my badly behaved topic, my vulgar topic, my outrageous topic, my aging topic, my topic that is out of the question and anyway still can't spell, in its oversized coat and worn winter boots, scuttling along the sidewalk as if it were flesh and blood, hunting for what's out there, an avocado, an alderman, an adjective, hungry as ever.

2

The basic Female Body comes with the following accessories: garter belt, panti-girdle, crinoline, camisole, bustle, brassiere, stomacher, chemise, virgin zone, spike heels, nose ring, veil, kid gloves, fishnet stockings, fichu, bandeau, Merry Widow, weepers, chokers, barrettes, bangles, beads, lorgnette, feather boa, basic black, compact, Lycra stretch one-piece with modesty panel, designer peignoir, flannel nightie, lace teddy, bed, head.

3

The Female Body is made of transparent plastic and lights up when you plug it in. You press a button to illuminate the different systems. The circulatory system is red, for the heart and arteries, purple for the veins; the respiratory system is blue; the lymphatic system is yellow; the digestive system is green, with liver and kidneys in aqua. The nerves are done in orange and the brain is pink. The skeleton, as you might expect, is white.

The reproductive system is optional, and can be removed. It comes   5
with or without a miniature embryo. Parental judgment can thereby be exercised. We do not wish to frighten or offend.

4

He said, I won't have one of those things in the house. It gives a   6
young girl a false notion of beauty, not to mention anatomy. If a real woman was built like that she'd fall on her face.

She said, If we don't let her have one like all the other girls she'll   7
feel singled out. It'll become an issue. She'll long for one and she'll long to turn into one. Repression breeds sublimation. You know that.

He said, It's not just the pointy plastic tits, it's the wardrobes. The   8
wardrobes and that stupid male doll, what's his name, the one with the underwear glued on.

She said, Better to get it over with when she's young. He said, All   9
right, but don't let me see it.

She came whizzing down the stairs, thrown like a dart. She was   10
stark naked. Her hair had been chopped off, her head was turned back to front, she was missing some toes and she'd been tattooed all over her body with purple ink in a scrollwork design. She hit the potted azalea, trembled there for a moment like a botched angel, and fell.

He said, I guess we're safe.   11

5

The Female Body has many uses. It's been used as a door knocker,   12
a bottle opener, as a clock with a ticking belly, as something to hold up lampshades, as a nutcracker, just squeeze the brass legs together and out comes your nut. It bears torches, lifts victorious wreaths, grows copper wings and raises aloft a ring of neon stars; whole buildings rest on its marble heads.

It sells cars, beer, shaving lotion, cigarettes, hard liquor; it sells diet   13
plans and diamonds, and desire in tiny crystal bottles. Is this the face that launched a thousand products? You bet it is, but don't get any funny big ideas, honey, that smile is a dime a dozen.

It does not merely sell, it is sold. Money flows into this country or   14
that country, flies in, practically crawls in, suitful after suitful, lured by all those hairless pre-teen legs. Listen, you want to reduce the national debt, don't you? Aren't you patriotic? That's the spirit. That's my girl.

She's a natural resource, a renewable one luckily, because those   15 things wear out so quickly. They don't make 'em like they used to. Shoddy goods.

6

One and one equals another one. Pleasure in the female is not a re- [16] quirement. Pair-bonding is stronger in geese. We're not talking about love, we're talking about biology. That's how we all got here, daughter.

Snails do it differently. They're hermaphrodites, and work in [17] threes.

7

Each Female Body contains a female brain. Handy. Makes things [18] work. Stick pins in it and you get amazing results. Old popular songs. Short circuits. Bad dreams.

Anyway: each of these brains has two halves. They're joined to- [19] gether by a thick cord; neural pathways flow from one to the other, sparkles of electric information washing to and fro. Like light on waves. Like a conversation. How does a woman know? She listens. She listens in.

The male brain, now, that's a different matter. Only a thin connec- [20] tion. Space over here, time over there, music and arithmetic in their own sealed compartments. The right brain doesn't know what the left brain is doing. Good for aiming through, for hitting the target when you pull the trigger. What's the target? Who's the target? Who cares? What matters is hitting it. That's the male brain for you. Objective.

This is why men are so sad, why they feel so cut off, why they [21] think of themselves as orphans cast adrift, footloose and stringless in the deep void. What void? she asks. What are you talking about? The void of the universe, he says, and she says Oh and looks out the window and tries to get a handle on it, but it's no use, there's too much going on, too many rustlings in the leaves, too many voices, so she says, Would you like a cheese sandwich, a piece of cake, a cup of tea? And he grinds his teeth because she doesn't understand, and wanders off, not just alone but Alone, lost in the dark, lost in the skull, searching for the other half, the twin who could complete him.

Then it comes to him: he's lost the Female Body! Look, it shines in [22] the gloom, far ahead, a vision of wholeness, ripeness, like a giant melon, like an apple, like a metaphor for "breast" in a bad sex novel; it shines like a balloon, like a foggy noon, a watery moon, shimmering in its egg of light.

Catch it. Put it in a pumpkin, in a high tower, in a compound, in a [23] chamber, in a house, in a room. Quick, stick a leash on it, a lock, a chain, some pain, settle it down, so it can never get away from you again.

Purpose and Meaning

1. How does the short excerpt preceding the essay work to announce Atwood's tone and thesis? What assumptions can you make about the letter's origin?

2. Considering Atwood's unorthodox style in this essay, how effective is her decision to break the essay into several sections? How does she use them: as transitional markers, or as topical shifts? Explain your answer.

3. What is Atwood's attitude toward her topic? What is her thesis?

4. What can you assume about Atwood's intended audience?

Language and Style

1. Atwood's style in this essay differs substantially from her other essays represented in this collection. How effective and appropriate is the style in terms of its relation to the subject?

2. Paragraph 2 has a single sentence that repeats the term *topic* and its referent eighteen times. How effective is that repetition? What does it contribute to the essay?

3. Examine Atwood's use of figurative language in paragraph 23. What is its effect on the essay as a whole?

4. Read the essay aloud, and listen to Atwood's diction. List the different poetic devices you recognize. What does the diction contribute to the essay?

Strategy and Structure

1. Why does Atwood choose to structure this essay nontraditionally? How effectively does her strategy support the essay's content?

2. In section 7, Atwood shifts strategy. What organizational pattern does she use? Considering the essay's subject, how effective is this shift in strategy?

3. Note the sentence structure of the concluding paragraph. How effective is it? Considering the overall design of the essay, how appropriate are these sentences as a conclusion?

Thinking and Writing

1. In an essay or in class discussion, consider the use of female bodies as "staples" to sell other products. Has the denigration of females as objects changed significantly as a result of the women's movement? If not, why? What cultural changes must take place to remedy the situation?

2. Read Stephen Jay Gould's "Women's Brains" and develop an argumentative essay supporting or refuting Atwood's assertions in section 7.

3. Write an essay in which you analyze the current tensions between males and females as another "hot topic."

MAXINE HONG KINGSTON

With the publication of *The Woman Warrior: Memoirs of a Girlhood Among Ghosts* (1976), Maxine Hong Kingston took her place as one of the most distinctive contemporary prose stylists. Kingston's account of growing up female and Chinese American in California revealed her as a writer not only driven to tell her stories but fascinated with the power of language itself. In his review of *The Woman Warrior*, John Leonard of the *New York Times* wrote that it was "a poem turned into a sword." Throughout her career, Kingston has been preoccupied with words and their unique power—through rhythm, sound, association, and sense—to create, and destroy, worlds.

Kingston's world begins in Stockton, California, where she was born in 1940, the eldest of six children, to Chinese immigrants who operated a laundry. In a 1989 interview, Kingston observed, "We used to run all over Stockton. We were real urchins." With her "pressed duck voice," she did not fit in in high school, a fact amusingly evident in "High School Reunion." The conflict of learning two cultures at once is the dominant theme in *The Woman Warrior* and its sequel, *China Men* (1980), which won the American Book Award. Just as her first book examined the lives of Kingston's mother and female relatives (the first section of which is excerpted here), so *China Men* presents the epic Chinese-American story from the viewpoint of her embittered male protagonist. Even outside California, as we see in "The Wild Man of the Green Swamp," racial and gender differences are the foundations of cultural conflict.

Kingston's latest publication, *Tripmaster Monkey: His Fake Book* (1989), is a fictive extension of *China Men* and indeed of Kingston's own life. It is a weave of literary fictions, Chinese and American, revealed in the life of a twenty-three-year-old Chinese-American male named Wittman Ah Sing. Curiously Kingston's hero is very much like herself—a 1960s Berkeley graduate and counterculture rebel addicted to "talk stories." Kingston graduated from the University of California at Berkeley in 1962, returned a year later to obtain a teaching certificate, and subsequently taught high school and college English, largely in Hawaii, where she lived with her husband and son for seventeen years. Today she lives in Oakland, California.

In all her work, Maxine Hong Kingston has the rare ability to make—as the critic Michiko Kakutani declares—a dazzling leap of "imaginative sympathy" in which she projects her life into those of her characters. In her own words, Kingston is interested in "building worlds, inventing selves." She tells her stories with the eye of a child who sees monsters as soon as the lights go out.

No Name Woman

"You must not tell anyone," my mother said, "what I am about to   1
tell you. In China your father had a sister who killed herself. She jumped
into the family well. We say that your father has all brothers because it is
as if she had never been born.

"In 1924 just a few days after our village celebrated seventeen   2
hurry-up weddings—to make sure that every young man who went 'out
on the road' would responsibly come home—your father and his brothers and your grandfather and his brothers and your aunt's new husband
sailed for America, the Gold Mountain. It was your grandfather's last
trip. Those lucky enough to get contracts waved good-bye from the
decks. They fed and guarded the stowaways and helped them off in
Cuba, New York, Bali, Hawaii. 'We'll meet in California next year,' they
said. All of them sent money home.

"I remember looking at your aunt one day when she and I were   3
dressing; I had not noticed before that she had such a protruding melon
of a stomach. But I did not think, 'She's pregnant,' until she began to
look like other pregnant women, her shirt pulling and the white tops of
her black pants showing. She could not have been pregnant, you see, because her husband had been gone for years. No one said anything. We
did not discuss it. In early summer she was ready to have the child, long
after the time when it could have been possible.

"The village had also been counting. On the night the baby was to   4
be born the villagers raided our house. Some were crying. Like a great
saw, teeth strung with lights, files of people walked zigzag across our
land, tearing the rice. Their lanterns doubled in the disturbed black
water, which drained away through the broken bunds. As the villagers
closed in, we could see that some of them, probably men and women we
knew well, wore white masks. The people with long hair hung it over
their faces. Women with short hair made it stand up on end. Some had
tied white bands around their foreheads, arms, and legs.

"At first they threw mud and rocks at the house. Then they threw   5
eggs and began slaughtering our stock. We could hear the animals
scream their deaths—the roosters, the pigs, a last great roar from the ox.
Familiar wild heads flared in our night windows; the villagers encircled
us. Some of the faces stopped to peer at us, their eyes rushing like
searchlights. The hands flattened against the panes, framed heads, and
left red prints.

"The villagers broke in the front and the back doors at the same   6
time, even though we had not locked the doors against them. Their

knives dripped with the blood of our animals. They smeared blood on the doors and walls. One woman swung a chicken, whose throat she had slit, splattering blood in red arcs about her. We stood together in the middle of our house, in the family hall with the pictures and tables of the ancestors around us, and looked straight ahead.

"At that time the house had only two wings. When the men came [7] back, we would build two more to enclose our courtyard and a third one to begin a second courtyard. The villagers pushed through both wings, even your grandparents' rooms, to find your aunt's, which was also mine until the men returned. From this room a new wing for one of the younger families would grow. They ripped up her clothes and shoes and broke her combs, grinding them underfoot. They tore her work from the loom. They scattered the cooking fire and rolled the new weaving in it. We could hear them in the kitchen breaking our bowls and banging the pots. They overturned the great waist-high earthenware jugs; duck eggs, pickled fruits, vegetables burst out and mixed in acrid torrents. The old woman from the next field swept a broom through the air and loosed the spirits-of-the-broom over our heads. 'Pig.' 'Ghost.' 'Pig,' they sobbed and scolded while they ruined our house.

"When they left, they took sugar and oranges to bless themselves. [8] They cut pieces from the dead animals. Some of them took bowls that were not broken and clothes that were not torn. Afterward we swept up the rice and sewed it back up into sacks. But the smells from the spilled preserves lasted. Your aunt gave birth in the pigsty that night. The next morning when I went for the water, I found her and the baby plugging up the family well.

"Don't let your father know that I told you. He denies her. Now [9] that you have started to menstruate, what happened to her could happen to you. Don't humiliate us. You wouldn't like to be forgotten as if you had never been born. The villagers are watchful."

Whenever she had to warn us about life, my mother told stories [10] that ran like this one, a story to grow up on. She tested our strength to establish realities. Those in the emigrant generations who could not reassert brute survival died young and far from home. Those of us in the first American generations have had to figure out how the invisible world the emigrants built around our childhood fits in solid America.

The emigrants confused the gods by diverting their curses, mis- [11] leading them with crooked streets and false names. They must try to confuse their offspring as well, who, I suppose, threaten them in similar ways—always trying to get things straight, always trying to name the unspeakable. The Chinese I know hide their names; sojourners take new names when their lives change and guard their real names with silence.

Chinese-Americans, when you try to understand what things in [12] you are Chinese, how do you separate what is peculiar to childhood, to poverty, insanities, one family, your mother who marked your growing with stories, from what is Chinese? What is Chinese tradition and what is the movies?

If I want to learn what clothes my aunt wore, whether flashy or or-   13
dinary, I would have to begin, "Remember Father's drowned-in-the-well sister?" I cannot ask that. My mother has told me once and for all the useful parts. She will add nothing unless powered by Necessity, a river-bank that guides her life. She plants vegetable gardens rather than lawns; she carries the odd-shaped tomatoes home from the fields and eats food left for the gods.

Whenever we did frivolous things, we used up energy; we flew   14
high kites. We children came up off the ground over the melting cones our parents brought home from work and the American movie on New Year's Day—*Oh, You Beautiful Doll* with Betty Grable one year, and *She Wore a Yellow Ribbon* with John Wayne another year. After the one carnival ride each, we paid in guilt; our tired father counted his change on the dark walk home.

Adultery is extravagance. Could people who hatch their own   15
chicks and eat the embryos and the heads for delicacies and boil the feet in vinegar for party food, leaving only the gravel, eating even the gizzard lining—could such people engender a prodigal aunt? To be a woman, to have a daughter in starvation time was a waste enough. My aunt could not have been the lone romantic who gave up everything for sex. Women in the old China did not choose. Some man had commanded her to lie with him and be his secret evil. I wonder whether he masked himself when he joined the raid on her family.

Perhaps she had encountered him in the fields or on the mountain   16
where the daughters-in-law collected fuel. Or perhaps he first noticed her in the marketplace. He was not a stranger because the village housed no strangers. She had to have dealings with him other than sex. Perhaps he worked an adjoining field, or he sold her the cloth for the dress she sewed and wore. His demand must have surprised, then terrified her. She obeyed him; she always did as she was told.

When the family found a young man in the next village to be her   17
husband, she had stood tractably beside the best rooster, his proxy, and promised before they met that she would be his forever. She was lucky that he was her age and she would be the first wife, an advantage secure now. The night she first saw him, he had sex with her. Then he left for America. She had almost forgotten what he looked like. When she tried to envision him, she only saw the black and white face in the group photograph the men had had taken before leaving.

The other man was not, after all, much different from her husband.   18
They both gave orders: she followed. "If you tell your family, I'll beat you. I'll kill you. Be here again next week." No one talked sex, ever. And

she might have separated the rapes from the rest of living if only she did not have to buy her oil from him or gather wood in the same forest. I want her fear to have lasted just as long as rape lasted so that the fear could have been contained. No drawn-out fear. But women at sex hazarded birth and hence lifetimes. The fear did not stop but permeated everywhere. She told the man, "I think I'm pregnant." He organized the raid against her.

On nights when my mother and father talked about their life back   19
home, sometimes they mentioned an "outcast table" whose business they still seemed to be settling, their voices tight. In a commensal tradition, where food is precious, the powerful older people made wrongdoers eat alone. Instead of letting them start separate new lives like the Japanese, who could become samurais and geishas, the Chinese family, faces averted but eyes glowering sideways, hung on to the offenders and fed them leftovers. My aunt must have lived in the same house as my parents and eaten at an outcast table. My mother spoke about the raid as if she had seen it, when she and my aunt, a daughter-in-law to a different household, should not have been living together at all. Daughters-in-law lived with their husbands' parents, not their own; a synonym for marriage in Chinese is "taking a daughter-in-law." Her husband's parents could have sold her, mortgaged her, stoned her. But they had sent her back to her own mother and father, a mysterious act hinting at disgraces not told me. Perhaps they had thrown her out to deflect the avengers.

She was the only daughter; her four brothers went with her father,   20
husband, and uncles "out on the road" and for some years became western men. When the goods were divided among the family, three of the brothers took land, and the youngest, my father, chose an education. After my grandparents gave their daughter away to her husband's family, they had dispensed all the adventure and all the property. They expected her alone to keep the traditional ways, which her brothers, now among the barbarians, could fumble without detection. The heavy, deep-rooted women were to maintain the past against the flood, safe for returning. But the rare urge west had fixed upon our family, and so my aunt crossed boundaries not delineated in space.

The work of preservation demands that the feelings playing about   21
in one's guts not be turned into action. Just watch their passing like cherry blossoms. But perhaps my aunt, my forerunner, caught in a slow life, let dreams grow and fade and after some months or years went toward what persisted. Fear at the enormities of the forbidden kept her desires delicate, wire and bone. She looked at a man because she liked the way the hair was tucked behind his ears, or she liked the question-mark line of a long torso curving at the shoulder and straight at the hip. For warm eyes or a soft voice or a slow walk—that's all—a few hairs, a line,

a brightness, a sound, a pace, she gave up family. She offered us up for a charm that vanished with tiredness, a pigtail that didn't toss when the wind died. Why, the wrong lighting could erase the dearest thing about him.

It could very well have been, however, that my aunt did not take 22 subtle enjoyment of her friend, but, a wild woman, kept rollicking company. Imagining her free with sex doesn't fit, though. I don't know any women like that, or men either. Unless I see her life branching into mine, she gives me no ancestral help.

To sustain her being in love, she often worked at herself in the mir- 23 ror, guessing at the colors and shapes that would interest him, changing them frequently in order to hit on the right combination. She wanted him to look back.

On a farm near the sea, a woman who tended her appearance 24 reaped a reputation for eccentricity. All the married women blunt-cut their hair in flaps about their ears or pulled it back in tight buns. No nonsense. Neither style blew easily into heart-catching tangles. And at their weddings they displayed themselves in their long hair for the last time. "It brushed the backs of my knees," my mother tells me. "It was braided, and even so, it brushed the backs of my knees."

At the mirror my aunt combed individuality into her bob. A bun 25 could have been contrived to escape into black streamers blowing in the wind or in quiet wisps about her face, but only the older women in our picture album wear buns. She brushed her hair back from her forehead, tucking the flaps behind her ears. She looped a piece of thread, knotted into a circle between her index fingers and thumbs, and ran the double strand across her forehead. When she closed her fingers as if she were making a pair of shadow geese bite, the string twisted together catching the little hairs. Then she pulled the thread away from her skin, ripping the hairs out neatly, her eyes watering from the needles of pain. Opening her fingers, she cleaned the thread, then rolled it along her hairline and the tops of her eyebrows. My mother did the same to me and my sisters and herself. I used to believe that the expression "caught by the short hairs" meant a captive held with a depilatory string. It especially hurt at the temples, but my mother said we were lucky we didn't have to have our feet bound when we were seven. Sisters used to sit on their beds and cry together, she said, as their mothers or their slave removed the bandages for a few minutes each night and let the blood gush back into their veins. I hope that the man my aunt loved appreciated a smooth brow, that he wasn't just a tits-and-ass man.

Once my aunt found a freckle on her chin, at a spot that the al- 26 manac said predestined her for unhappiness. She dug it out with a hot needle and washed the wound with peroxide.

More attention to her looks than these pullings of hairs and pick- 27 ings at spots would have caused gossip among the villagers. They owned work clothes and good clothes, and they wore good clothes for feasting the new seasons. But since a woman combing her hair hexes beginnings, my aunt rarely found an occasion to look her best. Women looked like great sea snails—the corded wood, babies, and laundry they carried were the whorls on their backs. The Chinese did not admire a bent back; goddesses and warriors stood straight. Still there must have been a marvelous freeing of beauty when a worker laid down her burden and stretched and arched.

Such commonplace loveliness, however, was not enough for my aunt. She dreamed of a lover for the fifteen days of New Year's, the time for families to exchange visits, money, and food. She plied her secret comb. And sure enough she cursed the year, the family, the village, and herself.   28

Even as her hair lured her imminent lover, many other men looked at her. Uncles, cousins, nephews, brothers would have looked, too, had they been home between journeys. Perhaps they had already been restraining their curiosity, and they left, fearful that their glances, like a field of nesting birds, might be startled and caught. Poverty hurt, and that was their first reason for leaving. But another, final reason for leaving the crowded house was the never-said.   29

She may have been unusually beloved, the precious only daughter, spoiled and mirror gazing because of the affection the family lavished on her. When her husband left, they welcomed the chance to take her back from the in-laws; she could live like the little daughter for just a while longer. There are stories that my grandfather was different from other people, "crazy ever since the little Jap bayoneted him in the head." He used to put his naked penis on the dinner table, laughing. And one day he brought home a baby girl, wrapped up inside his brown western-style greatcoat. He had traded one of his sons, probably my father, the youngest, for her. My grandmother made him trade back. When he finally got a daughter of his own, he doted on her. They must have all loved her, except perhaps my father, the only brother who never went back to China, having once been traded for a girl.   30

Brothers and sisters, newly men and women, had to efface their sexual color and present plain miens. Disturbing hair and eyes, a smile like no other, threatened the ideal of five generations living under one roof. To focus blurs, people shouted face to face and yelled from room to room. The immigrants I know have loud voices, unmodulated to American tones even after years away from the village where they called their friendships out across the fields. I have not been able to stop my mother's screams in public libraries or over telephones. Walking erect (knees straight, toes pointed forward, not pigeon-toed, which is Chinese-feminine) and speaking in an inaudible voice, I have tried to turn myself   31

American-feminine. Chinese communication was loud, public. Only sick people had to whisper. But at the dinner table, where the family members came nearest one another, no one could talk, not the outcasts nor any eaters. Every word that falls from the mouth is a coin lost. Silently they gave and accepted food with both hands. A preoccupied child who took his bowl with one hand got a sideways glare. A complete moment of total attention is due everyone alike. Children and lovers have no singularity here, but my aunt used a secret voice, a separate attentiveness.

She kept the man's name to herself throughout her labor and dying; she did not accuse him that he be punished with her. To save her inseminator's name she gave silent birth. 32

He may have been somebody in her own household, but intercourse with a man outside the family would have been no less abhorrent. All the village were kinsmen, and the titles shouted in loud country voices never let kinship be forgotten. Any man within visiting distance would have been neutralized as a lover—"brother," "younger brother," "older brother"—one hundred and fifteen relationship titles. Parents researched birth charts probably not so much to assure good fortune as to circumvent incest in a population that has but one hundred surnames. Everybody has eight million relatives. How useless then sexual mannerisms, how dangerous. 33

As if it came from an atavism deeper than fear, I used to add "brother" silently to boys' names. It hexed the boys, who would or would not ask me to dance and made them less scary and as familiar and deserving of benevolence as girls. 34

But, of course, I hexed myself also—no dates. I should have stood up, both arms waving, and shouted out across libraries, "Hey, you! Love me back." I had no idea, though, how to make attraction selective, how to control its direction and magnitude. If I made myself American-pretty so that the five or six Chinese boys in the class fell in love with me, everyone else—the Caucasian, Negro, and Japanese boys—would too. Sisterliness, dignified and honorable, made much more sense. 35

Attraction eludes control so stubbornly that whole societies designed to organize relationships among people cannot keep order, not even when they bind people to one another from childhood and raise them together. Among the very poor and the wealthy, brothers married their adopted sisters, like doves. Our family allowed some romance, paying adult brides' prices and providing dowries so that their sons and daughters could marry strangers. Marriage promises to turn strangers into friendly relatives—a nation of siblings. 36

In the village structure, spirits shimmered among the live creatures, balanced and held in equilibrium by time and land. But one human being flaring up into violence could open up a black hole, a maelstrom that pulled in the sky. The frightened villagers, who de- 37 pended on one another to maintain the real, went to my aunt to show her a personal, physical representation of the break she had made in the "roundness." Misallying couples snapped off the future, which was to be embodied in true offspring. The villagers punished her for acting as if she could have a private life, secret and apart from them.

If my aunt betrayed the family at a time of large grain yields and   38
peace, when many boys were born, and wings were being built on many houses, perhaps she might have escaped such severe punishment. But the men—hungry, greedy, tired of planting in dry soil—had been forced to leave the village in order to send food-money home. There were ghost plagues, bandit plagues, wars with the Japanese, floods. My Chinese brother and sister had died of an unknown sickness. Adultery, perhaps only a mistake during good times, became a crime when the village needed food.

The round moon cakes and round doorways, the round tables of   39
graduated size that fit one roundness inside another, round windows and rice bowls—these talismans had lost their power to warn this family of the law: a family must be whole, faithfully keeping the descent line by having sons to feed the old and the dead, who in turn look after the family. The villagers came to show my aunt and her lover-in-hiding a broken house. The villagers were speeding up the circling of events because she was too shortsighted to see that her infidelity had already harmed the village, that waves of consequences would return unpredictably, sometimes in disguise, as now, to hurt her. This roundness had to be made coin-sized so that she would see its circumference: punish her at the birth of her baby. Awaken her to the inexorable. People who refused fatalism because they could invent small resources insisted in culpability. Deny accidents and wrest fault from the stars.

After the villagers left, their lanterns now scattering in various di-   40
rections toward home, the family broke their silence and cursed her. "Aiaa, we're going to die. Death is coming. Death is coming. Look what you've done. You've killed us. Ghost! Dead ghost! Ghost! You've never been born." She ran out into the fields, far enough from the house so that she could no longer hear their voices, and pressed herself against the earth, her own land no more. When she felt the birth coming, she thought that she had been hurt. Her body seized together. "They've hurt me too much," she thought. "This is gall, and it will kill me." With forehead and knees against the earth, her body convulsed and then relaxed. She turned on her back, lay on the ground. The black well of sky and stars went out and out and out forever; her body and her complexity seemed to disappear. She was one of the stars, a bright dot in blackness, without home, without a companion, in eternal cold and silence. An agoraphobia rose in her, speeding higher and higher, bigger and bigger; she would not be able to contain it; there would be no end to fear.

Flayed, unprotected against space, she felt pain return, focusing   41 her body. This pain chilled her—a cold, steady kind of surface pain. Inside, spasmodically, the other pain, the pain of the child, heated her. For hours she lay on the ground, alternately body and space. Sometimes a vision of normal comfort obliterated reality: she saw the family in the evening gambling at the dinner table, the young people massaging their elders' backs. She saw them congratulating one another, high joy on the mornings the rice shoots came up. When these pictures burst, the stars drew yet further apart. Black space opened.

She got to her feet to fight better and remembered that old-fash- 42
ioned women gave birth in their pigsties to fool the jealous, pain-dealing gods, who do not snatch piglets. Before the next spasms could stop her, she ran to the pigsty, each step a rushing out into emptiness. She climbed over the fence and knelt in the dirt. It was good to have a fence enclosing her, a tribal person alone.

Laboring, this woman who had carried her child as a foreign 43
growth that sickened her every day, expelled it at last. She reached down to touch the hot, wet, moving mass, surely smaller than anything human, and could feel that it was human after all—fingers, toes, nails, nose. She pulled it up on to her belly, and it lay curled there, butt in the air, feet precisely tucked one under the other. She opened her loose shirt and buttoned the child inside. After resting, it squirmed and thrashed and she pushed it up to her breast. It turned its head this way and that until it found her nipple. There, it made little snuffling noises. She clenched her teeth at its preciousness, lovely as a young calf, a piglet, a little dog.

She may have gone to the pigsty as a last act of responsibility: she 44
would protect this child as she had protected its father. It would look after her soul, leaving supplies on her grave. But how would this tiny child without family find her grave when there would be no marker for her anywhere, neither in the earth nor the family hall? No one would give her a family hall name. She had taken the child with her into the wastes. At its birth the two of them had felt the same raw pain of separation, a wound that only the family pressing tight could close. A child with no descent line would not soften her life but only trail after her, ghostlike, begging her to give it purpose. At dawn the villagers on their way to the fields would stand around the fence and look.

Full of milk, the little ghost slept. When it awoke, she hardened her 45
breasts against the milk that crying loosens. Toward morning she picked up the baby and walked to the well.

Carrying the baby to the well shows loving. Otherwise abandon it. 46
Turn its face into the mud. Mothers who love their children take them along. It was probably a girl; there is some hope of forgiveness for boys.

"Don't tell anyone you had an aunt. Your father does not want to 47
hear her name. She has never been born." I have believed that sex was

unspeakable and words so strong and fathers so frail that "aunt" would do my father mysterious harm. I have thought that my family, having settled among immigrants who had also been their neighbors in the ancestral land, needed to clean their name, and a wrong word would incite the kinspeople even here. But there is more to this silence: they want me to participate in her punishment. And I have.

In the twenty years since I heard this story I have not asked for details nor said my aunt's name; I do not know it. People who can comfort the dead can also chase after them to hurt them further—a reverse ancestor worship. The real punishment was not the raid swiftly inflicted by the villagers, but the family's deliberately forgetting her. Her betrayal so maddened them, they saw to it that she would suffer forever, even after death. Always hungry, always needing, she would have to beg food from other ghosts, snatch and steal it from those whose living descendants give them gifts. She would have to fight the ghosts massed at crossroads for the buns a few thoughtful citizens leave to decoy her away from village and home so that the ancestral spirits could feast unharassed. At peace, they could act like gods, not ghosts, their descent lines providing them with paper suits and dresses, spirit money, paper houses, paper automobiles, chicken, meat, and rice into eternity— essences delivered up in smoke and flames, steam and incense rising from each rice bowl. In an attempt to make the Chinese care for people outside the family, Chairman Mao encourages us now to give our paper replicas to the spirits of outstanding soldiers and workers, no matter whose ancestors they may be. My aunt remains forever hungry. Goods are not distributed evenly among the dead. 48

My aunt haunts me—her ghost drawn to me because now, after fifty years of neglect, I alone devote pages of paper to her, though not origamied into houses and clothes. I do not think she always means me well. I am telling on her, and she was a spite suicide, drowning herself in the drinking water. The Chinese are always very frightened of the drowned one, whose weeping ghost, wet hair hanging and skin bloated, waits silently by the water to pull down a substitute. 49

1976

Purpose and Meaning

1. Some of the themes in Kingston's essay are Chinese-American cultural differences, storytelling, the distortion of facts, male and female positions in Chinese society, and the importance of names and naming. Examine the essay's five opening lines, and discuss how many of these themes are foreshadowed. What overarching thesis emerges from these themes?

2. What are some of the differences between Chinese and American culture,

as depicted by Kingston, concerning attitudes toward women, sex, and family? What insights does she want to convey to her audience?

3. Read again paragraphs 31 through 33. What are some of the mores that have formed in Chinese society as a result of the tradition of families living together over several generations?

Language and Style

1. Kingston's narrative opens with the shocking revelation that her aunt "jumped into the family well." Following this revelation, she recounts how villagers "threw mud and rocks at the house, . . . began slaughtering [the] stock, . . . smeared blood on the doors and walls." And still later she tells in graphic detail how her aunt gave birth and then committed suicide. What overall effect does this vivid description have on the reader's response to the narrative and perhaps to the writer?

2. Kingston's writing is highly imagistic. Nearly every line contains an image. One could say the images actually tell the story for Kingston. Comb Kingston's story for its images, choose five to ten that particularly strike you, and discuss what each one tells. You may want to refer to the themes mentioned in question 1 under "Purpose and Meaning."

3. Kingston is fond of recurring images or motifs, such as ghosts (see paragraphs 4, 7, 40, 45, 48, and 49) and the unnamed or "unspeakable" (see paragraphs 1, 2, 11, 32, 44, 47, and 48 and the essay's title.) How do these repeated references help to give order to both the form and content of the essay?

Strategy and Structure

1. Kingston begins the essay not in the narrator's voice but in her mother's. How does this approach prepare the reader for certain themes in the essay? How does it shift authority away from the narrator? Why might Kingston wish to shift authority in this way?

2. In paragraphs 15 through 33, Kingston tells several possible versions of her aunt's sexual encounter. It may have been rape, tender love, a passionate affair, an interlude with a relative. Since Kingston cannot know, neither can the reader. How does this uncertainty help to further themes about storytelling, cultural differences, and the distortion of facts?

3. Why does Kingston wait until the final paragraphs to discuss her identity as a writer struggling to tell her family history? Would the story have been strengthened or weakened if she had begun with the focus on her efforts to tell the stories of her ancestry? Why does she include this insight into herself at all, instead of leaving such information to a preface or introduction to the work?

Thinking and Writing

1. Kingston peppers her tale with references to rituals peculiar to Chinese culture, such as the "outcast table" (paragraph 19) and the plucking of hairs (paragraph 25). Describe three American rituals that may sound equally peculiar to people from other cultures.

2. Write about some incident in your family's history that is well known to all family members and has been elevated almost to the point of myth. What does your narrative reveal about your family and your own personal development?

3. Choose one of the following schemas and write three different scenarios for it (as Kingston does when she describes her aunt's sexual encounter):

    (a) A young woman writes poetry in relative secret all her life. After her death, she is recognized as a genius. Explain why she lived in isolation.

    (b) A man is found in his home, a gun in his hand, weeping beside the bed of his fatally shot wife. Describe what happened.

o━o━o━o━o━o━o━o━o━o━o━o━o━o━o

High School Reunion

I just opened an envelope in the mail to find a mimeograph sheet smelling like a school test and announcing the twentieth-year high school reunion. No Host Cocktail Party. Buffet Dinner. Family Picnic, Dancing. In August. Class of '58. Edison High. Stockton. The lurches in my stomach feel like doubt about the strength to stay grown up.

I had not gone to the tenth-year reunion; the friends I really wanted to see, I was seeing. But I've been having dreams about the people in high school, and sit up with an urge to talk to them, find out how they turned out. "Did you grow up?" There are emotions connected with those people that I don't feel for friends I've made since.

"When I think of you, I remember the hateful look you gave me on the day we signed yearbooks. That face pops into my mind a few times a year for twenty years. Why did you look at me that way?" I'd like to be able to say that at the No Host Cocktail. And to someone else, "I remember you winking at me across the physics lab."

I dreamed that the girl who never talked in all the years of school spoke to me: "Your house has moles living in it." Then my cat said, "I am a cat and not a car. Quit driving me around." High school is a component of the American subconscious.

Another reason I hadn't gone to the tenth was an item in the regis-   5
tration form: "List your publications." (The reunion committee must be
the kids who grew up to be personnel officers at universities.) To make a
list, it takes more than an article and one poem. Cutthroat competitors in
that class. With no snooty questions asked, maybe the people with interesting jail records would come. We were not the class to be jailed for our
politics or white-collar crimes but for burglary, armed robbery and
crimes of passion. "Reunions are planned by the people who were popular. They want the chance to put us down again," says a friend (Punahou
Academy '68), preparing for her tenth.

But surely I am not going to show up this year just because I have a   6
"list." And there is more to the questionnaire: "What's the greatest happiness you've had in the last twenty years?" "What do you regret the
most?" it asks. I'm going to write across the paper, "These questions are
too hard. Can I come anyway?" No, you can't write, "None of your business." It is their business; these are the special people that formed your
growing up.

I have a friend (Roosevelt High '62) who refused to go to his tenth   7
because he had to check "married," "separated," "divorced" or "single."
He could not bear to mark "divorced." Family Picnic.

But another divorced friend's reunion (Roosevelt '57) was so much   8
fun that the class decided to have another one the very next weekend—
without the spouses, a come-without-spouse party. And my brother
(Edison '60) and sister-in-law (Edison '62) went to her class reunion,
where they had an Old Flames Dance; you asked a Secret Love to dance.
Working out the regrets, people went home with other people's spouses.
Fifteen divorces and remarriages by summer's end.

At my husband Earll's (Bishop O'Dowd '56) reunion, there was an   9
uncomfortableness whether to call the married priests Father or Mister
or what.

What if you can't explain yourself over the dance music? Twenty   10
years of transcendence blown away at the No Host Cocktail. Cocktails—
another skill I haven't learned, like the dude in the old cowboy movies
who ordered milk or lemonade or sarsaparilla. They'll have disco dancing. Never been to a disco either. Not cool after all these years.

There will be a calling to account. That's why it's hard to go. A   11
judgment by one's real peers. We're going to judge whether The Most
Likely to Succeed succeeded.

In high school we did not choose our friends. I ended up with cer-   12
tain people, and then wondered why we went together. If she's the
pretty one, then I must be the homely one. (When I asked my sister,
Edison '59, she told me, "Well, when I think of the way you look in the
halls, I picture you with your slip hanging." Not well groomed.) We

were incomplete, and made complementary friendships, like Don Quixote and Sancho Panza. Or more like the Cisco Kid and Pancho. Friendships among equals is a possibility I have found as an adult.

No, my motive for going would not be because of my "list." I was 13 writing in high school. Writing did not protect me then, and it won't start protecting me now. I came from a school—no, it's not the school— it's the times; we are of a time when people don't read.

There's a race thing too. Suddenly the colored girls would walk up, 14 and my colored girlfriend would talk and move differently. Well, they're athletes, I thought; they go to the same parties. Some years, the only place I ever considered sitting for lunch was the Chinese table. But there were more of us than places at that table. Hurry and get there early, or go late when somebody may have finished and left. Not eat. Who will eat with whom at the Buffet Dinner?

I notice that the chairman of the reunion went to Chinese school, 15 too; maybe seeing her name, the Chinese-Americans will come. I will have people to eat with—unless they're mad at me for having written about them. I keep claiming our mutual material. They will have recognized themselves in the writing, and not like me for it. That people don't read is only my own wishful thinking.

And Earll says he may have to work in August and may not be 16 able to escort me. Alone at the Dance. Again.

One day a popular girl, who had her own car, stamped her foot 17 and shouted to a friend who was walking home with me. "Come here!" she ordered. "We go home with one another." To be seen going home alone was bad. They drove off. "I remember you shouting her away from me," I could say at the reunion, not, I swear, to accuse so much as to get the facts straight. Nobody came out and said that there were groups. I don't even know whether the friendships had a name; they were not called groups or crowds or gangs or cliques or anything ("Clicks," the kids today say.) "Were there groups?" I could ask at last. "Which one was I in?"

My son, who is a freshman (Class of '81), says he can't make 18 friends outside his group. "My old friends feel iced out, and then they ice me out."

What a test of character the reunion would be. I'm not worried 19 about looks. I and every woman of my age know that we look physically better at thirty-eight than eighteen. I'll have objective proof of the superiority of older women when I see the women who are eighteen in my dreams.

John Gregory Dunne (Portsmouth Priory '50) said to his wife, Joan 20 Didion (McClatchy High '52), "It is your obligation as an American writer to go to your high school reunion." And she went. She said she dreamed about the people for a long time afterward.

I have improved: I don't wear slips anymore; I got tired of hanging around with homely people. It would be nice to go to a reunion where we look at one another and know without explanations how much we all grew in twenty years of living. And know that we ended up at thirty-eight the way we did partly because of one another, psyches and memories intertwining, companions in time for a while, lucky to meet again. I wouldn't miss such a get-together for anything.

1978

Purpose and Meaning

1. Kingston writes that "high school is a component of the American subconscious" (paragraph 4). In what ways does she consider this to be so?

2. Throughout this essay, Kingston makes references to herself in high school as an outsider. How does this gain the interest and perhaps the sympathy of the reader, as well as further her purpose in writing the piece?

3. As Margaret Atwood does in some of her essays, Kingston refers to herself in this essay and in "No Name Woman" as a writer (see paragraph 15). What do you think is her purpose in such self-referential writing?

Language and Style

1. In this essay, as in "No Name Woman," Kingston often lets images tell her story. What is the significance of opening an essay about a high school with a smell, as opposed to a sight? What effect do smells have on memory?

2. Kingston's essay is very funny at times (note paragraphs 5, 10, 12). How does the humor help to shape the narrator's voice and balance an otherwise serious theme?

3. Kingston makes repeated reference to the invitation items listed in the first paragraph of the essay. She also capitalizes certain phrases, such as Secret Love (paragraph 8), The Most Likely to Succeed (paragraph 11), and Alone at the Dance (paragraph 16). What tone does this device help to create? How might it be considered schoolgirlish to capitalize these words?

Strategy and Structure

1. Kingston begins somewhat unconventionally by listing the items from her high school reunion announcement. In what other ways is this essay like a list or catalog?

2. What does Kingston accomplish in following every reference to a friend or family member with the high school name and year of graduation? How does this device affect the tone and the organization?

3. In the final paragraph, Kingston's tone shifts rather abruptly. Why does she make this shift? What final impressions does it leave with the reader?

Thinking and Writing

1. Kingston's writing is similar to Atwood's for her interest in how individual identity is shaped and defined. Write an essay in which you compare and contrast these two writers' approaches to the subject of identity.

2. High school reunions are a conventional topic, but Kingston manages—with wit and unconventional writing style—to make the essay fresh. Choose one of the following topics and through a fresh approach in tone, perspective, and writing style, develop an original essay on the subject:

   (a) high school graduation

   (b) moving away from home

   (c) first job.

The Wild Man
of the Green Swamp

For eight months in 1975, residents on the edge of Green Swamp, Florida, had been reporting to the police that they had seen a Wild Man. When they stepped toward him, he made strange noises as in a foreign language and ran back into the saw grass. At first, authorities said the Wild Man was a mass hallucination. Man-eating animals lived in the swamp, and a human being could hardly find a place to rest without sinking. Perhaps it was some kind of a bear the children had seen.

In October, a game officer saw a man crouched over a small fire, but as he approached, the figure ran away. It couldn't have been a bear because the Wild Man dragged a burlap bag after him. Also, the fire was obviously man-made.

The fish-and-game wardens and the sheriff's deputies entered the swamp with dogs but did not search for long; no one could live in the swamp. The mosquitoes alone would drive him out.

The Wild Man made forays out of the swamp. Farmers encoun- 4
tered him taking fruit and corn from the turkeys. He broke into a house
trailer, but the occupant came back, and the Wild Man escaped out a
window. The occupant said that a bad smell came off the Wild Man.
Usually, the only evidence of him were his abandoned campsites. At one
he left the remains of a four-foot-long alligator, of which he had eaten
the feet and tail.

In May a posse made an air and land search; the plane signaled 5
down to the hunters on the ground, who circled the Wild Man. A fish-
and-game warden "brought him down with a tackle," according to the
news. The Wild Man fought, but they took him to jail. He looked
Chinese, so they found a Chinese in town to come translate.

The Wild Man talked a lot to the translator. He told him his name. 6
He said he was thirty-nine years old, the father of seven children, who
were in Taiwan. To support them, he had shipped out on a Liberian
freighter. He had gotten very homesick and asked everyone if he could
leave the ship and go home. But the officers would not let him off. They
sent messages to China to find out about him. When the ship landed,
they took him to the airport and tried to put him on an airplane to some
foreign place. Then, he said, the white demons took him to Tampa
Hospital, which is for insane people, but he escaped, just walked out
and went into the swamp.

The interpreter asked how he lived in the swamp. He said he ate 7
snakes, turtles, armadillos, and alligators. The captors could tell how he
lived when they opened up his bag, which was not burlap but a pair of
pants with the legs knotted. Inside, he had carried a pot, a piece of
sharpened tin, and a small club, which he had made by sticking a railroad spike into a section of aluminum tubing.

The sheriff found the Liberian freighter that the Wild Man had 8
been on. The ship's officers said that they had not tried to stop him from
going home. His shipmates had decided that there was something
wrong with his mind. They had bought him a plane ticket and arranged
his passport to send him back to China. They had driven him to the airport, but there he began screaming and weeping and would not get on
the plane. So they had found him a doctor, who sent him to Tampa
Hospital.

Now the doctors at the jail gave him medicine for the mosquito 9
bites, which covered his entire body, and medicine for his stomachache.
He was getting better, but after he'd been in jail for three days, the U.S.
Border Patrol told him they were sending him back. He became hysteri-
cal. That night, he fastened his belt to the bars, wrapped it around his
neck, and hung himself.

In the newspaper picture he did not look very wild, being led by 10
the posse out of the swamp. He did not look dirty, either. He wore a

checkered shirt unbuttoned at the neck, where his white undershirt showed; his shirt was tucked into his pants; his hair was short. He was surrounded by men in cowboy hats. His fingers stretching open, his wrists pulling apart to the extent of the handcuffs, he lifted his head, his eyes screwed shut, and cried out.

There was a Wild Man in our slough too, only he was a black man.   11
He wore a shirt and no pants, and some mornings when we walked to school, we saw him asleep under the bridge. The police came and took him away. The newspaper said he was crazy; it said the police had been on the lookout for him for a long time, but we had seen him every day.

1980

Purpose and Meaning

1. What expectations does Kingston arouse in the reader with the title of this essay? Would you be more or less interested in the essay if it were titled, "A Chinese Man Confronts American Culture"? How does this writing tactic help to further Kingston's thesis about the Wild Man?

2. In the opening paragraph, Kingston writes, "He made strange noises as in a foreign language . . . and ran back into the saw grass." What does this description suggest about language and culture? If the Wild Man spoke English, would he be considered quite so wild?

3. In paragraph 6, Kingston writes that the Wild Man said, "The white demons took him to Tampa Hospital." Who are the white demons? What does this suggest about cultural perspective and Kingston's relationship to her readers?

Language and Style

1. Why might Kingston choose to capitalize the words "Wild Man" and to use them as a name to refer to the Chinese immigrant? What was your initial response to this term?

2. Time and again, Kingston focuses on extraordinary details: "Man-eating animals lived in the swamp" (paragraph 1); "he left the remains of a four-foot-long alligator" (paragraph 4); "mosquito bites . . . covered his entire body" (paragraph 9). How does this help to make the readers participants in cultural arrogance? What else might it reveal about us and our interests?

3. Kingston seems fond of lists. There are two lists of items in paragraph 7. Sometimes, as in paragraph 10, the sentences are short and read like lists of observations. Since lists contain condensed information, how is this stylistic device representative of Kingston's overall writing style? How is it similar to her use of imagery?

4. Examine Kingston's use of verb tenses. How does she manipulate them to suggest events in time?

Strategy and Structure

1. The first sentence of this essay contains the date, place, and subject. What tone does this journalistic opening create? How does it make us less like readers of an essay and more like participants in an event as it is happening? What pattern do you detect in this narrative sequencing of events?

2. Paragraph 10 contains an image completely contrary to that of the Wild Man depicted earlier. What strategic effect does it have for Kingston to save this information for last?

3. The final paragraph is almost a parable. Analyze it and describe the "moral of the story." Why would Kingston end her essay with such a moral tone?

Thinking and Writing

1. In all three of Kingston's essays, there is a common theme of individuals who are outsiders as a result of their actions, some physical abnormality, or a relative cultural oddity. Write an essay in which you compare this theme in the three essays.

2. Write an essay describing a way in which you are, or might be considered, out of the ordinary. Use the third-person perspective. In other words, as you describe yourself, pretend that you are someone else and write from his or her point of view.

3. Recall those people with whom you come into frequent contact and consider as "outsiders." Why are they "outsiders"? What "insider" values or behaviors don't they share? Write an essay on the topic.

STEPHEN JAY GOULD

With his wit, clarity, and accessible writing style, Stephen Jay Gould has gained an extraordinary reputation as a popularizer of difficult scientific theories. Over the course of his highly distinguished career as an evolutionary biologist, professor, and writer, he has received dozens of awards and honors—from the American Book Award in science (for *The Panda's Thumb*) to a Distinguished Service Award from the American Geological Institute to a MacArthur Fellowship—as well as more than twenty honorary degrees from colleges and universities.

Gould was born September 10, 1941, in New York City, "not far from Tyrannosaurus," he writes, alluding to the Museum of Natural History and his West Side origins. He received a B.A. degree from Antioch College in 1963 and a doctorate from Columbia University in 1967. He is married with two sons and is currently teaching at Harvard University.

Along with a monthly column, "This View of Life," published in *Natural History*, Gould has written and collaborated on numerous books and essay collections. In *The Panda's Thumb: More Reflections in Natural History* (1980), perhaps his most widely read work, Gould explores his favorite subject: the miracle of evolution. What is miraculous about evolution is not the perfect design of a divine creator but the imperfect evolution of living things as they adjust—or fail to adjust—to their environment. As codeveloper of an evolutionary theory called "punctuated equilibrium," which proposes that evolution is not a gradual process but a series of relatively rapid changes affecting isolated groups, Gould explains these evolutionary accidents in a way Darwin could not.

Gould has devoted much of his writing to clarifying the arguments that uphold creationism and evolutionary theory. Unlike most other scientific prose, however, Gould's writing often reaches a high emotional pitch, especially when the subject is creationism, for the misleading claims of creationists infuriate him in his quest for clarity.

What sets Gould apart from much of the scientific community and makes his writing so accessible is his insistence that science is culturally embedded, a theme he strikes in "Counters and Cable Cars." He once said, "Science is not a heartless pursuit of objective information, it is a creative human activity." Time and again—in *Ever Since Darwin* (1977), *Hen's Teeth and Horse's Toes* (1983), *The Flamingo's Smile* (1985), and *Eight Little Piggies* (1993), his newest collection, as well as in other books—Gould concerns himself with the abuse and misuse of scientific information. He has written on issues such as sterilization among the mentally ill and racist and sexist misuse of conclusions falsely drawn from studies of brain size, as in "Women's Brains." At the same time, he can reveal his own sensitivity and humanity by laughing at his own inaccurate memories, as he does in "Muller Bros. Moving & Storage."

Gould's contributions go beyond the pure pleasure of insightful, humorous informative reading. He has helped to blur the line between scientist and layperson, science and society. Noted reviewer Ashley Montague calls Gould "one of the most brilliant of our younger biologists, gifted, among other things, with the ability to write."

Women's Brains

In the prelude to *Middlemarch*, George Eliot lamented the unful- 1
filled lives of talented women:

> Some have felt that these blundering lives are due to the inconvenient in-
> definiteness with which the Supreme Power has fashioned the natures of
> women: if there were one level of feminine incompetence as strict as the
> ability to count three and no more, the social lot of women might be
> treated with scientific certitude.

Eliot goes on to discount the idea of innate limitation, but while 2
she wrote in 1872, the leaders of European anthropometry were trying
to measure "with scientific certitude" the inferiority of women.
Anthropometry, or measurement of the human body, is not so fashionable a field these days, but it dominated the human sciences for much of
the nineteenth century and remained popular until intelligence testing
replaced skull measurements as a favored device for making invidious
comparisons among races, classes, and sexes. Craniometry, or measurement of the skull, commanded the most attention and respect. Its un-
questioned leader, Paul Broca (1824–80), professor of clinical surgery at
the Faculty of Medicine in Paris, gathered a school of disciples and imi-
tators around himself. Their work, so meticulous and apparently ir-
refutable, exerted great influence and won high esteem as a jewel of
nineteenth-century science.

Broca's work seemed particularly invulnerable to refutation. Had 3
he not measured with the most scrupulous care and accuracy? (Indeed,
he had. I have the greatest respect for Broca's meticulous procedure. His
numbers are sound. But science is an inferential exercise, not a catalog of
facts. Numbers, by themselves, specify nothing. All depends upon what
you do with them.) Broca depicted himself as an apostle of objectivity, a
man who bowed before facts and cast aside superstition and sentimentality. He declared that "there is no faith, however respectable, no interest, however legitimate, which must not accommodate itself to the
progress of human knowledge and bend before truth." Women, like it or
not, had smaller brains than men and, therefore, could not equal them in
intelligence. This fact, Broca argued, may reinforce a common prejudice
in male society, but it is also a scientific truth. L. Manouvrier, a black
sheep in Broca's fold, rejected the inferiority of women and wrote with

feeling about the burden imposed upon them by Broca's numbers:

> Women displayed their talents and their diplomas. They also invoked philosophical authorities. But they were opposed by *numbers* unknown to Condorcet or to John Stuart Mill. These numbers fell upon poor women like a sledge hammer, and they were accompanied by commentaries and sarcasms more ferocious than the most misogynist imprecations of certain church fathers. The theologians had asked if women had a soul. Several centuries later, some scientists were ready to refuse them a human intelligence.

Broca's argument rested upon two sets of data: the larger brains of men in modern societies, and a supposed increase in male superiority through time. His most extensive data came from autopsies performed personally in four Parisian hospitals. For 292 male brains, he calculated an average weight of 1,325 grams; 140 female brains averaged 1,144 grams for a difference of 181 grams, or 14 percent of the male weight. Broca understood, of course, that part of this difference could be attributed to the greater height of males. Yet he made no attempt to measure the effect of size alone and actually stated that it cannot account for the entire difference because we know, a priori, that women are not as intelligent as men (a premise that the data were supposed to test, not rest upon):

> We might ask if the small size of the female brain depends exclusively upon the small size of her body. Tiedemann has proposed this explanation. But we must not forget that women are, on the average, a little less intelligent than men, a difference which we should not exaggerate but which is, nonetheless, real. We are therefore permitted to suppose that the relatively small size of the female brain depends in part upon her physical inferiority and in part upon her intellectual inferiority.

In 1873, the year after Eliot published *Middlemarch*, Broca measured the cranial capacities of prehistoric skulls from L'Homme Mort cave. Here he found a difference of only 99.5 cubic centimeters between males and females, while modern populations range from 129.5 to 220.7. Topinard, Broca's chief disciple, explained the increasing discrepancy through time as a result of differing evolutionary pressures upon dominant men and passive women:

> The man who fights for two or more in the struggle for existence, who has all the responsibility and the cares of tomorrow, who is constantly active in combating the environment and human rivals, needs more brain than the woman whom he must protect and nourish, the sedentary women, lacking any interior occupations, whose role is to raise children, love, and be passive.

In 1879, Gustave Le Bon, chief misogynist of Broca's school, used 6
these data to publish what must be the most vicious attack upon women
in modern scientific literature (no one can top Aristotle). I do not claim
his views were representative of Broca's school, but they were published
in France's most respected anthropological journal. Le Bon concluded:

> In the most intelligent races, as among the Parisians, there are a large num-
> ber of women whose brains are closer in size to those of gorillas than to
> the most developed male brains. This inferiority is so obvious that no one
> can contest it for a moment; only its degree is worth discussion. All psy-
> chologists who have studied the intelligence of women, as well as poets
> and novelists, recognize today that they represent the most inferior forms
> of human evolution and that they are closer to children and savages than
> to an adult, civilized man. They excel in fickleness, inconstancy, absence of
> thought and logic, and incapacity to reason. Without doubt there exist
> some distinguished women, very superior to the average man, but they
> are as exceptional as the birth of any monstrosity, as, for example, of a go-
> rilla with two heads; consequently, we may neglect them entirely.

Nor did Le Bon shrink from the social implications of his views. 7
He was horrified by the proposal of some American reformers to grant
women higher education on the same basis as men:

> A desire to give them the same education, and, as a consequence, to pro-
> pose the same goals for them, is a dangerous chimera. . . . The day when,
> misunderstanding the inferior occupations which nature has given her,
> women leave the home and take part in our battles; on this day a social
> revolution will begin, and everything that maintains the sacred ties of the
> family will disappear.

Sound familiar?*

I have reexamined Broca's data, the basis for all this derivative pro- 8
nouncement, and I find his numbers sound but his interpretation ill-
founded, to say the least. The data supporting his claim for increased
difference through time can be easily dismissed. Broca based his contention on the samples from L'Homme Mort alone—only seven male
and six female skulls in all. Never have so little data yielded such far
ranging conclusions.

In 1888, Topinard published Broca's more extensive data on the 9
Parisian hospitals. Since Broca recorded height and age as well as brain
size, we may use modern statistics to remove their effect. Brain weight

---

*When I wrote this essay, I assumed that Le Bon was a marginal, if color-
ful, figure. I have since learned that he was a leading scientist, one of the
founders of social psychology, and best known for a seminal study on crowd behavior, still cited today (*La psychologie des foules*, 1895), and for his work on unconscious motivation.

decreases with age, and Broca's women were, on average, considerably older than his men. Brain weight increases with height, and his average man was almost half a foot taller than his average woman. I used multiple regression, a technique that allowed me to assess simultaneously the influence of height and age upon brain size. In an analysis of the data for women, I found that, at average male height and age, a woman's brain would weigh 1,212 grams. Correction for height and age reduces Broca's measured difference of 181 grams by more than a third, to 113 grams.

I don't know what to make of this remaining difference because I   10
cannot assess other factors known to influence brain size in a major way. Cause of death has an important effect: degenerative disease often entails a substantial diminution of brain size. (This effect is separate from the decrease attributed to age alone.) Eugene Schreider, also working with Broca's data, found that men killed in accidents had brains weighing, on average, 60 grams more than men dying of infectious diseases. The best modern data I can find (from American hospitals) records a full 100-gram difference between death by degenerative arteriosclerosis and by violence or accident. Since so many of Broca's subjects were very elderly women, we may assume that lengthy degenerative disease was more common among them than among the men.

More importantly, modern students of brain size still have not   11
agreed on a proper measure for eliminating the powerful effect of body size. Height is partly adequate, but men and women of the same height do not share the same body build. Weight is even worse than height, because most of its variation reflects nutrition rather than intrinsic size— fat versus skinny exerts little influence upon the brain. Manouvrier took up this subject in the 1880s and argued that muscular mass and force should be used. He tried to measure this elusive property in various ways and found a marked difference in favor of men, even in men and women of the same height. When he corrected for what he called "sexual mass," women actually came out slightly ahead in brain size.

Thus, the corrected 113-gram difference is surely too large; the true   12
figure is probably close to zero and may as well favor women as men. And 113 grams, by the way, is exactly the difference between a 5 foot 4 inch and a 6 foot 4 inch male in Broca's data. We would not (especially us short folks) want to ascribe greater intelligence to tall men. In short, who knows what to do with Broca's data? They certainly don't permit any confident claim that men have bigger brains than women.

To appreciate the social role of Broca and his school, we must rec-   13
ognize that his statements about the brains of women do not reflect an isolated prejudice toward a single disadvantaged group. They must be weighed in the context of a general theory that supported contemporary social distinctions as biologically ordained. Women, blacks, and poor people suffered the same disparagement, but women bore the brunt of

Broca's argument because he had easier access to data on women's brains. Women were singularly denigrated but they also stood as surrogates for other disenfranchised groups. As one of Broca's disciples wrote in 1881: "Men of the black races have a brain scarcely heavier than that of white women." This juxtaposition extended into many other realms of anthropological argument, particularly to claims that, anatomically and emotionally, both women and blacks were like white children—and that white children, by the theory of recapitulation, represented an ancestral (primitive) adult stage of human evolution. I do not regard as empty rhetoric the claim that women's battles are for all of us.

Maria Montessori did not confine her activities to educational reform for young children. She lectured on anthropology for several years at the University of Rome, and wrote an influential book entitled *Pedagogical Anthropology* (English edition, 1913). Montessori was no egalitarian. She supported most of Broca's work and the theory of innate criminality proposed by her compatriot Cesare Lombroso. She measured the circumference of children's heads in her schools and inferred that the best prospects had bigger brains. But she had no use for Broca's conclusions about women. She discussed Manouvrier's work at length and made much of his tentative claim that women, after proper correction of the data, had slightly larger brains than men. Women, she concluded, were intellectually superior, but men had prevailed heretofore by dint of physical force. Since technology has abolished force as an instrument of power, the era of women may soon be upon us: "In such an epoch there will really be superior human beings, there will really be men strong in morality and in sentiment. Perhaps in this way the reign of women is approaching, when the enigma of her anthropological superiority will be deciphered. Woman was always the custodian of human sentiment, morality and honor."

This represents one possible antidote to "scientific" claims for the constitutional inferiority of certain groups. One may affirm the validity of biological distinctions but argue that the data have been misinterpreted by prejudiced men with a stake in the outcome, and that disadvantaged groups are truly superior. In recent years, Elaine Morgan has followed this strategy in her *Descent of Woman*, a speculative reconstruction of human prehistory from the woman's point of view—and as farcical as more famous tall tales by and for men.

I prefer another strategy. Montessori and Morgan followed Broca's philosophy to reach a more congenial conclusion. I would rather label the whole enterprise of setting a biological value upon groups for what it is: irrelevant and highly injurious. George Eliot well appreciated the special tragedy that biological labeling imposed upon members of disadvantaged groups. She expressed it for people like herself—women of extraordinary talent. I would apply it more widely—not only to those whose dreams are flouted but also to those who never realize that they may dream—but I cannot match her prose. In conclusion, then, the rest of Eliot's prelude to *Middlemarch:*

> The limits of variation are really much wider than anyone would imagine from the sameness of women's coiffure and the favorite love stories in prose and verse. Here and there a cygnet is reared uneasily among the ducklings in the brown pond, and never finds the living stream in fellowship with its own oary-footed kind. Here and there is born a Saint Theresa, foundress of nothing, whose loving heartbeats and sobs after an unattained goodness tremble off and are dispersed among hindrances instead of centering in some long-recognizable deed.

1980

Purpose and Meaning

1. Stephen Jay Gould, a well-respected scientist and writer, establishes his thesis that brain size is irrelevant to intelligence in part by discrediting the opposition. What does he mean when he argues (paragraph 4) that Paul Broca's premise "women are not as intelligent as men" is "a premise the data were supposed to test, not rest upon"?

2. Gould writes (paragraph 13) that Broca was not singling women out when he argued that they have biologically inferior brains. Does Gould mean that Broca was not motivated by any prejudice against women? What exactly is Gould's purpose here? What is his tone or attitude toward his subject?

3. Discuss how the following statement by Le Bon is similar to arguments put forward today by some conservatives: "The day when . . . women leave the home and take part in our [men's] battles . . . everything that maintains the sacred ties of the family will disappear" (paragraph 7). What counterarguments can you make to Le Bon's claim?

Language and Style

1. How does Gould's frequent use of scientific terminology create the tone of his essay? Is such language appropriate to the topic?

2. At times, Gould uses scientific language sarcastically, turning it back on itself: "I have the greatest respect for Broca's meticulous procedure . . . [but] numbers, by themselves, specify nothing" (paragraph 3); "we know, a priori, that women are not as intelligent as men" (paragraph 4); "Gustave Le Bon, chief misogynist . . ." (paragraph 6). How does this playfulness influence the reader's response and the strength of Gould's argument?

3. Gould does not write in jargon, nor does he simplify his arguments or condescend to his readers. Does this make his essay more or less readable? How? What aspects of style make the essay accessible to readers?

Strategy and Structure

1. Gould's essay is entirely an argument. Outline the steps in his argument. What principle governs his structure?

2. Gould has a point of view that he wants his readers to sympathize and perhaps agree with. Since his topic is women's brains, as the title indicates, of what strategic importance is opening and closing the essay with a quotation from a woman, the writer George Eliot?

3. Gould roots his argument in history. How does he present chronology and narrative to strengthen his major and minor propositions?

4. What techniques of refutation does Gould employ? How effective are they?

5. What is the effect of the extended quotations in this essay? How does Gould make them an organic part of the essay's structure?

Thinking and Writing

1. Write an essay in which you elaborate on Gould's statement that "women's battles are for all of us" (paragraph 13).

2. Reread and analyze George Eliot's prelude to *Middlemarch*, quoted in two parts at the beginning and end of Gould's essay. Relate Eliot's lament to Gould's argument.

3. In the essay, Gould alludes to the " 'scientific' claims for the constitutional inferiority of certain groups" (paragraph 15). Think of instances when false or misapplied science has led to controversy and crisis in recent history. Write an essay on the topic.

Counters and Cable Cars

San Francisco, October 11, 1989

In a distinctive linguistic regionalism, New Yorkers like me stand "on line," while the rest of the nation waits patiently "in line." Actually, I spend a good part of my life trying to avoid that particular activity altogether, no matter what preposition it may bear. I am a firm supporter of the Yogi Berra principle regarding once fashionable restaurants: "No one goes there anymore; it's too crowded."

Consequently, in San Francisco this morning, I awoke before sunrise in order to get my breakfast of Sears's famous eighteen pancakes (marvel not, they're very small) before the morning crush of more amenable hours rendered the restaurant uninhabitable on Berra's maxim. Then out the door by 7:30 to the cable car stop at Union Square for a ride that thrills me no less in middle life than on my first trip as a boy. What moment in public transportation could possibly surpass that final steep descent down Russian Hill? (For a distant second and third in America, I nominate the Saint Charles streetcar of New Orleans, last of the old-time trolley lines, as it passes by the antebellum houses of the garden district; and the Staten Island Ferry, only a nickel in my youth and the world's most distinguished cheap date, as it skirts the Statue of Liberty by moonlight.) I travel during the last minutes of comfort and accessibility. By 9 a.m., long lines of tourists will form and no one will want to ride anymore.

We paleontologists are driven, almost by professional definition, to an abiding respect for items and institutions that have prevailed and prospered with integrity in an unending sea of change (although I trust that we can also welcome, even foster, intellectual innovation). I love Sears restaurant with its familiar, uniformly excellent, and utterly nonyuppie breakfast menu. And I adore those Victorian cars with their wooden seats and their distinctive sounds—the two-clang signal to move, the hum of the cable perpetually running underground, the grasp of the grip as it takes hold to pull the passive car along.

As I ride, I ponder a psychological puzzle that has long intrigued me: why does authenticity—as a purely conceptual theme—exert such a hold upon us? An identical restaurant with the same food, newly built in the San Francisco segment of a Great Cities Theme Park, would supply me with nothing but calories; a perfect replica of a cable car, following an even hillier route in Disneyland, would be a silly bauble.

Authenticity has many guises, each contributing something essential to our calm satisfaction with the truly genuine. Authenticity of *object* fascinates me most deeply because its pull is entirely abstract and conceptual. The art of replica making has reached such sophistication that only the most astute professional can now tell the difference between, say, a genuine dinosaur skeleton and a well-made cast. The real and the replica are effectively alike in all but our abstract knowledge of authenticity, yet we feel awe in the presence of bone once truly clothed in dinosaur flesh and mere interest in fiberglass of identical appearance.

If I may repeat, because it touched me so deeply, a story on this subject told once before in this forum (November 1984). A group of blind visitors met with the director of the Air and Space Museum in Washington to discuss greater accessibility, especially of the large objects hanging from the ceiling of the great atrium and perceptible only by sight. The director asked his guests whether a scale model of Lindbergh's *Spirit of St. Louis*, mounted and fully touchable, might alleviate the frustration of nonaccess to the real McCoy. The visitors replied that such a solution would be most welcome, but only if the model was placed directly beneath the invisible original. Simple knowledge of the imperceptible presence of authenticity can move us to tears.

We also respect an authenticity of *place*. Genuine objects out of context and milieu may foster intrigue, but rarely inspiration. London Bridge dismantled and reassembled in America becomes a mere curiosity. I love to watch giraffes in zoo cages, but their jerky, yet somehow graceful, progress over the African veld provokes a more satisfying feeling of awe.

Yet, until today, I had not appreciated the power of a third authenticity, that of *use*. Genuine objects in their proper place can be devalued by altered use—particularly when our avid appetite for casual and ephemeral leisure overwhelms an original use in the honorable world of daily work.

Lord knows, being one myself, I have no right to complain about tourists mobbing cable cars. Visitors have an inalienable right to reach Fisherman's Wharf and Ghirardelli Square by any legal means sanctioned and maintained by the city of San Francisco. Still, I love to ride incognito at 7:30 a.m. with native San Franciscans using the cable car as a public conveyance to their place of work—Asian students embarking on their way to school as the car skirts by Chinatown; smartly dressed executives with their monthly transit passes.

But I write this essay because I experienced a different, unanticipated, and most pleasant example of authenticity of use in Sears this morning. (I could not have asked for a better context. The Bay Area, this week, is experiencing a bonanza in authenticity of place—as the Oakland A's and the San Francisco Giants prepare for the first single-area World Series since 1956, when the seventh and last "subway series" of ten glorious childhood years in New York, 1947 to 1956, produced Don Larsen's perfect game and the revenge of my beloved Yankees for their only defeat, the year before, by the Dodgers in their true home in Brooklyn. Think what we would lose if, in deference to October weather and a misplaced sense of even opportunity, the World Series moved from the home cities of full-season drama to some neutral turf in balmy Miami or New Orleans.)

I have always gone to Sears with other people and sat at a table. This time I went alone and ate at the counter. I had not known that the counter is a domain of regulars, native San Franciscans on their way to work. One man gets up and says to the waitress, "Real good, maybe I'll come back again sometime." "He's in here every morning," whispers the waitress to me. Another man takes the empty seat, saying "Hi, honey" to the woman on the next stool. "You're pretty early today," she replies. "The works!" he says as the waitress passes by. "You got it," she replies. A few minutes later, she returns with a plate of pancakes and a dish of scrambled eggs. But first she slides the eggs off the plate onto a napkin, blotting away the butter. "No good for him," she explains. He begins a discussion on the relative merits of cloth napkins and paper towels in such an enterprise. Good fellowship in authenticity of use; people taking care of each other in small ways of enduring significance.

As I present talks on evolutionary subjects all around America, I   12 can be sure of certain questions following any speech: Where is human evolution going? What about genetic engineering? Are blacks really better at basketball? (Both the dumb and the profound share this character of inevitability.) High on the list of these perennial inquiries, I must rank the ecological question, usually asked with compassion but sometimes with pugnacity: Why do we need to save all these species anyway?

I know the conventional answers rooted in practicality. I even be-   13 lieve in them: you never know what medical or agricultural use might emerge from species currently unknown or ignored; beneficial diversity of gene pools in cultivated species can often be fostered by interbreeding with wild relatives; interconnectedness of ecological webs may lead to dire and unintended consequences for "valued" species when "insignificant" creatures are rubbed out. Still, I prefer to answer with an ethical, more accurately a viscerally aesthetic, statement espoused by nearly all evolutionary biologists as a virtual psychic necessity for wanting to enter the field in the first place: we relish diversity; we love every slightly different way, every nuance of form and behavior; and we know that the loss of a significant fraction of this gorgeous variety will quench our senses and our satisfactions for any future worth contemplating in human terms (potential recovery of diversity several million years down the road is too abstract and conjectural for this legitimately selfish argument). What in the world could possibly be more magnificent than the fact that beetle anatomy presents itself in more than half a million separate packages called species?

I have always been especially wary of "soft" and overly pat analo-   14 gies between biological evolution and human cultural change. (Some comparisons are apt and informative, for all modes of change must hold features in common; but the mechanisms of biological evolution and cultural change are so different that close analogies usually confuse far more than they enlighten.) Nonetheless, aesthetic statements may claim a more legitimate universality, especially when an overt form rather than the underlying mechanism of production becomes the subject of our consideration. If you feel aesthetic pleasure in proportions set by the "golden section," then you may gain similar satisfaction from a nautilus shell or a Greek building despite their maximally different methods and causes of construction. I do, therefore, feel justified in writing an essay on the moral and aesthetic value of diversity both in natural and in human works—and in trying to link the genesis and defense of diversity with various meanings of authenticity. (In addition, *Natural History* has been breaking ground within its genre for many years by including the diversity of human works under its mantle, and by recognizing that the life of modern cities belongs as firmly to natural history as the overphotographed and overromanticized ways of the few human groups still living as hunters and gatherers in pristine habitats.)

(Finally, if I may make a terrible confession for a working biologist   15
and a natural historian: I grew up on the streets of New York, and I suppose that one never loses a primary affection for things first familiar—call it authenticity of place if you wish. I do think that America's southwestern desert, in the four corners region around Monument Valley, is the most sublime spot on earth. But when I crave diversity rather than majesty, I choose cities and the products of human labor, as they resist conformity and embody authenticity of object, place, and use. My motto must be the couplet of Milton's "L'Allegro" and "Il Penseroso"—from the happy rather than the pensive side: "Towered cities please us then / And the busy hum of men." Several years ago I visited India on a trip sponsored by Harvard's natural history museum. My colleagues delighted in arising at 4 a.m., piling into a bus, driving to a nature reserve, and trying to spot the dot of a tiger at some absurd distance, rendered only slightly more interesting by binoculars. I yearned to be let off the bus alone in the middle of any bazaar in any town.)

Natural diversity exists at several levels. Variety permeates any   16
nonclonal population from within. Even our tightest genealogical groups contain fat people and thin people, tall and short. The primal folk wisdom of the ages proclaims the enormous differences in temperament among siblings of a single family. But the greatest dollop of natural diversity arises from our geographical divisions—the differences from place to place as we adapt to varying environments and accumulate our distinctiveness by limited contact with other regions. If all species, like rats and pigeons, lived all over the world, our planet would contain but a tiny fraction of its actual diversity.

I therefore tend to revel most in the distinctive diversity of geo-   17
graphical regions when I contemplate the aesthetic pleasure of differences. Since I am most drawn to human works, I find my greatest joy in learning to recognize local accents, regional customs of greeting and dining, styles of architecture linked to distinctive times and places. I also, at least in my head if not often enough in overt action, think of myself as a watchdog for the preservation of this fragile variety and an implacable foe of standardization and homogenization.

I recognize, of course, that official programs of urban layout and   18 road building must produce more elements of commonality than a strict aesthetic of maximal diversity might welcome. After all, criteria of design have a universality that becomes more and more pressing at upper limits of size and speed. If you have to move a certain number of cars through a given region at a stated speed, the road can't meander along the riverbanks or run through the main streets of old market towns. Public buildings and city street grids beg for an optimal efficiency that imposes some acceptable degree of uniformity.

But the sacred task of regionalism must be to fill in the spaces between with a riotous diversity of distinctive local traditions—preferably of productive work, not only of leisure. With this model of a potentially standardized framework for roads and public spaces filled in, softened, and humanized by local products made by local people for local purposes—authenticity of object, place, and use—I think that I can finally articulate why I love the Sears counter and the cable cars in the early morning. They embody all the authenticities, but they also welcome the respectful stranger. (Again, nature and human life jibe in obedience to basic principles of structural organization. Ecological rules and principles—flow of energy across trophic levels, webs of interaction that define the "balance of nature"—have generality corresponding to permissible uniformity in the framework of public space. But local diversity prevails because different organisms embody the rules from place to place—lions or tigers or bears as predictable carnivores of three separate continents—just as uniquely local businesses should fill the slots within a more uniform framework.)

I also now understand, with an intellectual argument to back a previous feeling, what I find so troubling about the drive for standardization, on either vernacular (McDonald's) or boutique levels (Ghirardelli Square or Harborside or Quincy Market or how can you tell which is where when all have their gourmet chocolate chip cookie cart and their Crabtree & Evelyn soap store). I cannot object to the homogenization per se, for I accept such uniformity in the essential framework of public spaces. But McDonald's introduces standardization at the wrong level, for it usurps the smaller spaces of immediate and daily use, the places that cry out for local distinction and its attendant sense of community. McDonald's is a flock of pigeons ordering all endemic birds to the block, a horde of rats wiping out all the mice, gerbils, hamsters, chinchillas, squirrels, beavers, and capybaras. The Mom-and-Pop chain stores of Phoenix and Tucson are almost a cruel joke, a contradiction in terms.

I grew up in Queens, next to a fine establishment called the T-Bone Diner (it is still there, *mirabile dictu*). The contrast between railroad-car-style diners of my youth and McDonald's of my mid-life brings us to the heart of the dilemma. Diners were manufactured in a few standardized sizes and shapes—many by the Worcester Car Company in my adopted state—and then shipped to their prospective homes. Owners then took their standard issue and proceeded to cultivate the distinctness that defines this precious item of American culture: menus abounding with local products and suited to the skills and tastes of owners; waiters and waitresses with a flair for uniqueness, even eccentricity, of verve, sassiness, or simple friendliness; above all, a regular clientele forged into a community of common care. McDonald's works in precisely the opposite way and becomes perverse in its incongruity. It enters the small-scale domain of appropriate uniqueness within the interstices of an allowable uniform framework. It even occupies spaces of widely differing designs, placements, and previous uses. It then forges this diversity into a crushing uniformity that permits not a millimeter of variation in the width of a fry from Oakland to Ogunquit.

But we are not defeated. Uniqueness has a habit of crawling back   22
in and around the uniformities of central planning. Uniqueness also has staying power against all the practical odds of commercial culture because authenticities speak to the human soul. Many of those old diners are still flourishing in New England. I am at least a semiregular at one of the finest. On my last visit, the counter lady pointed to a jar with dollar bills. A regular customer, she told me, had a sick child in need of an operation, and everyone was kicking in, if only as a symbol of support and community. No one even mentioned the jar to casual customers on that particular morning; but I was simply told to contribute. No pleas, no harangues, no explanations beyond the simple facts of the case. Our communities are many, overlapping, and of various strengths. I am proud to be part of this aggregate, forged to a coherent species by a common place of local integrity. So long as these tiny communities continue to form in the interstices of conformity, I will remain optimistic about the power of diversity. And I will remember Elijah's discovery during his flight from Jezebel (I Kings 19:11–12): "After the wind an earthquake. . . . And after the earthquake a fire. . . . And after the fire a still, small voice."

Postscript: As the dateline indicates, I wrote this essay just a week   23
before the great San Francisco earthquake of October 17. This violently altered circumstance has converted my closing line into an utterance that, if intended after the fact rather than written unwittingly before, might seem overly pointed, if not verging on cruel. In using Elijah to reemphasize my central contrast between small-scale, local, and distinctive diversity (the "still, small voice") and global effects (well represented by general catastrophes), I was, I freely confess, also trying to make a small joke about San Francisco as the location of my essay—for the 1906 earthquake did wreak its main destruction with a tremor followed by fire.

Little did I know that my attempt at humor would soon be turned   24
so sour by nature. I could, of course, just change the ending, sink this
postscript, and fudge a fine fit with history—the virtue of working with
a magazine's three-month, rather than newspaper's one-day, lead time.
But I would rather show what I wrote originally—appropriate to its moment, but not a week later—as a testimony to nature's continuing power
over our fortunes, and as a working example of another theme so often
addressed in this series: the quirky role of unique historical events both
in nature and in human life.

The earthquake has also illuminated several other points that I   25
raised about authenticity and local diversity. The World Series, although
delayed, was not moved to neutral turf but was played by honoring
baseball's powerful tradition for authenticity of place, despite the practical difficulties. My line about "people taking care of each other in small
ways of enduring significance," although meant only as a comment
about the Sears counter, soon extended to the whole region. Every fire or
flood provokes endless rumination and pious commentary about why
we seem to need disaster to bring out the best in us. But clichés are hackneyed because they are true; and the framework of this essay does put a
different twist upon a commonplace: just as McDonald's marks the dark
side by bringing the allowable conformity of large-scale public space
into the inappropriate arena of local distinctiveness, human kindness
after disaster, on the bright side, has a precisely opposite effect, for it
promotes the usual caring of small and local communities to the large
and overt domain of anonymity and callousness. Now how can this still,
small voice be heard and felt at all scales all the time?

1989

Purpose and Meaning

1. As the title of this essay suggests, Gould seems to be concerned with two
   major ideas. What are they? How and where does he link them?

2. How does the postscript affect the essay as a whole? Would the essay have
   suffered in any way if it had been omitted? Why does Gould choose to end
   the postscript with a question?

3. In paragraph 4, Gould asks: "Why does authenticity—as a purely conceptual theme—exert such a hold on us?" Answer his question using examples from your own experience.

4. Why is Gould "wary" of drawing "overly pat analogies between biological
   evolution and human cultural change" (paragraph 14)? How is the realization of the differences between the two essential to the essay's purpose?

Language and Style

1. Stylistically, this essay is informed by two voices. What are they? Where does the shift from one to the other occur? In what ways is the shift of voice reflected in Gould's word choice?

2. Paragraphs 2, 10, 14, and 15 contain long sections enclosed in parentheses. How do these sections affect the essay's stylistic design? Considering the essay's purpose, is Gould's use of parenthetical information an appropriate addition to his purpose?

3. In paragraph 14, Gould claims that he is wary of soft analogies. Why? What is the primary problem with using them?

Strategy and Structure

1. What is the organizational pattern used in paragraphs 1 through 12? How does paragraph 12 function in the overall design of the essay?

2. What is the organizational strategy used in paragraph 21? What other types of strategy are evident in the essay?

Thinking and Writing

1. Write an essay confirming or refuting the "appeal of the authentic" in today's world. Use examples from your own experience to support your view.

2. Think of instances where using pat or false analogies to support an idea resulted in more confusion than enlightenment. Write an essay on this topic.

3. In his postscript, Gould points out that clichés are hackneyed because they are true. Select several clichés whose truths might serve as testimony to the goodness of human nature in times of crisis, and develop an essay focusing on relevant truths illustrated by clichés.

Muller Bros. Moving & Storage

I own many old and beautiful books, classics of natural history bound in leather and illustrated with hand-colored plates. But no item in my collection comes close in personal value to a modest volume, bound in gray cloth and published in 1892: *Studies of English Grammar*, by J. M.

Greenwood, Superintendent of Schools in Kansas City. The book belonged to my grandfather, a Hungarian immigrant. He wrote on the title page, in an elegant European hand: "Prop. of Joseph A. Rosenberg, New York." Just underneath, he added in pencil the most eloquent of all possible lines: "I have landed. Sept. 11, 1901."

Papa Joe died when I was thirteen, before I could properly distill   2
his deepest experiences, but long enough into my own ontogeny for the precious gifts of extensive memory and lasting influence. He was a man of great artistic sensibility and limited opportunity for expression. I am told that he sang beautifully as a young man, though increasing deafness and a pledge to the memory of his mother (never to sing again after her death) stilled his voice long before my birth. He never used his remarkable talent for drawing in any effort of fine arts, though he marshaled these skills to rise from cloth-cutting in the sweatshops to middle-class life as a brassiere and corset designer. (The content of his chosen expression titillated me as a child, but I now appreciate the primary theme of economic emancipation through the practical application of artistic talent.) Yet, above all, he expressed his artistic sensibilities in his personal bearing—in elegance of dress (a bit on the foppish side, perhaps), grace of movement, beauty of handwriting, ease of mannerism.

I well remember one manifestation of this rise above the ordinary,   3
both because we repeated the act every week and because the junction of locale and action seemed so incongruous, even to a small child of five or six. Every Sunday morning, Papa Joe and I would take a stroll to the corner store on Queens Boulevard to buy the paper and a half-dozen bagels. We then walked to the great world-class tennis stadium of Forest Hills, where McEnroe and his ilk still cavort. A decrepit and disused side entrance sported a rusty staircase of three or four steps. With his unfailing deftness, Papa Joe would take a section of the paper that we never read and neatly spread several sheets over the lowermost step (for the thought of a rust flake or speck of dust in contact with his trousers filled him with horror). We would then sit down and have the most wonderful man-to-man talk about the latest baseball scores, the rules of poker, or the results of the Friday night fights.

I retain a beautiful vision of this scene: The camera pans back and   4
we see a tiny staircase, increasingly dwarfed by the great stadium. Two little figures sit on the bottom step—a well-dressed elderly man gesturing earnestly, a little boy listening with adoration.

Certainty is both a blessing and a danger. Certainty provides   5
warmth, solace, security, an anchor in the unambiguously factual events of personal observation and experience. I know that I sat on those steps with my grandfather because I was there, and no external power of suggestion has ever played havoc with this most deeply personal and private experience.

But certainty is also a great danger, giving the notorious fallibil- 6
ity—and unrivaled power—of the human mind. How often have we
killed on vast scales for the "certainties" of nationhood and religion?
How often have we condemned the innocent because the most prestigious form of supposed certainty—eyewitness testimony—bears all the
flaws of our ordinary fallibility?

Primates are visual animals par excellence, and we therefore grant 7
special status to personal observation, to being there and seeing directly.
But all sights must be registered in the brain and stored somehow in its
intricate memory. And the human mind is both the greatest marvel of
nature and the most perverse of all tricksters: Einstein and Loge inextri-
cably combined.

This special (but unwarranted) prestige accorded to direct observa- 8
tion has led to a serious popular misunderstanding about science. Since
science is often regarded as the most objective and truth-directed of
human enterprises, and since direct observation is supposed to be the favored route to factuality, many people equate respectable science with
visual scrutiny—just the facts ma'am, and palpably before my eyes. But
science is a battery of observational and inferential methods, all directed
to the testing of propositions that can, in principle, be definitely proven
false. A restriction of compass to matters of direct observation would
stymie the profession intolerably. Science must often transcend sight to
win insight. At all scales, from smallest to largest, quickest to slowest,
many well-documented conclusions of science lie beyond the strictly
limited domain of direct observation. No one has ever seen an electron
or a black hole, the events of a picosecond or a geological eon.

One of the phoniest arguments raised for rhetorical effect by "cre- 9
ation scientists" tried to deny scientific status to evolution because its results take so much time to unfold and therefore can't be seen directly.
But if science required such immediate vision, we could draw no conclusions about any subject that studies the past—no geology, no cosmology,
no human history (including the strength and influence of religion) for
that matter. We can, after all, be reasonably sure that Henry V prevailed
at Agincourt even though no photos exist and no one has survived more
than five hundred years to tell the tale. And dinosaurs really did snuff it
tens of millions of years before any conscious observer inhabited our
planet. Evolution suffers no special infirmity as a science because its
grandest events took so long to unfold during an unobservable past.

Moreover, eyewitness accounts do not deserve their conventional 10
status as ultimate arbiters even when testimony of direct observation
can be marshaled in abundance. In her sobering book, *Eyewitness
Testimony* (1979), Elizabeth Loftus debunks, largely in a legal context, the
notion that visual observation confers some special claim for veracity.
She identifies three levels of potential error in supposedly direct and ob-

jective vision: misperception of the event itself, and the two great tricksters of passage through memory before later disgorgement—retention and retrieval.

In one experiment, for example, Loftus showed 40 students a three- 11 minute videotape of a classroom lecture disrupted by 8 demonstrators (a relevant subject for a study from the early 1970s!). She gave the students a questionnaire and asked half of them, "Was the leader of the 12 demonstrators . . . a male?"; and the other half, "Was the leader of the 4 demonstrators . . . a male?" One week later, in a follow-up questionnaire, she asked all the students, "How many demonstrators did you see entering the classroom? Those who had previously received the question about 12 demonstrators reported seeing an average of 8.9 people; those told of 4 demonstrators claimed an average of 6.4. All had actually seen 8, but formed a later judgment as a compromise between their actual observation and the largely subliminal power of suggestion in the first questionnaire.

People can even be induced to "see" totally illusory objects. In an- 12 other experiment, Loftus showed a film of an accident, followed by a misleading question: "How fast was the white sports car going when it passed the barn while traveling along the country road?" (The film showed no barn, and a control group received a more accurate question: "How fast was the white sports car going while traveling along the country road?") A week later, 17 percent of students in the first group stated that they had seen the nonexistent barn; only 3 percent of the controls reported a barn.

Thus, we are easily fooled on all fronts of both eye and mind: see- 13 ing, storing, and recalling. The eye tricks us badly enough; the mind is even more perverse. What remedy can we possibly suggest but constant humility, and eternal vigilance and scrutiny? Trust your memory as you would your poker buddy (one of my grandfather's mottos from the steps).

With this principle in mind, I went searching for those steps last 14 year after more than thirty years of absence from my natal turf. I exited the subway at 67th Avenue, walked to my first apartment at 98-50, and then set off on my grandfather's route for Queens Boulevard and the tennis stadium.

I was walking in the right direction, but soon realized that I had 15 made a serious mistake. The tennis stadium stood at least a mile down the road, too far for those short strolls with a bag of bagels in one hand and a five-year-old boy attached to the other. In increasing puzzlement, I walked down the street and, at the very next corner, saw the steps and felt the jolt and flood of memory that drives our *recherches des temps perdus*.

My recall of the steps was entirely accurate—three modest flag- 16 stone rungs, bordered by rusty iron railings. But the steps are not attached to the tennis stadium; they form the side entrance to a modest brick building, now crumbling, padlocked, and abandoned, but still announcing its former use with a commercial sign, painted directly on the brick in the old industrial style—"Muller Bros. Moving & Storage"— with a telephone number below from the age before all-digit dialing: ILlinois 9-9200.

Obviously, I had conflated the most prominent symbol of my old 17
neighborhood, the tennis stadium, with an important personal place, and had constructed a juxtaposed hybrid for my mental image. Yet my memory of the tennis stadium soaring above the steps remains strong, even now in the face of conclusive correction.

I might ask indulgence on the grounds of inexperience and relative 18
youth, for my failure as an eyewitness at the Muller Bros. steps. After all, I was only an impressionable lad of five or so, when even a modest six-story warehouse might be perceived as big enough to conflate with something truly important.

But I have no excuses for a second story. Ten years later, at a 19
trustable age of fifteen, my family made a western trip by automobile: I have specially vivid memories of an observation at Devil's Tower, Wyoming (the volcanic plug made most famous as a landing site for aliens in *Close Encounters of the Third Kind*). We approach from the east. My father tells us to look for the tower from tens of miles away, for he has read in a guidebook that it rises, with an awesome near-verticality, from the dead-flat Great Plains, and that pioneer families used the tower as a landmark and beacon on their westward trek. We see the tower, first as a tiny projection, almost square in outline, at the horizon. It gets larger and larger as we approach, assuming its distinctive form and finally revealing its structure as a conjoined mat of hexagonal basalt columns. I have never forgotten the two features that inspired my rapt attention: the maximal rise of verticality from flatness, forming a perpendicular junction, and the steady increase in size from a bump on the horizon to a looming, almost fearful giant of a rock pile.

Now I know, I absolutely *know* that I saw this visual drama, as de- 20
scribed. The picture in my mind of that distinctive profile, growing in size, is as strong as any memory I possess. I *see* the tower as a little dot in the distance, as a midsized monument, as a full field of view. I have told the story to scores of people, comparing this natural reality with a sight of Chartres as a tiny toy tower twenty miles from Paris, growing to the overarching symbol and skyline of its medieval city.

In 1987, I revisited Devil's Tower with my family—the only return 21
since my first close encounter thirty years before. I planned the trip to approach from the east, so that they would see the awesome effect—and I told them my story, of course.

In the context of this essay, my dénouement will be anticlimactic in   22
its predictability, however acute my personal embarrassment. The terrain around Devil's Tower is mountainous; the monument cannot be
seen from more than a few miles away in any direction. I bought a booklet on pioneer trails westward, and none passed anywhere near Devil's
Tower. We enjoyed our visit, but I felt like a perfect fool. Later, I checked
my old log book for that high school trip. The monument that rises from
the plain, the beacon of the pioneers, is Scottsbluff, Nebraska—not
nearly so impressive a pile of stone as Devil's Tower.

And yet I still *see* Devil's Tower in my mind when I think of that   23
growing dot on the horizon. I see it as clearly and as surely as ever,
though I now know that the memory is false.

This has been a long story for a simple moral. Papa Joe, the wise   24
old peasant in a natty and elegant business suit, told me on those steps
to be wary of all blandishments and to trust nothing that cannot be
proved. We must extend his good council to our own interior certainties,
particularly those that we never question because we regard eyewitness-
ing as paramount in veracity.

Of course we must treat the human mind with respect, for nature   25
has fashioned no more admirable instrument. But we must also struggle
to stand back and to scrutinize our own mental certainties. This last line
poses an obvious paradox, if not an outright contradiction, and I have no
resolution to offer. Yes, step back and scrutinize your own mind. But
with what?

1993

Purpose and Meaning

1. How is Gould's thesis related to the two personal anecdotes that he recounts? What is his central point?

2. Gould concludes the essay with a short question. What are some of the implications of this question?

3. What is Gould's purpose in citing Elizabeth Loftus's book in paragraphs 10
through 12? What does recounting her experiments contribute to the
essay? If the citations were removed or paraphrased, would the essay gain
or lose impact? Why?

4. In your opinion, does the essay's title effectively reflect the thesis? Would
another choice of title better reflect Gould's central concern?

Language and Style

1. What does Gould's careful selection of concrete details in the anecdotes
contribute to the essay? Does it matter, for instance, whether the steps
upon which he and his grandfather sat were flagstone or whether the step
railings were rusty iron? Explain your answer.

2. In this essay, Gould's style is marked by short paragraphs and traditional transitional devices. Compare his style in this essay with that which he employs in "Women's Brains." What differences are there? What assumptions can you make about Gould's style?

3. Examine paragraphs 4 and 5 carefully. What differences can you find in voice and tone between the two? What is Gould's stylistic purpose in shifting tone and voice?

Strategy and Structure

1. How does Gould link the personal anecdotes to his thesis? Why does he separate the two stories? Discuss the effectiveness of such a strategy.

2. How effective is Gould's concluding paragraph? Would a more theoretical explanation have been a better strategy? Explain your answer.

3. How does the structure of the essay reinforce the thesis?

4. What evidence of humor can you find in this selection? Discuss the appropriateness of humor within a scientifically based essay.

Thinking and Writing

1. Write an essay on the topic that certainty is both a blessing and a danger. Support your thesis with personal observation and experience.

2. In paragraph 10, Gould notes that Elizabeth Loftus classifies three levels of potential errors of observation. Using her categories, write an essay in which you discuss personal misperceptions and their effects.

RICHARD RODRIGUEZ

"I am a journalist," declares Richard Rodriguez modestly, for he is also a fine prose stylist. Rodriguez was born July 31, 1944, in San Francisco, California. He was educated at Stanford, Columbia, and the University of California at Berkeley, receiving a Fulbright fellowship in 1972 to study in London. Rodriguez is a writer by profession, primarily of essays and journalistic pieces. His major work is an autobiography, *Hunger of Memory; The Education of Richard Rodriguez* (1982), and *Mexico's Children* (1990). His newest work, *Days of Obligation: an argument with my Mexican father*, was published in 1992 and nominated for a National Book Award.

In *Hunger of Memory*, from which "Complexion" is taken, Rodriguez writes about his upbringing as the son of Mexican-American immigrants. He vividly recounts his education in the United States school system and explores the issues of bilingual education and assimilation. He attacks bilingual education for failing to help children assimilate and instead causing painful identity confusion between the "public" individual and the "private" individual. One's own family language, he contends, gives one a sense of belonging. When one loses that language to the public language, one's identity is lost as well. Rodriguez's straightforward and at times angry prose gives his account a raw emotional power. In the early stages of the memoir, he writes, "This is what matters to me: the story of the scholarship boy who returns home one summer from college to discover bewildering silence, facing his parents." His advanced education and studies of English Renaissance literature as a Fulbright scholar left him feeling like an "anthropologist in the family kitchen." The loss of his private self through the gradual linguistic drift from Spanish to English caused this terrible separation between himself and his family. That is why he writes, "This autobiography . . . is a book about language."

Since publishing *Hunger of Memory*, Rodriguez has worked primarily as a journalist and specialist in Hispanic affairs. He has published numerous articles on such subjects as AIDS in "Late Victorians" and cultural assimilation in "Children of a Marriage." He writes for magazines as diverse as *Time, Mother Jones, Harper's*, and *Reader's Digest*. In an interview, Rodriguez once remarked that as a journalist he is concerned with "separating the prosaic world from the poetic world." But his writing is not only about language; it is about the world as well: "I try to write about everyday concerns—an educational issue say, or the problems of the unemployed—but to write them as powerfully, as richly, as well as I can."

Rodriguez's own loss of ethnicity as recorded in *Hunger of Memory* is evident also in his essays and articles on Hispanic-American culture. His personal experience of assimilation and conflicts of language and culture, combined with a keen ear for the poetry and power of language, often move his writing beyond reportage into the realm of excellent prose.

Complexion

Complexion. My first conscious experience of sexual excitement   1
concerns my complexion. One summer weekend, when I was around
seven years old, I was at a public swimming pool with the whole family.
I remember sitting on the damp pavement next to the pool and seeing
my mother, in the spectators' bleachers, holding my younger sister on
her lap. My mother, I noticed, was watching my father as he stood on a
diving board, waving to her. I watched her wave back. Then saw her radiant, bashful, astonishing smile. In that second I sensed that my mother
and father had a relationship I knew nothing about. A nervous excitement encircled my stomach as I saw my mother's eyes follow my father's figure curving into the water. A second or two later, he emerged. I
heard him call out. Smiling, his voice sounded, buoyant, calling me to
swim to him. But turning to see him, I caught my mother's eye. I heard
her shout over to me. In Spanish she called through the crowd: 'Put a
towel on over your shoulders.' In public, she didn't want to say why. I
knew.

That incident anticipates the shame and sexual inferiority I was to   2
feel in later years because of my dark complexion. I was to grow up an
ugly child. Or one who thought himself ugly. (Feo.) One night when I
was eleven or twelve years old, I locked myself in the bathroom and
carefully regarded my reflection in the mirror over the sink. Without
any pleasure I studied my skin. I turned on the faucet. (In my mind I
heard the swirling voices of aunts, and even my mother's voice, whispering incessantly about lemon juice solutions and dark, feo children.)
With a bar of soap, I fashioned a thick ball of lather. I began soaping my
arms. I took my father's straight razor out of the medicine cabinet.
Slowly, with steady deliberateness, I put the blade against my flesh,
pressed it as close as I could without cutting, and moved it up and down
across my skin to see if I could get out, somehow lessen, the dark. All I
succeeded in doing, however, was in shaving my arms bare of their hair.
For as I noted with disappointment, the dark would not come out. It remained. Trapped. Deep in the cells of my skin.

Throughout adolescence, I felt myself mysteriously marked.   3
Nothing else about my appearance would concern me so much as the
fact that my complexion was dark. My mother would say how sorry she
was that there was not money enough to get braces to straighten my
teeth. But I never bothered about my teeth. In three-way mirrors at department stores, I'd see my profile dramatically defined by a long nose,
but it was really only the color of my skin that caught my attention.

I wasn't afraid that I would become a menial laborer because of my   4
skin. Nor did my complexion make me feel especially vulnerable to
racial abuse. (I didn't really consider my dark skin to be a racial characteristic. I would have been only too happy to look as Mexican as my
light-skinned older brother.) Simply, I judged myself ugly. And, since
the women in my family had been the ones who discussed it in such
worried tones, I felt my dark skin made me unattractive to women.

Thirteen years old. Fourteen. In a grammar school art class, when   5
the assignment was to draw a self-portrait, I tried and tried but could
not bring myself to shade in the face on the paper to anything like my
actual tone. With disgust then I would come face to face with myself in
mirrors. With disappointment I located myself in class photographs—
my dark face undefined by the camera which had clearly described the
white faces of classmates. Or I'd see my dark wrist against my long-
sleeved white shirt.

I grew divorced from my body. Insecure, overweight, listless. On   6
hot summer days when my rubber-soled shoes soaked up the heat from
the sidewalk, I kept my head down. Or walked in the shade. My mother
didn't need anymore to tell me to watch out for the sun. I denied myself
a sensational life. The normal, extraordinary, animal excitement of feeling my body alive—riding shirtless on a bicycle in the warm wind created by furious self-propelled motion—the sensations that first had excited in me a sense of my maleness, I denied. I was too ashamed of my
body. I wanted to forget that I had a body because I had a brown body. I
was grateful that none of my classmates ever mentioned the fact.

I continued to see the *braceros*, those men I resembled in one way   7
and in another way, didn't resemble at all. On the watery horizon of a
Valley afternoon, I'd see them. And though I feared looking like them, it
was with silent envy that I regarded them still. I envied them their physical lives, their freedom to violate the taboo of the sun. Closer to home I
would notice the shirtless construction workers, the roofers, the sweating men tarring the street in front of the house. And I'd see the Mexican
gardeners. I was unwilling to admit the attraction of their lives. I tried to
deny it by looking away. But what was denied became strongly desired.

In high school physical education classes, I withdrew, in the regu-   8
lar company of five or six classmates, to a distant corner of a football
field where we smoked and talked. Our company was composed of bodies too short or too tall, all graceless and all—except mine—pale. Our
conversation was usually witty. (In fact we were intelligent.) If we referred to the athletic contests around us, it was with sarcasm. With savage scorn I'd refer to the 'animals' playing football or baseball. It would
have been important for me to have joined them. Or for me to have
taken off my shirt, to have let the sun burn dark on my skin, and to have
run barefoot on the warm wet grass. It would have been very important.

Too important. It would have been too telling a gesture—to admit the desire for sensation, the body, my body.

Fifteen, sixteen. I was a teenager shy in the presence of girls. Never   9
dated. Barely could talk to a girl without stammering. In high school I went to several dances, but I never managed to ask a girl to dance. So I stopped going. I cannot remember high school years now with the parade of typical images: bright drive-ins or gliding blue shadows of a Junior Prom. At home most weekend nights, I would pass evenings reading. Like those hidden, precocious adolescents who have no real-life sexual experiences, I read a great deal of romantic fiction. 'You won't find it in your books,' my brother would playfully taunt me as he prepared to go to a party by freezing the crest of the wave in his hair with sticky pomade. Through my reading, however, I developed a fabulous and sophisticated sexual imagination. At seventeen, I may not have known how to engage a girl in small talk, but I had read *Lady Chatterley's Lover*.

It annoyed me to hear my father's teasing: that I would never   10
know what 'real work' is; that my hands were so soft. I think I knew it was his way of admitting pleasure and pride in my academic success. But I didn't smile. My mother said she was glad her children were getting their educations and would not be pushed around like *los pobres*. I heard the remark ironically as a reminder of my separation from *los braceros*. At such times I suspected that education was making me effeminate. The odd thing, however, was that I did not judge my classmates so harshly. Nor did I consider my male teachers in high school effeminate. It was only myself I judged against some shadowy, mythical Mexican laborer—dark like me, yet very different.

Language was crucial. I knew that I had violated the ideal of the   11
macho by becoming such a dedicated student of language and literature. *Machismo* was a word never exactly defined by the persons who used it. (It was best described in the 'proper' behavior of men.) Women at home, nevertheless, would repeat the old Mexican dictum that a man should be *feo, fuerte, y formal*. 'The three F's,' my mother called them, smiling slyly. *Feo* I took to mean not literally ugly so much as ruggedly handsome. (When my mother and her sisters spent a loud, laughing afternoon determining ideal male good looks, they finally settled on the actor Gilbert Roland, who was neither too pretty nor ugly but had looks 'like a man.') *Fuerte*, 'strong,' seemed to mean not physical strength as much as inner strength, character. A dependable man is *fuerte*. *Fuerte* for that reason was a characteristic subsumed by the last of the three qualities, and the one I most often considered—*formal*. To be *formal* is to be steady. A man of responsibility, a good provider. Someone *formal* is also constant. A person to be relied upon in adversity. A sober man, a man of high seriousness.

I learned a great deal about being *formal* just by listening to the   12
way my father and other male relatives of his generation spoke. A man
was not silent necessarily. Nor was he limited in the tones he could
sound. For example, he could tell a long, involved, humorous story and
laugh at his own humor with high-pitched giggling. But a man was not
talkative the way a woman could be. It was permitted a woman to be
gossipy and chatty. (When one heard many voices in a room, it was usually women who were talking.) Men spoke much less rapidly. And often
men spoke in monologues. (When one voice sounded in a crowded
room, it was most often a man's voice one heard.) More important than
any of this was the fact that a man never verbally revealed his emotions.
Men did not speak about their unease in moments of crisis or danger. It
was the woman who worried aloud when her husband got laid off from
work. At times of illness or death in the family, a man was usually quiet,
even silent. Women spoke up to voice prayers. In distress, women always sounded quick ejaculations to God or the Virgin; women prayed in
clearly audible voices at a wake held in a funeral parlor. And on the subject of love, a woman was verbally expansive. She spoke of her yearning
and delight. A married man, if he spoke publicly about love, usually did
so with playful, mischievous irony. Younger, unmarried men more often
were quiet. (The *macho* is a silent suitor. *Formal*.)

At home I was quiet, so perhaps I seemed *formal* to my relations   13
and other Spanish-speaking visitors to the house. But outside the
house—my God!—I talked. Particularly in class or alone with my teachers, I chattered. (Talking seemed to make teachers think I was bright.) I
often was proud of my way with words. Though, on other occasions, for
example, when I would hear my mother busily speaking to women, it
would occur to me that my attachment to words made me like her. Her
son. Not *formal* like my father. At such times I even suspected that my
nostalgia for sounds—the noisy, intimate Spanish sounds of my past—
was nothing more than effeminate yearning.

High school English teachers encouraged me to describe very per-   14
sonal feelings in words. Poems and short stories I wrote, expressing sorrow and loneliness, were awarded high grades. In my bedroom were
books by poets and novelists—books that I loved—in which male writers published feelings the men in my family never revealed or acknowledged in words. And it seemed to me that there was something un-
manly about my attachment to literature. Even today, when so much
about the myth of the *macho* no longer concerns me, I cannot altogether
evade such notions. Writing these pages, admitting my embarrassment
or my guilt, admitting my sexual anxieties and my physical insecurity, I
have not been able to forget that I am not being *formal*.

So be it.   15

1982

Purpose and Meaning

1. From one incident in his childhood—when his mother told him to cover his shoulders with a towel—Richard Rodriguez unfolds all of his teen years up to adulthood. "That incident," he writes, "anticipates the shame and sexual inferiority I was to feel in later years because of my dark complexion" (paragraph 1). What does this suggest about the power of a mother's words? about the fragility of one's psyche? about society's attitudes toward skin color?

2. What is Rodriguez's purpose in devoting most of the last half of this essay to a discussion of the male ideal in Hispanic society? How did the three F's of masculinity conflict with Rodriguez's interests in words, both written and spoken?

3. Is the thesis of this essay stated or implied? Explain your answer.

Language and Style

1. Complexion is the first word, and the first sentence, of Rodriguez's essay. How does this one-word beginning characterize Rodriguez's direct writing style? Does he use many words with which you are not familiar? What relationship does this help to establish between writer and reader?

2. Although this essay suggests a great deal about cultural attitudes toward skin color and about male and female roles, Rodriguez does not spell out what those attitudes are. He, like many of the writers in this collection, allows the images he creates to do the telling. What does the following dual image tell about men, women, and power: "When one heard many voices in a room, it was usually women who were talking. . . . When one voice sounded in a crowded room, it was most often a man's voice one heard" (paragraph 12)? How is this method more effective than direct commentary? How does it involve the reader?

3. Throughout the essay, Rodriguez uses Spanish terminology. What are some stylistic reasons he might do this? What are some personal reasons he, as a Hispanic, might do this?

Strategy and Structure

1. Rodriguez begins paragraphs 5 and 9 with sentence fragments which mark his age. How does this give this essay a "linear" shape? Is a linear approach a logical one to take? Explain.

2. In the early part of the essay, Rodriguez describes himself—his insecurities, his "abnormality," his failure to "fit in." In paragraphs 7 and 8 he contrasts himself with *los braceros*. Is this comparison effective? In what way does it caricature both Rodriguez and the *braceros* and consequently make both look ridiculous?

3. Because of Rodriguez's linear approach and in part because of actual circumstances, readers are left seeing his talents as a writer emerging almost directly from his dark skin. In what ways does Rodriguez employ definition to explore his development as a Hispanic American and a writer?

Thinking and Writing

1. Write an autobiography of your life from the age of six to sixteen in which you focus on some particular development, such as a talent, career interest, or personal quality. Details the events or influences—in society as well as at home—that led to this development.

2. Teenagers often are pressured by their peers to fit in—to wear the right clothes, say the right things, have the right look. However, many creative people in the arts and sciences were in fact "outcasts" in their teens. In an essay, analyze what social and personal factors may influence this phenomenon.

3. Compare and contrast concepts of masculinity or feminity in American culture and one other culture that you are familiar with.

◦━◦━◦━◦━◦━◦━◦━◦━◦━◦━◦━◦━◦━◦━◦━◦

Children of a Marriage

What is culture? 1

The immigrant shrugs. Latin American immigrants come to the 2 United States with only the things they need in mind—not abstractions like culture. Money. They need dollars. They need food. Maybe they need to get out of the way of bullets.

Most of us who concern ourselves with Hispanic-American cul- 3 ture, as painters, musicians, writers—or as sons and daughters—are the children of immigrants. We have grown up on this side of the border, in the land of Elvis Presley and Thomas Edison; our lives are prescribed by the mall, by the DMV and the Chinese restaurant. Our imaginations yet vacillate between an Edenic Latin America (the blue door)—which nevertheless betrayed our parents—and the repellent plate glass of a real American city—which has been good to us.

Hispanic-American culture is where the past meets the future. 4 Hispanic-American culture is not an Hispanic milestone only, not simply a celebration at the crossroads. America transforms into pleasure what America cannot avoid. Is it any coincidence that at a time when Americans are troubled by the encroachment of the Mexican desert, Americans discover a chic in cactus, in the decorator colors of the Southwest? In sand?

Hispanic-American culture of the sort that is now showing (the teen movie, the rock song) may exist in an hourglass; may in fact be irrelevant to the epic. The US Border Patrol works through the night to arrest the flow of illegal immigrants over the border, even as Americans wait in line to get into "La Bamba." Even as Americans vote to declare, once and for all, that English shall be the official language of the United States, Madonna starts recording in Spanish.

But then so is Bill Cosby's show irrelevant to the 10 o'clock news, where families huddle together in fear on porches, pointing at the body of the slain boy bagged in tarpoline. Which is not to say that Bill Cosby or Michael Jackson are irrelevant to the future or without neo-Platonic influence. Like players within the play, they prefigure, they resolve. They make black and white audiences aware of a bond that may not yet exist.

Before a national TV audience, Rita Moreno tells Geraldo Rivera that her dream as an actress is to play a character rather like herself: "I speak English perfectly well . . . I'm not dying from poverty . . . I want to play *that* kind of Hispanic woman, which is to say, an American citizen." This is an actress talking, these are sho-biz pieties. But Moreno expresses as well the general Hispanic-American predicament. Hispanics want to belong to America without betraying the past.

Hispanics fear losing ground in any negotiation with the American city. We come from an expansive, an intimate culture that has been judged second-rate by the United States of America. For reasons of pride, therefore, as much as of affection, we are reluctant to give up our past. Hispanics often express a fear of "losing" culture. Our fame in the United States has been our resistance to assimilation.

The symbol of Hispanic culture has been the tongue of flame— Spanish. But the remarkable legacy Hispanics carry from Latin America is not language—an inflatable skin—but breath itself, capacity of soul, an inclination to live. The genius of Latin America is the habit of synthesis.

We assimilate. Just over the border there is the example of Mexico, the country from which the majority of US Hispanics come. Mexico is mestizo—Indian and Spanish. Within a single family, Mexicans are light-skinned and dark. It is impossible for the Mexican to say, in the scheme of things, where the Indian begins and the Spaniard surrenders.

In culture as in blood, Latin America was formed by a rape that became a marriage. Due to the absorbing generosity of the Indian, European culture took on new soil. What Latin America knows is that people create one another as they marry. In the music of Latin America you will hear the litany of bloodlines—the African drum, the German accordion, the cry from the minaret.

The United States stands as the opposing New World experiment.   12
In North America the Indian and the European stood apace. Whereas Latin America was formed by a medieval Catholic dream of one world—of meltdown conversion—the United States was built up from Protestant individualism. The American melting pot washes away only embarrassment; it is the necessary initiation into public life. The American faith is that our national strength derives from separateness, from "diversity." The glamour of the United States is a carnival promise: You can lose weight, get rich as Rockefeller, tough up your roots, get a divorce.

Immigrants still come for the promise. But the United States wa-   13
vers in its faith. As long as there was space enough, sky enough, as long as economic success validated individualism, loneliness was not too high a price to pay. (The cabin on the prairie or the Sony Walkman.)

As we near the end of the American century, two alternative cul-   14
tures beckon the American imagination—both highly communal cultures—the Asian and the Latin American. The United States is a literal culture. Americans devour what we might otherwise fear to become. Sushi will make us corporate warriors. Combination Plate #3, smothered in mestizo gravy, will burn a hole in our hearts.

Latin America offers passion. Latin America has a life—I mean   15
life—big clouds, unambiguous themes, death, birth, faith, that the United States, for all its quality of life, seems without now. Latin America offers communal riches: an undistressed leisure, a kitchen table, even a full sorrow. Such is the solitude of America, such is the urgency of American need, Americans reach right past a fledgling, homegrown Hispanic-American culture for the real thing—the darker bottle of Mexican beer; the denser novel of a Latin American master.

For a long time, Hispanics in the United States withheld from the   16
United States our Latin American gift. We denied the value of assimilation. But as our presence is judged less foreign in America, we will produce a more generous art, less timid, less parochial. Carlos Santana, Luis Valdez, Linda Ronstadt—Hispanic Americans do not have a "pure" Latin American art to offer. Expect bastard themes, expect ironies, comic conclusions. For we live on this side of the border, where Kraft manufactures bricks of "Mexican style" Velveeta, and where Jack in the Box serves "Fajita Pita."

The flame-red Chevy floats a song down the Pan American Highway: 17
From a rolled-down window, the grizzled voice of Willie Nelson rises in disembodied harmony with the voice of Julio Iglesias. Gabby Hayes and Cisco are thus resolved.

Expect marriage. We will change America even as we will be   18
changed. We will disappear with you into a new miscegenation.

Along the border, real conflicts remain. But the ancient tear sepa-   19
rating Europe from itself—the Catholic Mediterranean from the
Protestant north—may yet heal itself in the New World. For generations,
Latin America has been the place—the bed—of a confluence of so many
races and cultures that Protestant North America shuddered to imagine
it.

Imagine it.   20

1988

Purpose and Meaning

1. What aspects of "Complexion" may have made you a better audience for
   the thesis of this essay?

2. In much of his writing, Rodriguez pursues a dominant theme, that of immigrants seeking refuge in the United States—primarily for jobs, to pursue
   dreams, to partake of the "land of plenty." In this essay, however,
   Rodriguez reverses those roles somewhat. What does he say Hispanics
   have to give to the United States?

3. Analyze the last line of this essay. What does Rodriguez want imagined?
   Who does he want to imagine it, and why?

Language and Style

1. While Rodriguez's language is largely concrete in "Complexion," this
   essay alternates between concrete imagery and abstract reflections. Locate
   examples of this procedure. How effective is the contrast? What tone does
   the more abstract, reflective language create?

2. Other contrasts are at work in this essay as well, such as in this sentence
   from paragraph 5: "The U.S. Border Patrol works through the night to arrest the flow of illegal immigrants over the border, even as Americans
   stand patiently in line for *La Bamba*." This is a contrast of a different kind
   however. What is its purpose? What point is Rodriguez making about the
   two cultures when he juxtaposes them syntactically in this way?

3. Rodriguez sometimes attributes human characteristics to abstractions. He
   uses this approach in "Children of a Marriage" when he writes about the
   "genius of Latin America" (paragraph 9) and when he writes that "Latin
   America knows . . . people create one another" (paragraph 11). How does
   this personification strengthen Rodriguez's characterizations?

4. Adjectives abound in this essay. Latin America, for example, has "passion," a "full sorrow, " "darker" beer, and "denser" novels. How do these
   emphatic words help Rodriguez to make his point? What culture suffers
   from the depravity of no passion, light beer, thinner novels?

Strategy and Structure

1. Rodriguez begins his essay with a giant question. Does he expect an absolute answer? Why does he provoke the reader with such an abstraction? How does the very difficulty of answering such a question help to support his thesis and lead into his extended definition?

2. Throughout this essay Rodriguez develops a series of contrasts. What are they, and where do they occur? What principle holds them together?

3. How might this essay be considered an argumentative one? What is Rodriguez's main proposition? What are his key supporting reasons?

4. Why does Rodriguez end his essay with a one-sentence paragraph? What is the effect? Does it end his argument?

Thinking and Writing

1. Characterize U.S. culture today. Is our "culture" the same in every part of the United States? Write your essay as a presentation to a group of visitors from various countries around the world.

2. Evaluate Rodriguez's evolving vision of United States and Hispanic culture in these two essays. What, ultimately, would he wish for these two cultures in terms of the American experience?

◦●◦●◦●◦●◦●◦●◦●◦●◦

Late Victorians

St. Augustine writes from his cope of dust that we are restless   1
hearts, for earth is not our true home. Human unhappiness is evidence
of our immortality. Intuition tells us we are meant for some other city.

Elizabeth Taylor, quoted in a magazine article of twenty years ago,   2
spoke of cerulean Richard Burton days on her yacht, days that were nevertheless undermined by the elemental private reflection: This must end.

On a Sunday in summer, ten years ago, I was walking home from   3
the Latin mass at St. Patrick's, the old Irish parish downtown, when I
saw thousands of people on Market Street. It was the Gay Freedom Day
parade—not the first, but the first I ever saw. Private lives were becoming public. There were marching bands. There were floats. Banners
blocked single lives thematically into a processional mass, not unlike the
consortiums of the blessed in Renaissance paintings, each saint cherish-

ing the apparatus of his martyrdom: GAY DENTISTS. BLACK AND WHITE LOVERS. GAYS FROM BAKERSFIELD. LATINA LESBIANS. From the foot of Market Street they marched, east to west, following the mythic American path toward optimism.

I followed the parade to Civic Center Plaza, where flags of routine   4
nations yielded sovereignty to a multitude. Pastel billows flowed over all.

Five years later, another parade. Politicians waved from white con-   5
vertibles. "Dykes on Bikes" revved up, thumbs-upped. But now banners bore the acronyms of death. AIDS. ARC. Drums were muffled as passing, plum-spotted young men slid by on motorized cable cars.

Though I am alive now, I do not believe an old man's pessimism is   6
necessarily truer than a young man's optimism simply because it comes after. There are things a young man knows that are true and are not yet in the old man's power to recollect. Spring has its sappy wisdom. Lonely teenagers still arrive in San Francisco aboard Greyhound buses. The city can still seem, by comparison with where they came from, paradise.

Four years ago on a Sunday in winter—a brilliant spring after-   7
noon—I was jogging near Fort Point while overhead a young woman was, with difficulty, climbing over the railing of the Golden Gate Bridge. Holding down her skirt with one hand, with the other she waved to a startled spectator (the newspaper next day quoted a workman who was painting the bridge) before she stepped onto the sky.

To land like a spilled purse at my feet.   8

Serendipity has an eschatological tang here. Always has. Few   9
American cities have had the experience, as we have had, of watching the civic body burn even as we stood, out of body, on a hillside, in a movie theater. Jeanette MacDonald's loony scatting of "San Francisco" has become our go-to-hell anthem. San Francisco has taken some heightened pleasure from the circus of final things. To Atlantis, to Pompeii, to the Pillar of Salt, we add the Golden Gate Bridge, not golden at all, but rust red. San Francisco toys with the tragic conclusion.

For most of its brief life, San Francisco has entertained an idea of it-   10
self as heaven on earth, whether as Gold Town or City Beautiful or the Haight-Ashbury.

San Francisco can support both comic and tragic conclusions be-   11
cause the city is geographically *in extremis*, a metaphor for the farthest-flung possibility, a metaphor for the end of the line. Land's end.

To speak of San Francisco as land's end is to read the map from   12
one direction only—as Europeans would read it or as the East Coast has always read. In my lifetime San Francisco has become an Asian city. To speak, therefore, of San Francisco as land's end is to betray parochialism. My parents came here from Mexico. They saw San Francisco as the

North. The West was not west for them. They did not share the Eastern traveler's sense of running before the past—the darkening time zone, the lowering curtain.

I cannot claim for myself the memory of a skyline such as the one 13 César saw. César came to San Francisco in middle age; César came here as to some final place. He was born in South America; he had grown up in Paris; he had been everywhere, done everything; he assumed the world. Yet César was not condescending toward San Francisco, not at all. Here César saw revolution, and he embraced it.

Whereas I live here because I was born here. I grew up ninety 14 miles away, in Sacramento. San Francisco was the nearest, the easiest, the inevitable city, since I needed a city. And yet I live here surrounded by people for whom San Francisco is the end of quest.

I have never looked for utopia on a map. Of course I believe in 15 human advancement. I believe in medicine, in astrophysics, in washing machines. But my compass takes its cardinal point from tragedy. If I respond to the metaphor of spring, I nevertheless learned, years ago, from my Mexican father, from my Irish nuns, to count on winter. The point of Eden for me, for us, is not approach but expulsion.

After I met César in 1984, our friendly debate concerning the hal- 16 cyon properties of San Francisco ranged from restaurant to restaurant. I spoke of limits. César boasted of freedoms.

It was César's conceit to add to the gates of Jerusalem, to add to the 17 soccer fields of Tijuana, one other dreamscape hoped for the world over. It was the view from a hill, through a mesh of tram wires, of an urban neighborhood in a valley. The vision took its name from the protruding wedge of a theater marquee. Here César raised his glass without discretion: To the Castro.

There were times, dear César, when you tried to switch sides, if 18 only to scorn American optimism, which, I remind you, had already become your own. At the high school where César taught, teachers and parents had organized a campaign to keep kids from driving themselves to the junior prom, in an attempt to forestall liquor and death. Such a scheme momentarily reawakened César's Latin skepticism.

Didn't the Americans know? (His tone exaggerated incredulity.) 19 Teenagers will crash into lampposts on their way home from proms, and there is nothing to be done about it. You cannot forbid tragedy.

By California standards I live in an old house. But not haunted. 20 There are too many tall windows, there is too much salty light, especially in winter, though the windows rattle, rattle in summer when the fog flies overhead, and the house creaks and prowls at night. I feel myself immune to any confidence it seeks to tell.

To grow up homosexual is to live with secrets and within secrets. 21

In no other place are those secrets more closely guarded than within the family home. The grammar of the gay city borrows metaphors from the nineteenth-century house. "Coming out of the closet" is predicated upon family laundry, dirty linen, skeletons.

I live in a tall Victorian house that has been converted to four   22
apartments; four single men.

Neighborhood streets are named to honor nineteenth-century men   23
of action, men of distant fame. Clay. Jackson. Scott. Pierce. Many Victorians in the neighborhood date from before the 1906 earthquake and fire.

Architectural historians credit the gay movement of the 1970s with   24
the urban restoration of San Francisco. Twenty years ago this was a borderline neighborhood. This room, like all the rooms of the house, was painted headache green, apple green, boardinghouse green. In the 1970s, homosexuals moved into black and working-class parts of the city, where they were perceived as pioneers or as block-busters, depending.

Two decades ago, some of the least expensive sections of San   25
Francisco were wooden Victorian sections. It was thus a coincidence of the market that gay men found themselves living within the architectural metaphor for family. No other architecture in the American imagination is more evocative of family than the Victorian house. In those same years—the 1970s—and within those same Victorian houses, homosexuals were living rebellious lives to challenge the foundations of domesticity.

Was "queer-bashing" as much a manifestation of homophobia as a   26
reaction against gentrification? One heard the complaint, often enough, that gay men were as promiscuous with their capital as otherwise, buying, fixing up, then selling and moving on. Two incomes, no children, described an unfair advantage. No sooner would flower boxes begin to appear than an anonymous reply was smeared on the sidewalk out front: KILL FAGGOTS.

The three-or four-story Victorian house, like the Victorian novel,   27
was built to contain several generations and several classes under one roof, behind a single oaken door. What strikes me at odd moments is the confidence of Victorian architecture. Stairs, connecting one story with another, describe the confidence that bound generations together through time—confidence that the family would inherit the earth. The other day I noticed for the first time the vestige of a hinge on the topmost newel of the staircase. This must have been the hinge of a gate that kept infants upstairs so many years ago.

If Victorian houses assert a sturdy optimism by day, they are also   28
associated in our imaginations with the Gothic—with shadows and cobwebby gimcrack, long corridors. The nineteenth century was remarkable for escalating optimism even as it excavated the backstairs, the descending architecture of nightmare—Freud's labor and Engels's.

I live on the second story, in rooms that have been rendered as 29
empty as Yorick's skull—gutted, unrattled, in various ways unlocked—
added skylights and new windows, new doors. The hallway remains the
darkest part of the house.

This winter the hallway and lobby are being repainted to resemble 30
an eighteenth-century French foyer. Of late we had walls and carpet of
Sienese red; a baroque mirror hung in an alcove by the stairwell. Now
we are to have enlightened austerity—black-and-white marble floors
and faux masonry. A man comes in the afternoons to texture the walls
with a sponge and a rag and to paint white mortar lines that create an illusion of permanence, of stone.

The renovation of Victorian San Francisco into dollhouses for lib- 31
ertines may have seemed, in the 1970s, an evasion of what the city was
actually becoming. San Francisco's rows of storied houses proclaimed a
multigenerational orthodoxy, all the while masking the city's unconventional soul. Elsewhere, meanwhile, domestic America was coming un-
done.

Suburban Los Angeles, the prototype for a new America, was char- 32
acterized by a more apparently radical residential architecture. There
was, for example, the work of Frank Gehry. In the 1970s, Gehry ex-
ploded the nuclear-family house, turning it inside out intellectually and
in fact. Though, in a way, Gehry merely completed the logic of the post-
war suburban tract house—with its one story, its sliding glass doors,
Formica kitchen, two-car garage. The tract house exchanged privacy for
mobility. Heterosexuals opted for the one-lifetime house, the freeway,
the birth-control pill, minimalist fiction.

The age-old description of homosexuality is of a sin against nature. 33
Moralistic society has always judged emotion literally. The homosexual
was sinful because he had no kosher place to stick it. In attempting to
drape the architecture of sodomy with art, homosexuals have lived for
thousands of years against the expectations of nature. Barren as Shakers
and, interestingly, as concerned with the small effect, homosexuals have
made a covenant against nature. Homosexual survival lay in artifice, in
plumage, in lampshades, sonnets, musical comedy, couture, syntax, religious ceremony, opera, lacquer, irony.

I once asked Byron, an interior decorator, if he had many homosex- 34
ual clients. "*Mais non,*" said he, flexing his eyelids. "Queers don't need
decorators. They were born knowing how. All this ASID stuff—tests and
regulations—as if you can confer a homosexual diploma on a suburban
housewife by granting her a discount card."

A knack? The genius, we are beginning to fear in an age of AIDS, is 35
irreplaceable—but does it exist? The question is whether the darling
affinities are innate to homosexuality or whether they are compensatory.

Why have so many homosexuals retired into the small effect, the ineffectual career, the stereotype, the card shop, the florist? *Be gentle with me?* Or do homosexuals know things others do not?

This way power lay. Once upon a time, the homosexual appropriated to himself a mystical province, that of taste. Taste, which is, after all, the insecurity of the middle class, became the homosexual's licentiate to challenge the rule of nature. (The fairy in his blood, he intimated.) 36

Deciding how best to stick it may be only an architectural problem or a question of physics or of engineering or of cabinetry. Nevertheless, society's condemnation forced the homosexual to find his redemption outside nature. *We'll put a little skirt here.* The impulse is not to create but to re-create, to sham, to convert, to sauce, to rouge, to fragrance, to prettify. No effect is too small or too ephemeral to be snatched away from nature, to be ushered toward the perfection of artificiality. *We'll bring out the highlights there.* The homosexual has marshaled the architecture of the straight world to the very gates of Versailles—that great Vatican of fairyland—beyond which power is tyrannized by leisure. 37

In San Francisco in the 1980s, the highest form of art became interior decoration. The glory hole was thus converted to an eighteenth-century foyer. 38

I live away from the street, in a back apartment, in two rooms. I use my bedroom as a visitor's room—the sleigh bed tricked up with shams into a sofa—whereas I rarely invite anyone into my library, the public room, where I write, the public gesture. 39

I read in my bedroom in the afternoon because the light is good there, especially now, in winter, when the sun recedes from the earth. 40

There is a door in the south wall that leads to a balcony. The door was once a window. Inside the door, inside my bedroom, are twin green shutters. They are false shutters, of no function beyond wit. The shutters open into the room; they have the effect of turning my apartment inside out. 41

A few months ago I hired a man to paint the shutters green. I wanted the green shutters of Manet—you know the ones I mean—I wanted a weathered look, as of verdigris. For several days the painter labored, rubbing his paints into the wood and then wiping them off again. In this way he rehearsed for me decades of the ravages of weather. Yellow enough? Black? 42

The painter left one afternoon, saying he would return the next, leaving behind his tubes, his brushes, his sponges and rags. He never returned. Someone told me he has AIDS. 43

A black woman haunts California Street between the donut shop and the cheese store. She talks to herself—a debate, wandering, never 44 advancing. Pedestrians who do not know her give her a wide berth. Somebody told me her story; I don't know whether it's true. Neighborhood merchants tolerate her presence as a vestige of dispirited humanity clinging to an otherwise dispiriting progress of "better" shops and restaurants.

Repainted façades extend now from Jackson Street south into what was once the heart of the "Mo"—black Fillmore Street. Today there are watercress sandwiches at three o'clock where recently there had been loudmouthed kids, hole-in-the-wall bars, pimps. Now there are tweeds and perambulators, matrons and nannies. Yuppies. And gays. 45

The gay-male revolution had greater influence on San Francisco in the 1970s than did the feminist revolution. Feminists, with whom I include lesbians—such was the inclusiveness of the feminist movement— were preoccupied with career, with escape from the house in order to create a sexually democratic city. Homosexual men sought to reclaim the house, the house that traditionally had been the reward for heterosexuality, with all its selfless tasks and burdens. 46

Leisure defined the gay-male revolution. The gay political movement began, by most accounts, in 1969 with the Stonewall riots in New York City, whereby gay men fought to defend the nonconformity of their leisure. 47

It was no coincidence that homosexuals migrated to San Francisco in the 1970s, for the city was famed as a playful place, more Catholic than Protestant in its eschatological intuition. In 1975, the state of California legalized consensual homosexuality, and about that same time Castro Street, southwest of downtown, began to eclipse Polk Street as the homosexual address in San Francisco. Polk Street was a string of bars. The Castro was an entire district. The Castro had Victorian houses and churches, bookstores and restaurants, gyms, dry cleaners, supermarkets, and an elected member of the Board of Supervisors. The Castro supported baths and bars, but there was nothing furtive about them. On Castro Street the light of day penetrated gay life through clear plate-glass windows. The light of day discovered a new confidence, a new politics. Also a new look—a noncosmopolitan, Burt Reynolds, butch-kid style: beer, ball games, Levi's, short hair, muscles. 48

Gay men who lived elsewhere in the city, in Pacific Heights or in the Richmond, often spoke with derision of "Castro Street clones," describing the look, or scorned what they called the ghettoization of homosexuality. To an older generation of homosexuals, the blatancy of Castro Street threatened the discreet compromise they had negotiated with a tolerant city. 49

As the Castro district thrived, Folsom Street, south of Market, also began to thrive, as if in contradistinction to the utopian Castro. Folsom Street was a warehouse district of puddled alleys and deserted corners. 50

Folsom Street offered an assortment of leather bars—an evening's regress to the outlaw sexuality of the fifties, the forties, the nineteenth century, and so on—an eroticism of the dark, of the Reeperbahn, or of the guardsman's barracks.

The Castro district implied that sexuality was more crucial, that 51 homosexuality was the central fact of identity. The Castro district, with its ice-cream parlors and hardware stores, was the revolutionary place.

Into which carloads of vacant-eyed teenagers from other districts 52 or from middle-class suburbs would drive after dark, cruising the neighborhood for solitary victims.

The ultimate gay-basher was a city supervisor named Dan White, 53 ex-cop, ex-boxer, ex-fireman, ex-altar boy. Dan White had grown up in the Castro district; he recognized the Castro revolution for what it was. Gays had achieved power over him. He murdered the mayor and he murdered the homosexual member of the Board of Supervisors.

Katherine, a sophisticate if ever there was one, nevertheless dis- 54 misses two men descending the aisle at the Opera House: "All so sleek and smooth-jowled and silver-haired—they don't seem real, poor darlings. It must be because they don't have children."

Lodged within Katherine's complaint is the perennial heterosexual 55 annoyance with the homosexual's freedom from childrearing, which does not so much place the homosexual beyond the pale as it relegates the homosexual outside "responsible" life.

It was the glamour of gay life, after all, as much as it was the femi- 56 nist call to career, that encouraged heterosexuals in the 1970s to excuse themselves from nature, to swallow the birth-control pill. Who needs children? The gay bar became the paradigm for the singles bar. The gay couple became the paradigm for the selfish couple—all dressed up and everywhere to go. And there was the example of the gay house in illustrated life-style magazines. At the same time that suburban housewives were looking outside the home for fulfillment, gay men were reintroducing a new generation in the city—heterosexual men and women—to the complaisancies of the barren house.

Puritanical America dismissed gay camp followers as yuppies; the 57 term means to suggest infantility. Yuppies were obsessive and awkward in their materialism. Whereas gays arranged a decorative life against a barren state, yuppies sought early returns—lives that were not to be all toil and spin. Yuppies, trained to careerism from the cradle, wavered in their pursuit of the Northern European ethic—indeed, we might now call it the pan-Pacific ethic—in favor of the Mediterranean, the Latin, the Catholic, the Castro, the Gay.

The international architectural idioms of Skidmore, Owings & 58

Merrill, which defined the skyline of the 1970s, betrayed no awareness of any street-level debate concerning the primacy of play in San Francisco or of any human dramas resulting from urban redevelopment. The repellent office tower was a fortress raised against the sky, against the street, against the idea of a city. Offices were hives where money was made, and damn all.

In the 1970s, San Francisco divided between the interests of down-   59
town and the pleasures of the neighborhoods. Neighborhoods asserted idiosyncrasy, human scale, light. San Francisco neighborhoods perceived downtown as working against their influence in determining what the city should be. Thus neighborhoods seceded from the idea of a city.

The gay movement rejected downtown as representing "straight"   60
conformity. But was it possible that heterosexual Union Street was related to Castro Street? Was it possible that either was related to the Latino Mission district? Or to the Sino-Russian Richmond? San Francisco, though complimented world-wide for holding its center, was in fact without a vision of itself entire.

In the 1980s, in deference to the neighborhoods, City Hall would   61
attempt a counterreformation of downtown, forbidding "Manhattanization." Shadows were legislated away from parks and playgrounds. Height restrictions were lowered beneath an existing skyline. Design, too, fell under the retrojurisdiction of the city planner's office. The Victorian house was presented to architects as a model of what the city wanted to uphold and to become. In heterosexual neighborhoods, one saw newly built Victorians. Downtown, postmodernist prescriptions for playfulness advised skyscrapers to wear party hats, buttons, comic mustaches. Philip Johnson yielded to the dollhouse impulse to perch angels atop one of his skyscrapers.

I can see downtown from my bedroom window. But days pass and   62
I do not leave the foreground for the city. Most days my public impression of San Francisco is taken from Fillmore Street, from the anchorhold of the Lady of the Donut Shop.

She now often parades with her arms crossed over her breasts in   63
an "X," the posture emblematic of prophecy. And yet gather her madness where she sits on the curb, chain-smoking, hugging her knees, while I disappear down Fillmore Street to make Xerox copies, to mail letters, to rent a video, to shop for dinner. I am soon pleased by the faint breeze from the city, the slight agitation of the homing crowds of singles, so intent upon the path of least resistance. I admire the prosperity of the corridor, the shop windows that beckon inward toward the perfected life-style, the little way of the City of St. Francis.

Turning down Pine Street, I am recalled by the prickly silhouette of   64

St. Dominic's Church against the scrim of the western sky. I turn, instead, into the Pacific Heights Health Club.

In the 1970s, like a lot of men and women in this city, I joined a 65
gym. My club, I've even caught myself calling it.

In the gay city of the 1970s, bodybuilding became an architectural 66
preoccupation of the upper middle class. Bodybuilding is a parody of
labor, a useless accumulation of the laborer's bulk and strength. No useful task is accomplished. And yet there is something businesslike about
habitués, and the gym is filled with the punch-clock logic of the workplace. Machines clank and hum. Needles on gauges toll spent calories.

The gym is at once a closet of privacy and an exhibition gallery. All 67
four walls are mirrored.

I study my body in the mirror. Physical revelation—nakedness—is 68
no longer possible, cannot be desired, for the body is shrouded in meat
and wears itself.

The intent is some merciless press of body against a standard, per- 69
fect mold. Bodies are "cut" or "pumped" or "buffed" as on an assembly
line in Turin. A body becomes so many extrovert parts. Delts, pecs, lats,
traps.

I harness myself in a Nautilus cage. 70

Lats become wings. For the gym is nothing if not the occasion for 71
transcendence. From homosexual to autosexual . . .

I lift weights over my head, baring my teeth like an animal with 72
the strain.

. . . to nonsexual. The effect of the overdeveloped body is the 73
miniaturization of the sexual organs—of no function beyond wit. Behold
the ape become Blakean angel, revolving in an empyrean of mirrors.

The nineteenth-century mirror over the fireplace in my bedroom 74
was purchased by a decorator from the estate of a man who died last
year of AIDS. It is a top-heavy piece, confusing styles. Two ebony-
painted columns support a frieze of painted glass above the mirror. The
frieze depicts three bourgeois graces and a couple of free-range cherubs.
The lake of the mirror has formed a cataract, and at its edges it is beginning to corrode.

Thus the mirror that now draws upon my room owns some bright 75
curse, maybe—some memory not mine.

As I regard this mirror, I imagine St. Augustine's meditation 76
slowly hardening into syllogism, passing down through centuries to
confound us: evil is the absence of good.

We have become accustomed to figures disappearing from our 77
landscape. Does this not lead us to interrogate the landscape?

With reason do we invest mirrors with the superstition of memory, 78
for they, though glass, though liquid captured in a bay, are so often less

fragile than we are. They—bright ovals, or rectangles, or rounds—bump down unscathed, unspilled through centuries, whereas we . . .

The man in the red baseball cap used to jog so religiously on Marina Green. By the time it occurs to me that I have not seen him for months, I realize he may be dead—not lapsed, not moved away. People come and go in the city, it's true. But in San Francisco death has become as routine an explanation for disappearance as Mayflower Van Lines. 79

AIDS, it has been discovered, is a plague of absence. Absence opened in the blood. Absence condensed into the fluid of passing emotion. Absence shot through opalescent tugs of semen to deflower the city. 80

And then AIDS, it was discovered, is a nonmetaphorical disease, a disease like any other. Absence sprang from substance—a virus, a hairy bubble perched upon a needle, a platter of no intention served round: fever, blisters, a death sentence. 81

At first I heard only a few names—names connected, perhaps, with the right faces, perhaps not. People vaguely remembered, as through the cataract of this mirror, from dinner parties or from intermissions. A few articles in the press. The rumored celebrities. But within months the slow beating of the blood had found its bay. 82

One of San Francisco's gay newspapers, the *Bay Area Reporter*, began to accept advertisements from funeral parlors and casket makers, inserting them between the randy ads for leather bars and tanning salons. The *Reporter* invited homemade obituaries—lovers writing of lovers, friends remembering friends and the blessings of unexceptional life. 83

Peter. Carlos. Gary. Asel. Perry. Nikos. 84

Healthy snapshots accompany each annal. At the Russian River. By the Christmas tree. Lifting a beer. In uniform. A dinner jacket. A satin gown. 85

He was born in Puerto La Libertad, El Salvador. 86

He attended Apple Valley High School, where he was their first male cheerleader. 87

From El Paso. From Medford. From Germany. From Long Island. 88

I moved back to San Francisco in 1979. Oh, I had had some salad days elsewhere, but by 1979 I was a wintry man. I came here in order not to be distracted by the ambitions or, for that matter, the pleasures of others but to pursue my own ambition. Once here, though, I found the company of men who pursued an earthly paradise charming. Skepticism became my demeanor toward them—I was the dinner-party skeptic, a firm believer in Original Sin and in the limits of possibility. 89

Which charmed them. 90

He was a dancer. 91

He settled into the interior-design department of Gump's, where he   92
worked until his illness.

He was a teacher.   93

César, for example.   94

César had an excellent mind. César could shave the rind from any   95
assertion to expose its pulp and jelly. But César was otherwise ruled by
pulp. César loved everything that ripened in time. Freshmen. Bordeaux.
César could fashion liturgy from an artichoke. Yesterday it was not
ready (cocking his head, rotating the artichoke in his hand over a pot of
cold water). Tomorrow will be too late (Yorick's skull). Today it is perfect (as he lit the fire beneath the pot). We will eat it now.

If he's lucky, he's got a year, a doctor told me. If not, he's got two.   96

The phone rang. AIDS had tagged a friend. And then the phone   97
rang again. And then the phone rang again. Michael had tested positive.
Adrian, well, what he had assumed were shingles. . . . Paul was back in
the hospital. And César, dammit, César, even César, especially César.

That winter before his death, César traveled back to South   98
America. On his return to San Francisco, he described to me how he had
walked with his mother in her garden—his mother chafing her hands as
if she were cold. But it was not cold, he said. They moved slowly. Her
summer garden was prolonging itself this year, she said. The cicadas
will not stop singing.

When he lay on his deathbed, César said everyone else he knew   99
might get AIDS and die. He said I would be the only one spared—
"spared" was supposed to have been chased with irony, I knew, but his
voice was too weak to do the job. "You are too circumspect," he said
then, wagging his finger upon the coverlet.

So I was going to live to see that the garden of earthly delights was,   100
after all, only wallpaper—was that it, César? Hadn't I always said so? It
was then I saw that the greater sin against heaven was my unwillingness
to embrace life.

César said he found paradise at the baths. He said I didn't under-   101
stand. He said if I had to ask about it, I might as well ask if a wife will
spend eternity with Husband #1 or Husband #2.

The baths were places of good humor, that was Number One; there   102
was nothing demeaning about them. From within cubicles men would
nod at one another or not, but there was no sting of rejection, because
one had at last entered a region of complete acceptance. César spoke of
floating from body to body, open arms yielding to open arms in an angelic round.

The best night. That's easy, he said, the best night was spent in the   103
pool with an antiques dealer—up to their necks in warm water—their

two heads bobbing on an ocean of chlorine green, bawling Noël Coward songs.

But each went home alone? 104

Each satisfied, dear, César corrected. And all the way home San 105 Francisco seemed to him balmed and merciful, he said. He felt weight-lessness of being, the pavement under his step as light as air.

It was not as in some Victorian novel—the curtains drawn, the pil- 106 lows plumped, the streets strewn with sawdust. It was not to be a matter of custards in covered dishes, steaming possets, *Try a little of this, my dear*. Or gathering up the issues of *Architectural Digest* strewn about the bed. Closing the biography of Diana Cooper and marking its place. Or the unfolding of discretionary screens, morphine, parrots, pavilions.

César experienced agony. 107

Four of his high-school students sawed through a Vivaldi quartet 108 in the corridor outside his hospital room, prolonging the hideous gar-den.

In the presence of his lover Gregory and friends, Scott passed from this 109 *life. . . .*

He died peacefully at home in his lover Ron's arms. 110

Immediately after a friend led a prayer for him to be taken home and while 111 *his dear mother was reciting the 23rd Psalm, Bill peacefully took his last breath.*

I stood aloof at César's memorial, the kind of party he would 112 enjoy, everyone said. And so for a time, César lay improperly buried, unconvincingly resurrected in the conditional: would enjoy. What else could they say? César had no religion beyond aesthetic bravery.

Sunlight remains. Traffic remains. Nocturnal chic attaches to some 113 discovered restaurant. A new novel is reviewed in *The New York Times*. And the mirror rasps on its hook. The mirror is lifted down.

A priest friend, a good friend, who out of naïveté plays the cynic, 114 tells me—this is on a bright, billowy day; we are standing outside—"It's not as sad as you may think. There is at least spectacle in the death of the young. Come to the funeral of an old lady sometime if you want to feel an empty church."

I will grant my priest friend this much: that it is easier, easier on 115 me, to sit with gay men in hospitals than with the staring old. Young men talk as much as they are able.

But those who gather around the young man's bed do not see 116 Chatterton. This doll is Death. I have seen people caressing it, staring Death down. I have seen people wipe its tears, wipe its ass; I have seen people kiss Death on his lips, where once there were lips.

Chris was inspired after his own diagnosis in July 1987 with the truth 117 *and reality of how such a terrible disease could bring out the love, warmth, and support of so many friends and family.*

Sometimes no family came. If there was family, it was usually   118
Mother. Mom. With her suitcase and with the torn flap of an envelope in
her hand.

Brenda. Pat. Connie. Toni. Soledad.   119

Or parents came but then left without reconciliation, some prefer-   120
ring to say "cancer."

But others came. They walked Death's dog. They washed his   121
dishes. They bought his groceries. They massaged his poor back. They
changed his bandages. They emptied his bedpan.

Men who sought the aesthetic ordering of existence were recalled   122
to nature. Men who aspired to the mock-angelic settled for the shirt of
hair. The gay community of San Francisco, having found freedom, consented to necessity—to all that the proud world had for so long held up
to them, withheld from them, as "real humanity."

And if gays took care of their own, they were not alone. AIDS was   123
a disease of the entire city. Nor were Charity and Mercy only male, only
gay. Others came. There were nurses and nuns and the couple from next
door, co-workers, strangers, teenagers, corporations, pensioners. A community was forming over the city.

Cary and Rick's friends and family wish to thank the many people who   124
provided both small and great kindnesses.

He was attended to and lovingly cared for by the staff at Coming Home   125
Hospice.

And the saints of this city have names listed in the phone book,   126
names I heard called through a microphone one cold Sunday in Advent
as I sat in Most Holy Redeemer Church. It might have been any of the
churches or community centers in the Castro district, but it happened at
Most Holy Redeemer at a time in the history of the world when the
Roman Catholic Church pronounced the homosexual a sinner.

A woman at the microphone called upon volunteers from the AIDS   127
Support Group to come forward. Throughout the church, people stood
up, young men and women, and middle-aged and old, straight, gay, and
all of them shy at being called. Yet they came forward and assembled in
the sanctuary, facing the congregation, grinning self-consciously at one
another, their hands hidden behind them.

I am preoccupied by the fussing of a man sitting in the pew di-   128
rectly in front of me—in his seventies, frail, his iodine-colored hair
combed forward and pasted upon his forehead. Fingers of porcelain
clutch the pearly beads of what must have been his mother's rosary. He
is not the sort of man any gay man would have chosen to become in the
1970s. He is probably not what he himself expected to become.
Something of the old dear about him, wizened butterfly, powdered old
pouf. Certainly he is what I fear becoming. And then he rises, this old
monkey, with the most beatific dignity, in answer to the microphone,

and he strides into the sanctuary to take his place in the company of the Blessed.

So this is it—this, what looks like a Christmas party in an insurance   129
office, and not as in Renaissance paintings, and not as we had always
thought, not some flower-strewn, some sequined curtain call of grease-
painted heroes gesturing to the stalls. A lady with a plastic candy cane
pinned to her lapel. A Castro clone with a red bandana exploding from
his hip pocket. A perfume-counter lady with an Hermès scarf mantled
upon her shoulder. A black man in a checkered sports coat. The pink-
haired punkess with a jewel in her nose. Here, too, is the gay couple in
middle age; interchangeable plaid shirts and corduroy pants. Blood and
shit and Mr. Happy Face. These know the weight of bodies.

Bill died.   130

. . . Passed on to heaven.   131

. . . Turning over in his bed one night and then gone.   132

These learned to love what is corruptible, while I, barren skeptic,   133
reader of St. Augustine, curator of the earthly paradise, inheritor of the
empty mirror, I shift my tailbone upon the cold, hard pew.

1990

Purpose and Meaning

1. This essay begins and ends with references to St. Augustine. How do these
   references reveal Rodriguez's primary theme? What is his main concern in
   the essay?

2. The essay purports to be about three interrelated topics. What are they?
   How does Rodriguez weave the three concerns into a coherent whole?

3. What is Rodriguez's perspective in the essay? In the essay's context, what
   does he mean that his sin is his unwillingness to embrace life?

Language and Style

1. What is the tone of paragraphs 70–77 and paragraphs 78–96? Does it differ
   from previous sections? Is Rodriguez's desired effect heightened or less-
   ened by his use of italicized elements?

2. How do Rodriguez's style and sentence arrangement affect the story of the
   suicide he relates in paragraphs 7–8? Does the figurative language make
   the point more effectively than literal language would have?

3. Study the language and style of paragraphs 66–69. How are these paragraphs typical of Rodriguez's style in general? What effects does he gain
   by using the techniques he does? As a reader, do you find the style effective? Why?

Strategy and Structure

1. What does the essay's structure gain (or lose) by its being divided into sections? Is such division an appropriate device for this essay? Explain your answer.

2. What is Rodriguez's purpose and strategy of inserting chronological references throughout the essay?

3. What is the function of paragraph 36? How effective is it?

Thinking and Writing

1. This essay concerns the tragedy of AIDS from the point of view of a member of the gay community. AIDS, Rodriguez points out, is "a disease like any other." Write an essay on the tragedy associated with another life-threatening disease.

2. Raised as a Roman Catholic, Rodriguez writes that his life compass's cardinal point is the tragic sense of life. Is this view a more sensible view of life than another? Write an essay on this topic.

3. Rodriguez deals with several attributes of the "straight culture" toward homosexuals, including the "theory" that homosexuality is a "sin" against nature. In light of the increasing scientific evidence that human sexual orientation is influenced significantly by genetic factors and is not exclusively a result of either upbringing or "life-style choice," is it possible to continue to argue that homosexuality is a sin against nature? Write an essay on this topic.

ALICE WALKER

Alice Walker's fiction, poetry, and essays have earned her a reputation as a clear and provocative voice for African Americans, particularly black American women. Her book *The Color Purple* (1982) received both the Pulitzer Prize and the American Book Award. Widely read and debated, it was made into a feature film in 1985 that received several Academy Award nominations. The panorama of characters in the novel are almost archetypal in the way they define the African-American experience.

Walker was born February 9, 1944, in Eatonton, Georgia, into a sharecropping family. She studied at Spellman and Sarah Lawrence colleges and upon graduation became active in the civil rights movement. Walker married a civil rights lawyer in 1967 and was divorced from him in 1976. She has one child, a daughter, Rebecca Grant.

Walker often remembers her mother, as well as her father and her childhood, in her writing. One of her earliest volumes of poetry, *Goodnight, Willie Lee, I'll See You in the Morning* (1979), contains her father's name in the title, and one essay presented here, "Father," deals with him. The essay "In Search of Our Mothers' Gardens" is essentially a tribute to her mother. But it is through her own past that Walker speaks of the collective past of black Americans. She does not, nor do her characters, live in isolation from historical and societal influences. For this reason, her novels—*The Color Purple, Meridian* (1976), and her most recent work, *The Temple of My Familiar* (1989)—are in many ways regarded as historical records. Of *Meridian*, Gloria Steinem has remarked that it "is often cited as the best novel of the civil rights movement, and it is taught as part of some American history as well as literature courses."

In her early writings, Walker's particular concern was black women in America. In 1973, she published a collection of short stories, *In Love and Trouble: Stories of Black Women*. This focus continues in her novels and a second collection of short stories, *You Can't Keep a Good Woman Down* (1981). However, in later writings, such as the collection *Living by the Word: Selected Writings* (1973–1987), Walker's concerns are universalized to include the suffering and survival of humanity as a whole. She considers issues as diverse as racism in China, Native Americans, and the nuclear arms threat. In essays like "Am I Blue?" she writes eloquently and with metaphorical subtlety about animal nature and its human implications. Always she seeks to expose faults in the American landscape. "I was brought up to try to see what was wrong, and right it. Since I am a writer, writing is how I right it." Walker once described the characters in *The Color Purple* as "all parts of myself, composites and memories and reconstructions" for which she created a "place where they could be free." She is haunted by these yearning, loving spirits. This sense of the characters and writings of Alice Walker coming from a wellspring of memory released into the present is what makes her work so richly alive and deeply rooted in history.

In Search
of Our Mothers' Gardens

> I described her own nature and temperament. Told
> how they needed a larger life for their expression. . . .
> I pointed out that in lieu of proper channels, her emo-
> tions had overflowed into paths that dissipated them.
> I talked, beautifully I thought, about an art that
> would be born, an art that would open the way for
> women the likes of her. I asked her to hope, and build
> up an inner life against the coming of that day. . . . I
> sang, with a strange quiver in my voice, a promise
> song.
>
> Jean Toomer, "Avey,"
> *CANE*

The poet speaking to a prostitute who falls asleep while he's talking—   1

When the poet Jean Toomer walked through the South in the early   2
twenties, he discovered a curious thing: black women whose spirituality
was so intense, so deep, so *unconscious*, that they were themselves unaware of the richness they held. They stumbled blindly through their
lives: creatures so abused and mutilated in body, so dimmed and confused by pain, that they considered themselves unworthy even of hope.
In the selfless abstractions their bodies became to the men who used
them, they became more than "sexual objects," more even than mere
women: they became "Saints." Instead of being perceived as whole persons, their bodies became shrines: what was thought to be their minds
became temples suitable for worship. These crazy Saints stared out at
the world, wildly, like lunatics—or quietly, like suicides; and the "God"
that was in their gaze was as mute as a great stone.

Who were these Saints? These crazy, loony, pitiful women?   3
Some of them, without a doubt, were our mothers and grandmothers.   4
In the still heat of the post-Reconstruction South, this is how they   5
seemed to Jean Toomer: exquisite butterflies trapped in an evil honey,
toiling away their lives in an era, a century, that did not acknowledge
them, except as "the *mule* of the world." They dreamed dreams that no
one knew—not even themselves, in any coherent fashion—and saw visions no one could understand. They wandered or sat about the coun-

tryside crooning lullabies to ghosts, and drawing the mother of Christ in charcoal on courthouse walls.

They forced their minds to desert their bodies and their striving 6 spirits sought to rise, like frail whirlwinds from the hard red clay. And when those frail whirlwinds fell, in scattered particles, upon the ground, no one mourned. Instead, men lit candles to celebrate the emptiness that remained, as people do who enter a beautiful but vacant space to resurrect a God.

Our mothers and grandmothers, some of them: moving to music 7 not yet written. And they waited.

They waited for a day when the unknown thing that was in them 8 would be made known; but guessed, somehow in their darkness, that on the day of their revelation they would be long dead. Therefore to Toomer they walked, and even ran, in slow motion. For they were going nowhere immediate, and the future was not yet within their grasp. And men took our mothers and grandmothers, "but got no pleasure from it." So complex was their passion and their calm.

To Toomer, they lay vacant and fallow as autumn fields, with har- 9 vest time never in sight: and he saw them enter loveless marriages, without joy; and become prostitutes, without resistance; and become mothers of children, without fulfillment.

For these grandmothers and mothers of ours were not Saints, but 10 Artists; driven to a numb and bleeding madness by the springs of creativity in them for which there was no release. They were Creators, who lived lives of spiritual waste, because they were so rich in spirituality— which is the basis of Art—that the strain of enduring their unused and unwanted talent drove them insane. Throwing away this spirituality was their pathetic attempt to lighten the soul to a weight their workworn, sexually abused bodies could bear.

What did it mean for a black woman to be an artist in our grand- 11 mothers' time? In our great-grandmothers' day? It is a question with an answer cruel enough to stop the blood.

Did you have a genius of a great-great-grandmother who died 12 under some ignorant and depraved white overseer's lash? Or was she required to bake biscuits for a lazy backwater tramp, when she cried out in her soul to paint watercolors of sunsets, or the rain falling on the green and peaceful pasturelands? Or was her body broken and forced to bear children (who were more often than not sold away from her)— eight, ten, fifteen, twenty children—when her one joy was the thought of modeling heroic figures of rebellion, in stone or clay?

How was the creativity of the black woman kept alive, year after 13 year and century after century, when for most of the years black people have been in America, it was a punishable crime for a black person to read or write? And the freedom to paint, to sculpt, to expand the mind with action did not exist. Consider, if you can bear to imagine it, what might have been the result if singing, too, had been forbidden by law. Listen to the voices of Bessie Smith, Billie Holiday, Nina Simone, Roberta Flack, and Aretha Franklin, among others, and imagine those voices muzzled for life. Then you may begin to comprehend the lives of our "crazy," "Sainted" mothers and grandmothers. The agony of the lives of women who might have been Poets, Novelists, Essayists, and Short-Story Writers (over a period of centuries), who died with their real gifts stifled within them.

And, if this were the end of the story, we would have cause to cry   14
out in my paraphrase of Okot p'Bitek's great poem:

> O, my clanswomen
> Let us all cry together!
> Come,
> Let us mourn the death of our mother,
> The death of a Queen
> The ash that was produced
> By a great fire!
> O, this homestead is utterly dead
> Close the gates
> With *lacari* thorns,
> For our mother
> The creator of the Stool is lost!
> And all the young women
> Have perished in the wilderness!

But this is not the end of the story, for all the young women—our   15
mothers and grandmothers, *ourselves*—have not perished in the wilderness. And if we ask ourselves why, and search for and find the answer, we will know beyond all efforts to erase it from our minds, just exactly who, and of what, we black American women are.

One example, perhaps the most pathetic, most misunderstood one,   16
can provide a backdrop for our mothers' work: Phillis Wheatley, a slave in the 1700s.

Virginia Woolf, in her book *A Room of One's Own*, wrote that in   17
order for a woman to write fiction she must have two things, certainly: a room of her own (with key and lock), and enough money to support herself.

What then are we to make of Phillis Wheatley, a slave, who owned   18
not even herself? This sickly, frail black girl who required a servant of her own at times—her health was so precarious—and who, had she been white, would have been easily considered the intellectual superior of all the women and most of the men in the society of her day.

Virginia Woolf wrote further, speaking of course not of our Phillis,   19 that "any woman born with a great gift in the sixteenth century [insert "eighteenth century," insert "black woman," insert "born or made a slave"] would certainly have gone crazed, shot herself, or ended her days in some lonely cottage outside the village, half witch, half wizard [insert "Saint"], feared and mocked at. For it needs little skill and psychology to be sure that a highly gifted girl who had tried to use her gift for poetry would have been so thwarted and hindered by contrary instincts [add "chains, guns, the lash, the ownership of one's body by someone else, submission to an alien religion"], that she must have lost her health and sanity to a certainty."

The key words, as they relate to Phillis, are "contrary instincts." 20 For when we read the poetry of Phillis Wheatley—as when we read the novels of Nella Larsen or the oddly false-sounding autobiography of that freest of all black women writers, Zora Hurston—evidence of "contrary instincts" is everywhere. Her loyalties were completely divided, as was, without question, her mind.

But how could this be otherwise? Captured at seven, a slave of 21 wealthy, doting whites who instilled in her the "savagery" of the Africa they "rescued" her from. . .one wonders if she was even able to remember her homeland as she had known it, or as it really was.

Yet, because she did try to use her gift for poetry in a world that 22 made her a slave, she was "so thwarted and hindered by. . .contrary instincts, that she . . . lost her health. . . ." In the last years of her brief life, burdened not only with the need to express her gift but also with a penniless, friendless "freedom" and several small children for whom she was forced to do strenuous work to feed, she lost her health, certainly. Suffering from malnutrition and neglect and who knows what mental agonies, Phillis Wheatley died.

So torn by "contrary instincts" was black, kidnapped, enslaved 23 Phillis that her description of "the Goddess"—as she poetically called the Liberty she did not have—is ironically, cruelly humorous. And, in fact, has held Phillis up to ridicule for more than a century. It is usually read prior to hanging Phillis's memory as that of a fool. She wrote:

> The Goddess comes, she moves divinely fair,
> Olive and laurel binds her *golden* hair.
> Wherever shines this native of the skies,
> Unnumber'd charms and recent graces rise. [My italics]

It is obvious that Phillis, the slave, combed the "Goddess's" hair 24 every morning; prior, perhaps, to bringing in the milk, or fixing her mistress's lunch. She took her imagery from the one thing she saw elevated above all others.

With the benefit of hindsight we ask, "How could she?" 25

But at last, Phillis, we understand. No more snickering when your   26
stiff, struggling, ambivalent lines are forced on us. We know now that
you were not an idiot or a traitor; only a sickly little black girl, snatched
from your home and country and made a slave; a woman who still
struggled to sing the song that was your gift, although in a land of barbarians who praised you for your bewildered tongue. It is not so much
what you sang, as that you kept alive, in so many of our ancestors, *the
notion of song*.

Black women are called, in the folklore that so aptly identifies one's   27
status in society, "the *mule* of the world," because we have been handed
the burdens that everyone else—*everyone* else—refused to carry. We
have also been called "Matriarchs," "Superwomen," and "Mean and
Evil Bitches." Not to mention "Castraters" and "Sapphire's Mama."
When we have pleaded for understanding, our character has been distorted; when we have asked for simple caring, we have been handed
empty inspirational appellations, then stuck in the farthest corner. When
we have asked for love, we have been given children. In short, even our
plainer gifts, our labors of fidelity and love, have been knocked down
our throats. To be an artist and a black woman, even today, lowers our
status in many respects, rather than raises it: and yet, artists we will be.

Therefore we must fearlessly pull out of ourselves and look at and   28
identify with our lives the living creativity some of our great-grandmothers were not allowed to know. I stress *some* of them because it is
well known that the majority of our great-grandmothers knew, even
without "knowing" it, the reality of their spirituality, even if they didn't
recognize it beyond what happened in the singing at church—and they
never had any intention of giving it up.

How they did it—those millions of black women who were not   29
Phillis Wheatley, or Lucy Terry or Frances Harper or Zora Hurston or
Nella Larsen or Bessie Smith; or Elizabeth Catlett, or Katherine Dunham,
either—brings me to the title of this essay, "In Search of Our Mothers'
Gardens," which is a personal account that is yet shared, in its theme
and its meaning, by all of us. I found, while thinking about the far-reach-
ing world of the creative black woman, that often the truest answer to a
question that really matters can be found very close.

In the late 1920s my mother ran away from home to marry my fa-   30
ther. Marriage, if not running away, was expected of seventeen-year-old
girls. By the time she was twenty, she had two children and was pregnant with a third. Five children later, I was born. And this is how I came
to know my mother: she seemed a large, soft, loving-eyed woman who
was rarely impatient in our home. Her quick, violent temper was on

view only a few times a year, when she battled with the white landlord who had the misfortune to suggest to her that her children did not need to go to school.

She made all the clothes we wore, even my brothers' overalls. She made all the towels and sheets we used. She spent the summers canning vegetables and fruits. She spent the winter evenings making quilts enough to cover all our beds. 31

During the "working" day, she labored beside—not behind—my father in the fields. Her day began before sunup, and did not end until late at night. There was never a moment for her to sit down, undisturbed, to unravel her own private thoughts; never a time free from interruption—by work or the noisy inquiries of her many children. And yet, it is to my mother—and all our mothers who were not famous—that I went in search of the secret of what has fed that muzzled and often mutilated, but vibrant, creative spirit that the black woman has inherited, and that pops out in wild and unlikely places to this day. 32

But when, you will ask, did my overworked mother have time to know or care about feeding the creative spirit? 33

The answer is so simple that many of us have spent years discovering it. We have constantly looked high, when we should have looked high—and low. 34

For example: in the Smithsonian Institute in Washington, D.C., there hangs a quilt unlike any other in the world. In fanciful, inspired, and yet simple and identifiable figures, it portrays the story of the Crucifixion. It is considered rare, beyond price. Though it follows no known pattern of quilt-making, and though it is made of bits and pieces of worthless rags, it is obviously the work of a person of powerful imagination and deep spiritual feeling. Below this quilt I saw a note that says it was made by "an anonymous Black woman in Alabama, a hundred years ago." 35

If we could locate this "anonymous" black woman from Alabama, she would turn out to be one of our grandmothers—an artist who left her mark in the only materials she could afford, and in the only medium her position in society allowed her to use. 36

As Virginia Woolf wrote further, in *A Room of One's Own:* 37

Yet genius of a sort must have existed among women as it must have existed among the working class. [Change this to "slaves" and "the wives and daughters of sharecroppers."] Now and again an Emily Brontë or a Robert Burns [change this to "a Zora Hurston or a Richard Wright"] blazes out and proves its presence. But certainly it never got itself on to paper. When, however, one reads of a witch being ducked, of a woman possessed by devils [or "Sainthood"], of a wise woman selling herbs [our root workers], or even a very remarkable man who had a mother, then I think we are on the track of a lost novelist, a suppressed poet, of some mute and inglorious Jane Austen. . . . Indeed, I would venture to guess that Anon, who wrote so many poems without signing them, was often a woman. . . .

And so our mothers and grandmothers have, more often than not anonymously, handed on the creative spark, the seed of the flower they themselves never hoped to see: or like a sealed letter they could not plainly read.   38

And so it is, certainly, with my own mother. Unlike "Ma" Rainey's songs, which retained their creator's name even while blasting forth from Bessie Smith's mouth, no song or poem will bear my mother's name. Yet so many of the stories that I write, that we all write, are my mother's stories. Only recently did I fully realize this: that through years of listening to my mother's stories of her life, I have absorbed not only the stories themselves, but something of the manner in which she spoke, something of the urgency that involves the knowledge that her stories—like her life—must be recorded. It is probably for this reason that so much of what I have written is about characters whose counterparts in real life are so much older than I am.   39

But the telling of these stories, which came from my mother's lips as naturally as breathing, was not the only way my mother showed herself as an artist. For stories, too, were subject to being distracted, to dying without conclusion. Dinners must be started, and cotton must be gathered before the big rains. The artist that was and is my mother showed itself to me only after many years. This is what I finally noticed: 40

Like Mem, a character in *The Third Life of Grange Copeland*, my mother adorned with flowers whatever shabby house we were forced to live in. And not just your typical straggly country stand of zinnias, either. She planted ambitious gardens—and still does—with over fifty different varieties of plants that bloom profusely from early March until late November. Before she left home for the fields, she watered her flowers, chopped up the grass, and laid out new beds. When she returned from the fields she might divide clumps of bulbs, dig a cold pit, uproot and replant roses, or prune branches from her taller bushes or trees—until night came and it was too dark to see.   41

Whatever she planted grew as if by magic, and her fame as a grower of flowers spread over three counties. Because of her creativity with her flowers, even my memories of poverty are seen through a screen of blooms—sunflowers, petunias, roses, dahlias, forsythia, spirea, delphiniums, verbena . . . and on and on.   42

And I remember people coming to my mother's yard to be given cuttings from her flowers; I hear again the praise showered on her because whatever rocky soil she landed on, she turned into a garden. A garden so brilliant with colors, so original in its design, so magnificent   43 with life and creativity, that to this day people drive by our house in Georgia—perfect strangers and imperfect strangers—and ask to stand or walk among my mother's art.

I notice that it is only when my mother is working in her flowers   44
that she is radiant, almost to the point of being invisible—except as Creator: hand and eye. She is involved in work her soul must have. Ordering the universe in the image of her personal conception of Beauty.

Her face, as she prepares the Art that is her gift, is a legacy of re-   45
spect she leaves to me, for all that illuminates and cherishes life. She has handed down respect for the possibilities—and the will to grasp them.

For her, so hindered and intruded upon in so many ways, being an   46
artist has still been a daily part of her life. This ability to hold on, even in very simple ways, is work black women have done for a very long time.

This poem is not enough, but it is something, for the woman who   47
literally covered the holes in our walls with sunflowers:

> They were women then
> My mama's generation
> Husky of voice—Stout of
> Step
> With fists as well as
> Hands
> How they battered down
> Doors
> And ironed
> Starched white
> Shirts
> How they led
> Armies
> Headragged Generals
> Across mined
> Fields
> Booby-trapped
> Kitchens
> To discover books
> Desks
> A place for us
> How they knew what we
> *Must* know
> Without knowing a page
> Of it
> Themselves.

Guided by my heritage of a love of beauty and a respect for   48
strength—in search of my mother's garden, I found my own.

And perhaps in Africa over two hundred years ago, there was just such a mother; perhaps she painted vivid and daring decorations in oranges and yellows and greens on the walls of her hut; perhaps she sang—in a voice like Roberta Flack's—*sweetly* over the compounds of her village; perhaps she wove the most stunning mats or told the most ingenious stories of all the village storytellers. Perhaps she was herself a poet—though only her daughter's name is signed to the poems that we know. 49

Perhaps Phillis Wheatley's mother was also an artist. 50

Perhaps in more than Phillis Wheatley's biological life is her mother's signature made clear. 51

1974

Purpose and Meaning

1. In the title of this essay, Alice Walker uses the possessive pronoun *our*. To whom does *our* refer? What is her purpose in writing the essay? Later in the essay, she writes of her own mother's garden. What do the gardens symbolize?

2. Why do the women Walker writes of force "their minds to desert their bodies" (paragraph 6)? How are their bodies "shrines" (paragraph 2)? What is the effect on a human being when she is made into a shrine or temple?

3. Compare George Eliot's prelude, quoted in Stephen Jay Gould's essay "Women's Brains," with these words from paragraph 10: "For these grandmothers and mothers of ours were not Saints, but Artists; driven to a numb and bleeding madness by the springs of creativity in them for which there was no release."

Language and Style

1. Strongly emotional language characterizes Walker's style early in the essay—for example, "exquisite butterflies trapped in an evil honey" (paragraph 5); "they dreamed dreams that no one knew" (paragraph 5); "their striving spirits sought to rise" (paragraph 6). Locate other instances of emotional language. What effect does such language have on the reader? Why does she write in such a lyrical, emotional voice?

2. Beginning in paragraph 13, Walker's voice becomes somewhat less lyrical and more biting. Paragraphs 19 and 37 in particular have no talk of souls or dreams or butterflies. Instead she takes a piece from Virginia Woolf, already sharp in tone, and sharpens it further with her own insertions. What effect might this have on white male readers? What effect might an essay expressive of such anger have on black women? Who is Walker probably writing for?

3. Walker uses many names to describe the black American woman: saint, "the mule of the world," artist, creator. She also lists what they might have

been: poets, novelists, essayists (paragraph 13). Why does she capitalize all the names? In paragraph 27, she lists yet more names. What is their significance? What power do names have in language? Recall Maxine Hong Kingston's "No Name Woman." Do Walker's women have individual, given names? Why not?

Strategy and Structure

1. Why does Walker begin by quoting Jean Toomer? How does this quotation relate to her later quotation from Virginia Woolf? How do these quotations help to universalize Walker's thesis? What common experiences do black women share with other women? Are hidden or uncultivated gardens unique to black women? What is the essence of Walker's argument?

2. Identify the key examples that Walker uses to organize the essay. Which two examples are more extended than the others?

3. Why does Walker wait until nearly the end of this essay to introduce her own mother? Does she want this to be an essay only about her personal search?

Thinking and Writing

1. Walker paraphrases a poem in paragraph 14 and supplies one of her own poems in paragraph 47. Analyze the meaning and effectiveness of these poems. How do they add to, or detract from, the essay?

2. Interview your mother, grandmother, or another woman close to you. Ask them whether they ever had a "garden," a talent they would like to have cultivated had their lives been different. Ask whether they *did* cultivate their talents and what advantages they had if they did; or ask what inhibited them if they did not. Take notes on your conversations and compile these notes into an organized form. Give your work a title.

3. Write your own extended definition of what it means to be a woman in American society. How does that definition change when you ask what it means to be a black woman in society?

○●○●○●○●○●○

Am I Blue?

"Ain't these tears in these eyes tellin' you?"

For about three years my companion and I rented a small house in the country that stood on the edge of a large meadow that appeared to run from the end of our deck straight into the mountains. The moun-   1 tains, however, were quite far away, and between us and them there was, in fact, a town. It was one of the many pleasant aspects of the house that you never really were aware of this.

It was a house of many windows, low, wide, nearly floor to ceiling in the living room, which faced the meadow, and it was from one of these that I first saw our closest neighbor, a large white horse, cropping grass, flipping its mane, and ambling about—not over the entire meadow, which stretched well out of sight of the house, but over the five or so fenced-in acres that were next to the twenty-odd that we had rented. I soon learned that the horse, whose name was Blue, belonged to a man who lived in another town, but was boarded by our neighbors next door. Occasionally, one of the children, usually a stocky teen-ager, but sometimes a much younger girl or boy, could be seen riding Blue. They would appear in the meadow, climb up on his back, ride furiously for ten or fifteen minutes, then get off, slap Blue on the flanks, and not be seen again for a month or more.

There were many apple trees in our yard, and one by the fence that Blue could almost reach. We were soon in the habit of feeding him apples, which he relished, especially because by the middle of summer the meadow grasses—so green and succulent since January—had dried out from lack of rain, and Blue stumbled about munching the dried stalks half-heartedly. Sometimes he would stand very still just by the apple tree, and when one of us came out, he would whinny, snort loudly, or stamp the ground. This meant, of course: I want an apple.

It was quite wonderful to pick a few apples, or collect those that had fallen to the ground overnight, and patiently hold them, one by one, up to his large, toothy mouth. I remained as thrilled as a child by his flexible dark lips, huge, cubelike teeth that crunched the apples, core and all, with such finality, and his high broad-breasted *enormity*; beside which, I felt small indeed. When I was a child, I used to ride horses, and was especially friendly with one named Nan until the day I was riding and my brother deliberately spooked her and I was thrown, head first, against the trunk of a tree. When I came to, I was in bed and my mother was bending worriedly over me; we silently agreed that perhaps horseback riding was not the safest sport for me. Since then I have walked, and prefer walking to horseback riding—but I had forgotten the depth of feeling one could see in horses' eyes.

I was therefore unprepared for the expression in Blue's. Blue was lonely. Blue was horribly lonely and bored. I was not shocked that this should be the case; five acres to tramp by yourself, endlessly, even in the most beautiful of meadows—and his was—cannot provide many interesting events, and once rainy season turned to dry that was about it. No, I was shocked that I had forgotten that human animals and nonhuman animals can communicate quite well; if we are brought up around animals as children we take this for granted. By the time we are adults we no longer remember. However, the animals have not changed. They are in fact *completed* creations (at least they seem to be, so much more than we) who are not likely *to* change; it is their nature to express themselves. What else are they going to express? And they do. And, generally speaking, they are ignored.

After giving Blue the apples, I would wander back to the house, aware that he was observing me. Were more apples not forthcoming then? Was that to be his sole entertainment for the day? My partner's small son had decided he wanted to learn how to piece a quilt; we worked in silence on our respective squares as I thought . . .   6

Well, about slavery: about white children, who were raised by black people, who knew their first all-accepting love from black women, and then, when they were twelve or so, were told they must "forget" the deep levels of communication between themselves and "mammy" that they knew. Later they would be able to relate quite calmly, "My old mammy was sold to another good family." "My old mammy was _____." Fill in the blank. Many more years later a white woman would say: "I can't understand these Negroes, these blacks. What do they want? They're so different from us."   7

And about the Indians, considered to be "like animals" by the "settlers" (a very benign euphemism for what they actually were), who did not understand their description as a compliment.   8

And about the thousands of American men who marry Japanese, Korean, Filipina, and other non-English-speaking women and of how happy they report they are, *"blissfully,"* until their brides learn to speak English, at which point the marriages tend to fall apart. What then did the men see, when they looked into the eyes of the women they married, before they could speak English? Apparently only their own reflections.   9

I thought of society's impatience with the young. "Why are they playing the music so loud?" Perhaps the children have listened to much of the music of oppressed people their parents danced to before they were born, with its passionate but soft cries for acceptance and love, and they have wondered why their parents failed to hear.   10

I do not know how long Blue had inhabited his five beautiful, boring acres before we moved into our house; a year after we had arrived— and had also traveled to other valleys, other cities, other worlds—he was still there.   11

But then, in our second year at the house, something happened in Blue's life. One morning, looking out the window at the fog that lay like a ribbon over the meadow, I saw another horse, a brown one, at the other end of Blue's field. Blue appeared to be afraid of it, and for several days made no attempt to go near. We went away for a week. When we   12 returned, Blue had decided to make friends and the two horses ambled or galloped along together, and Blue did not come nearly as often to the fence underneath the apple tree.

When he did, bringing his new friend with him, there was a differ- 13
ent look in his eyes. A look of independence, of self-possession, of inalienable *horse*ness. His friend eventually became pregnant. For months and months there was, it seemed to me, a mutual feeling between me and the horses of justice, of peace. I fed apples to them both. The look in Blue's eyes was one of unabashed, "this is *it*ness."

It did not, however, last forever. One day, after a visit to the city, I 14
went out to give Blue some apples. He stood waiting, or so I thought, though not beneath the tree. When I shook the tree and jumped back from the shower of apples, he made no move. I carried some over to him. He managed to half-crunch one. The rest he let fall to the ground. I dreaded looking into his eyes—because I had of course noticed that Brown, his partner, had gone—but I did look. If I had been born into slavery, and my partner had been sold or killed, my eyes would have looked like that. The children next door explained that Blue's partner had been "put with him" (the same expression that old people used, I had noticed, when speaking of an ancestor during slavery who had been impregnated by her owner) so that they could mate and she conceive. Since that was accomplished, she had been taken back by her owner, who lived somewhere else.

Will she be back? I asked 15

They didn't know. 16

Blue was like a crazed person. Blue *was*, to me, a crazed person. He 17
galloped furiously, as if he were being ridden, around and around his five beautiful acres. He whinnied until he couldn't. He tore at the ground with his hooves. He butted himself against his single shade tree. He looked always and always toward the road down which his partner had gone. And then, occasionally, when he came up for apples, or I took apples to him, he looked at me. It was a look so piercing, so full of grief, a look so *human*. I almost laughed (I felt too sad to cry) to think there are people who do not know that animals suffer. People like me who have forgotten, and daily forget, all that animals try to tell us. "Everything you do to us will happen to you; we are your teachers, as you are ours. We are one lesson" is essentially it, I think. There are those who never once have even considered animals' rights: those who have been taught that animals actually want to be used and abused by us, as small children "love" to be frightened, or women "love" to be mutilated and raped. . . . They are the great-grandchildren of those who honestly thought, because someone taught them this: "Women can't think," and "niggers can't faint." But most disturbing of all, in Blue's large brown

eyes was a new look, more painful than the look of despair: the look of disgust with human beings, with life, the look of hatred. And it was odd what the look of hatred did. It gave him, for the first time, the look of a beast. And what that meant was that he had put up a barrier within to protect himself from further violence; all the apples in the world wouldn't change that fact.

And so Blue remained, a beautiful part of our landscape, very   18
peaceful to look at from the window, white against the grass. Once a friend came to visit and said, looking out on the soothing view: "And it *would* have to be a *white* horse; the very image of freedom." And I thought, yes, the animals are forced to become for us merely "images" of what they once so beautifully expressed. And we are used to drinking milk from containers showing "contented" cows, whose real lives we want to hear nothing about, eating eggs and drumsticks from "happy" hens, and munching hamburgers advertised by bulls of integrity who seem to command their fate.

As we talked of freedom and justice one day for all, we sat down to   19
steaks. I am eating misery, I thought, as I took the first bite. And spit it out.

1986

Purpose and Meaning

1. If this essay were simply a description of a horse in a meadow, would it have been as interesting: Does it have a meaning beyond pure description? What comment is Walker making on societal attitudes toward animals (paragraph 5), young people (paragraph 10), and people of other cultures (paragraphs 8 and 9)?

2. Walker writes that some people "have been taught that animals actually want to be used and abused by us, as small children `love' to be frightened, or women `love' to be mutilated and raped" (paragraph 17). What happens to Blue that leads Walker to say this? What is the connection between this isolated incident and Walker's more general condemnation? Is she justified in making this generalization? How does she expect her audience to respond to this assumption?

Language and Style

1. The first sentence in paragraph 2 is six lines long. Many of the sentences are long series of dependent clauses that ramble along. How is this pattern of sentence structure similar to speech? Would a formal structure have been more effective? What relationship does this establish between writer and reader?

2. The first several paragraphs of this essay are descriptive. Here, Walker writes in a rather gentle manner. How does this voice compare to the opening of "In Search of Our Mothers' Gardens"? How is the language plainer and less dramatic?

3. By paragraph 5, language with a moral message enters the essay—a prominent characteristic seen also in "In Search of Our Mothers' Gardens." Walker discusses the ability of animals to communicate and the ability of human beings to ignore their communications. Would her essay have been more or less effective without this commentary? Would you have discerned the same message about human beings and animals without Walker's explications?

Strategy and Structure

1. Why does Walker delay getting to her commentary until later in the essay? If she had begun with a statement about how human beings fail to learn from other species, would the reader have stayed interested? In what ways is this piece more effective because of the focus on a particular horse?

2. As in many of the other essays in this collection, the author begins by establishing the reader's perspective. Walker describes the setting and gives us a sense of place. How does this make the reader feel and why?

3. Walker takes great care to describe Blue: how he stomped for an apple (paragraph 3), relished the apples she fed to him (paragraph 3), the expression in his eyes (paragraph 5), and how he observed her walking away from him (paragraph 6). In what way does this description help us to "identify" with Blue? What effect does our identification with him have on our feelings toward him? How does it prepare us for the disturbing climax in paragraph 17?

Thinking and Writing

1. In the final paragraphs of this essay, Walker raises an important issue about human beings and our conflicting attitudes toward animals. On the one hand, we love our pets and we admire animals in zoos and the wilderness. On the other hand, many people condescend to them, hunt them for sport, and kill them for food. Write an essay stating your opinion on this issue. Are we inconsistent in our treatment of other species, or are we not? Do we have a natural right to use animals as we please? Do we have an obligation—moral or otherwise—to treat them with respect and care?

2. Argue for or against one of these practices: (a) hunting, (b) eating meat, (c) keeping animals in zoos.

०●○●○●○●○●○

Father

Though it is more difficult to write about my father than about my   1
mother, since I spent less time with him and knew him less well, it is
equally as liberating. Partly this is because writing about people helps us
to understand them, and understanding them helps us to accept them as
part of ourselves. Since I share so many of my father's characteristics,
physical and otherwise, coming to terms with what he has meant to my
life is crucial to a full acceptance and love of myself.

I'm positive my father never understood why I wrote. I wonder   2
sometimes if the appearance, in 1968, of my first book, *Once*, poems
largely about my experiences in the Civil Rights movement and in other
countries, notably African and Eastern European, surprised him. It is
frustrating that, because he is now dead, I will never know.

In fact, what I regret most about my relationship with my father is   3
that it did not improve until after his death. For a long time I felt so shut
off from him that we were unable to talk. I hadn't the experience, as a
younger woman, to ask the questions I would ask now. These days I feel
we are on good terms, spiritually (my dreams of him are deeply loving
and comforting ones), and that we both understand our relationship was
a casualty of exhaustion and circumstances. My birth, the eighth child,
unplanned, must have elicited more anxiety than joy. It hurts me to
think that for both my parents, poor people, my arrival represented
many more years of backbreaking and spirit-crushing toil.

I grew up to marry someone very unlike my father, as I knew   4
him—though I feel sure he had these qualities himself as a younger
man—someone warm, openly and spontaneously affectionate, who
loved to talk to me about everything, including my work. I now share
my life with another man who has these qualities. But I would give a lot
to be able to talk grownup to grownup with Daddy. I'd like to tell him
how hard I am working to understand. And about the humor and solace
I occasionally find (while writing *The Color Purple*, for instance, in which
some of his early life is imagined) in the work.

> My father
> (back blistered)
> beat me
> because I
> could not
> stop crying.

He'd had
enough "fuss"
he said
for one damn
voting day.

In my heart, I have never wanted to be at odds with my father, but   5
I have felt, over the years, especially when I was younger, that he gave
me no choice. Perhaps if I could have relaxed and been content to be his
favorite, there would have been a chance for closeness, but because a sister whom I loved was clearly not favorite material I did not want to be
either. When I look back over my life, I see a pattern in my relationships
going back to this, and in my love relationships I have refused men who
loved me (at least for a time) if they in turn were loved by another
woman but did not love her in return. I am the kind of woman who
could positively forbid a married lover to leave his wife.

The poem above is one of my earliest as an adult, written after an   6
abortion of which my father would not have approved, in which I felt
that visceral understanding of a situation that for a poet can mean a
poem. My father far away in the South, me in college in the North—how
far away from each other! Yet in the pain of the moment and the illumination of some of what was wrong between us, how close. If he ever
read the poem, I wonder what he thought. We never discussed my
work, though I thought he tended to become more like some of my
worst characters the older he got. I remember going home once and
being told by my mother of some of the curses he was capable of, and
hardly believing her, since the most I'd ever heard my father say was
"God damn!" and I could count the number of times on toes and fingers.
(In fact, his favorite curse, when a nail refused to go in straight or he
dropped the hammer on his sore corn was "God damn the goddam luck
to the devil!" which always sounded rather ineffectual and humorous to
me, and which, thinking of it, I hear him say and see his perspiring dark
face.)

Did he actually beat me on voting day? Probably not. I suppose the   7
illegal abortion caused me to understand what living under other people's politics can force us to do. The only time I remember his beating
me was one day after he'd come home tired and hungry from the dairy
(where he and my brothers milked a large herd of cows morning and afternoon), and my brother Bobby, three years older than me and a lover
of chaos, and I were fighting. He had started it, of course. My mother,
sick of our noise, spoke to my father about it, and without asking questions he took off his belt and flailed away, indiscriminately, at the two of
us.

Why do certain things stick in the mind? I recall a scene, much ear-   8
lier, when I was only three or so, in which my father questioned me

about a fruit jar I had accidentally broken. I felt he knew I had broken it; at the same time, I couldn't be sure. Apparently breaking it was, in any event, the wrong thing to have done. I could say, Yes, I broke the jar, and risk a whipping for breaking something valuable, or, No, I did not break it, and perhaps bluff my way through.

I've never forgotten my feeling that he really wanted me to tell the   9
truth. And because he seemed to desire it—and the moments during which he waited for my reply seemed quite out of time, so much so I can still feel them, and, as I said, I was only three, if that—I confessed. I broke the jar, I said. I think he hugged me. He probably didn't, but I still feel as if he did, so embraced did I feel by the happy relief I noted on his face and by the fact that he didn't punish me at all, but seemed, instead, pleased with me. I think it was at that moment that I resolved to take my chances with the truth, although as the years rolled on I was to break more serious things in his scheme of things than fruit jars.

It was the unfairness of the beating that keeps it fresh in my mind.   10
(And this was thirty-seven years ago!) And my disappointment at the deterioration of my father's ethics. And yet, since I am never happy in my heart when estranged from my father, any more than I would be happy shut off from sunlight, in writing this particular poem I tried to see my father's behavior in a context larger than our personal relationship.

Actually, my father was two fathers.   11

To the first four of his children he was one kind of father, to the   12
second set of four he was another kind. Whenever I talk to the elder set I am astonished at the picture they draw, for the man they describe bears little resemblance to the man I knew. For one thing, the man they knew was physically healthy, whereas the man I knew was almost always sick; not sick enough to be in bed, or perhaps he was but with so many children to feed he couldn't afford to lie down, but "dragging-around" sick, in the manner of the very poor. Overweight, high blood pressure, diabetes, or, as it was called, "sugar," rotten teeth. There are certain *facts*, however, that identify our father as the same man; one of which is that, in the 1930s, my father was one of the first black men to vote in Eatonton, Georgia, among a group of men like himself he helped organize, mainly poor sharecroppers with large families, totally at the mercy of the white landlords. He voted for Roosevelt. He was one of the leading supporters of the local one-room black school, and according to everyone who knew him then, including my older brothers and sister, believed in education above all else. Years later, when I knew him, he seemed fearful of both education and politics and disappointed and resentful as well.

And why not? Though he risked his life and livelihood to vote   13
more than once, nothing much changed in his world. Cotton prices con-

tinued low. Dairying was hard. White men and women continued to run things, badly. In his whole life my father never had a vacation. (Of course my mother had less of one: she could not even get in the car and drive off to town, as he could.) Education merely seemed to make his children more critical of him. When I went south in the mid-sixties to help register voters, I stopped by our house to say hello but never told either of my parents what I planned to do. I didn't want them to worry about my safety, and it never occurred to me that they cared much about the vote. My father was visibly ill, paranoid, complaining the whole time of my mother's religious activities (she had become a Jehovah's Witness). Then, for no apparent reason, he would come out with one of those startlingly intelligent comments about world affairs or some absolutely clear insight into the deficiencies of national leaders, and I would be reminded of the father I didn't know.

For years I have held on to another early memory of my life between the ages of two and four. Every afternoon a tired but jolly very black man came up to me with arms outstretched. I flew into them to be carried, to be hugged, to be kissed. For years I thought this black man was my father. But no. He was my oldest brother, Fred, whose memories of my father are, surprisingly, as painful as *my* memories of him, because as my father's first child, and a son, he was subjected to my father's very confused notions of what constituted behavior suitable for a male. And of course my father himself didn't really know. He was in his late teens, a child himself, when he married. His mother had been murdered, by a man who claimed to love her, when he was eleven. His father, to put it very politely, drank, and terrorized his children. 14

My father was so confused that when my sister Ruth appeared in the world and physically resembled his mother, and sounded like his mother, and had similar expressions, he rejected her and missed no opportunity that I ever saw to put her down. I, of course, took the side of my sister, forfeiting my chance to be my father's favorite among the second set of children, as my oldest sister, Mamie, was favorite among the first. In her case the favoritism seemed outwardly caused by her very light color, and of course she was remarkably intelligent as well. In my case, my father seemed partial to me because of my "smartness" and forthrightness, but more obviously because of my hair, which was the longest and "best" in the family. 15

And yet, my father taught me two things that have been important to me: he taught me not to bother telling lies, because the listener might be delighted with the truth, and he told me never to cut my hair. Though I have tried not to lie, the sister he rejected and I loved became a beautician, and one of the first things she did—partly in defiance of him—was to cut my shoulder-blade-length hair. I did not regret it so much while in high school and college (everyone kept their hair short, it 16 seemed), but years later, after I married, I grew it long again, almost as long as it had been when I was growing up. I'd had it relaxed to feathers. When I walked up to my father, as he was talking to a neighbor, I stooped a little and placed his hand on my head. I thought he'd be pleased. "A woman's hair is her glory," he'd always said. He paid little attention. When the black power movement arrived, with its emphasis on cropped natural hair, I did the job myself, filling the face bowl and bathroom floor with hair and shocking my husband when he arrived home.

Only recently have I come to believe he was right in wanting me to   17
keep my hair. After years of short hair, of cutting my hair back each time it raised its head, so to speak, I have begun to feel each time as if I am mutilating my antennae (which is how Rastafarians, among others, think of hair) and attenuating my power. It seems imperative not to cut my hair anymore.

I didn't listen to my father because I assumed he meant that in the   18
eyes of a *man*, in his eyes, a woman's hair is her glory (unfortunately, he wore his own head absolutely clean-shaven all his life); and that is probably what he did mean. But now I begin to sense something else, that there is power (would an ancient translation of glory *be* power?) in uncut hair itself. The power (and glory) perhaps of the untamed, the undomesticated; in short, the wild. A wildness about the head, as the Rastas have discovered, places us somehow in the loose and spacious freedom of Jah's universe. Hippies, of course, knew this, too.

As I write, my own hair reaches just below my ears. It is at the dan-   19
gerous stage at which I usually butt my forehead against the mirror and in resignation over not knowing "what to do with it" cut it off. But this time I have thought ahead and have encased it in braids made of someone else's hair. I expect to wear them, braces for the hair, so to speak, until my own hair replaces them. Eventually I will be able, as I was when a child, to tie my hair under my chin. But mostly I would like to set it free.

My father would have loved Jesse Jackson. On the night Jesse ad-   20
dressed the Democratic convention I stayed close to my radio. In my backwoods cabin, linked to the world only by radio, I felt something like my father must have, since he lived most of his life before television and far from towns. He would have appreciated Jesse's oratorical gift, and, unlike some newscasters who seemed to think of it primarily as technique, he would have felt, as I did, the transformation of the spirit of the man implicit in the words he chose to say. He would have felt, as I did, that in asking for forgiveness as well as votes and for patience as well as commitment to the Democratic party, Jackson lost nothing and won almost everything: a cleared conscience and peace of mind.

My father was never able to vote for a black candidate for any national or local political office. By the time black people were running for office and occasionally winning elections, in the late sixties and early seventies, he was too sick to respond with the exhilaration he must have felt. On the night of Jackson's speech, I felt it for him; along with the grief that in neither of our lifetimes is the United States likely to choose the best leadership offered to it. This is the kind of leader, the kind of ever-growing, ever-expanding spirit *you* might have been, Daddy, I thought—and damn it, I love you for what you might have been. And thinking of you now, merging the two fathers that you were, remembering how tightly I hugged you as a small child returning home after two long months at a favorite aunt's, and with what apparent joy you lifted me beside your cheek; knowing now, at forty, what it takes out of body and spirit to go and how much more to stay, and having learned, too, by now, some of the pitiful confusions in behavior caused by ignorance and pain, I love you no less for what you were.

1984

Purpose and Meaning

1. Walker notes in the opening paragraph that "writing about people helps us to understand them." How is this so? She continues, "understanding them helps us to accept them as a part of ourselves." How is this similar to Margaret Atwood's thesis in "Travels Back"? What, specifically, is Walker's thesis?

2. Recall Richard Rodriguez's account of his mother telling him to cover his dark skin with a towel ("Complexion"). Rodriguez associates that incident with his growth as an individual and as a writer. Walker tells of an incident that was just as significant in her development. She breaks a fruit jar and subsequently tells her father the truth about it, anticipating his delight with her honesty (paragraphs 8 and 9). How does this incident affect her as an individual? How does her need to tell the truth come through in her writing?

3. In paragraph 12, as Walker struggles to describe her and her siblings' father, she writes, "There are certain *facts*, however, that identify our fathers as the same man." What is the difference between the "facts" and the rest of her description? How much, if anything, can we know of other people that is pure fact?

Language and Style

1. In this essay there is very little imagery or metaphor. Walker's language is direct and unembellished. Is the absence of metaphor notable? How does it affect the style and the reader's response?

2. In what ways is Walker's writing in this essay more conversational than in many of the other essays in this collection?

Strategy and Structure

1. At the beginning of the essay, Walker announces that she is writing about her father in an effort to understand him. Is this opening effective? What reason could she have for avoiding a more leisurely or more poetic introduction?

2. This essay is obviously not fiction, but neither is it purely autobiographical. It is closer to journal writing than anything else. What makes this writing journal-like? Why is this an appropriate approach for Walker's subject?

3. Walker alternates between discussion of herself as a child and as an adult. How does this juxtaposition aid the reader in understanding both Walker and her father? If we were limited to insights about her early relationship with him, would our understanding be as deep? Of whom do we have a better, more rounded understanding—Walker or her father? Why?

4. Beginning in paragraph 14, Walker takes a long diversion about hair and its social and political power. Is this an appropriate diversion? Why or why not?

Thinking and Writing

1. Adopting Walker's journal-like method of writing, explore your relationship with your father. As she did, make reference to both your past and present, and give your readers factual information about your father.

2. Examine the relationship of style, subject matter, and the reader's response in "Father."

3. Compare Walker's writing in this essay with Maxine Hong Kingston's in "No Name Woman." Consider writing styles, such as the use of figurative language and directness of speech. Also consider issues of content, such as cultural backgrounds and attitudes toward telling the truth.

ANNIE DILLARD

Annie Dillard was born April 30, 1945, in Pittsburgh, Pennsylvania. She received a B.A. from Hollins College in 1967 and an M.A. the following year. In 1974, she published a collection of poetry, *Tickets for a Prayer Wheel*, and her highly acclaimed *Pilgrim at Tinker Creek*, for which she received a Pulitzer Prize for nonfiction. Since then, Dillard has published several other books, including the essay collection *Teaching a Stone to Talk* (1982); a personal memoir, *An American Childhood* (1987); and *A Writing Life* (1989). Dillard's philosophically based nature writing, which stems from her fascination with the natural world and its mysteries, has been compared by many to that of Henry David Thoreau's masterpiece, *Walden*.

Echoes of Thoreau's vow to "live life to the bone" and to "suck out all its marrow" can be heard in Dillard's "Living Like Weasels" when she says, "I would like to live as I should, as the weasel lives as he should. And I suspect that for me the way is like the weasel's: open to time and death painlessly, noticing everything, remembering nothing, choosing the given with a fierce and pointed will." And in her nature writing, she does notice and examine everything intensely, whether her topic is an old snakeskin, a total eclipse, or a weasel. Interwoven with these observations is a fascination with mystery as a manifestation of God. Typically, in essays like "Singing with the Fundamentalists," Dillard finds that all of life is holy. One critic has written that "Dillard brings to her work an artist's eye, a scientist's curiosity, a metaphysician's mind, all woven together in what might be called, essentially, a theologian's quest." Dillard herself admits, "I am a wanderer with a background in theology and a penchant for quirky facts."

Not only does Dillard work as a writer and teach writing, but she also writes about the writing process. In an interview, she lamented the mistaken impression some readers have that "you just sit on a tree stump and take dictation from some little chipmunk!" Instead, she cautions, writing is "hard, conscious, terribly frustrating work!" The rich, poetic journey into nature, its mystery and wonder, that Dillard takes in *Pilgrim at Tinker Creek*, was written over an eight-month period at a pace of fifteen to sixteen hours a day, seven days a week—in a library, not in the wilderness. A voracious reader and researcher, Dillard has collected some fifty volumes of notes from her readings. She lives six months of each year near Bellingham, Washington, the locale of her Northwest frontier novel, *The Living* (1992).

"Writing is work" is one message that is clear from Dillard's mounting list of publications. She is a painstaking researcher, writer, and reviser. But there is also present in her writing the unmistakable mark of inspiration.

An American Childhood

One Sunday afternoon Mother wandered through our kitchen, where Father was making a sandwich and listening to the ball game. The Pirates were playing the New York Giants at Forbes Field. In those days, the Giants had a utility infielder named Wayne Terwilliger. Just as Mother passed through, the radio announcer cried—with undue drama—"Terwilliger bunts one!" 1

"Terwilliger bunts one?" Mother cried back, stopped short. She turned. "Is that English?" 2

"The player's name is Terwilliger," Father said. "He bunted." 3

"That's marvelous," Mother said. " 'Terwilliger bunts one.' No wonder you listen to baseball. 'Terwilliger bunts one.' " 4

For the next seven or eight years, Mother made this surprising string of syllables her own. Testing a microphone, she repeated, "Terwilliger bunts one"; testing a pen or a typewriter, she wrote it. If, as happened surprisingly often in the course of various improvised gags, she pretended to whisper something else in my ear, she actually whispered, "Terwilliger bunts one." Whenever someone used a French phrase, or a Latin one, she answered solemnly, "Terwilliger bunts one." If Mother had had, like Andrew Carnegie, the opportunity to cook up a motto for a coat of arms, hers would have read simply and tellingly, "Terwilliger bunts one." (Carnegie's was "Death to Privilege.") 5

She served us with other words and phrases. On a Florida trip, she repeated tremulously, "That . . . is a royal poinciana." I don't remember the tree; I remember the thrill in her voice. She pronounced it carefully, and spelled it. She also liked to say "portulaca." 6

The drama of the words "Tamiami Trail" stirred her, we learned on the same Florida trip. People built Tampa on one coast, and they built Miami on another. Then—the height of visionary ambition and folly—they piled a slow, tremendous road through the terrible Everglades to connect them. To build the road, men stood sunk in muck to their armpits. They fought off cottonmouth moccasins and six-foot alligators. They slept in boats, wet. They blasted muck with dynamite, cut jungle with machetes; they laid logs, dragged drilling machines, hauled dredges, heaped limestone. The road took fourteen years to build up by the shovelful, a Panama Canal in reverse, and cost hundreds of lives from tropical, mosquito-carried diseases. Then, capping it all, some genius thought of the word Tamiami: they called the road from Tampa to Miami, this very road under our spinning wheels, the Tamiami Trail. Some called it Alligator Alley. Anyone could drive over this road without a thought. 7

Hearing this, moved, I thought all the suffering of road building   8
was worth it (it wasn't my suffering), now that we had this new thing to
hang these new words on—Alligator Alley for those who liked things
cute, and, for connoisseurs like Mother, for lovers of the human drama
in all its boldness and terror, the Tamiami Trail.

Back home, Mother cut clips from reels of talk, as it were, and   9
played them back at leisure. She noticed that many Pittsburghers confuse "leave" and "let." One kind relative brightened our morning by
mentioning why she'd brought her son to visit: "He wanted to come
with me, so I left him." Mother filled in Amy and me on locutions we
missed. "I can't do it on Friday," her pretty sister told a crowded dinner
party, "because Friday's the day I lay in the stores."

(All unconsciously, though, we ourselves used some pure   10
Pittsburghisms. We said "tele pole," pronounced "telly pole," for that
splintery sidewalk post I loved to climb. We said "slippy"—the side-
walks are "slippy." We said, "That's all the farther I could go." And we
said, as Pittsburghers do say, "This glass needs washed," or "The dog
needs walked"—a usage our father eschewed; he knew it was not standard English, nor even comprehensible English, but he never let on.)

"Spell 'poinsettia,'" Mother would throw out at me, smiling with   11
pleasure. "Spell 'sherbet.'" The idea was not to make us whizzes, but,
quite the contrary, to remind us—and I, especially, needed reminding—
that we didn't know it all just yet.

"There's a deer standing in the front hall," she told me one quiet   12
evening in the country.

"Really?"   13

"No. I just wanted to tell you something once without your saying,   14
'I know.'"

Supermarkets in the middle 1950s began luring, or bothering, cus-   15
tomers by giving out Top Value Stamps or Green Stamps. When, shopping with Mother, we got to the head of the checkout line, the checker,
always a young man, asked, "Save stamps?"

"No," Mother replied genially, week after week, "I build model   16
airplanes." I believe she originated this line. It took me years to determine where the joke lay.

Anyone who met her verbal challenges she adored. She had   17
surgery on one of her eyes. On the operating table, just before she
conked out, she appealed feelingly to the surgeon, saying, as she had
been planning to say for weeks, "Will I be able to play the piano?" "Not
on me," the surgeon said. "You won't pull that old one on me."

It was, indeed, an old one. The surgeon was supposed to answer,   18
"Yes, my dear, brave woman, you will be able to play the piano after
this operation," to which Mother intended to reply, "Oh, good, I've always wanted to play the piano." This pat scenario bored her; she loved

having it interrupted. It must have galled her that usually her acquaintances were so predictably unalert; it must have galled her that, for the length of her life, she could surprise everyone so continually, so easily, when she had been the same all along. At any rate, she loved anyone who, as she put it, saw it coming, and called her on it.

She regarded the instructions on bureaucratic forms as straight   19
lines. "Do you advocate the overthrow of the United States government by force or violence?" After some thought she wrote, "Force." She regarded children, even babies, as straight men. When Molly learned to crawl, Mother delighted in buying her gowns with drawstrings at the bottom, like Swee'pea's, because, as she explained energetically, you could easily step on the drawstring without the baby's noticing, so that she crawled and crawled and crawled and never got anywhere except into a small ball at the gown's top.

When we children were young, she mothered us tenderly and de-   20
pendably; as we got older, she resumed her career of anarchism. She collared us into her gags. If she answered the phone on a wrong number, she told the caller, "Just a minute," and dragged the receiver to Amy or me, saying, "Here, take this, your name is Cecile," or, worse, just, "It's for you." You had to think on your feet. But did you want to perform well as Cecile, or did you want to take pity on the wretched caller?

During a family trip to the Highland Park Zoo, Mother and I were   21
alone for a minute. She approached a young couple holding hands on a bench by the seals, and addressed the young man in dripping tones: "Where have you been? Still got those baby-blue eyes; always did slay me. And this"—a swift nod at the dumbstruck young woman, who had removed her hand from the man's—"must be the one you were telling me about. She's not so bad, really, as you used to make out. But listen, you know how I miss you, you know where to reach me, same old place. And there's Ann over there—see how she's grown? See the blue eyes?"

And off she sashayed, taking me firmly by the hand, and leading   22
us around briskly past the monkey house and away. She cocked an ear back, and both of us heard the desperate man begin, in a high-pitched wail, "I swear, I never saw her before in my life . . ."

On a long, sloping beach by the ocean, she lay stretched out sun-   23
ning with Father and friends, until the conversation gradually grew tedious, when without forethought she gave a little push with her heel and rolled away. People were stunned. She rolled deadpan and apparently effortlessly, arms and legs extended and tidy, down the beach to the distant water's edge, where she lay at ease just as she had been, but half in the surf, and well out of earshot.

She dearly loved to fluster people by throwing out a game's rules   24 at whim—when she was getting bored, losing in a dull sort of way, and when everybody else was taking it too seriously. If you turned your back, she moved the checkers around on the board. When you got them all straightened out, she denied she'd touched them; the next time you turned your back, she lined them up on the rug or hid them under your chair. In a betting rummy game called Michigan, she routinely played out of turn, or called out a card she didn't hold, or counted backward, simply to amuse herself by causing an uproar and watching the rest of us do double takes and have fits. (Much later, when serious suitors came to call, Mother subjected them to this fast card game as a trial by ordeal; she used it as an intelligence test and a measure of spirit. If the poor man could stay a round without breaking down or running out, he got to marry one of us, if he still wanted to.)

She excelled at bridge, playing fast and boldly, but when the stakes   25
were low and the hands dull, she bid slams for the devilment of it, or raised her opponents' suit to bug them, or showed her hand, or tossed her cards in a handful behind her back in a characteristic swift motion accompanied by a vibrantly innocent look. It drove our stolid father crazy. The hand was over before it began, and the guests were appalled. How do you score it, who deals now, what do you do with a crazy person who is having so much fun? Or they were down seven, and the guests were appalled. "Pam!" "Dammit, Pam!" He groaned. What ails such people? What on earth possesses them? He rubbed his face.

She was an unstoppable force; she never let go. When we moved   26
across town, she persuaded the U.S. Post Office to let her keep her old address—forever—because she'd had stationery printed. I don't know how she did it. Every new post office worker, over decades, needed to learn that although the Doaks' mail is addressed to here, it is delivered to there.

Mother's energy and intelligence suited her for a greater role in a   27
larger arena—mayor of New York, say—than the one she had. She followed American politics closely; she had been known to vote for Democrats. She saw how things should be run, but she had nothing to run but our household. Even there, small minds bugged her; she was smarter than the people who designed the things she had to use all day for the length of her life.

"Look," she said. "Whoever designed this corkscrew never used   28
one. Why would anyone sell it without trying it out?" So she invented a better one. She showed me a drawing of it. The spirit of American enterprise never faded in Mother. If capitalizing and tooling up had been as interesting as theorizing and thinking up, she would have fired up a new factory every week, and chaired several hundred corporations.

"It grieves me," she would say, "it grieves my heart," that the com-   29
pany that made one superior product packaged it poorly, or took the

wrong tack in its advertising. She knew, as she held the thing mournfully in her two hands, that she'd never find another. She was right. We children wholly sympathized, and so did Father; what could she do, what could anyone do, about it? She was Samson in chains. She paced.

She didn't like the taste of stamps so she didn't lick stamps; she licked the corner of the envelope instead. She glued sandpaper to the sides of kitchen drawers, and under kitchen cabinets, so she always had a handy place to strike a match. She designed, and hounded workmen to build against all norms, doubly wide kitchen counters and elevated bathroom sinks. To splint a finger, she stuck it in a lightweight cigar tube. Conversely, to protect a pack of cigarettes, she carried it in a Band-Aid box. She drew plans for an over-the-finger toothbrush for babies, an oven rack that slid up and down, and—the family favorite—Lendalarm. Lendalarm was a beeper you attached to books (or tools) you loaned friends. After ten days, the beeper sounded. Only the rightful owner could silence it.

She repeatedly reminded us of P. T. Barnum's dictum: You could sell anything to anybody if you marketed it right. The adman who thought of making Americans believe they needed underarm deodorant was a visionary. So, too, was the hero who made a success of a new product, Ivory soap. The executives were horrified, Mother told me, that a cake of this stuff floated. Soap wasn't supposed to float. Anyone would be able to tell it was mostly whipped-up air. Then some inspired adman made a leap: Advertise that it floats. Flaunt it. The rest is history.

She respected the rare few who broke through to new ways. "Look," she'd say, "here's an intelligent apron." She called upon us to admire intelligent control knobs and intelligent pan handles, intelligent andirons and picture frames and knife sharpeners. She questioned everything, every pair of scissors, every knitting needle, gardening glove, tape dispenser. Hers was a restless mental vigor that just about ignited the dumb household objects with its force.

Torpid conformity was a kind of sin; it was stupidity itself, the mighty stream against which Mother would never cease to struggle. If you held no minority opinions, or if you failed to risk total ostracism for them daily, the world would be a better place without you.

Always I heard Mother's emotional voice asking Amy and me the same few questions: "Is that your own idea? Or somebody else's?" "*Giant* is a good movie," I pronounced to the family at dinner. "Oh, really?" Mother warmed to these occasions. She all but rolled up her sleeves. She knew I hadn't seen it. "Is that your considered opinion?"

She herself held many unpopular, even fantastic, positions. She was scathingly sarcastic about the McCarthy hearings while they took place, right on our living-room television; she frantically opposed

Father's wait-and-see calm. "We don't know enough about it," he said. "I do," she said. "I know all I need to know."

She asserted, against all opposition, that people who lived in trailer parks were not bad but simply poor, and had as much right to settle on beautiful land, such as rural Ligonier, Pennsylvania, as did the oldest of families in the finest of hidden houses. Therefore, the people who owned trailer parks, and sought zoning changes to permit trailer parks, needed our help. Her profound belief that the country-club pool sweeper was a person, and that the department-store saleslady, the bus driver, telephone operator, and house-painter were people, and even in groups the steelworkers who carried pickets and the Christmas shoppers who clogged intersections were people—this was a conviction common enough in democratic Pittsburgh, but not altogether common among our friends' parents, or even, perhaps, among our parents' friends.   36

Opposition emboldened Mother, and she would take on anybody on any issue—the chairman of the board, at a cocktail party, on the current strike; she would fly at him in a flurry of passion, as a songbird selflessly attacks a big hawk.   37

"Eisenhower's going to win," I announced after school. She lowered her magazine and looked me in the eyes: "How do you know?" I was doomed. It was fatal to say, "Everyone says so." We all knew well what happened. "Do you consult this Everyone before you make your decisions? What if Everyone decided to round up all the Jews?" Mother knew there was no danger of cowing me. She simply tried to keep us all awake. And in fact it was always clear to Amy and me, and to Molly when she grew old enough to listen, that if our classmates came to cruelty, just as much as if the neighborhood or the nation came to madness, we were expected to take, and would be each separately capable of taking, a stand.   38

1987

Purpose and Meaning

1. What does learning about Annie Dillard's mother tell us about Annie Dillard? What influences can you detect in Dillard's writing that may have come from her mother's curious sense of humor and excellent ear?

2. In paragraph 5, Dillard recounts how her mother repeated the phrase, "Terwilliger bunts one" for years after she first heard it, and at the most outrageous moments. In paragraphs 7 and 8, she discusses the names of a road and the effect they had on her and others. In paragraphs 9 and 10, she writes about various "Pittsburghisms." How do these examples characterize the

power of language to amuse, place, and even separate people? How is this essay in some ways more about language than about Dillard's mother?

3. What is the thesis of this essay?

Language and Style

1. What is phonetically appealing about "Terwilliger bunts one" (paragraph 1), "royal poinciana" (paragraph 6), "Tamiami Trail" (paragraph 7)? Read the phrases out loud as you consider sound here. What makes these combinations of sound appealing?

2. Notice the powerful mixing of nouns and verbs in this series of sentences: "men stood sunk in muck to their armpits. . . . They blasted muck with dynamite, cut jungle with machetes; they laid logs, dragged drilling machines, hauled dredges, heaped limestone" (paragraph 7). How does the mixing of contrasting sounds, hard images, active verbs, and one-or two-syllable words invigorate the writing? Find other examples of this stylistic method.

3. Another feature of Dillard's writing is its specificity. The men were not using an explosive; they used *dynamite*. The machines were *drilling* machines. The rock was *limestone*. Choose any paragraph in the essay and notice how specific her references are. Why is Dillard so careful to be specific?

4. What stylistic device does Dillard employ to create a humorous tone in this essay?

Strategy and Structure

1. While Dillard is interested in characterizing her mother, her subject is an American childhood, *her* childhood. Still, she focuses on her mother for many pages. We learn indirectly about Dillard's interest in language, her "know-it-all" attitude, her conditioning toward intellectual rigor and a questioning mind, as well as some of her politics. How effective is this approach? Why is her mother such a good model for Dillard's self-revelations?

2. Why doesn't Dillard ever tell us her mother's name? Is she failing to see her mother as an individual? What effect does not naming her have on the readers' point of view?

3. Dillard separates her essay into segments through spatial breaks. How many are there? What is in each segment? How do the segments finally cohere?

4. It is often said the people tend to remember best what comes first or last—in a poem, a movie, or a story. Since Dillard ends her essay with an account of her mother's insistence on a questioning, think-for-yourself kind of mind, she probably wants her readers particularly to remember this. Why? What is its significance to Dillard the writer?

Thinking and Writing

1. Analyze the literary influences Dillard may have gained from her mother. Consider content as well as style.

2. Adopt Dillard's approach and write an essay about your own mother or about someone you considered as a mother. Focus on those qualities and occurrences that most strongly affected you.

3. Pretend you are a child again and from that perspective describe an incident, or two or three related incidents, that involved your mother. Use the first person.

Living Like Weasels

A weasel is wild. Who knows what he thinks? He sleeps in his underground den, his tail draped over his nose. Sometimes he lives in his den for two days without leaving. Outside, he stalks rabbits, mice, muskrats, and birds, killing more bodies than he can eat warm, and often dragging the carcasses home. Obedient to instinct, he bites his prey at the neck, either splitting the jugular vein at the throat or crunching the brain at the base of the skull, and he does not let go. One naturalist refused to kill a weasel who was socketed into his hand deeply as a rattlesnake. The man could in no way pry the tiny weasel off, and he had to walk half a mile to water, the weasel dangling from his palm, and soak him off like a stubborn label.   1

And once, says Ernest Thompson Seton—once, a man shot an eagle out of the sky. He examined the eagle and found the dry skull of a weasel fixed by the jaws to his throat. The supposition is that the eagle had pounced on the weasel and the weasel swiveled and bit as instinct taught him, tooth to neck, and nearly won. I would like to have seen that eagle from the air a few weeks or months before he was shot: was the whole weasel still attached to his feathered throat, a fur pendant? Or did the eagle eat what he could reach, gutting the living weasel with his talons before his breast, bending his beak, cleaning the beautiful airborne bones?   2

I have been reading about weasels because I saw one last week. I startled a weasel who startled me, and we exchanged a long glance.   3

Twenty minutes from my house, through the woods by the quarry   4 and across the highway, is Hollins Pond, a remarkable piece of shallow-ness, where I like to go at sunset and sit on a tree trunk. Hollins Pond is also called Murray's Pond; it covers two acres of bottomland near Tinker Creek with six inches of water and six thousand lily pads. In winter, brown-and-white steers stand in the middle of it, merely dampening their hooves; from the distant shore they look like miracle itself, complete with miracle's nonchalance. Now, in summer, the steers are gone. The water lilies have blossomed and spread to a green horizontal plane that is terra firma to plodding blackbirds, and tremulous ceiling to black leeches, crayfish, and carp.

This is, mind you, suburbia. It is a five-minute walk in three directions to rows of houses, though none is visible here. There's a 55 mph highway at one end of the pond, and a nesting pair of wood ducks at the other. Under every bush is a muskrat hole or a beer can. The far end is an alternating series of fields and woods, fields and woods, threaded everywhere with motorcycle tracks—in whose bare clay wild turtles lay eggs. 5

So. I had crossed the highway, stepped over two low barbed-wire fences, and traced the motorcycle path in all gratitude through the wild rose and poison ivy of the pond's shoreline up into high grassy fields. Then I cut down through the woods to the mossy fallen tree where I sit. This tree is excellent. It makes a dry, upholstered bench at the upper, marshy end of the pond, a plush jetty raised from the thorny shore between a shallow blue body of water and a deep blue body of sky. 6

The sun had just set. I was relaxed on the tree trunk, ensconced in the lap of lichen, watching the lily pads at my feet tremble and part dreamily over the thrusting path of a carp. A yellow bird appeared to my right and flew behind me. It caught my eye; I swiveled around—and the next instant, inexplicably, I was looking down at a weasel, who was looking up at me. 7

Weasel! I'd never seen one wild before. He was ten inches long, thin as a curve, a muscled ribbon, brown as fruitwood, soft-furred, alert. His face was fierce, small and pointed as a lizard's; he would have made a good arrowhead. There was just a dot of chin, maybe two brown hairs' worth, and then the pure white fur began that spread down his underside. He had two black eyes I didn't see, any more than you see a window. 8

The weasel was stunned into stillness as he was emerging from beneath an enormous shaggy wild rose bush four feet away. I was stunned into stillness twisted backward on the tree trunk. Our eyes locked, and someone threw away the key. 9

Our look was as if two lovers, or deadly enemies, met unexpectedly on an overgrown path when each had been thinking of something 10 else: a clearing blow to the gut. It was also a bright blow to the brain, or a sudden beating of brains, with all the charge and intimate grate of rubbed balloons. It emptied our lungs. It felled the forest, moved the fields, and drained the pond; the world dismantled and tumbled into that black hole of eyes. If you and I looked at each other that way, our skulls would split and drop to our shoulders. But we don't. We keep our skulls. So.

He disappeared. This was only last week, and already I don't re- 11 member what shattered the enchantment. I think I blinked, I think I re- trieved my brain from the weasel's brain, and tried to memorize what I was seeing, and the weasel felt the yank of separation, the careening splashdown into real life and the urgent current of instinct. He vanished under the wild rose. I waited motionless, my mind suddenly full of data and my spirit with pleadings, but he didn't return.

Please do not tell me about "approach-avoidance conflicts." I tell 12 you I've been in that weasel's brain for sixty seconds, and he was in mine. Brains are private places, muttering through unique and secret tapes—but the weasel and I both plugged into another tape simultane- ously, for a sweet and shocking time. Can I help it if it was a blank?

What goes on in his brain the rest of the time? What does a weasel 13 think about? He won't say. His journal is tracks in clay, a spray of feath- ers, mouse blood and bone: uncollected, unconnected, loose-leaf, and blown.

I would like to learn, or remember, how to live. I come to Hollins 14 Pond not so much to learn how to live as, frankly, to forget about it. That is, I don't think I can learn from a wild animal how to live in particu- lar—shall I suck warm blood, hold my tail high, walk with my footprints precisely over the prints of my hands?—but I might learn something of mindlessness, something of the purity of living in the physical senses and the dignity of living without bias or motive. The weasel lives in ne- cessity and we live in choice, hating necessity and dying at the last ig- nobly in its talons. I would like to live as I should, as the weasel lives as he should. And I suspect that for me the way is like the weasel's: open to time and death painlessly, noticing everything, remembering nothing, choosing the given with a fierce and pointed will.

I missed my chance. I should have gone for the throat. I should 15 have lunged for that streak of white under the weasel's chin and held on, held on through mud and into the wild rose, held on for a dearer life. We could live under the wild rose wild as weasels, mute and un- comprehending. I could very calmly go wild. I could live two days in the den, curled, leaning on mouse fur, sniffing bird bones, blinking, lick- ing, breathing musk, my hair tangled in the roots of grasses. Down is a good place to go, where the mind is single. Down is out, out of your ever-loving mind and back to your careless senses. I remember muteness as a prolonged and giddy fast, where every moment is a feast of utterance received. Time and events are merely poured, unremarked, and ingested directly, like blood pulsed into my gut through a jugular vein. Could two live that way? Could two live under the wild rose, and explore by the pond, so that the smooth mind of each is as everywhere present to the other, and as received and as unchallenged, as falling snow?

We could, you know. We can live any way we want. People take   16
vows of poverty, chastity, and obedience—even of silence—by choice. The thing is to stalk your calling in a certain skilled and supple way, to locate the most tender and live spot and plug into that pulse. This is yielding, not fighting. A weasel doesn't "attack" anything; a weasel lives as he's meant to, yielding at every moment to the perfect freedom of single necessity.

I think it would be well, and proper, and obedient, and pure, to   17
grasp your one necessity and not let it go, to dangle from it limp wherever it takes you. Then even death, where you're going no matter how you live, cannot you part. Seize it and let it seize you up aloft even, till your eyes burn out and drop; let your musky flesh fall off in shreds, and let your very bones unhinge and scatter, loosened over fields, over fields and woods, lightly, thoughtless, from any height at all, from as high as eagles.

1982

Purpose and Meaning

1. How does the essay's title reflect Dillard's purpose? What is the quality that weasels possess from which Dillard suggests humans can learn? What is the natural principle by which the weasel lives? What is its fascination for Annie Dillard?

2. Why does Dillard describe the location of Hollins Pond so specifically? How does that description relate to her thesis?

3. How do the anecdotes about weasels that open the essay contribute to it?

Language and Style

1. As she does in much of her other writing, Dillard here often uses poetic techniques such as alliteration and assonance. Select several instances of these techniques, such as in paragraph 7, and discuss the importance of word choice and sound.

2. In paragraphs 8 and 9, Dillard makes use of a number of similes and metaphoric comparisons. How do these comparisons allow us to understand better her experience of seeing the weasel?

3. Paragraph 6 begins with a one-word sentence: "So." Paragraph 10 ends the same way. How do these sentences function?

Strategy and Structure

1. Discuss Dillard's general design in this essay. How does she link her observations to her main purpose? How effective is that strategy?

2. Dillard acknowledges the impossibility of living literally like a weasel in paragraph 14. Yet in her next paragraph, she says she could "live two days in the den, curled, leaning on mouse fur, sniffing bird bones." What is her purpose? Does this strategy clarify or confuse the reader?

3. Notice the shifting of subject pronouns in the closing paragraph. What does such shifting contribute to the essay's overall design? If the shift were removed, would the essay gain or lose in impact as a result?

Thinking and Writing

1. Dillard says in paragraph 14 that we "live in choice, hating necessity and dying ignobly in its talons." This echoes Henry David Thoreau's famous maxim that "most men lead lives of quiet desperation." Is living with singleness of purpose a truly practical approach to living? Write an essay that supports or refutes the call to "live deliberately" and with the singleness of the weasel.

2. Using figurative language where possible, develop an essay in which you use your own observations of an animal as a springboard to discuss the quality of human life.

Singing with the Fundamentalists

It is early spring. I have a temporary office at a state university on the West Coast. The office is on the third floor. It looks down on the Square, the enormous open courtyard at the center of the campus. From my desk I see hundreds of people moving between classes. There is a large circular fountain in the Square's center.

Early one morning, on the first day of spring quarter, I hear   2
singing. A pack of students has gathered at the fountain. They are
singing something which, at this distance, and through the heavy window, sounds good.

I know who these singing students are: they are the   3
Fundamentalists. This campus has a lot of them. Mornings they sing on
the Square; it is their only perceptible activity. What are they singing?
Whatever it is, I want to join them, for I like to sing; whatever it is, I
want to take my stand with them, for I am drawn to their very absurdity, their innocent indifference to what people think. My colleagues
and students here, and my friends everywhere, dislike and fear
Christian fundamentalists. You may never have met such people, but
you've heard what they do: they pile up money, vote in blocs, and elect
right-wing crazies; they censor books; they carry handguns; they fight
fluoride in the drinking water and evolution in the schools; probably
they would lynch people if they could get away with it. I'm not sure my
friends are correct. I close my pen and join the singers on the Square.

There is a clapping song in progress. I have to concentrate to fol-   4
low it:

> Come on, rejoice,
> And let your heart sing,
> Come on rejoice,
> Give praise to the king.
>
> Singing alleluia—
> He is the king of kings;
> Singing alleluia—
> He is the king of kings.

Two song leaders are standing on the broad rim of the fountain; the
water is splashing just behind them. The boy is short, hardfaced, with a
moustache. He bangs his guitar with the backs of his fingers. The blonde
girl, who leads the clapping, is bouncy; she wears a bit of makeup. Both
are wearing blue jeans.

The students beside me are wearing blue jeans too—and athletic   5
jerseys, parkas, football jackets, turtlenecks, and hiking shoes or jogging
shoes. They all have canvas or nylon book bags. They look like any random batch of seventy or eighty students at this university. They are
grubby or scrubbed, mostly scrubbed; they are tall, fair, or red-headed in
large proportions. Their parents are white-collar workers, blue-collar
workers, farmers, loggers, orchardists, merchants, fishermen; their
names are, I'll bet, Olsen, Jensen, Seyersen, Hansen, Klokker, Sigurdsen.

Despite the vigor of the clapping song, no one seems to be giving it   6
much effort. And no one looks at anyone else; there are no sentimental

glances and smiles, no glances even of recognition. These kids don't seem to know each other. We stand at the fountain's side, out on the broad, bricked Square in front of the science building, and sing the clapping song through three times.

It is quarter to nine in the morning. Hundreds of people are crossing the Square. These passersby—faculty, staff, students—pay very little attention to us; this morning singing has gone on for years. Most of them look at us directly, then ignore us, for there is nothing to see; no animal sacrifices, no lynchings, no collection plate for Jesse Helms, no seizures, snake handling, healing, or glossolalia. There is barely anything to hear. I suspect the people glance at us to learn if we are really singing: How could so many people make so little sound? My fellow singers, who ignore each other, certainly ignore passersby as well. Within a week, most of them will have their eyes closed anyway.

We move directly to another song, a slower one.

> He is my peace
> Who has broken down every wall;
> He is my peace,
> He is my peace.
>
> Cast all your cares on him,
> For he careth for you—oo—oo
> He is my peace,
> He is my peace.

I am paying strict attention to the song leaders, for I am singing at the top of my lungs and I've never heard any of these songs before. They are not the old American low-church Protestant hymns; they are not the old European high-church Protestant hymns. These hymns seem to have been written just yesterday, apparently by the same people who put out lyrical Christian greeting cards and bookmarks.

"Where do these songs come from?" I ask a girl standing next to me. She seems appalled to be addressed at all, and startled by the question. "They're from the praise albums!" she explains, and moves away.

The songs' melodies run dominant, subdominant, dominant, tonic, dominant. The pace is slow, about the pace of "Tell Laura I Love Her," and with that song's quavering, long notes. The lyrics are simple and repetitive; there are very few of them to which a devout Jew or Mohammedan could not give wholehearted assent. These songs are similar to the things Catholics sing in church these days. I don't know if any studies have been done to correlate the introduction of contemporary songs into Catholic churches with those churches' decline in membership, or with the phenomenon of Catholic converts' applying to enter cloistered monasteries directly, without passing through parish churches.

> I'm set free to worship,
> I'm set free to praise him,
> I'm set free to dance before the Lord . . .

At nine o'clock sharp we quit and scatter. I hear a few quiet "see   12
you"s. Mostly the students leave quickly, as if they didn't want to be
seen. The Square empties.

The next day we show up again, at twenty to nine. The same two   13
leaders stand on the fountain's rim; the fountain is pouring down behind them.

After the first song, the boy with the moustache hollers, "Move on   14
up! Some of you guys aren't paying attention back there! You're talking
to each other. I want you to concentrate!" The students laugh, embarrassed for him. He sounds like a teacher. No one moves. The girl breaks
into the next song, which we join at once:

> In my life, Lord,
> Be glorified, be glorified, be glorified;
> In my life, Lord.
> Be glorified, be glorified, today.

At the end of this singularly monotonous verse, which is straining my
tolerance for singing virtually anything, the boy with the moustache
startles me by shouting, "Classes!"

At once, without skipping a beat, we sing, "In my classes, Lord, be   15
glorified, be glorified . . ." I give fleet thought to the class I'm teaching
this afternoon. We're reading a little "Talk of the Town" piece called
"Eggbag," about a cat in a magic store on Eighth Avenue.
"Relationships!" the boy calls. The students seem to sing "In my relationships, Lord," more easily than they sang "classes." They seemed embarrassed by "classes." In fact, to my fascination, they seemed embarrassed by almost everything. Why are they here? I will sing with the
Fundamentalists every weekday morning all spring; I will decide, tentatively, that they come pretty much for the same reasons I do: Each has a
private relationship with "the Lord" and will put up with a lot of junk
for it.

I have taught some Fundamentalist students here, and know a bit   16
of what they think. They are college students above all, worried about
their love lives, their grades, and finding jobs. Some support moderate
Democrats; some support moderate Republicans. Like their classmates,
most support nuclear freeze, ERA, and an end to the draft. I believe they
are divided on abortion and busing. They are not particularly political.

They read *Christianity Today* and *Campus Life* and *Eternity*—moderate, sensible magazines, I think; they read a lot of C. S. Lewis. (One such student, who seemed perfectly tolerant of me and my shoddy Christianity, introduced me to C. S. Lewis's critical book on Charles Williams.) They read the Bible. I think they all "believe in" organic evolution. The main thing about them is this: There isn't any "them." Their views vary. They don't know each other.

Their common Christianity puts them, if anywhere, to the left of 17 their classmates. I believe they also tend to be more able than their classmates to think well in the abstract, and also to recognize the complexity of moral issues. But I may be wrong.

In 1980, the media were certainly wrong about television evange- 18 lists. Printed estimates of Jerry Falwell's television audience ranged from 18 million to 30 million people. In fact, according to Arbitron's actual counts, fewer than 1.5 million people were watching Falwell. And, according to an Emory University study, those who did watch television evangelists didn't necessarily vote with them. Emory University sociologist G. Melton Mobley reports, "When that message turns political, they cut it off." Analysis of the 1982 off-year election turned up no Fundamentalist bloc voting. The media were wrong, but no one printed retractions.

The media were wrong, too, in a tendency to identify all funda- 19 mentalist Christians with Falwell and his ilk, and to attribute to them, across the board, conservative views.

Someone has sent me two recent issues of *Eternity: The Evangelical* 20 *Monthly*. One lead article criticizes a television preacher for saying that the United States had never used military might to take land from another nation. The same article censures Newspeak, saying that government rhetoric would have us believe in a "clean bomb," would have us believe that we "defend" America by invading foreign soil, and would have us believe that the dictatorships we support are "democracies." "When the President of the United States says that one reason to support defense spending is because it creates jobs," this lead article says, "a little bit of *1984* begins to surface." Another article criticizes a "heavy-handed" opinion of Jerry Falwell Ministries—in this case a broadside attack on artificial insemination, surrogate motherhood, and lesbian motherhood. Browsing through *Eternity*, I find a double crosstic. I find an intelligent, analytical, and enthusiastic review of the new London Philharmonic recording of Mahler's second symphony—a review which stresses the "glorious truth" of the Jewish composer's magnificent work, and cites its recent performance in Jerusalem to celebrate the recapture of the Western Wall following the Six Day War. Surely, the evangelical Christians who read this magazine are not bookburners. If by chance they vote with the magazine's editors, then it looks to me as if they vote with the American Civil Liberties Union and Americans for Democratic Action.

Every few years some bold and sincere Christian student at this university disagrees with a professor in class—usually about the professor's out-of-hand dismissal of Christianity. Members of the faculty, outraged, repeat the stories of these rare and uneven encounters for years on end, as if to prove that the crazies are everywhere, and gaining ground. The notion is, apparently, that these kids can't think for themselves. Or they wouldn't disagree. 21

Now again the moustached leader asks us to move up. There is no harangue, so we move up. (This will be a theme all spring. The leaders want us closer together. Our instinct is to stand alone.) From behind the tall fountain comes a wind; on several gusts we get sprayed. No one seems to notice. 22

We have time for one more song. The leader, perhaps sensing that no one likes him, blunders on, "I want you to pray this one through," he says. "We have a lot of people here from a lot of different fellowships, but we're all one body. Amen?" They don't like it. He gets a few polite Amens. We sing: 23

> Bind us together, Lord,
> With a bond that can't be broken;
> Bind us together, Lord,
> With love.

Everyone seems to be in a remarkably foul mood today. We don't like this song. There is no one here under seventeen, and, I think, no one here who believes that love is a bond that can't be broken. We sing the song through three times; then it is time to go.

The leader calls after our retreating backs, "Hey, have a good day! Praise Him all day!" The kids around me roll up their eyes privately. Some groan; all flee. 24

The next morning is very cold. I am here early. Two girls are talking on the fountain's rim; one is part Italian. She says, "I've got the Old Testament, but I can't get the New. I screw up the New." She takes a breath and rattles off a long list, ending with "Jonah, Micah, Nahum, Habakkuk, Zephaniah, Haggai, Zechariah, Malachi." The other girl produces a slow, sarcastic applause. I ask one of the girls to help me with the words to a song. She is agreeable, but says, "I'm sorry, I can't. I just became a Christian this year, so I don't know all the words yet." 25

The others are coming; we stand and separate. The boy with the 26 moustache is gone, replaced by a big, serious fellow in a green down jacket. The bouncy girl is back with her guitar; she's wearing a skirt and wool knee socks. We begin without any preamble, by singing a song that has so few words that we actually stretch one syllable over eleven separate notes. Then we sing a song in which the men sing one phrase and the women echo it. Everyone seems to know just what to do. In the context of our vapid songs, the lyrics of this one are extraordinary:

> I was nothing before you found me.
> Heartache! Broken people! Ruined lives
> Is why you died on Calvary.

The last line rises in a regular series of half-notes. Now at last some people are actually singing; they throw some breath into the business. There is a seriousness and urgency to it: "Heartache! Broken people! Ruined lives . . . I was nothing."

We don't look like nothing. We look like a bunch of students of 27 every stripe, ill-shaven or well-shaven, dressed up or down, but dressed warmly against the cold: jeans and parkas, jeans and heavy sweaters, jeans and scarves and blow-dried hair. We look ordinary. But I think, quite on my own, that we are here because we know this business of nothingness, brokenness, and ruination. We sing this song over and over.

Something catches my eye. Behind us, up in the science building, 28 professors are standing alone at opened windows.

The long brick science building has three upper floors of faculty of- 29 fices, thirty-two windows. At one window stands a bearded man, about forty; his opening his window is what caught my eye. He stands full in the open window, his hands on his hips, his head cocked down toward the fountain. He is drawn to look, as I was drawn to come. Up on the building's top floor, at the far right window, there is another: An Asian-American professor, wearing a white shirt, is sitting with one hip on his desk, looking out and down. In the middle of the row of windows, another one, an old professor in a checked shirt, stands sideways to the open window, stands stock-still, his long, old ear to the air. Now another window cranks open, another professor—or maybe a graduate student—leans out, his hands on the sill.

We are all singing, and I am watching these five still men, my col- 30 leagues, whose office doors are surely shut—for that is the custom here: five of them alone in their office in the science building who have opened their windows on this very cold morning, who motionless hear the Fundamentalists sing, utterly unknown to each other.

We sing another four songs, including the clapping song, and one 31 which repeats, "This is the day which the Lord hath made; rejoice and be glad in it." All the professors but one stay by their opened windows, figures in a frieze. When after ten minutes we break off and scatter, each cranks his window shut. Maybe they have nine o'clock classes too.

I miss a few sessions. One morning of the following week, I rejoin   32 the Fundamentalists on the Square. The wind is blowing from the north; it is sunny and cold. There are several new developments.

Someone has blown up rubber gloves and floated them in the   33 fountain. I saw them yesterday afternoon from my high office window, and couldn't quite make them out: I seemed to see hands in the fountain waving from side to side, like those hands wagging on springs which people stick in the back windows of their cars. I saw these many years ago in Quito and Guayaquil, where they were a great fad long before they showed up here. The cardboard hands said, on their palms, HOLA GENTE, hello people. Some of them just said HOLA, hello, with a little wave to the universe at large, in case anybody happened to be looking. It is like sending radio signals to planets in other galaxies: HOLA, if anyone is listening. Jolly folk, these Ecuadorians, I thought.

Now, waiting by the fountain for the singing, I see that these par-   34 ticular hands are long surgical gloves, yellow and white, ten of them tied off at the cuff. They float upright and they wave, *hola, hola, hola*; they mill around like a crowd, bobbing under the fountain's spray and back again to the pool's rim, *hola*. It is a good prank. It is far too cold for the university's maintenance crew to retrieve them without turning off the fountain and putting on rubber boots.

From all around the Square, people are gathering for the singing.   35 There is no way I can guess which kids, from among the masses crossing the Square, will veer off to the fountain. When they get here, I never recognize anybody except the leaders.

The singing begins without ado as usual, but there is something   36 different about it. The students are growing prayerful, and they show it this morning with a peculiar gesture. I'm glad they weren't like this when I first joined them, or I never would have stayed.

Last night there was an educational television special, part of   37 "Middletown." It was a segment called "Community of Praise," and I watched it because it was about Fundamentalists. It showed a Jesus-loving family in the Midwest; the treatment was good and complex. This family attended the prayer meetings, healing sessions, and church services of an unnamed sect—a very low-church sect, whose doctrine and culture were much more low-church than those of the kids I sing with. When the members of this sect prayed, they held their arms over their heads and raised their plams, as if to feel or receive a blessing or energy from above.

Now today on the Square there is a new serious mood. The leaders   38 are singing with their eyes shut. I am impressed that they can bang their guitars, keep their balance, and not fall into the pool. It is the same bouncy girl and earnest boy. Their eyeballs are rolled back a bit. I look around and see that almost everyone in this crowd of eighty or so has his eyes shut and is apparently praying the words of this song or praying some other prayer.

Now as the chorus rises, as it gets louder and higher and simpler in   39
melody—

> I exalt thee,
> I exalt thee,
> I exalt thee,
> Thou art the Lord—

then, at this moment, hands start rising. All around me, hands are going up—that tall girl, that blond boy with his head back, the red-headed boy up front, the girl with the MacDonald's jacket. Their arms rise as if pulled on strings. Some few of them have raised their arms very high over their heads and are tilting back their palms. Many, many more of them, as inconspicuously as possible, have raised their hands to the level of their chins.

What is going on? Why are these students today raising their   40
palms in this gesture, when nobody did it last week? Is it because the leaders have set a prayerful tone this morning? Is it because this gesture always accompanies this song, just as clapping accompanies other songs? Or is it, as I suspect, that these kids watched the widely publicized documentary last night just as I did, and are adopting, or trying out, the gesture?

It is a sunny morning, and the sun is rising behind the leaders and   41
the fountain, so those students have their heads tilted, eyes closed, and palms upraised toward the sun. I glance up at the science building and think my own prayer: Thank God no one is watching this.

The leaders cannot move around much on the fountain's rim. The   42
girl has her eyes shut; the boy opens his eyes from time to time, glances at the neck of his guitar, and closes his eyes again.

When the song is over, the hands go down, and there is some   43
desultory chatting in the crowd, as usual: Can I borrow your library card? And, as usual nobody looks at anybody.

All our songs today are serious. There is a feudal theme to them, or   44
a feudal analogue:

> I will eat from abundance of your household.
> I will dream beside your streams of righteousness.
>
> You are my king.

Enter his gates
with thanksgiving in your heart;
come before his courts with praise.
He is the king of kings.

Thou art the Lord.

All around me, eyes are closed and hands are raised. There is no ⁴⁵ social pressure to do this, or anything else. I've never known any group to be less cohesive, imposing fewer controls. Since no one looks at anyone, and since passersby no longer look, everyone out here is inconspicuous and free. Perhaps the palm-raising has begun because the kids realize by now that they are not on display; they're praying in their closets, right out here on the Square. Over the course of the next weeks, I will learn that the palm-raising is here to stay.

The sun is rising higher. We are singing our last song. We are praying. We are alone together. ⁴⁶

He is my peace
Who has broken down every wall . . .

When the song is over, the hands go down. The heads lower, the ⁴⁷ eyes open and blink. We stay still a second before we break up. We have been standing in a broad current; now we have stepped aside. We have dismantled the radar cups; we have closed the telescope's vault. Students gather their book bags and go. The two leaders step down from the fountain's rim and pack away their guitars. Everyone scatters. I am in no hurry, so I stay after everyone is gone. It is after nine o'clock, and the Square is deserted. The fountain is playing to an empty house. In the pool the cheerful hands are waving over the water, bobbing under the fountain's veil and out again in the current, *hola*.

1984

Purpose and Meaning

1. In this essay, Dillard considers prejudicial opinions about fundamentalist Christians. How do her actions support her opinion that we should take a closer look at people before we judge them? What expectations does she have of her audience? To what things does she respond besides these fundamentalist views?

2. In paragraph 16, Dillard writes that the fundamentalist singers are "college students above all" and that "they are not particularly political." What point is she making in this paragraph? Why is this point important to our overall understanding of the essay and Dillard's experience?

3. How does Dillard anticipate and deal with her audience's possible objection to her position?

Language and Style

1. The sentences in this essay tend to be short and to begin with the basic subject-verb pattern. How does the language differ from the first two Dillard essays? What tone does this style create?

2. Generally, the language in this essay is plainer than in Dillard's other work. Still, she employs imagery and resonating sounds to inform her subject. Lists are a common feature: "athletic jerseys, parkas, football jackets, turtle-necks" (paragraph 5), "white-collar workers, blue-collar workers, farmers, loggers, orchardists . . . Olsen, Jensen, Seversen, Hansen, Klokker" (paragraph 5). Find other examples. What do lists add to a piece of writing?

3. Considering Dillard's subject and its potential for controversy, what reason could she have for writing in a plain, unaffected style?

4. What is unusual about Dillard's point of view in this essay?

Strategy and Structure

1. Dillard begins this essay with a view of the Christian singers from a distance, from her third-floor office window. Why might she begin this way? How does Dillard involve the reader in getting to know the singers?

2. How does Dillard organize the body of the essay? Is she consistent in her rhetorical approach? Explain.

3. How does Dillard's writing contrast with the quoted lyrics of the fundamentalist songs? Why would she want to create this contrast?

4. When Dillard decided to write an essay about her experience with the fundamentalist singers, she had the choice to begin and end her account at any point. Why do you suppose she chose to end after the description of the morning when students had begun to raise their arms to the sky in emulation of some evangelicals in a television documentary? That day, she writes, all the songs were "serious" (paragraph 38). What effect is this final image likely to have on readers' evaluation of the group and Dillard's experience?

Thinking and Writing

1. Although metaphorical language is rare in this essay, the final paragraph contains several metaphors. Dillard writes: "We have been standing in a broad current; now we have stepped aside. We have dismantled the radar cups; we have closed the telescope's vault." Analyze the meaning of these metaphors, and explain their relation to the rest of the essay.

2. Write about a religious or spiritual experience you have had or have observed. Following Dillard's lead, write effectively, but do not sensationalize.

○●○●○●○●○

Push It

People love pretty much the same things best. A writer looking for subjects inquires not after what he loves best, but after what he alone loves at all. Strange seizures beset us. Frank Conroy loves his yo-yo tricks, Emily Dickinson her slant of light; Richard Selzer loves the glistening peritoneum, Faulkner the muddy bottom of a little girl's drawers visible when she's up a pear tree. "Each student of the ferns," I once read, "will have his own list of plants that for some reason or another stir his emotions."

Why do you never find anything written about that idiosyncratic thought you advert to, about your fascination with something no one else understands? Because it is up to you. There is something you find interesting, for a reason hard to explain. It is hard to explain because you have never read it on any page; there you begin. You were made and set here to give voice to this, your own astonishment.

Write as if you were dying. At the same time, assume you write for an audience consisting solely of terminal patients. That is, after all, the case. What would you begin writing if you knew you would die soon? What could you say to a dying person that would not enrage by its triviality?

Write about winter in the summer. Describe Norway as Ibsen did, from a desk in Italy; describe Dublin as James Joyce did, from a desk in Paris. Willa Cather wrote her prairie novels in New York City; Mark Twain wrote "Huckleberry Finn" in Hartford. Recently scholars learned that Walt Whitman rarely left his room.

The writer studies literature, not the world. She lives in the world; she cannot miss it. If she has ever bought a hamburger, or taken a commercial airplane flight, she spares her readers a report of her experience. She is careful of what she reads, for that is what she will write. She is careful of what she learns, because that is what she will know.

The writer knows her field—what has been done, what could be done, the limits—the way a tennis player knows the court. And like that expert, she, too, plays the edges. That is where the exhilaration is. She hits up the line. In writing, she can push the edges. Beyond this limit, here, the reader must recoil. Reason balks, poetry snaps; some madness enters, or strain. Now gingerly, can she enlarge it, can she nudge the bounds? And enclose what wild power?

A well-known writer got collared by a university student who   7
asked, "Do you think I could be a writer?"

"Well," the writer said, "I don't know. . . . Do you like sentences?"   8

The writer could see the student's amazement. Sentences? Do I like   9
sentences? I am 20 years old and do I like sentences? If he had liked sentences, of course, he could begin, like a joyful painter I knew. I asked him how he came to be a painter. He said, "I liked the smell of the paint."

Hemingway studied, as models, the novels of Knut Hamsun and   10
Ivan Turgenev. Isaac Bashevis Singer, as it happened, also chose Hamsun and Turgenev as models. Ralph Ellison studied Hemingway and Gertrude Stein. Thoreau loved Homer; Eudora Welty loved Chekhov. Faulkner described his debt to Sherwood Anderson and Joyce; E. M. Forster, his debt to Jane Austen and Proust. By contrast, if you ask a 21-year-old poet whose poetry he likes, he might say, unblushing, "Nobody's." He has not yet understood that poets like poetry, and novelists like novels; he himself likes only the role, the thought of himself in a hat. Rembrandt and Shakespeare, Bohr and Gauguin, possessed powerful hearts, not powerful wills. They loved the range of materials they used. The work's possibilities excited them; the field's complexities fired their imaginations. The caring suggested the tasks; the tasks suggested the schedules. They learned their fields and then loved them. They worked, respectfully, out of their love and knowledge, and they produced complex bodies of work that endure. Then, and only then, the world harassed them with some sort of wretched hat, which, if they were still living, they knocked away as well as they could, to keep at their tasks.

It makes more sense to write one big book—a novel or nonfiction   11
narrative—than to write many stories or essays. Into a long, ambitious project you can fit or pour all you possess and learn. A project that takes five years will accumulate those years' inventions and richnesses. Much of those years' reading will feed the work. Further, writing sentences is difficult whatever their subject. It is no less difficult to write sentences in a recipe than sentences in "Moby Dick." So you might as well write "Moby Dick." Similarly, since every original work requires a unique form, it is more prudent to struggle with the outcome of only one form—that of a long work—than to struggle with the many forms of a collection.

Every book has an intrinsic impossibility, which its writer discov-   12
ers as soon as his first excitement dwindles. The problem is structural; it is insoluble; it is why no one can ever write this book. Complex stories,

essays and poems have this problem, too—the prohibitive structural defect the writer wishes he had never noticed. He writes it in spite of that. He finds ways to minimize the difficulty; he strengthens other virtues; he cantilevers the whole narrative out into thin air and it holds.

Why are we reading, if not in hope of beauty laid bare, life height- 13
ened and its deepest mystery probed? Can the writer isolate and vivify all in experience that most deeply engages our intellects and our hearts? Can the writer renew our hopes for literary forms? Why are we reading, if not in hope that the writer will magnify and dramatize our days, will illuminate and inspire us with wisdom, courage and the hope of meaningfulness, and press upon our minds the deepest mysteries, so we may feel again their majesty and power? What do we ever know that is higher than that power which, from time to time, seizes our lives, and which reveals us startlingly to ourselves as creatures set down here bewildered? Why does death so catch us by surprise, and why love? We still and always want waking. If we are reading for these things, why would anyone read books with advertising slogans and brand names in them? Why would anyone write such books? We should mass half-dressed in long lines like tribesmen and shake gourds at each other, to wake up; instead we watch television and miss the show.

No manipulation is possible in a work of art, but every miracle is. 14
Those artists who dabble in eternity, or who aim never to manipulate but only to lay out hard truths, grow accustomed to miracles. Their sureness is hard won. "Given a large canvas," said Veronese, "I enriched it as I saw fit."

The sensation of writing a book is the sensation of spinning, 15
blinded by love and daring. It is the sensation of a stunt pilot's turning barrel rolls, or an inchworm's blind rearing from a stem in search of a route. At its worst, it feels like alligator wrestling, at the level of the sentence.

At its best, the sensation of writing is that of any unmerited grace. 16
It is handed to you, but only if you look for it. You search, you break your fists, your back, your brain, and then—and only then—it is handed to you. From the corner of your eye you see motion. Something is moving through the air and headed your way. It is a parcel bound in ribbons and bows; it has two white wings. It flies directly at you; you can read your name on it. If it were a baseball, you would hit it out of the park. It is that one pitch in a thousand you see in slow motion; its wings beat slowly as a hawk's.

One line of a poem, the poet said—only one line, but thank God for 17
that one line—drops from the ceiling. Thornton Wilder cited this unnamed writer of sonnets: one line of a sonnet falls from the ceiling, and you tap in the others around it with a jeweler's hammer. Nobody whispers it in your ear. It is like something you memorized once and forgot.

Now it comes back and rips away your breath. You find and finger a phrase at a time, you lay it down as if with tongs, restraining your strength, and wait suspended and fierce until the next one finds you: yes, this; and yes, praise be, then this.

Einstein likened the generation of a new idea to a chicken's laying   18
an egg: *"Kieks—auf einmal ist es da."* Cheep—and all at once there it is. Of course, Einstein was not above playing to the crowd.

Push it. Examine all things intensely and relentlessly. Probe and   19
search each object in a piece of art; do not leave it, do not course over it, as if it were understood, but instead follow it down until you see it in the mystery of its own specificity and strength. Giacometti's drawings and paintings show his bewilderment and persistence. If he had not acknowledged his bewilderment, he would not have persisted. A master of drawing, Rico Lebrun, discovered that "the draftsman must aggress; only by persistent assault will the live image capitulate and give up its secret to an unrelenting line." Who but an artist fierce to know—not fierce to seem to know—would suppose that a live image possessed a secret? The artist is willing to give all his or her strength and life to probing with blunt instruments those same secrets no one can describe any way but with the instruments' faint tracks.

Admire the world for never ending on you as you would admire   20
an opponent, without taking your eyes off him, or walking away.

One of the few things I know about writing is this: spend it all,   21
shoot it, play it, lose it, all, right away, every time. Do not hoard what seems good for a later place in the book, or for another book; give it, give it all, give it now. The impulse to save something for a better place later is the signal to spend it now. Something more will arise for later, something better. These things fill from behind, from beneath, like well water. Similarly, the impulse to keep to yourself what you have learned is not only shameful, it is destructive. Anything you do not give freely and abundantly becomes lost to you. You open your safe and find ashes.

After Michelangelo died, someone found in his studio a piece of   22
paper on which he had written a note to his apprentice, in the handwriting of his old age: "Draw, Antonio, draw, Antonio, draw and do not waste time."

1989

Purpose and Meaning

1. What is Dillard's purpose in writing this essay? What assumptions does she make about her audience?

2. In paragraph 5, Dillard writes, "The writer studies literature, not the world. She lives in the world; she cannot miss it." What do you think Dillard means by this, specifically? Do you agree with her? Does everyone "living in the world" really experience it?

3. Dillard seems to be writing to her audience in several voices. Identify these multiple voices, and explain their effect.

Language and Style

1. Dillard begins using the pronoun *he* to refer to the writer. The next time she refers to the writer, in paragraph 5, she uses *she*. Why does she alternate her usage and why does she continue with the altered usage? What reasons could she have—both ideological and stylistic—for this usage?

2. Commands appear frequently in this essay: "Write as if you were dying" (paragraph 3); "Write about winter in the summer" (paragraph 4); "Examine all things intensely and relentlessly" (paragraph 19); "Probe and search each object" (paragraph 19); "Admire the world for never ending on you" (paragraph 20). What tone is generated by these commands?

3. Some of Dillard's sentences are exceedingly compact, reminiscent of an Emily Dickinson poem: "Strange seizures beset us" (paragraph 1); "Reason balks, poetry snaps; some madness enters, or strain" (paragraph 6). What is poetic about such language?

4. Many of the metaphors Dillard has chosen liken writing to a physical experience—for instance, "The writer knows her field . . . the way a tennis player knows the court" (paragraph 6). Cite additional examples of this technique. What effect do these metaphors produce? In what way are they more effective than a nonfigurative explanation of writing? Why does she choose such physical imagery?

Strategy and Structure

1. For the first twelve paragraphs, Dillard's approach is direct. In paragraph 13, she becomes questioning. Why does she shift her tone at this point?

2. Beginning in paragraph 15, Dillard shifts her approach again and becomes rather lyrical. Why is a lyric tone appropriate now? What shift has occurred in the discussion?

3. For most of the essay, Dillard has been writing as an authority. She is a widely read, Pulitzer–Prize winning author who knows her subject well. However, at the end of the essay, she begins paragraph 21 by saying, "One of the few things I know about writing is this." Why does she affect modesty at this point? Is it effective, or does it sound false?

Thinking and Writing

1. In paragraph 16, Dillard writes: "You search, you break your fists, your back, your brain, and then—and only then—it is handed to you. From the corner of your eye you see motion. Something is moving through the air

and headed your way. It is a parcel bound in ribbons and bows; it has two white wings. It flies directly at you; you can read your name on it. If it were a baseball, you would hit it out of the park. It is that one pitch in a thousand you see in slow motion; its wings beat slowly as a hawk's." Analyze this passage for meaning and effectiveness. Evaluate those features that are characteristic of Dillard's writing in all four essays—both in style and content.

2. Choose an activity you know well and write an essay instructing your readers on how to do it best. Try to imitate some of Dillard's techniques.

3. Write an extended essay on the role and mission of writers and artists in modern times, drawing on relevant essays and essayists in this anthology. Consult, for example, Orwell's "Why I Write" and Didion's essay by the same title; Baldwin's "Autobiographical Notes"; and Selzer's "The Pen and the Scalpel."

BARRY LOPEZ

Barry Holstun Lopez was born in New York in 1945 but spent most of his first ten years in southern California's San Fernando Valley, which at that time was still rural and "before it became a caricature of itself," as he once put it. He received his B.A. from the University of Notre Dame in 1966 and an M.A.T. from the University of Oregon in 1968. He did further graduate work at Oregon for a year before turning to a full-time writing career. "I never thought I would be able to make a living as a writer," he once confessed, and "that I would probably be a teacher and would write, like everyone else did, on the side."

Lopez's early articles and essays in such periodicals as *National Geographic*, *Antaeus*, *Orion Nature Quarterly*, *Wilderness*, *Science*, and *Harper's* quickly established him as an authoritative voice in natural history and environmental subjects. His first book of fiction, *Desert Notes: Reflections in the Eye of a Raven* (1976), and his collection of Coyote Trickster stories, *Giving Birth to Thunder, Sleeping with His Daughter: Coyote Builds North America* (1977), found only a limited appreciative audience, but his first major nonfiction work, *Of Wolves and Men* (1978), brought him national acclaim, an American Book Award nomination, and the John Burroughs medal for nature writing. His subsequent ventures into fiction, *River Notes: The Dance of Herons* (1979) and *Winter Count* (1980), were critically well received, and *Arctic Dreams: Imagination and Desire in a Northern Landscape* (1986), his second work of nonfiction, gained him a prominent place among major contemporary writers. His first collection of essays, *Crossing Open Ground*, appeared in 1988.

Lopez considers himself a storyteller in the way the term is used among aboriginal cultures: the storyteller's responsibility is to create an atmosphere in which the wisdom of the work can reveal itself and "make the reader feel a part of something." The underpinnings of that "something" are philosophical and moral inquiry, focusing particularly upon the interrelationship of humans and the natural world. "Writers work with metaphors," he once said in an interview with *Contemporary Authors*. "Mine are natural history, anthropology, geology." Lopez's approach is to give himself over to a place and try to pass on some of what he sees as a trained observer. "The story, whether it's non-fiction or fiction, has a power to elevate or to heal or to illuminate, to provide hope, to . . . give an individual life greater dimension."

Lopez bases his style upon his felt need to clarify for the reader and to "make the language work beautifully." The result is deceivingly simple and highly effective, as demonstrated in "The Stone Horse." He begins with a conscious realization that to be successful, he—as "a worthy illuminator of the world for the reader"—must withdraw from the scene at some point to enable the reader to gain another understanding. "By the time the reader finishes a book or essay," Lopez says, "he's really thinking about his own thoughts with regard to that subject, or that place . . . and not so much about the writer's. The initial step (establishing himself as a distinct personality) is an act of ego, the next step a loss of ego, a sort of disappearance." The reader is then able to leave the story "feeling the wisdom, the power, the life-blood, if you will, of whatever the reader and the writer were involved in together. For me that's very important."

The fabric of language with which Lopez weaves his stories is simple, musical, and quietly powerful. In his own words, his work is "written with a respect for both the source and the reader and with an understanding of why the human heart and the land have been brought together." That respect and understanding can be felt in such works as "The American Geographies" and marks Lopez as a master of the contemporary essay.

The Stone Horse

The deserts of southern California, the high, relatively cooler and wetter Mojave and the hotter, dryer Sonoran to the south of it, carry the signatures of many cultures. Prehistoric rock drawings in the Mojave's Coso Range, probably the greatest concentration of petroglyphs in North America, are at least three thousand years old. Big game hunting cultures that flourished six or seven thousand years before that are known from broken spear tips, choppers, and burins left scattered along the shores of great Pleistocene lakes, long since evaporated. Weapons and tools discovered at China Lake may be thirty thousand years old; and worked stone from a quarry in the Calico Mountains is, some argue, evidence that human beings were here more than two hundred thousand years ago.

Because of the long-term stability of such arid environments, much of this prehistoric stone evidence still lies exposed on the ground, accessible to anyone who passes by—the studious, the acquisitive, the indifferent, the merely curious. Archaeologists do not agree on the sequence of cultural history beyond about twelve thousand years ago, but it is clear that these broken bits of chalcedony, chert, and obsidian, like the animal drawings and geometric designs etched on walls of basalt throughout the desert, anchor the earliest threads of human history, the first record of human endeavor here.

Western man did not enter the California desert until the end of the eighteenth century, 250 years after Coronado brought his soldiers into the Zuni pueblos in a bewildered search for the cities of Cibola. The earliest appraisals of the land were cursory, hurried. People traveled *through* it, en route to Santa Fe or the California coastal settlements. Only miners tarried. In 1823 what had been Spain's became Mexico's and in 1848 what had been Mexico's became America's; but the bare, jagged mountains and dry lake beds, the vast and uniform plains of creosote bush and yucca plants, remained as obscure as the northern Sudan until the end of the nineteenth century.

Before 1940 the tangible evidence of twentieth-century man's passage here consisted of very little—the hard tracery of travel corridors; the widely scattered, relatively insignificant evidence of mining operations; and the fair expanse of irrigated fields at the desert's periphery. In the space of a hundred years or so the wagon roads were paved, railroads were laid down, and canals and high-tension lines were built to bring water and electricity across the desert to Los Angeles from the Colorado River. The dark mouths of gold, talc, and tin mines yawned from the bony flanks of desert ranges. Dust-encrusted chemical plants stood at work on the lonely edges of dry lake beds. And crops of grapes, lettuce, dates, alfalfa, and cotton covered the Coachella and Imperial valleys, north and south of the Salton Sea, and the Palo Verde Valley along the Colorado.

These developments proceeded with little or no awareness of earlier human occupations by cultures that preceded those of the historic Indians—the Mohave, the Chemehuevi, the Quechan. (Extensive irrigation began to actually change the climate of the Sonoran Desert, and human settlements, the railroads, and farming introduced many new, successful plants and animals into the region.)

During World War II, the American military moved into the desert in great force, to train troops and to test equipment. They found the clear weather conducive to year-round flying, the dry air, and isolation very attractive. After the war, a complex of training grounds, storage facilities, and gunnery and test ranges was permanently settled on more than three million acres of military reservations. Few perceived the extent or significance of the destruction of aboriginal sites that took place during tank maneuvers and bombing runs or in the laying out of highways, railroads, mining districts, and irrigated fields. The few who intuited that something like an American Dordogne Valley lay exposed here were (only) amateur archaeologists; even they reasoned that the desert was too vast for any of this to matter.

After World War II, people began moving out of the crowded Los Angeles basin into homes in Lucerne, Apple, and Antelope valleys in the western Mojave. They emigrated as well to a stretch of resort land at the foot of the San Jacinto Mountains that included Palm Springs, and farther out to old railroad and military towns like Twentynine Palms and Barstow. People also began exploring the desert, at first in military-surplus jeeps and then with a variety of all-terrain and off-road vehicles that became available in the 1960s. By the mid-1970s, the number of people using such vehicles for desert recreation had increased exponentially. Most came and went in innocent curiosity; the few who didn't wreaked a havoc all out of proportion to their numbers. The disturbance of previously isolated archaeological sites increased by an order of magnitude. Many sites were vandalized before archaeologists, themselves late to the desert, had any firm grasp of the bounds of human history in the desert. It was as though in the same moment an Aztec library had been discovered intact various lacunae had begun to appear.

The vandalism was of three sorts: the general disturbance usually caused by souvenir hunters and by the curious and the oblivious; the wholesale stripping of a place by professional thieves for black-market sale and trade; and outright destruction, in which vehicles were actually used to ram and trench an area. By 1980, the Bureau of Land

Management estimated that probably thirty-five percent of the archaeological sites in the desert had been vandalized. The destruction at some places by rifles and shotguns, or by power winches mounted on vehicles, was, if one cared for history, demoralizing to behold.

In spite of public education, land closures, and stricter law enforcement in recent years, the BLM estimates that, annually, about one percent of the archaeological record in the desert continues to be destroyed or stolen.   9

2

A BLM archaeologist told me, with understandable reluctance,   10
where to find the intaglio. I spread my Automobile Club of Southern California map of Imperial County out on his desk, and he traced the route with a pink felt-tip pen. The line crossed Interstate 8 and then turned west along the Mexican border.

"You can't drive any farther than about here," he said, marking a   11
small x. "There's boulders in the wash. You walk up past them."

On a separate piece of paper he drew a route in a smaller scale that   12
would take me up the arroyo to a certain point where I was to cross back east, to another arroyo. At its head, on higher ground just to the north, I would find the horse.

"It's tough to spot unless you know it's there. Once you pick it   13
up . . ." He shook his head slowly, in a gesture of wonder at its existence.

I waited until I held his eye. I assured him I would not tell anyone   14
else how to get there. He looked at me with stoical despair, like a man who had been robbed twice, whose belief in human beings was offered without conviction.

I did not go until the following day because I wanted to see it at   15
dawn. I ate breakfast at 4 a.m. in El Centro and then drove south. The route was easy to follow, though the last section of road proved difficult, broken and drifted over with sand in some spots. I came to the barricade of boulders and parked. It was light enough by then to find my way over the ground with little trouble. The contours of the landscape were stark, without any masking vegetation. I worried only about rattlesnakes.

I traversed the stone plain as directed, but, in spite of the frankness   16
of the land, I came on the horse unawares. In the first moment of recognition I was without feeling. I recalled later being startled, and that I held my breath. It was laid out on the ground with its head to the east, three times life size. As I took in its outline I felt a growing concentration of all my senses, as though my attentiveness to the pale rose color of the morning sky and other peripheral images had now ceased to be impor-

tant. I was aware that I was straining for sound in the windless air and I felt the uneven pressure of the earth hard against my feet. The horse, outlined in a standing profile on the dark ground, was as vivid before me as a bed of tulips.

I've come upon animals suddenly before, and felt a similar tension,   17 a precipitate heightening of the senses. And I have felt the inexplicable but sharply boosted intensity of a wild moment in the bush, where it is not until some minutes later that you discover the source of electricity— the warm remains of a grizzly bear kill, or the still moist tracks of a wolverine.

But this was slightly different. I felt I had stepped into an unoccu-   18 pied corridor. I had no familiar sense of history, the temporal structure in which to think: This horse was made by Quechan people three hundred years ago. I felt instead a headlong rush of images: people hunting wild horses with spears on the Pleistocene veld of southern California; Cortés riding across the causeway into Montezuma's Tenochtitlán; a short-legged Comanche, astride his horse like some sort of ferret, slashing through cavalry lines of young men who rode like farmers. A hoof exploding past my face one morning in a corral in Wyoming. These images had the weight and silence of stone.

When I released my breath, the images softened. My initial feeling,   19 of facing a wild animal in a remote region, was replaced with a calm sense of antiquity. It was then that I became conscious, like an ordinary tourist, of what was before me, and thought: This horse was probably laid out by Quechan people. But when, I wondered? The first horses they saw, I knew, might have been those that came north from Mexico in 1692 with Father Eusebio Kino. But Cocopa people, I recalled, also came this far north on occasion, to fight with their neighbors, the Quechan. And *they* could have seen horses with Melchior Díaz, at the mouth of the Colorado River in the fall of 1540. So, it could be four hundred years old. (No one in fact knows.)

I still had not moved. I took my eyes off the horse for a moment to   20 look south over the desert plain into Mexico, to look east past its head at the brightening sunrise, to situate myself. Then, finally, I brought my trailing foot slowly forward and stood erect. Sunlight was running like a thin sheet of water over the stony ground and it threw the horse into relief. It looked as though no hand had ever disturbed the stones that gave it its form.

The horse had been brought to life on ground called desert pave-   21 ment, a tight, flat matrix of small cobbles blasted smooth by sand-laden winds. The uniform, monochromatic blackness of the stones, a patina of iron and magnesium oxides called desert varnish, is caused by long-term exposure to the sun. To make this type of low-relief ground glyph, or intaglio, the artist either selectively turns individual stones over to their lighter side or removes areas of stone to expose the lighter soil underneath, creating a negative image. This horse, about eighteen feet from brow to rump and eight feet from withers to hoof, had been made in the latter way, and its outline was bermed at certain points with low ridges of stone a few inches high to enhance its three-dimensional qualities. (The left side of the horse was in full profile; each leg was extended at 90 degrees to the body and fully visible, as though seen in three-quarter profile.)

I was not eager to move. The moment I did I would be back in the   22 flow of time, the horse no longer quivering in the same way before me. I did not want to feel again the sequence of quotidian events—to be drawn off into deliberation and analysis. A human being, a four-footed animal, the open land. That was all that was present—and a "thought-less" understanding of the very old desires bearing on this particular animal: to hunt it, to render it, to fathom it, to subjugate it, to honor it, to take it as a companion.

What finally made me move was the light. The sun now filled the   23 shallow basin of the horse's body. The weighted line of the stone berm created the illusion of a mane and the distinctive roundness of an equine belly. The change in definition impelled me. I moved to the left, circling past its rump, to see how the light might flesh the horse out from various points of view. I circled it completely before squatting on my haunches. Ten or fifteen minutes later I chose another view. The third time I moved, to a point near the rear hooves, I spotted a stone tool at my feet. I stared at it a long while, more in awe than disbelief, before reaching out to pick it up. I turned it over in my left palm and took it between my fingers to feel its cutting edge. It is always difficult, especially with something so portable, to rechannel the desire to steal.

I spent several hours with the horse. As I changed positions and as   24 the angle of the light continued to change I noticed a number of things. The angle at which the pastern carried the hoof away from the ankle was perfect. Also, stones had been placed within the image to suggest, at precisely the right spot, the left shoulder above the foreleg. The line that joined thigh and hock was similarly accurate. The muzzle alone seemed distorted—but perhaps these stones had been moved by a later hand. It was an admirably accurate representation, but not what a breeder would call perfect conformation. There was the suggestion of a bowed neck and an undershot jaw, and the tail, as full as a winter coyote's, did not appear to be precisely to scale.

The more I thought about it, the more I felt I was looking at an in-   25 dividual horse, a unique combination of generic and specific detail. It was easy to imagine one of Kino's horses as a model, or a horse that ran off from one of Coronado's columns. What kind of horses would these have been, I wondered? In the sixteenth century the most sought-after horses in Europe were Spanish, the offspring of Arabian stock and Barbary horses that the Moors brought to Iberia and bred to the older, eastern European strains brought in by the Romans. The model for this horse, I speculated, could easily have been a palomino, or a descendant of horses trained for lion-hunting in North Africa.

A few generations ago, cowboys, cavalry quarter-masters, and draymen would have taken this horse before me under consideration and not let up their scrutiny until they had its heritage fixed to their satisfaction. Today, the distinction between draft and harness horses is arcane knowledge, and no image may come to mind for a blue roan or a claybank horse. The loss of such refinement in everyday conversation leaves me unsettled. People praise the Eskimo's ability to distinguish among forty types of snow but forget the skill of others who routinely differentiate between overo and tobiano pintos. Such distinctions are made for the same reason. You have to do it to be able to talk clearly about the world. 26

For parts of two years I worked as a horse wrangler and packer in Wyoming. It is dim knowledge now; I would have to think to remember if a buckskin was a kind of dun horse. And I couldn't throw a double-diamond hitch over a set of panniers—the packer's basic tie-down—without guidance. As I squatted there in the desert, however, these more personal memories seemed tenuous in comparison with the sweep of this animal in human time. My memories had no depth. I thought of the Hittite cavalry riding against the Syrians 3500 years ago. And the first of the Chinese emperors, Ch'in Shih Huang, buried in Shensi Province in 210 BC with thousands of life-size horses and soldiers, a terra-cotta guardian army. What could I know of what was in the mind of whoever made this horse? Was there some racial memory of it as an animal that had once fed the artist's ancestors and then disappeared from North America? And then returned in this strange alliance with another race of men? 27

Certainly, whoever it was, the artist had observed the animal very closely. Certainly the animal's speed had impressed him. Among the first things the Quechan would have learned from an encounter with Kino's horses was that their own long-distance runners—men who could run down mule deer—were no match for this animal. 28

From where I squatted I could look far out over the Mexican plain. Juan Bautista de Anza passed this way in 1774, extending El Camino Real into Alta California from Sinaloa. He was followed by others, all of them astride the magical horse; *gente de razón*, the people of reason, coming into the country of *los primitivos*. The horse, like the stone animals of 29

Egypt, urged these memories upon me. And as I drew them up from some forgotten corner of my mind—huge horses carved in the white chalk downs of southern England by an Iron Age people; Spanish horses rearing and wheeling in fear before alligators in Florida—the images seemed tethered before me. With this sense of proportion, a memory of my own—the morning I almost lost my face to a horse's hoof—now had somewhere to fit.

I rose up and began to walk slowly around the horse again. I had taken the first long measure of it and was looking now for a way to depart, a new angle of light, a fading of the image itself before the rising sun, that would break its hold on me. As I circled, feeling both heady and serene at the encounter, I realized again how strangely vivid it was. It had been created on a barren bajada between two arroyos, as nondescript a place as one could imagine. The only plant life here was a few wands of ocotillo cactus. The ground beneath my shoes was so hard it wouldn't take the print of a heavy animal even after a rain. The only sounds I had heard here were the voices of quail. 30

The archaeologist had been correct. For all its forcefulness, the horse is inconspicuous. If you don't care to see it you can walk right past it. That pleases him, I think. Unmarked on this bleak shoulder of the plain, the site signals to no one; so he wants no protective fences here, no informative plaque, to act as beacons. He would rather take a chance that no motorcyclist, no aimless wanderer with a flair for violence and a depth of ignorance, will ever find his way here. 31

The archaeologist had given me something before I left his office that now seemed peculiar—an aerial photograph of the horse. It is widely believed that an aerial view of an intaglio provides a fair and accurate description. It does not. In the photograph the horse looks somewhat crudely constructed; from the ground it appears far more deftly rendered. The photograph is of a single moment, and in that split second the horse seems vaguely impotent. I watched light pool in the intaglio at dawn; I imagine you could watch it withdraw at dusk and sense the same animation I did. In those prolonged moments its shape and so, too, its general character changed—noticeably. The living quality of the image, its immediacy to the eye, was brought out by the light-in-time, not, at least here, in the camera's frozen instant. 32

Intaglios, I thought, were never meant to be seen by gods in the sky above. They were meant to be seen by people on the ground, over a long period of shifting light. This could even be true of the huge figures on the Plain of Nazca in Peru, where people could walk for the length of a day beside them. It is our own impatience that leads us to think otherwise. 33

This process of abstraction, almost unintentional, drew me gradually away from the horse. I came to a position of attention at the edge of 34 the sphere of its influence. With a slight bow I paid my respects to the horse, its maker, and the history of us all, and departed.

3

A short distance away I stopped the car in the middle of the road 35
to make a few notes. I had not been able to write down what I was thinking when I was with the horse. It would have seemed disrespectful, and it would have required another kind of attention. So now I patiently drained my memory of the details it had fastened itself upon. The road I'd stopped on was adjacent to the All American Canal, the major source of water for the Imperial and Coachella valleys. The water flowed west placidly. A disjointed flock of coots, small, dark birds with white bills, was paddling against the current, foraging in the rushes.

I was peripherally aware of the birds as I wrote, the only move- 36
ment in the desert; and of a series of sounds from a village a half-mile away. The first sounds from this collection of ramshackle houses in a grove of cottonwoods were the distracted dawn voices of dogs. I heard them intermingled with the cries of a rooster. Later, the high-pitched voices of children calling out to each other came disembodied through the dry desert air. Now, a little after seven, I could hear someone practicing on the trumpet, the same rough phrases played over and over. I suddenly remembered how as children we had tried to get the rhythm of a galloping horse with hands against our thighs, or by fluttering our tongues against the roofs of our mouths.

After the trumpet, the impatient calls of adults, summoning chil- 37
dren. Sunday morning. Wood smoke hung like a lens in the trees. The first car starts—a cold, eight-cylinder engine, of Chrysler extraction perhaps, goosed to life, then throttled back to murmur through dual mufflers, the obbligato music of a shade-tree mechanic. The rote bark of mongrel dogs at dawn, the jagged outcries of men and women, an engine coming to life. Like a thousand villages from West Virginia to Guadalajara.

I finished my notes—where was I going to find a description of the 38
horses that came north with the conquistadors? Did their manes come forward prominently over the brow, like this one's, like the forelocks of Blackfeet and Assiniboine men in nineteenth-century paintings? I set the notes on the seat beside me.

The road followed the canal for a while and then arced north, to- 39
ward Interstate 8. It was slow driving and I fell to thinking how the desert had changed since Anza had come through. New plants and animals—the MacDougall cottonwood, the English house sparrow, the chukar from India—have about them now the air of the native-born. Of the native species, some—no one knows how many—are extinct. The

populations of many others, especially the animals, have been sharply reduced. The idea of a desert impoverished by agricultural poisons and varmint hunters, by off-road vehicles and military operations, did not seem as disturbing to me, however, as this other horror, now that I had been those hours with the horse. The vandals, the few who crowbar rock art off the desert's walls, who dig up graves, who punish the ground that holds intaglios, are people who devour history. Their self-centered scorn, their disrespect for ideas and images beyond their ken, create the awful atmosphere of loose ends in which totalitarianism thrives, in which the past is merely curious or wrong.

I thought about the horse sitting out there on the unprotected plain. I enumerated its qualities in my mind until a sense of its vulnerability receded and it became an anchor for something else. I remembered that history, a history like this one, which ran deeper than Mexico, deeper than the Spanish, was a kind of medicine. It permitted the great breadth of human expression to reverberate, and it did not urge you to locate its apotheosis in the present. 40

Each of us, individuals and civilizations, has been held upside down like Achilles in the River Styx. The artist mixing his colors in the dim light of Altamira; an Egyptian ruler lying still now, wrapped in his byssus, stored against time in a pyramid; the faded Dorset culture of the Arctic; the Hmong and Samburu and Walbiri of historic time; the modern nations. This great, imperfect stretch of human expression is the clarification and encouragement, the urging and the reminder, we call history. And it is inscribed everywhere in the face of the land, from the mountain passes of the Himalayas to a nameless bajada in the California desert. 41

Small birds rose up in the road ahead, startled, and flew off. I prayed no infidel would ever find that horse. 42

1986

Purpose and Meaning

1. What is Lopez's primary purpose in this essay? How does its title relate to that purpose?

2. What assumptions is Lopez making about his audience? Explain your answer.

3. What does Lopez mean in paragraph 41 when he says, "Each of us, individuals and civilizations, has been held upside down like Achilles in the River Styx"? How does this statement relate to his comments about history?

Language and Style

1. How would you characterize the tone of this essay? Does the tone remain constant or change? Connect the tone with Lopez's thesis.

2. What stylistic techniques does Lopez use to relate the stone horse's effect on him? Give examples to explain your answer.

3. How does Lopez use his personal memories in part 2 of the essay? Considering his purpose in this section, is their usage appropriate? Explain your answer.

Strategy and Structure

1. Lopez chooses to divide this essay into three sections. Why is that decision appropriate to his strategy? How does the structure relate to overall style?

2. Most of the essay's second section is devoted to describing the stone horse's effect on Lopez as an observer. How does that discussion relate to his purpose?

3. The concluding paragraph of the essay is composed of two short sentences. Is this an effective closing, or is it too abrupt? Explain your answer.

Thinking and Writing

1. This essay echoes points made by E. B. White in "Walden" concerning the treatment of special places. Develop an essay in which you discuss this topic.

2. Develop an essay in which you argue for or against public access to archeological sites, using the propositions of the public's right to access and the documented wanton destruction of those sites as premises.

3. Observe a larger-than-life work of art on your own. Write an essay in which you not only describe the work itself, but also its effect on you as an observer.

The American Geographies

It has become commonplace to observe that Americans know little   1
of the geography of their country, that they are innocent of it as a land-scape of rivers, mountains, and towns. They do not know, supposedly, the location of the Delaware Water Gap, the Olympic Mountains, or the Piedmont Plateau; and, the indictment continues, they have little conception of the way the individual components of this landscape are imperiled, from a human perspective, by modern farming practices or industrial pollution.

I do not know how true this is, but it is easy to believe that it is   2 truer than most of us would wish. A recent Gallup Organization and National Geographic Society survey found Americans woefully ignorant of world geography. Three out of four couldn't locate the Persian Gulf. The implication was that we knew no more about our own homeland, and that this ignorance undermined the integrity of our political processes and the efficiency of our business enterprises.

As Americans, we profess a sincere and fierce love for the   3
American landscape, for our rolling prairies, free-flowing rivers, and "purple mountains' majesty"; but it is hard to imagine, actually, where this particular landscape is. It is not just that a nostalgic landscape has passed away—Mark Twain's Mississippi is now dammed from Illinois to Louisiana and the prairies have all been sold and fenced. It is that it's always been a romantic's landscape. In the attenuated form in which it is presented on television today, in magazine articles and in calendar photographs, the essential wildness of the American landscape is reduced to attractive scenery. We look out on a familiar, memorized landscape that portends adventure and promises enrichment. There are no distracting people in it and few artifacts of human life. The animals are all beautiful, diligent, one might even say well behaved. Nature's unruliness, the power of rivers and skies to intimidate, and any evidence of disastrous human land management practices are all but invisible. It is, in short, a magnificent garden, a colonial vision of paradise imposed on a real place that is, at best, only selectively known.

The real American landscape is a face of almost incomprehensible   4
depth and complexity. If one were to sit for a few days, for example, among the ponderosa pine forests and black lava fields of the Cascade Mountains in western Oregon, inhaling the pines' sweet balm on an evening breeze from some point on the barren rock, and then were to step off to the Olympic Peninsula in Washington, to those rain forests with sphagnum moss floors soft as fleece underfoot and Douglas firs too big around for five people to hug, and then head south to walk the ephemeral creeks and sun-blistered playas of the Mojave Desert in southern California, one would be reeling under the sensations. The contrast is not only one of plants and soils, a different array, say, of brilliantly colored beetles. The shock to the senses comes from a different shape to the silence, a difference in the very quality of light, in the weight of the air. And this relatively short journey down the West Coast would still leave the traveler with all that lay to the east to explore—the anomalous sand hills of Nebraska, the heat and frog voices of Okefenokee Swamp, the fetch of Chesapeake Bay, the hardwood copses and black bears of the Ozark Mountains.

No one of these places, of course, can be entirely fathomed, biologi-   5
cally or aesthetically. They are mysteries upon which we impose names.

Enchantments. We tick the names off glibly but lovingly. We mean no disrespect. Our genuine desire, though we may be skeptical about the time it would take and uncertain of its practical value to us, is to actually know these places. As deeply ingrained in the American psyche as the desire to conquer and control the land is the desire to sojourn in it, to sail up and down Pamlico Sound, to paddle a canoe through Minnesota's boundary waters, to walk on the desert of the Great Salt Lake, to camp in the stony hardwood valleys of Vermont.

To do this well, to really come to an understanding of a specific 6
American geography, requires not only time but a kind of local expertise, an intimacy with place few of us ever develop. There is no way around the former requirement: if you want to know you must take the time. It is not in books. A specific geographical understanding, however, can be sought out and borrowed. It resides with men and women more or less sworn to a place, who abide there, who have a feel for the soil and history, for the turn of leaves and night sounds. Often they are glad to take the outlander in tow.

These local geniuses of American landscape, in my experience, are 7
people in whom geography thrives. They are the antithesis of geographical ignorance. Rarely known outside their own communities, they often seem, at the first encounter, unremarkable and anonymous. They may not be able to recall the name of a particular wildflower—or they may have given it a name known only to them. They might have forgotten the precise circumstances of a local historical event. Or they can't say for certain when the last of the Canada geese passed through in the fall, or can't differentiate between two kinds of trout in the same creek. Like all of us, they have fallen prey to the fallacies of memory and are burdened with ignorance; but they are nearly flawless in the respect they bear these places they love. Their knowledge is intimate rather than encyclopedic, human but not necessarily scholarly. It rings with the concrete details of experience.

America, I believe, teems with such people. The paradox here, be- 8
tween a faulty grasp of geographical knowledge for which Americans are indicted and the intimate, apparently contradictory familiarity of a group of largely anonymous people, is not solely a matter of confused scale. (The local landscape is easier to know than a national landscape—and many local geographers, of course, are relatively ignorant of a national geography.) And it is not simply ironic. The paradox is dark. To be succinct: the politics and advertising that seek a national audience must project a national geography; to be broadly useful that geography must, inevitably, be generalized and it is often romantic. It is therefore frequently misleading and imprecise. The same holds true with the entertainment industry, but here the problem might be clearer. The same films, magazines, and television features that honor an imaginary

American landscape also tout the worth of the anonymous men and women who interpret it. Their affinity for the land is lauded, their local allegiance admired. But the rigor of their local geographies, taken as a whole, contradicts a patriotic, national vision of unspoiled, untroubled land. These men and women are ultimately forgotten, along with the details of the landscapes they speak for, in the face of more pressing national matters. It is the chilling nature of modern society to find an ignorance of geography, local or national, as excusable as an ignorance of hand tools; and to find the commitment of people to their home places only momentarily entertaining. And finally naive.

If one were to pass time among Basawara people in the Kalahari   9
Desert, or with Kreen-Akrora in the Amazon Basin, or with Pitjantjatjara Aborigines in Australia, the most salient impression they might leave is of an absolutely stunning knowledge of their local geography—geology, hydrology, biology, and weather. In short, the extensive particulars of their intercourse with it.

In forty thousand years of human history, it has only been in the   10
last few hundred years or so that a people could afford to ignore their local geographies as completely as we do and still survive. Technological innovations from refrigerated trucks to artificial fertilizers, from sophisticated cost accounting to mass air transportation, have utterly changed concepts of season, distance, soil productivity, and the real cost of drawing sustenance from the land. It is now possible for a resident of Boston to bite into a fresh strawberry in the dead of winter; for someone in San Francisco to travel to Atlanta in a few hours with no worry of how formidable might be crossings of the Great Basin Desert or the Mississippi River; for an absentee farmer to gain a tax advantage from a farm that leaches poisons into its water table and on which crops are left to rot. The Pitjantjatjara might shake their heads in bewilderment and bemusement, not because they are primitive or ignorant people, not because they have no sense of irony or are incapable of marveling, but because they have not (many would say not yet) realized a world in which such manipulation of the land—surmounting the imperatives of distance it imposes, for example, or turning the large-scale destruction of forests and arable land into wealth—is desirable or plausible.

In the years I have traveled through America, in cars and on horse-   11
back, on foot and by raft, I have repeatedly been brought to a sudden state of awe by some gracile or savage movement of animal, some odd wrapping of a tree's foliage by the wind, an unimpeded run of dew-laden prairie stretching to a horizon flat as a coin where a pin-dot sun pales the dawn sky pink. I know these things are beyond intellection, that they are the vivid edges of a world that includes but also transcends the human world. In memory, when I dwell on these things, I know that

in a truly national literature there should be odes to the Triassic reds of the Colorado Plateau, to the sharp and ghostly light of the Florida Keys, to the aeolian soils of southern Minnesota and the Palouse in Washington, though the modern mind abjures the literary potential of such subjects. (If the sand and floodwater farmers of Arizona and New Mexico were to take the black loams of Louisiana in their hands they would be flabbergasted, and that is the beginning of literature.) I know there should be eloquent evocations of the cobbled beaches of Maine, the plutonic walls of the Sierra Nevada, the orange canyons of the Kaibab Plateau. I have no doubt, in fact, that there are. They are as numerous and diverse as the eyes and fingers that ponder the country—it is that only a handful of them are known. The great majority are to be found in drawers and boxes, in the letters and private journals of millions of workaday people who have regarded their encounters with the land as an engagement bordering on the spiritual, as being fundamentally linked to their state of health.

One cannot acknowledge the extent and the history of this kind of testimony without being forced to the realization that something strange, if not dangerous, is afoot. Year by year, the number of people with firsthand experience in the land dwindles. Rural populations continue to shift to the cities. The family farm is in a state of demise, and government and industry continue to apply pressure on the native peoples of North America to sever their ties with the land. In the wake of this loss of personal and local knowledge, the knowledge from which a real geography is derived, the knowledge on which a country must ultimately stand, has come something hard to define but I think sinister and unsettling—the packaging and marketing of land as a form of entertainment. An incipient industry, capitalizing on the nostalgia Americans feel for the imagined virgin landscapes of their fathers, and on a desire for adventure, now offers people a convenient though sometimes incomplete or even spurious geography as an inducement to purchase a unique experience. But the line between authentic experience and a superficial exposure to the elements of experience is blurred. And the real landscape, in all its complexity, is distorted even further in the public imagination. No longer innately mysterious and dignified, a ground from which experience grows, it becomes a curiously generic backdrop on which experience is imposed.

In theme parks the profound, subtle, and protracted experience of running a river is reduced to a loud, quick, safe equivalence, a pleasant distraction. People only able to venture into the countryside on annual vacations are, increasingly, schooled in the belief that wild land will, and should, provide thrills and exceptional scenery on a timely basis. If it does not, something is wrong, either with the land itself or possibly with the company outfitting the trip.

People in America, then, face a convoluted situation. The land it- 14
self, vast and differentiated, defies the notion of a national geography. If
applied at all it must be applied lightly, and it must grow out of the concrete detail of local geographies. Yet Americans are daily presented
with, and have become accustomed to talking about, a homogenized national geography, one that seems to operate independently of the land, a
collection of objects rather than a continuous bolt of fabric. It appears in
advertisements, as a background in movies, and in patriotic calendars.
The suggestion is that there *can* be a national geography because the
constituent parts are interchangeable and can be treated as commodities.
In day-to-day affairs, in other words, one place serves as well as another
to convey one's point. On reflection, this is an appalling condescension
and a terrible imprecision, the very antithesis of knowledge. The idea
that either the Green River in Utah or the Salmon River in Idaho will do,
or that the valleys of Kentucky and West Virginia are virtually interchangeable, is not just misleading. For people still dependent on the soil
for their sustenance, or for people whose memories tie them to those
places, it betrays a numbing casualness, a utilitarian, expedient, and
commercial frame of mind. It heralds a society in which it is no longer
necessary for human beings to know where they live, except as those
places are described and fixed by numbers. The truly difficult and lifelong task of discovering where one lives is finally disdained.

If a society forgets or no longer cares where it lives, then anyone 15
with the political power and the will to do so can manipulate the landscape to conform to certain social ideals or nostalgic visions. People may
hardly notice that anything has happened, or assume that whatever happens—a mountain stripped of timber and eroding into its creeks—is for
the common good. The more superficial a society's knowledge of the
real dimensions of the land it occupies becomes, the more vulnerable the
land is to exploitation, to manipulation for short-term gain. The land,
virtually powerless before political and commercial entities, finds itself
finally with no defenders. It finds itself bereft of intimates with indispensable, concrete knowledge. (Oddly, or perhaps not oddly, while
American society continues to value local knowledge as a quaint part of
its heritage, it continues to cut such people off from any real political
power. This is as true for small farmers and illiterate cowboys as it is for
American Indians, native Hawaiians, and Eskimos.)

The intense pressure of imagery in America, and the manipulation 16
of images necessary to a society with specific goals, means the land will
inevitably be treated like a commodity; and voices that tend to contradict the proffered image will, one way or another, be silenced or discred-
ited by those in power. This is not new to America; the promulgation in
America of a false or imposed geography has been the case from the beginning. All local geographies, as they were defined by hundreds of sep-

arate, independent native traditions, were denied in the beginning in favor of an imported and unifying vision of America's natural history. The country, the landscape itself, was eventually defined according to dictates of Progress like Manifest Destiny, and laws like the Homestead Act which reflected a poor understanding of the physical lay of the land.

When I was growing up in southern California, I formed the rudi- 17 ments of a local geography—eucalyptus trees, February rains, Santa Ana winds. I lost much of it when my family moved to New York City, a move typical of the modern, peripatetic style of American life, responding to the exigencies of divorce and employment. As a boy I felt a hunger to know the American landscape that was extreme; when I was finally able to travel on my own, I did so. Eventually I visited most of the United States, living for brief periods of time in Arizona, Indiana, Alabama, Georgia, Wyoming, New Jersey, and Montana before settling twenty years ago in western Oregon.

The astonishing level of my ignorance confronted me everywhere I 18 went. I knew early on that the country could not be held together in a few phrases, that its geography was magnificent and incomprehensible, that a man or woman could devote a lifetime to its elucidation and still feel in the end that he had but sailed many thousands of miles over the surface of the ocean. So I came into the habit of traversing landscapes I wanted to know with local tutors and reading what had previously been written about, and in, those places. I came to value exceedingly novels and essays and works of nonfiction that connected human enterprise to real and specific places, and I grew to be mildly distrustful of work that occurred in no particular place, work so cerebral and detached as to be refutable only in an argument of ideas.

These sojourns in various corners of the country infused me, some- 19 what to my surprise on thinking about it, with a great sense of hope. Whatever despair I had come to feel at a waning sense of the real land and the emergence of false geographies—elements of the land being manipulated, for example, to create erroneous but useful patterns in advertising—was dispelled by the depth of a single person's local knowledge, by the serenity that seemed to come with that intelligence. Any harm that might be done by people who cared nothing for the land, to whom it was not innately worthy but only something ultimately for sale, I thought, would one day have to meet this kind of integrity, people with the same dignity and transcendence as the land they occupied. So when I traveled, when I rolled my sleeping bag out on the shores of the Beaufort Sea or in the high pastures of the Absaroka Range in Wyoming, or at the bottom of the Grand Canyon, I absorbed those particular testaments to life, the indigenous color and songbird song, the smell of sunbleached rock, damp earth, and wild honey, with some crude appreciation of the singular magnificence of each of those places. And the reassurance I felt expanded in the knowledge that there were, and would likely always be, people speaking out whenever they felt the dignity of the earth imperiled in these places.

The promulgation of false geographies, which threaten the fundamental notion of what it means to live somewhere, is a current with a stable and perhaps growing countercurrent. People living in New York City are familiar with the stone basements, the cratonic geology, of that island and have a feeling for birds migrating through in the fall, their sequence and number. They do not find the city alien but human, its attenuated natural history merely different from that of rural Georgia or Kansas. I find the countermeasure, too, among Eskimos who cannot read but who might engage you for days on the subtleties of sea-ice topography. And among men and women who, though they have followed in the footsteps of their parents, have come to the conclusion that they cannot farm or fish or log in the way their ancestors did; the finite boundaries to this sort of wealth have appeared in their lifetime. Or among young men and women who have taken several decades of book-learned agronomy, zoology, silviculture, and horticulture, ecology, ethnobotany, and fluvial geomorphology and turned it into a new kind of local knowledge, who have taken up residence in a place and sought, both because of and in spite of their education, to develop a deep intimacy with it. Or they have gone to work, idealistically, for the National Park Service or the fish and wildlife services or for a private institution like The Nature Conservancy. They are people to whom the land is more than politics or economics. These are people for whom the land is alive. It feeds them, directly, and that is how and why they learn its geography.

In the end, then, if one begins among the blue crabs of Chesapeake Bay and wanders for several years, down through the Smoky Mountains and back to the bluegrass hills, along the drainages of the Ohio and into the hill country of Missouri, where in summer a chorus of cicadas might drown out human conversation, then up the Missouri itself, reading on the way the entries of Meriwether Lewis and William Clark and musing on the demise of the plains grizzly and the sturgeon, crosses west into the drainage of the Platte and spends the evenings with Gene Weltfish's *The Lost Universe*, her book about the Pawnee who once thrived there, then drops south to Palo Duro Canyon and the irrigated farms of the Llano Estacado in Texas, turns west across the Sangre de Cristo, southern-most of the Rocky Mountain ranges, and moves north and west up onto the slickrock mesas of Utah, those browns and oranges, the ocherous hues reverberating in the deep canyons, then goes north, swinging west to the insular ranges that sit like battleships in the pelagic space of

Nevada, camps at the steaming edge of sulphur springs in the Black Rock Desert, where alkaline pans are glazed with a ferocious light, a heat to melt iron, then crosses the northern Sierra Nevada, waist-deep in summer snow in the passes, to descend to the valley of the Sacramento, and rises through groves of elephantine redwoods in the Coast Range, to arrive at Cape Mendocino, before Balboa's Pacific, cormorants and gulls, gray whales headed north for Unimak Pass in the Aleutians, the winds crashing down on you, facing the ocean over the blue ocean that gives the scene its true vastness, making this crossing, having been so often astonished at the line and the color of the land, the ingenious lives of its plants and animals, the varieties of its darknesses, the intensity of the stars overhead, you would be ashamed to discover, then, in yourself, any capacity to focus on ravages in the land that left you unsettled. You would have seen so much, breathtaking, startling, and outsize, that you might not be able for a long time to break the spell, the sense, especially finishing your journey in the West, that the land had not been as rearranged or quite as compromised as you had first imagined.

After you had slept some nights on the beach, however, with that [22] finite line of the ocean before you and the land stretching out behind you, the wind first battering then cradling you, you would be compelled by memory, obligated by your own involvement, to speak of what left you troubled. To find the rivers dammed and shrunken, the soil washed away, the land fenced, a tracery of pipes and wires and roads laid down everywhere, blocking and channeling the movement of water and animals, cutting the eye off repeatedly and confining it—you had expected this. It troubles you no more than your despair over the ruthlessness, the insensitivity, the impetuousness of modern life. What underlies this obvious change, however, is a less noticeable pattern of disruption: acidic lakes, skies empty of birds, fouled beaches, the poisonous slags of industry, the sun burning like a molten coin in ruined air.

It is a tenet of certain ideologies that man is responsible for all that [23] is ugly, that everything nature creates is beautiful. Nature's darkness goes partly unreported, of course, and human brilliance is often perversely ignored. What is true is that man has a power, literally beyond his comprehension, to destroy. The lethality of some of what he manufactures, the incompetence with which he stores it or seeks to dispose of it, the cavalier way in which he employs in his daily living substances that threaten his health, the leniency of the courts in these matters (as though products as well as people enjoyed the protection of the Fifth Amendment), and the treatment of open land, rivers, and the atmosphere as if, in some medieval way, they could still be regarded as disposal sinks of infinite capacity, would make you wonder, standing face to in the wind at Cape Mendocino, if we weren't bent on an errand of madness.

The geographies of North America, the myriad small landscapes   24
that make up the national fabric, are threatened—by ignorance of what
makes them unique, by utilitarian attitudes, by failure to include them in
the moral universe, and by brutal disregard. A testament of minor
voices can clear away an ignorance of any place, can inform us of its special qualities; but no voice, by merely telling a story, can cause the poisonous wastes that saturate some parts of the land to decompose, to evap-
orate. This responsibility falls ultimately to the national community, a
vague and fragile entity to be sure, but one that, in America, can be ferocious in exerting its will.

Geography, the formal way in which we grapple with this areal   25
mystery, is finally knowledge that calls up something in the land we recognize and respond to. It gives us a sense of place and a sense of community. Both are indispensable to a state of well-being, an individual's
and a country's.

One afternoon on the Siuslaw River in the Coast Range of Oregon,   26
in January, I hooked a steelhead, a sea-run trout, that told me, through
the muscles of my hands and arms and shoulders, something of the nature of the thing I was calling "the Siuslaw River." Years ago I had stood
under a pecan tree in Upson County, Georgia, idly eating the nuts, when
slowly it occurred to me that these nuts would taste different from
pecans growing somewhere up in South Carolina. I didn't need a sharp
sense of taste to know this, only to pay attention at a level no one had
ever told me was necessary. One November dawn, long before the sun
rose, I began a vigil at the Dumont Dunes in the Mojave Desert in
California, which I kept until a few minutes after the sun broke the horizon. During that time I named to myself the colors by which the sky
changed and by which the sand itself flowed like a rising tide through
grays and silvers and blues into yellows, pinks, washed duns, and fallow beiges.

It is through the power of observation, the gifts of eye and ear, of   27
tongue and nose and finger, that a place first rises up in our mind, afterwards it is memory that carries the place, that allows it to grow in depth
and complexity. For as long as our records go back, we have held these
two things dear, landscape and memory. Each infuses us with a different kind of life. The one feeds us, figuratively and literally. The other
protects us from lies and tyranny. To keep landscapes intact and the
memory of them, our history in them, alive, seems as imperative a task
in modern time as finding the extent to which individual expression can
be accommodated, before it threatens to destroy the fabric of society.

If I were to now visit another country, I would ask my local com-   28
panion, before I saw any museum or library, any factory or fabled town,
to walk me in the country of his or her youth, to tell me the names of

things and how, traditionally, they have been fitted together in a community. I would ask for the stories, the voice of memory over the land. I would ask to taste the wild nuts and fruits, to see their fishing lures, their bouquets, their fences. I would ask about the history of storms there, the age of the trees, the winter color of the hills. Only then would I ask to see the museums. I would want first the sense of a real place, to know that I was not inhabiting an idea. I would want to know the lay of the land first, the real geography, and take some measure of the love of it in my companion before I stood before the paintings or read works of scholarship. I would want to have something real and remembered against which I might hope to measure their truth.

1989

Purpose and Meaning

1. What is Lopez's concern in this essay? What does he mean by "real" geography as opposed to "unreal" geography?

2. What is the danger of adhering to what Lopez calls a "national geography"?

3. What, according to Lopez, is one of our culture's most imperative tasks? How can the task be accomplished? How can the idea of a "false" geography be reversed?

Language and Style

1. In paragraph 8, Lopez discusses a paradox. How does the paradox function in relation to the essay's general design?

2. In paragraph 10, Lopez uses specific locales with descriptive characteristics. How does he use them? What is their function? Are they objective or subjective? Explain your answer.

3. Lopez uses few personal pronouns until the last paragraph. How does restricting their usage contribute to the essay's main purpose? What effect does the use of them in the last paragraph have on Lopez's central concern?

Strategy and Structure

1. What technique does Lopez use to support his argument? How effective are they in terms of his argument?

2. How does the repetition of the same subject-verb combination, "I would ask," affect the strength of his argument? If the repetition were removed, would the essay gain or lose in impact? Why?

3. What organization pattern does Lopez use to distinguish between a "homogenized" landscape and the "real" American landscape?

Thinking and Writing

1. How intimate are you with the characteristics of your native landscape? Write an essay which through observation evokes the uniqueness and complexity of a specific locale.

2. Filmmakers often intentionally use beautiful but incorrectly identified landscapes strictly for visual effect, and few moviegoers notice the change. Adopting Lopez's point of view, write an essay in which you argue the inappropriateness of taking such liberties with landscapes, regardless of the audience's inability to recognize the substitution.

○●○●○●○●○●○●○●○●○●○●○●○●○●○●○●○●○

Renegotiating the Contracts

In an essay in *Harper's* magazine several years ago, Lewis Lapham   1
wrote that democracy was an experiment, a flawed enterprise that required continued human attention if it was going to serve us well. The philosophy behind our relationship with animals in the Western world is also flawed, and in need of continued attention.

To put this in the most basic terms, our relationships with wild ani-   2
mals were once contractual—principled agreements, established and maintained in a spirit of reciprocity and mythic in their pervasiveness. Among hunting peoples in general in the northern hemisphere, these agreements derived from a sense of mutual obligation and courtesy.

Over the past two decades, in particular, our contemporary rela-   3
tionships with wild animals have been energetically scrutinized by anthropologists, moral philosophers, and field biologists. A renewed interest in the mythologies and values of hunting peoples has caused us to question the moral basis for a continuation of hunting by industrialized cultures. Tests to determine the lethal dosages of consumer products and the corrosiveness of cosmetics in animal laboratories, the commercial harvest of infant harp seals, and research on cetacean brains have all provoked heated debate over animal rights. A proliferation of animal images in advertising, and their dominant presence in children's stories, have brought thinkers such as Paul Shepard to wonder how animals affect the very way we conceptualize.

We once thought of animals as not only sentient but as congruent   4
with ourselves in a world beyond the world we can see, one structured
by myth and moral obligation, and activated by spiritual power. The departure from the original conception was formalized in Cartesian dual-
ism—the animal was a soulless entity with which people could not have
a moral relationship—and in Ruskin's belief that to find anything but
the profane and mechanistic in the natural world was to engage in a pathetic fallacy. Both these ideas seem short-sighted and to have not
served us well.

Today, commerce raises perhaps the most strenuous objection to   5
the interference of animals—their mere presence, their purported
rights—in human activity. Wilderness areas the world over, the only
places where animals are free of the social and economic schemes of
men, are consistently violated for their wealth of timber, minerals, and
hydrocarbons; and to fill zoos. Fundamentalist religions and reductionist science deny—or persist in regarding as "outdated"—the aboriginal
aspects of our relationships with animals; and deny that animals themselves have any spiritual dimension.

If we have embarked on a shared path in reevaluating this situa-   6
tion as humanists and scientists, it has been to inquire how we are going
to repair the original contracts. These agreements were abrogated during the agricultural, scientific, and industrial revolutions with a determined degradation of the value of animal life. Acts once indefensible became, over the centuries, only what was acceptable or expeditious. Such
a reconsideration bears sharply on the fate of zoos and the future of animal experimentation, but it is also fundamentally important to us as
creatures. Whatever wisdom we have shown in deriving a science of
ecology, whatever insight we have gained from quantum mechanics into
the importance of *relationships* (rather than the mere existence of *things*),
urges us to consider these issues without calculation and passionately.
We must examine a deep and long-lived insult.

I believe there are two failures to face. I speak with the view of   7
someone who regards human beings as a Pleistocene species rather than
a twentieth-century phenomenon; and who also believes that to set aside
our relationships with wild animals as inconsequential is to undermine
our regard for the other sex, other cultures, other universes. Animals
exist apart from us, and the balance here between self-esteem and a prejudice directed toward what is different is one of the most rarefied and
baffling issues in anthropology. Our own direction as a culture has been
to enhance self-esteem *and* to dismantle prejudice by eradicating ignorance. No culture, however, including our own, with its great admiration for compassion and the high value it places on a broad education,
has erased prejudice. (No one for that matter has proved it a worthless
aspect of cultural evolution and survival.) What is required—or our

Western venture is for naught—is to rise above prejudice to a position of respectful regard toward everything that is different from ourselves and not innately evil.

The two ways we have broken with animals are clear and could easily be the focus of our repair. One is that we have simply lost contact with them. Our notions of animal life are highly intellectualized, and no longer checked by daily contact with their environs. Our conceptions of them are not only bookish but stagnant, for, once discovered, we do not permit them to evolve as cultures. We allow them very little grace, enterprise, or individual variation. On the basis of even my own meager field experience—with wolves in Alaska, with mountain lion in Arizona, and with muskoxen, polar bear, and narwhal in the Canadian Arctic—this is a major blind spot in our efforts to erase ignorance. By predetermining categories of relevant information, by dismissing what cannot be easily quantified, by designing research to flatter the predilection of sponsors or defeat the political aims of a special interest group—field biologists have complained to me of both—we have produced distorted and incomplete images of animals.

We have created, further, mathematical models of ecosystems we only superficially grasp and then set divisions of government to managing the lives of the affected animals on the basis of these abstractions. We come perilously close in this to the worst moments of our history, to events we regret most deeply: the subjugation of races, the violent persecution of minority beliefs, the waging of war. With animals, all that saves us here is Descartes' convenience. Of course, some believe him right and regard this as firm ethical ground. But we skirt such imperious condescension here, such hubris, that we cannot help but undermine our principles of behavior toward ourselves, toward each other.

Some doubt the validity or the pertinence of these themes. But I have often heard, at grave and hopeful meetings, eloquent talk of the intellectual and social crises of our times—suppression of personality in a patriarchal society; the inhumane thrust of industry; the colonial designs of Russian or American foreign policy. With the change of only a word or two people could have been speaking of animals. The prejudices inform each other.

If the first failure is one of principle, where our attitudes toward animals have become those of owners and our knowledge skewed because we no longer meet with them and rarely enter their landscapes, the second is a failure of imagination. We have largely lost our understanding of where in an adult life to fit the awe and mystery that animals excite. This sensibility is still maintained in some fashion, however, by many aboriginal peoples and I would suggest, again on the basis of my own short time with Eskimos, that to step beyond a superficial acquaintance with such people is to enter a realm of understanding where what has meant human survival for the past 40,000 years remains clear. Here the comprehension of fundamental human needs and their application—how to live a successful life—is revealed continuously in story, often in stories of human encounters with animals. These stories employ the prosaic to announce the profound, the profound to reveal the ineffable. They balance reassuringly the unfathomable and the concrete. In our age we prefer analysis, not awe; but historically, human beings have subsisted as much on the mystery and awe inspired by animals as they have on the actual flesh of the caribou or the salmon. They have actively sought them in the hunting experience and have preserved them in their oral literatures.

The cultivation of mystery and awe keeps the human capacity for 12 metaphor alive. And a capacity for metaphor allows us to perceive several layers of meaning in a story about, say, a polar bear; to perceive animals not only as complex physiological organisms but as part of a coherent and shared landscape.

Our second failure with animals, then, has been to banish them from 13 our minds, as though they were not capable of helping us with our predicaments, the myriad paradoxes of our existence. It is as though we had told the polar bear that his solitary life and the implacable hunger that makes him a persistent and resourceful hunter have no meaning for us. I believe this is a false sophistication of mind, and ultimately destructive.

A convenience of rational thought allows me to say there are but 14 two places where our relationships with animals have been severed; audacity perhaps moves me to state that we must repair these breaks. I say so out of years of coming and going in a world inhabited largely by animals and aboriginal peoples, and out of repeated contact with human despair and loneliness in my own culture. What we do to animals troubles us—the horror of laboratory experiment, trophy shooting, factory farming; and our loss of contact with them leaves us mysteriously bereaved. If we could establish an atmosphere of respect in our relationships, simple awe for the complexities of animals' lives, I think we would feel revived as a species. And we would know more, deeply more, about what we are fighting for when we raise our voices against tyranny of any sort.

I am aware of having written here without reference to the inci- 15 dents of day-to-day life by which most of us corroborate our beliefs. I think of several images. There is a group of sea ducks called scoters. They are dark, thick-bodied birds. With the exception of the males, who have bright, oddly shaped bills, they are of undistinguished coloration. The casual spring visitor to Cape Cod or to Cape Flattery would very likely see a few, but we know little about them. Like the ribbon seal and the narwhal, we cannot easily find them again once they leave these accustomed meeting places. So they are not really known to us.

Taxonomists took years to finally differentiate the spotted seal   16
(Phoca largha) from the harbor seal *(Phoca vitulina)*. They distrusted the
statements of Eskimos in the same Bering Sea region who had always
separated the two seals on the basis of their ice-related behavior. Now
the scientists speak like Yup'ik men about the matter.

A marine biologist, armed with a prestigious grant, went to Hawaii   17
to study a certain crab. The animal's behavior was so utterly different
from what he had imagined it would be (from reading the literature)
that his research proposal made no sense. To maintain his credibility he
abandoned the experiment rather than restructure his conception of the
animal.

One morning, walking through fresh snow, looking for mountain   18
lion tracks on the north rim of the Grand Canyon, a biologist with years
of this behind him said to me suddenly, "It's not in the data." I looked at
him. "It's not in the data," he reiterated. With his hands he made a motion to indicate his head, his chest. "It's here. What I know is here." We
went on in silence. "But as a field biologist," I said, "you must offer data
or ——." "We are not biologists," he answered. "We are historians."

A final moment. In the Sea of Labrador one summer a sperm whale   19
approached our ship head-on. I was standing in the bow with a retired
Danish master mariner. The calm green sea broke over the whale's brow
as he closed on us at ten or twelve knots. His approach was unwavering.
I wondered out loud to my companion if they were aware on the bridge
of our collision course. The whale surged past suddenly to port, crashing across our bow wave. I turned around—the mate shrugged from the
superstructure several hundred feet away: who knows? The retired captain had not moved. He had not loosened the tenacious grip he had on
the ship's rail. He slowly began to tell me a story about a convoy in the
North Atlantic in 1942, the night they were torpedoed.

If we are to locate animals again at the complicated ethical and   20
conceptual level of our ancestors, where they seem to have such a bearing on our state of mental health, we must decide what obligations and
courtesies we will be bound by. The hunting contracts of our ancestors
are no longer appropriate, just as their insight into natural history is no
longer superior to our own at every point. These are to be new contracts.
They must represent a new decorum, born of our aboriginal attachment
to ancestral landscapes, our extraordinary learning, and the evolution of
our culture from Altamira and Lascaux to the chambers of Washington,
D.C. and the corridors of the Metropolitan Museum of Art.

Enormous as these steps are to contemplate, we seem in diverse   21
ways to have firm hold of a beginning. The best of our books and films
reflect a wider-than-Western, wider-than-purely scientific, more-than-
utilitarian view of animals. Moral philosophers are at work in a schol-

arly remodeling of Western philosophy in this area. And some people choose now to vacation among snow geese in northern California or among egrets and roseate spoonbills in Florida, as well as among the pyramids, or creations of the Medici.

However new agreements are drawn up, they must reflect as the old ones did an atmosphere of mutual regard, some latitude for mystery, and a sense of hope. As a European people we have taken great intellectual risks and made at various times penetrating insights— Leibnitz's calculus, Darwin's theory of natural selection, Heisenberg's uncertainty principle, Levi-Strauss's anthropology. We have in common with all other people in the world an understanding of how animals inform our intellectual, physical, aesthetic, and spiritual lives. From this reservoir of knowledge and sensitivity we could hope to forge a new covenant, fiercely honest, with other creatures.   22

In the time I have spent with native peoples in North America I have observed a deceptively simple event—how superstition, a slight, seemingly irrational prohibition, will be used to undercut arrogance in a young, headstrong hunter. To see it once is to be reminded forever that all life is a great gamble; wisdom is not simply erudition; and to behave in an irrational manner can, in fact, be life-enhancing. We tore up the animal contracts when the animals got in the way of our agriculture, our husbandry, and our science. We are now tearing up and rewriting our contracts with native peoples, because they block our political and industrial development. We cannot keep doing this. We will find ourselves with a false and miserable existence, a hollow probity, isolated far from our roots.   23

We will never find a way home until we find a way to look the caribou, the salmon, the lynx, and the white-throated sparrow in the face, without guile, with no plan of betrayal. We have to decide, again, after a long hiatus, how we are going to behave. We have to decide again to be impeccable in our dealings with the elements of our natural history.   24

1983

Purpose and Meaning

1. Why does Lopez refer so often to several major philosophers? How do their philosophies relate to the essay's thesis? What is Lopez's thesis?

2. In paragraph 4, Lopez mentions "pathetic fallacy." What does the term mean, and how does it relate to Lopez's developing thesis?

3. What does Lopez feel is wrong with our images of animals? How do those images relate to and affect other social and cultural problems?

Language and Style

1. Paragraphs 6 and 11 contain sentences utilizing parallel structures. What do such structures lend to the success of the essay?

2. Characterize the tone of this essay: Is it formal and objective, or informal and subjective? Is the tone appropriate to the subject? Explain your view.

3. Lopez begins this essay with an analogy. How effective is it as an opening? Would another opening have been more effective? Why? Explain your response.

Strategy and Structure

1. Discuss the various techniques Lopez uses to advance his argument. Are they appropriate in terms of the essay's content? Why or why not?

2. What organizational pattern does Lopez use in paragraphs 7 through 13? How does paragraph 14 function?

3. How are paragraphs 15 through 19 organized? How does the chosen technique relate to the essay's major point?

Thinking and Writing

1. Lopez maintains that the fate of animal experimentation and the fate of zoos are important to us as creatures. Develop an essay on this topic.

2. Using methods similar to Lopez, develop an essay in which you argue for or against keeping animals in zoos.

3. Experimenting on animals is a controversial issue, even among scientists. Develop an essay in which you argue for or against animal experimentation, using documented evidence wherever possible.

GLOBAL VOICES

OCTAVIO PAZ

◦━◦━◦━◦━◦━◦━◦━◦━◦━◦━◦━◦━◦━◦━◦━◦

Hygiene and Repression

Octavio Paz, the 1990 winner of the Nobel Prize in literature, was born in Mexico City in 1914 and has lived in Japan, North America, France, and India. He was Mexico's ambassador to India from 1962 to 1968. Although known internationally primarily as a writer of fiction and poetry, Paz has published several nonfiction works as well. The following essay, which analyzes American culture through its cuisine, was written while he was teaching at Harvard University.

Traditional American cooking is a cuisine without mystery: simple, nourishing, scantily seasoned foods. No tricks: a carrot is a homely, honest carrot, a potato is not ashamed of its humble condition, and a steak is a big, bloody hunk of meat. This is a transubstantiation of the democratic virtues of the Founding Fathers: a plain meal, one dish following another like the sensible, unaffected sentences of a virtuous discourse. Like the conversation among those at table, the relation between substances and flavors is direct: sauces that mask tastes, garnishes that entice the eye, condiments that confuse the taste buds are taboo. The separation of one food from another is analogous to the reserve that characterizes the relations between sexes, races, and classes. In our countries food is communion, not only between those together at table but between ingredients; Yankee food, impregnated with Puritanism, is based on exclusions. The maniacal preoccupation with the purity and origin of food products has its counterpart in racism and exclusivism. The American contradiction—a democratic universalism based on ethnic, cultural, religious, and sexual exclusions—is reflected in its cuisine. In this culinary tradition our fondness for dark, passionate stews such as moles, for thick and sumptuous red, green, and yellow sauces, would be scandalous, as would be the choice place at our table of *huitlacoche*, which not only is made from diseased young maize but is black in color. Likewise our love for hot peppers, ranging from parakeet green to ecclesiastical purple, and for ears of Indian corn, their grains varying from golden yellow to midnight blue. Colors as violent as their tastes. Americans adore

1

fresh, delicate colors and flavors. Their cuisine is like watercolor painting or pastels.

American cooking shuns spices as it shuns the devil, but it wallows in slews of cream and butter. Orgies of sugar. Complementary opposites: the almost apostolic simplicity and soberness of lunch, in stark contrast to the suspiciously innocent, pregenital pleasures of ice cream and milkshakes. Two poles: the glass of milk and the glass of whiskey. The first affirms the primacy of home and mother. The virtues of the glass of milk are twofold: it is a wholesome food and it takes us back to childhood. Fourier detested the family repast, the image of the family in civilized society, a tedious daily ceremony presided over by a tyrannical father and a phallic mother. What would he have said of the cult of the glass of milk? As for whiskey and gin, they are drinks for loners and introverts. For Fourier, Gastrosophy was the science of combining not only foods but guests at table: matching the variety of dishes is the variety of persons sharing the meal. Wines, spirits, and liqueurs are the complement of a meal, hence their object is to stimulate the relations and unions consolidated round a table. Unlike wine, pulque, champagne, beer, and vodka, neither whiskey nor gin accompanies meals. Nor are they apéritifs or digestifs. They are drinks that accentuate uncommunicativeness and unsociability. In a gastrosophic age they would not enjoy much of a reputation. The universal favor accorded them reveals the situation of our societies, ever wavering between promiscuous association and solitude.

Ambiguity and ambivalence are resources unknown to American cooking. Here, as in so many other things, it is the diametrical opposite of the extremely delicate French cuisine, based on nuances, variations, and modulations—transitions from one substance to another, from one flavor to another. In a sort of profane Eucharist, even a glass of water is transfigured into an erotic chalice:

> Ta lèvre contre le cristal
> Gorgée à gorgée y compose
> Le souvenir pourpre et vital
> De la moins éphémère rose.*

It is the contrary as well of Mexican and Hindu cuisine, whose secret is the shock of tastes: cool and piquant, salt and sweet, hot and tart, pungent and delicate. Desire is the active agent, the secret producer of changes, whether it be the transition from one flavor to another or the contrast between several. In gastronomy as in the erotic, it's desire that

---

*Your lip against the crystal / Sip by sip forms therein / The vital deep crimson memory / Of the least ephemeral rose.—Stéphane Mallarmé, "Verre d'eau."

sets substances, bodies, and sensations in motion; this is the power that rules their conjunction, commingling, and transmutation. A reasonable cuisine, in which each substance is what it is and in which both variations and contrasts are avoided, is a cuisine that has excluded desire.

Pleasure is a notion (a sensation) absent from traditional Yankee cuisine. Not pleasure but health, not correspondence between savors but the satisfaction of a need—these are its two values. One is physical and the other moral; both are associated with the idea of the body as work. Work in turn is a concept at once economic and spiritual: production and redemption. We are condemned to labor, and food restores the body after the pain and punishment of work. It is a real *reparation*, in both the physical and the moral sense. Through work the body pays its debt; by earning its physical sustenance, it also earns its spiritual recompense. Work redeems us and the sign of this redemption is food. An active sign in the spiritual economy of humanity, food restores the health of body and soul. If what we eat gives us physical and spiritual health, the exclusion of spices for moral and hygienic reasons is justified: they are the signs of desire, and they are difficult to digest. 4

Health is the condition of two activities of the body, work and sports. In the first, the body is an agent that produces and at the same time redeems; in the second, the sign changes: sports are a wasteful expenditure of energy. This is a contradiction in appearance only, since what we have here in reality is a system of communicating vessels. Sports are a physical expenditure that is precisely the contrary of what happens in sexual pleasure, since sports in the end become productive— an expenditure that produces health. Work in turn is an expenditure of energy that produces goods and thereby transforms biological life into social, economic, and moral life. There is, moreover, another connection between work and sports: both take place within a context of rivalry; both are competition and emulation. The two of them are forms of Fourier's "Cabalist" passion. In this sense, sports possess the rigor and gravity of work, and work possesses the gratuity and levity of sports. The play element of work is one of the few features of American society that might have earned Fourier's praise, though doubtless he would have been horrified at the commercialization of sports. The preeminence of work and sports, activities necessarily excluding sexual pleasure, has the same significance as the exclusion of spices in cuisine. If gastronomy and eroticism are unions and conjunctions of substances and tastes or of bodies and sensations, it is evident that neither has been a central preoccupation of American society—as ideas and social values, I repeat, not as more or less secret realities. In the American tradition the body is not a source of pleasure but of health and work, in the material and the moral sense. 5

The cult of health manifests itself as an "ethic of hygiene." I use the 6 word ethic because its prescriptions are at once physiological and moral. A despotic ethic: sexuality, work, sports, and even cuisine are its domains. Again, there is a dual concept: hygiene governs both the corporeal and the moral life. Following the precepts of hygiene means obeying not only rules concerning physiology but also ethical principles: temperance, moderation, reserve. The morality of separation gives rise to the rules of hygiene, just as the aesthetics of fusion inspires the combinations of gastronomy and erotics. In India I frequently witnessed the obsession of Americans with hygiene. Their dread of contagion seemed to know no bounds; anything and everything might be laden with germs: food, drink, objects, people, the very air. These preoccupations are the precise counterpart of the ritual preoccupations of Brahmans fearing contact with certain foods and impure things, not to mention people belonging to a caste different from their own. Many will say that the concerns of the American are justified, whereas those of the Brahman are superstitions. Everything depends on the point of view: for the Brahman the bacteria that the American fears are illusory, while the moral stains produced by contact with alien people are real. These stains are stigmas that isolate him: no member of his caste would dare touch him until he had performed long and complicated rites of purification. The fear of social isolation is no less intense than that of illness. The hygienic taboo of the American and the ritual taboo of the Brahman have a common basis: the concern for purity. This basis is religious even though, in the case of hygiene, it is masked by the authority of science.

In the last analysis, the cult of hygiene is merely another expression of the principle underlying attitudes toward sports, work, cuisine, sex, and races. The other name of purity is separation. Although hygiene is a social morality based explicitly on science, its unconscious root is religious. Nonetheless, the form in which it expresses itself, and the justifications for it, are rational. In American society, unlike in ours, science from the very beginning has occupied a privileged place in the system of beliefs and values. The quarrel between faith and reason never took on the intensity that it assumed among Hispanic peoples. Ever since their birth as a nation, Americans have been modern; for them it is natural to believe in science, whereas for us this belief implies a negation of our past. The prestige of science in American public opinion is such that even political disputes frequently take on the form of scientific polemics, just as in the Soviet Union they assume the guise of quarrels about Marxist orthodoxy. Two recent examples are the racial question and the feminist movement: are intellectual differences between races and sexes genetic in origin or a historico-cultural phenomenon?

The universality of science (or what passes for science) justifies the development and imposition of collective patterns of normality. Obviating the necessity for direct coercion, the overlapping of science and Puritan morality permits the imposition of rules that condemn peculiarities, exceptions, and deviations in a manner no less categorical and implacable than religious anathemas. Against the excommunications of science, the individual has neither the religious recourse of abjuration nor the legal one of *habeas corpus*. Although they masquerade as hygiene and science, these patterns of normality have the same function in the realm of eroticism as "healthful" cuisine in the sphere of gastronomy: the extirpation or the separation of what is alien, different, ambiguous, impure. One and the same condemnation applies to blacks, Chicanos, sodomites, and spices.

1987

Making Connections

1. This essay's title hints at Paz's major thematic concern. What is his thesis? From your reading of the essay, do you find any indications that he is not being entirely serious? Explain your answer.

2. In this essay, Paz links America's concern with hygiene to its zenophobic attitudes in general. What similarities do you find between Paz's statements and those of James Baldwin in "Autobiographical Notes," "Stranger in the Village," or "The Discovery of What It Means to Be an American"?

DORIS LESSING

◦●◦●◦●◦●◦●◦●◦●◦●◦●◦

My Father

Born in 1919 to British parents living in Persia (now Iran), Doris Lessing, author of more than thirty books of fiction, poetry, and nonfiction, spent twenty-five years in Africa before moving to England in 1949. Africa provides her with the focus for examining elements of the British colonial experience, a central concern in many of her books. The following essay, a sensitive portrait of her father, reflects the stylistic brilliance for which she is so well known.

We use our parents like recurring dreams, to be entered into when   1
needed; they are always there for love or for hate; but it occurs to me
that I was not always there for my father. I've written about him before,
but novels, stories, don't have to be "true." Writing this article is difficult
because it has to be "true." I knew him when his best years were over.

There are photographs of him. The largest is of an officer in the   2
1914–18 war. A new uniform—buttoned, badged, strapped, tabbed—
confines a handsome, dark young man who holds himself stiffly to confront what he certainly thought of as his duty. His eyes are steady, serious, and responsible, and show no signs of what he became later. A photograph at sixteen is of a dark, introspective youth with the same intent
eyes. But it is his mouth you notice—a heavily-jutting upper lip contradicts the rest of a regular face. His moustache was to hide it: "Had to do
something—a damned fleshy mouth. Always made me uncomfortable,
that mouth of mine."

Earlier a baby (eyes already alert) appears in a lace waterfall that   3
cascades from the pillowy bosom of a fat, plain woman to her feet. It is
the face of a head cook. "Lord, but my mother was a practical female—
almost as bad as you!" as he used to say, or throw at my mother in moments of exasperation. Beside her stands, or droops, arms dangling, his
father, the source of the dark, arresting eyes, but otherwise masked by a
long beard.

The birth certificate says: Born 3rd August, 1886, Walton Villa,   4
Creffield Road, S. Mary at the Wall, R.S.D. Name, Alfred Cook. Name
and surname of Father: Alfred Cook Tayler. Name and maiden name of

Mother: Caroline May Batley. Rank or Profession: Bank Clerk. Colchester, Essex.

They were very poor. Clothes and boots were a problem. They "made their own amusements." Books were mostly the Bible and *The Pilgrim's Progress*. Every Saturday night they bathed in a hip-bath in front of the kitchen fire. No servants. Church three times on Sundays. "Lord, when I think of those Sundays! I dreaded them all week, like a nightmare coming at you full tilt and no escape." But he rabbited with ferrets along the lanes and fields, bird-nested, stole fruit, picked nuts and mushrooms, paid visits to the blacksmith and the mill and rode a farmer's carthorse.

They ate economically, but when he got diabetes in his forties and subsisted on lean meat and lettuce leaves, he remembered suet puddings, treacle puddings, raisin and currant puddings, steak and kidney puddings, bread and butter pudding, "batter cooked in the gravy with the meat," potato cake, plum cake, butter cake, porridge with treacle, fruit tarts and pies, brawn, pig's trotters and pig's cheek and home-smoked ham and sausages. And "lashings of fresh butter and cream and eggs." He wondered if this diet had produced the diabetes, but said it was worth it.

There was an elder brother described by my father as: "Too damned clever by half. One of those quick, clever brains. Now I've always had a slow brain, but I get there in the end, damn it!"

The brothers went to a local school and the elder did well, but my father was beaten for being slow. They both became bank clerks in, I think, the Westminster Bank, and one must have found it congenial, for he became a manager, the "rich brother," who had cars and even a yacht. But my father did not like it, though he was conscientious. For instance, he changed his writing, letter by letter, because a senior criticised it. I never saw his unregenerate hand, but the one he created was elegant, spiky, careful. Did this mean he created a new personality for himself, hiding one he did not like, as he hid his "damned fleshy mouth"? I don't know.

Nor do I know when he left home to live in Luton or why. He found family life too narrow? A safe guess—he found everything too narrow. His mother was too down-to-earth? He had to get away from his clever elder brother?

Being a young man in Luton was the best part of his life. It ended in 1914, so he had a decade of happiness. His reminiscences of it were all of pleasure, the delight of physical movement, of dancing in particular. All his girls were "a beautiful dancer, light as a feather." He played billards and ping-pong (both for his country); he swam, boated, played cricket and football, went to picnics and horse races, sang at musical evenings. One family of a mother and two daughters treated him "like a son only better. I didn't know whether I was in love with the mother or the daughters, but oh I did love going there; we had such good times." He was engaged to one daughter, then, for a time, to the other. An engagement was broken off because she was rude to a waiter. "I could not marry a woman who allowed herself to insult someone who was defenceless." He used to say to my wryly smiling mother: "Just as well I didn't marry either of *them*; they would never have stuck it out the way you have, old girl."

Just before he died he told me he had dreamed he was standing in 11 a kitchen on a very high mountain holding X in his arms. "Ah, yes, that's what I've missed in my life. Now don't you let yourself be cheated out of life by the old dears. They take all the colour out of everything if you let them."

But in that decade—"I'd walk 10, 15 miles to a dance two or three 12 times a week and think nothing of it. Then I'd dance every dance and walk home again over the fields. Sometimes it was moonlight, but I liked the snow best, all crisp and fresh. I loved walking back and getting into my digs just as the sun was rising. My little dog was so happy to see me, and I'd feed her, and make myself porridge and tea, then I'd wash and shave and go off to work."

The boy who was beaten at school, who went too much to church, 13 who carried the fear of poverty all his life, but who nevertheless was filled with the memories of country pleasures; the young bank clerk who worked such long hours for so little money, but who danced, sang, played, flirted—this naturally vigorous, sensuous being was killed in 1914, 1915, 1916. I think the best of my father died in that war, that his spirit was crippled by it. The people I've met, particularly the women, who knew him young, speak of his high spirits, his energy, his enjoyment of life. Also of his kindness, his compassion and—a word that keeps recurring—his wisdom. "Even when he was just a boy he understood things that you'd think even an old man would find it easy to condemn." I do not think these people would have easily recognised the ill, irritable, abstracted, hypochondriac man I knew.

He "joined up" as an ordinary soldier out of a characteristically 14 quirky scruple: it wasn't right to enjoy officers' privileges when the Tommies had such a bad time. But he could not stick the communal latrines, the obligatory drinking, the collective visits to brothels, the jokes about girls. So next time he was offered a commission he took it.

His childhood and young man's memories, kept fluid, were added 15 to, grew, as living memories do. But his war memories were congealed in stories that he told again and again, with the same words and gestures, in stereotyped phrases. They were anonymous, general, as if they had come out of a communal war memoir. He met a German in no-man's-land, but both slowly lowered their rifles and smiled and walked away. The Tommies were the salt of the earth, the British fighting men the best in the world. He had never known such comradeship. A certain brutal officer was shot in a sortie by his men, but the other officers, recognising rough justice, said nothing. He had known men intimately who saw the Angels at Mons. He wished he could force all the generals on both sides into the trenches for just one day, to see what the common soldiers endured . . . *that* would have ended the war at once.

There was an undercurrent of memories, dreams, and emotions much deeper, more personal. This dark region in him, fate-ruled, where nothing was true but horror, was expressed inarticulately, in brief, bitter exclamations or phrases of rage, incredulity, betrayal. The men who went to fight in that war believed it when they said it was to end war. My father believed it. And he was never able to reconcile his belief in his country with his anger at the cynicism of its leaders. And the anger, the sense of betrayal, strengthened as he grew old and ill. 16

But in 1914 he was naive, the German atrocities in Belgium inflamed him, and he enlisted out of idealism, although he knew he would have a hard time. He knew because a fortuneteller told him. (He could be described as uncritically superstitious or as psychically gifted.) He would be in great danger twice, yet not die—he was being protected by a famous soldier who was his ancestor. "And sure enough, later I heard from the Little Aunties that the church records showed we were descended the backstairs way from the Duke of Wellington, or was it Marlborough? Damn it, I forget. But one of them would be beside me all through the war, she said." (He was romantic, not only about this solicitous ghost, but also about being a descendant of the Huguenots, on the strength of the "e" in Tayler; and about "the wild blood" in his veins from a great uncle who, sent unjustly to prison for smuggling, came out of a ten-year sentence and earned it, very efficiently, along the coasts of Cornwall until he died.) 17

The luckiest thing that ever happened to my father, he said, was getting his leg shattered by shrapnel ten days before Passchendaele. His whole company was killed. He knew he was going to be wounded because of the fortuneteller, who had said he would know. "I did not understand what she meant, but both times in the trenches, first when my appendix burst and I nearly died, and then just before Passchendaele, I felt for some days as if a thick, black velvet pall was settled over me. I can't tell you what it was like. Oh, it was awful, awful, and the second time it was so bad I wrote to the old people and told them I was going to be killed." 18

His leg was cut off at mid-thigh, he was shell-shocked, he was very ill for many months, with a prolonged depression afterwards. "You should always remember that sometimes people are all seething under- 19 neath. You don't know what terrible things people have to fight against. You should look at a person's eyes, that's how you tell. . . . When I was like that, after I lost my leg, I went to a nice doctor man and said I was going mad, but he said, don't worry, everyone locks up things like that. You don't know—horrible, horrible, awful things. I was afraid of myself, of what I used to dream. I wasn't myself at all."

In the Royal Free Hospital was my mother, Sister McVeagh. He [20] married his nurse which, as they both said often enough (though in different tones of voice), was just as well. That was 1919. He could not face being a bank clerk in England, he said, not after the trenches. Besides, England was too narrow and conventional. Besides, the civilians did not know what the soldiers had suffered, they didn't want to know, and now it wasn't done even to remember "The Great Unmentionable." He went off to the Imperial Bank of Persia, in which country I was born.

The house was beautiful, with great stone-floored high-ceilinged [21] rooms whose windows showed ranges of snow-streaked mountains. The gardens were full of roses, jasmine, pomegranates, walnuts, Kermanshah he spoke of with liking, but soon they went to Teheran, populous with "Embassy people," and my gregarious mother created a lively social life about which he was irritable even in recollection.

Irritableness—that note was first struck here, about Persia. He did [22] not like, he said, "the graft and the corruption." But here it is time to try and describe something difficult—how a man's good qualities can also be his bad ones, or if not bad, a danger to him.

My father was honourable—he always knew exactly what that [23] word meant. He had integrity. His "one does not do that sort of thing," his "no, it is *not* right," sounded throughout my childhood and were final for all of us. I am sure it was true he wanted to leave Persia because of "the corruption." But it was also because he was already unconsciously longing for something freer, because as a bank official he could not let go into the dream-logged personality that was waiting for him. And later in Rhodesia, too, what was best in him was also what prevented him from shaking away the shadows: it was always in the name of honesty or decency that he refused to take this step or that out of the slow decay of the family's fortunes.

In 1925 there was leave from Persia. That year in London there was [24] an Empire Exhibition, and on the Southern Rhodesian stand some very fine maize cobs and a poster saying that fortunes could be made on maize at 25/-a bag. So on an impulse, turning his back forever on England, washing his hands of the corruption of the East, my father collected all his capital, £800, I think, while my mother packed curtains from Liberty's, clothes from Harrods, visiting cards, a piano, Persian rugs, a governess and two small children.

Soon, there was my father in a cigar-shaped house of thatch and   25
mud on the top of a kopje that overlooked in all directions a great system of mountains, rivers, valleys, while overhead the sky arched from
horizon to empty horizon. This was a couple of hundred miles south
from the Zambesi, a hundred or so west from Mozambique, in the district of Banket, so called because certain of its reefs were of the same formation as those called *banket* on the Rand. Lomagundi—gold country,
tobacco country, maize country—wild, almost empty. (The Africans had
been turned off it into reserves.) Our neighbours were four, five, seven
miles off. In front of the house . . . no neighbours, nothing; no farms, just
wild bush with two rivers but no fences to the mountains seven miles
away. And beyond these mountains and bush again to the Portuguese
border, over which "our boys" used to escape when wanted by the police for pass or other offences.

And then? There was bad luck. For instance, the price of maize   26
dropped from 25/- to 9/- a bag. The seasons were bad, prices bad, crops
failed. This was the sort of thing that made it impossible for him ever to
"get off the farm," which, he agreed with my mother, was what he most
wanted to do.

It was an absurd country, he said. A man could "own" a farm for   27
years that was totally mortgaged to the Government and run from the
Land Bank, meanwhile employing half-a-hundred Africans at 12/-a
month and none of them knew how to do a day's work. Why, two farm
labourers from Europe could do in a day what twenty of these ignorant
black savages would take a week to do. (Yet he was proud that he had a
name as a just employer, that he gave "a square deal.") Things got
worse. A fortuneteller had told him that her heart ached when she saw
the misery ahead for my father: this was the misery.

But it was my mother who suffered. After a period of neurotic ill-   28
ness, which was a protest against her situation, she became brave and
resourceful. But she never saw that her husband was not living in a real
world, that he had made a captive of her common sense. We were always about to "get off the farm." A miracle would do it—a sweepstake,
a goldmine, a legacy. And then? What a question! We would go to
England where life would be normal with people coming in for musical
evenings and nice supper parties at the Trocadero after a show. Poor
woman, for the twenty years we were on the farm, she waited for when
life would begin for her and for her children, for she never understood
that what was a calamity for her was for them a blessing.

Meanwhile my father sank towards his death (at 61). Everything   29
changed in him. He had been a dandy and fastidious, now he hated to
change out of shabby khaki. He had been sociable, now he was misan-
thropic. His body's disorders—soon diabetes and all kinds of stomach
ailments—dominated him. He was brave about his wooden leg, and

even went down mine shafts and climbed trees with it, but he walked clumsily and it irked him badly. He greyed fast, and slept more in the day, but would be awake half the night pondering about. . . .

It could be gold divining. For ten years he experimented on private   30
theories to do with the attractions and repulsions of metals. His whole soul went into it but his theories were wrong or he was *unlucky*—after all, if he had found a mine he would have had to leave the farm. It could be the relation between the minerals of the earth and of the moon; his decision to make infusions of all the plants on the farm and drink them himself in the interests of science; the criminal folly of the British Government in not realising that the Germans and the Russians were conspiring as Anti-Christ to . . . the inevitability of war because no one would listen to Churchill, but it would be all right because God (by then he was a British Israelite) had destined Britain to rule the world; a prophecy said 10 million dead would surround Jerusalem—how would the corpses be cleared away?; people who wished to abolish flogging should be flogged; the natives understood nothing but a good beating; hanging must not be abolished because the Old Testament said "an eye for an eye and a tooth for a tooth. . . ."

Yet, as this side of him darkened, so that it seemed all his thoughts   31
were of violence, illness, war, still no one dared to make an unkind comment in his presence or to gossip. Criticism of people, particularly of women, made him more and more uncomfortable till at last he burst out with: "It's all very well, but no one has the right to say that about another person."

In Africa, when the sun goes down, the stars spring up, all of them   32
in their expected places, glittering and moving. In the rainy season, the sky flashed and thundered. In the dry season, the great dark hollow of night was lit by veld fires: the mountains burned through September and October in chains of red fire. Every night my father took out his chair to watch the sky and the mountains, smoking, silent, a thin shabby fly-away figure under the stars. "Makes you think—there are so many worlds up there, wouldn't really matter if we did blow ourselves up—plenty more where we came from."

The Second World War, so long foreseen by him, was a bad time.   33
His son was in the Navy and in danger, and his daughter a sorrow to him. He became very ill. More and more often it was necessary to drive him into Salisbury with him in a coma, or in danger of one, on the back seat. My mother moved him into a pretty little suburban house in town near the hospitals, where he took to his bed and a couple of years later died. For the most part he was unconscious under drugs. When awake he talked obsessively (a tongue licking a nagging sore place) about "the old war." Or he remembered his youth. "I've been dreaming—Lord, to see those horses come lickety-split down the course with their necks

stretched out and the sun on their coats and everyone shouting. . . . I've been dreaming how I walked along the river in the mist as the sun was rising. . . . Lord, lord, lord, what a time that was, what good times we all had then, before the old war."

1963

Making Connections

1. How does Lessing's introductory paragraph express the essay's central purpose? Are there any indications of how she is using her father at the time of the writing?

2. Compare Lessing's opening paragraph of this essay with those of Alice Walker in the first paragraph of her essay, "Father." Are they saying essentially the same thing about parents? Discuss your response.

NADINE GORDIMER

○━●○━●○━●○━●○━●○━●○━●○━●○━●○━●○━●○━●○

Where Do Whites Fit In?

Nadine Gordimer, the 1991 winner of the Nobel Prize in literature, was born in South Africa in 1923 and educated there. Although known primarily as a writer of novels and short stories, Gordimer has regularly published essays in newspapers and magazines in both North America and abroad. "Where Do Whites Fit In?" is reflective of her lifelong concern with civil liberties, particularly in South Africa.

Where do whites fit in in the New Africa? *Nowhere*, I'm inclined to say, in my gloomier and least courageous moods; and I do believe that it is true that even the gentlest and most westernised Africans would like the emotional idea of the continent entirely without the complication of the presence of the white man for a generation or two. But *nowhere*, as an answer for us whites, is in the same category as remarks like *What's the use of living?* in the face of the threat of atomic radiation. We are living; we are in Africa. *Nowhere* is the desire to avoid painful processes and accept an ultimate and final solution (which doesn't exist in the continuous process that is life itself); the desire to have over and done with; the death wish, if not of the body, at least of the spirit.

For if we're going to fit in at all in the new Africa, it's going to be sideways, where-we-can, wherever-they'll-shift-up-for-us. This will not be comfortable; indeed, it will be hardest of all for those of us (I am one myself) who want to belong in the new Africa as we never could in the old, where our skin-colour labelled us as oppressors to the blacks and our views labelled us as traitors to the whites. We want merely to be ordinary members of a multi-coloured, any-coloured society, freed both of the privileges and the guilt of the white sins of our fathers. This seems to us perfectly reasonable and possible and, in terms of reason, it is. But belonging to a society implies two factors which are outside reason: the desire to belong, on the one part, and acceptance, on the other part. The new Africa may, with luck, grant us our legal rights, full citizenship and the vote, but I don't think it will accept us in the way we're hankering

1

2

425

after. If ever, it will take the confidence of several generations of jealous independence before Africa will feel that she can let us belong.

There is nothing so damaging to the ego as an emotional rebuff of   3
this kind. (More bearable by far the hate-engendered hate that the apartheiders must expect.) And you don't have to be particularly thin-skinned in order to feel this rebuff coming in Africa. Africans are prickling with the desire to be off on their own; the very fact that you welcome the new Africa almost as fervently as they do seems an intrusion in itself. They have had so much of us—let's not go through the whole list again, from tear-gas and taxes to brotherly advice—that all they crave is to have no part of us.

You'll understand that I'm not speaking in economic or even politi-   4
cal, but purely in human or, if you prefer it, psychological terms. For the purposes of what I have to say it may be true that in South Africa, for example, foreign capital and skills would have to be retained, in order to keep the mines and industry going, by wide concessions given by any black independent government with its head screwed on the right way. But the fact that we might go on living in our comfortable houses in the suburbs of Johannesburg under a black republic just as we do under a white near-republic, does not mean that we should feel ourselves accepted as part of the homogeneous society of the new Africa. For a long time to come any white South African must expect to find any black man, from any African territory, considered by the black South African as more of a brother than the white South African himself. No personal bonds of loyalty, friendship or even love will change this; it is a nationalism of the heart that has been brought about by suffering. There is no share in it we can hope to have. I for one can read this already in the faces, voices and eloquently regretful but firm handclasps of my own African friends.

Make no mistake, those moderate African political leaders who   5
offer us whites—with sincerity, I believe—full participation in the new life of Africa offer us only the tangibles of existence. The intangibles that make up emotional participation and the sense of belonging cannot be legislated for.

What are we to do? Shall we go? Shall we leave Africa? For those   6
small white communities who are truly foreign to the African territories in which they live, 'sent out' from a homeland in Europe for a spell of duty on administrative jobs or as representatives of commercial firms, there can't be much question of staying on. But in those territories, such as South Africa and the Rhodesias, where there is a sizeable and settled white population whose *home* is Africa, there is no easy answer; sometimes, it seems no answer at all. I do not attempt to speak, of course, for the stubborn mass that will continue, like a Napoleon in a mad house, to see itself as the undisputed master and make no attempt to consider the

reality of living another role. I do not even try to guess what will happen to them; what *can* happen to them in a situation that they find unthinkable. I can only fear that events will deal with them grimly, as events usually do with people who refuse to think. I speak for people like myself, who think almost too much about the whole business and hope to arrive at an honest answer, without self-pity for the whites or sentiment about the blacks.

Some of us in South Africa want to leave; a few of us have gone already. And certainly, when one comes to Europe on a visit, one becomes a little uneasy at the number of friends (well-informed friends with a good perspective on the swerves and lurches of the way the world is going) who take one aside and ask whether one isn't planning to leave Africa? Which brings me to the reasons why some people have left and why these friends in Europe think one should pack up, too. A few have left because they cannot bear the guilt and ugliness of the white man's easy lot here; a few have left because they are afraid of the black man; and most, I should say, have left because of a combination of the two. I doubt if any consciously have left for the long-term reason I have elaborated here—the growing unwelcomeness of the white man in Africa. Yet I feel that if the white man's lot were to become no better and no worse than anyone else's tomorrow and the fear of violence at the hands of the black man (which we all have) were to have been brought to the test and disproved, unwelcomeness might still remain as the factor that would, in the end, decide many of us to give up our home and quit Africa.

I myself fluctuate between the desire to be gone—to find a society for myself where my white skin will have no bearing on my place in the community—and a terrible, obstinate and fearful desire to stay. I feel the one desire with my head and the other with my guts. I know that there must be many others who feel as I do, and who realise that generally the head is the more sensible guide of the two. Those of us who stay will need to have the use of our heads in order to sustain the emotional decision that home is not necessarily where you belong ethnogenically, but rather the place you were born to, the faces you first saw around you, and the elements of the situation among your fellow men in which you found yourself and with which you have been struggling, politically, personally or artistically, all your life.

The white man who wants to fit in in the new Africa must learn a number of hard things. He'd do well to regard himself as an immigrant to a new country; somewhere he has never lived before, but to whose life he has committed himself. He'll have to forget the old impulses to leadership, and the temptation to give advice backed by the experience and culture of Western civilisation—Africa is going through a stage when it passionately prefers its own mistakes to successes (or mistakes) that are not its own. This is an absolutely necessary stage in all political,

7

8

9

sociological and spiritual growth, but it is an uncomfortable and disillu-sioning one to live through. And giving up the impulse to advise and interfere and offer to resume responsibility may not be as easy as we whites think. Even those of us who don't want to be boss (or *baas*, rather) have become used to being bossy. We've been used to assuming leadership or at least tutorship, even if it's only been in liberal campaigns to secure the rights of the Africans to vote and speak for themselves. Out of our very concern to see Africans make a go of the new Africa, we may—indeed, I know we shall—be tempted to offer guidance when we haven't been consulted. The facts that we'll be well-meaning and that the advice may be good and badly-needed do not count; the sooner we drum that into our egos the better. What counts is the need of Africa to acquire confidence through the experience of picking itself up, dusting itself down, and starting all over again; and the quickening marvel of often getting things right into the bargain.

It's hard to sit quiet when you think you can tell how a problem   10 may be solved or a goal accomplished, but it may be even harder to give help without recriminations or, worse, smugness when it is sought. If we want to fit in anywhere in Africa, that is what we'll have to teach ourselves to do; answer up, cheerfully and willingly, when we're called upon and shut up when we're not. Already I notice that the only really happy whites I know in Africa—the only ones who are at peace with themselves over their place in the community—are some South African friends of mine who have gone to live in Ghana, and who have an educational job to do on contract from the Government. They are living as equals among the Africans, they have no say in the affairs of the country for the Africans to resent and they are contributing something useful and welcome to the development of Africa. In other words, they are in the position of foreign experts, employed at the Government's pleasure. I can positively feel my fellow-whites in Africa swelling with indignance at this extreme picture of the white man's future life on the continent; and it makes me feel rather indignant myself. But I think we've got to accept the home truth of the picture, whether we like it or not, and whether or not what we see there seems fair. All that the new Africa will really want from us will be what we can give as 'foreign experts'—the technical, scientific and cultural knowledge that white civilisation has acquired many hundreds of years before black civilisation, and on which, whether the Africans like it or not, their own aspirations are based.

I suppose we may get over being a minority minority instead of the   11 majority minority we've been used to being all these past years, but I don't know whether that valuable change of attitude will actually bring us much nearer the integration we seek. Will intermarriage help us? It

would, of course, on a large scale, but personally I don't believe that it
will happen on a large scale in Africa. Intermarriage has always been regarded as a social stigma by whites, even in those territories where, unlike South Africa, it is not actually a crime, but I have never been able to
find out whether, among blacks, it is regarded as a stigma or a step up in
the world. (Most whites assume it is regarded as a deeply desired privilege, of course.) I know that, for example, in South Africa many Africans
who are not Bechuanas, and have nothing whatever to do with the people of Bechuanaland, have on their walls a picture of Ruth and Seretse
Khama. It is difficult to say whether this means that they take pride in
the fact that a white woman chose to marry an important African, or
whether the picture simply gives them a chance to identify themselves
with the ex-chief's successful defiance of white taboo and authority.

Once the social stigma is removed—in the new Africa marriage 12
with an African will be marrying into the ruling class, remember, and no
one can measure how much of colour-prejudice is purely class-preju-
dice, in a country where there has been a great gap between the living
standards of black and white—and once (in the case of South Africa)
there are no legal disabilities in mixed marriages, I think that intermarriage will increase at two extreme levels of the social scale, but scarcely
at all in between. Intellectuals will intermarry because they feel closer to
intellectuals, whatever their race or colour, than to the mass, and the
humbler and poorly-adjusted fringes of both the black and white
masses, who have not found acceptance in their own societies, will intermarry in order to find a home somewhere—if not within the confines of
their own background, then in someone else's. But I don't think we can
hope for intermarriage on an effective scale between ordinary people,
and I shouldn't be surprised if independent black Africa frowned upon
it, in an unofficial but firm way. Especially in a country like South
Africa, where there might remain whites in sufficiently large numbers to
create an unease at the possibility that they might try to close their
hands once again on those possessions of power from which their fingers had been prised back one by one. It is quite likely that there will be
a social stigma, among ordinary people whose sense of nationalism is
well stoked up, attached to marrying whites; it may be considered un-
African. (Nkrumah has set the official precedent already, by choosing
not a Ruth Williams, but a girl who 'belongs' to the continent—a bride
from Nasser's Egypt.) If white numbers do not dwindle in those areas of
the continent which are heavily white-populated, and there is integration in schools and universities and no discrimination against white children, the picture will change in a few generations, of course. I do not see
those young people as likely to regard parental race prejudice on either
side as anything but fuddy-duddy. But will the whites remain, stick it

out anywhere in Africa in sufficient numbers for this to come about? Isn't it much more likely that they will dwindle to small, socially isolated communities, whites in the diaspora?

If one will always have to feel white first, and African second, it   13 would be better not to stay in Africa. It would not be worth it for this. Yet, although I claim no mystique about Africa, I fear that like one of those oxen I sometimes read about in the Sunday papers, I might, dumped somewhere else and kindly treated, continually plod blindly back to where I came from.

1959

Making Connections

1. In your own words, summarize Gordimer's response to the question posed in the essay's title. How realistic are her answers? Are there other alternatives that she does not consider? Explain your answer.

2. Compare Gordimer's comments about minority populations with those of George Orwell. What similarities can you find? What differences?

CHINUA ACHEBE

◦●◦●◦●◦●◦●◦●◦●◦●◦●◦●◦

Named for Victoria, Queen of England

Recognized as one of Nigeria's most gifted writers, Chinua Achebe was born in eastern Nigeria in 1930. The recipient of many international awards, Achebe has published novels, short stories, essay, poetry, and children's books. The following memoir deals with his family and his devout Anglican upbringing.

I was born in Ogidi in Eastern Nigeria of devout Christian parents. 1 The line between Christian and non-Christian was much more definite in my village forty years ago than it is today. When I was growing up I remember we tended to look down on the others. We were called in our language "the people of the church" or "the association of God." The others we called, with the conceit appropriate to followers of the true religion, the heathen or even "the people of nothing."

Thinking about it today I am not so sure that it isn't they who 2 should have been looking down on us for our apostasy. And perhaps they did. But the bounties of the Christian God were not to be taken lightly—education, paid jobs and many other advantages that nobody in his right senses could underrate. And in fairness we should add that there was more than naked opportunism in the defection of many to the new religion. For in some ways and in certain circumstances it stood firmly on the side of humane behavior. It said, for instance, that twins were not evil and must no longer be abandoned in the forest to die. Think what that would have done for that unhappy woman whose heart torn to shreds at every birth could now hold on precariously to a new hope.

There was still considerable evangelical fervour in my early days. 3 Once a month in place of the afternoon church service we went into the village with the gospel. We would sing all the way to the selected communal meeting place. Then the pastor or catechist or one of the elders having waited for enough heathen people to assemble would address them on the evil futility of their ways. I do not recall that we made even one conversion. On the contrary, I have a distinct memory of the preacher getting into serious trouble with a villager who was apparently notorious for turning up at every occasion with a different awkward question. As you would expect, this was no common villager but a fallen Christian, technically known as a *backslider*. Like Satan, a spell in heaven had armed him with unfair insights.

My father had joined the new faith as a young man and risen   4
rapidly in its ranks to become an evangelist and church teacher. His maternal uncle, who had brought him up (his own parents having died early), was a man of note in the village. He had taken the highest-but-one title that a man of wealth and honour might aspire to, and the feast he gave the town on his initiation became a byword for open-handedness bordering on prodigality. The grateful and approving community called him henceforth Udo Osinyi—Udo who cooks more than the whole people can eat.

From which you might deduce that my ancestors approved of os-   5
tentation. And you would be right. But they would probably have argued if the charge was made by their modern counterparts that in their day wealth could only be acquired honestly, by the sweat of a man's brow. They would probably never have given what I believe was the real but carefully concealed reason, namely that given their extreme republican and egalitarian world-view it made good sense for the community to encourage a man acquiring more wealth than his neighbours to squander it and thus convert a threat of material power into harmless honorific distinction, while his accumulated riches flowed back into the commonwealth.

Apparently the first missionaries who came to my village went to   6
Udo Osinyi to pay their respects and seek support for their work. For a short while he allowed them to operate from his compound. He probably thought it was some kind of circus whose strange presence added lustre to his household. But after a few days he sent them packing again. Not, as you might think, on account of the crazy theology they had begun to propound but on the much more serious grounds of musical aesthetics. Said the old man: "Your singing is too sad to come from a man's house. My neighbours might think it was my funeral dirge."

So they parted—without rancour. When my father joined the mis-   7
sionaries the old man does not seem to have raised any serious objections. Perhaps like Ezeulu he thought he needed a representative in their camp. Or perhaps he thought it was a modern diversion which a young man might indulge in without coming to too much harm. He must have had second thoughts when my father began to have ideas about converting him. But it never came to an open rift; apparently not even a quarrel. They remained very close to the end. I don't know it for certain, but I

think the old man was the very embodiment of tolerance, insisting only that whatever a man decided to do he should do it with style. I am told he was very pleased when my father, a teacher now, had a wedding to which white missionaries (now no longer figures of fun) came in their fineries, their men and their women, bearing gifts. He must have been impressed too by the wedding feast, which might not have approached his own legendary performance but was by all accounts pretty lavish.

Before my father died, he had told me of a recent dream in which   8 his uncle, long long dead, arrived at our house like a traveller from a distant land come in for a brief stop and rest and was full of admiration for the zinc house my father had built. There was something between those two that I find deep, moving and perplexing. And of those two generations—defectors and loyalists alike—there was something I have not been able to fathom. That was why the middle story in the Okonkwo trilogy as I originally projected it never got written. I had suddenly become aware that in my gallery of ancestral heroes there is an empty place from which an unknown personage seems to have departed.

I was baptized Albert Chinualumogu. I dropped the tribute to   9 Victorian England when I went to the university although you might find some early acquaintances still calling me by it. The earliest of them all—my mother—certainly stuck to it to the bitter end. So if anyone asks you what Her Britannic Majesty Queen Victoria had in common with Chinua Achebe, the answer is: They both lost their Albert! As for the second name, which in the manner of my people is a full-length philosophical statement, I simply cut it in two, making it more businesslike without, I hope, losing the general drift of its meaning.

I have always been fond of stories and intrigued by language—first   10 Igbo, spoken with such eloquence by the old men of the village, and later English, which I began to learn at about the age of eight. I don't know for certain, but I have probably spoken more words in Igbo than English but I have definitely written more words in English than Igbo. Which I think makes me perfectly bilingual. Some people have suggested that I should be better off writing in Igbo. Sometimes they seek to drive the point home by asking me in which language I dream. When I reply that I dream in both languages they seem not to believe it. More recently I have heard an even more potent and metaphysical version of the question: In what language do you have an orgasm? That should settle the matter if I knew.

We lived at the crossroads of cultures. We still do today; but when   11 I was a boy one could see and sense the peculiar quality and atmosphere of it more clearly. I am not talking about all that rubbish we hear of the spiritual void and mental stresses that Africans are supposed to have, or the evil forces and irrational passions prowling through Africa's heart of darkness. We know the racist mystique behind a lot of that stuff and should merely point out that those who prefer to see Africa in those lurid terms have not themselves demonstrated any clear superiority in sanity or more competence in coping with life.

But still the crossroads does have a certain dangerous potency;   12 dangerous because a man might perish there wrestling with multiple-headed spirits, but also he might be lucky and return to his people with the boon of prophetic vision.

On one arm of the cross we sang hymns and read the Bible night   13 and day. On the other my father's brother and his family, blinded by heathenism, offered food to idols. That was how it was supposed to be anyhow. But I knew without knowing why that it was too simple a way to describe what was going on. Those idols and that food had a strange pull on me in spite of my being such a thorough little Christian that often at Sunday services at the height of the grandeur of "Te Deum Laudamus" I would have dreams of a mantle of gold falling on me as the choir of angels drowned our mortal song and the voice of God Himself thundering: This is my beloved son in whom I am well pleased. Yet, despite those delusions of divine destiny I was not past taking my little sister to our neighbor's house when our parents were not looking and partaking of heathen festival meals. I never found their rice and stew to have the flavour of idolatry. I was about ten then. If anyone likes to believe that I was torn by spiritual agonies or stretched on the rack of my ambivalence, he certainly may suit himself. I do not remember any undue distress. What I do remember is a fascination for the ritual and the life on the other arm of the crossroads. And I believe two things were in my favour—that curiosity, and the little distance imposed between me and it by the accident of my birth. The distance becomes not a separation but a bringing together like the necessary backward step which a judicious viewer may take in order to see a canvas steadily and fully.

I was lucky in having a few old books around the house when I   14 was learning to read. As the fifth in a family of six children and with parents so passionate for their children's education, I inherited many discarded primers and readers. I remember *A Midsummer Night's Dream* in an advanced stage of falling apart. I think it must have been a prose adaptation, simplified and illustrated. I don't remember whether I made anything of it. Except the title. I couldn't get over the strange beauty of it. "A Midsummer Night's Dream." It was a magic phrase—an incantation that conjured up scenes and landscapes of an alien, happy and unattainable land.

I remember also my mother's *Ije Onye Kraist* which must have been   15 an Igbo adaptation of *Pilgrim's Progress*. It could not have been the whole book; it was too thin. But it had some frightening pictures. I recall in particular a most vivid impression of the valley of the shadow of death. I thought a lot about death in those days. There was another little book which frightened and fascinated me. It had drawings of different parts of the human body. But I was primarily interested in what my elder sister told me was the human heart. Since there is a slight confusion in Igbo between heart and soul I took it that that strange thing looking almost like my mother's iron cooking pot turned upside down was the very thing that flew out when a man died and perched on the head of the coffin on the way to the cemetery.

I found some use for most of the books in our house but by no means all. There was one arithmetic book I smuggled out and sold for half a penny which I needed to buy the tasty *elele* some temptress of a woman sold in the little market outside the school. I was found out and my mother, who had never had cause till then to doubt my honesty—laziness, yes, but not theft—received a huge shock. Of course she redeemed the book. I was so ashamed when she brought it home that I don't think I ever looked at it again, which was probably why I never had much use for mathematics.   16

My parents' reverence for books was almost superstitious; so my action must have seemed like a form of juvenile simony. My father was much worse than my mother. He never destroyed any paper. When he died we had to make a bonfire of all the hoardings of his long life. I am the very opposite of him in this. I can't stand paper around me. Whenever I see a lot of it I am seized by a mild attack of pyromania. When I die my children will not have a bonfire.   17

The kind of taste I acquired from the chaotic literature in my father's house can well be imagined. For instance, I became very fond of those aspects of ecclesiastical history as could be garnered from *The West African Churchman's Pamphlet*—a little terror of a booklet prescribing interminable Bible readings morning and night. But it was a veritable gold mine for the kind of information I craved in those days. It had the date of consecration for practically every Anglican bishop who ever served in West Africa; and even more intriguing, the dates of their death. Many of them didn't last very long. I remember one pathetic case (I forget his name) who arrived in Lagos straight from his consecration at St. Paul's Cathedral and was dead within days, and his wife a week or two after him. Those were the days when West Africa was truly the white man's grave, when those great lines were written of which I was at that time unaware: 18

> Bight of Benin! Bight of Benin!
> Where few come out though many go in!

But the most fascinating information I got from *Pamphlet*, as we called it, was this cryptic entry: "Augustine, Bishop of Hippo, died 430." It had that elusive and eternal quality, a tantalizing unfamiliarity which I always found moving.

I did not know that I was going to be a writer because I did not really know of the existence of such creatures until fairly late. The folk stories my mother and elder sister told me had the immemorial quality of the sky and the forests and the rivers. Later, when I got to know that the European stories I read were written by known people, it still didn't help much. It was the same Europeans who made all the other marvellous things like the motor car. We did not come into it at all. We made nothing that wasn't primitive and heathenish.   19

The nationalist movement in British West Africa after the Second World War brought about a mental revolution which began to reconcile us to ourselves. It suddenly seemed that we too might have a story to tell. "Rule Britannia!" to which we had marched so unselfconsciously on Empire Day now stuck in our throat.   20

At the university I read some appalling novels about Africa (including Joyce Cary's much praised *Mister Johnson*) and decided that the story we had to tell could not be told for us by anyone else no matter how gifted or well intentioned.   21

Although I did not set about it consciously in that solemn way, I now know that my first book, *Things Fall Apart*, was an act of atonement with my past, the ritual return and homage of a prodigal son. But things happen very fast in Africa. I had hardly begun to bask in the sunshine of reconciliation when a new cloud appeared, a new estrangement. Political independence had come. The nationalist leader of yesterday (with whom it had not been too difficult to make common cause) had become the not so attractive party boss. And then things really got going. The party boss was chased out by the bright military boys, new idols of the people. But the party boss knows how to wait, knows by heart the counsel Mother Bedbug gave her little ones when the harassed owner of the bed poured hot water on them: "Be patient," said she, "for what is hot will in the end be cold." What is bright can also get tarnished, like the military boys.   22

One hears that the party boss is already conducting a whispering campaign: "You done see us chop," he says, "now you see *dem* chop. Which one you like pass?" And the people are truly confused.   23

In a little nondescript coffee shop where I sometimes stop for a hamburger in Amherst there are some unfunny inscriptions hanging on the walls, representing a one-sided dialogue between management and staff. The unfunniest of them all reads—poetically: 24

> Take care of your boss
> The next one may be worse.

The trouble with writers is that they will often refuse to live by such rationality.

1973

Making Connections

1. How is the essay organized? Is this method of organization appropriate for the essay's content? Explain your answer.

2. Contrast Achebe's comments about his childhood with those of James Baldwin. What differences can you distinguish? What similarities? What different cultural priorities become obvious? Explain your response.

V. S. NAIPAUL

Columbus and Crusoe

The author of nearly two dozen works of both fiction and non-fiction, V. S. Naipaul was born in Trinidad of Indian parents in 1932 and has lived in India, Africa, the Middle East, and South America. He currently lives and writes in England. The following essay, though purporting to be a review of Björn Landström's book *Columbus*, focuses on the qualities of the discoverer that lie beyond the scope of the book. The essay aptly demonstrates Naipaul's powerful prose style.

The adventure of Columbus is like *Robinson Crusoe*. No one can imaginatively possess the whole; everything beyond the legend is tedious and complicating. It is so even in Björn Landström's book, *Columbus*, which makes the difficult adventure as accessible as it can be made. The text itself is a retelling from the usual sources. The maps and illustrations are more important. The maps make medieval ideas of geography clear. The illustrations, a true labour of love, are numerous and exact: ships, the islands, the people, the weather, the vegetation, and even the Flemish hawk's bell which delighted the natives until it became a measure of the gold dust the discoverer required them to collect.

In the legend Columbus is persecuted by many enemies; he goes back to Spain white-haired, in chains, and he dies in poverty and disgrace. It is Columbus's own picture: he had a feeling for theatre. His concern for gold exceeded his sovereign's: he expected to get a tenth of all that was found. The chains were not necessary; he was begged to take them off. He wore them for effect, just as, after the previous disaster, he had returned in the Franciscan habit. That disaster had its profitable side. He had sent back slaves, as he had always intended. He claimed, or his son claimed for him, that he had got rid of two-thirds of the natives of Hispaniola in two years; the remainder had been set to gathering gold dust. (This was an exaggeration: he had only got rid of a third.) Even after his disgrace he fussed about his coat-of-arms, appropriating a red field for the castle of Castile, as on the royal coat-of-arms. He complained to the end about his poverty, but one of his personal gold shipments, again after his disgrace, amounted to 405 pounds. His father was a weaver; his sister married a cheesemonger; his son married a lady of royal blood. And at his death Spain hadn't gained very much. Mexico was thirteen years away; and the Indies, the source of his gold, where he thought he had discovered the Terrestrial Paradise, had become, largely through his example, *anus mundi*.

It is a story of extended horror. But it isn't only the horror that numbs response. Nor is it that the discoverer deteriorates so steadily after the discovery. It is the banality of the man. He was looking less for America or Asia than for gold; and the banality of expectation matches a continuing banality of perception. At the heart of the seamanship, the toughness, the avarice, the vindictiveness and the brutality, there is only this:

> 16 September. Here the Admiral says that on that day and all succeeding days they met with very mild breezes, and the mornings were very sweet, with naught lacking save the song of the nightingale. He adds: 'And the weather was like April in Andalusia.'

> 29 September. The air was very sweet and refreshing, so that the only thing lacking was the song of the nightingale; the sea was as calm as a river.

This is from *The Book of the First Voyage*, when he was at his most alert. The concrete details are deceptive. The sea and its life are observed, but mainly for signs of the nearness of land; just as, at the moment of discovery, the natives are studied, but only by a man 'vigilant'—his own word—for gold. 'Their hair is not curly . . . they are not at all black.' Not an anthropological interest, not the response of wonder—disappointment rather: Columbus believed that where Negroes were, there was gold. Beyond this vigilance the words and the perceptions fail. The nightingale, April in Andalusia: the props of a banal poetry are used again and again until they are without meaning. They are at an even lower level than the recent astronaut's 'Wow'—there is nothing like this pure cry of delight in Columbus. After the discovery, his gold-seeking seaman's banalities become repetitive, destroying romance and making the great adventure trivial. A book about Columbus needs to have pictures, and this is why Mr. Landström's book is so valuable.

The medieval mind? But Queen Isabella wrote during the second voyage to find out what the climate was like. April in Andalusia wasn't enough: she wanted pictures, and the romance. Marco Polo, whom Columbus had read, dealt in romance; and Amerigo Vespucci, after whom the continent is not unfairly named. Vespucci thought it worth mentioning that the natives of the islands and the Main pissed casually into the hot sand during conversation, without turning aside; that the women were wanton and used a certain animal poison, sometimes last-ingly fatal to virility, to increase the size of the male member. Perhaps he made this up; but though he too was vigilant and his own voyage ended in profitable slave-trading, he sought in the tradition of travel-romance to awaken wonder at the fact of the New World.

The facts about Columbus have always been known. In his own writings and in all his actions his egoism is like an exposed deformity; he condemns himself. But the heroic gloss, which is not even his own, has come down through the centuries. When the flagship ran aground at Haiti on the first voyage, the Indians were more than helpful: they wept to show their sympathy. Columbus was vigilant: he noted that it would be easy to subdue this 'cowardly' unarmed race. This was what he presently did. Mr Landström suggests that it was unfortunate and not really meant: it is the traditional gloss. On the third voyage Columbus thought he had discovered the Terrestrial Paradise. Mr Landström, again following the gloss, says that Columbus wasn't very well at the time. But it was just this sort of geography that had made him attempt the Ocean Sea.

In this adventure, as in today's adventures in space, the romance is something we ourselves have to supply. The discovery needs a hero; the contempt settles on the country that, in the legend, betrays the hero. The discovery—and it would have come without Columbus—could not but be horrible. Primitive people, once exposed, have to be subdued and uti-lized and somehow put down, in the Indies, Australasia, the United States, Southern Africa; even India has its aboriginal problems. Four hundred years after the great Spanish debate, convened by the Emperor, on the treatment of primitive people, Rhodesia is an imperial issue. The parallel is there; only the contemporary debate, conducted before a mass-electorate on one side and a dispossessed but indifferent primitive people on the other, is necessarily more debased.

There is no Australian or American black legend; there is at the most a romantic, self-flattering guilt. But the black legend of Spain will persist, as will the heroic legend of Columbus. The dream of the un-touched, complete world, the thing for ourselves alone, the dream of Shangri-la, is an enduring human fantasy. It fell to the Spaniards to have the unique experience. Generosity and romance, then, to the discoverer; but the Spaniards will never be forgiven. And even in the violated New World the Spaniards themselves remained subject to the fantasy. The quest for El Dorado became like a recapitulation of the whole New World adventure, a wish to have it all over again; more men and money were expended on this in twenty expeditions than on the conquest of Mexico, Peru and New Granada.

Robinson Crusoe, in its essential myth-making middle part, is an as-pect of the same fantasy. It is a monologue; it is all in the mind. It is the dream of being the first man in the world, of watching the first crop grow. Not only a dream of innocence: it is the dream of being suddenly, just as one is, in unquestionable control of the physical world, of possessing 'the first gun that had been fired there since the creation of the world.' It is the dream of total power. 'First, I made him know his name should be Friday, which was the day I saved his life. I called him so for the memory of the time. I likewise taught him to say master, and then let him know that was to be my name.' Friday is awkward about religion; Crusoe cannot answer. Power brings problems. Crusoe sees some cannibals about to kill and eat a man. He runs to liberate. But then he stops. What is his right to interfere? Is it just the gun? Some Spaniards are to be rescued. How will his freedom and power continue? How will they obey? Where do sanctions start in the empty world? They must sign a contract. But there is no pen, no paper: a difficulty as particular and irrational as in a nightmare. It is from more than a desert island that he is rescued. The issues can never be resolved.

Later Crusoe makes good, in that very New World, but in the settled, beaten-down slave society of Brazil. The horror of the discovery, of being the first totally powerful man in the world: that happened a long time before.

1967

Making Connections

1. What are the main strategies Naipaul uses to structure this essay? What kinds of evidence are offered for support of his generalizations? How reliable is that evidence? Why?

2. In this essay, Naipaul briefly discusses the responsibilities and options that accompany power, a concern also voiced by George Orwell in "Shooting an Elephant." What do their comments have in common? How are they different?

UMBERTO ECO

○━●━○━●━○━●━○━●━○━●━○━●━○━●━○━●━○

The City of Robots

> Most widely known in the United States as the author of the
> international best-selling novel *The Name of the Rose*, Umberto Eco,
> born in Italy in 1932, is a professor of semiotics (the study of signs
> and symbols) at the University of Bologna. In his professional writ-
> ing, Eco analyzes cultural symbols and their meanings in very tech-
> nical terms; however, he also writes regularly for newspapers and
> magazines on the same subjects in much simpler language. In the
> following essay, Eco reflects on his impressions of America's "theme
> cities."

In Europe, when people want to be amused, they go to a "house"   1
of amusement (whether a cinema, theater, or casino); sometimes a
"park" is created, which may seem a "city," but only metaphorically. In
the United States, on the contrary, as everyone knows, there exist
amusement cities. Las Vegas is one example; it is focused on gambling
and entertainment, its architecture is totally artificial, and it has been
studied by Robert Venturi as a completely new phenomenon in city
planning, a "message" city, entirely made up of signs, not a city like the
others, which communicate in order to function, but rather a city that
functions in order to communicate. But Las Vegas is still a "real" city,
and in a recent essay on Las Vegas, Giovanni Brino showed how, though
born as a place for gambling, it is gradually being transformed into a
residential city, a place of business, industry, conventions. The theme of
our trip—on the contrary—is the Absolute Fake; and therefore we are interested only in absolutely fake cities. Disneyland (California) and
Disney World (Florida) are obviously the chief examples, but if they existed alone they would represent a negligible exception. The fact is that
the United States is filled with cities that imitate a city, just as wax museums imitate painting and the Venetian palazzos or Pompeiian villas imitate architecture. In particular there are the "ghost towns," the Western
cities of a century and more ago. Some are reasonably authentic, and the
restoration or preservation has been carried out on an extant, "archeological" urban complex; but more interesting are those born from nothing, out of pure imitative determination. They are "the real thing."

442

There is an embarrassment of riches to choose from: You can have   2
fragments of cities, as at Stone Mountain near Atlanta, where you take a
trip on a nineteenth-century train, witness an Indian raid, and see sheriffs at work, against the background of a fake Mount Rushmore. The Six
Guns Territory, in Silver Springs, also has train and sheriffs, a shoot-out
in the streets and French can-can in the saloon. There is a series of ran-
chos and Mexican missions in Arizona; Tombstone with its OK Corral,
Old Tucson, Legend City near Phoenix. There is the Old South Bar-b-Q
Ranch at Clewison, Florida, and so on. If you venture beyond the myth
of the West, you have cities like the Magic Mountain in Valencia,
California, or Santa Claus Village, Polynesian gardens, pirate islands,
Astroworlds like the one in Kirby, Texas, and the "wild" territories of
the various Marinelands, as well as ecological cities, which we will discuss elsewhere.

There are also the ship imitations. In Florida, for example, between   3
Tampa and St. Petersburg, you can board the *Bounty*, anchored at the
edge of a Tahitian village, faithfully reconstructed according to the
drawings preserved by the Royal Society in London, but with an eye
also on the old film with Charles Laughton and Clark Gable. Many of
the nautical instruments are of the period, some of the sailors are wax-
works, one officer's shoes are those worn by the actor who played the
part, the historical information on the various panels is credible, the
voices that pervade the atmosphere come from the sound track of the
movie. But we'll stick to the Western myth and take as a sample city the
Knott's Berry Farm of Buena Park, Los Angeles.

Here the whole trick seems to be exposed; the surrounding city   4
context and the iron fencing (as well as the admission ticket) warn us
that we are entering not a real city but a toy city. But as we begin walking down the first streets, the studied illusion takes over. First of all,
there is the realism of the reconstruction: the dusty stables, the sagging
shops, the offices of the sheriff and the telegraph agent, the jail, the saloon are life size and executed with absolute fidelity; the old carriages
are covered with dust, the Chinese laundry is dimly lit, all the buildings
are more or less practical, and the shops are open, because Berry Farm,
like Disneyland, blends the reality of trade with the play of fiction. And
if the dry-goods store is fake nineteenth-century and the shopgirl is
dressed like a John Ford heroine, the candies, the peanuts, the pseudo-
Indian handicrafts are real and are sold for real dollars, just as the soft
drinks, advertised with antique posters, are real, and the customer finds
himself participating in the fantasy because of his own authenticity as a
consumer; in other words, he is in the role of the cowboy or the gold-
prospector who comes into town to be fleeced of all he has accumulated
while out in the wilds.

Furthermore the levels of illusion are numerous, and this increases   5 the hallucination—that is to say, the Chinese in the laundry or the prisoner in the jail are wax dummies, who exist, in realistic attitudes, in settings that are equally realistic, though you can't actually enter them; but you don't realize the room in question is a glass display case, because it looks as if you could, if you chose, open the door or climb through the window; and then the next room, say, which is both the general store and the justice of the peace's office, looks like a display case but is actually practical, and the justice of the peace, with his black alpaca jacket and his pistols at his hips, is an actual person who sells you his merchandise. It should be added that extras walk about the streets and periodically stage a furious gun battle, and when you realize that the average American visitor is wearing blue jeans not very different from the cowboys', many of the visitors become confused with the extras, increasing the theatricality of the whole. For example, the village school, reconstructed with hyperrealistic detail, has behind the desk a schoolmarm wearing a bonnet and an ample checked skirt, but the children on the benches are little passing visitors, and I heard one tourist ask his wife if the children were real or "fake" (and you could sense his psychological readiness to consider them, at will, extras, dummies, or moving robots of the sort we will see in Disneyland).

Apparently ghost towns involve a different approach from that of wax museums or museums for copies of works of art. In the first nobody expects the wax Napoleon to be taken for real, but the hallucination serves to level the various historical periods and erase the distinction between historical reality and fantasy; in the case of the works of art what is culturally, if not psychologically, hallucinatory is the confusion between copy and original, and the fetishization of art as a sequence of famous subjects. In the ghost town, on the contrary, since the theatricality is explicit, the hallucination operates in making the visitors take part in the scene and thus become participants in that commercial fair that is apparently an element of the fiction but in fact represents the substantial aim of the whole imitative machine.

In an excellent essay on Disneyland as "degenerate utopia" ("a degenerate utopia is an ideology realized in the form of myth"), Louis Marin analyzed the structure of that nineteenth-century frontier city street that receives entering visitors and distributes them through the various sectors of the magic city. Disneyland's Main Street seems the first scene of the fiction whereas it is an extremely shrewd commercial reality. Main Street—like the whole city, for that matter—is presented as at once absolutely realistic and absolutely fantastic, and this is the advantage (in terms of artistic conception) of Disneyland over the other toy cities. The houses of Disneyland are full-size on the ground floor, and on a two-thirds scale on the floor above, so they give the impression of being inhabitable (and they are) but also of belonging to a fantastic past that we can grasp with our imagination. The Main Street façades are presented to us as toy houses and invite us to enter them, but their interior is always a disguised supermarket, where you buy obsessively, believing that you are still playing.

In this sense Disneyland is more hyperrealistic than the wax museum, precisely because the latter still tries to make us believe that what we are seeing reproduces reality absolutely, whereas Disneyland makes it clear that within its magic enclosure it is fantasy that is absolutely reproduced. The Palace of Living Arts presents its Venus de Milo as almost real, whereas Disneyland can permit itself to present its reconstructions as masterpieces of falsification, for what it sells is, indeed, goods, but genuine merchandise, not reproductions. What is falsified is our will to buy, which we take as real, and in this sense Disneyland is really the quintessence of consumer ideology.

But once the "total fake" is admitted, in order to be enjoyed it must seem totally real. So the Polynesian restaurant will have, in addition to a fairly authentic menu, Tahitian waitresses in costume, appropriate vegetation, rock walls with little cascades, and once you are inside nothing must lead you to suspect that outside there is anything but Polynesia. If, between two trees, there appears a stretch of river that belongs to another sector, Adventureland, then that section of stream is so designed that it would not be unrealistic to see in Tahiti, beyond the garden hedge, a river like this. And if in the wax museums wax is not flesh, in Disneyland, when rocks are involved, they are rock, and water is water, and a baobab a baobab. When there is a fake—hippopotamus, dinosaur, sea serpent—it is not so much because it wouldn't be possible to have the real equivalent but because the public is meant to admire the perfection of the fake and its obedience to the program. In this sense Disneyland not only produces illusion, but—in confessing it—stimulates the desire for it: A real crocodile can be found in the zoo, and as a rule it is dozing or hiding, but Disneyland tells us that faked nature corresponds much more to our daydream demands. When, in the space of twenty-four hours, you go (as I did deliberately) from the fake New Orleans of Disneyland to the real one, and from the wild river of Adventureland to a trip on the Mississippi, where the captain of the paddle-wheel steamer says it is possible to see alligators on the banks of the river, and then you don't see any, you risk feeling homesick for Disneyland, where the wild animals don't have to be coaxed. Disneyland tells us that technology can give us more reality than nature can.

In this sense I believe the most typical phenomenon of this universe is not the more famous Fantasyland—an amusing carousel of fantastic journeys that take the visitor into the world of Peter Pan or Snow White, a wondrous machine whose fascination and lucid legitimacy it would be foolish to deny—but the Caribbean Pirates and the Haunted

Mansion. The pirate show lasts a quarter of an hour (but you lose any sense of time, it could be ten minutes or thirty); you enter a series of caves, carried in boats over the surface of the water, you see first abandoned treasures, a captain's skeleton in a sumptuous bed of moldy brocade, pendent cobwebs, bodies of executed men devoured by ravens, while the skeleton addresses menacing admonitions to you. Then you navigate an inlet, passing through the crossfire of a galleon and the cannon of a fort, while the chief corsair shouts taunting challenges at the beleaguered garrison; then, as if along a river, you go by an invaded city which is being sacked, with the rape of the women, theft of jewels, torture of the mayor; the city burns like a match, drunken pirates sprawled on piles of kegs sing obscene songs; some completely out of their heads, shoot at the visitors; the scene degenerates, everything collapses in flames, slowly the last songs die away, you emerge into the sunlight. Everything you have seen was on human scale, the vault of the caves became confused with that of the sky, the boundary of this underground world was that of the universe and it was impossible to glimpse its limits. The pirates moved, danced, slept, popped their eyes, sniggered, drank—really. You realize that they are robots, but you remain dumbfounded by their verisimilitude. And, in fact, the "Audio-Animatronic" technique represented a great source of pride for Walt Disney, who had finally managed to achieve his own dream and reconstruct a fantasy world more real than reality, breaking down the wall of the second dimension, creating not a movie, which is illusion, but total theater, and not with anthropomorphized animals, but with human beings. In fact, Disney's robots are masterpieces of electronics; each was devised by observing the expressions of a real actor, then building models, then developing skeletons of absolute precision, authentic computers in human form, to be dressed in "flesh" and "skin" made by craftsmen, whose command of realism is incredible. Each robot obeys a program, can synchronize the movements of mouth and eyes with the words and sounds of the audio, repeating ad infinitum all day long his established part (a sentence, one or two gestures) and the visitor, caught off guard by the succession of events, obliged to see several things at once, to left and right and straight ahead, has no time to look back and observe that the robot he has just seen is already repeating his eternal scenario.

The "Audio-Animatronic" technique is used in many other parts of [11] Disneyland and also enlivens a review of presidents of the United States, but in the pirates' cave, more than anywhere else, it demonstrates all its miraculous efficacy. Humans could do no better, and would cost more, but the important thing is precisely the fact that these are not humans and we know they're not. The pleasure of imitation, as the ancients knew, is one of the most innate in the human spirit; but here we not only enjoy a perfect imitation, we also enjoy the conviction that imitation has reached its apex and afterwards reality will always be inferior to it.

Similar criteria underlie the journey through the cellars of the   12
Haunted Mansion, which looks at first like a rundown country house,
somewhere between Edgar Allan Poe and the cartoons of Charles
Addams; but inside, it conceals the most complete array of witchcraft
surprises that anyone could desire. You pass through an abandoned
graveyard, where skeletal hands raise gravestones from below, you
cross a hill enlivened by a witches' sabbath complete with spirits and
beldams; then you move through a room with a table all laid and a
group of transparent ghosts in nineteenth-century costume dancing
while diaphanous guests, occasionally vanishing into thin air, enjoy the
banquet of a barbaric sovereign. You are grazed by cobwebs, reflected in
crystals on whose surface a greenish figure appears, behind your back;
you encounter moving candelabra. . . . In no instance are these the cheap
tricks of some tunnel of love; the involvement (always tempered by the
humor of the inventions) is total. As in certain horror films, detachment
is impossible; you are not witnessing another's horror, you are inside the
horror through complete synesthesia; and if there is an earthquake the
movie theater must also tremble.

I would say that these two attractions sum up the Disneyland phi-   13
losophy more than the equally perfect models of the pirate ship, the
river boat, and the sailing ship *Columbia*, all obviously in working order.
And more than the Future section, with the science-fiction emotions it
arouses (such as a flight to Mars experienced from inside a spacecraft,
with all the effects of deceleration, loss of gravity, dizzying movement
away from the earth, and so on). More than the models of rockets and
atomic submarines, which prompted Marin to observe that whereas the
fake Western cities, the fake New Orleans, the fake jungle provide life-
size duplicates of organic but historical or fantastic events, these are re-
duced-scale models of mechanical realities of today, and so, where
something is incredible, the full-scale model prevails, and where it is
credible, the reduction serves to make it attractive to the imagination.
The Pirates and the Ghosts sum up all Disneyland, at least from the
point of view of our trip, because they transform the whole city into an
immense robot, the final realization of the dreams of the eighteenth-century mechanics who gave life to the Writer of Neuchâtel and the Chess-
playing Turk of Baron von Kempelen.

Disneyland's precision and coherence are to some extent disturbed   14
by the ambitions of Disney World in Florida. Built later, Disney World is
a hundred fifty times larger than Disneyland, and proudly presents itself
not as a toy city but as the model of an urban agglomerate of the future.
The structures that make up California's Disneyland form here only a
marginal part of an immense complex of construction covering an area
twice the size of Manhattan. The great monorail that takes you from the
entrance to the Magic Kingdom (the Disneyland part proper) passes artificial bays and lagoons, a Swiss village, a Polynesian village, golf courses

and tennis courts, an immense hotel: an area dedicated, in other words, to organized vacationing. So you reach the Magic Kingdom, your eyes already dazzled by so much science fiction that the sight of the high medieval castle (far more Gothic than Disneyland: a Strasbourg Cathedral, let's say, compared to a San Miniato) no longer stirs the imagination. Tomorrow, with its violence, has made the colors fade from the stories of Yesterday. In this respect Disneyland is much shrewder; it must be visited without anything to remind us of the future surrounding it. Marin has observed that, to enter it, the essential condition is to abandon your car in an endless parking lot and reach the boundary of the dream city by special little trains. And for a Californian, leaving his car means leaving his own humanity, consigning himself to another power, abandoning his own will.

An allegory of the consumer society, a place of absolute iconism,   15
Disneyland is also a place of total passivity. Its visitors must agree to behave like its robots. Access to each attraction is regulated by a maze of metal railings which discourages any individual initiative. The number of visitors obviously sets the pace of the line; the officials of the dream, properly dressed in the uniforms suited to each specific attraction, not only admit the visitor to the threshold of the chosen sector, but, in successive phases, regulate his every move ("Now wait here please, go up now, sit down please, wait before standing up," always in a polite tone, impersonal, imperious, over the microphone). If the visitor pays this price, he can have not only "the real thing" but the abundance of the reconstructed truth. Like the Hearst Castle, Disneyland also has no transitional spaces; there is always something to see, the great voids of modern architecture and city planning are unknown here. If America is the country of the Guggenheim Museum or the new skyscrapers of Manhattan, then Disneyland is a curious exception and American intellectuals are quite right to refuse to go there. But if America is what we have seen in the course of our trip, then Disneyland is its Sistine Chapel, and the hyperrealists of the art galleries are only the timid voyeurs of an immense and continuous "found object."

1983

Making Connections

1. According to Eco, what is "hyperrealistic" about America's "theme cities," such as Knott's Berry Farm and Disneyland? What does he mean when he calls Disneyland "allegorical"?

2. Compare Eco's comments about the "absolute fake" to Stephen Jay Gould's remarks about authenticity in "Counters and Cable Cars." What do the remarks of both writers reveal about American culture?

VED MEHTA

•○•○•○•○•○•○•○•○•○•○•○•

Pom's Engagement

Born in 1934 and blind from the age of three, Ved Mehta grew up in Lahore, a city in northern India. His family sent him to the United States when he was fifteen, and he later earned degrees from Pomona College and Harvard University. He is currently a staff writer for the *New Yorker*. In addition to his magazine writing, Mehta has published several works on Indian culture and political history, as well as collections of interviews with international theologians, historians, and philosophers. The following essay reflects the changing traditions within Indian culture.

Before we moved to Lahore, Daddyji had gone to Mussoorie, a hill 1
station in the United Provinces, without telling us why he was going out of the Punjab. Now, several months after he made that trip, he gathered us around him in the drawing room at 11 Temple Road while Mamaji mysteriously hurried Sister Pom upstairs. He started talking as if we were all very small and he were conducting one of our "dinner-table-school" discussions. He said that by right and tradition the oldest daughter had to be given in marriage first, and that the ripe age for marriage was nineteen. He said that when a girl approached that age her parents, who had to take the initiative, made many inquiries and followed many leads. They investigated each young man and his family background, his relatives, his friends, his classmates, because it was important to know what kind of family the girl would be marrying into, what kind of company she would be expected to keep. If the girl's parents decided that a particular young man was suitable, then his people also had to make their investigations, but, however favorable their findings, their decision was unpredictable, because good, well-settled boys were in great demand and could afford to be choosy. All this took a lot of time. "That's why I said nothing to you children about why I went to Mussoorie," he concluded. "I went to see a young man for Pom. She's already nineteen."

We were stunned. We have never really faced the idea that Sister 2
Pom might get married and suddenly leave, I thought.

"We won't lose Pom, we'll get a new family member," Daddyji 3
said, as if reading my thoughts.

Then all of us started talking at once. We wanted to know if Sister 4
Pom had been told; if she'd agreed; whom she'd be marrying.

"Your mother has just taken Pom up to tell her," Daddyji said. 5
"But she's a good girl. She will agree." He added, "The young man in
question is twenty-eight years old. He's a dentist, and so has a profession."

"Did you get a dentist because Sister Pom has bad teeth?" Usha 6
asked. Sister Pom had always been held up to us as an example of someone who, as a child, had spurned greens and had therefore grown up
with a mouthful of poor teeth.

Daddyji laughed. "I confess I didn't think of anyone's teeth when I 7
chose the young man in question."

"What is he like?" I asked. "What are we to call him?" 8

"He's a little bit on the short side, but he has a happy-go-lucky na- 9
ture, like Nimi's. He doesn't drink, but, unfortunately, he does smoke.
His father died at an early age of a heart attack, but he has a nice mother,
who will not give Pom any trouble. It seems that everyone calls him
Kakaji."

We all laughed. Kakaji, or "youngster," was what very small boys 10
were called.

"That's what he must have been called when he was small, and the 11
name stuck," Daddyji said.

In spite of myself, I pictured a boy smaller than I was and imag- 12
ined him taking Sister Pom away, and then I imagined her having to
keep his pocket money, to arrange his clothes in the cupboards, to comb
his hair. My mouth felt dry.

"What will Kakaji call Sister Pom?" I asked. 13

"Pom, silly—what else?" Sister Umi said. 14

Mamaji and Sister Pom walked into the room. Daddyji made a 15
place for Sister Pom next to him and said, "Now, now, now, no reason to
cry. Is it to be yes?"

"Whatever you say," Sister Pom said in a small voice, between 16
sobs.

"Pom, how can you say that? You've never seen him," Sister Umi 17
said.

"Kakaji's uncle, Dr. Prakash Mehrotra, himself a dentist, has 18
known our family from his student days in Lahore," Daddyji said. "As a
student dentist, he used to be welcomed in Babuji's Shahalmi Gate
house. He would come and go as he pleased. He has known for a long
time what kind of people we are. He remembered seeing you, Pom,
when we went to Mussoorie on holiday. He said yes immediately, and
his approval seemed to be enough for Kakaji."

"You promised me you wouldn't cry again," Mamaji said to Sister   19
Pom, patting her on the back, and then, to Daddyji, "She's agreed."

Daddyji said much else, sometimes talking just for the sake of talk-   20
ing, sometimes laughing at us because we were sniffling, and all the
time trying to make us believe that this was a happy occasion. First,
Sister Umi took issue with him: parents had no business arranging marriages; if she were Pom she would run away. Then Sister Nimi: all her
life she had heard him say to us children, "Think for yourself—be independent," and here he was not allowing Pom to think for herself.
Brother Om took Daddyji's part: girls who didn't get married became a
burden on their parents, and Daddyji had four daughters to marry off,
and would be retiring in a few years. Sisters Nimi and Umi retorted:
they hadn't gone to college to get married off, to have some young man
following them around like a leech. Daddyji just laughed. I thought he
was so wise, and right.

"Go and bless your big sister," Mamaji said, pushing me in the di-   21
rection of Sister Pom.

"I don't want to, " I said. "I don't know him."   22

"What'll happen to Sister Pom's room?" Usha asked. She and   23
Ashok didn't have rooms of their own. They slept in Mamaji's room.

"Pom's room will remain empty, so that any time she likes she can   24
come and stay in her room with Kakaji," Daddyji said.

The thought that a man I never met would sleep in Pom's room   25
with Sister Pom there made my heart race. A sob shook me. I ran outside.

The whole house seemed to be in an uproar. Mamaji was shouting   26
at Gian Chand, Gian Chand was shouting at the bearer, the bearer was
shouting at the sweeper. There were the sounds of the kitchen fire being
stoked, of the drain being washed out, of water running in bathrooms.
From behind whichever door I passed came the rustle of saris, salwars,
and kemises. The house smelled of fresh flowers, but it had a ghostly
chill. I would climb to the landing of Sister Pom's room and thump
down the stairs two at a time. Brother Om would shout up at me, "Stop
it!" Sister Umi would shout down at me, "Don't you have anything better to do?" Sister Nimi would call to me from somewhere, "You're giving Pom a headache." I wouldn't heed any of them. As soon as I had
thumped down, I would clatter to the top and thump my way down
again.

Daddyji went past on the back veranda. "Who's coming with   27
Kakaji?" I asked. Kakaji was in Lahore to buy some dental equipment,
and in a few minutes he was expected for tea, to meet Sister Pom and
the family.

"He's coming alone," Daddyji said, over his shoulder. "He's come   28 from very far away." I had somehow imagined that Kakaji would come with at least as many people as we had in our family, because I had started thinking of the tea as a kind of cricket match—the elevens facing off.

I followed Daddyji into the drawing room. "Will he come alone for his wedding, too?" 29

"No. Then he'll come with the bridegroom's party." 30

We were joined by everyone except Mamaji and Sister Pom, who from the moment we got the news of Sister Pom's marriage had become inseparable. 31

Gian Chand came in, the tea things rattling on his tray. 32

Later, I couldn't remember exactly how Kakaji had arrived, but I remember noticing that his footfall was heavy, that his greeting was affectionate, and that his voice seemed to float up with laughter. I don't know what I'd expected, but I imagined that if I had been in his place I would have skulked in the *gulli*, and perhaps changed my mind and not entered at all. 33

"Better to have ventured and lost than never to have ventured at all," Daddyji was saying to Kakaji about life's battles. 34

"Yes, Daddyji, just so," he said, with a little laugh. I had never heard anybody outside our family call my father Daddyji. It sounded odd. 35

Sister Pom was sent for, and she came in with Mamaji. Her footsteps were shy, and the rustle of her sari around her feet was slow, as if she felt too conscious of the noise she was making just in walking. Daddyji made some complimentary remark about the silver border on her sari, and told her to sit next to Kakaji. Kakaji and Sister Pom exchanged a few words about a family group photograph on the mantelpiece, and about her studies. There was the clink of china as Sister Pom served Kakaji tea. 36

"Won't you have some tea yourself?" Kakaji asked Sister Pom. 37

Sister Pom's sari rustled over her shoulder as she turned to Daddyji. 38

"Kakaji, none of my children have ever tasted tea or coffee," Daddyji said. "We consider both to be bad habits. My children have been brought up on hot milk, and lately Pom has been taking a little ghi in her milk at bedtime, for health reasons." 39

We all protested at Daddyji's broadcasting family matters. 40

Kakaji tactfully turned the conversation to a visit to Mussoorie that our family was planning. 41

Mamaji offered him onion, potato, and cauliflower pakoras. He accepted, remarking how hot and crisp they were. 42

"Where will Sister Pom live?" Usha asked. 43

"In the summer, my practice is in Mussoorie," Kakaji said, "but in   44
the winter it's in Dehra Dun."

It struck me for the first time that after Sister Pom got married peo-   45
ple we didn't know, people she didn't know, would become more important to her than we were.

Kakaji had left without formally committing himself. Then, four   46
days later, when we were all sitting in the drawing room, a servant
brought a letter to Mamaji. She told us that it was from Kakaji's mother,
and that it asked if Sister Pom might be engaged to Kakaji. "She even
wants to know if Pom can be married in April or May," Mamaji said excitedly. "How propitious! That'll be the fifth wedding in the family in
those two months." Cousins Prakash and Dev, Cousin Pushpa (Bhaji
Ganga Ram's adopted daughter), and Auntie Vimla were all due to be
married in Lahore then.

"You still have time to change your mind," Daddyji said to Sister   47
Pom. "What do you really think of him?"

Sister Pom wouldn't say anything.   48

"How do you expect her to know what her mind is when all that   49
the two talked about was a picture and her bachelor's exam in May?"
Sister Umi demanded. "Could she have fallen in love already?"

"Love, Umi, means something very different from 'falling in love,' "   50
Daddyji said. "It's not an act but a lifelong process. The best we can do as
Pom's parents is to give her love every opportunity to grow."

"But doesn't your 'every opportunity' include knowing the person   51
better than over a cup of tea, or whatever?" Sister Umi persisted.

"Yes, of course it does. But what we are discussing here is a simple   52
matter of choice—not love," Daddyji said. "To know a person, to love a
person, takes years of living together."

"Do you mean, then, that knowing a person and loving a person   53
are the same thing?" Sister Umi asked.

"Not quite, but understanding and respect are essential to love,   54
and that cannot come from talking together, even over a period of days
or months. That can come only in good time, through years of experience. It is only when Pom and Kakaji learn to consider each other's problems as one and the same that they will find love."

"But, Daddyji, look at the risk you're taking, the risk you're mak-   55
ing Pom take," Sister Nimi said.

"We are trying to minimize the risk as much as we can by finding   56
Pom a family that is like ours," Daddyji said. "Kakaji is a dentist, I am a
doctor. His life and way of thinking will be similar to mine. We are from
the same caste, and Kakaji's family originally came from the Punjab.
They eat meat and eggs, and they take religion in their stride, and don't

pray every day and go to temples, like Brahmans. Kakaji knows how I walk into a club and how I am greeted there. The atmosphere in Pom's new home will be very much the same as the atmosphere here. Now, if I were to give Pom in marriage to a Brahman he'd expect Pom to live as he did. That would really be gambling."

"Then what you're doing is perpetuating the caste system," Sister Nimi said. She was the political rebel in the family. "You seem to presuppose that a Kshatriya should marry only a Kshatriya, that a Brahman should marry only a Brahman. I would just as soon marry a shopkeeper from the Bania caste or an Untouchable, and help to break down caste barriers."   57

"That day might come," Daddyji said. "But you will admit, Nimi, that by doing that you'd be increasing the odds."   58

"But for a cause I believe in," Sister Nimi said.   59

"Yes, but that's a whole other issue," Daddyji said.   60

"Daddyji, you say that understanding and respect are necessary for love," Sister Umi said. "I don't see why you would respect a person more because you lived with him and shared his problems."   61

"In our society, we think of understanding and respect as coming only through sacrifice," Daddyji said.   62

"Then you're advocating the subservience of women," Sister Nimi said, "because it's not Kakaji who will be expected to sacrifice—it's Pom. That's not fair."   63

"And why do you think that Pom will learn to respect Kakaji because she sacrifices for him?" Sister Umi said, pressing her point.   64

"No, Umi, it is the other way around," Daddyji said. "It is Kakaji who will respect Pom because she sacrifices for him."   65

"But that doesn't mean that Pom will respect Kakaji," Sister Umi persisted.   66

"But if Kakaji is moved by Pom's sacrifices he will show more consideration for her. He will grow to love her. I know in my own case I was moved to the depths to see Shanti suffer so because she was so ill-prepared to be my wife. It took me long enough—too long, I believe—to reach that understanding, perhaps because I had broken away from the old traditions and had given in to Western influences."   67

"So you admit that Pom will have to suffer for years," Sister Umi said.   68

"Perhaps," Daddyji said. "But all that time she will be striving for ultimate happiness and love. Those are precious gifts that can only be cultivated in time."   69

"You haven't told us what this ultimate happiness is," Sister Umi said. "I don't really understand it."   70

"It is a uniting of ideals and purposes, and a merging of them. This is the tradition of our society, and it is the means we have adopted to make our marriages successful and beautiful. It works because we believe in the   71 goodness of the individuals going into the marriage and rely on the strength of the sacred bond."

"But my ideal is to be independent," Sister Nimi said. "As you say, 72 'Think for yourself.' "

"But often you have to choose among ideals," Daddyji said. "You 73 may have to choose between being independent and being married."

"But aren't you struck by the fact that all the suffering is going to be 74 on Pom's part? Shouldn't Kakaji be required to sacrifice for their happiness, too?" Sister Nimi said, reverting to the old theme.

"There has to be a start," Daddyji said. "Remember, in our tradition 75 it's her life that is joined with his; it is she who will forsake her past to build a new future with him. If both Pom and Kakaji were to be obstinate, were to compete with each other about who would sacrifice first, who would sacrifice more, what hope would there be of their ever getting on together, of their ever finding love?"

"Daddyji, you're evading the issue," Sister Nimi said. "Why should- 76 n't he take the initiative in this business of sacrifice?"

"He would perhaps be expected to if Pom were working, too, as in 77 the West, and, though married, leading a whole different life from his. I suppose more than this I really can't say, and there may be some injustice in our system, at that. In the West, they go in for romantic love, which is unknown among us. I'm not sure that that method works any better than our method does."

Then Daddyji said to Sister Pom, "I have done my best. Even after 78 you marry Kakaji, my responsibility for you will not be over. I will always be there in the background if you should need me."

"I respect your judgment, Daddyji," Sister Pom said obediently. "I'll 79 do what you say."

Mamaji consulted Shambu Pandit. He compared the horoscopes of 80 Sister Pom and Kakaji and set the date of the marriage for the eleventh of May.... " That's just three days after she finishes her B.A. finals!" we cried. "When will she study? You are sacrificing her education to some silly superstition."

But Shambu Pandit would not be budged from the date. "I am only 81 going by the horoscopes of the couple," he said. "You might as well protest to the stars."

We appealed to Daddyji, but he said that he didn't want to interfere, 82 because such matters were up to Mamaji. That was as much as to say that Shambu Pandit's date was a settled thing.

I recall that at about that time there was an engagement ceremony. 83 We all—Daddyji, Mamaji, Sister Pom, many of our Mehta and Mehra relatives—sat cross-legged on the floor of the front veranda around Shambu Pandit. He recited the Gayatri Mantra, the simple prayer he used to tell us

to say before we went to sleep, and made a thank offering of incense and
ghi to a fire in a brazier, much as Mamaji did—behind Daddyji's back—
when one of us was going on a trip or had recovered from a bout of illness. Servants passed around a platter heaped up with crumbly sweet
balls. I heard Kakaji's sister, Billo, saying something to Sister Pom; she
had just come from Dehra Dun bearing a sari, a veil, and the engagement ring for Sister Pom, after Romesh Chachaji, one of Daddyji's brothers, had gone to Dehra Dun bearing some money, a silver platter and silver bowls, and sweetmeats for Kakaji. It was the first time that I was
able to think of Kakaji both as a remote and frightening dentist who was
going to take Sister Pom away and as someone ordinary like us, who
had his own family. At some point, Mamaji prodded me, and I scooted
forward, crab fashion, to embrace Sister Pom. I felt her hand on my
neck. It had something cold and metallic on it, which sent a shiver
through me. I realized that she was wearing her engagement ring, and
that until then Mamaji was the only one in our family who had worn a
ring.

In the evening, the women relatives closeted themselves in the   84
drawing room with Sister Pom for the engagement singsong. I crouched
outside with my ear to the door. The door pulsated with the beat of a
barrel drum. The pulse in my forehead throbbed in sympathy with the
beat as I caught snatches of songs about bedsheets and henna, along
with explosions of laughter, the songs themselves rising and falling like
the cooing of the doves that nested under the eaves of the veranda. I
thought that a couple of years earlier I would have been playing somewhere outside on such an occasion, without knowing what I was missing, or been in the drawing room clapping and singing, but now I was
crouching by the door like a thief, and was feeling ashamed even as I
was captivated.

1984

Making Connections

1. What is Mehta's purpose underlying this essay's lively narrative? Is Mehta
   being objective in his appraisal of Indian custom? How do you know?

2. Through his narrative, Mehta focuses on India's marriage ritual and Indian
   cultural traditions. In "Marrying Absurd," Joan Didion focuses on one
   form of the American marriage ritual. Compare and contrast these two essays, and discuss the interpretations of marriage in the two cultures.

VACLAV HAVEL

Second Wind

Vaclav Havel, the former president of Czechoslovakia, was born in 1936 and educated in his homeland. Havel, internationally known as a playwright, is also the author of numerous essays on dissent within totalitarian societies, a topic with which he is intimately familiar. An outspoken advocate of Czech human rights, Havel was imprisoned for several years for his involvement in the Czech civil rights movement. "Second Wind" remains one of the few autobiographical statements he has made.

When a writer is twenty, something we might call his initial experience of the world usually begins to ripen within him, and becomes a source he will draw on for a long time to come. It is about this age, after a lot of initial groping, that he comes to a more serious understanding of himself, looks about the world with his own eyes, and discovers his own way of bearing witness to it, and to himself. Then it takes roughly ten years for him to investigate, think through, and exhaust this initial experience of the world from all angles. It is an important ten years: a time of getting under way, of heroic self-discovery, a time of relative bravery and relative optimism.

I do not belong to that fortunate class of authors who write constantly, quickly, easily, and always well, whose imaginations never tire and who—unhampered by doubts or inhibitions—are by nature open to the world. Whatever they touch, it is always exactly right. That I do not belong in such company, of course, bothers me, and sometimes even upsets me: I am ambitious and I'm angry with myself for having so few ideas, for finding it so difficult to write, for having so little faith in myself, and for thinking so much about everything that I often feel crippled by it.

And yet I must admit in my writing too, there was something like that first "heroic" period when—self-confident, uninhibited, without a lot of overblown ambition—I was simply mapping out my initial experience of the world. Of course, I didn't see it that way at the time and I'm well aware today that it was only relatively true: even then, after all, I

rewrote everything a hundred times, I groped in the dark and suc-
cumbed to despair. Still, with the passing of time, it seems to me that
everything was easier then, and my first plays were—on their own
level—in many ways more masterful than much of what I wrote later.

This relatively confident start of mine, of course, was influenced—   4
and I've only really become fully aware of this today—by a fortunate in-
terplay of several quite accidental circumstances.

Thanks to the apparent disadvantage of coming from a bourgeois   5
background and growing up in a communist state, I had the opportunity, right from the start, of seeing the world "from below," that is, as it
really is. This helped me to escape certain eventual illusions and mystifi-
cations. Of course I don't think that, had I grown up in a different state
with the same background, I would necessarily have become a capitalist,
any more than, had I grown up in the same state with a different background, I would necessarily have become a party functionary. In either
case, I would probably still have become a writer. But I'm well aware
that because in both those cases I would have been, in some ways, exter-
nally better off, internally I'd have been far worse off, because I'd have
been denied that initial experience of the world "from below," which
probably gave me more than I was willing to admit at the time. If I displayed—as they used to write about me—a certain sensitivity for the absurd dimensions of the world, then it was not just because of my temperament, but also because of my experience: as we know, the absurd
and comic dimensions of the world are always best seen from below.

I was twenty in 1956. It was the time of the famous revelations, the   6
first widespread collapse of illusions, and the first efforts to reconstruct
them again in a more or less "renewed" or "reformist" shape.
Historically, it was a fascinating period; for the first time in our part of
the world the merry-go-round of hope and disappointment, of half-
baked remedies and their half-baked liquidation, of renewed ideals and
their renewed betrayal, began to turn. For the first time, that peculiar dialectical dance of truth and lies began its whirl in society and in people's
minds, of truth alienated by lies and the phony manipulation of hopes
that we know so intimately today and which is brought home to us in
such an original way by one of the basic themes of modern art: the
theme of human identity and existential schizophrenia.

Naturally, I don't know how I'd have written if I'd turned twenty   7
earlier, in 1950, for instance, but I feel that the chronological coincidence
of my first serious attempt at self-definition with that particular historical moment was for me—as a writer—most fortunate. Equipped with
my view "from below," the experience of Franz Kafka and the French
theatre of the absurd, and somewhat obsessed with a tendency to elaborate on things rationally to the point of absurdity, I found in those remarkable social conditions (hitherto unprecedented and therefore unde-

scribed) a wonderful horizon for my writing. I am not claiming that in my first plays there was nothing more going on, or that my only concern was describing the dialectical mechanisms behind those pseudo-reforms and the irresistible decay of the system that was trying to bring them about, but I can scarcely imagine having written them without the inspiration provided by that particular background.

There are several reasons, some deep and some accidental, why I [8] began to write plays in the late fifties after several years of trying to write poetry, but none are important in this connection. What is important is that it is far harder to store a play away in your desk drawer than it is poetry or prose. Once written, a play is only half done, and it is never complete and itself until it has been performed in a theatre. Theatre is an art form so social that, more than any other art form, it depends on having a public existence, and that means it is at the mercy of cultural conditions. (Whereas one can imagine a movie shot for audiences in the future, theatre either exists in the present or not at all.)

The fortunate way in which my own "bioliterary" time meshed [9] with historical time gave me another tremendous advantage: my early beginnings as a playwright coincided with the 1960s, a remarkable and relatively favorable era in which my plays, despite being so different from what had been permitted until then, could actually reach the stage, something that would have been impossible both before and after that. I don't suppose I need emphasize how important this was for my writing. It was not just the formal fact that my plays were permitted; there was something deeper and more essential here: that society was capable of accepting them, that they resonated with the general state of mind, that the intellectual and social climate of the time, open to new self-knowledge and hungry for it, not only tolerated them, but—if I may say so—actually wanted them. And of course every such act of social self-awareness—that is, every genuine and profound acceptance of a new work, identification with it, and the integration of it into the spiritual reality of the time—immediately and inevitably opens the way for even more radical acts. With each new work, the possibilities of the repressive system were weakened; the more we were able to do, the more we did, and the more we did, the more we were able to do. It was a state of accelerated metabolism between art and its time, and it is always inspiring and productive for phenomena as social as theatre. (Of course many of my generation active in other areas were blessed with the same fortunate coincidence of the times with their first artistic efforts: the whole "new wave" of Czech film, for instance.)

The final circumstance that had a positive influence on the first [10] stage of my writing was the fact that in 1960—again as a result of many fortunate coincidences—I found myself working in the Theatre on the Balustrade in Prague. Here was a theatre with a specific artistic profile.

Its ambition was not to become a part of the country's cultural industry, as one of the institutions that helped to keep the world of appearances running smoothly; it was to be something essentially different: a place where that unsettling process of social self-awareness could occur. In other words, it was precisely the kind of theatre I believe in and which inspires me. I was not only an author who occasionally came up with a new play, I was able to take part in the everyday running of the theatre in all kinds of ways: I could help influence its profile, be a part of its organism, test my work in it from day to day, and—last but certainly not least—enjoy the dramaturgical assistance of Jan Grossman. At the Balustrade, there was something happening—and throughout the sixties, this created extraordinarily favorable conditions for my writing: I knew why I was writing, and who I was writing for. [. . .]

Sooner or later, however, a writer (or at least a writer of my type)   11
finds himself at a crossroads: he has exhausted his initial experience of the world and the ways of expressing it and he must decide how to proceed from there. He can, of course, seek ever more brilliant ways of saying the things he has already said; that is, he can essentially repeat himself. Or he can rest in the position he achieved in his first burst of creativity, subordinate everything he learned to the interests of consolidating that position, and thus assure himself a place on Parnassus.

But he has a third option: he can abandon everything proven, step   12
beyond his initial experience of the world, with which he is by now all too familiar, liberate himself from what binds him to his own tradition, to public expectation and to his own established position, and try for a new and more mature self-definition, one that corresponds to his present and authentic experience of the world. In short, he can find his "second wind." Anyone who chooses this route—the only one (if one wishes to go on writing) that genuinely makes sense—will not, as a rule, have an easy time of it. At this stage in his life, a writer is no longer a blank sheet of paper, and some things are hard to part with. His original élan, self-confidence, and spontaneous openness have gone, but genuine maturity is not yet in sight; he must, in fact, start over again, but in essentially more difficult conditions.

I found myself at this crossroads in the late 1960s, and I'm afraid   13
I'm still looking for my second wind. In my case, the search is harder not just because of what I am, but also because the very factors that favored me in the past are now working against me.

First of all, when I arrived at this point, my external situation had   14
also changed for the worse. I lost the possibility not only of working in the Theatre on the Balustrade, but of having anything to do with Czech theatre whatsoever. And as an author, I was one of the ones most completely prohibited. True, they couldn't stop my plays from being produced abroad, but that wasn't much use to me; I had become too accus-

tomed to writing from a particular social situation, for a particular theatre, and a particular audience; in other words, I'd become too used to that special interaction between the time and my writing to be able to write just for the sake of writing, for "the world in general," and then send the play somewhere without knowing how, by whom, why, or for whom it would be produced. I had learned to understand a play as something that could fly into the world only from a specific home that alone could breathe specific meaning into the play; it was not something you tossed experimentally into the air in the hopes that it would land somewhere, catch on, and only then gain some kind of meaning. And if my older plays were performed in so many countries, it wasn't because I'd planned them to be "world-class," but because the charge of energy given to them by their maternal environment was obviously capable of being discharged elsewhere. So, for a long time, the search for that second wind meant trying to overcome a feeling of emptiness and futility.

Even more serious, however, was the fact that I was standing at 15 this inner crossroads at a time of deep change in the surrounding world. August 1968 did not just mean the routine replacement of a more liberal regime with a more conservative one; it was not just the usual freeze after a thaw. It was something more: it was the end of an era; the disintegration of a spiritual and social climate; a profound mental dislocation. The seriousness of the events that caused this transformation and the profound experiences that came with it seemed to alter our prospects completely. It was not just that the carnival-like elation of 1968 had come to an end; the whole world crumbled, a world in which we had all learned to live well and move with some ease, a world that had, as it were, weaned us—the peaceful, somewhat comic, somewhat disjointed, and very Biedermeier world of the 1960s. For a while, the nerves of society were still strung as taut as piano wire, but the tension could not last, and out of the rubble of the old world a sinister new world grew, one that was intrinsically different, merciless, gloomily serious, Asiatic, hard. The fun was definitely over, and things began to get tough.

In my earlier plays, I had said enough about the seesaw of libera 16 tors and liquidators that one might have thought I'd be prepared for this new reversal. And yet I was not: everything was suddenly too different, too serious, too dramatic and tragic, and I was experiencing it all too much as a participator to be able to deal with it in my traditional manner—with irony, a wry grin, or a cool piece of analysis. Suddenly, my position as a distant, amused observer "from below" seemed inadequate, a relic of the past, and yes, even somewhat evasive. The new world into which we entered began to touch each one of us too insistently, and it had a far different existential dimension than the one we were used to. After all, not only did it arrive bathed in the glow of a human torch, but Jan Palach's act of self-immolation was immediately understood by the whole of society. No, this had nothing whatsoever in common with the sixties. Certainly, once again people's spines were bent, and lying, cheating, and betrayal became common; once again, the theme of human identity and existential schizophrenia was everywhere—but now, it all seemed to take place on a completely different level: the time of oral juggling was over and it became increasingly obvious that human existence itself was at stake. Suddenly, instead of laughing, one felt like shouting.

1976
Tr. Paul Wilson

Making Connections

1. What is Havel referring to by the title of the essay? How does it connect to his thesis?

2. Compare Havel's statements about writing to those of George Orwell. What similarities are apparent?

CLIVE JAMES

The Kid from Kogarah

Known by *London Observer* readers for his wit and fluid style, Clive James was born in Australia in 1936 and educated there and at Cambridge University, in England. Primarily a feature writer in the area of literary criticism, James is also well known for his media criticism, and appears regularly on BBC television. In addition to his autobiographical *Unreliable Memoirs* (1980), James has published a collection of travel essays, a novel, and nearly a dozen collections of critical essays.

I was born in 1939. The other big event of that year was the outbreak of the Second World War, but for the moment that did not affect me. Sydney in those days had all of its present attractions and few of the drawbacks. You can see it glittering in the background of the few photographs in which my father and I are together. Stocky was the word for me. Handsome was the word for him. Without firing a shot, the Japanese succeeded in extricating him from my clutches. Although a man of humble birth and restricted education, he was smart enough to see that there would be war in the Pacific. Believing that Australia should be ready, he joined up. That was how he came to be in Malaya at the crucial moment. He was at Parit Sulong bridge on the day when a lot of senior officers at last found out what their troops had guessed long before—that the Japanese army was better led and better equipped than anything we had to pit against it. After the battle my father walked all the way south to Singapore and arrived just in time for the surrender. If he had waited to be conscripted, he might have been sent to the Western Desert and spent a relatively happy few months fighting the kind of Germans whose essential decency was later to be portrayed on the screen by James Mason and Marlon Brando. As it was, he drew the short straw.

This isn't the place to tell the story of my mother and father—a story which was by no means over, even though they never saw one another again. I could get a lot of mileage out of describing how the good-looking young mechanic wooed and won the pretty girl who left school at fourteen and worked as an upholsterer at General Motors Holden. How the Depression kept them so poor that they had to wait years to get married and have me. How fate was cruel to both of them beyond measure. But it would be untrue to them. It was thirty years or more before I even began to consider what my parents must have meant to each other. Before that I hardly gave them a thought, except as vague occurrences on the outskirts of a solipsistic universe. I can't remember my father at all. I can remember my mother only through a child's eyes. I don't know which fact is the sadder.

Anyway, my mother let our little house in Kogarah and we went to stay with my Aunt Dot in Jannali, another half hour down the Illawarra line. This move was made on the advice of my father, who assumed that the centre of Sydney would be flattened by Japanese bombs about two hours after the whistle blew. The assumption proved to be ill-founded, but the side effects were beneficial, since Jannali was a perfect spot to grow up in. There were only a dozen or so streets in the whole area. Only one of them was paved. The railway line ran through a cutting somewhere in the middle. Everything else was bush. 3

The houses were made of either weatherboard or fibro. Ours was weatherboard. Like all the others, it was surrounded by an area of land which could be distinguished from the bush only because of its even more lavish concentrations of colour. Nasturtiums and honeysuckle proliferated, their strident perfumes locked in perpetual contention. Hydrangeas grew in reefs, like coral in a sea of warm air. At the bottom of the back yard lay an air-raid trench full of rainwater. I fell into it within minutes of arriving. Hearing a distant splash, Aunt Dot, who was no sylph, came through the back door like a train out of a tunnel and hit the lawn running. The door, a fly-screen frame with a return spring, made exactly the same sound as one of those punching-bags you try your strength on. Aunt Dot was attired in a pink corset but it didn't slow her down. She covered the ground like Marjorie Jackson, the girl who later became famous as the Lithgow Flash. The earth shook. I was going down for the third time but I can distinctly remember the moment she launched herself into the air, describing a parabolic trajectory which involved, at one point, a total eclipse of the sun. She landed in the trench beside me. Suddenly we were sitting together in the mud. All the water was outside on the lawn. 4

Usually my mother was first to the rescue. This time she was second. She had to resuscitate both of us. She must have been in front of the house looking after my grandfather. He needed a lot of looking after. Later on my mother told me that he had always been a selfish man. She and Aunt Dot had given a good part of their lives to waiting on him. Mentally, he had never left England. I remember him as a tall, barely articulate source of smells. The principal smells were of mouldy cloth, 5 mothballs, seaweed, powerful tobacco and the tars that collect in the stem of a very old pipe. When he was smoking he was invisible. When he wasn't smoking he was merely hard to pick out in the gloom. You could track him down by listening for his constant, low-pitched, incoherent mumble. From his carpet slippers to his moustache was twice as high as I could reach. The moustache was saffron with nicotine. Everywhere else he was either grey or tortoise-shell mottle. His teeth were both.

I remember he bared them at me one Christmas dinner. It was because he was choking on a coin in a mouthful of plum pudding. It was the usual Australian Christmas dinner, taking place in the middle of the day. Despite the temperature being 100°F. in the shade, there had been the full panoply of ragingly hot food, topped off with a volcanic plum pudding smothered in scalding custard. My mother had naturally spiced the pudding with six-pences and threepenny bits, called zacs and trays respectively. Grandpa had collected one of these in the esophagus. He gave a protracted, strangled gurgle which for a long time we all took to be the beginning of some anecdote. Then Aunt Dot bounded out of her chair and hit him in the back. By some miracle she did not snap his calcified spine. Coated with black crumbs and custard, the zac streaked out of his mouth like a dum-dum and ricocheted off a tureen.

Grandpa used to take me on his knee and read me stories, of which I could understand scarcely a word, not because the stories were over my head but because his speech by that stage consisted entirely of impediments. 'Once upon a mpf,' he would intone, 'there wah ngung mawg blf . . .' My mother got angry with me if I was not suitably grateful to Grandpa for telling me stories. I was supposed to dance up and down at the very prospect. To dodge this obligation, I would build cubby-holes. Collecting chairs, cushions, bread-boards and blankets from all over the house, I would assemble them into a pill-box and crawl in, plugging the hole behind me. Safe inside, I could fart discreetly while staring through various eye-slits to keep track of what was going on. From the outside I was just a pair of marsupial eyeballs in a heap of household junk, topped off with a rising pall of sulphuretted hydrogen. It was widely conjectured that I was hiding from ghosts. I was, too, but not as hard as I was hiding from Grandpa. When he shuffled off to bed, I would unplug my igloo and emerge. Since my own bed-time was not long after dark, I suppose he must have been going to bed in the late afternoon. Finally he went to bed altogether.

With Grandpa laid up, I was the man of the house, except when Uncle Vic or Ray came home on leave. Uncle Vic was Aunt Dot's husband and Ray was her son, therefore my cousin. Uncle Vic was an infantry corporal stationed in New Guinea. Sometimes when he got leave he would bring his Owen gun home, minus the bolt. I was allowed to play with the gun. It was huge. I stumbled around pointing it at bull-ants' nests. The bull-ants, however, didn't bluff so easily. The only argument they understood was a few gallons of boiling water poured down their central stair-well. I once saw Uncle Vic administer this treatment, in revenge after half a dozen bull-ants stung me on the right foot. They were the big red kind with the black bag at the back. When that size bull-ant stings you, you stay stung. My foot came up like a loaf of bread. I just lay in the road and screamed. The same foot got into even worse trouble later on, as I shall relate.

While I staggered around blasting the nasturtiums, Uncle Vic did a ⁹ lot of enigmatic smiling. One day I struggled all the way down to the railway cutting so that I could show the gun to some local children I hoped to impress. They hadn't waited. I could see them climbing the hill on the other side of the railway line. I shouted to them, holding the gun up as high as I could, which I suppose was no height at all. They couldn't hear me. I think it was the first big disappointment of my life. When I came back dragging the gun through the dirt, Uncle Vic did a bit more of his enigmatic smiling. Talking to him years later, I realised why he was so quiet at the time. It was because he wasn't too thrilled about what he had seen in New Guinea. Japanese scouts used to sneak up on our sentries through the thick white morning jungle mist and punch meat-skewers through their heads from ear to ear.

Ray was more forthcoming, until he got sick. He was a fitter with ¹⁰ the RAAF somewhere up there but after his first leave he never went back. He just stayed around the house in his dressing-gown, getting thinner. He used to let me stand on his feet while he walked me around. The game was called Giant Steps. I loved it. Then the day came when he didn't want to play it any more. My mother told me he wasn't strong enough. I got into trouble at the dinner table when I asked him why he was holding his fork with both hands.

So really my mother was the only pillar of strength available. One ¹¹ parent is enough to spoil you but discipline takes two. I got too much of what I wanted and not enough of what I needed. I was a child who was picked up. The effects have stayed with me to this day, although in the last few years I have gradually learned to blame myself instead of circumstances. My mother had a strong will but she would have had to be Fabius Cunctator to cope with my tantrums when I didn't feel like going to school. Every second day I played sick and stayed home. Her only alternative was to see how far she could drag me. She would have had a better chance of dragging a dead horse through soft sand. The school room was a single-room wooden hut with twelve desks. Painted cream, it sat in half an acre of dirt playground about a mile from our house. Bushfires burned it down every couple of years but unfortunately it was easy to replace. The first year of school wasn't so bad. I liked Miss Dear.

Usually I got more questions right than anybody else and was awarded first choice of blocks. I chose the set with the arches and the columns. I would go off on my own into a corner of the playground and build structures akin to the Alhambra or the Escorial, throwing a fit if any other child tried to interfere.

Even the best set of school blocks wasn't as good as the set I had at home. Passed on to me by Grandpa, they were satin-smooth Victorian creations of inch-by-inch oak, every length from one to twelve inches, plus arches, Doric columns, metopes, triglyphs and sundry other bits and pieces. With them I could build a tower much taller than myself. The usual site was the middle of the lounge room. A length of cotton could be tied to one of the lower columns, so that I could retire into hiding and collapse the tower by remote control at the precise moment when Aunt Dot lumbered into range. It made a noise like Valhalla falling. She would have one of her turns—these needed plenty of space—and demand that I be sent to school next day.

Toys were scarce. A few crude lead soldiers were still produced so that children could go on poisoning themselves but otherwise there was almost nothing. It was a big event when my mother bought me a little painted lead cow. Presumably it was English. I took it to school and lost it. Next day she came with me to school, wanting to find out what had happened to it. My carelessness with everything she bought me went on hurting her for years. She construed it, accurately, as ingratitude. From the sensitivity angle I was about as obtuse as a child can be. I was sensitive enough about myself, but that's a different thing.

School, passable for the first year, became unbearable in the second, when the kind Miss Dear was supplanted by a hard case called Miss Turnbull. Dark, cold and impatient, Miss Turnbull might have been the firm hand I needed, but already I was unable to cope with authority. I still can't today, tending to oscillate between nervous flippancy and overly solicitous respect. In those days, when I was about a third of my present height and a quarter of the weight, there was nothing to do except duck. I did everything to get out of facing up to Miss Turnbull. I had Mondayitis every day of the week. As my mother dragged me down the front path, I would clutch my stomach, cross my eyes, stick out my tongue, cough, choke, scream and vomit simultaneously.

But there were some occasions when I ended up at school no matter what I did. It was then revealed that I had Dropped Behind the Class. Words I could not recognise would come up on the spelling wheel. The spelling wheel was a thick card with a window in it and a cardboard disc behind. As you turned the disc, words appeared one at a time in the window. I remember not being able to pronounce the word 'the'. I pronounced it 'ter-*her*'. The class had collective hysterics. They were rolling around on the floor with their knees up. I suppose one of the reasons why I grew up feeling the need to cause laughter was perpetual fear of being its unwitting object.

From the start of Miss Turnbull's reign until the day we left 16 Jannali, every morning I would shout the house down. For my mother, the path leading from the front porch to the front gate became a Via Dolorosa. My act reached ever new heights of extravagance. Either it worked or it didn't. If it didn't I would sit in school praying for the bushfires to come early and incinerate the place. If it did I would either hang around the house or go and play with Ron, a truant of my own age who lived next to Hally the butcher down near the station. Ron was a grub. I was always being warned off him because he was so filthy. He and I used to squat under his house tweaking each other's ding, watching each other pee, and so on. I can't remember it all now. I suppose I have repressed it. If there was any sexual excitement, it took the form of intense curiosity, just as I was curious about my mother when we were in the bath together. I remember the shock of seeing Ray undressed. He looked as if he had a squirrel hanging there. I had an acorn.

Ron's wreck of a mother used to give us buttered bread with hun- 17 dreds and thousands on it. It was like being handed a slice of powdered rainbow. They must have been a poor family but I remember my visits to them as luxuries. As well as the Technicolor bread and butter, there were vivid, viscid green drinks made from some kind of cordial. Ron's place would have been Beulah Land except for one drawback. They had a cattle dog called Bluey. A known psychopath, Bluey would attack himself if nothing else was available. He used to chase himself in circles trying to bite his own balls off. To avert instant death, I was supposed to call out from the front gate when I arrived and not open it until I was told that Bluey had been chained up. One day I opened it too early and Bluey met me on the front path. I don't know where he had come from—probably around the side of the house—but it was as if he had come up out of the ground on a lift. He was nasty enough when chained up but on the loose he was a bad dream. Barking from the stomach, he opened a mouth like a great, wet tropical flower. When he snapped it shut, my right foot was inside it.

If Bluey hadn't been as old as the hills, my foot would have come 18 right off. Luckily his teeth were in ruins, but even so I was only a few tendons short of becoming an amputee. Since Bluey's spittle obviously contained every bacterium known to science, my frantic mother concluded that the local doctor would not be enough. I think I went to some kind of hospital in Sutherland. Needles were stuck into me while she had yet another case of heart failure. Bluey was taken away to be destroyed. Looking back on it, I can see that this was tough on Bluey, who had grown old in the belief that biting ankles was the thing to do. At the time I was traumatised. I loathed dogs from that day forward. They could sense my terror from miles away. Any dog could back me against a wall for hours. Eventually I learned not to show fear. The breakthrough came when I managed to walk away from a dog who had me bailed up against the door of a garage. Admittedly he was only a Pekinese about eight inches long, but it was still a triumph. That was more than a year ago.

Making Connections

1. One of the techniques James uses to achieve his purpose in this memoir of childhood is *hyperbole*, the intentional exaggeration of qualities or characteristics. Select two or more passages that rely upon this device, and discuss how their usage contributes to the overall success of the essay.

2. Compare James's recollection of elementary school years with E. B. White's comments concerning his son's school days in "Education." Are there any similarities? What major differences can you find? Which seems to be the more realistic? Why?

LUISA VALENZUELA

◦●■●◦●◦●◦●◦●◦●◦●◦●◦●◦●◦●◦●◦●◦●■◦●

Writing with the Body

Luisa Valenzuela was born in Buenos Aires in 1938. After studying at the University of Buenos Aires, she worked as a journalist and media writer in Paris for three years. She lives in the United States, where she has been writer-in-residence at several universities. Primarily a fiction writer, Valenzuela has published two novels and several collections of short stories. "Writing with the Body" reveals her vibrant style, her personal approach to the act of writing, and her regard for the psychological forces affecting women as writers.

As I leave the ambassador's residence in Buenos Aires early one morning in 1977, at the height of my country's military dictatorship, and walk through the dark, tree-lined streets, I think I am being followed. I have been hearing political testimony from people who sought asylum in the Mexican embassy. Enemies of the de facto government. I think that I can be abducted at any moment. Yet I feel immensely vital, filled with an inexplicable strength that may come from my having reached some kind of understanding. I walk back home through those streets that appear to be empty, and take all the precautions I can to make sure that I'm not being followed, that I'm not being aimed at from some doorway, and I feel alive. I would say happy. 1

Now I know why. 2

The answer is simple, now, so many years later. I felt—at this moment, I feel—happy because I was—am—writing with the body. Writing that lingers in the memory of my pores. Writing with the body? Yes. I am aware of having done this throughout my life, at intervals, although it may be almost impossible for me to describe. I'm afraid that it's a matter of a secret action or a mode of being that may be ineffable. 3

But I don't believe in the ineffable. The struggle of every person who writes, of every true writer, is primarily against the demon of that which resists being put into words. It is a struggle that spreads like an oil stain. Often, to surrender to the difficulty is to triumph, because the best text can sometimes be the one that allows words to have their own liberty. 4

While writing with the body one also works with words, some- 5
times completely formed in one's mind, sometimes barely suggested.
Writing with the body has nothing to do with "body language." It implies being fully committed to an act which is, in essence, a literary act.

At the Mexican embassy that night in 1977, I had just spoken at 6
length with an ex-president who was a political refugee, as well as with
a terrorist who had also sought asylum. Both men were sitting at the
same table; we were all somewhat drunk and, because of that, more sincere. Then I walked down the streets and as I was walking, I was writing
with the body. And not just because of a letter that I was mentally addressing to my friend, Julio Cortázar. I was telling him in the letter—because I knew that I was risking my life and was afraid—that I don't
want to play "duck": when I get into the water, I choose to get wet.

I was writing with the body, and fear had much to do with this. 7

Fear. 8

I was the kind of child who always poked around wherever there 9
was fear: to see what kind of a creature fear was. I played at being a
snake, a snail, or a hippopotamus in a warm African river. Among the
animals I avoided was the ostrich. I wanted nothing to do with hiding
my head in the sand. I don't know what crazy, morbid impulse made
me run through the dark long hallways to the foyer at the entrance of
my house in the middle of the night, when the clock—controlled by
witches—struck the hour. Nor do I know what made me go to the ter-
race where there was supposed to be a two-headed eagle, or behind the
house where all kinds of dangers were lurking. I would have preferred
hiding my head under the covers. But then who would reassure me?
How could my eyes face daylight if they couldn't face shadows in the
night? This is why I would go to look, and maybe because I looked came
the need, sometime much later, to tell what I had seen.

Why? 10

Because of surprise

Because of adventure

Because of a question, and a gut rejection of any answers.

You tend to task yourself why write with your entire body when 11
you have that simple upper extremity which, thanks to the evolution of
the species, has an opposable thumb especially made for holding a pen.

You also ask yourself—and this is really overwhelming—why 12
write at all? In my case, I belong, body and soul and mind, to the so-
called Third World where certain needs exist that are not at all literary.

Then other responses (or perhaps they are excuses) come to mind. 13
The need to preserve collective memory is undoubtedly one of them.

There is yet another good excuse: writing as one's destined voca-   14
tion. But I don't know if literature was my destiny. I wanted to be a physi-
cist, or a mathematician, and, before that, an archaeologist or anthropologist, and for a long time I wanted to be a painter. Because I was raised in a
house full of writers and that wasn't for me. No, ma'am. No thanks.

Fernando Alegría now describes that moment and place as the   15
Buenos Aires Bloomsbury and this description isn't as crazy as it may
appear. In our old house in the Belgrano section of town, the habitués
were named Borges, Sábato, Mallea. My mother, the writer Luisa
Mercedes Levinson, was the most sociable person in the world when she
wasn't in bed, writing.

When I was a child, I would look from the door of her room and   16
she would be in her bed surrounded by papers, all day until sunset
when the others arrived. I would watch her with admiration and with
the conviction that that life wasn't for me. I wanted a different future.

Disguises I chose for Carnivals: 17

Aviatrix

Woman Explorer

Robin Hood

Those were the masks that belonged to the official Carnival. But   18
other masks at other times also took the shape of exploration and adventure. I would climb onto the roofs of the neighboring houses to try and
reach the end of the block, something which was impossible to do because of the gardens in between. On those days when I felt really daring,
I would climb up to a stone angel that clung to a column and that
needed my presence, because otherwise no one would ever see it. I
would also sneak into empty lots, or explore an abandoned house
around the block. I was always looking for treasures that changed according to my ambitions: colorful figurines, stamps, coins. There was an
old guard at the abandoned house who would let us in and was our
friend. Until one afternoon, after exploring the basement looking for secret passages—at that time we pretended that the house belonged to
German spies or was it a smuggler's hideout?—the old guard greeted us
with his fly open and all those strange things hanging out. I ran away
with my best friend in tow. I never went back, but years, thousands of
years later, I wondered if that was the treasure for which we searched.

Now I know: with that small adventure around the block and with   19
those big stories I made up, I began the slow learning process of writing
with the body

> Because
> pores or ink, it is the same thing
> the same stakes.

Clarice Lispector knew it and in her books focused on that love-   20
hate, that happiness-misfortune we call literature. Her novels appear to
be about love and the search for knowledge but they are also different
ways of speaking about writing.

One's happiness is greatest when the story flows like a stream of   21
clear water, even if the worst abominations are being narrated. It is only
during the reading of those passages that the fear of what has flowed
from one's own pen takes over.

There is another misfortune in writing and it is perhaps the most   22
painful. It is inscribed during times of silence, when nothing is written
with the body or mind or hand. Periods of drought which seem to be of
nonexistence.

This is why I say sometimes that writing is a full-time curse.   23

I also say that, in its best moments, writing a novel is a euphoric   24
feeling, like being in love.

And to think that my mother, the writer, is to blame for all of this.   25
Not because of the example she set, nor because of my emulation of her,
which I acknowledge. She is to blame because when I was in the sixth
grade in elementary school, my teacher asked her to help me with my
compositions. "Your daughter is so bright in science," my teacher told
her, "it's a shame that her grade should go down because she can't
write." So my mother, overzealous in trying to help me, write a compo-
sition as she thought a tender eleven-year-old would.

I didn't think it was a very dignified text. From that moment on, I   26
decided to assume the responsibility of my own writings. And that's
how things are.

Because writing is the path that leads to the unknown. The way   27
back is made of reflection, trying to come to terms with yourself and
with that which has been produced. I strongly believe in the fluctuation
from intuition to understanding. Placing ourselves right there

> at the border
> between two currents
> at the center of the whirlpool,
> the eye of the tornado?

"You are too intelligent to be beautiful" is what many of us have   28
been told at some time by a man we've loved. Or, supposing literature is
your profession: "You are too intelligent to be a good writer."
Contrasting, of course, that ugly, masculine thing which is intelligence
with female intuition. You wouldn't tell that to Susan Sontag is what
someone with clearer ideas would reply. But those marks were made on
young and tender skin, and from that moment on, one will always have
a feeling of inadequacy.

Incapable, inactive, unproductive. I think all of us, from the time   29
we're very young, feel at some time what could be called a nostalgia for
imprisonment: the crazy, romantic fantasy that a prisoner has all the
time to herself, to write. Only later do we realize that writing is an exercise of liberty.

From exigencies and from temptations, the stuff of literature is   30
made. And from reflection, also. From everything. There is no unworthy
material, although a great deal must be discarded.

When I was seventeen years old, I started working in journalism.   31
For many years it was the perfect combination, one that allowed me to
be part of all the disciplines, to go everywhere, and, at the same time, to
write. A gift of ubiquity wrapped in words. I had the tremendous luck,
almost a miracle, of having a boss who was a true teacher. Ambrosio
Vencino was not a journalist; he was a displaced man of letters. To him I
owe my obsessive precision with language.

I owe my travels to myself, to my need to touch the world with my   32
own hands. I never paid attention to the premise that you don't have to
leave your own bedroom to know the world. I traveled, I continue traveling, and I sometimes think that in all those displacements, parts of my
self are being left behind.

Rodolfo Walsh, the Argentine writer and activist, once told me   33
when I was complaining about how much I went from one place to the
next and how little I wrote: "Your writing is also made from your travels."

Many years later, my writing was also made from another of   34
Rodolfo Walsh's lessons to which I didn't pay much attention at the
time. One day he showed me the difficult physical exercises that Cuban
guerrillas practiced then in the Sierra Maestra. That physical guerrilla
wisdom seemed to stand me in good stead in 1975 and 1976, when I sat
in the cafes of Buenos Aires, devastated by state terrorism, and wrote
stories that were, in a way, guerrilla exercises.

I put my body where my words are.   35

The physical loss hasn't been as great for me as it has been for oth-   36
ers. I haven't been tortured, beaten, or persecuted. Knock on wood. I've
been spared, perhaps because my statements aren't frontal; they are visions from the corner of my eye, oblique. I think we must continue writing about the horrors so that memory isn't lost and history won't repeat
itself.

As a teenager, I was a voracious reader and I bragged about it but   37
there were two books that I read in secret: *Freud* by Emil Ludwig and
The Devil in the Flesh (Le Diable au Corps) by Raymond Radiguet. With
these two books I may not have gone very far in terms of pornographic
material but it's clear that my libido was already acting up.

That writing with the body known as the act of love happened   38 later, as it should have, and turned out quite well, with great style, but with more of an inclination toward the short story than the novel.

I love the short story for being round, suggestive, insinuating, microcosmic. The story has both the inconvenience and the fascination of new beginnings. 39

The novel, on the other hand, requires more concentration, more time, a state of grace. I love it because of the joy in opening new paths as words progress. 40

Paths to the unknown, the only interesting ones. 41

What I already know bores me, makes me repetitive. This is why whenever I have had a good plot that was clearly thought out, I was forced to give it up or at least to compress it, trying to squeeze out the juice that wasn't visible at first sight. 42

If I had to write my creed, I would first mention humor: 43

I believe in having a sense of humor at all costs
I believe in sharp, black humor
I believe in the absurd
in the grotesque

in everything which allows us to move beyond our limited thinking, beyond self-censorship and the censorship by others, which tends to be much more lethal. Taking a step to one side to observe the action as it is happening. A necessary step so that the vision of political reality is not contaminated by dogmas or messages.

I have nothing to say. 44

With luck, something will be said through me, despite myself, and I might not even realize it. 45

It is said that women's literature is made of questions. 46

I say that women's literature consequently is much more realistic. 47

Questions, uncertainties, searches, contradictions. 48

Everything is fused, and sometimes confused, and implicates us. The true act of writing with the body implies being fully involved. I am my own bet; I play myself, as though lying on the roulette table, calling out "All or nothing!" 49

What is interesting about the literary wager is that we do wager everything, but we don't know against what. 50

They say that women's literature is made of fragments. 51

I repeat that it is a matter of realism. 52

It is made of rips, shreds of your own skin which adhere to the paper but are not always read or even legible. Shreds that can be of laughter, of sheer delight. 53

Sometimes while writing, I have to get up to dance, to celebrate the flow of energy transforming itself into words. Sometimes the energy be- 54 comes words that are not printed, not even with the delicate line of a fountain pen, which is the most voluptuous in the act of writing. You must always celebrate when—whether in a cafe or subway—a happy combination of words, a fortuitous allusion, elicits associations that unwind the mental thread of writing without a mark. The mark comes next. And I will do my best to retain the freshness of that first moment of awe and transformation.

1991
Translated from the Spanish
by Cynthia Ventura and Janet Sternburg

Making Connections

1. How does this essay's title reflect Valenzuela's major concern? What is her thesis? What qualities does Valenzuela associate with "writing with the body"?

2. Compare Valenzuela's comments about writing with those of Virginia Woolf and Joan Didion. What similarities can you discern? What differences?

Acknowledgements

Chinua Achebe, "Named for Victoria, Queen of England." From *Hopes and Impediments* by Chinua Achebe. Copyright © 1988 by Chinua Achebe. Used by permission of Doubleday, a division of Bantam Doubleday Dell Publishing Group, Inc. and Harold Ober Associates Incorporated.

Margaret Atwood, "Travels Back." From Second Words by Margaret Atwood. Copyright © 1982 by O. W. Toad, Limited. Reprinted by permission of Beacon Press and Stoddart Publishing Company Limited. "Great Unexpectations." Originally published in Ms Magazine. Reprinted with permission of author. "The Female Body." © 1992 O. W. Toad Ltd. Reprinted from Good Bones by permission Coach House Press.

James Baldwin, "Autobiographical Notes." From *Notes of a Native Son* by James Baldwin. Copyright © 1955, renewed 1988 by James Baldwin. Reprinted by permission of Beacon Press. "Fifth Avenue, Uptown: A Letter from Harlem." From *Nobody Knows My Name* by James Baldwin, © 1961, copyright renewed 1989. Published by Vintage Books. Reprinted by permission of the James Baldwin Estate. "Stranger in the Village." From *Notes of a Native Son* by James Baldwin. Copyright © 1955, renewed 1983 by James Baldwin. Reprinted by permission of Beacon Press. "If Black English Isn't a Language, Then Tell Me, What Is?" From *The New York Times*, July 29, 1979 (op-ed). Copyright © 1979 by The New York Times Company. Reprinted by permission.

Joan Didion, "Marrying Absurd" and "On Self-Respect" from *Slouching Towards Bethlehem* by Joan Didion. Copyright © 1961, 1967, 1968 by Joan Didion. Reprinted by permission of Farrar, Straus & Giroux, Inc. "In Bed" and "Georgia O'Keeffe" from *The White Album* by Joan Didion. Copyright © 1979 by Joan Didion. Reprinted by permission of Farrar, Straus & Giroux, Inc. "Why I Write." Reprinted by permission of Joan Didion. Copyright © 1976 by Joan Didion. First appeared in *The New York Times Book Review*, December 5, 1976.

Annie Dillard, "An American Childhood." From *An American Childhood* by Annie Dillard. Copyright © 1987 by Annie Dillard. Reprinted by permission of HarperCollins Publishers, Inc. "Living Like Weasels" from *Teaching a Stone to Talk* by Annie Dillard. Copyright © 1982 by Annie Dillard. Reprinted by permission of HarperCollins Publishers, Inc. "Singing with the Fundamentalists." Reprinted by permission of the author and Blanche C. Gregory, Inc. Copyright © 1984 by Annie Dillard. "Push It" from *The Writing Life* by Annie Dillard. Copyright © 1989 by Annie Dillard. Reprinted by permission of HarperCollins Publishers, Inc.

Umberto Eco, "City of Robots" from *Travels in Hyperreality* by Umberto Eco, copyright © 1983, 1976, 1973 by Gruppo Editoriale Fabbri-Bompiani, Sonzogno, Etas S.p.A., English translation copyright © 1986 by Harcourt Brace & Company, copyright © 1986, 1967 by Umberto Eco, reprinted by permission of Harcourt Brace & Company.

Nadine Gordimer, "Where Do Whites Fit In?" From *The Essential Gesture* by Nadine Gordimer and Stephen Clingman. Copyright © 1988 by Felix B.V.I.O. Reprinted by permission of Alfred A. Knopf, Inc.

Stephen Jay Gould, "Women's Brains." Reprinted from *The Panda's Thumb, More Reflections in Natural History*, by Stephen Jay Gould, by permission of W. W. Norton & Company, Inc. Copyright © 1980 by Stephen Jay Gould. "Muller Bros. Moving & Storage" and "Counters and Cable Cars." Reprinted from *Eight Little Piggies: Reflections in Natural History*, by Stephen Jay Gould, by permission of W. W. Norton & Company, Inc. Copyright © 1993 by Stephen Jay Gould.

Vaclav Havel, "Second Wind." From *Open Letters* by Vaclav Havel, trans., P. Wilson. Copyright © 1991 by Václav Havel and Paul Wilson. Reprinted by permission of Alfred A. Knopf, Inc.

Clive James, "The Kid from Kogarah." From *Unreliable Memoirs* by Clive James. Copyright © 1980 by Clive James. Reprinted by permission of Alfred A. Knopf, Inc.

Maxine Hong Kingston, "No Name Woman." From *The Woman Warrior* by Maxine Hong Kingston. Copyright © 1975, 1976 by Maxine Hong Kingston. Reprinted by permission of Alfred A. Knopf, Inc. "High School Reunion." © 1978 by Maxine Hong Kingston. Reprinted by permission of the Schaffner Literary Agency. "The Wild Man of the Green Swamp." From *China Men* by Maxine Hong Kingston. Copyright © 1980 by Maxine Hong Kingston. Reprinted by permission of Alfred A. Knopf, Inc.

Doris Lessing, "My Father." © 1963 Doris Lessing. (First appeared in *The Sunday Telegraph*, 1.9.63.) Reprinted by permission of Jonathan Clowes Ltd., London, on behalf of Doris Lessing.

Barry Lopez, "The Stone Horse" is reprinted with the permission of Charles Scribner's Sons, an imprint of Macmillan Publishing Company from *Crossing Open Ground* by Barry Lopez. Copyright © 1988 Barry Lopez. (First appeared in *Antaeus*, Autumn 1986.) "The American Geographies." Reprinted by permission of Sterling Lord Literistic, Inc. Copyright © 1989 by Barry Lopez. "Renegotiating the Contracts." Reprinted from *Parabola, The Magazine of Myth and Tradition*, Vol. VIII, No. 2 (Spring, 1983). Reprinted by permission of Sterling Lord Literistic, Inc. Copyright © 1983 by Barry Lopez.

Ved Mehta, "Pom's Engagement." Reprinted from *The Ledge Between the Streams* by Ved Mehta, by permission of W. W. Norton & Company, Inc. Copyright © 1982, 1983, 1984 by Ved Mehta.

V. S. Naipaul, "Columbus and Crusoe." Reprinted from *The Overcrowded Barracoon* by permission of V. S. Naipaul. © 1972 V. S. Naipaul.

George Orwell, "A Hanging," "Shooting an Elephant," and "Politics and the English Language" from *Shooting an Elephant and Other Essays* by George Orwell, copyright 1950 by Sonia Brownell Orwell and renewed 1978 by Sonia Pitt-Rivers, reprinted by permission of Harcourt Brace and Company, the estate of the late Sonia Brownell Orwell and Martin Secker & Warburg Ltd. "Antisemitism in Britain" from *The Collected Essays, Journalism and Letters of George Orwell, Volume III, As I Please, 1943–1945*, copyright © 1968 by Sonia Brownell Orwell, reprinted by permission of Harcourt Brace & Company and the estate of the late Sonia Brownell Orwell and Martin Secker & Warburg Ltd. "Why I Write" from *Such, Such Were the Joys* by George Orwell, copyright 1953 by Sonia Brownell Orwell and renewed 1981 by Mrs. George K. Perutz, Mrs. Miriam Gross, Dr. Michael Dickson, Executors of the Estate of Sonia Brownell Orwell, reprinted by permission of Harcourt Brace & Company, the estate of the late Sonia Brownell Orwell and Martin Secker & Warburg Ltd.

Cynthia Ozick, "The Seam of the Snail." From *Metaphor and Memory* by Cynthia Ozick. Copyright © 1989 by Cynthia Ozick. Reprinted by permission of Alfred A. Knopf, Inc. "A Drugstore in Winter." From *Art & Ardor* by Cynthia Ozick. Copyright © 1983 by Cynthia Ozick. Reprinted by permission of Alfred A. Knopf, Inc. "Of Christian Heroism." Originally appeared in *Partisan Review*, volume 59, number 1, 1992. Reprinted by permission of Cynthia Ozick and her agents Raines & Raines, 71 Park Avenue, New York, N.Y. 10016. Copyright © 1992 by Cynthia Ozick.

Octavio Paz, "Hygiene and Repression" from *Convergences, Essays on Art and Literature* by Octavio Paz, copyright © 1973 by Editorial Joaquín Moritz, copyright © 1984, 1983, 1979 by Editorial Seix Barral, S. A., English translation copyright © 1987 by Harcourt Brace & Company, reprinted by permission of Harcourt Brace & Company.

Richard Rodriguez, "Complexion." From *Hunger of Memory* by Richard Rodriguez. Copyright © 1982 by Richard Rodriguez. Reprinted by permission of David R. Godine, Publisher. "Children of a Marriage" by Richard Rodriguez. Reprinted by permission of Georges Borchardt, Inc. for the author. Copyright © 1974 by Richard Rodriguez. "Late Victorians: San Francisco, AIDS and the Homosexual Stereotype," from *Days of Obligation* by Richard Rodriguez. Copyright © 1992 by Richard Rodriguez. Used by permission of Viking Penguin, a division of Penguin Books USA Inc.

Richard Selzer, "Lessons from the Art." Copyright © 1974, 1975, 1976, 1987 by Richard Selzer. Reprinted by permission of Simon & Schuster, Inc. "The Masked Marvel's Last Toehold." Copyright © 1979 by Richard Selzer. Reprinted by permission of John Hawkins & Associates, Inc. "A Mask on the Face of Death." Copyright © 1987 by Richard Selzer. Reprinted by permission of Georges Borchardt, Inc. for the author. "The Pen and the Scalpel" from *The New York Times*, August 21, 1988. Copyright © 1988 by The New York Times Company. Reprinted by permission.

Lewis Thomas, "Computers," copyright © 1973 by The Massachusetts Medical Society, from *The Lives of a Cell* by Lewis Thomas. Used by permission of Viking Penguin, a division of Penguin Books USA Inc. "The Tucson Zoo," copyright © 1977 by Lewis Thomas, from *The Medusa and the Snail* by Lewis Thomas. Used by permission of Viking Penguin, a division of Penguin Books USA Inc. "Notes on Punctuation," copyright © 1979 by Lewis Thomas, from *The Medusa and the Snail* by Lewis Thomas. Used by permission of Viking Penguin, a division of Penguin Books USA Inc. "Becoming a Doctor." Reprinted with the permission of Charles Scribner's Sons, an imprint of Macmillan Publishing Company from *The Fragile Species* by Lewis Thomas. Copyright © 1992 by Lewis Thomas.

Luisa Valenzuela, "Writing with the Body." Reprinted by permission of Harold Ober Associates Incorporated. Copyright © 1991 by Janet Sternburg.

Alice Walker, "In Search of Our Mothers' Gardens" from *In Search of Our Mothers' Gardens: Womanist Prose*, copyright © 1974 by Alice Walker, reprinted by permission of Harcourt Brace & Company. "Women" from *Revolutionary Petunias & Other Poems*, copyright © 1970 by Alice Walker, reprinted by permission of Harcourt Brace & Company. "Am I Blue?" from *Living by the Word: Selected Writings 1973–1987*, copyright © 1986 by Alice Walker, reprinted by permission of Harcourt Brace & Company. "Father" from *Living by the Word: Selected Writings 1973–1987*, copyright © 1985 by Alice Walker, reprinted by permission of Harcourt Brace & Company. "The Democratic Order, Such Things in Twenty Years I Understood" from *Once*, copyright © 1968 by Alice Walker, reprinted by permission of Harcourt Brace & Company.

E. B. White, "Farewell, My Lovely!" from *Essays of E. B. White* (Harper & Row); © 1936, 1964 The New Yorker Magazine, Inc. Originally published in *The New Yorker* in 1936 over the pseudonym "Lee Strout White." Richard L. Strout had submitted a manuscript on the Ford, and White, with his collaboration, rewrote it. "Once More to the Lake" and

Photo Credits

Rhetorical Index

CAUSE AND EFFECT

CLASSIFICATION

COMPARISON AND CONTRAST

DEFINITION

DESCRIPTION

HUMOR, IRONY, SATIRE

ILLUSTRATION

NARRATION

PROCESS ANALYSIS